EXPERIMENTAL PSYCHOLOGY

BURTON G. ANDREAS
Associate Professor of Psychology
University of Rochester

EXPERIMENTAL PSYCHOLOGY

New York · London, John Wiley & Sons, Inc

THIRD PRINTING, APRIL, 1963

To Jan

Preface

Initially as a student and later as a teacher and research worker, I experienced a strong appreciation of the ongoing nature of the scientific enterprise as we see it in psychology. Indebted though we are to workers of earlier decades, there seems to be a recent maturing in methodological development that marks the present as a time of promise in our attempts to delineate behavior principles. I hope that this textbook offers to students a mixture of sophistication in methods and motivation for investigation that will stimulate them to join actively in our effort even while they are still growing toward achieving competence in research.

I would not defend the proposition that there is a particular subject matter that should be rightfully called "experimental psychology." Tradition has applied this label to a diverse group of problem areas, but the accent has been on the experimental approach rather than on the specific realms of study. I have retained—hopefully even emphasized—the methodological accent while departing slightly from tradition in making the forced choices of topics to be treated. Consideration of the chemical and cutaneous senses has been omitted. This is more than offset, I feel, by the inclusion of chapters dealing with perceptual-motor behavior and with social processes.

More important than the choice of content is the approach that is taken. Again, however, there are constraints. I have purposely omitted lengthy historical reviews, physiological mechanisms, and particular theoretical positions. I have stressed research methods, general and specific, and illustrative reviews of experimental studies which show how research has answered some of our questions while revealing much that needs yet to be investigated. The instructor may choose to treat historical, physiological, or theoretical matters in order to intensify certain parts of the course.

Since beginning to teach experimental psychology in 1951 I have assigned different chapters in the various textbooks I have used, with the intent of strengthening the laboratory work of the students. Similarly, I hope that selections from this book will be chosen to undergird the experiments that are performed. The two-part division of the book is not intended to demand sequential reading. On the contrary, it is expected that students will draw from both parts concurrently as their course of study proceeds. Part 1 attempts to guide the student in considering numerous elements of a scientific approach to behavior study—the formulating of hypotheses, the designing and conducting of experiments, the treatment of data, and the reporting of research. The relationship of empirical investigation to theory construction is also treated, as are the general methods of psychophysics and psychological scaling. I hope that the student may exhibit benefit from these considerations in a more mature approach to the laboratory work which is central in experimental psychology. Part 2 offers background information and research models for many areas of investigation. The illustrative studies all involve human subjects rather than animals. This choice is a deliberate one, attempting to provide suggestions for student research in the many colleges and universities where undergraduate use of experimental animals is not possible.

My students and I have enjoyed trying to pattern some of our experiments after research reported in the psychology journals of recent decades. Our efforts, with modified techniques being used, have not always led to the expected results, but it has been gratifying to carry out the investigations within the rules as we understand them. Even more satisfying to the students have been their ventures into independent research projects. Although the level of confidence sought for the experimental hypothesis has not always been attained, I have been pleased with the level of maturity which has been shown by students in planning and executing these studies. I hope this textbook will help other students to reach this subgoal of maturity in behavioral research while pursuing the distant goal of completing their education.

BURTON G. ANDREAS

Rochester
February, 1960

Acknowledgments

Evidence is abundant in this book that a host of people contributed indirectly to its writing. Scores of original research papers are cited and I wish to acknowledge the help of their authors. I have tried to incorporate their scientific reports in a treatise that may aid in the training of future research workers. Less evident, but still recalled with gratitude, are the contributions made by many investigators, reviewers, and theorists whose writings were a source of stimulation to me even though they could not be cited in the final draft of the manuscript.

The antecedent conditions for the writing of this textbook are many and varied, which is merely to express an axiom of behavior science. If there be any scholarship here, the sources of inspiration are my teachers from years past. I particularly wish to acknowledge the training I received from my professors at the State University of Iowa: H. P. Bechtoldt, A. L. Benton, G. Bergmann, P. Blommers, J. S. Brown, I. E. Farber, J. R. Knott, D. Lewis, E. F. Lindquist, and K. W. Spence. The advanced offerings of these men in statistics, quantitative methods, experimental design, animal research, philosophy of science, systematic psychology, and theory construction are unfortunately represented only slightly in this textbook for beginning experimentalists. Their books and papers constitute an excellent library for the advanced student.

An indirect contributor to the development of this textbook was my first instructor in psychology, K. U. Smith. I shall never forget how he demonstrated stimulus-response pyschology by shouting for all class members to stand up until even the last rebel sheepishly obeyed. I should acknowledge early encouragement from two others of my undergraduate teachers, S. D. S. Spragg and G. R. Wendt. They contributed to this book in another way, too, by permitting me to practice the experimental art on their research projects over a number of years.

Since my efforts here have grown out of the teaching of the undergraduate course in experimental psychology, there is another group
who made a strong contribution. I wish to thank D. A. Buchanan,
A. Finck, B. W. Harleston, D. C. Hodge, G. L. Kandel, C. L. Kling-
berg, R. A. Monty, D. M. Pomeranz, W. Riss, S. Smith, J. F. Sturr,
and M. W. Wagner, all laboratory section instructors with whom I
was privileged to work at the University of Rochester. I enjoyed an
active exchange of ideas with these men, now widely scattered in
teaching and research positions, and I hope that they also derived
benefit from our work together.

I wish to give heartfelt thanks to my wife, Jan, for constant encouragement of my writing efforts. I thank her, too, for typing the
manuscript and helping with proofreading and indexing. The best
part of such arduous work, she will undoubtedly agree, is looking
back on it. My appreciation goes to my daughter, Cherie, for many
suggestions on what to include in this book, and for a number of
other helps including the not-watching of television during much of
the continuing crisis that is authorship. I am grateful to Mother and
Father for motivating my education—another indirect contribution
to this book.

For permission to quote and to use graphic and tabular materials
from other sources, I am grateful to numerous individuals and organ-
izations: American Psychological Association; Professor R. F. Bales;
Professor Karl M. Dallenbach, Editor, *The American Journal of Psychology;* Professor Charles Haig; Henry Holt and Company; John
Wiley & Sons; The Journal Press; McGraw-Hill Book Company; National Academy of Sciences—National Research Council; The Rocke-
feller Institute Press; Professor George Wald; and Yale University
Press. I am indebted to Professor Sir Ronald A. Fisher, F.R.S., Cambridge, and to Dr. Frank Yates, F.R.S., Rothamsted, also to Messrs.
Oliver & Boyd Ltd., Edinburgh, for permission to reprint Table B,
Appendix, from their book *Statistical Tables for Biological, Agricultural and Medical Research.*

Final thanks go to a number of kind people who have helped me
in many ways to carry out this project. I am indebted to friends
on the River Campus—staff members, students, secretaries, and shop
superintendent—for assistance and encouragement.

BURTON G. ANDREAS

Rochester
February, 1960

Contents

PART 1

Introduction and General Methods

CHAPTER 1

Psychology as the Science of Behavior

A fundamental assumption in all of science is that certain regular relationships exist in nature. The common aim of science is to formulate laws which express these regularities that occur among different aspects of natural phenomena. The biologist, for example, seeks a formula that will relate plant growth to temperature, to humidity, to amount of light, and to the chemical composition of the soil. The chemist plots the course of a reaction as it depends on temperature and on the strength of the chemical solutions involved. The work of these scientists exemplifies the constructing of precise descriptive laws on the foundation of careful observations. This commonly shared aim of science is matched by the widespread use of a general mode of approach that has become known as the scientific method. Later in this chapter we shall explore some aspects of this method in the context of psychological research.

If their basic methodology and aims are the same, why do we have many different sciences? Why do not the astronomer and the physicist, the biologist and the chemist all cooperate in one grand science? The answer, of course, is that they do. These various divisions of science merely represent interests in different sorts of natural occurrences with accompanying differences in technical method used for their study. Biology, for example, is interested in the growth and reproduction of living organisms. Its techniques range from microscopic observation of intracellular processes to the restructuring of chromosomal materials in the fruit fly. These particular methods of the biologist are specific instances of the more general scientific method. It is in the sharing of the general method that the sciences are one, no matter how varied are their special approaches to their tasks.

The Aim of Psychological Science

Psychology seeks to express the laws of behavior. It makes the assumption that all aspects of behavior, like other natural phenomena, are dependent on the conditions under which the behavior occurs. Just as the biologist assumes that plant growth depends on genetic and environmental factors, the psychologist assumes, for example, that the development of a child's personality depends on his heredity and environment. Psychology seeks to describe the dependence of the activities of people or animals on their environments and their states of being. Psychology's place in the unity of science is delineated by this particular goal and the special techniques devised for striving toward it. As we examine specific aims and methods of psychology later, it will be well to remember that they are concrete instances of the general endeavor of science.

BEHAVIOR LAWS AND HYPOTHESES

Psychology shares the assumption common to all of science that the phenomena it studies are lawful. A few examples may remind us of the diverse sorts of behavioral laws that psychologists have formulated:

1. Meaningful verbal material is more readily learned than is material which is relatively devoid of meaning.
2. When he is hungry, a normal infant becomes active and vociferous.
3. Strong illumination results in a constriction of the pupil of the eye.
4. The amount of learned material which is retained decreases with the passage of time.
5. Reaction time to an auditory stimulus is briefer than reaction time to a visual stimulus.

These varied examples serve to bear out the assumption that behavior is related in regular ways to environmental stimulation and to the state of the reacting individual.

Law and Hypothesis

Although we seek behavior laws, much of our research activity centers around the formulating and testing of hypotheses. As we shall employ the terms, an hypothesis and a law differ only in the extent of scientific confirmation which has been accomplished. An hypothesis is a tentative law awaiting initial test or requiring further checking before it can be regarded as a law. A law is an hypothesis which has received a relatively high degree of confirmation. Both are conditional statements in their format, stating that *if* certain conditions are established, *then* particular behavioral consequences will follow.

A scientist may hypothesize that "if a line segment is presented in vertical orientation, then it will be judged longer than when it is presented horizontally." If several experiments are performed and it is consistently found that the line-judging behavior of a number of people conforms to his formulation, then his hypothesis may be regarded as a law of perception. The law might be stated in exactly the same words that the hypothesis was. The close correspondence between hypothesis and law, in phrasing as well as in form, thus bears out our definition of an hypothesis as a tentative statement of a law.

Strictly speaking, an experiment does not lead to the absolute confirmation of an hypothesis but only to a considerable increase of confidence in its tenability (assuming it is not rejected on the basis of the experimental observations). The laws of science may be considered, then, as hypotheses in which great confidence has been placed as a result of repeated observations and testing. Research leads from hypothesis to law by increasing the confidence that anyone may have that the stated formulation is indeed tenable. Alternatively, the outcome of research may force the scientist to reformulate the hypothesis so that it is still in agreement with his observations and then to retest it. We shall need to say more in Chapter 2 about the forming and testing of hypotheses in behavior science.

A Model for the Form of a Law or Hypothesis

Despite the diversity of ways in which they were stated, all the examples of behavior laws we cited may be paraphrased to correspond to a single form, represented by the model: if A, then B. This model or paradigm will help us to understand just what is meant by a behavior law or hypothesis. As a matter of fact, this paradigm, if A, then B, can be considered as a model for a law formulated in any discipline of science. Let us concentrate here on how we may reformulate some of our psychological laws to fit it. "Strong illumination results in a constriction of the pupil" becomes "*If* the eye is strongly illuminated, *then* the pupil constricts"—if A, then B. *If* material studied is meaningful, *then* learning is facilitated. *If* the stimulus is an auditory one, *then* the reaction time will be shorter than if the stimulus had been visual. Maybe you can think of other laws of behavior that might be expressible in the form of our model: if A, then B.

There is more utility to this paradigm for a scientific law than just its mere application to paraphrasing statements of dependence or relationship. Applying the model, if A, then B, helps to show clearly what the essence of the relationship actually is. Would you approve, for instance, of this reformulation of the law relating hunger and vocal activity?—"If hungry, then the normal infant becomes active and vociferous." Is our application of the model correct in this instance? It might have been better to say, "if hungry, and if normal, then the infant becomes active and vociferous." We put normalcy as well as hunger in the conditional clause, where both rightly belong, since both are conditions under which the behavior will occur.

Since an hypothesis, like a law, is a conditional statement of the dependence of an event upon preceding and surrounding conditions, it may also be structured like our model: if A, then B. The model serves as a guide as we formulate hypotheses for experimental testing. The "if" clause demands that we specify the conditions surrounding the behavior; the "then" clause requires us to state what effect on behavior is expected or to tell the response measurements we shall take to see if there has *been* an effect.

EXPANSION OF THE MODEL. A little reflection will convince us that scientific laws often contain numerous factors in their conditional clauses. There are several things besides meaningfulness, for example, that contribute to the memorizing of verbal material. "If A, then B" becomes "if A_1 and if A_2 and if A_3 . . . and if A_n, then B." One aim of behavioral science is to discover *all* of the factors that govern a particular activity. Such an aim is, of course, more of a challenge to ingenuity in carrying out research than it is an attainable goal. More realistically, our goal is to determine the role played by a few of the factors in governing a bit of behavior. This will permit the formulation of a law that applies to most cases. The limitation to "most cases" does not mean that the formulation is now and then invalid, but rather that it is imperfect in identifying all factors that may be operative in certain instances.

THE MODEL IN QUANTITATIVE EXPRESSION. It may have occurred to you that many of the disciplines of science feature quantitative laws. Psychology also attempts to quantify relationships among variables. As applied to such a formulation, our paradigm is merely replicated: if illumination is 1.0 millilambert (abbreviated mL), then pupillary area is 20 sq mm; if illumination is 10.0 mL, then pupillary area is 13 sq mm; if 100.0 mL, then 7 sq mm. If A, then B has now been expanded to a quantitative relationship that is expressible as a mathematical function. A law in this form is called a *functional relationship*. It represents a more precisely stated law than does a nonquantified statement like "Strong illumination results in constriction of the pupil." The functional relationship precludes such questions about the law as "What do you mean by constriction?" and "How strong is 'strong'?"

THE FUNCTIONAL RELATIONSHIP AS AN ALTERNATE MODEL. Most attempts to state behavioral laws are attempts to specify functional relationships. The experimental approach to behavioral law, then, is to vary quantitatively any factors considered relevant and to look for co-variation in some measure of the behavior. If it is observed, this co-variation may be expressed as a mathematical equation or functional relationship. When this is done, the paradigm for the law may be changed from "if A, then B" to "$B = f(A)$." This may be read "B *is a function of* A" or "B is quantitatively dependent upon A." Besides being expressible as a mathematical equation, a functional relationship lends itself readily to graphic portrayal.

Dependent and Independent Variables

When a psychologist gathers data to use in formulating a behavioral law, especially in the form of a functional relationship, he regards the measurements of behavior that he makes as *depending* on values of the conditions under which the behavior has occurred. Any behavior measure is therefore termed the *dependent variable* in the formula, $B = f(A)$. The functional relationship is a mathematical expression of the dependence of the behavioral data, B, upon the values of the antecedent conditions, A. With B representing behavior and A standing for antecedent conditions, you can see that B is also the dependent variable in our first paradigm—if A, then B. Thus, pupillary size, a behavior measure, can be regarded as depending on antecedent conditions of illumination no matter how we choose to express the relationship, whether as a functional relationship or patterned after the "if, then" model which we examined first.

We are considering that behavior, B, is determined by antecedent conditions, A. Under this term "antecedent conditions" we must include both environmental factors and various states of the reacting organism which we earlier indicated to be the determinants of behavior. Antecedent conditions are called *independent variables* in formulations of behavioral laws. In seeking to formulate behavioral laws we can often assign numerical values to these factors or variables. Sometimes we assign them by measuring some aspect of the environment or some state of the organism; at other times we may experimentally manipulate an environmental factor or a state of the subject. In either case, the data on these factors are regarded as independent of the behavior that occurs, thus accounting for the term, independent variables. Our models or paradigms for behavior laws, "if A, then B" or "$B = f(A)$," are seen to contain terms for both the dependent variable, B, which is the measurement of behavior that is taken, and the independent variables, A, which are the data describing the antecedent conditions.

ANTECEDENT CONDITIONS AS DETERMINANTS OF BEHAVIOR

The domain of natural events that we call "behavior" is extremely broad, ranging from the blink of an eye to the spirited cheering of the crowd at a game. Accounting for the determinants of behavioral phenomena is a monumental undertaking. Behavior scientists appreciate the enormity of the task and the impossibility of its completion. But they realize, too, that the essence of science is the working toward the goal rather than the attainment of it. No matter how remote ultimate success may be, we know that the stuff of which science is being made is the descriptive formulation of relationships among dependent and independent variables. In behavior science, it is in specifiable antecedent conditions that we seek to account for the aspects of behavior that we consider as the dependent variables. Considering the tremendous diversity of factors which might affect behavior, we can see that the expression "antecedent conditions" must be very broadly interpreted if it is to include everything that would be a possible determinant of the actions of an organism. It would be futile to attempt a mere catalog listing of antecedents of behavior but it may be helpful to discuss further the part that these independent variables play in testing behavioral hypotheses. Even a single response may have numerous determinants.

A Sample Behavioral Phenomenon

Let us consider a classical laboratory experiment, the determination of a person's reaction time, to see how great a variety of factors might affect even so simple a bit of behavior as releasing a telegraph key as quickly as possible in response to the sound of a buzzer. With a clock or timer calibrated in hundredths of a second, a student experimenter, E, might find that the response of his subject, S, took 0.18 sec on one trial and 0.24 sec on the next, the time being measured from the onset of the sound to the instant of release of the key.* In the usual investigation such trial-to-trial variability in the response measurements would be no cause for concern. However, we have been assuming that behavior is determined by antecedent conditions and even so slight a change in response might be presumed to have its reasons. To find them in an actual instance would call for detective work worthy of your favorite fictional sleuth. Our student investigator would hardly be motivated to attempt to pin this "crime" on any antecedent condition. Nor can *we* solve the mystery without all the facts in the case. What we *can* do is to suggest a variety of factors that might possibly have been responsible for the 0.06 sec difference in successive measures of reaction time, RT. Our consideration of this matter will emphasize the important fact that even the simplest sort of response measure is likely to yield values that are dependent jointly on several different determinants. We shall illustrate, too, that these determining factors may be conveniently considered as falling in one of two categories, environmental factors or states of the person.

Multiple Determinants of Behavior

If we can show that such a simple response measure as speed of releasing a key in the RT experiment is dependent for its value on numerous antecedent conditions, we should be going a long way toward demonstrating that any measurement of behavior of a more complex sort is similarly likely to be based on a multiplicity of determinants. The principle of multiple determination of phenomena is one that any investigator should keep in mind in planning research or in interpreting data that have been obtained. To return to our example, what factors would you list among the determinants of RT? As measured by our student researcher, RT might have been dependent on:

* The abbreviations used here—E for *experimenter* and S for *subject*—are conventional in psychological writing. O is often used to stand for *observer*.

1. Intensity of sound.
2. Length of foreperiod (interval from warning signal of "Ready" to the onset of the stimulus).
3. Motivation of subject.
4. Force required to hold response key down.
5. Number of previous trials.
6. Acuity of S's hearing.

There is reason to believe that any and all these independent variables might be determiners of RT, the dependent variable. Our paradigm for a behavioral law, $B = f(A)$, needs to be expanded if it is to represent the dependence of even simple RT upon antecedent conditions:

$$RT = f(I, L, M, F, N, A)$$

The model suggests that the equation relating RT to these several factors would contain many terms. Only one or two of these conditions would be of primary interest in a particular study; these might be systematically varied while others were kept constant. Such experimental considerations will concern us in Chapter 2.

If we were to single out any variable listed in accounting for the two different RT values that we were discussing, we might suggest that the second factor listed might be a likely source of trial-to-trial differences in response. This independent variable, length of foreperiod, is typically varied from trial to trial whereas the others would tend to remain constant. The others might be more likely to account for differences in RT from subject to subject or from experiment to experiment.

Environmental Factors and States of the Person as Determinants of Behavior

Behavior of almost any sort may be considered to depend jointly on two classes of determinant: environmental or situational factors, and the states of the responding person. How might we divide our list of six determinants of RT into two such groups? We could consider that Nos. 1, 2, and 4 are characteristic of the situation surrounding performance, whereas Nos. 3, 5, and 6 represent states of the subject which might be reflected in the speed with which he reacted to the auditory stimulus.

The fifth variable in our list, number of previous trials, may provide an example of the two ways we can look at an independent variable. With E administering as many trials as he wishes to S, it might seem that we should classify the number of trials as an environmental variable. As a determinant of behavior, however, this antecedent condition would be considered to have an effect on RT by way of the state it might have produced in S. Thus, many trials in close succession might have induced a fatigue state that would lead to greater RT values. On the other hand, repeated trials might have led to a practice effect that would shorten RT. In either case the variable might be regarded as producing a state in S which then served as a determinant of behavior. Our willingness to tolerate ambiguity in the classification of the determinants of behavior should not discourage you. This classification is only arbitrary, attempted as an aid to our thinking and our formulating of hypotheses. Such a classification schema is *not* the essence of scientific enterprise.

The Manipulation of Antecedent Conditions

In this discussion of the RT experiment we have seen that E can not only manipulate environmental variables, but can also exert some influence on those antecedent conditions which were classed as states of the person. To suggest another example, S's motivational state might be altered by special instructions or by placing two Ss in competition with one another. Thus research involving organic states need not be approached with physiological techniques. We can treat these states as hypothetical, defining them in terms of the operations used in creating them. In considering any behavioral law or hypothesis, it is necessary to be sure of the definition—the operational definition—of the variables involved in the formulation. In relating RT to M, then, hypothetical motivational levels might be defined by specifying different sorts of instructions employed. It should be noted that this indirect operational approach to organic states does not rule out their more direct manipulation, as, for example, by way of administering a substance like caffeine. The definition of the state remains operational, but the operations differ markedly. Both direct and indirect, the operations that define antecedent conditions play a key role in testing hypotheses. Operational definition will therefore require our attention again in Chapter 2.

Our RT example offers another important fact about the determinants of response data. Some of the antecedent conditions are very amenable to manipulation by E. Readily varied in RT study, for example, are intensity of stimulus and length of foreperiod. In other cases, independent variables defy manipulation and demand special selection of Ss as the way to search for a functional relationship.

As an example of the latter technique, Ss might be grouped into three or four classes on the basis of tests of auditory acuity and then might have their *RT* measured with tones of fairly low intensities.

In the search for some kinds of functional relationships it might be possible neither to manipulate the values of an independent variable nor to select Ss on such a basis. If we were investigating the effect of interest in the task, for example, on the accuracy of sorting colors, it might be necessary to have a group of judges rate Ss on their manifest level of interest while they were actually engaged in the sorting task. We could then look for a mathematical dependence of accuracy scores on judged level of interest.

TEMPORAL RELATIONS OF ANTECEDENT CONDITIONS TO BEHAVIOR. From our several examples it can be seen that antecedent conditions are often very unlike one another in the time that they precede the response they influence. In the *RT* investigation the foreperiod preceded the response by only a few seconds, whereas stimulus intensity plays its role only in the split second before the making of the response. Contrastingly, the acuity of *S*'s hearing as a factor may date back to a childhood illness or even to his genetic inheritance. Motivation may similarly be based in part upon experience of earlier years or it may be affected by the stimulus intensity, a very closely antecedent condition. We see that in their temporal placement the independent variables are about as diversified as they are in their qualitative nature.

THE MEASUREMENT OF BEHAVIOR
OR DEPENDENT VARIABLES

Having manipulated antecedent conditions so as to produce the desired values of independent variables, we must complete our search for a functional relationship by measuring the behavior that is presumed to be the dependent variable in the situation. Even a very simple instance of behavior has several measurable aspects, but one or two of them are usually singled out to be measured. The choice of what behavioral measure to take is dictated by the hypothesis that is being tested. If the hypothesis states that speed of response will be determined by the factor that is being manipulated, then of course response speed is the measurement that is taken, as in the *RT* experiment. If we were seeking to examine the curve of forgetting, we might use as the index of retention the number of words correctly recalled after varying intervals. Speed of response or number of words correct on a recall test are just two indices or measurements that might enter into behavioral laws. We need to consider these and several other dependent variable measurements in order to see that the possibilities for determining functional relationships are almost as numerous on the response side as they are in the realm of antecedent conditions.

Response Latency

Reaction time studies occupy so prominent a place in classical laboratory psychology that RT is often treated as though it were a kind of behavior rather than a behavioral measure. The usual RT experiment is indeed a particular kind of experiment, but the measurement that is taken is useful in a wide variety of studies. As the interval between a stimulus change and the occurrence of a response, it is given the general designation of response latency. We mentioned a stimulus change, you may note, because any kind of environmental change may initiate the period designated as latency even though it is usually the onset of a stimulus that is used.

The use of response latency, as we have said, is by no means confined to the RT experiment where a simple motor response is being studied. It is possible to obtain latency measures for some of the discrete responses that occur while a person is engaged in a very complex adjustive task such as keeping a pointer aligned with a moving target. But again this is a motor response, so we must provide another example to show further what a useful measure response latency may be. Suppose we are investigating the hypothesis that preferences for certain hues are strengthened when the preferred hue is presented in a more deeply saturated form. For various pairs of hues we request S to give us his judgment which is preferred, the red or the blue? We might measure the time taken to respond and consider it as an index of the strength of the preference. If the preference is strong, the subject, S, will probably take a very short time to report it; if it is a weak preference, he may take somewhat longer before making his response. Thus, response latency may serve as an index of even the complex sort of behavior that is represented in esthetic judgment. Of course, this way of measuring strength of esthetic preference is valid only for relative comparisons within the data of individual Ss; we would not expect the technique to yield values useful in comparing preferences between individuals.

Response Duration

In some studies of behavior we may find the duration of the response to be a more appropriate measurement than latency. Some investigations call for response time measurements to be taken for each of several components in a behavior sequence. The time occupied in making numerous adjustments on a panel of control knobs or switches, for example, has been fractionated into travel time from unit to unit and manipulation time occupied by the actual making of the control settings. In a rather different context, response time has often been used as an index of behavioral proficiency. We measure how long it takes a person to solve a problem, for example, under different conditions of instruction. You may be able to think of other instances where behavior is timed to provide an index of comparative skill.

Amount or Amplitude of Response

The amount of any behavior that occurs or the amplitude of a response that is made provides another sort of dependent variable. Amount of saliva secreted was an index of behavior in Pavlov's researches with dogs. The same measure has also been used in salivary conditioning studies employing human subjects. Other reflex types of response have also been commonly measured by their amount or amplitude. The patellar reflex, or knee jerk, is measured by the amount of kick produced or by the amount of thickening in the quadriceps muscle in the thigh. Pupillary constriction or dilation is indexed by the amount of change taking place in the pupil's diameter. This type of index, like temporal measures, is applicable in a great variety of situations. A psychologist might measure the amount of work done at a routine task in a specified time as a means of assessing the motivation of the subject.

Response Error

A special sort of behavioral measure that is useful in numerous situations is a measure of the amount by which a response is in error when there is some way of specifying what a perfect response would be. We are all familiar with this way of assessing proficiency in target shooting. The distance from the bull's-eye of any shot is the index of skill for that particular attempt. Error measurement is by no means confined to target shooting tasks. It is often used in describing perceptual performance where a setting of a stimulus which a subject makes is compared to a physical standard to determine the direction and size of error. This approach is used, for example, in assessing depth perception where S has to align a movable pin with a fixed reference pin. The error he makes is an index of his perception of distance under the particular conditions governing that trial. Another example of error measurement occurs in the study of time perception where S is required to estimate or to duplicate the passage of a period of time. In addition to the size of errors made in such a task, their sign—plus or minus—is an important measure indicating any tendency for the passage of the time period to be overestimated or underestimated.

Frequency of Response

A measure of widespread applicability in social science is the frequency of occurrence of a particular response in a given number of persons. An applied psychologist may wish to test the efficacy of two different advertising campaigns for the promotion of a product. After choosing two comparable cities, he runs one campaign in each city and then uses sales figures or consumer survey data to estimate the number of persons responding to each method of advertising. These data are a response frequency measure that is the dependent variable in this applied experiment. Frequency measures are commonly used in a variety of basic laboratory experiments also. For example, an experimenter may tally the number of Ss "voting" for each item in a study of esthetic preferences. In a different kind of investigation E may count the Ss who turn a crank clockwise when told to move a pointer to the right, comparing this number with the number of those who make a counterclockwise response. This sort of frequency measurement might be made for a number of different arrangements of the crank and the pointer which it controls.

Instead of counting the number of persons making a particular response, it is common, in other types of investigations, to count the number of responses of a certain sort made by each S over a series of trials. This type of frequency measure is commonly used in testing sensory or perceptual abilities to discriminate between stimuli. The question "How discriminable are two lines whose lengths differ by a specified amount?" becomes "How many times is the longer of the two lines actually reported as longer by the subject?" The frequency or per cent of correct responses, or of errors, is an index of the discrimination. This counting of the frequency of errors contrasts with size of error as a behavior measure.

Rate of Response

Still another measure of performance is a count of the number of occurrences of a response in a given amount of time. We see that this actually defines rate of response, commonly used as a behavioral index. Rate of response is a very appropriate measure of repetitive actions of a simple motor sort, like tapping. More complex perceptual-motor performance also lends itself to this index. It was employed, for example, to assess the acquisition of skill in a classical study of telegraphers' rates of sending and receiving of Morse code.

Complex Response Measures

Certain behavioral phenomena require more complex measurement techniques than the simple timing or counting of responses. As an example we may consider a conventional approach to measuring memory or retention of learned material. First E records the number of trials in the original session that each S requires to memorize the material, perhaps a list of words. Then after a lapse of a period of time, S is tested with the same list. If the retention interval has been long, it may be assumed that S remembers little of the list. He is therefore required to relearn the words. It should not require as many trials for mastery this time because S is aided by whatever he has retained from the original learning. The number of trials he saves in relearning, compared to original learning, is an index of his retention. Often the ratio of trials saved to trials originally needed is expressed as a per cent savings score.

The savings score, used to measure retention or memory, is just one example of the complex measuring techniques that psychologists have devised to meet their needs in assessing the dependent variables that they observe. We shall be considering special measurement methods in nearly every chapter of this book. Many of them, you will find, are elaborations of some of those we have listed here. In a few instances, specialized and interrelated methods of measurement or scaling have become so important as research tools that we devote entire chapters to them. We refer to Chapter 5, "Psychophysical Methods"; and Chapter 6, "Psychological Scaling."

Although there are several conventional measurement techniques in psychology as we have noted, research in this field rarely permits their application in stereotyped fashion. As you begin doing experiments you will find it necessary to adapt the methods to the problem under investigation. In this connection you will benefit from a knowledge of the fundamental measures we have reviewed and from an introduction to the philosophy of measurement or scaling which forms a part of Chapter 3, "Measurement and Statistics."

ASPECTS OF SCIENTIFIC METHOD

In discussing the manipulation of antecedent conditions and the measurement of behavior we have been proceeding toward our major goal—the understanding of experimentation as a means of formulating psychological laws.   Before we go further in our study of how experiments are designed and carried out, it is well to pause for a consideration of the scientific method in general.   Later we shall see that behavioral research involves special applications of this method.

The Scientific Method in Conventional Form

As usually outlined, the scientific method begins with observations that lead the scientist to formulate a tentative hypothesis.   Then the hypothesis is checked through further systematic observation.   It may be rejected as a result of such testing or it may be found tenable; very likely it will be found to require some modification or refinement. After reformulating his hypothesis the scientist again puts it to empirical or observational test.   We see that in its essence the scientific method does not necessarily require experimentation, just careful observation or measurement and precise description or formation of hypotheses to be tested.   No one ever did an experiment with the moons of Jupiter, but we have laws describing their motion.   Most applications of the scientific method, however, involve performing experiments.   Such an investigative technique involves isolation and control of a number of relevant independent variables and the measurement of dependent variables.

Laboratory Experiments and Field Observation

Laboratory studies have the great advantage over field observation that the scientist can exclude some factors and vary others systematically as the independent variables in the hypothesis he is testing. Further, he is in a position to measure the dependent variable accurately since he knows exactly which aspects of the phenomenon demand such quantitative description if the hypothesis is to be tested. In psychology, as in other disciplines of science, both field observation of events as they happen and laboratory experiments where responses are made to occur when and where the investigator wishes are each a useful expression of the scientific method.   In a field study an investigator might test the hypothesis that frustration leads to aggression by counting the number of fist fights in New Haven on a Saturday evening after Yale has just lost to Harvard.   Control data would come from the same city on another occasion when Yale had beaten Harvard (and after the Harvard rooters had left town). Our facetious example is perhaps realistic enough to hint at the many uncontrolled factors that make field studies a difficult path to the formulation of behavior laws.   Many excellent field studies have been done, however, and they have yielded valuable information about psychological processes. Having noted this, we devote the greater part of this textbook to considering the role that experimentation can play in contributing to our understanding of behavior.

Basic Processes of Scientific Method

At the heart of the scientific method are two related processes, observation and description, each complementary to the other. We shall see later that these processes are greatly refined when they are employed by scientific investigators, but we need to consider first their essential nature. Anything less than this fundamental approach may lead us to misidentify specific techniques in science as *the* scientific method. We said earlier that the aim of science is to formulate the relationships that occur regularly in natural phenomena. These formulations are essentially descriptive, and if they are to represent events faithfully they must be based on observation.

There seem to be many scientific workers whose work is primarily concerned with observation, others whose endeavors are principally descriptive. But even in a cooperative enterprise where the work is divided, the researcher who observes must describe, no matter how elementarily. And the scientist who describes must observe, however indirectly. The team approach to research depends greatly on communication. The observer reports his observations and this description constitutes the material to be "observed" by the scientist who will formulate the law. Modern science is a team effort on a grand scale. Some scientists are primarily engaged in theory construction, the ultimate in description. Others are primarily engaged in collecting data, making the observations which become the building stones employed by the theorist. Communication, the writing of scientific reports, is the all-important tie between these two kinds of worker.

REFINEMENTS OF OBSERVATION. Observation and description are no longer the simple processes that they were in the days of that pre-eminent natural scientist, Aristotle. Observational techniques have become refined and descriptive methods have been elaborated almost infinitely. Let us add the refinements and elaborations to the fundamental activities until modern science becomes recognizable. The first refinement of observation is repetition. If a phenomenon is observed only once it may be difficult to decide which aspects of it need to be described for inclusion in a statement of the law. Repeated observation permits the scientist to identify the essential elements in a situation and to ignore those which occurred only fortuitously. It may be important for observations to be repeated for the simple reason that sensory factors in the observer might distort a single observation. Such factors might be presumed not to affect observations that are repeated, especially after a lapse of time. Another important form taken by the repetition of observation is the checking of one scientist's perceptions by another, the assumption being that two or more observers minimize subjective sources of error that might bias a report made by one person. As our consideration of experimental methods unfolds we shall encounter still more reasons for making repeated observations.

A great aid to observation is the laboratory experiment. When we bring behavior into the laboratory we are putting it under the "microscope" of controlled conditions that enable us to examine it more closely than we could otherwise do. We exert control over at least a few of the antecedent conditions and place ourselves in the most advantageous position for viewing the resultant behavior. Like the user of the microscope we may first dissect the material we wish to examine; even behavior may be dissected. If we take behavior apart we may destroy some of the tissue of which it is composed, but the closer look that we gain should enable us to formulate more accurate descriptions of behavioral processes. From these we may construct a theory of behavior that might never have been created without the controlled analysis that laboratory research represents. Most of the chapters of this book are devoted to helping you learn to make the controlled analyses of behavior that we call psychological experiments. Even if you do not become a research worker, you will benefit by an understanding of how behavioral hypotheses are formulated and tested.

REFINEMENTS OF DESCRIPTION. Descriptive techniques in science, like observational methods, have been greatly improved since Aristotle's time. A primary advance in description occurs when scientists measure different aspects of the phenomena they study. We may briefly define measurement here as numerical description. The measurement of both independent variables, A, and dependent variables, B, is a necessary step in the establishing of functional relationships of the form $B = f(A)$ which represent mathematical descriptions. A verbal description could rarely approach the precision of such a quantitative formulation.

Closely related to measurement in sharpening description are the statistical methods the scientist employs in treating the data he collects. A multitude of measurements becomes a mean or a median and the scientist has effected a great economy in describing his findings. After calculating the standard deviation he may go on to estimate how precisely he can determine a value for the population mean. Certain statistical tests of data permit inferences to be drawn about behavior under different experimental conditions. Measures of behavior and their statistical analysis, then, are key parts of formulating behavior laws.

The growth of science has been characterized by another kind of refinement of description. Precise definition of terms has become almost synonymous with a scientific approach to a problem. Here, then, we have verbal techniques quite as useful as the numerical techniques of measurement. A law relating vaguely defined states or events is almost no law at all. Thinking about it for a moment you will see that careful definition of terms is necessary before we can test an hypothesis by collecting data.

Defining a term that is descriptive of behavior is a process of abstraction. The descriptive term is not the behavior itself; it is, rather, a verbal creation abstracted from the behavioral event, perhaps by specifying the way in which the behavior was observed and measured. These specifications may indicate that the term or concept is not very far removed from the behavior it represents. On the other hand, science is filled with concepts that represent a considerable degree of abstraction from the direct observations of phenomena that a scientist makes. We may cite, for example, such concepts as biological mutation, chemical valence, or the psychological concept of the IQ. The utility of these constructs in formulating hypotheses or laws is a tribute to the inventive daring of the scientists who are willing to let their descriptive enterprise range far from their direct observations. Observation and description remain the central processes of science but they are linked very flexibly. The development of abstract concepts from raw observational data is something that must be undertaken very carefully, with the rules of logic being rigorously followed. This process, a part of theory construction, is something that demands our further attention in Chapter 8, "Theory and Research."

The Design of Experiments

If we recall that the aim of research is to test an hypothesis which may be stated in the form "if A, then B" or in the form "$B = f(A)$," we can readily see that the essential requirements for conducting an experiment are to set up the antecedent conditions, A, and to measure the behavior, B, that occurs. The general plan for setting up a test of one or more hypotheses is called the *design* of the experiment. An investigator has considerable latitude in designing an experiment. Beyond this he may choose from a wide variety of special techniques to employ within the broad framework of the experimental design. We shall be learning many of the details of such techniques as they are used in psychological investigations. For example, we shall become acquainted with the psychophysical methods for assessing sensory and perceptual capacities of our laboratory subjects. We shall learn, too, of numerous ways of measuring memory as it is affected by different factors. Such specific study of technical methodology in experimental psychology will occupy entire chapters of this book. Here we must merely acquaint ourselves with some examples of designs of experiments.

SAMPLE DESIGNS BY STUDENT EXPERIMENTERS. Suppose that applied psychologists have formulated the hypothesis that listening to music will increase the amount of work that a typist can accomplish. Restated in our familiar form, this becomes: if music, then increased typing productivity. This might appear to be a simple hypothesis to test experimentally. It poses problems, however, that will serve to acquaint us with the difficulties of designing an experiment that will really accomplish its purpose. Let us first consider some faulty experimental designs; considerable benefit can be derived from a study of errors in research.

A student who wanted to test the hypothesis that music increases typing productivity enlisted fellow students as subjects and succeeded in borrowing enough typewriters to provide one for each subject. Apparently this experimenter was efficient in meeting some of the practical problems of doing research, but what of the experimental design he chose? Here is how he conducted the study. After assembling his Ss in the laboratory he instructed them to do as speedy and accurate a job of typing as possible. Then he had them type for 5 min, an interval which he measured very carefully. He collected their papers and then set them immediately to typing again, this time to the accompaniment of the lilting strains of "The Blue Danube." Collecting their papers again, he thanked them for their participation and hurried off to the nearest desk calculator to analyze the data. The results were most gratifying. He discovered that without music his subjects had averaged a mere 22.3 words per minute, whereas with the music their performance had increased to a healthy 31.7 words per minute. He concluded that his original hypothesis was tenable.

While the experiment we have just reviewed was being conducted, another student experimentalist was investigating the same hypothesis in a laboratory on a rival campus. His procedure was only slightly different. The initial performance of his Ss, without the music, lasted 30 min. After collecting their papers he immediately asked them to type again, this time with a stirring march blaring from the record player. When the data were analyzed, this E found the mean score to be 28.7 words per minute for the typing without music and only 24.1 words per minute with music. He reluctantly concluded that his original hypothesis must be rejected and went on, in fact, to formulate the hypothesis that music is detrimental to typing. Which experimenter was right?

There is considerable reason to suspect that neither student had adequately tested the original hypothesis and that both their conclusions were unjustified. The second student's result might have been due to the fatigue that his Ss experienced in the second half of an hour's typing. In his experimental design the music condition was confounded with the unintended fatigue condition. What might we suspect about the first experimenter's results? Even though the hypothesis was found tenable, the design of the first experiment may be criticized on similar grounds. In the first case, however, we might point to a warm-up effect that was confounded with the music in the second 5-min period. The superior scores may have been due to the Ss' becoming adjusted to the typing task rather than being attributable to the music.

A PROPER DESIGN OF THE EXPERIMENT. The faulty design of each of the experiments that we reviewed consisted in allowing other factors to co-vary with the condition that was specified in the hypothesis. When the hypothesis cites a particular independent variable, then that factor alone must be varied to determine its effect on the dependent variable. This is a fundamental principle of simple experimental design. Often it is difficult to apply directly, but in the present case we can readily suggest how the students might have taken it into account. They might have divided the available subjects into two groups, either randomly selected or equated on the basis of typing ability. The randomization or the equating of groups is something we shall discuss in a subsequent chapter.

Having established the two groups, E has one group perform the typing task over a moderate time interval to the accompaniment of music. This would conventionally be designated the *experimental* group since it was subjected to the experimental variable, music. The other group, typing without music, is called the *control* group because it serves as a control for all other variables, such as age, training in typing, and motivation, which might affect typing scores. A comparison of the scores made by the experimental and control groups should indicate if the music had affected productivity in typing.

Adopting this design for the experiment does not guarantee an adequate test of the hypothesis. There are many procedural errors which might be made. What might they be? What if one group had been tested in the middle of the morning and the other at four in the afternoon? Could this affect the results?

The hypothesis relating typing performance to music might be tested in experiments of several different designs. Although each of them might be appropriate, each would be likely to entail special procedural difficulties. There are several other faulty approaches to this investigation also, in addition to the two we examined. But additional consideration of good and poor designs for research studies will be deferred until our next chapter, in which we shall also examine some procedural details in psychological research.

OPPORTUNITIES IN PSYCHOLOGICAL RESEARCH

Psychology may be regarded as the newest of the major disciplines of science. Intensive scientific study of behavior began, as you probably know, about a century ago. Considerable progress has been made in formulating behavioral laws but, as is true in all of science, there is much more to be done. Facilities and trained research workers are not available in sufficient numbers to carry out needed study of many important and interesting problems.

Psychology is a discipline that should be particularly attractive to beginners in research. Although many studies require complicated techniques and elaborate instrumentation, there are some equally fascinating problems that may be attacked with far simpler methods. Simple procedures, however, must be supported by just as rigorous experimental design as more complex investigations require. Simple techniques must be very carefully administered, too, if they are to test adequately the desired hypothesis. If the research is conscientiously conducted, experiments performed by graduate students and by undergraduates may contribute importantly to our knowledge of behavioral processes.

It is as true in psychological research as elsewhere that we learn by doing. You will learn some of the many experimental skills by actually designing and conducting experiments. To supplement your practical experience the chapters of this book offer guidance and information. You will find a further discussion of behavior measurement in Chapter

3, along with the rules and formulas for the statistical analysis of experimental data. In Chapters 5 and 6 we shall learn about the employment of some scaling methods, psychophysical and psychological. In Chapter 7 you will find guidance in writing acceptable reports of experiments, the conventional forms that are employed in scientific communication. In many other chapters you will learn of special techniques applied to particular problems by examining some of the investigations that psychologists have conducted. Before we perform many experiments, we probably need to become more familiar with the essential aspects of laboratory research. We continue our mastery of fundamentals in Chapter 2, "Designing and Conducting Experiments."

SUMMARY

Psychology shares the general assumption and aim of science as it seeks to formulate laws which represent behavioral phenomena. The paradigm, if A, then B, serves as a model for any conditional statement which indicates the dependence of behavior, B, on antecedent conditions, A. The paradigm must be expanded to provide for multiple determinants and quantitative expression. The functional relationship may serve as an alternate model in many cases.

As the independent variables in hypotheses or laws about behavior, antecedent conditions may be classified as environmental factors or as states of the person whose responses are being studied. Variables in both of these classes may affect behavior, as an analysis of a study of reaction time showed. The two-part classification is not a rigid one; many experimental operations can be considered as manipulating either an environmental factor or a state of the person. Some research may not permit a particular variable to be manipulated but may call for the selection of subjects on some classified basis or the scaling of some aspect of an experimental situation.

Behavior measurements have been employed in wide variety to complete the formulation of psychological hypotheses and laws. A brief survey included response latency, duration, amplitude, and error. In addition to these possible aspects of a single response which might be measured, frequency or rate of making repeated responses were noted as additional behavior indices. Complex response measurement was illustrated by the savings score for retention, just one example of the many techniques of psychological assessment which are treated in later chapters.

An empirical or observational basis for hypotheses and laws was seen to be one aspect of scientific method. Field observation was recognized as a source of information, but laboratory experimentation will be stressed in this book. The process of observation is refined in the controlled situation of the laboratory and the description of behavior is sharpened by the techniques of measurement and statistics which may be used. The careful definition of abstract terms was also noted as a refinement of description.

To the basic processes of observation and description we added proper experimental design as a requirement of useful experimentation. Improperly designed student experiments were seen to lead to erroneous interpretation and to permit no firm conclusion at all. An appropriate design or plan for investigating the hypothesis was seen to involve testing two groups of subjects instead of giving two treatments consecutively to just one group of subjects.

Many opportunities exist in psychological research for those who will make the effort to master fundamentals. Even the simplest of techniques must be carefully administered in combination with good research design if valid conclusions are to be reached. This book offers guidance and information to the student of experimental psychology, but the learning of research methods will be completed only through actual practice.

ADDITIONAL READINGS

Brown, C. W., & Ghiselli, E. E. *Scientific method in psychology.* New York: McGraw-Hill, 1955.

Kaufmann, F. *Methodology of the social sciences.* New York: Oxford, 1944.

CHAPTER 2

Designing and Conducting Experiments

Just as psychology shares the aims and general methods of other disciplines of science, we shall see that it also involves some of the major aspects of experimentation. In behavior study these include setting up certain controlled conditions and measuring some selected aspect of the behavior exhibited by the subjects. Within this format, of course, procedural details may vary greatly.

You may have had experience as a subject in a psychological study. This may have given you some acquaintance with the experimenter's giving of instructions, presenting stimulus material, and requiring some specified performance. All these phases of conducting research may be readily apparent to participants. The design or plan of the study may not be as easily discerned, however, by the individual subject. Both designing and conducting experiments occupy us in this chapter. The many special technicalities that we must crowd into subsequent chapters will prevent much reiteration of the general rules that we shall consider here, so master them now and retain them for use in the studies you will be carrying out.

THE HYPOTHESIS GUIDES THE EXPERIMENTAL DESIGN

To design an experiment is to plan just how the hypothesis is to be tested. As one of the creative activities of the scientist, the designing of a study can be even more fun than conducting it. We see evidence of this when professors design research but let their graduate assistants work to carry it out.

It may appear in some investigations that there is no hypothesis at all. The investigator may be unwilling to predict what the effect is expected to be. We should note, however, that he is usually betting his time and somebody's money that there will *be* an effect. It is *this* consideration that leads us to assert that *all* experiments test hypotheses. The assertion is made with full knowledge that there are vast differences in how the hypotheses are generated, how precisely they are stated, and how adequately they are tested. The hypothesis to be tested, whether formally worded or not, is an important determiner of many parts of the experimental plan that is chosen.

Sources of Hypotheses

We initiate our study of experimental design by considering where we get hypotheses which may be a starting point for one or more investigations.

PAST RESEARCH. Science is a growing enterprise. The results of one investigation raise many problems and suggest numerous hypotheses for testing. Current investigations are motivated by past findings and are often possible only because of contributions to knowledge achieved through past discoveries. A research worker need never lack for problems to investigate if he will keep in close touch with the literature in his field.

FIELD OBSERVATIONS. In behavioral science as well as in other disciplines it is possible for laws to be formulated on the basis of observations made outside the laboratory. An observer might be stationed at a street intersection, for example, to record the actions of motorists and pedestrians under different traffic conditions. He might see in his data on behavior in rush hour traffic a principle that could be stated quite broadly: "Frustration leads to aggression." This hypothesis has actually been advanced and experimentally tested by psychologists. Here we are merely imagining that it might have first arisen in our traffic survey. Had this been the case, a possible step would be to take this formulation from the field situation to the laboratory. Stated broadly, it is not limited to traffic jams as the source of frustration nor to the honking of automobile horns as the aggressive behavior. Some situation that we create in the laboratory may qualify as frustrating and get us started on testing the hypothesis.

PRACTICAL PROBLEMS. Topics for investigation in the behavior laboratory may arise in a somewhat different way. Hypotheses may be generated from problems which confront applied psychologists. Faced with the problem of dial-reading errors by aircraft pilots, the applied psychologist may hypothesize that numerals designed for their legibility would reduce the frequency of such errors. Testing this hypothesis under field conditions, that is, by installing new instruments in aircraft to be tested in actual operations, would be very costly. Instead, having formed his hypothesis as the "best guess" answer to a practical problem, the psychologist could test it in a laboratory experiment. Such an investigation might be an applied study and, at the same time, contribute importantly to fundamental knowledge about such a process as perception.

THEORY. A theory may be defined as a set of stated interrelationships among measurable variables and abstract concepts that are indirectly defined in terms of observations or measurements. From the broader formulations which appear in a theory it is often possible to generate specific theorems by deduction. In science we do not rely on the rigor of the deductive logic to assure us of the tenability of the deduced theorem or hypothesis but we go on to put it to empirical test. We are not testing our powers of logical reasoning, of course. What we are testing indirectly is the broad generalization from which the deduction was made.

Kinds of Hypotheses

Perhaps the simplest sort of hypothesis is one that states that a particular independent variable or condition will have an effect on behavior without stating the magnitude of the effect or even its direction. For example, consider the hypothesis that music affects studying. Some students maintain it helps them to study; others maintain that it is a distraction that hampers concentration. If someone neutral in the controversy were to try to resolve it by research, then he might formulate the hypothesis, at least implicitly, that music does have an effect on studying without stating whether the effect would be helpful or detrimental.

It is far commoner to undertake an experiment with some notion as to the direction of the effect that will occur than it is to seek an effect with no expectation of its direction. Most experiments, in other words, are tests of predictions. The prediction states whether the effect of a condition on performance will be facilitating or inhibiting; it may omit stating the expected magnitude of the effect.

A prediction that an effect will occur is given greater specificity when the magnitude of the effect is also stated. Such a quantitative prediction is usually possible only when the scientist has a considerable body of related research or a fairly well established theory to use as the basis for a quantified hypothesis. With such a basis for prediction he may go beyond the mere specifying of a value of an expected effect;

he may predict a functional relationship or mathematical curve that will describe the relationship between independent and dependent variables.

The Formulation of Hypotheses for Testing

If the purpose of every experiment is to test an hypothesis, then the way in which the investigation is conducted is going to depend on how the hypothesis is stated. Indeed, the way in which it is stated may determine whether it can be tested experimentally at all. Since the design of the study depends rather closely on how the hypothesis is structured, we shall be learning much about the design of experiments as we examine the formulation of hypotheses.

It would be well if we were able to read a number of reports of experiments to see how the hypotheses were stated so that we could keep them in mind as models for our own research. In the journal articles reporting psychological studies, however, we find that a considerable part of the forming of the hypothesis is done implicitly. Usually there will be an explicit statement of the problem under investigation that indicates the major aspect of the hypothesis, but other facets of the hypothesis may be left unsaid, to be revealed only in the design or plan of the experiment. Rather than try to identify implicit features of hypotheses that are hidden among procedural details, let us try to make explicit the different aspects of hypotheses. A considered approach to the formulating of hypotheses will lead us to the design of better experiments.

SPECIFICITY. To be testable an hypothesis must be stated quite specifically. How could we test the hypothesis that students loaf too much? *Students loaf too much* is an hypothesis which contains, unfortunately, three terms that are not specific enough to permit the formulation to be tested. These terms are: "students," "loaf," and "too much." Do we mean high school students or college students? If college students, do we mean those on this campus, or those less fortunate who attend elsewhere? What do we mean by loaf? Is this what is meant by college-bred, made with father's dough? And how much loafing is too much loafing? This is a value judgment in essence, not subject to experimental testing. So much for one ill-fated hypothesis.

Let us turn now to a more seriously offered hypothesis, one which is stated extremely broadly: "The existence of frustration always leads to some form of aggression" (Dollard, Doob, Miller, Mowrer, & Sears, 1939, p. 1). Despite the generality of its phrasing, this hypothesis is unequivocal in stating that aggressive behavior will always follow frustration. We are offered wide latitude in setting up a frustrating situation and there are numerous forms of aggression, the occurrence of which would confirm the hypothesis. In addition to experimental testing, we might seek to verify this formulation through field observation—looking for frustrating situations and noting whether they lead to aggression.

We have stated that hypotheses must be specific to be tested, yet we have just been suggesting that one formulated in the broadest of terms is testable. How do we resolve this apparent contradiction? Its resolution lies in the fact that prior to its actual testing the general formulation must be reduced to specific terms. Situations must be sought that can be acceptably defined as frustrating, and there must be agreement as to kinds of behavior that are encompassed by the term "aggression." The authors who offered this hypothesis provided definitions and examples of these key terms which offered guidance to anyone wishing to verify the statement empirically (Dollard et al., 1939).

PRACTICALITY. It is possible for a formulation to be stated quite specifically yet in such a way as to defy empirical test for practical reasons. We are not likely to find such a statement in the experimental literature, so let us make one up: Eighty per cent of psychotic patients would show improvement in three months if taken out of institutions and placed in private homes. Stated with reasonable specificity, this hypothesis is testable in principle but its testing in actual practice would encounter great difficulty. The statement may be rephrased, however, to permit practical experimentation without doing violent injustice to the original formulation: If placed in a homelike atmosphere, given extended satisfaction of affiliative needs and some of the experiences of family life, 80 per cent of psychotic patients would show improvement in three months. Even though it contains a degree of compromise, this statement, if confirmed experimentally within the institutional setting, would offer support to the first hypothesis which we judged to be practically untestable.

IDENTIFICATION OF THE POPULATION. Some hypotheses about behavior are intended to apply to practically all living creatures. *Frustration leads to aggression* is a formulation that has been tested with both human and animal subjects. Within the human species its applicability is assumed, of course, for children and adults, for both sexes, for every IQ level, *etc.*

More common in psychology are hypotheses that apply only to a particular group—preschool children or white rats or college students. A group identifiable by specified characteristics is often called a *population.* It is the population to be included in a formulation that must be specified if the hypothesis is to be considered complete. Often the population to which an hypothesis refers is not specifically stated but is identified implicitly in the statement offered. If the hypothesis is a tentative law that concerns verbal behavior, for example, we may assume that human beings are considered to be the population although the legalistic among us might demand to know if talking birds were to be included or not. Hypotheses about verbal learning are usually offered without placing age limits on the intended population although obviously a principle that governs the memorizing of a poem is not assumed to apply to a lisping two-year-old of very limited vocabulary.

One fault that sometimes has been noted in research is not very different in principle from the foregoing example. Investigators on the campus occasionally have seemed to assume that the college sophomore was an appropriate representative of the human race for purposes of psychological research. With no disparagement of sophomores intended, we may join those who gently suggest that this may not be so. The college student differs demonstrably from the general population in IQ, in sensory and motor abilities, and in patterns of motivation and attitude. Thus, hypotheses that purport to be generalizations about people in general are not adequately tested with college students as subjects. We must quickly add that there are numerous areas of research where information about the reaction of college students can be used to formulate principles whose wider applicability cannot be doubted.

We should be careful to notice that our insistence on identification of the population to which an hypothesis applies is not a special condition that we are imposing on the hypothesis from outside, as it were. The specifying of the population is an important part of the conditional clause of the hypothesis when it is stated in complete form. *If a ten-word list is memorized to the point of one perfect recitation, 4.8 words will be retained one week later* is stated more adequately when we expand the conditional clause to read . . . *memorized by college sophomores.* . . . Reports of research do not often include specific reference to the pertinent population in a formal statement but the population is implied in some way, even if only in the description of the group of subjects used in the study.

OPERATIONAL DEFINITION OF TERMS. Let us examine an hypothesis that might be offered for experimental testing by a college junior proposing an original research project in experimental psychology: *Environmental noise decreases hand steadiness.* Rephrased in *If-then* form, it becomes: *If there is noise in the environment, then subjects' hands will be less steady than under quiet conditions.* In proposing this hypothesis for test, the experimenter probably has something more specific in mind than he has revealed in stating the hypothesis. At least we hope he has. There are many questions we would want to ask before approving his project. His answers need to be incorporated in a more specific framing of the hypothesis. Central in our questioning would be these two queries: What do you mean by noise? and what do you mean by hand steadiness?

In asking for a definition of the independent variable, noise, and the dependent variable, hand steadiness, we want more than mere verbal description. We want specifications of the operations we would have to perform to test this experimenter's hypothesis to his satisfaction. In other words, we want *operational definitions* of the key terms in the hypothesis. When we ask "What kind of noise?" we cannot be satisfied with the reply, "A loud noise." We want detailed instructions as to what sound source is to be used and what the loudness level and duration of the noise must be. Similarly, we want detailed guidance as to the operations to be performed in measuring the hand steadiness of the subjects. Is there some standard test for hand steadiness that can be administered according to prescribed procedures? Or will the student devise some special technique for assessing steadiness in this research? What, precisely, are the operations to be used in quantifying hand steadiness?

In reported psychological research it is common to find that the hypothesis purportedly being tested is stated in very general terms as in the example we have just been discussing. The experimenter relies on his description of the procedure employed to inform the reader of the report just what operational definition he gives to the terms he used in his statement of the problem. Thus the report of the study may involve two hypotheses—the one stated in very broad terms and the one tested with specific techniques. If the latter hypothesis is confirmed, the experimenter sometimes makes the mistake of discussing the outcome of the investigation as if the broadly stated relationship had been explored thoroughly and found to hold true. The conclusions reported should reflect the particular relationship tested, not the general relationship which the study sought to explore partially. Extrapolations or generalizations may be offered, but this should be done with a recognition of the need for further testing. To avoid the danger of overgeneralizing from specific tests, a good rule is to state the hypothesis specifically in the first place, defining each term operationally.

ADDITIONAL ASSUMPTIONS. Earlier, we recognized that a behavioral event has many determinants. To state it differently, any measure of behavior is a function of many independent variables. When a simple hypothesis is proposed for experimental testing by the manipulation of a single variable, numerous assumptions are being made about the action of other variables which could affect performance. It should be recognized that these assumptions are being tested concurrently with the major hypothesis that was proposed for verification. For example, in testing the formulation that hand steadiness is affected by noise in the environment, we make the assumption, without stating it, that the level of illumination provided in the laboratory is adequate for the visually guided performance of the steadiness test.

Other assumptions, often unknowingly incorporated in an experimental design, may not be so harmless. In testing the effect of noise on steadiness, an experimenter might assume that it did not matter whether the subjects had been smoking just before the experiment. If negative results were obtained, it might not be due to the untenability of the noise hypothesis but to the untenability of the assumption that smoking has no effect on hand steadiness.

DESIGNING THE EXPERIMENT

As we have seen, the complete formulation of an hypothesis goes a long way toward suggesting how an experiment should be carried out to test it. The hypothesis tends to dictate several important aspects of the investigation, but some equally important questions about the design of the experiment must be answered by the experimenter on other grounds. After examining the design problem from both viewpoints—dictation by the hypothesis and decision by the experimenter—we shall go on to suggest some guiding factors that should help an investigator in his planning.

Factors Dictated by the Hypothesis

SUBJECTS. Hypotheses about behavior may be so broadly formulated that they seem applicable to a wide variety of possible experimental subjects. When an hypothesis is made more specific in order to put it to a test, however, part of the narrowing process will be to specify the population to which it applies. In reports of studies you may read, you may not find reference to a particular population or group of subjects in the stated hypothesis or problem. A description elsewhere in the report of the groups of subjects used may be regarded as an extension of the statement of the problem.

INDEPENDENT VARIABLES. An hypothesis contains an identification of one or more independent variables which must be manipulated in conducting the experiment. The independent variable may be just a single dimension of stimulus material to be presented to the subject. For example, we might think of the hypothesis that if advertisements are colored, as opposed to black and white, they will be remembered better. A student experimenter is free to choose the size of advertisement used, even to using a variety of sizes, but he *must* use the colored and the black and white material as dictated by the hypothesis. Whatever decision he makes as to size becomes a part of the hypothesis that his experimental design is testing whether he consciously reformulates it or not.

DEPENDENT VARIABLES. The statement of an hypothesis will usually indicate, at least in general terms, what the dependent variable in an experimental test will have to be. The experimenter may have considerable leeway, though, in deciding just what measures of performance to take and how they are to be taken. Consider the hypothesis that the level of room illumination affects typing speed. Try to decide what you would regard as an appropriate measure of "typing speed." You might, for example, decide on the number of words typed from standard copy in 3 min as a good index of typing speed. Would you impose a penalty for errors? Would a 10-min session be preferable to a 3-min test? What effect might this have on the results you obtained? We see that the operational definition that we give to typing speed adds specificity to the formulation we are testing. We might even get negative results on the specific hypothesis under test, whereas the general hypothesis is still tenable if interpreted in a slightly different way. We must exercise great care in designing an experiment to avoid testing a generally phrased hypothesis inadequately because of our faulty translation of its terms into operational definitions.

Factors Decided by the Experimenter

GROUPING OF SUBJECTS AND CONDITIONS. Consider the commonly encountered experiment where the effects on behavior of two different conditions, or two values of the independent variable, are to be compared. A key problem is whether to administer the two conditions to the same group of subjects or to separate groups. In the first case, the score that a person makes under one condition can be compared with his score under the other condition or treatment. The comparing of group average scores made under each condition is possible too, of course. In a second possible design, where an individual is given only one of the two treatments, the comparison of a person with himself is impossible, naturally, and the comparison of group averages constitutes the usual test of the hypothesis that the two treatments affected performance differentially.

A third possibility for grouping the subjects for the different treatments is to give a preliminary test that is related to the performance under investigation and then to match persons in equivalent pairs on the basis of scores made. Then members of each pair are assigned, one to each treatment group, at random. Now, although each person receives just one of the two treatments, it is still possible to compare individual scores, within matched pairs, to find out more about the effect of the treatments, perhaps, than would be revealed by merely comparing group averages. We might discover, for example, that two treatments were more potent in separating the higher scoring subjects than in their effect on the low scorers. Such a finding would not have been possible had the subjects not been pretested and assigned to matched pairs.

VALUES OF ADDITIONAL VARIABLES. Besides the experimental variable whose manipulation is largely dictated by the hypothesis under test, there are many other variables in an experimental situation that may take on particular values at the discretion of the experimenter. To illustrate the handling of additional variables let us consider a study of the hypothesis that under short-exposure viewing geometrical grouping of dots makes their number more perceptible than random arrangement does. The geometrically grouped dots and some randomly arranged dots might be located on different slides for projected presentation in brief exposures of about a twenty-fifth of a second to a classroom group of subjects. The measure of performance taken in such studies is often the per cent of subjects correctly identifying the number of dots projected under each stimulus condition. While the grouping or random arrangement of the dots constitutes the independent variable in this investigation, there are several additional variables that may be considered intimately related to these since they are also dimensions of the stimulus presentation. These related variables include the number of dots chosen for the test, the brightness contrast at the projection screen, the portion of the visual field occupied by the stimulus material, and the exposure time. All these might possibly affect performance and the test of the hypothesis.

There are several possible ways of dealing with a variable that is not involved directly in the test of the hypothesis. Such a variable may be held constant, it may be assigned a series of particular values, or it may be allowed to vary at random. For example, in our illustrative experiment the number of dots placed on different slides might range in a series from about five to about twenty-five. The brightness contrast might be held constant at a fixed value. The visual field might be permitted to vary at random in accordance with the distance of each subject from the screen. The exposure time might be held at a particular value determined in preliminary research, or several values might be used as the slides were repeatedly employed in an increasing series of exposure times. An investigator must make choices from among many such procedural possibilities.

A variable in our illustrative experiment which might affect perform- ance even though it is not closely associated with the independent variable would be room temperature. This might or might not be controllable by the experimenter, depending on the weather and the whims of the boys in the boiler room. (An air-conditioned, tempera- ture-controlled psychology laboratory cannot be promised to every college at this time.) Over a considerable range, temperature would not be likely to affect perceptual performance. An uncomfortably warm room might make the subjects less motivated, however, thus reducing the number of correct perceptions they would achieve.

NUMBER OF TRIALS OR DURATION OF TREATMENTS. Except for experi- ments on special problems like fatigue, the statement of a problem will rarely dictate a procedural detail like how many trials should be given to the subjects. The decision about the number of trials or the duration of any continuous treatment needs to be made by the experi- menter on the basis of what is known about the behavior under investi- gation. Some general principles should be kept in mind. First, the session should be long enough to permit the independent variable to have an effect on the dependent variable. Second, performance should be measured often enough or over a long enough period of time to obtain a reliable assessment. Third, a session should not be so long as to permit unwanted fatigue or boredom to affect performance.

How would these principles govern the design of an experiment to determine the effect of room illumination on performance on a test of finger dexterity where the subject has to place small pegs in the holes of a pegboard? Suppose we were to give one trial of 10 sec duration under each of three levels of illumination. Such a brief trial under the lowest illumination might not be long enough to develop the eyestrain that might be typical of more prolonged per- ceptual-motor effort. The results of the experiment might thus be negative merely because the conditions were operative too briefly. In addition to providing little opportunity for the independent variable to take effect, such a brief trial would permit an uncontrolled factor like a momentary distraction of the subject to play too great a role in determining the score. In a much longer trial uncontrolled factors tend to cancel each other; a momentary heightening of motivation might be balanced by a momentary lapse of attention. Longer trials thus yield a more reliable measure of the effect of the variables that are being tested. However, trials can obviously be made too long. If we tried to keep subjects at the task in this experiment for 30 min under each condition, we would encounter a rebellion that would be likely to invalidate the results completely. Even when subjects are not moved to protest openly, their performance is likely to suffer and to detract from the effectiveness of the experiment. A compromise is evidently needed between samples of performance that are too brief and sessions that are too long.

The duration of the measured or observed performance that is required of subjects is something that must be determined after a consideration of all that can be known about the behavior in question. No duration of trials can be suggested that will be appropriate for all investigations. A rule of some general applicability, however, is to divide the gathering of performance data into several trials instead of using just one. The intertrial rest periods will help to stave off the development of fatigue or boredom, and a trial-to-trial comparison of performance scores will help later to detect any change in performance that did occur during the session.

METHOD OF STIMULUS PRESENTATION. Several kinds of psychological research call for particular kinds of stimulus material, like words or geometric designs, but do not dictate any particular way in which these have to be presented to the subjects. This is left to the discretion of the experimenter. The stimuli may be projected on the screen or may be printed in booklets, to be studied by an entire group of subjects at once. Or the subjects may be run individually with the stimuli presented on cards or by means of special exposure devices. It might seem that the techniques to deliver the stimulation to subjects should be chosen merely on the basis of practical considerations. These, of course, are important. In emphasizing the design of the experiment, however, we need to point out that the technical means selected for stimulus presentation must be scrutinized for any effect it may have on the subjects' performance. If slides were so smudged by fingerprints as to obscure projected words or if a memory drum shutter were so noisy as to make subjects jump, then optimal performance could hardly be expected.

MATERIALS TO BE USED. The statement of an hypothesis may dictate the selection of stimulus material with respect to one of its dimensions.

This specification may still permit the experimenter a wide choice of particular materials to be employed in a study. In making that choice he must consider other dimensions of the stimulus materials as they may affect performance. As an example we may take the hypothesis that nouns, since they often represent objects which may be visualized, are more easily memorized than are verbs. It might seem that the experimenter merely has to draw up a list of twenty nouns and a list of twenty verbs in order to prepare to test this hypothesis. We must realize, however, that words have other dimensions besides their part of speech, like noun or verb. Words differ in length and they differ in familiarity or frequency of usage. For this experiment we need a list of nouns and list of verbs that are equivalent on these dimensions, which could conceivably affect ease of learning.

An experimenter must also employ enough stimulus items to be sure of accurately representing the population of stimulus material identified in the hypothesis. The process of choosing the items must be safeguarded against the introduction of bias which might take place unknowingly. A useful rule is to draw up a long list of items that meet the specifications and then to select from the list at random the smaller number of items needed in the study.

MEASUREMENT OF THE RESPONSE. The dependent variable identified in the hypothesis determines the measure of behavior that is taken in a psychological experiment. If the hypothesis states that the experimental conditions will affect speed of response, then response speed will naturally have to be measured. If accuracy is indicated as the dependent variable, then accuracy of response must be measured. There are detailed questions about the index of behavior to be employed, however, that the hypothesis in its broad original form would probably not answer. If typing speed is the performance measure, should a warm-up or practice period be given before the actual data of the study are taken? To what extent should the occurrence of error be penalized by subtracting from the score? The experimenter must answer questions like these on the basis of the best information available to him. In deciding on particular procedures for response measurement, he must realize that he may be making implicit changes in the hypothesis that is actually being tested and he must satisfy himself that this is the specific experimental test that he actually wishes to make.

An important principle in behavior measurement is that the measuring technique must not interfere unduly with the response being measured. We must exercise care in how many threads and recording wires we attach to a subject who is performing the task that is under study. Suppose that we wish to determine whether a person can move his right hand more quickly to the right or to the left in moving a sliding control knob along a horizontal metal bar. An excess amount of friction between the slider and the bar would naturally slow down the motion and make subjects appear to be somewhat slow. We probably would try to minimize friction, then, but it cannot be eliminated completely.

Once friction had been minimized, we would no longer consider it to interfere with the response. Rather, it becomes part of our operational definition of the response that we are measuring. However, if the friction were unequal for right and left movements of the slider on the bar we would consider it an unwanted distortion of the response measures being taken. This sort of distortion would bias the outcome of the experiment whereas equal frictions in each direction would not.

Guides to the Experimenter

Designing an experiment is a creative activity. The designing of a study is one of the points at which a sort of artistic endeavor is found in science. Perhaps it would be more correct to say that planning an experiment calls for inventive ingenuity. Artist or inventor, you will probably need all the help you can get when you face the problem of just how to go about testing a behavioral hypothesis in the laboratory. Let us consider, then, some of the guides that may help you and some of the practical considerations that may be a limiting influence as you carry out the design phase of an investigation.

PAST RESEARCH ON THE SAME PROBLEM. It sometimes happens that an investigator will wish to study further a problem which has already been studied before. In your reading in textbooks, handbooks, and psychology journals you will encounter many hypotheses which may have been partially confirmed by experimentation but which deserve further exploration. When an experimenter decides to test a generally stated hypothesis in a specific study he will usually find that there have been previous experiments testing the same broad hypothesis with techniques somewhat different than those he intends to use. These previous studies are a great help in the designing of his investigation.

Reports of any such prior studies should be read very carefully before undertaking the designing of an experiment. They will contain suggestions that are pertinent to many aspects of the design problem: sharpening the hypothesis, operationally defining the variables, planning administrative procedures, and measuring the responses. Special attention should be paid to any difficulties in conducting the study that may be mentioned. Avoiding the mistakes made in earlier research calls for inventive ingenuity. Our challenge is to design ever better experiments.

DETERMINANTS OF THE BEHAVIOR BEING STUDIED. In addition to past research which was aimed at testing very similar hypotheses, studies which identify some of the determinants of the behavior in question provide valuable guidance in designing an experiment. We have seen that there are many variables that may affect performance besides the ones that are designated as the independent variables in a study. How will these other variables affect the responses that the subjects make? Past studies where these responses were measured under a variety of experimental conditions should provide some answers.

Suppose we wanted to test the effect of high environmental temperature on the learning of a list of words. We may have decided that we ought to keep our volunteer subjects in the overheated experimental chamber for only about five minutes. Should we give them a ten-word list or a hundred-word list to memorize? To answer the question we would hope to find a research report which would indicate the time taken to learn lists of different lengths with the same method of presenting the words as we propose to use. Such data would enable us to select a list of appropriate length for our purposes. As often as not, we do not find the precise information we are seeking in the research literature. We find experimental results that are of some relevance, however, and from these we deduce the answers we need.

INFORMATION ON BEHAVIORAL PROCESSES. When an experimenter provides for an experimental session of sufficient duration to yield reliable data on the behavior being studied, he must be aware that the measures he obtains may be affected by factors arising out of the performance itself. During a long session scores may improve due to learning or they may deteriorate due to fatigue. Of course, some kinds of performance are more susceptible to one factor, others to another. Repetitive tapping with a stylus on a metal plate, for example, would not be expected to benefit much from learning, but it would definitely show a drop in rate as fatigue set in. Solving a series of puzzles based on a similar principle might exhibit a learning effect but would probably not evidence much fatigue. Some tasks, like sorting numbered cards into a sorting tray, would be subject to both learning and fatigue effects operating concurrently, with one possibly outweighing the other.

Assuming that he does not want to study the learning or fatigue processes themselves, an experimenter must nevertheless consider what their effects on performance may be. Considering the problem of learning, he must formulate the hypothesis he is testing so as to indicate clearly whether it applies to subjects who have had little practice at the task or to highly skilled persons. One possible way of handling the problem of learning is to give all subjects enough pre-liminary practice so that they have reached their peak performance before the experiment proper is begun. In recognition of a possible fatigue problem, an experimenter must plan a work and rest schedule which will reveal and not obscure the influence of his independent variable. Procedures may be planned to minimize the development of fatigue by giving liberal rest intervals to the subjects.

Another common way of dealing with learning or fatigue is to take repeated measurements during a session so that the occurrence of these processes in the performance can be studied in the data along with the effects of the independent variable which was of primary interest in the investigation. The effects of this major variable may thus be studied at different stages of practice, a desirable feature of many well-designed experiments.

STATISTICAL ANALYSIS OF THE DATA. The statistical analysis which he intends to apply to the data he collects is an important consideration for the experienced investigator when he is designing an experiment. To the novice the data, or response measures taken, are too often something to be considered only after the study is all over. At that point it is too late to amend the study to provide the data that are now seen to be necessary for an adequate test of the hypothesis. The experi-menter should have carefully examined the research problem, and the plan of the study while he was designing it, to see if the data he pro-posed to collect would bear on the hypothesis when they were statisti-cally analyzed.

PRACTICAL CONSIDERATIONS. As in all the affairs of this world, practi-cal considerations loom large when we attempt to design an experi-ment. We need to realize that trying different solutions to the practical problems of an investigation actually changes the specific hypothesis which will be tested. We must be ingenious enough to get around practical procedural difficulties without jeopardizing the test of the hypothesis that is our goal.

DESIGN PROBLEMS IN A
REPRESENTATIVE EXPERIMENT

We have used varied examples to illustrate some of the problems encountered in designing experiments. We have discussed other aspects of experimental design without benefit of illustration. At this point it would be well to consider a single experiment, noting how different problems may be treated as we attempt to formulate a precise hypothesis and to test it. Many of these problems will have been mentioned before. We shall see how these might be solved in this particular experiment, and we shall introduce a few new thoughts about experimental design as well. The experiment that we may take as our model will be one to determine the effect of environmental noise on memorizing verbal material.

Formulating the Hypothesis

DEFINING "ENVIRONMENTAL NOISE." Our designing of this experiment begins when we decide on an operational definition of noise. Should we play symphonic music? Should we turn the radiators on and off to provide a cacophony of hissing and banging? Since we are not suggesting that this noisy investigation actually be carried on, we need not arrive at a firm decision. We know that the kind of noise and the sound level at which it is played need to be specified.

DEFINING "VERBAL MATERIAL." Shall we have subjects memorize a poem? A prose passage? A list of Turkish words? A list of English words? Numerous considerations might guide our selection of the material. Poems might be considered too likely to be familiar to some of the subjects. A list of Turkish words might call more for problem-solving behavior on how they should be spelled than for rote memorization. Suppose we decide on a list of English words. Several questions still need to be answered. We need to decide on such dimensions of this verbal task as the length of list and the familiarity level of the words included. We must make these decisions in the full knowledge that the specific hypothesis then being tested may be somewhat narrower than the one stated at the outset. We can only extrapolate tentatively beyond the narrow conclusions that the study enables us to reach directly. If we desire to arrive at broader conclusions, we would have to broaden the experiment accordingly.

DEFINING "MEMORIZING." It might seem that "memorizing" should hardly need defining by anyone undertaking psychological research. Yet there are numerous ways in which we could have subjects attempt a memory task and several methods by which we could measure their performance. We must cite these details as a means of operationally defining what we mean by memorization in this study. We need to state, for example, whether the words will be projected individually on a screen or presented as a complete list printed on paper. These are but two of the many modes of presentation we might employ.

How shall we test the memorization accomplished by the subjects? Shall we ask them to write down as many words as they can recall or shall we have them check as many as they recognize in a much longer list of words? These might seem to be mere procedural details which might well be settled arbitrarily, but the needed decisions should be made with as much knowledge gleaned from earlier research as possible.

DESCRIBING THE POPULATION. The odds are great that the subjects in our experiment will be college students. The group will be restricted as to age range and range of IQ. They may or may not be experienced in rote verbal learning. Whatever the characteristics of the subject group, the conclusions that we reach in the experiment will be applicable rigorously only to the population of which this group may be considered a sample. Thus subjects, too, are part of the design of our study.

ASSUMPTIONS. When we conduct this experiment we shall have to assume that the instructions we give subjects to memorize the words will motivate them in this task. If we administer a different list of words under each condition—a noisy and a quiet environment—to the same group of subjects, we shall have to assume that the lists are equally difficult to learn. If we use two different groups of subjects, one under each condition, we must assume that the two groups do not differ significantly from each other. Possibly we may be quite confident of the tenability of these several assumptions. They could technically be regarded, though, as being under test along with the main hypothesis. If two groups are used and significantly different scores are made under noisy and quiet conditions, we may conclude that these conditions affected performance differentially or we *could* conclude that the groups differed in their memorizing abilities. We can conclude that the conditions were responsible for the difference only if we are willing to *assume* that there was no significant difference in learning skill between the groups.

Universal Aspects of Design

We have seen that particular attention must be given to specific aspects of every hypothesis that is proposed for experimental testing. We shall also see that each new experiment involves its own procedural problems. There are, however, some features of design that will be found in almost every psychological experiment employing human subjects. We shall identify these in the context of our experiment testing the effect of environmental noise on verbal memorization.

INSTRUCTIONS TO INFORM AND MOTIVATE. Having assembled a group of willing subjects we would begin our study by instructing them as to their task. As we inform them that they will be presented with verbal material to memorize we will also be motivating them. Simply assigning a task is, in our culture, something of a challenge for people to perform it to the best of their ability. We should probably find it unnecessary to offer any special inducements to the subjects, although money bonuses and other rewards are occasionally used in psychological research.

It might seem a very simple thing to tell people to learn a list of words, but student experimenters have been known to make serious mistakes with even this elementary aspect of a study. Should subjects be told to memorize the list of words in the order of presentation? Should they be informed as to how and when their memory is to be tested? How we answer questions like these may affect the achievement levels of our subjects. We should therefore give great thought to the instructions, preparing them in writing and delivering them verbatim to the groups participating. It is obviously quite important for the success of any study that the subjects know exactly what is expected of them. We cannot afford to discard data because instructions were not understood. Besides clarity of expression, good instructions will usually include enough repetition of key points to insure that each participant knows what is expected of him.

REPEATED MEASUREMENTS. Experimenters in psychology are rarely satisfied to measure a subject's performance on a single trial. Taking only a single measurement runs the risk of having a momentary uncontrolled factor distort the datum. Repeating measurements tends to insure a reliable estimate of performance level as it reflects the experimental conditions. Important as reliability is, it is by no means the only reason for making several separate assessments of behavior. In our experiment on memorization we are investigating a process, memory, that is closely related to another measurable variable, passage of time. In our study, then, we might be interested in testing the subjects' retention of the word list at two or even three times following the study period. We might test retention immediately after the presentation of the list under the noisy or quiet conditions, and then we might test it again a day later, and perhaps again after a week had passed. These repeated measures could then be examined to see how the noisy environment had affected long-term memory as well as immediate memory when compared to the effects of the quiet condition.

CONTROL VALUES. In our study are we more concerned with determining the effect of quiet or the effect of noise on memorizing? Since a quiet environment would seem to be the normal surroundings for concentrating on a memory task, it would appear that we are more interested in determining what the effect of a special condition, noise, would be. If our particular interest is the effect of noise, why do we bother to take any data under the quiet condition? Obviously, we do it for purposes of comparison. The quiet environment is the *control* condition. The control data that it provides form a baseline for assessing the relative effect on performance of the *experimental* condition, the noisy environment.

Almost every kind of psychological study provides control data of some sort. In fatigue studies, to consider a different type of example, the performance data from the early part of a session might be used as control values in measuring the decrement in work performed by the subjects as they kept at the task for a long period. One exception to using control data for assessing behavior might be those studies in which the subjects' scores were compared with a physical standard, as in target shooting. Even in this sort of situation, many investigations would compare performance under different conditions, one of which might be considered as the control.

PLANNED STATISTICAL ANALYSIS. Most psychological experiments turn behavior into numbers. From the numbers we draw inferences about behavior. As you probably know, there are numerous technicalities in the proper treatment of the data that we gather. We shall not discuss them at any length here. They must be considered, though, in the planning stages of experimentation.

Let us examine two of the simpler problems that are illustrated in our memory experiment. The first is absurdly simple. Should we use just one subject in our experiment or should we run a group of subjects? Using only one subject would obviously be a risky way to test any hypothesis. In fact, there are technical reasons why we could not draw any valid conclusions from the scores of one person. At best we might draw conclusions about that particular person, but these would hardly be the generalizations toward which science aims. If just one person were tested, there are a number of factors which might affect his performance besides the noise and quiet of the environment. If we make a list of these possible influences, we may think of some that would show up in the scores of almost an entire group. Any such factors would have to be guarded against by procedural controls in our study or else treated as independent variables to be manipulated along with noise or quiet in a more complex experimental design.

Another statistical problem is anticipated in the design phase of research when we consider the scale of measurement that we are going to apply to performance. Assume that we had chosen a ten-word list to be memorized in our study. If our retention test is scored for number of words correct, a ten-word list may yield scores ranging from zero to ten, an eleven-point scale. Suppose we found that under the quiet condition fourteen out of twenty subjects had memorized the entire list perfectly in a single study effort. These performance data do not tell us much about how good a job of memorizing might have been indicated if our measurement scale, the list of words, had permitted its measurement more adequately. Since so many subjects reached the ceiling imposed by the scale, we do not actually have control values that will be helpful in assessing performance under the noise condition. Even if subjects do worse under noise we will have no way of deciding how *much* worse these scores are than the scores which *might* have been made under the quiet condition had those measures been better indicators.

Alternative Designs

Having reviewed some of the common aspects of experimentation that would appear in our model experiment, we must now go on to examine several different possibilities of design for the study. We shall consider the plan of arranging the subject groups and the conditions. Such consideration is required in designing most psychological studies.

ONE GROUP PER CONDITION. One possible design for our study of memorization under noise and quiet conditions would be to test one group of subjects under the quiet condition and a different group under the noisy environment, these subjects being designated as the control and experimental groups, respectively. The key question in using separate groups is whether they may be considered equal, as groups, in memorizing ability. Unless we can give an affirmative answer to this question we cannot consider our experiment a test of the two conditions as we want it to be. We can state with some confidence that the groups are equal in memorizing ability if they are of fair size and if the individuals were assigned to them at random. "At random" means that each individual had an equal chance of assignment to either group. If the number of persons available were very small, say a total of only six, then we could not be quite so sure that the two groups of three that we randomly designated would be equivalent in memory skill. The three best memorizers might end up, just by chance, in one group.

Rather than assigning available people to the groups at random, we might prefer the alternate design that calls for pretesting these persons on memorizing ability, matching them in pairs, and then putting one member of each pair in each group. This matched group technique is particularly useful when only a small number of participants is available. It is not necessary that subjects be matched on a pretest of the performance that will be required in the experiment. If memorizing is to be required in the study, we might match subjects on some measure that we know is related to memory, like IQ.

SINGLE GROUP. Rather than run the risk that group differences would distort the conclusions we might reach in our study, we might decide to use just one group of subjects, asking them to do some memorizing under noise and under quiet conditions. The question of memorizing ability practically disappears. Each person contributes both control data and experimental data or, as we say, each subject serves as his own control. We can examine the data collected in this design of our study to see if some persons showed a marked difference in scores made under the two conditions, whereas others showed little or no difference. This design, then, yields some estimate of individual differences in susceptibility to distraction by noise in a memorizing task. We can examine the averages of the sets of scores to determine the general magnitude of the difference in scores attributable to the experimental condition compared to the control condition.

Special Design Problems and Techniques

EXAMPLE OF A PROBLEM: PRACTICE EFFECT. We can see a possible difficulty if we use the design that tests a single group of subjects under both conditions. During the first experimental session they might learn how to go about this task of memorizing so that in the second session they might be better memorizers, even though required to study a completely different list of words. Suppose we ran the subjects in the quiet condition first and then in the noisy environment. The noise might be detrimental to their performance in the second session, but their added skill in memorizing, a benefit gained during the first session, might offset the negative effect of the noise.

It would be no solution to this problem to conduct the noisy session first and the quiet one second. True, it might be a way of obtaining higher scores under the quiet condition, which is the experimental result we might have predicted. But our prediction was based on the hypothesis that a difference in performance would result from the environmental conditions, and not from any practice effect. Our problem is to design an experiment in which such a learning effect will not be confounded with the effect of the experimental treatment.

SOLUTION TO THE PROBLEM: COUNTERBALANCING. One way we might

suggest for dealing with the practice effect in designing our study would be to divide our group of subjects into two groups. One group would be run first in the noisy environment and then under the quiet condition, memorizing a new list. The other group would be given the quiet environment first, then the noisy condition. Every subject would still be contributing to both the control data and the experimental data. For half of them, however, any practice effect that augmented their scores in the second session would raise the control score whereas for the other half of the subjects the experimental score would be raised. The mean score calculated for the quiet condition would thus be based on a number of scores, half of them elevated by the practice effect and half of them not increased by it. The average calculated for the noise condition would be similarly based on data of which half would reflect the practice effect and half would not. A comparison of the mean values for the two conditions should thus show the general effect of the noisy environment on the memorizing process. Running one group of subjects in the noise-quiet sequence and the other group in the quiet-noise order of presentation of conditions is called *counterbalancing*.

Counterbalancing is a technique of experimental design that is often used to equalize the contribution of an ongoing process like the practice effect to the data of each condition being studied. With the counterbalanced design we can compare the effects of noise and quiet on memorization without a bias due to the practice effect. An additional benefit accrues from this design, too, if we make a second analysis of the data. Suppose we compute a mean performance score from the data from all subjects for the first session and a similar average score for the second session. Remember, for each session half the subjects were given the quiet condition and half the noisy environment. With both experimental treatments represented in the means we have computed, these means will reveal, when they are evaluated statistically, whether there *is* any practice effect evident in the performances of our subjects. If a significant practice effect is revealed, we can be glad that we counterbalanced the experiment to prevent it from distorting our conclusions concerning the effect of noise on memorization. If no practice effect seems to have taken place, no harm will have been done by our counterbalancing.

PROCEDURAL DETAILS IN CONDUCTING RESEARCH

Having considered some of the broad aspects of the design of experiments, we need to get closer to the laboratory situation to discuss a few of the procedural problems common to many psychological investigations. In later chapters we shall discuss particular techniques appropriate to specific problem areas.

Values for the Independent Variable

The variety of factors which may appear as independent variables in behavior research is great. Experimenters vary such things as stimulus intensities, physical work loads imposed on subjects, time permitted for performance, length of word lists, or complexity of problems to be solved. We must next examine some of the considerations that might guide us in selecting particular quantitative values for independent variables to use in an experiment.

ADEQUATE SEPARATION. We select an independent variable for study because we believe it is one of the determinants of behavior. We test different values of it because we think they will affect performance differentially. If we expect that such a difference will appear in the measures of the dependent variable, we need to select values for the independent variable that are themselves different enough to produce a demonstrable behavioral difference. How brave is the student experimenter who predicts that the length of word list is a determinant of the time needed for rote memorization and then proceeds to look for the effect with lists of sixteen words compared with lists of eighteen words! Despite the plausibility of his hypothesis, he is unlikely to find statistical support for it with values of the independent variable so near to each other. Fortunately, few students are as brave, and as naively hopeful, as this. We can take this fictitious experimenter, however, as a horrible example to remind us to use values of our independent variables that are different enough to produce a significant effect.

AVOIDANCE OF EXTREMES. While separating the values of the independent variable to demonstrate their effect on performance, we do not want to go to such an extreme that we complicate the relationship we are studying. For example, if we were seeking to measure the improvement that occurs in typing as illumination is increased, we would not want to include in our choice of values a luminance so intense that it would cause glare in reflections from many surfaces and half-blind the subjects. The introduction of glare would be an unwanted complication for the aims of our study. Of course, if our hypothesis demanded a study of typing under such extremely strong illumination, then such a high luminance value would be appropriate.

SEEKING A FUNCTIONAL RELATIONSHIP. As in many aspects of the planning of research, our best guide to setting values for the independent variable in a study may come from past investigations of the same behavioral phenomenon. A number of values of the experimental variable may already have been employed in different experiments. If we are altering some condition, but are otherwise repeating an earlier study, we may want to choose the same values that the previous experimenter used so that our results will be directly comparable with his. If we are seeking to establish a functional relationship between independent and dependent variables, however, we may choose values intermediate to those employed earlier in order to delineate better the mathematical function over this range of values. Quite possibly we may wish to extend the functional relationship by using greater values of the independent variable than have been used before.

PRACTICAL APPLICATIONS. Suppose we are undertaking a study of the effect of page format or layout on the retention of prose material. We need to specify certain dimensions of the task such as the length of the prose passages to be employed and their difficulty level. We would be guided in part by technical considerations like the need for reliable and discriminating performance measures, which might set a minimal length for the material to be studied. In planning such research, however, there is no harm in selecting values that approximate those encountered in real situations—provided, of course, that such selections are congruent with the test of the hypothesis that we wish to make. Thus, we might use a passage that would be the length of a normal study unit and of a usual difficulty level for the scholastic group serving as subjects. Basic research may thus have an applied, or at least an applicable, feature which need not invalidate its contribution to behavioral science.

Instructions to Subjects

Human beings are more complex than the molecules studied by physical scientists. In psychological research we usually begin by asking the cooperation of the subject and then instructing him as to what he is required to do. We cannot ignore the fact that among the determinants of what he will do or how he will perform are the very instructions given him. We need to give thought to the phrasing and delivery of the instructions so that they will have the desired effect.

MOTIVATION. Subjects in psychological research sometimes arrive at the experimental session with no strong interest in participating. They may be members of a class group whose participation has been requested by the instructor. As you well know, this is no guarantee of individual interest. A student may volunteer to serve as subject for a fraternity brother. Again, personal motivation may not be high. It needs to be aroused by the instructions. One way to arouse interest is to state as much about the purpose of the study as may be revealed. Most people will take seriously a task that they can regard as a contribution to a scientific investigation. Sometimes it may be particularly appealing if we can indicate possible practical application of the results.

It may be possible to arouse the competitive aspect of motivation in college students if we can tell them that students at another institution have performed very well on the task we are assigning. Or we may create a competitive spirit within the group we are employing, perhaps by indicating that scores will be posted. However, we need to ask ourselves if such a technique will actually motivate *all* the subjects.

DIRECTIVE CLARITY. Subjects must perform in the manner we intend them to if the data are to reward our research effort. We may have been thinking about so many details of an experiment that when it is time to write the instructions we may write from the point of view of one who knows all about the study instead of from the subject's viewpoint, who may not have the slightest idea of what he is to do. To be sure that instructions indicate clearly what subjects are to do, it is well to pretest their wording on a preliminary group. Without pretesting we run the risk of having to discard data because 10 or 20 per cent of the subjects obviously did not understand the instructions. We may be even worse off when their misunderstanding is not detectable and yet is a factor that influenced the experimental results. It is common practice to ask if there are any questions after we read instructions to subjects, but it must be remembered that people are often reluctant to reveal that they did not understand. They may remain silent, hoping to grasp what is expected of them after the experiment gets under way. It is obviously desirable to avoid this by making instructions clear in the first place.

REPETITION FOR EMPHASIS. We know enough about the principles of human behavior to realize that some points in our instructions will have to be emphasized if we expect subjects to comply. This applies particularly to those parts of the instructions that call for a way of performing that might be antagonistic to established habits. For example, if our experiment requires that subjects leave no margins on the paper when performing a handwriting task, the warning to leave no margins ought to be repeated once or twice in the instructions since people will be inclined by training to leave space at the left and right of each line. It is well to repeat such a key part of the instructions just before the first trial begins.

INTERPROCEDURAL INSTRUCTIONS. Although instructions to subjects are often presented in their entirety before the experimental task begins, it is well to think of some of the values to be gained through delivering part of the instructions at a later point in the procedure. This may be useful to restore motivation when the subject's interest in the task may be flagging or when motivation needs to be brought to a peak just before the critical data are to be taken.

Sometimes it may help to alternate practice periods and additional instructions which may serve to extend the subject's knowledge of what is expected of him. A subject, for example, might be given some practice at reading as quickly as possible the adjectives that appeared on a screen. Then he might be given the additional instruction to read the adjective silently and to state aloud its opposite as quickly as possible. The preliminary reading of the words might have been used to establish baseline reaction times, to acquaint the subjects with the words being used, or merely to help them adjust to the experimental situation before the critical task of naming opposites was introduced.

ADJUNCTIVE INSTRUCTIONAL TECHNIQUES. An experimenter need not rely solely on the verbal instructions given the subjects to motivate them and inform them of what they are expected to do. Some guidance may be provided by means of the material employed. The warning that appears in some test booklets, not to turn the page until told to do so, is a familiar example. Experimental apparatus may be constructed to flash a warning to a subject if he does something wrong. More simply, the experimenter may give such a warning if the plan of the study calls for it. Information as to how well he is doing may be given to a subject in some studies as a supplement to the instructions he was given. Such knowledge of results may be both motivational and informative, depending on what is presented and how it is related to the task being performed. Individual responses are sometimes identified for subjects as right or wrong through the use of appropriate cues. This type of adjunct to formal instructions may even include actual punishment, like a mild electric shock, for a wrong response.

Presentation of Treatments

The procedural heart of any behavioral experiment may be variously described as presenting the treatments to the subjects, administering the experimental conditions to them, or requiring the performance of the assigned task from them. All these are encompassed, too, in the vernacular phrase from psychological experimentation, "running the subjects." This aspect of conducting research is no less important than several others we have discussed. It is in the treatment of the subjects that we shall find the diversity of special methods that will occupy us in many subsequent chapters. Here, we turn our attention to two general problems encountered in running subjects.

PRELIMINARY PRACTICE. The statement of an hypothesis may call for the collecting of data from subjects who are practiced at a task or at least quite familiar with it. The experiment may therefore be designed to give preliminary practice to the subjects. This may sometimes be done informally with the experimenter watching the subject's performance and perhaps offering suggestions that will aid performance. It is important to realize how this practice may affect the analysis of the formal part of the study, administered later. The assessment of any practice effect in the data of the latter portion of the experiment will not be very meaningful if subjects have been given different opportunities to benefit by practice in the preliminary part. It may be suggested, therefore, that everything about the preliminary part of a study, both treatment and performance, be made a matter of record so that it may be analyzed later if necessary.

OCCLUDING EXTRANEOUS STIMULI. Shutting out unwanted stimulation is commonly required in psychological research since the aim of such studies is so often to determine the effect of particular stimuli on performance. The task of the experimenter is to see to it that these desired stimuli, and nothing but these stimuli, impinge upon the subjects. While this requirement is of paramount importance in most studies of sensory and perceptual processes, it is almost never absent from behavioral investigations. The laboratory or research room is generally situated and constructed to isolate the subjects from unwanted noise and visual distractions. Other solutions to the problem include blindfolding the subject when the study calls for no visual cues and delivering auditory stimuli through earphones when it is desired to minimize interference from noise in the room.

SUMMARY

There are numerous principles and practical rules which may be followed in planning and conducting research in psychology. Designing an experiment means formulating a plan for adequately testing an hypothesis. A knowledge of the general aspects of carrying out behavioral research is a great aid in undertaking specific studies.

Research begins with the formulation of hypotheses drawn from past research, field observations, or theory. Hypotheses may vary widely in their formality of statement and the specificity of predictions which they contain or imply. Great care should be exercised in stating an hypothesis for testing, so that it actually bears upon the problem we intend to investigate. We must pay close attention to operational definitions of terms, to the population involved, and to assumptions.

In the design of an experiment, the hypothesis to be tested will usually dictate the subjects to be used and the dependent and independent variables. Other details of the study are decided upon by the experimenter in the light of his experience and knowledge of earlier investigations. Among the points to be covered may be the grouping of subjects, the selection and presentation of stimulus material, and the specific response measurements to be made.

Almost every experiment in psychology which employs human subjects will require carefully worded instructions. Universally required also are repeated measures, control data, and planned statistical analysis.

Most problems requiring research permit considerable latitude in choosing an experimental design. For some studies it may be best to give each treatment to all subjects. In other investigations it may be preferable to run a different group of subjects under each condition. Counterbalancing may be employed in different ways to prevent data from being biased by some factor like a practice effect.

A number of procedural points need to be given close attention if behavioral experiments are to be successful. A thoughtful choice of values for the independent variable is desirable. We need to motivate subjects carefully and be sure they know what is expected of them. Preliminary practice at a task should be planned and conducted carefully. Whenever possible, we occlude extraneous stimuli which might either distract the subject or give him information which he is not supposed to have.

REFERENCE

Dollard, J., Doob, L. W., Miller, N. E., Mowrer, O. H., & Sears, R. R. *Frustration and aggression*. New Haven: Yale Univer. Press, 1939.

ADDITIONAL READINGS

Slack, C. W. Trial design in human experiments. *Psychol. Rev.*, 1958, 65, 92–102.

Tinker, M. A., & Russell, W. A. *Introduction to methods in experimental psychology.* (3rd ed.) New York: Appleton-Century-Crofts, 1958.

Underwood, B. J. *Psychological research.* New York: Appleton-Century-Crofts, 1957.

Wilson, E. B. *An introduction to scientific research.* New York: McGraw-Hill, 1952.

CHAPTER 3

Measurement
and
Statistics

Much of laboratory experimentation in psychology is aimed at finding functional relationships between independent and dependent variables. In many cases, the independent variables are physical stimulus dimensions that are quantified in accordance with conventional physical scales, like the Centigrade scale for temperature or a decibel scale for sound intensity. In other cases, stimulus materials may involve dimensions which have previously been subjected to psychological scaling procedures, our topic of study in Chapter 6. Aspects of behavior which we select as dependent variables are also quantifiable by applying a variety of scales. These may be identical with scales used by the physicist, as when we measure the duration of a response in seconds or determine the force, in kilograms, with which a subject squeezes a dynamometer. We may also use more complex measures of behavior like the number of trials required to memorize ten words or the per cent of subjects able to detect a tone of a given low intensity.

We obtain experimental data by using different measurement techniques. With measurement occupying so central a place in research, we need to become acquainted with various kinds of scales by which we may quantify behavior. These behavioral data are treated statistically in order to achieve an orderly quantitative description of the behavior. In this chapter we explore the nature of measurement, the kinds of scales which we may use, the descriptive uses of statistics, and certain computational formulas. In Chapter 4 we consider how statistical manipulations help us to assess the likelihood that the data support the hypothesis being tested.

MEASUREMENT SCALES

Definition of Measurement

Our examination of how research workers in psychology quantify behavior will begin with a consideration of just what measurement is —in any part of science or in everyday life. "Measurement is the assignment of numerals to objects or events according to rules" says Stevens (1951, p. 1), paraphrasing Campbell. Let us see if this concise definition really applies to varied examples of measuring which come to mind. When we measure the width of a laboratory work table with a meter stick, are we assigning a numeral according to rules? There are, indeed, several rules which must be followed to make this physical measurement in valid fashion. The meter stick must cross the table squarely. The end of the stick, or some cardinal point on the stick, must be aligned with one edge of the table. We must observe from an appropriate angle to note the nearest gradua-tion mark corresponding to the other edge of the table. We must subtract the meter stick readings aligned with the two edges to get the width of the table. Our rules may prescribe that we take the datum to the nearest centimeter, or may require a reading to the nearest millimeter. The really complete definition of this physical measure-ment is even more elaborate than this, involving reference to our conventionally graduated meter stick, and in turn to the standard meter of the metric system. It appears, then, that the measurement of the width of the table does indeed involve assigning a numeral according to the rules.

In measuring a person's reaction time, RT, are we also assigning a numeral according to rules? Our first step in using a chronometer is to check its calibration, if we are very rigorous in our approach to temporal quantification. With the soundness of the instrument as-sured, we next follow certain rules in placing it in the circuit of the RT apparatus. We make sure that the chronometer starts at the instant that the stimulus is presented and that it stops simultaneously with the making of the reaction. In reading the timer we take precautions not to distort the obtained value by viewing it from the wrong angle. All these steps are part of the series of operations we perform in quantifying the behavioral event represented in the RT experiment. When we describe the sequential steps we take in obtaining RT, then, we are prescribing rules for its measurement. At the same time, we are operationally defining what we mean by *RT*. Thus, measurement of a behavioral event and its operational definition are practically identical. Consider additional facets of the experiment. When we instruct a subject to respond as quickly as possible, and when we take the average *RT* over many trials, we are further expanding our rules for *RT* measurement and our operational definition of this concept. No matter how we *verbally* define a dependent variable, be it *RT* or memory or esthetic judgment, our procedures for measuring it constitute the *operational* definition of it. This is the meaningful definition as we seek empirical functional relationships, or behavioral laws.

Types of Measurement Scales

Whenever we are confronted with behavioral data we need to ask exactly how the data were obtained. Although some aspects of behavior are measurable through the use of meter sticks and chronometers, many data in psychological research stem from elaborate techniques which constitute a complex scale. A scale may be defined as a prescribed series of steps employed in assigning a numeral to an object or event. Conventional measuring instruments like meter sticks and chronometers represent a consolidation of several steps in the complete series, thus offering a great economy of effort through reducing the number of remaining steps. We find that different classes or types of measurement scales are defined by different characteristics of the magnitudes being measured. In turn, these types of scales determine what statistical manipulations are appropriately applicable to the data they yield. We now turn to an examination of different types of scales and the numerical manipulations applicable to the data they give us.

SCALE-DEFINING OPERATIONS. Different types of measurement scales are defined by the kind of operation which can validly be performed on the dimension under study. We shall use the physical dimension, length, to illustrate the various operations in question. It would be extremely difficult to portray the application of these operations to behavioral dimensions. However, if we can see them applied to length, we may be better able to appreciate the meaning of these operations and the scales to which they give rise.

In Figure 3.1A we see four different line segments to which we successively apply the scale-defining operations in other parts of the figure. These different operations are performed on the physical dimension, length, itself. They may be paralleled by mathematical

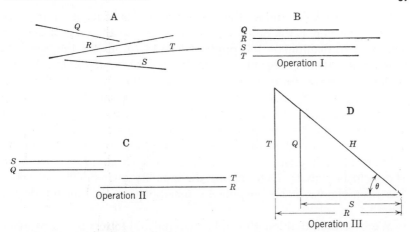

Fig. 3.1. The application of three different scale-defining operations to the physical dimension of length as represented by line segments Q, R, S, and T. (See text for explanation.)

operations performed on measurements which we might take of each line segment.

Operation I is the determination of greater, less, or equality. The way this operation is performed on physical length is illustrated in Figure 3.1B where we see the line segments arranged in parallel fashion with their left end points aligned. It is readily apparent that none of the segments is equal in length. S is greater in length than Q, T is of lesser length than R, etc. The operation of aligning the ends of the segments after making them parallel has revealed their different orders of magnitude.

Operation II is the determination of equality or inequality of differences. Is the difference between Q and S the same as the difference between R and T? To determine this by physical manipulation, we may align the segments as shown in Figure 3.1C. We have arranged them so as to bring into alignment the two differences in which we are interested. By bringing Q and S into correspondence at the left and R and T into correspondence at the right, we can examine the differences, $S - Q$ and $R - T$, in direct physical comparison. When we examine the center part of this configuration we see that the difference between R and T is greater than that between S and Q. Our manipulation of the lengths has demonstrated the inequality of these differences. Our operation has revealed that the physical dimension of length is one for which it is possible to determine the equality or inequality of differences.

Operation III determines the equality of ratios of magnitudes. We ask the question, is the ratio of Q to S the same as the ratio of T to R? One way to manipulate the physical lengths to answer this question is to employ them as legs of a right triangle. In Figure 3.1D we see T and R utilized to form such a triangle with the angle θ having T/R as its tangent. By placing the lengths S and Q as shown, to form a similar right triangle, we see that Q/S is also the tangent value for the same angle, θ. The hypotenuse of the smaller triangle coincides completely with that of the larger one, indicated by H in the figure. As tangents of the same angle, θ, the ratios Q/S and T/R have been shown to be equal. Determining the equality or inequality of ratios has been shown to be possible by manipulating the magnitudes of length.

We have seen that length can be manipulated to test for three kinds of equality:

1. Equality of magnitudes, by Operation I.
2. Equality of differences, by Operation II.
3. Equality of ratios, by Operation III.

Of course, we might have measured the four line segments in Figure 3.1A and used the measurements obtained to check for these equalities. The mathematical process of subtraction could have been appropriately applied to these data to parallel Operations I and II, represented in Figures 3.1B and 3.1C, respectively. The processes of division and then subtraction could have been successively applied in a parallel to Operation III to determine the equality of ratios, Q/S and T/R. Such mathematical processes are readily applicable to data of all sorts. Measurement theory, however, dictates that such computations are appropriate only when the dimension in question permits similar operations to be performed on the corresponding magnitudes themselves. Thus, a ratio of two measured lengths may be calculated because the ratio of the two physical lengths has meaning in certain geometrical configurations, as we saw in Figure 3.1D. Different types of measurement scales are determined by the kinds of operation that can be performed on the magnitudes in question.

RATIO SCALES. A ratio scale is one applicable to magnitudes that permit us to perform Operations I, II, and III, previously described. We illustrated these with the example of physical length. This, then, is one dimension that we measure with a ratio scale. For other kinds of dimensions the three operations indicating the applicability of a ratio scale might be performed in other ways, suited to the dimension in question.

A ratio scale always has a zero point, either hypothetical or empirically determinable. When such a scale is used to obtain measurements, it is appropriate to speak of ratios which exist among the data. We may take an example from the temporal scale used to measure RT. Time is measured on a ratio scale. Although conventional techniques guard against obtaining RT measures of zero magnitude, we may consider that a response simultaneous with the stimulus presentation is hypothetically possible. A zero reading on a chronometer might even be obtained empirically, although not validly, if a subject took his cue for responding from the warning signal and timed his reaction to coincide with the stimulus. Having seen that the temporal scale of RT has a zero point, let us see the implications of a ratio scale for interpretation of the data obtained.

Suppose that a certain subject, No. 17, has demonstrated a simple RT, under "normal" conditions, of 180 msec. Suppose also that the corresponding datum for another subject, No. 22, is 190 msec. When we now test them after 48 continuous waking hours, we may find that No. 17 shows an RT of 198 msec and No. 22 gives us an RT of 209 msec. Under this amount of sleep deprivation, the RT values obtained exhibit a ratio of 11:10 when compared to "normal" RT. This equality of ratios, the 10 per cent increase of RT shown by both subjects, may be appropriately noted because we are dealing with a ratio scale. If Subject No. 17 had shown an RT of 189 msec under the experimental condition, we would be able to say that the sleep deprivation had led to a 5 per cent increase in RT. Our statements have meaning for the behavioral dimension, RT, as well as for the numerical data.

The fact that ratios and per cents are appropriately considered only with respect to ratio scales—those with a meaningful zero point—may become clearer if we consider data obtained with a scale that is not a ratio scale. Suppose that we had tested our subjects in the sleep deprivation experiment by a conventional hand steadiness test. The apparatus consists of a stylus which must be inserted, without touching, into holes drilled with a series of decreasing diameters in a brass plate. A series of numbers, assigned to these holes in order, provides a measurement scale. The smaller the hole into which the stylus is successfully inserted, the greater the score. Suppose that Subject No. 17 scored 5 under "normal" conditions and only 4 after sleep deprivation. The 5:4 ratio of these numbers does *not* mean a 20 per cent decrease in hand steadiness. The way in which the test apparatus was designed to assess steadiness does not permit such a reference to a ratio or per cent, since without a zero point and without meaningful expressions of ratio the series of possible scores does not constitute a ratio scale.

Returning to positive examples of ratio scales, we may note that in the study of motor performance we may borrow other scales, besides the temporal scale, from the physicist. In studying positioning movements, we borrow the dimension of length or angular displacement. Measuring responses in terms of centimeters for linear positioning or degrees for angular positioning, we may properly refer to an error being found to be 13 per cent greater, for example, under one condition than another. A positioning reaction, or an error in positioning, of zero magnitude is perfectly possible. The physical scales of length or angular displacement are true ratio scales.

Psychology, like other disciplines within empirical science, borrows the ratio scale of *numerosity* from mathematics. Whenever we assign numerals to objects or events by counting, we are employing this scale. For example, we might determine the number of subjects who are able to maintain a standing posture within prescribed limits on a body sway test. We might find that only half as many succeed in passing the test when blindfolded as when vision is permitted. It is appropriate to take note of this ratio of frequencies since we are dealing with a scale which has a possible zero point. Under certain conditions no one might be able to pass the test. Frequency measurements refer to a dimension of numerosity which permits the defining operations for a ratio scale.

Besides counting subjects who exhibit some behavior, we may use the ratio scale of numerosity by counting the responses which a subject makes during a given period. This turns simple frequency into a measure of rate, but the potential zero point—no responses occurring—is maintained. When we have measured rates of response under different conditions, it is appropriate to compare them as ratios or to state that a particular per cent of difference was observed. When making such statements about the data taken by means of any scale of measurement, the complete operational definition of the scale must be kept in mind. Let us assume that a fifty per cent increase is found in the number of words understood in a speech intelligibility test when a particular change in condition is made. This ratio of improvement must be regarded as specific to the type of words chosen as test material, as well as to numerous other factors in the study. The ratio scale of numerosity is as subject to the limitations of a particular operational definition as are other scales of measurement in psychological research.

An area of psychological research where the construction of ratio scales has been attempted with some success is the measurement of sensory magnitudes. The operations for determining the equality of ratios are often centered in the responses of the subject when he attempts to adjust a comparison stimulus to make its sensory magnitude half as great as that aroused by a standard stimulus. For example, a subject might have to adjust a comparison tone until it seemed just half as loud as a standard tone. Ratios of 2:1 may thus be established using many standard tone magnitudes, and we may assume that all loudness ratios judged to be 2:1 are equal in experience to each other. In making a judgment like half as loud, the subject may be assumed to be utilizing a judged zero point as one end of the interval he is bisecting. This zero point and the equality of ratios as operationally defined satisfy the requirements for a ratio scale.

INTERVAL SCALES. An interval scale is one that may be applied to dimensions within which we can perform Operations I and II. We can determine the equality or inequality of magnitudes and of differences, but we cannot determine the equality of ratios. This Operation III is ruled out due to the lack of a true zero point.

One approach to interval scaling in psychology resembles the ratio scaling of sensory magnitudes. Just as dimensions like loudness may be scaled by direct manipulations of ratios, other dimensions may lend themselves to the direct determination of intervals in the responses given by experimental subjects. For example, we might ask a subject to indicate, by marks placed along a line, the distances he judges to separate samples of handwriting on a dimension of legibility. A subject might presumably manage this direct indicating of scale differences even though ratio scaling, requiring a notion of zero legibility, might not be easily accomplished.

ORDINAL SCALES. We are said to be working with an ordinal scale when the dimension in question permits us to apply only Operation I, determining equality or inequality of magnitudes, whether one is equal to, greater than, or less than, another. An example of this is the conventional hand steadiness measurement. We saw that the scores, determined by the size of hole into which the stylus could be inserted without touching, would not justify reference to ratios of hand steadiness. Even the comparison of intervals, Operation II, is not valid. We cannot say that the difference between scores of 4 and 5 represent the same increment in steadiness as the difference between scores of 7 and 8. The operational definition of hand steadiness does permit us to state, however, that greater steadiness is shown by successful insertion of the stylus into the smaller holes. A score of 5 represents steadier performance than a score of 4, since the hole numbered 5 is the smaller of the two and therefore represents a more exacting task.

A different instance of ordinal scaling in psychology is found in our requiring subjects to rank or rate various stimulus items on some continuum for which there is no simple physical correlate. For example, we might ask a group of people to rank several samples of floor tile on the esthetic appeal of their color combinations. Which set of colors is most pleasing to the eye? Which is next most attractive, and so on? We find that, as a psychological dimension, esthetic appeal—call it beauty or pleasantness, if you will—can be readily handled by Operation I. Subjects find it easy to judge different sample items with reference to one another. For many complex attributes like beauty, however, they would find it difficult or impossible to express ratio judgments—this one is twice as beautiful as that. Our measurement of numerous aspects of perceptual and evaluative experience, then, is limited to ordinal scaling.

PERMISSIBLE TREATMENTS OF DATA. The nature of the different kinds of scales we have discussed—ratio, interval, and ordinal—imposes certain limitation on the ways in which the data they yield may be treated. If the operations which yield the conventional ordinal scale of hand steadiness, for example, do not permit any manipulations to demonstrate the magnitude of a difference between two scale points, then it is meaningless to treat the two scores which correspond to these points as if they could yield a meaningful difference value. The subtraction of the numbers reveals that one magnitude of steadiness exceeds the other but does not validly indicate the size of the behavioral difference when an ordinal scale is involved. Such restrictions on treatment of data are reflected in the statistics which may legitimately be computed for numbers derived from the various types of scales. We shall indicate the applicability of different statistical analyses, referring to statistics which are possibly familiar to you or are presented for your study later in this chapter.

From data obtained from ordinal scales we may calculate the median and percentiles, as well as order correlation with similar sets of data. As the midmost item in a series of values, the median is identifiable even though we do not know the magnitudes of the differences separating the various values. By definition, we know the order of items that have been ordinally scaled, and it is its place in an ordered series that defines the median as well. Percentiles are calculated on the basis of cumulative frequencies of cases which fall in successive ordered intervals. As long as they are ordinally arranged, the magnitude of these intervals does not affect our computing of the number of cases included up to the end point of any interval. Order correlation, a measure of the relationship between two sets of paired ordinally scaled values, is similarly free from any restraint based on size of intervals between magnitudes. The computation is based only on rank order of the items, which is provided by ordinal scaling.

Interval scale values may be used in computing the three statistics just mentioned, and they permit us to use several additional statistics as well. For data obtained through interval scale measurement we may compute the mean and the standard deviation. If we have two sets of interval data on the same persons or items, we may compute a correlation of the product-moment type. These three statistics have meaning when the separations of the different values along the scale have meaning. Ordinal scale values, on the other hand, indicate no meaningful intervals of separation and therefore should not be treated with these statistics.

Ratio scales permit the application of all the statistics we have mentioned, from the median to the product-moment correlation. In addition, our knowledge of ratio scaled magnitudes with respect to an absolute zero point allows us to compute statistics like the geometric mean, not very often used in psychology.

DESCRIPTIVE STATISTICS

A statistic is a number which represents some aspect of a group of data. If we run a group of subjects under a particular experimental condition it would be laborious as well as confusing to recite a long list of numerical scores in attempting to communicate our findings. If our measurements of the behavior can be summarized meaningfully by using descriptive statistics, a great economy in the reporting of research results can be accomplished. Our own thinking about our findings is facilitated, too, by a summary form of numerical description. By developing a working acquaintance with some conventionally employed statistics we can improve our own presentation of experimental outcomes, and we can sharpen our ability to profit from reading the research literature of psychology and other fields.

Our consideration of statistics in this textbook is definitely delimited. It is offered merely as an adjunct to a laboratory course in experimental psychology. In both range and depth it will not be the equivalent of the material you find in textbooks on statistics. The more thorough treatments of topics which those books present are an extra dividend for the student who accompanies or precedes his experimental work with a course in statistics. For that student, as well as for those retaining a knowledge of some statistics from courses like introductory psychology, the following pages may serve in part to provide a convenient reference for basic facts and computational formulas. Anyone who may suffer from "formulaphobia" will find that the symbols and computational steps provided have been tamed to the point where even the rank amateur can make them perform.

One aspect of a group of data which we often wish to summarize and report is the *central tendency* of the values. Some sort of average value is a convenient description of this general characteristic of a set of numbers. The set of values may range closely or widely around any such average, and so we can usefully employ a second kind of statistic, a measure of *variability*. In the remainder of this chapter, we will find a working guide to various statistics which are descriptive of central tendency and variability.

Measures of Central Tendency

For describing the typical outcome of an experimental treatment as represented in a group of data, either the *mean* or the *median* is commonly employed. Rigorous adherence to principles of measurement permits the mean to be employed only for interval and ratio scale data, whereas the median can be used to describe data from an ordinal scale as well. Measurements of the ordinal type are sometimes assumed to meet the criteria for interval scales, so that we may find means being computed more widely than formal rules would permit.

THE MEAN. The term *mean* is applied most commonly to the statistic obtained by summing a set of values and then dividing by the number of data in the set. Strictly speaking, this average should be called the *arithmetic mean* to contrast it with others such as the geometric mean, differently defined. However, it may generally be understood that the designation *mean* standing alone refers to this simple averaging of the data.

Since the computation of such an average as the mean is widely understood, we may find it useful in considering the symbolic notation employed in statistical formulas. The usual way of presenting the formula for the mean is:

$$M_X = \frac{\Sigma X}{N} \qquad\qquad \text{Formula 3.1}$$

where M_X = the mean of a set of data.

X = each individual datum in the set.

Σ = the summation operation to be performed in computing the mean; it directs us to sum the data, each X value being included in the summation.

N = the number of data in the set.

In a verbal statement, the formula directs us to calculate the mean by first getting the sum of the values and then dividing this by the number of values which have been added. The numerical examples of Table 3.1 renew our acquaintance with this familiar statistic. The two simple illustrations in the table are useful in pointing out a few facts in addition to the computational steps. In presenting the mean reaction time on the left, we used the subscript RT on the symbol M instead of writing M_X as in the general formula. The notation, M_{RT}, illustrates a useful way of keeping track of the performance measure being cited as well as of the statistic that has been computed. On the right we have utilized a sub-subscript, E, as a notation that the data for which this is M_X were obtained under the experimental condition as opposed to a control condition, the mean of which might be noted as M_{X_C}. It may also be noted that, in both examples, we have followed the convention of carrying the computation of the means to one more decimal place than was found in the data being summarized.

TABLE 3.1

Numerical Examples of the Computation of the Mean

Mean Reaction Time for Six Subjects	Mean Constant Error in an Adjustment Task ($N = 5$)
X (msec)	X (cm)
182	+3.3
191	−0.8
173	−1.4
176	+1.7
234	+2.7
185	$\Sigma X = +5.5$
$\Sigma X = 1141$	$M_{X_E} = +1.10$ cm
$M_{RT} = 190.2$ msec	

The right-hand column of data in Table 3.1 suggests another point to be made. In any task where both positive and negative values are obtained, we have an opportunity to compute two different means, to be given somewhat different interpretations. In our illustrative calculation we summed algebraically, taking the positive and negative signs into account. Dividing the resulting positive sum by N we obtained a statistic called the *mean constant error*. If we had averaged the magnitudes of error *without* regard for their algebraic sign, we would have obtained a mean value of 1.98, designated as the *average error*, the central tendency of the error magnitudes. If this mean is to be computed, the formula may be written as follows:

$$M = \frac{\Sigma|X|}{N}$$
                                                                    Formula 3.2

where the vertical lines on either side of the X indicate that the summation is to be made with algebraic sign of the different values ignored.

Whereas this average error indicates how large the errors have been, discounting their direction, the mean constant error represents the central tendency of the errors as they range along the response scale both above and below zero. We often find it useful to compute a mean constant error for each individual subject, an index of his tendency to err either positively or negatively in responding. We may then wish to average these values to obtain a mean constant error for a group, an index of a general tendency which may be induced by various factors in the experiment. Individual and group analyses of error data may be similarly performed using the average error statistic with a different interpretation to be given.

THE MEDIAN. We define the *median* as that point on the scale above and below which half of the obtained data fall. This statistic divides the set of data into two equally numerous subsets, a half of the values exceeding the median, a half of the values being less. The median may or may not coincide with one of the data in the set.

How the median is determined may first be illustrated by referring to the sets of data (Table 3.1) for which we computed means. There are six values in the set of *RT* data so that the median will be a point on the scale between the third highest and the fourth highest of the obtained values, 185 and 182, respectively. It is customary to consider the median to fall exactly halfway between these two midmost values in an even-numbered set of cases. Our example thus yields a median of 183.5, halfway between 182 and 185, a value which does indeed separate the data into two subsets with $N/2$ cases in each. If a set of data contains an odd number of cases, the median is considered to fall at the value of the midmost case, with half of the remaining data above and below it. In the case of our positive and negative error values this midmost datum is +1.7, so this is taken as the value of the median.

When there are several identical values at the midpoint of a set of data, whether the number of cases in the set is odd or even, we may employ a refinement in computing the median. Consider, for example, the following set of 18 hand steadiness scores:

$$1, 2, 2, 3, 4, 4, 4, 4, 4, 4, 4, 5, 5, 5, 6, 6, 7, 8$$

Counting from the lower end of the set, we find that the ninth and tenth values are both 4. To report this value as the median, however, would be somewhat misleading. It is not really a midpoint since only 4 scores are below it while 7 scores exceed it. To refine our determination of the median in such a case, we assume that the interval from 3.5 to 4.5 on our scale is actually divided into 7 segments, each occupied by one of the scores of 4. By considering these 7 scores to be spread out in this fashion, we can count 9 cases from the top and bottom of our set of data to find the dividing point between the ninth and tenth cases, our definition of the median when N is 18. Up to 3.5 on the scale we have 4 cases, so we need to proceed up through 5 of the 7 segments between 3.5 and 4.5 to reach the desired median value. Five-sevenths of 1.0 is 0.71, so we add this to 3.5 to obtain 4.21 as the point on the scale below which half of the cases lie. As a check on our calculation we may proceed downward from the top of the distribution. Down to 4.5 we accumulate 7 cases so we need to continue down through 2 of the 7 segments between 4.5 and 3.5 to reach the midpoint or median. Two-sevenths of 1.0 is 0.29, a value which we subtract from the upper limit of 4.5 of the interval containing all the 4's. This gives us 4.21 as the median value, checking our other computation. The refined median value of 4.21 reflects the fact that a few more scores were above 4 than were below it.

USING THE MEAN AND MEDIAN. We need to know some general guide rules concerning when to employ the mean as a measure of central tendency, and when to employ a different statistic such as the median. The mean should be used when we want the most reliable index of central tendency, that is, the statistic which will vary least as different samples of data are studied. The use of the mean applies particularly when the set of scores is fairly symmetrical around the central tendency, without extreme values at one end of the distribution of measures. We would want to know the mean when we intend to study the variability of the data around this central value. This is often the case when we proceed with a complete statistical analysis of data collected in an experiment.

It is usually considered better to calculate the median as well as the mean when the set of data contains extreme values, either very high or very low, which are not balanced out by values at the opposite end of the set. The mean is unduly affected by the magnitude of such extreme values whereas the median is not. By presenting both these statistics, we can indicate something of the nature and magnitude of the *skewness* of the set of scores, its departure from symmetry due to the extreme values at one end of the set. The mean will exceed the median if the extreme values are at the high end of the scale, a positive skewness. When the extreme values which introduce asymmetry are low, a negative skewness, the mean will be lower in value than the median.

It is also preferable to calculate the median when some of the data are indeterminate, as in the case of time scores for performance when some subjects are prevented from completing the task because a time limit is imposed. Not knowing how long these subjects would have taken, we cannot compute a valid mean. The median, however, can usually be found satisfactorily. The median is also the appropriate measure of central tendency for ordinal scale values, as opposed to data obtained with interval or ratio scales which permit the calculation of the arithmetic mean.

Measures of Variability

The statistical description of a set of data is never complete if only a measure of central tendency is given. We require some index to indicate how the data vary above and below the typical values. There are numerous measures of variability which may be used in describing a set of data just as there are several measures of central tendency. Again we shall be selective, treating only those statistics which are especially useful in analyzing the outcome of an experiment. We shall see later that a consideration of variability in different sets of data is important as we draw statistical inferences from research results. Our present discussion, however, will center on the descriptive aspect of measures of variability. We shall define and calculate the *average deviation,* the *standard deviation,* and the *variance.* Strictly speaking, these descriptive statistics should be taken only from sets of data which are interval or ratio scale values, as we also mentioned for the mean.

THE AVERAGE DEVIATION. This index of how the data spread out along the measurement scale is defined as the arithmetic mean of the amounts by which the individual data differ from the mean of the set, the signs of these differences being disregarded. The computational formula is this:

$$AD = \frac{\Sigma|x|}{N}$$
Formula 3.3

where AD = the average deviation.

Σ = the summation sign.

$|x|$ = the deviation of each score from the mean $(x = X - M)$ with algebraic sign to be disregarded.

N = the number of values in the set, including those, if any, where $X = M$ so that $x = 0$.

To employ the computational formula, we begin with the mean of the set of raw scores. We subtract this mean, in turn, from each of the values in the set of raw data. This gives us a set of deviations from the mean, some of them computed to be positive and some of them negative. Each deviation may be represented by x, as the formula indicated. Disregarding their signs, we summate these deviations and divide the sum by the number of measures in the set. This yields the value of AD. This statistic tells us, on the average, how far the data were above and below the mean. It serves chiefly as a descriptive statistic. We turn next to another measure of variability which is also descriptive and has additional usefulness in the statistical analysis of research data.

THE STANDARD DEVIATION. This index of how a set of data vary about their mean is abbreviated as SD or σ. The SD is calculated in a fashion that resembles, at the outset, the computation of the AD. That is, we begin by finding the deviation, x, of each measure from the group mean. Each deviation is defined, as before, according to the formula, $x = X - M$. We write x, instead of $|x|$ as in computing the AD, since the signs of the deviations may be usefully employed in a check on our arithmetic. If we retain signs and obtain the algebraic summation, Σx, we should find this sum equal to zero. In other words, the sum of the negative deviations should equal the sum of the positive deviations so that the algebraic sum is zero. This computation serves as a check on the correctness of the values obtained for the mean and for the deviations from it. With allowances made for slight error due to rounding the value of the mean, Σx should always equal zero. In the case of the SD, it is not Σx but Σx^2 that we use in obtaining this measure of variability. The formula to be used is as follows:

$$SD = \sqrt{\frac{\Sigma x^2}{N}}$$ Formula 3.4

where
   SD = the standard deviation, also written as σ.
   Σ = the summation sign.
   x^2 = the square of each deviation from the mean: $x^2 = (X - M)^2$.
   N = the number of values in the set, including those, if any, where
       $X = M$ so that x and $x^2 = 0$.

Our computation of the SD begins with the mean of the set of raw
scores. We find how each individual value deviates from this mean,
using the formula, $x = X - M$. We check our work by seeing that Σx,
the algebraic sum of the deviations, is zero. We square each deviation
to obtain a set of x^2 values, all positive in sign because of the squaring.
Next, we add these squared deviations together to get Σx^2. This
value is divided by N, yielding the average squared deviation. Finally
we extract the square root. This is the SD or σ. Having described
its calculation, we may see the steps as they are worked out in a
simple numerical example. To illustrate the calculations needed, we
have computed in Table 3.2 the SD of the RT data for which the
mean value of 190.2 was found in an earlier exercise (p. 67). We
found each x value in the table by using the formula $x = X - M$.

As a pure descriptive statistic the SD is perhaps no more informa-

TABLE 3.2

**Numerical Example of the Computation of the SD of Reaction Times
for Six Subjects**

$M = 190.2$ msec

X	x	x^2
182	−8.2	67.24
191	+0.8	0.64
173	−17.2	295.84
176	−14.2	201.64
234	+43.8	1918.44
185	−5.2	27.04
	+44.6	$\Sigma x^2 = 2510.84$
	−44.8	
Check Sum: $\Sigma x =$	−0.2	

$$SD = \sqrt{\frac{\Sigma x^2}{N}} = \sqrt{\frac{2510.84}{6}} = \sqrt{418.47} = 20.5$$

tive than the AD. The SD tends to give more weight, in portraying variability, to extremely high or low values in the set, due to the squaring of their deviations from the mean. The SD is considered more stable or reliable as different samples of measurements are taken under the same conditions. The chief reason for preferring to compute the SD instead of the AD, however, is its usefulness in the further statistical analysis of experimental measurements or other data. We shall see this to be true when we discuss statistical inference in Chapter 4.

COMPUTATIONAL FORMULA FOR THE STANDARD DEVIATION. A raw score formula for the standard deviation is based on the fact that each deviation, x, may be written in terms of raw scores thus:

$$x = X - M \qquad \text{or} \qquad x = X - \frac{\Sigma X}{N}$$

Using this relationship, it is found that Formula 3.4 for SD, p. 72, may be replaced by the following computational formula:

$$SD = \frac{1}{N} \sqrt{N\Sigma X^2 - (\Sigma X)^2} \qquad \text{Formula 3.5}$$

where $SD =$ the standard deviation.
          $N =$ the number of values in the set.
          $\Sigma X^2 =$ the sum of the squares of all the scores or measures, one for each individual subject.
          $(\Sigma X)^2 =$ the square of the sum of the scores or measures.

This formula makes it unnecessary to find the deviation, x, of each subject's score from the mean of the set. It does require us to square each subject's score to obtain a set of X^2 values which are summed to get ΣX^2 in the first term of the expression for SD. Note carefully that this *sum of squares* differs from the *square of the sum*, found in the second term under the radical. $(\Sigma X)^2$ represents the square of the summation of all the scores. Since the standard deviation is intended to represent the variability due to individual differences in behavioral measurement, it is to be based on one score per individual subject. If several measurements are taken on each person, these should be summed or averaged into one value per person which may then be considered to be represented by X in the formula. The value of the SD obtained by using Formula 3.5 is equivalent to the value found when Formula 3.4 is employed. It can therefore be used when we wish to proceed to a determination of the standard error of the mean, using Formula 4.1, p. 83, Chapter 4.

THE VARIANCE. Occasionally we may encounter reference in research reports to the *variance,* a statistic used in describing variability and in analysis of research results. The variance is the square of the standard deviation of a set of data. It is usually symbolized, therefore, by the notation, σ^2. Since the last step in calculating a standard deviation is extracting the square root, the prior value is actually the variance. The formula for this statistic is therefore as follows:

$$\sigma^2 = \frac{\Sigma x^2}{N} \qquad\qquad \text{Formula 3.6}$$

Conventionally, we would go on to compute σ for descriptive purposes. Our acquaintance with the variance will serve us primarily as we may find it mentioned in the experimental literature. One advanced technique for assessing the operation of various factors in an experiment is called *analysis of variance.*

SUMMARY

Our search for quantified behavioral relationships is aided by a knowledge of the nature of measurement and an acquaintance with the descriptive uses of statistics.

Measurement involves following certain prescribed rules in order to assign numbers to phenomena such as behavioral events. Different kinds of measurement scales are determined by the operations which may be performed on the dimension being studied. The types of scales which hold interest for research in psychology include the ratio scale, the interval scale, and the ordinal scale. An important aspect of measurements determined with these different types of scales is the limitations which are imposed on the statistical treatment of the data they yield.

Descriptive statistics offer a useful way of thinking about and reporting the results of research. Both the central tendency and the variability of a set of data may each be represented by several statistics.

In considering the arithmetic mean we found a convenient approach to computational formulas, especially to the summation sign, Σ, which appears in the formulas for numerous statistics. The mean constant error and the average error, computed with and without regard for algebraic sign, respectively, are special uses of the mean which we examined. Besides the mean, we found the median to be a major index of central tendency, useful when treating ordinal scale values or skewed distributions of measures.

Measures of variability which we can compute include the average deviation, the standard deviation, and the variance of a set of data. The standard deviation is often preferred since it may enter into further statistical analysis of experimental results.

REFERENCE

Stevens, S. S. Mathematics, measurement, and psychophysics. In S. S. Stevens (Ed.), *Handbook of experimental psychology.* New York: Wiley, 1951. Pp. 1–49.

ADDITIONAL READINGS

Churchman, C. W., & Ratoosh, P. *Measurement: definitions and theories.* New York: Wiley, 1959.

Edwards, A. L. *Statistical methods for the behavioral sciences.* New York: Rinehart, 1954.

Lewis, D. *Quantitative methods in psychology.* New York: McGraw-Hill, 1960.

Underwood, B. J., Duncan, C. P., Taylor, Janet A., & Cotton, J. W. *Elementary statistics.* New York: Appleton-Century-Crofts, 1954.

CHAPTER 4

Statistical
Inference

In our consideration of statistics as an adjunct to experimentation, we have seen in Chapter 3 how the outcome of a study may be summarized through the use of measures of central tendency and of variability. These descriptive statistics are an aid to communication in science. We shall now go on to examine how statistical analysis can assist us with another aspect of the scientific enterprise, arriving at a decision concerning the tenability of an hypothesis. Using statistical techniques to guide such decision-making is called *statistical inference*.

Sampling

As we seek to discover behavior laws it is obviously impossible to examine everyone's behavior. We must be content to use a sample of people as our experimental subjects. When we have subjected this small group of persons to our experimental procedures, we want to know how probable it is that the result obtained is a typical one, a result that would recur in repeated samples of subjects who were similarly treated. The topic of sampling looms large in any discussion of statistical inference.

SAMPLE AND POPULATION. A *population* may be considered to be a group defined by specified characteristics. In psychology the populations which interest us will often be groups of *people* with specific attributes, but this might not always be the case. For example, we might be interested in populations defined as "handwriting specimens written by emotionally disturbed children" or "articles published in popular magazines during the 1950's." In laboratory experimentation, a population to which our attention could be directed might be "hand steadiness scores made by college students under Condition I." Notice that it is a specified group of behavior data, not just a group of people, which constitutes the population toward which the research is oriented. The term "college students" is just one of the specifications of this population.

If it were practically possible to test the hand steadiness of *all* college students under Condition I, then descriptive statistics could be computed which would provide definite answers to any question we might ask about this set of data. Since it is impossible to test all members of this vast group we must be content with sampling it. Instead of summary data on the entire population, called *parameters,* we must be content with statistics that are descriptive only of the sample. From these sample statistics we may draw inferences about the population parameters like the hypothetical mean and standard deviation of the population. Such inferences must be drawn if we wish to relate our hypotheses and laws to the population and not merely to the sample on which we have actual measurements.

For our purposes, an exploration of the logical and mathematical foundations of statistical inference will not be required. It will be sufficient to use certain prescribed definitions and computational formulas in testing hypotheses through the use of experimentally collected data. We need not adopt these techniques in complete blind faith, however. Fortunately, the statistical approach to reaching conclusions is parallel at many points to what may be termed intuitive inference. By applying intuitive inference in trying to reach decisions on the basis of illustrative sample data, we shall appreciate the aim and general approach of statistical inference, if not its detailed characteristics. Our exercises will be concentrated on inferences concerning the central tendencies of populations of data since this represents one of the commoner aims of statistical analysis.

RANDOM SAMPLE. Statistical inference about population parameters, based on sample statistics, generally depends on the assumption that the sample was drawn at random from the population. An accepted definition of a *random sample* from a population is that it *consists of a group into which every member of the population had an equal chance of falling.* We shall see that a sample so drawn has a probability of being representative of the population that tends to increase as the size of the sample increases.

Suppose we consider a hypothetical population of tapping scores obtained under prescribed conditions. In the great majority of instances exact population parameters remain unknown, but we shall assume this population of 6000 data to have a mean of 100, a median also of 100, a standard deviation of 10, and a range of 60. Assuming that these parameters were not known, what is the probability that random sampling from this set of data will provide us with appropriate estimates of the central tendency of the population? It may be instructive to examine first an alternative question, what is the probability of occurrence of inappropriate estimates? We shall explore the question intuitively, using some very simple probability concepts.

One way that an inappropriate estimate of the population mean might arise would be through the drawing of a sample in which every datum was one which exceeded the population mean. Such a sample, which would inflate our estimate of the population mean, can conceivably arise through random drawing of data from the population. But how probable would this sample be? Knowing the population median to be 100, we know that half of the data are above this value and half below it, excluding data identical with the median. The probability of drawing a value at random which exceeds 100 is exactly equal to the probability of drawing a value lower than the median. If we assume that no values fall right at the median, the probability of either sort of selection of a value is .50. Knowing this, we can compute the probabilities that all the data drawn in a sample would be, for example, above the population mean and median. If a sample of 2 cases is drawn, this probability is .25, the product of the probabilities that each case would independently be taken at random from the upper half of the distribution. If 10 cases are randomly selected, the probability that every one of them comes from the top half of the population data is only .001, indicating a rare occurrence of this particular random selection when every datum in the population has an equal chance of being selected. Computations indicate that having 9 out of 10 cases fall above the population median and one below it should occur with a probability of .01, still a slight likelihood.

Less extreme divisions in a sample between data originating above and below the population median are much more likely to occur. The most probable occurrence is a 50:50 split, equal numbers of cases coming from above and below the median. The probabilities of getting sample statistics that are generally representative of the population increase as the size of random sample is increased. It is facts such as these that are represented in the calculations used in statistical inference. In our experimentation we strive for representative estimates of population means when we select sufficient numbers of cases at random.

Drawing a random sample of subjects from a population of persons can be accomplished in several ways. The prime requirement is that each member of the population must have an equal chance of being selected. We must take precautions to permit no subtle violation of this rule in the procedure for randomizing which we employ. Three techniques for drawing a random sample which we shall consider briefly are ordinal selection, mechanical randomization, and using a table of random numbers. For randomizing by ordinal selection we might begin by listing alphabetically all persons in the population. Then we would select as our sample those whose names fell at certain ordinal positions, say every tenth or twentieth name in the list. In using a mechanical way of randomizing, we might put each name on a slip of paper first. Placing all these slips in a hat and shaking it well, we might then reach in blindly and draw out the desired number of names.

The difficulty with the methods mentioned, ordinal selection or mechanical randomization, is that they may not actually provide an equal chance for the appearance of every person in the sample. An individual named Aab would have little opportunity to be chosen if we count down ten names in an alphabetized list in the ordinal selection method. If we decided to take the first, eleventh, twenty-first, etc., names, this person would probably have a better than average chance of being selected. Possible error in randomizing mechanically might stem from the possibility that the names which were last to go into the hat might have a better chance of being drawn than those buried at the bottom of the heap. Precautions against such errors may be taken of course, but a safer way to insure that a sample is truly random is to employ a table of random numbers. Such a set of numbers may be found in the Appendix, Table A. As the designation implies, this table is composed of numbers selected in a strictly random fashion. To draw a random sample using such a table, we first list in any order all members of the population from which the sample is to be taken. This initial listing may be done quite systematically. We then select any column of four-digit numbers in Table A, Appendix, and assign these numbers, in sequence as they appear in the table, to the members of the population that we have listed. We then set aside those members whose assigned numbers are the largest in magnitude, continuing until the desired size of sample is reached. These members constitute a sample that has been drawn entirely at random since the magnitudes of the numbers in Table A are ordered in completely random fashion.

As an example of using a table of random numbers, suppose we wish to designate randomly 40 members from a population of 80 persons to serve as experimental subjects, the remaining individuals to be used as a control group of subjects. We would begin by listing the population in any convenient way, perhaps alphabetically. We next blindly select a point in the table of random numbers. Working consecutively from that point, we assign to each person a four-digit number. When we reach the bottom of one column, we proceed down, or up, the next column. By thus taking the numbers in some spatially systematic way which we have prearranged in our planning, we insure that the order of magnitudes of the numbers is a random one. We designate as the experimental group the 40 members of the population who have received the 40 largest assigned numbers. The remaining 40 people become our control subjects.

BIASED SAMPLE. A *biased sample* is one drawn from a population in such a way that every member of the population does *not* have an equal chance of falling into it. Such a nonrandom sample is to be avoided in research, of course, because the procedures of statistical inference require that hypotheses concerning a population be tested with random samples from that population. A biased sample may yield statistics that are *not* representative of population parameters. The direction and extent of the bias or distortion entering into the sample statistics depend on the factors involved in the biasing and how these factors relate to the measurements being taken. In many instances, this relationship is not known, so that a biased sample would result in distortions of unknown magnitude.

We may be helped in avoiding biased samples if we consider a few of the guises in which we might encounter them in psychological research. We may note initially that a biased sample may occur at two points in most investigations. In the first place, the entire group of subjects used in any experiment will rarely be a random sample of people from any specified population. They will very often comprise what has been termed an *incidental sample,* yet to be discussed. Second, an investigator may introduce a bias as he assigns the available subjects to different experimental treatments. If this assignment is not made randomly, the data obtained cannot be considered to be a random sample from any hypothetical population of data. As a result, the drawing of statistical inferences cannot be accomplished on a sound basis.

One or two examples may illustrate how bias may enter into research data if subjects are not randomly assigned to treatments. Suppose a student experimenter calls for volunteers to participate in a study involving proficiency in mathematics. As some of his friends explore the question of serving in the experiment, they declare that they are "not very good in math." If the experimenter is not careful, he may respond gallantly by putting them in the condition which involves easier mathematical problems. Gallantry is not the same as skill in research, of course, so that this failure to randomize the assignment to treatments or conditions may bias the outcome of the study.

A different example will demonstrate that the ways in which bias may be allowed to creep into research results are very numerous. This time we may imagine that the experiment involves the visual perception of geometric forms to be projected on the screen at the front of the classroom. Let us suppose that the class is to be divided into two groups who must wait different lengths of time before attempting to draw the patterns they have seen. What would be wrong if the experimenter designated the three front rows of students as Group I— One-Minute Retention and the three back rows as Group II—Three-Minute Retention? Such a nonrandom division of the available subjects might influence the performance due to the different distances from which the two groups had to view the screen. A division into groups on the basis of a table of random numbers would avoid this source of bias.

INCIDENTAL SAMPLE. When a fairly large population has been defined, it is quite a task to draw a random sample from it. Persons designated randomly to serve in an experiment may not actually be available or willing to act as subjects. For such reasons, those doing behavioral research have often employed classroom groups or volunteers as subjects. These may be designated as *incidental samples*. They must be regarded as definitely biased, to an unknown degree, with respect to some behavioral measurements which may be sought. On the other hand, they may be the working equivalent of random samples from certain populations which might be cautiously defined. It is this equivalence which must be assumed in generalizing experimental findings beyond their applicability to the sample of subjects. A college class is practically known to be a biased sample of the population of citizens at large; such a class may be the equivalent of a defined population of college students, including those from some other institutions besides the one sampled. The latter assumption should always be made conservatively and somewhat tentatively. Its use weakens the investigator's ability to use statistical inference with the full power that random sampling would have permitted.

One point must be made clear. If we use a nonrandom group of persons, an incidental sample, as participants in a study, we may still assign them in randomly designated groups to treatments or conditions in the experiment. This random determination of subjects to receive particular treatments means that statistical inference may be used to test hypotheses applying to the larger group. In other words, the original incidental sample may be considered as a small population about which we can legitimately draw inferences from the experimental data. These inferences can be considered tenable at particular levels of confidence. We cannot be quite so precise, however, in stating the tenability of inferences as they might apply to a large population which resembled our incidental sample to a greater or lesser degree. In this effort to generalize our research results, statistical inference no longer serves as an exact yardstick for evaluating decisions, but as a less precise indicator for making shrewd guesses about hypotheses.

The Standard Error of a Mean

A central concept in statistical inference is the *standard error of a mean*, abbreviated SE, σ_M, or SE_M. It is the standard deviation of a number of sample means drawn at random from the same population. Since an experiment usually provides us with just one sample obtained under a particular set of conditions or, in other words, drawn from a particular population, we do not generally compute SE_M directly. We employ a formula for its estimation on the basis of the sample data. This estimated SE_M (the same symbol usually serves for an estimated standard error as for one computed from a group of sample means) is in effect an index of the variability in sample means that *would be expected* if the experiment *were repeated* numerous times with identical treatment of samples of this size.

By estimating how varied the quantified outcome of a study might be, and knowing the value of the sample mean obtained, we can assess the likelihood that a particular hypothesis about the population mean is tenable. For example, if we find the mean of a sample of measurements to be 62.8, and the SE_M is estimated from the data to be 4.3, then the hypothesis that the population mean is 65.0 is entirely tenable by conventional rules of statistical inference. Also tenable, of course, are hypotheses that this population parameter is 60.0, 61.0, 62.0, 63.0, or 64.0. Many other values might be cited as possibilities, too. Instead of listing all possible values, with their varied probabilities, the statistician would identify the limits within which he would consider the population mean to lie. In setting these limits, he would take into account the seriousness of risk involved in making the decision. Such considerations make up the intricacies of statistical inference, most of which we must forego in our brief discussion.

One fact of which we must be aware is that we gain precision in locating the possible values of the population mean as the SE_M decreases. Important related facts are the ways in which we can strive for small SE_M values in our experimentation. Clues to these facts may be found in the formula for this important statistic, which is as follows:

$$SE_M = \frac{SD}{\sqrt{N-1}}$$ Formula 4.1

where SE_M = the standard error of the mean of a sample of data.

SD = the standard deviation of that set of data, computed according to Formula 3.4, p. 72, or Formula 3.5, p. 73.

N = the number of cases in the set of data.

From the formula we see that we are contributing to the ultimate precision of our statements about possible means of the population when we keep SD small. In turn, we keep the SD small insofar as we exert experimental controls to prevent unwanted sources of variability from increasing the variance. Another way to work toward smaller SE_M values is to increase the size of the sample studied, thus increasing the denominator of the formula. Provided that SD remains the same, we can reduce SE_M by one-half if we increase N from 26 to 101, as substitution in the formula indicates. The desirability of effecting reductions in SE_M will become more apparent as we explore statistical inference further.

The Standard Error of a Difference between Uncorrelated Means

In many of our experiments we may be less interested in estimating population means than in interpreting the difference between two sample means obtained under different conditions. Again, our interpretation is directed toward projecting our result in a generalization that will be applicable not only to the samples we have studied but to similar samples which might be drawn from the same populations. We are going to be concerned first with investigating the stability, or reliability, of a difference between two means of independent samples. Such samples arise when two sets of data are taken from different groups of subjects, not paired in any way. Later on we shall deal with the experimental design involving the same, or matched, subjects under two different conditions, yielding two sets of data which may be correlated. Such a correlation alters the estimate of the reliability of the obtained difference.

If an experiment which gives means of two independent samples were repeated numerous times, we should expect the obtained sample means to vary to the extent indicated by an estimate of the standard error of each mean. As these means fluctuate from one replication of an experiment to another, the difference between them will also fluctuate over a range of values determined by the values occurring in the sample means. Just as we can estimate SE_M on the basis of a sample set of data, we can estimate the *standard error of the difference between uncorrelated means* on the basis of the samples of the two uncorrelated sets of measures.

The standard error of a mean difference between two uncorrelated means may be defined as the square root of the sum of the two squared SE_M values obtained from the two sets of sample data. Symbolized here as SE_{D_M}, this definition may be grasped more readily from an examination of the computational formula, as follows:

$$SE_{D_M} = \sqrt{SE_{M_1}^2 + SE_{M_2}^2} \qquad \text{Formula 4.2}$$

where SE_{D_M} = the standard error of the difference between two means.
 SE_{M1} = the standard error of the mean of the first sample of data, obtained under one condition.
 SE_{M2} = the standard error of the mean of the second sample of data, obtained under the second condition.

As the formula indicates, we first obtain the standard error estimates from the two sets of data separately, using Formula 4.1, page 83. Then we square each of these SE_M values, add the two squares together, and extract the square root. The resultant value of SE_{D_M} is an estimate of the standard deviation of values of D_M (difference between sample means) which would arise from numerous repetitions of the experiment. The SE_{D_M}, as we shall see, is used in drawing statistical inferences from the outcome of experiments involving two sets of data.

The Null Hypothesis

In arriving at a statistical inference from two sets of measurements obtained under different experimental conditions, it is common practice to make use of the *null hypothesis*. This is the hypothesis that there is no difference in the populations of measurements from which the two sample sets of data were drawn. It states in effect that the different experimental conditions actually have no differential effect on the behavior measurements that are obtained under them. An alternative way of defining this null hypothesis is to say that the two samples of data were drawn at random from the same hypothetical population of behavior measurements instead of from different populations of data.

The null hypothesis is the logical alternative to the hypothesis that the different experimental conditions or treatments *do* lead to different populations of data, from which the two sample sets of data were drawn. This latter hypothesis might be considered as the affirmative hypothesis that a difference does exist. Since the null hypothesis and the affirmative hypothesis about the population or populations are in logical opposition, a decision is required as to which is tenable with respect to the outcome of any experiment. If the null hypothesis is tenable, then the affirmative hypothesis must be rejected. If the null hypothesis may be rejected, the affirmative hypothesis may be considered tenable. The decision to reject an hypothesis on the basis of statistical analysis of the results of one experiment does not mean that this hypothesis is permanently excluded from further consideration. Nor does ruling an hypothesis to be tenable mean that it is to be considered proved to be completely valid. Decisions concerning hypotheses are made with greater or lesser confidence, based on the procedures of statistical inference.

Critical Ratio as a Test of the Null Hypothesis

The null hypothesis may be interpreted to state that the population mean difference corresponding to different experimental conditions is zero. When we obtain a particular difference between two sample means, we may ask how probable it is that such a difference has been obtained by random sampling when no mean difference exists between the two populations being sampled. If the obtained mean difference, D_M, is of a size which might occur fairly frequently in random samples drawn from a population with a parameter mean difference of zero, then we may assume the null hypothesis to be tenable. However, if D_M is so large as to indicate an extremely improbable random sample from a population with a mean difference of zero, then the null hypothesis may be considered to be rejected.

The determination of the probability of a particular D_M value, assuming the null hypothesis to hold for the population, is accomplished by comparing this sample statistic with the estimated standard error of the mean difference. The ratio which constitutes this approach to a statistical inference about the population is known as the *critical ratio*, abbreviated *CR*, or as the $\bar{z}$ *ratio*. The formula for computing the *CR* is as follows:

$$CR = \frac{D_M}{SE_{D_M}}$$ Formula 4.3

where CR = the critical ratio.
   D_M = the obtained difference between the two sample means.
   SE_{D_M} = the standard error of the mean difference, calculated as indicated in Formula 4.2, p. 84.

Study of the formula shows that the value of the CR will be increased as the mean difference, D_M, is increased or as the standard error of the mean difference, SE_{D_M}, is decreased. We may recall that the latter value reflects the variability in the two sets of data obtained.

The higher the value of the CR, as computed, the less probable it is that the null hypothesis is true. Assuming that 30 or more subjects have been run under each condition, a CR value of 2.58 indicates that there is only 1 chance in 100, $p = .01$, that the obtained difference arose by random sampling from a population of differences whose mean is actually zero. If a CR value of 2.58 or greater is obtained, it is conventional to reject the null hypothesis as untenable, too improbable to retain. This means that the affirmative hypothesis would be considered tenable if such a high CR value is calculated. The two different treatments of the study actually lead to two different populations of data, it would be concluded.

The t Ratio as a Test of the Null Hypothesis

In making a statistical analysis of the difference between two sample means, the CR has been supplanted in many instances by the t ratio. In its calculation, the t ratio can be obtained in precisely the same way as the CR, using Formula 4.3, p. 85. However, an alternative computational technique can be used to obtain the t ratio which gives more consideration to the meaning of the null hypothesis, as we shall see. In its interpretation, the t ratio demands more consideration for the size of the samples of data taken, especially as the value of N falls much below 25 or 30. It is as a small sample statistic that the t test has gained popularity in behavioral research.

We have noted that it is entirely proper to use the CR formula for computing a t ratio. If we do so, we compute separate values of SE_M for each sample and then combine these into an estimate of SE_{D_M}, the denominator of the ratio. Since we are testing the null hypothesis, however, we may wish to follow a different technique which combines the data into a single estimate of the variability of the population. This is done in view of the fact that the null hypothesis states that our two samples of data were drawn at random from a single population. The computational formula requires that we obtain Σx^2 separately for each set of data (where $x = X - M$ in each set). This obtaining of the sum of squared deviations, we recall, was a step in getting the SD of a set of values. These two sums of squared deviations are combined in finding an estimate of the standard error of the difference in means, as this formula indicates:

$$t = \frac{D_M}{\sqrt{\left(\dfrac{\Sigma x_1{}^2 + \Sigma x_2{}^2}{N_1 + N_2 - 2}\right)\left(\dfrac{N_1 + N_2}{N_1 N_2}\right)}} \qquad \text{Formula 4.4}$$

where t = the t ratio test for the significance of the difference between two means when samples are small.

D_M = the difference between the two uncorrelated sample means $(D_M = M_1 - M_2)$.

$\Sigma x_1{}^2$ = the summation of the squared deviations of one set of values from their mean, M_1 $(x_1 = X_1 - M_1)$.

$\Sigma x_2{}^2$ = the summation of the squared deviations of the other set of values from their mean, M_2 $(x_2 = X_2 - M_2)$.

N_1 = the number of subjects contributing to M_1.

N_2 = the number of subjects contributing to M_2.

When calculated, a t ratio must be interpreted by noting how it compares with tabled values which have been determined for samples of different size. Such a table is presented as Table B, Appendix. To use this table we first employ the values of N_1 and N_2 to determine the number of degrees of freedom appropriate to the analysis we are making. Degrees of freedom, often written df, is a statistical concept with meanings not essential to our discussion. We are concerned with df only as a key to locating the proper tabled values of t to interpret the outcome of a two-group experiment. The formula for df is as follows:

$$df = N_1 + N_2 - 2 \qquad \text{Formula 4.5}$$

where df = number of degrees of freedom.

N_1 = the number of subjects contributing to M_1.

N_2 = the number of subjects contributing to M_2.

Of course, if $N_1 = N_2$, the formula might be simplified to $df = 2(N - 1)$, where N symbolizes the number of subjects in either group. These formulas for t and df apply when we are dealing with separate, uncorrelated sets of data. Later we shall learn different formulas for t and df to be applied when treatments are given to the same, or to matched, subjects.

Having determined the df for our experiment, we locate this df value in Column 1 of Table B, Appendix. If the exact df number is not in the table, we may introduce only a moderate error if we use the nearest df value that we do find there. Corresponding to each df value, we see that Table B contains two t values. When the t ratio we have calculated from our experimental data exceeds the appropriate tabled value, this indicates that the null hypothesis is probably not tenable for our study. In other words, the affirmative hypothesis—that there is a statistically significant difference between the two means—is supported as tenable when the computed t ratio exceeds the appropriate tabled t value, from Column 2 or Column 3 depending on the level of confidence we demand for the interpretation of the experimental result.

We may describe the tabled values of the t ratio in a somewhat more exact way by referring to probability. For any value of df, the tabled t value in Column 2 is one which would be attained or exceeded on the average of 1 time in 20 if the experiment were repeated numerous times and if the null hypothesis were actually valid. With the null hypothesis truly applicable to the situation, most replications of the study (19 out of 20, on the average) would yield smaller computed t ratios than the tabled t value in Column 2. A larger value may be interpreted as indicating that the obtained sets of data represent rare random samples from the same population— the null hypothesis—or else that a difference in the sets of data is attributable to the experimental treatments. Since the former alternative has such a slim probability, $p = .05$, of being valid, the preferred alternative interpretation of a large t ratio is that it indicates the affirmative hypothesis to be tenable.

The values of t which we find in Column 2 of Table B are said to represent the five per cent level of confidence in rejecting the null hypothesis. This level of confidence has received wide usage in behavioral research. Some experimenters wish to be more stringent in accepting an affirmative hypothesis so they require a higher t value before rejecting the null hypothesis. Often they demand the one per cent level of confidence, a probability of only 1 in a 100 that the two sets of data came from the same population of measures. The t values of Column 3 of Table B, Appendix, represent this one per cent level of confidence. These greater t values serve as guides for decision-making for those investigators who have chosen this level as the point where they will abandon the null hypothesis in the light of the t ratio they have calculated. We shall have more to say about this process of statistical inference after we have examined the calculation of the t ratio for correlated sets of data.

The Standard Error of a Difference between Correlated Means

We saw earlier how to compute the standard error of a difference between means using Formula 4.2 when the two sets of data were taken from different groups of subjects, not paired in any way. We must now examine the computation of SE_{D_M} when the two sets of data are paired in such a way that a coefficient of correlation* between the two sets may be computed. This situation arises primarily in two experimental designs, one in which the same subjects are run under two conditions yielding two different means, and the other in which different groups of subjects are paired off on some variable related to the one under investigation. In either case there may be a correlation between the two sets of experimental data. The existence of such a correlation affects the value of SE_{D_M} and should be taken into account in its computation, as the following formula shows:

$$SE_{D_M} = \sqrt{SE_{M_1}^2 + SE_{M_2}^2 - 2r_{12} \cdot SE_{M_1} \cdot SE_{M_2}} \qquad \text{Formula 4.6}$$

where SE_{D_M} = the standard error of the difference between means.

$\quad SE_{M1}$ = the standard error of the mean of the first sample of data, obtained under one condition.

$\quad SE_{M2}$ = the standard error of the mean of the second, correlated sample of data, obtained under the second condition.

$\quad r_{12}$ = the Pearson coefficient of the correlation between the paired sets of measures obtained under the two conditions from the same or matched subjects. The subscript 12 merely indicates that Set 1 and Set 2 were correlated.

We may note that this formula differs from Formula 4.2 by the addition of a third term under the radical. An important factor in this term is the Pearson correlation coefficient between the two sets of data which have been collected. If this coefficient, r_{12}, is positive, then this third term has the effect of reducing the value of SE_{D_M}. Such a reduction is one advantage of using the same subjects in two experimental conditions or of administering the two treatments to subjects who have been paired on some matching test. These experimental designs cannot always be employed. Where they may be used, the smaller SE_{D_M} value obtained increases the probability of rejecting the null hypothesis by leading to a larger t ratio.

Computational Formula for the Standard Error of a Difference between Correlated Means

If we used Formula 4.6, to find the SE_{D_M} between two means when the data are paired and correlated, we have to compute a Pearson

* The meaning and computation of coefficients of correlation are discussed in statistics textbooks and in some introductory psychology textbooks. Although Formula 4.6 includes a coefficient of correlation, r_{12}, the standard error of a difference between correlated means can be calculated without using such a coefficient by employing Formula 4.7, p. 90.

coefficient of correlation, r, and the standard error of each mean as intermediate steps. These steps may be eliminated by using a formula which depends on first obtaining an algebraic difference, D, between the pair of measures obtained for each individual or for each matched pair of subjects. This formula is as follows:

$$SE_{D_M} = \frac{1}{N} \sqrt{\frac{N\Sigma D^2 - (\Sigma D)^2}{N - 1}} \qquad \text{Formula 4.7}$$

where SE_{D_M} = the standard error of a difference between means.

$\quad\quad$ N = the number of subjects, or number of matched pairs.

$\quad\quad$ ΣD^2 = the sum of the squares of the algebraic differences between the measures of each pair.

$\quad\quad$ $(\Sigma D)^2$ = the square of the sum of the algebraic differences.

A simple example may help to clarify how this formula is used. Let us suppose that we have reaction time data on ten subjects, each person having been tested under each of two conditions, designated

TABLE 4.1

Numerical Example of the Computation of SE_{D_M} of Reaction Times for Ten Subjects

S No.	X	Y	D	D^2
1	185	178	7	49
2	193	184	9	81
3	174	168	6	36
4	191	193	−2	4
5	206	197	9	81
6	179	182	−3	9
7	188	179	9	81
8	193	188	5	25
9	185	180	5	25
10	190	186	4	16
Σ:	1884	1835	49	407

$$SE_{D_M} = \frac{1}{10} \sqrt{\frac{10 \cdot 407 - 49^2}{9}}$$

$$= \frac{1}{10} \sqrt{\frac{4070 - 2401}{9}}$$

$$= \frac{1}{10} \sqrt{\frac{1669}{9}}$$

$$= \frac{1}{10} \sqrt{185.44} = \frac{13.6}{10} = 1.36$$

X and Y. The treatment of the data to obtain SE_{D_M} is indicated in the tabulations of Table 4.1. The value of SE_{D_M} as calculated here may be used as the denominator of a t ratio to test the significance of D_M, the difference between the mean RT values obtained under the two conditions. Formula 4.7 represents a great economy over Formula 4.6 which demanded several laborious preliminary calculations.

The t Ratio for Paired Measures

When we have employed Formula 4.7 to calculate the value of SE_{D_M} for two sets of paired measures, taking their correlation into account, we may use this value as the denominator of a t ratio. The numerator of the ratio, as before, is D_M, the difference between the two means of the measures obtained. In other words, we may use the same formula as in computing the CR, Formula 4.3. However, since we are considering this quotient as a t ratio, we must interpret its outcome on the basis of the tabled values of t.

To use Table B, Appendix, we may recall, we must know the number of degrees of freedom, df, applicable to our experiment. In the case of paired, correlated sets of data, df is computed with a different formula than we employed earlier. For paired measures this formula is as follows:

$$df = N - 1 \qquad \text{Formula 4.8}$$

where df = number of degrees of freedom.
N = the number of *pairs* of measures.

If 20 subjects had been run under two conditions or if 40 subjects had been matched on some variable and then used as two matched groups of 20 subjects each, the 20 pairs of data yielded in either case would mean that df was 19 for such a study. If the 40 subjects had been randomly divided into two experimental groups instead of being matched, then the t ratio for testing the mean difference would have involved a df value of 38, as indicated by Formula 4.5, p. 87. Pairing off available subjects by some matching procedure thus reduces df and therefore requires a higher t ratio for rejecting the null hypothesis than would be needed if two groups had been created randomly. However, matching often yields a higher calculated t ratio due to the reduction in SE_{D_M} that the correlation term affords. The degree to which a matching factor is correlated with the behavior measures to be taken determines to a great extent the correlation between the two sets of experimental measures that are obtained under the different conditions. This fact deserves close attention in deciding how much precision we may hope to gain in a study by using matched groups instead of groups designated randomly.

Precautions and Possibilities in Statistical Inference

In a textbook of experimental psychology such as this we have a limited opportunity to explore statistical inference. We must close this brief discussion with some cautions to be observed as we interpret the outcome of our experiments and with some suggestions for developing additional skill in statistical analysis.

TYPES OF ERROR IN STATISTICAL INFERENCE. A statistical test like the t ratio indicates how probable it is that the null hypothesis is valid with respect to two randomly drawn sets of data. The actual decision concerning acceptance or rejection of the null hypothesis remains for the investigator to make. As this decision is undertaken, two types of error may be made. A Type I error is the rejection of the null hypothesis when it is actually valid. A Type II error is the acceptance of the null hypothesis when it is not actually true. Normally, of course, we never know whether we are making one type of error or the other when we make a decision after statistical analysis. What we can do, however, is to set the levels of confidence which we demand in a study so as to lessen the risk of making a particular type of error, whichever type would be more damaging in the light of our research purposes. By demanding the one per cent level of confidence, for example, we cut the probability of a Type I error, false rejection of the null hypothesis, to one-fifth of what it would be if only the five per cent level of confidence were required. We do this by permitting only 1 chance in 100 instead of 5 in 100 that an acceptably large t ratio could arise when two samples of data were randomly drawn from the same population. Such a precaution against a Type I error might be quite appropriate if we were testing an affirmative hypothesis which we hoped might be regarded as a behavioral law. On the other hand, in exploratory research we might afford to be less stringent in setting the confidence level to be demanded. At this point in a program of investigation, a greater risk attaches to a Type II error, deciding that the null hypothesis is tenable when in fact it is not. This decision might block a potentially valuable series of studies. In such a situation this risk could be lessened by requiring only the five or the ten per cent level of confidence before rejecting the null hypothesis. It is generally advocated that this type of reasoning be conducted before data are gathered. With the level of confidence selected in advance, the null hypothesis can be accepted or rejected as soon as the statistical analysis is complete.

PROOF VS. TENABILITY OF HYPOTHESES. It is commonly pointed out that the null hypothesis can never be disproved. Our statistical tests may merely indicate that its validity in a given situation is highly improbable. On this basis we may decide to reject the null hypothesis as untenable. We have not disproved it by deciding to reject it.

Deciding that the null hypothesis is untenable is equivalent to deciding that some affirmative hypothesis is tenable. In general terms, the affirmative hypothesis indicated to be tenable when a sufficiently high t ratio is computed states that the two different conditions of the experiment represented sampling from two different populations of data. This is by no means the same as proving the validity of the hypothesis we set out to test in the study. At best we may have demonstrated this hypothesis to be tenable, providing that the experimental conditions actually used were a valid representation of this hypothesis. In many cases, the treatments to which subjects are exposed are complex enough to permit at least a few alternative hypotheses to be offered in explanation of a significant difference between two means. These alternative possibilities may have crept in through flaws in the experimental design or procedure or they may have been virtually unavoidable. In any case, a decision to reject the null hypothesis usually leaves us with possible conclusions whose specificity or generality must be carefully considered.

ASSUMPTIONS UNDERLYING THE t RATIO. We have considered the t ratio as a widely useful tool of statistical inference in behavioral research. In dealing with it we paid little attention to the formal assumptions underlying the use of this test, but we are going to give them passing attention at this time. The first assumption made in employing a t ratio is that the population or populations of values being sampled represent a normal distribution—symmetrical, with most cases falling near the point of central tendency and with deviations from this central tendency being increasingly rare, the larger their size. The second assumption is that if two different populations are involved as we randomly draw the two samples of data, these populations must have the same degree of variability or variance before we can consider the t ratio to evaluate the significance of the difference between the two means. A third assumption underlying the t ratio and many other statistical tests is that the sets of data being tested have been drawn at random from the population or populations.

We should do what we can to be sure these assumptions are met as we perform experiments and analyze the data they yield. When the samples of data we have are small, the statistical tests for normality of distribution and for homogeneity of variance, the first two assumptions, are not very sensitive. Their complexity and their limited usefulness preclude any consideration of such tests here. We often proceed with computing a t ratio without any demonstration that we have met these assumptions. If there is reason to suspect that the data we have collected have come from a population that is markedly skewed, we may wish to transform the data into a set for which normality may be assumed. We then use these transformed data in computing the t ratio to see if the null hypothesis may be rejected. Among the transformations which have proved useful for such a purpose are the *square root transformation* (extracting the square root of each value originally obtained), and the *logarithmic transformation* (taking the logarithm of each original value).

The assumption that sampling must be random is the one which should concern us most as we design our experiments. By keeping it in mind we may avoid letting various kinds of bias affect the data which we collect. Not only does biased sampling preclude the use of the standard statistical tests, but it effectively prevents us from reaching sound conclusions, even intuitively, when the experiment is finished. The need for random sampling in statistical inference is one way in which statistical considerations should influence our research in its planning stage.

OTHER APPROACHES TO STATISTICAL INFERENCE. The t ratio was selected for discussion because it is a tool in statistical inference which is likely to have applicability to some of the experimental results which we have to evaluate. We must be aware that there are numerous other techniques of statistical analysis which are also aids to decision-making. As a student, you may become acquainted with some of these through courses in statistics, statistical textbooks, and the help of your instructors in courses dealing with experimental psychology. A rule of paramount importance is to consider early in planning a study the statistical analysis that is to be made when the measurements have been taken. In our deliberations concerning the statistical testing of our hypotheses we must be sure that our data meet the assumptions which the technique being considered requires. If we find, for example, that our data have a skewed distribution, we may find it useful to normalize by some such numerical transformation as was suggested earlier in our discussion of the assumptions for the t ratio. Alternatively, we may decide to explore the possibility of using a *nonparametric test,* one which makes no assumptions regarding the form of the distribution of data. It must be repeated for emphasis that virtually all tests assume that the data have been randomly sampled from the populations for which inferences are to be drawn.

Our proficiency in behavioral research has another advantage to gain from our acquaintance with statistics. Besides using statistics in our own research, we may better understand the reports of experiments that we read. If an experimenter declines to regard a difference between two means as significant because a t ratio failed to reach the one per cent level of confidence, we shall understand that he decided upon this fairly stringent level on the basis of his research purposes. If we see that the t value he obtained exceeded the tabled value for the five per cent level of confidence, we ourselves may choose to regard the difference as significant in the light of the use we wish to make of his findings—perhaps as a guide to additional studies.

Our grasp of reported results of behavioral research may be strengthened by a nodding acquaintance with *analysis of variance,* a statistical test widely used. One of its applications is in assessing the outcome of studies in which several values of the independent variable were used instead of just employing two experimental conditions. In this instance the F ratio that is obtained by analysis of variance is an evaluation of the difference among several means instead of an assessment of the difference between just two means as accomplished by the t ratio. Like the t test, an F ratio may lead to the acceptance or rejection of the null hypothesis at a particular level of confidence when the calculated ratio is compared with the F value tabled for the appropriate number of degrees of freedom. If it is decided on the basis of the F test that there is a significant difference among the several means in general, t ratios may then be employed to see which particular differences between pairs of these means are themselves significant.

Another use of analysis of variance is in studies where more than one independent variable is manipulated. In such a case, a separate F ratio is computed for each independent variable to see if it had a significant effect on the values of the behavior measures that were obtained. It might happen that analysis of a three-variable study would show, for example, that two of the independent variables had exerted an effect on the behavior as revealed in significant F ratios. The third variable might not have led to a significant F ratio, indicating the tenability of the null hypothesis that this variable has no effect on the behavior measure in question.

SUMMARY

As a guide to understanding and describing the outcome of an experiment, statistical inference is of great help to the investigator. Since it depends generally on random sampling of data from the population for which inferences are to be drawn, we found it useful to consider the nature of random, biased, and incidental samples. When an experimenter uses an incidental sample of subjects, we saw that he may divide it randomly into smaller groups for the administration of the experimental conditions.

A cornerstone of statistical inference is the standard error of the mean. As usually employed, this statistic is an estimate of the hypothetical variability of sample means in replicated experiments. Its calculation is based on the variability of the data of the one sample of data that is typically available after a study has been run just once. From a knowledge of the obtained sample mean and the standard error of the mean we can estimate how probable it is that various values exist as the population mean.

Somewhat analogous to the standard error of the mean and related to it is the standard error of a difference between means. This is an estimate of how variable the obtained mean difference would be if a study were repeated numerous times. This SE_{D_M} is calculated somewhat differently when the two sets of data are uncorrelated or are correlated. In either case the computed value may serve as the denominator of a critical ratio or a t ratio with the difference between means as the numerator. Such a ratio may be interpreted to indicate the probability that such a difference might occur when the null hypothesis is actually valid. The null hypothesis states that the two samples of data were drawn from the same population or identical populations.

In attempting statistical inference based on some test like the t ratio, we must be aware of necessary cautions as well as of possibilities of interpreting our research results. In setting the level of confidence at which we reject the null hypothesis, we must consider the risks involved in making either type of error—false rejection or false acceptance. Accepting the null hypothesis does not prove that it is true, nor does rejecting it constitute a proof that the affirmative hypothesis of an experiment is the only valid explanation of the results.

As we employ statistical aids to inference we must be aware of the assumptions which are required if various statistical tests are to be properly used. Our experimental designs, our measurement techniques, and our manipulations of the data collected should be oriented toward the legitimate use of such tests. Sometimes we must be content to project our findings only to populations of limited size, from which our data may be said to have been randomly sampled.

Our discussion of statistical inference was a limited one, with the t ratio taken as our primary example. Statistics textbooks and other sources are available to broaden our acquaintance with additional aids to the interpretation of research outcomes. Knowledge of statistics will prove beneficial in understanding the experimentation of others as well as in conducting our own studies. The F ratio of analysis of variance, for example, is a statistical test which we find reported frequently in behavioral research.

ADDITIONAL READINGS

Edwards, A. L. *Statistical analysis.* (Rev. ed.) New York: Rinehart, 1958.

Guilford, J. P. *Fundamental statistics in psychology and education.* (3rd ed.) New York: McGraw-Hill, 1956.

Lindquist, E. F. *Design and analysis of experiments in psychology and education.* Houghton Mifflin, 1953.

McNemar, Q. *Psychological statistics.* (2nd ed.) New York: Wiley, 1955.

Senders, Virginia L. *Measurement and statistics.* New York: Oxford, 1958.

Siegel, S. *Nonparametric statistics for the behavioral sciences.* New York: McGraw-Hill, 1956.

CHAPTER 5

Psychophysical
Methods

The sensory experiences aroused by physical stimuli often initiate or alter behavior sequences. Just as we quantify the behavior that results from stimulation, we strive also to measure the sensation experienced by the organism. A scale is created for the measurement of sensation by performing certain operations with the physical stimuli and using physical measures as a convenient reference. The scaling operations to which we refer are called *psychophysical methods* because psychological sensory magnitudes are approached by manipulations of physical stimulus dimensions. Among the important aspects of such scaling of sensations are the identification of zero points and the determination of the smallest discriminable sensory differences.

Although psychophysical methods occupy a central place in the development of laboratory psychology, we shall not concern ourselves with their historical position but with their usefulness in modern experimental work. There is a versatility about these different methods that makes them applicable to a greater range of investigations than the studies for which they were originally devised. They can be employed in the study of complex perceptions as well as for investigating simpler sensory phenomena. Also, they lend themselves to applied experimentation as in determining the psychophysical aspects of particular man-machine systems.

Oriented as they are toward scaling or quantification, the psychophysical methods involve the statistical treatment of the collected data. In fact, many of the central constructs in psychophysics are statistically defined. Accurate specification of such constructs naturally demands a foundation of reliable data, carefully treated mathematically to yield valid information. The basis, in turn, for the reliability of the data we obtain is to be found in taking enough repeated measurements while every safeguard against experimental error is exercised.

EXPLORING SENSORY BOUNDARIES

The eye is sensitive only to a particular band of wavelengths of electromagnetic radiation, from about 400mμ to about 700mμ.* Hearing is limited to a frequency range between about 16$\sim$ and 16,000$\sim$.† On the energy dimension, too, there are values of physical intensity for both auditory and visual stimuli that are at the limit of sensation. Weaker physical energies than these threshold values are not experienced. There are boundaries to these modalities of sensation, then, within the broad extent of physical stimuli for both the dimensions of energy level and of wavelength or frequency. An important application of the psychophysical methods is to survey these boundaries.

THE ABSOLUTE THRESHOLD OR LIMEN. As we see how the methods are employed, we shall learn not only about the procedural techniques of psychophysics, but we shall become better acquainted with the concept of *absolute threshold* or *limen* at the same time. An absolute threshold may be defined as a boundary point in sensation, separating sensory experience from no such experience when physical stimulus values reach a particular point. "Limen" is the Latin word for the threshold of a door and it is generally used as a synonym for "threshold" in psychophysics. The often used abbreviation for the absolute threshold is *RL* taken from the German *Reiz Limen* which means *stimulus threshold*.

The Method of Limits

Most psychophysical methods have been known by more than one name. The *method of limits*, for example, is also called the *method of minimal changes*. If you can remember both names in this case, you will be aided in remembering the details of experimental procedure. To locate the absolute threshold, the experimenter gives a series of trials in which stimulation is *minimally changed* in successive steps along some physical dimension until the boundary of sensation

---

* The abbreviation, mμ, stands for millimicrons—units of wavelength measurement.

† The symbol, $\sim$, stands for cycles per second—units of vibratory frequency measurement.

is passed. That is, a series of stimulations which begins above the sensory threshold is continued until a physical stimulus value is reached which arouses no reported sensation. Or, a series beginning somewhat below threshold is continued until a stimulus value is reached that arouses a reported sensation. In either case, the occurrence of a change in report on the part of the subject is an indication that the *limit* or sensory boundary has been reached. The series of trials is terminated whenever the subject's report of sensation changes from "Yes" to "No" or from "No" to "Yes."

DETERMINING THE ABSOLUTE THRESHOLD; AN EXAMPLE. The method of limits is often used in audiometry—testing a person's hearing. The hearing specialist presents a series of tones that begins above threshold. Attenuation weakens the physical tone intensity with each stimulus presentation until it becomes so faint that it is not reported as heard. On other series of trials, the tone is initially below threshold and its intensity is increased in small steps until it can be heard. Several such series of trials, working down and up to the limit of hearing, permit the calculation of an average threshold value. In audiometry, the threshold is obtained for each of several frequency values so that a threshold curve or audiogram may be plotted. Such a curve is drawn in a rectangular coordinate plot with intensity level on the ordinate and frequency along the abscissa. A major use of all the psychophysical methods has been to establish normal limits of sensation based on data from large groups of subjects. Besides being employed in clinical audiometry, the method of limits may be used as a research technique to determine hearing thresholds under special conditions like environmental masking noise.

Returning to our example, let us examine the procedural details of the method of limits as it might be used to test one subject in a normative study of hearing thresholds. Assume we are testing with a tone of 8000 cycles per second at this point in the experiment. With the tone presented monaurally, the absolute threshold, RL, may fall about 55 db below a reference pressure level of 1 dyne/cm^2, or −55. Some of our series of trials might begin above this value, say at −45 or −50, and descend in 1 db steps until the subject could no longer hear the tone. These would be called *descending series*. Other series would begin below threshold, perhaps at −60 or −65, and be increased until reported as heard. These are termed *ascending series*. Most experimental work involves both descending and ascending series of trials with minimal changes being made in physical stimulus intensity until a limit of sensation is reached. We see that this psychophysical method employs *physical* changes in the physical stimulus to locate a boundary point on the *psychological* scale of sensation—a *psychophysical* procedure.

Our administration of the method of limits would be guided by a work sheet on which we would indicate the minimal change steps to be used and the starting points for the various descending and ascending series. Preliminary trials would have served to locate the threshold approximately. Table 5.1 shows a work sheet for

TABLE 5.1

Completed Work Sheet for Determination of Absolute Threshold for an 8000-Cycle Tone by the Method of Limits.
(The testing of one subject is represented)

*Stimulus Intensity	Type of Series					
	d	a	d	a	d	a
−44						
−45	†Yes					
−46	Yes				†Yes	
−47	Yes				Yes	
−48	Yes				Yes	
−49	Yes		†Yes		Yes	
−50	Yes		Yes		Yes	
−51	Yes		Yes		Yes	
−52	Yes		Yes		Yes	
−53	Yes		Yes		Yes	Yes
−54	Yes	Yes	Yes		Yes	No
−55	Yes	No	No		Yes	No
−56	No	No		Yes	Yes	No
−57		No		No	No	No
−58		No		No		No
−59		No		No		No
−60		No		No		†No
−61		No		No		
−62		†No		No		
−63				No		
−64				No		
−65				†No		
Series *RL*:	−55.5	−54.5	−54.5	−56.5	−56.5	−53.5

*In decibels below 1 dyne/cm² reference pressure level.
†Predetermined starting point for this series.

determining the intensity threshold for the 8000-cycle tone with three descending and three ascending series of trials. Also included in the table are the symbols which were used to tally the responses as the testing proceeded in this hypothetical study. Each column in the table, you see, represents one series of trials, either descending, d, or ascending, a. The scale at the left indicates the successive physical values that made up a series. Each column indicates that a series was terminated as soon as the subject made a change in judgment from "Yes" to "No" or from "No" to "Yes" in response to some visual signal meaning, "Do you hear the tone?" For each series of trials an estimate of the threshold value was taken to be the value halfway between the intensity that elicited a change in judgment and the preceding intensity of the series. These threshold estimates are indicated at the bottom of each column of Table 5.1. An averaging of these series RL estimates over several series of trials completes the operational definition of the threshold of hearing for this subject for an 8000-cycle tone. The liminal value, or RL, in our example is −55.17 db below the reference level of 1 dyne/cm².

PROCEDURAL DETAILS. Several procedural details should be noted in our example of the method of limits. The steps used in each series of stimulus presentations are small ones, approximating minimal changes. Much larger steps would give only a coarse estimate of the threshold on each series of trials. Ascending and descending series of trials were both used, in this case alternately. The use of both types of series tends to guard against certain errors as our later discussion will show. Different series in either category are begun at different points on the scale. This prevents a subject from falling into a habit of changing his judgment after a fixed number of stimulus presentations. The threshold estimates from several series are averaged to give a more reliable value for the limen than one or two series would yield.

EXAMPLE OF RESEARCH APPLICATION. The method of limits was employed by Mote, Briggs, and Michels (1954) in taking successive visual threshold measurements to plot a curve of dark adaptation as a function of time. This experimental use of the method differed in several respects from the hypothetical example in audiometry which we discussed. Since they were measuring dark adaptation, the investigators could not risk destroying the adaptation by presenting a descending series of light stimuli that started well above threshold. Consequently, each estimate of the threshold was based on an ascending series of trials. The threshold value was approached from below in steps of 0.01 to 0.03 logarithmic units of intensity. Each ascending series was continued until the stimulus was reported as visible for two successive presentations of the same intensity value. In other words, whenever the limit of visibility was crossed to yield a positive report, that intensity of stimulus was repeated as a reliability check on the sensation reported. If the positive report were not repeated, the ascending series would continue. This experiment deviates in several procedural respects from the method of limits as we outlined it earlier. This serves only to show, however, that the psychophysical methods can be varied to suit different research purposes.

Other Methods for Threshold Determination

We have cited two examples of determining absolute thresholds by the method of limits, also called the method of minimal changes. Various limens of sensation can also be determined by means of other psychophysical methods. We shall briefly indicate them here, while reserving a more complete discussion of these methods in another application, measuring discrimination.

THE METHOD OF ADJUSTMENT. If we recall the exploring of the auditory threshold by the method of limits, we remember that the experimenter moved the attenuator control in small steps to produce small changes in the stimulus intensity, making it either successively less or greater. This was continued until the limit of hearing was passed. This locating of the limit of a sensation can also be achieved by the *method of adjustment*. In this psychophysical method, the subject himself adjusts the control that regulates stimulus intensity; hence the name, method of adjustment. The subject regulates the control until the stimulus can just barely be sensed, having increased its intensity from below threshold. Or, starting above threshold, he reduces the stimulus intensity until the sensation just barely disappears. Thus the method permits both ascending and descending trials. The point from which the adjustment is originated is probably not too important in many cases since the subject is usually allowed to make adjustments back and forth when he gets to the boundary of sensation. Besides this active participation by the subject, it is the continuous change in stimulus that differentiates this method from the method of limits which employs small discrete steps in changing the stimulus. The liminal value, or *RL*, is determined in the method of adjustment by taking an average of a number of settings made by the subject.

THE METHOD OF CONSTANT STIMULI. Like the method of limits, the *method of constant stimuli* involves the presentation of discrete stimulus values. However, they are not presented in ascending or descending series but in a random or irregular order. The presentations are referred to as *constant stimuli* because they are not changed while being presented as they are in the method of adjustment.

If we do not present stimulus values in a regular series, how can we determine the boundary of sensation? In the method of constant stimuli the threshold value is computed somewhat more indirectly than in the other two methods. For each different stimulus value presented, we determine the per cent of times that it was detected by the subject. A stimulus that is well above threshold will naturally be detected 100 per cent of the time. Conversely, a stimulus that is quite far below threshold will never be sensed by the subject. Stimulus values that are near the threshold will be detected on varying per cents of the trials. If each stimulus intensity is presented enough times, we should find that the per cent of detection is an increasing function of the intensity value. The absolute threshold value, or *RL,* is arbitrarily defined as that stimulus intensity that is detected 50 per cent of the time. If no stimulus value yields exactly 50 per cent detection, interpolation may be used to calculate the limen.

Let us assume that our hypothetical experiment to determine the absolute threshold for an 8000-cycle tone had employed the method of constant stimuli. Nine different stimulus intensities might have been presented twenty times each, in random order. Table 5.2 indicates the data which might have been obtained. The more

TABLE 5.2

Tabulation Sheet for Determination of Absolute Threshold for an 8000-Cycle Tone by the Method of Constant Stimuli

*Stimulus Intensity	Per Cent of Trials Detected
−48	95
−50	90
−52	75
−54	60
−56	45
−58	30
−60	15
−62	10
−64	0

* In decibels below 1 dyne/cm² reference pressure level.

intense stimuli were detected a greater per cent of the time. One stimulus, at −64 db, was never sensed at all. What stimulus value was detected 50 per cent of the time? None of the intensities yielded this exact per cent of positive reports by the subject. The threshold apparently lies between −56 db which was detected 45 per cent of the time and −54 db which was sensed on 60 per cent of its presentations. Since 50 per cent is one-third of the distance from 45 to 60 per cent, we may use linear interpolation to fix the *RL* at a corresponding position on the stimulus intensity scale, −55.33 db.

MEASURING DISCRIMINATION

We have seen that the psychophysical methods can be used to determine absolute sensory thresholds. Next we shall find them used at stimulus values well above absolute threshold to find out how small a stimulus difference can be reliably detected. The difference between two stimuli that can just barely be differentiated from each other is variously called the *differential threshold, difference threshold,* or *DL* (for "difference limen"). We shall see that each one of the methods we have already discussed can be employed in determining the *DL*. More precisely, the concept of the *DL* is given a number of different operational definitions. The variations in these different sets of operations are both procedural and statistical. Besides the *DL* for intensity differences in any sense modality, we may determine *DL*s for other stimulus dimensions like the wavelength of chromatic visual stimuli or the frequency of tones.

THE JUST NOTICEABLE DIFFERENCE. Before seeing how the various psychophysical methods are used in determining the *DL*, we should become acquainted with a construct closely related to the *DL*, the *just noticeable difference* or *JND*.* The *JND* is the smallest difference between two stimuli which can be detected by an observer. Any stimulus, then, would have to be increased or decreased by one *JND* in order for the change to be detected. The determination of the magnitude of the *JND* is a key step in many of the methods for arriving at the *DL*. Often, in fact, the term *JND* is applied to instances where the calculation of the *DL* has actually been made.

Closely related to the *JND* is the *just unnoticeable difference*, or *JUD*. This is again a construct appearing in some methods for determining the *DL*. It may be defined as the largest difference in some

* Often abbreviated *j.n.d.*

physical stimulus dimension which cannot be detected by the observer. The magnitude of the *JUD*, then, is very slightly less than that of the *JND* for the same stimulus dimension. A *DL* is sometimes calculated, we shall see, by averaging *JND*s and *JUD*s.

WEBER'S LAW. Among the early psychophysical investigations were studies of the tactual and kinesthetic senses conducted by Ernst Weber and others. They sought to determine, for example, the *JND* for lifted weights. By what amount do two weights have to differ to feel just noticeably different when lifted? As a matter of fact, it was found that there was no *absolute* difference that represented the *JND*. Rather, the *JND* was found to be a *relative* quantity, proportional to the weights being judged. The *JND*, they discovered, was a constant proportion, about 1/30, of the weights under comparison. If the standard weight were 30 grams, a 31-gram weight would seem just noticeably heavier, the *JND* being 1 gram. However, if the standard weight were 60 grams, it would take a 2-gram difference to be reliably detected. Similarly, a standard weight of 90 grams would require 93 grams in the comparison stimulus for dependable discrimination, a *JND* of 3 grams. This proportionality of the *JND* to the standard stimulus was noted by Weber and became known as *Weber's law*. The constant of proportionality, about 1/30 in the case of lifted weights, became known as *Weber's constant*. Attempts were made to determine the value of this constant for a great number of stimulus dimensions in all of the sensory modalities. Evidence was gradually accumulated to show that there is no Weber's constant which holds over the entire range of stimulus values for any sensory dimension. Today, the determination of the *JND* or *DL* at any point on a stimulus continuum is regarded as an empirical problem rather than an attempt to verify or disprove Weber's law.

The Method of Adjustment or Average Error

One psychophysical approach to sensory or perceptual discrimination is the *method of adjustment*, sometimes referred to as the *method of average error* or the *method of reproduction*. All these names are descriptive of the procedure used in assessing the discriminatory abilities exhibited under the conditions of the experiment.

THE PROCEDURE. Earlier we saw how the method of adjustment could be used to locate absolute thresholds by having subjects manipulate some stimulus dimension until the boundary of sensation was reached. For measuring discrimination a similar performance is required of the subject except that, in addition to the *variable stimulus* under his control, a *standard stimulus* is provided. Instead of adjusting the variable stimulus to the boundary of sensation, he must regulate its value until he judges it to be equal in sensory magnitude to the standard stimulus. In other words, the subject must manipulate the variable stimulus until he reproduces the sensation level of the standard stimulus—hence the designation, method of reproduction. When the two stimuli are measured in physical terms, it will be found that only on rare trials does the subject match the variable to the standard stimulus with perfect accuracy. The occurrence of some small error on most trials indicates a failure to discriminate very small stimulus differences. Various averages of these errors provide indices of discriminating ability. These treatments of the psychophysical data give us the name—method of average error.

MEASURING VISUAL DISCRIMINATION. A hypothetical experiment measuring the perception of visual extents will serve to illustrate the method of adjustment. For this study we might employ the Galton bar, an apparatus that consists of a horizontal metal bar divided at the center. One side of the bar is stationary, the other adjustable. The subject's task on each trial is to adjust the movable side so that it appears to equal the stationary side of the bar in length or extent. The various settings of length of the variable stimulus bar constitute the psychophysical data of the experiment. The magnitudes of the errors of adjustment indicate the subject's ability at discriminating visual extents of the sort provided. One index of this discrimination might be the absolute mean error size. An index of consistency might be the SD of the errors. Still another measure that has been used in the probable error, PE, a value exceeded by the size of error made on 50 per cent of the trials, assuming the data to be normally distributed. Any of these measures has been selected at some time or other as an appropriate indicator of discrimination. In the absence of a fixed convention any one may be considered to represent a definition of the DL. We shall see later how other definitions of the DL arise from different psychophysical methods.

CONSTANT ERRORS. Besides permitting an approach to discrimination ability through the averaging of absolute error magnitudes, the method of adjustment often reveals tendencies to overestimate or to underestimate the standard stimulus in attempting to set the variable one equal to it. The *algebraic* mean of errors would reveal such a tendency. In our Galton bar study, for example, we might find that using only one arrangement of the apparatus in the experimental room led to repeated settings of the adjustable side at values longer than the standard. Such a positive constant error might be due to uneven room lighting or extraneous visual cues near the apparatus. In many psychophysical experiments we guard against unwanted constant errors by counterbalancing factors which may generate them. Thus, we would reverse the orientation of the Galton bar so that the standard length was on the left for half the trials and on the right for half. Constant errors arising from particular environmental factors should thus be canceled out.

In some studies, the measurement of constant errors may be of primary interest. Data gathered under different conditions may be analyzed separately to assess such errors and relate them to the conditions which gave rise to them. Constant errors are central enough in psychophysical work that we shall give them special attention after we have examined others of the basic psychophysical methods.

CHARACTERISTICS OF THE METHOD. Having seen that the method of adjustment can be used in assessing both absolute and differential thresholds, we may note its salient features before proceeding to discuss other techniques. A key feature of this method is the subject's direct control over the variable stimulus dimension. The manipulation of the variable is characterized by continuous rather than discrete changes in its value and by the possibility of ranging back and forth in the region of the final setting. It has been found that this "bracketing" procedure reduces the influence on the final setting of the point where the adjustment was started.

The Method of Limits

Having seen earlier how the method of limits or method of minimal changes could be used to determine the absolute threshold, or RL, we may now consider its use in determining the DL. A standard stimulus is held at a constant value and a comparison stimulus is varied in minimal steps forming either an ascending or descending series of values.

DL BY THE METHOD OF LIMITS; AN EXAMPLE. As a hypothetical study in psychophysics let us take the problem of finding the DL for loudness of an 8000-cycle tone at a standard level of 30 db above threshold. You will note that we must state the standard tone intensity level since Weber's law suggests that the magnitude of the DL will depend upon it. Our procedure might be to present the standard tone on each trial together with a comparison tone, asking the subject to state whether the latter was louder or softer than the standard, or apparently equal to it. Later we shall see that the order and the timing of this pair of stimuli pose important problems for the determination of the *DL*. On a descending series of trials our comparison tones might start at intensities well above that of the standard so that the first few judgments would be "louder." Finally, the *JND* would give way to the *JUD*, and the subject would change his judgments to "equal." These judgments of equality would presumably continue to the point of physical equality of the two tones and slightly beyond. That is, the comparison tone would continue to be called "equal" to the standard even after it had become weaker in physical intensity. This series of judgments would prevail as long as a *JUD* or less was the difference between the two physical intensities. As the descending series continued, the *JUD* would finally be passed and the stimulus difference would be at least a *JND* in sensory magnitude. The change in judgment to "softer" would indicate that the limit of the series had been reached.

In the method of limits as we have described it, each series of trials yields two estimates of the *DL*. Our descending series first yielded an estimate of the upper *DL* when judgments changed from "louder" to "equal." This change might also be described as a change from a stimulus difference value of a *JND* or more to a value of a *JUD* or less. By taking a mean of these two difference values for the upper *DL*, we are taking a sort of average between an upper *JND* and an upper *JUD*. After the descending series has proceeded through the "equal" judgments, a lower *DL* is reached where the responses change to "softer." This may be calculated as the mean of the last two stimulus values in the series, one representing a lower *JUD* or less, the other a lower *JND* or more. In some psychophysical work, the upper and lower *DLs* will be separately calculated and cited. In other cases, the upper and lower *DLs* are averaged to obtain a single value for the differential threshold.

Our determination of the *DL* for the loudness of an 8000-cycle tone might proceed as indicated in Table 5.3 which presents a completed work sheet from a hypothetical experiment. The intensity level of the standard tone is kept at 30 db above absolute threshold and the comparison tone is varied in one-quarter db steps. An estimate of an upper and a lower *DL* is obtained on each series of trials, either ascending or descending. The means for upper *DL* and lower *DL* are computed and a combined *DL* is calculated by taking the grand mean of all the upper and lower *DLs*, a value of 0.83 db. This value of the *DL* is determined for one subject at one reference intensity, 30 db above threshold, of the standard 8000-cycle tone. Most psychophysical studies involve taking many more data by utilizing more subjects and testing them with more standard stimuli at varying

TABLE 5.3

Completed Work Sheet for Determination of the Differential Intensity Threshold for an 8000-Cycle Tone at an Intensity Level 30 db above Absolute Threshold
(The testing of one subject is represented)

Comparison Stimulus Intensity*	Type of Series					
	Descending	Ascending	Descending	Ascending	Descending	Ascending
32.25						
32.00					Louder	
31.75			Louder		Louder	
31.50	Louder		Louder		Louder	
31.25	Louder		Louder	Louder	Louder	
31.00	Louder		Louder	Equal	Louder	
30.75	Louder	Louder	Equal	Equal	Equal	Louder
30.50	Equal	Equal	Equal	Equal	Equal	Equal
30.25	Equal	Equal	Equal	Equal	Equal	Equal
30.00	Equal	Equal	Equal	Equal	Equal	Equal
29.75	Equal	Equal	Equal	Equal	Equal	Equal
29.50	Equal	Equal	Equal	Softer	Equal	Equal
29.25	Equal	Softer	Equal	Softer	Equal	Equal
29.00	Softer	Softer	Equal	Softer	Equal	Equal
28.75		Softer	Softer	Softer	Softer	Softer
28.50		Softer		Softer		Softer
28.25				Softer		Softer
Upper DL:	0.62	0.62	0.88	1.12	0.88	0.62
Lower DL:	0.88	0.62	1.12	0.38	1.12	1.12

Mean upper $DL = 0.79$ Mean lower $DL = 0.87$

Grand mean $DL = 0.83$

* In decibels above absolute threshold for 8000-cycle tone.

intensity levels and, in the case of tonal stimuli, at different frequencies.

ERRORS OF ANTICIPATION AND HABITUATION. Participating as a subject in a psychophysical experiment, with its demands for the making of difficult judgments, is a complex behavioral process. There is danger that other aspects of the situation besides the stimuli being presented may affect the subject's responses and hence the data. The method of limits is particularly subject to two classes of error called *error of anticipation* and *error of habituation*. Both these errors may stem from the repeated responses which a subject must make as a series of trials proceeds. We can describe these two types of error with reference to our hypothetical determination of the *DL* for the 8000-cycle tone.

As a descending series of trials begins in our illustrative study, the subject repeatedly responds "louder" as each different comparison tone is paired with the standard tone. He knows that the comparison tone is approaching the standard one in intensity and that he will be unable to distinguish the two loudnesses after a few trials. This knowledge, together with his weariness at saying "louder" on every trial, may cause him to *anticipate* when the tones become indistinguishable in loudness. He may therefore begin saying "equal" when in fact he could still sense the comparison tone as louder, if he made the necessary effort. On a descending series of trials this error of anticipation will, of course, make the estimate of the upper *DL* somewhat larger than if the error were successfully avoided. In psychophysical experiments subjects must be instructed and trained to respond only on the basis of the stimuli presented to them on a given trial, ignoring their responses to stimuli earlier in the series.

What will be the effect of an error of anticipation if it occurs later in a descending series, when the subject has been responding "equal" to the paired stimuli on a number of trials? In our sample study, if he anticipates that the comparison tone is eventually going to be sensed as softer, the subject may change his report to "softer" when the two tones are in fact still indistinguishable to him in loudness. At this point in a descending series, the error of anticipation will cause an underestimate of the magnitude of the lower *DL*. This contrasts, you see, with the overestimate of the upper *DL* in a descending series due to anticipation.

In an *ascending* series, the error of anticipation will have opposite tendencies to affect the estimates of the lower *DL* and the upper *DL*. As we begin with a series of "softer" judgments, a premature response of "equal" will lead to an overestimated lower *DL* and an anticipation of the change to discriminably louder comparison tones will lead to an underestimation of the upper *DL*. These opposite effects in ascending series indicate one of the values of using both types of series in the method of limits. If a subject is prone to making errors of anticipation with some consistency, the effects of these on *DL* estimates will tend to cancel out, when the data for descending and ascending series are combined.

Some subjects may persevere in making one response as if by habit, so that this response may persist even beyond the point where their judgment would change if they were responding on the basis of their sensory discriminations alone. These errors of *habituation* have opposite effects from errors of anticipation in creating over-estimates or underestimates of upper or lower *DLs*. In ascending and descending series of trials the data will be distorted by the error of habituation in opposite ways that tend to cancel out in combined data.

It would be unlikely that individual subjects would make either anticipation or habituation errors so consistently as to yield final estimates of upper and lower *DLs* that were free from distortion. We need to aid our subjects in avoiding errors of either sort. Besides our use of instructions and training we help to do this by alternating descending and ascending series and by varying the starting points of each type of series. This helps to prevent the development of anticipations and habituations in the subject's responding.

The Method of Constant Stimulus Differences

In discussing absolute thresholds we saw how the method of constant stimuli could be used to determine a physical intensity that would be detected by subjects on 50 per cent of its presentations. A similar psychophysical technique can be used to determine the differential threshold or *DL*. The *DL* is computed with reference to some designated point on the stimulus continuum, of course, and so an application of this psychophysical method would begin by choosing such a value, termed the *standard stimulus*. With the stand-ard having been selected, a series of *comparison stimuli* is chosen which ranges closely on either side of the standard value. The actual selection of the comparison values may be based on earlier psychophysical data on the same or related stimulus dimensions. Sometimes the choice of these values is determined through pre-liminary work.

Each comparison stimulus is paired repeatedly with the standard stimulus, with the subject having to indicate on every trial which stimulus has the greater sensory value in his judgment. Since the fixed values of the comparison stimuli are selected to provide various fixed differences from the standard value, the technique is called the *method of constant stimulus differences*. How this method is employed to determine the *DL* will be indicated by considering a sample experiment.

A PROBLEM; TACTUAL DISCRIMINATION OF LENGTH. The pilot of an airplane must sometimes reach out to operate controls while his visual attention is directed elsewhere. To prevent errors in choosing which lever or switch to manipulate, the shape-coding of controls has been suggested as a result of human engineering studies. It has been found that control handles that are quite different in shape can be discriminated tactually. It is possible to distinguish a square handle from a round one, or even from a rectangular one. When it comes to identifying a rectangular shape tactually the problem becomes one of discriminating the lengths of the sides of the rectangle to be sure that one is not dealing with a square control. Out of such considerations we may generate a fundamental problem in tactual discrimination: How small a difference in physical stimulus length can be reliably detected tactually? This is a psychophysical question which we may attack with the method of constant stimulus differences. We may consider the problem as one which calls for basic research, not necessarily directed at solving the applied problems of control handle shapes.

EXPERIMENTAL MATERIALS. Let us suppose the problem to be specifically stated as the determination of the DL for tactual discrimination of the length of wooden pegs, based on a 2 in. standard length. To accompany this standard stimulus we might select a series of comparison pegs whose lengths, in inches, might be $1\frac{3}{4}$, $1\frac{13}{16}$, $1\frac{7}{8}$, $1\frac{15}{16}$, $2\frac{1}{16}$, $2\frac{1}{8}$, $2\frac{3}{16}$, and $2\frac{1}{4}$. This series of comparison pegs is graded in steps of $\frac{1}{16}$ in., four pegs being longer and four shorter than the standard. In conducting the study we might profitably employ a holder equipped with two small clips. In these clips we could put the two pegs to be presented on a particular trial, the standard peg and one of the comparison pegs. A data record sheet, prepared to guide us in our pairings of comparison stimuli with the standard, would complete the materials we employ.

PROCEDURE. Our experimental procedure actually begins when we prepare the record sheet since it outlines how the stimuli are to be paired in conducting the experiment. The sample data record sheet in Table 5.4 may be considered as a model one for any study employing the method of constant stimulus differences. By referring to this table we can note many procedural details.

The illustrative data record sheet provides for just 1 series of 16 trials. Several such series would be used in an actual experiment with the order of stimulus presentation varied from series to series. Careful examination of Table 5.4 will show you how the comparison stimuli are presented in an irregular order in the 16 trials of a series. Each comparison stimulus is presented once as the first stimulus of a pair, preceding the standard stimulus, and once as the second stimulus of the pair, following the standard. Column 2 and Column 3 of the record sheet, which we fill out in advance, are the guide we

TABLE 5.4

Data Record Sheet for Method of Constant Stimulus Differences

Problem: Determine DL for tactual discrimination of length
Standard value: 2-in. peg length
Comparison values: peg lengths of $1\frac{3}{4}$, $1\frac{13}{16}$, $1\frac{7}{8}$, $1\frac{15}{16}$, $2\frac{1}{16}$, $2\frac{1}{8}$, $2\frac{3}{16}$, $2\frac{1}{4}$ in.

Col. 1	Col. 2	Col. 3	Col. 4	Col. 5
Trial Number	First Stimulus	Second Stimulus	Response to Second Stimulus	Response to Comparison Stimulus
1	2	$2\frac{1}{8}$	L	L
2	2	$1\frac{13}{16}$	S	S
3	$2\frac{1}{16}$	2	S	L
4	$1\frac{3}{4}$	2	L	S
5	2	$1\frac{15}{16}$	L	L
6	$2\frac{1}{4}$	2	S	L
7	$1\frac{7}{8}$	2	L	S
8	2	$2\frac{3}{16}$	L	L
9	2	$2\frac{1}{16}$	S	S
10	$2\frac{3}{16}$	2	S	L
11	$1\frac{13}{16}$	2	L	S
12	2	$1\frac{3}{4}$	S	S
13	2	$2\frac{1}{4}$	L	L
14	2	$1\frac{7}{8}$	L	L
15	$2\frac{1}{8}$	2	S	L
16	$1\frac{15}{16}$	2	S	L

follow in presenting the pairs of stimuli. Before we discuss the recording of the subject's responses, let us consider some of the details of experimental procedure.

We shall learn something of the technique of gathering the data in our sample experiment if we first read the instructions that are given to the subject:

In this experiment we want to see how accurately you can perform a task that requires the tactual discrimination of peg lengths. The pegs will be presented to you in pairs. Keeping your eyes closed throughout the trials, you will use your thumb and forefinger to sample the length of the first peg and then the second. You must immediately state whether the second one is longer or shorter than the first. You must hold your hand still during the trials so the pegs can be easily presented to you. After sampling the length of the first peg for just a second, you must open your thumb and forefinger before receiving the second peg. Your decision about the second peg must be given immediately upon feeling its length. You must make a judgment on every trial despite any uncertainty you may experience. Do you have any questions? We shall take a few practice trials to be sure the procedure is clear.

In this psychophysical study, as in any experiment, the data we obtain will depend on the care with which we administer the trials. For each trial we select the comparison peg to be used and place it in the peg holder in which the standard peg is already located. We orient the holder for ease in presenting the two pegs in proper sequence. We place the pegs successively between the thumb and forefinger of the subject, allowing each to be sampled for just a second. Recording the subject's response as in Column 4 of Table 5.4 completes the trial. An entry of S or L means that the second peg was judged shorter or longer than the first. Column 5 is not filled out until later.

Since the performance of the experimenter and the subject on each trial must be coordinated, it is well to begin with practice trials. These may consist of a complete series of 16 trials with the data to be discarded later. Another possibility for practice is to use the largest and smallest comparison stimuli as a pair for 5 or 10 trials. When these two extreme values are used, the discrimination will be very easy for the subject and he can concentrate on learning to perform the task in the required fashion. When the actual trials begin, of course, the standard stimulus is always part of each pair. Thus the 2-inch peg in our sample study can be left in the peg holder once we begin collecting data.

As the trials are administered, the subject should not be informed of the correctness or error of his judgments. He should not be told which presentations involve the standard stimulus peg and which are the comparison pegs. If we make sure he keeps his eyes closed, it will help prevent his obtaining this sort of information inadvertently. If rest intervals are given after 16 or 32 trials, the subject should not be permitted to examine the experimental materials. Only his tactual experiencing of the stimuli should be permitted to influence his judgments in the study. Of course, in a laboratory experiment a student might serve as subject after having worked with the stimulus materials as experimenter.

TREATMENT OF THE DATA. Our determination of the DL by the method of constant stimulus differences requires that we know the per cent of times that each *comparison* stimulus peg was judged longer than the *standard* peg. As we administered the experiment, though, we required the subject to express his judgment of the *second* peg on each trial as it related to the *first*. He did not even know which peg was the standard and which was the comparison. It is necessary to express all the judgments as they pertain to the comparison pegs in relation to the standard. This is the use that we make of Column 5 in Table 5.4. After administering the entire experiment we fill out Column 5 by following a simple two-part rule: (1) For the trials on which any comparison peg was the second stimulus, we simply transfer the subject's stated response, S or L, from Column 4 to Column 5. (2) For all the trials on which the standard peg was the second stimulus, we convert the subject's judgment recorded in Column 4 to its opposite in Column 5. If you will look again at Table 5.4, you will see that we followed the first part of the rule in treating the data for Trials 1 and 2, for example. For Trials 3 and 4 we followed the second part of the rule because these were trials on which the standard peg has been used as the second stimulus. Notice that in the entire experiment, in recording the responses in Column 4 or in transferring them by the rule to Column 5, we never concerned ourselves with whether the responses were correct or erroneous judgments.

What we must tally from Column 5 is the number of times that each separate comparison peg was judged longer than the standard. Since we refer to each comparison peg in turn, it is Column 5 that provides the data; Column 4 is of no further use, having been used merely to insure correct recording of responses during the administration of the trials.

A tally of judgments based on only two presentations of each comparison stimulus would be useless. Let us suppose that we have administered 64 series of 16 trials each so that we have 128 presentations of each comparison stimulus to provide us with the psychophysical data. Proper administration of the method of constant stimulus differences requires a great many trials with each stimulus for serious determination of the *DL*. In our sample experiment we might consider that we have pooled the data from 16 subjects, each given 4 series of 16 trials. Our tally of responses, based on Column 5 of the record sheets, might yield data like those in Table 5.5.

DETERMINING THE DL. In our experiment on the tactual discrimination of length if we had used a comparison peg 2 in. long, the same as the standard peg, we might expect it to be called "longer" on about 50 per cent of the trials. Fifty per cent "longer" judgments would be expected on a chance basis for a stimulus value completely indiscriminable from the standard. On the other hand, a stimulus clearly longer than the standard, say 2½ in. in length, might be called longer on 100 per cent of its presentations. We do not demand such perfect discriminability in our definition of the *DL*. Rather, a value of 75 per cent is usually selected as denoting a *DL* since it falls halfway on the per cent scale between no discrimination and perfect discrimination. Looking at the data of Column 4 in Table 5.5 we see that the

TABLE 5.5

Distribution of "Longer" and "Shorter" Responses to Eight Comparison Stimuli, Each Presented 128 Times

Col. 1	Col. 2	Col. 3	Col. 4	Col. 5
Comparison Stimulus	No. of L Responses	No. of S Responses	Per Cent of L Responses	Per Cent of S Responses
$1\frac{3}{4}$ or 1.750 in.	5	123	4	96
$1\frac{13}{16}$ or 1.812	17	111	13	87
$1\frac{7}{8}$ or 1.875	31	97	24	76
$1\frac{15}{16}$ or 1.938	44	84	34	66
$2\frac{1}{16}$ or 2.062	86	42	67	33
$2\frac{1}{8}$ or 2.125	102	26	80	20
$2\frac{3}{16}$ or 2.188	114	14	89	11
$2\frac{1}{4}$ or 2.250	119	9	93	7

upper *DL* is indicated to correspond to a comparison stimulus value between $2\frac{1}{16}$ in. and $2\frac{1}{8}$ in. since 75 per cent of longer judgments would fall by interpolation between the 67 per cent longer judgments given to the $2\frac{1}{16}$ in. peg and the 80 per cent given to the $2\frac{1}{8}$ in. peg. The upper *DL* is more than $\frac{1}{16}$ in. and less than $\frac{1}{8}$ in. Using linear interpolation between these two values (0.0625 in. and 0.1250 in., expressed in decimals), we find the upper *DL* to be 0.1010 in. In other words, a comparison peg of 2.1010 in. long would be expected to be called longer than the 2 in. standard on 75 per cent of the trials.

The lower *DL* may be seen to have a value close to $\frac{1}{8}$ in. since the $1\frac{7}{8}$ in. comparison peg (1.875 in.) was judged shorter than the 2 in. standard on 76 per cent of the trials. Interpolating between the 66 per cent of shorter judgments corresponding to a difference from the standard of 0.0625 in. and the 76 per cent for a difference of 0.1250 in. we find that the value for the lower *DL* is 0.1188 in. A comparison peg of 1.8812 in., which is 0.1188 in. shorter than the standard, would be expected to be termed shorter than the standard on 75 per cent of the trials. We may note that this same linear interpolation could have been performed on the per cents given in Column 4 of Table 5.5.

In terms of those per cent of "longer" judgments, the lower DL is defined as yielding 25 per cent "longer" judgments. This, of course, is identical with the value yielding 75 per cent "shorter" judgments. The per cents in Columns 4 and 5 are naturally complementary for any comparison stimulus.

Having found the upper DL, 0.1010 in., and the lower DL, 0.1188 in., we may average them, if we wish, to obtain a single estimate of the DL, 0.1099 in. Obtaining the DLs by linear interpolation in the per cents of "longer" or "shorter" judgments is not regarded as the most appropriate computational technique. We shall examine two other methods.

Our second method for determining the DLs is a graphic one. In Figure 5.1 we have plotted the per cent of "longer" judgments taken from Column 4 of Table 5.5 as a function of the comparison stimulus values. The empirical data of the experiment are represented in the eight points on the graph. To these empirical data we have fitted by inspection an ogive curve. If we had fitted a curve by elaborate computations, we would have used an ogive that is the integral of the normal distribution curve. Such an ogive is called the *phi-gamma function*. The hypothesis that this curve is most appropriate for fitting the data from the method of constant stimulus

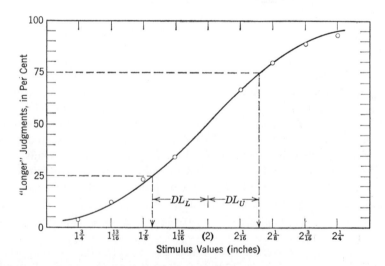

Fig. 5.1. Per cent "longer" judgments as a function of the comparison stimulus lengths. The ogive curve fitted by inspection to the plotted points permits the graphic determination of upper and lower DLs.

differences is called the *phi-gamma hypothesis*. The phi-gamma curve, integral of the normal curve, is an ogive very similar to the one we have drawn through the plotted points of Figure 5.1. We are now employing a graphic approach to determining upper and lower *DL*s which has the merit of reflecting all of the data of the experiment. In linear interpolation, you recall, we used only the data on either side of the region yielding 25 and 75 per cent "longer" judgments.

The dotted lines in Figure 5.1 show how a graphic determination of the upper and lower *DL*s is made. A horizontal line at the 75 per cent level intersects the ogive; at this point a perpendicular is dropped to the abscissa. This locates the terminus of the upper *DL* interval. A similar procedure for the 25 per cent value indicates the terminal point of the lower *DL*. The scale of the abscissa indicates the upper *DL* to be about 0.1022 in. and the lower *DL* to be about 0.1079 in. The values differ from those obtained by linear interpolation since the ogive was plotted to pass near all the empirical points so that they all contribute to the *DL* obtained by this graphical method. Thus, responses to all the comparison stimuli, rather than just two pairs of them, help to determine the *DL*s when we fit the ogive to the empirical data. The more elaborate methods for finding *DL*s by the method of constant stimulus differences involve computations that are analogous to curve-fitting with the phi-gamma function. The empirical data are specially weighted in these calculations with those nearer to the standard stimulus contributing more heavily to the *DL* values. Formulas for these detailed computational techniques are given by Johannsen (1941, p. 72 ff.).

The third method we shall consider for determining *DL*s is a graphic approach suggested by Guilford (1954, pp. 123–125) as a modification of a technique proposed by Newhall (1928). Curve-fitting by inspection is much easier in this method since a straight line rather than an ogive is the function fitted to plotted points. We begin by considering the per cent "longer" judgments in our sample experiment as per cent of area under the normal curve. Looking up these per cents in Column 1 of Table C of the Appendix, we obtain the corresponding values in sigma units (x/σ) from Column 2. (Per cents less than .50 are first subtracted from .50; the remainders yield sigma values that are to be considered negative. For a per cent greater than .50, we first subtract .50 from the per cent expressed as a decimal, then look up the remainder in Column 1; in such a case the corresponding sigma value is positive in sign.) Table 5.6 shows how the required transformation to sigma units from per cent "longer" judgments has been performed for the data of our sample experiment, with linear interpolation used where necessary.

TABLE 5.6

Conversion of Data of Sample Experiment from Per Cent* "Longer" Responses to Sigma Units by Use of Table C of Appendix

Col. 1	Col. 2	Col. 3	Col. 4
Comparison Stimulus (inches)	Per Cent of L Responses	Difference from 50 Per Cent*	Corresponding Sigma Value
1¾	.040	.460	−1.75
1¹³⁄₁₆	.130	.370	−1.13
1⅞	.240	.260	−0.71
1¹⁵⁄₁₆	.340	.160	−0.41
2¹⁄₁₆	.670	.170	0.44
2⅛	.800	.300	0.84
2³⁄₁₆	.890	.390	1.23
2¼	.930	.430	1.48

* Per cents are expressed in decimal form to correspond to data in Column 1 of Table C of the Appendix.

Having converted to sigma units we next employ a graphic plot of the new data with the sigma value scale on the ordinate and the stimulus value scale on the abscissa. The advantage of this plot is that it is to be fitted by a straight line rather than a curvilinear function. In Figure 5.2 you see that we have plotted the sigma values from Column 4 of Table 5.6. By inspection we fitted the straight line shown in the figure. Since 75 per cent "longer" judgments defines the upper DL we have located the sigma value, $+0.6745$, that corresponds to 0.750 (or 0.250) in Table C of the Appendix. We extended a horizontal line from this sigma value on the ordinate until it intersected the linear function and there we dropped a perpendicular to the abscissa. It falls about ³⁄₃₂ in. above the standard stimulus value of 2 in. so that our upper DL may be considered to have a value of ³⁄₃₂ in. or 0.0937 in. Our graphic determination of the lower DL begins at -0.6745 on the ordinate scale of sigma values. This corresponds to a lower DL on the abscissa of 0.1074 in. below the standard stimulus.

THE TIME ERROR; DEFINITION, CONTROL, AND MEASUREMENT. In our example of the method of constant stimulus differences as applied to tactual discrimination of length, each trial involved the presenting of two different pegs. The subject's task was to indicate whether the

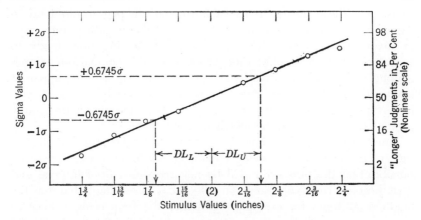

Fig. 5.2. Per cent "longer" judgments transformed to sigma units and plotted as a function of comparison stimulus lengths. A straight line fitted by inspection to the plotted points permits the graphic determination of upper and lower *DL*s.

second peg was judged longer or shorter than the first. He was comparing the sensation of length aroused by the second peg with the memory image of the length of the first peg, we might say. Thinking about this comparison, we see that there is danger of bias in the data we obtain. The memory image may fade very rapidly, reducing the stimulus magnitude with which the second peg is actually compared. This would tend to increase the number of "longer" judgments given during the experiment. If every trial consisted of first presenting the standard and then a comparison peg, the effect of this tendency would always "benefit" the comparison peg. The per cent of "longer" judgments for each comparison stimulus would be increased. Had this procedure been followed, then, the entire ogive curve of Figure 5.1 would have been raised on the graph with a resultant change in the magnitudes of the upper *DL* and the lower *DL*. In what directions would these two values change?

The bias which may arise when stimuli must be presented successively is known as the *time error*. In considering our hypothetical experiment we speculated that the first stimulus presented would suffer a loss in its apparent magnitude. This is termed a *negative time error,* leading to the overestimation of the second stimulus in comparison to the first. We saw how this would have affected the determination of *DL*s if all trials had involved presenting the standard stimulus first. Fortunately we planned for a counterbalanced design with a comparison stimulus preceding the standard peg on half of the

trials.   On those presentations each comparison peg would tend to
garner fewer "longer" judgments, assuming the negative time error
to favor the standard stimulus.   Counterbalancing thus tends to
cancel out the effect of a time error, with the comparison stimuli
gaining in apparent relative length on half the trials, losing apparent
length on the other half. Possible time errors must be reckoned with
in most psychophysical studies of auditory *DLs* since stimuli are usually
presented in succession rather than simultaneously.

Time errors may sometimes be *positive*, with the apparent magnitude of the first stimulus being enhanced as time elapses.   It is even
possible that the time error will be negative for a brief interval and
then become positive.   Such an effect has been suggested for the
loudness of tones for example.   Whether the time error is positive
or negative, or whether it changes as a function of time, it can be
controlled by counterbalancing, so that its net effect on psychophysical data is negligible.   Such control over possible time error is
useful in all the psychophysical methods where *DLs* are sought by
presenting two stimuli in succession to be judged by the subject.

Although the design of many studies calls for counterbalancing of
stimulus presentation to cancel out the effects of any time error, in
some studies it is desired to assess the magnitude of this effect for
the particular interstimulus interval being employed.   Considerable
light may be thrown on processes of sensation, perception, and discrimination by investigation of the time error.   Through its measure-

TABLE 5.7

**Distribution of "Longer" Responses to Eight Comparison Stimuli (1) on
All Trials (Col. 2), (2) on Trials with Standard First (Col. 3), and (3)
on Trials with Standard Second (Col. 4)**

Col. 1	Col. 2	Col. 3	Col. 4
Comparison Stimulus (inches)	Per Cent L Responses— All Trials	Per Cent L Responses— Standard First	Per Cent L Responses— Standard Second
$1\frac{3}{4}$ or 1.750	4	8	1
$1\frac{13}{16}$ or 1.812	13	20	7
$1\frac{7}{8}$ or 1.875	24	34	15
$1\frac{15}{16}$ or 1.938	34	46	22
$2\frac{1}{16}$ or 2.062	67	78	56
$2\frac{1}{8}$ or 2.125	80	89	64
$2\frac{3}{16}$ or 2.188	89	91	81
$2\frac{1}{4}$ or 2.250	93	94	88

ment we may be able to assign values to a hypothetical stimulus memory trace.

We may illustrate a quantitative approach to the time error by means of hypothetical data which we might imagine to have come from our sample experiment on tactual discrimination of length. The essential step in assessing the time error is to separate those data which were obtained on trials with the standard stimulus presented first from the data which came from the trials when the standard stimulus was second. Such a fractionation of the data from the sample study might yield the values given in Table 5.7.

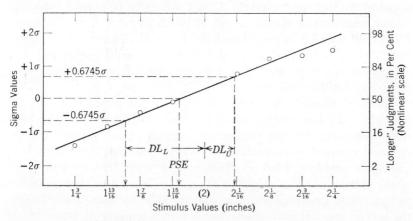

Fig. 5.3. A plot in sigma units of the transformed data of Column 3, Table 5.7. The graphic determination of the *DLs* and the *PSE*, as explained in the text, reveals that the hypothetical illustrative data contain evidence of a negative time error.

To see what happens when we take data only from trials on which the standard was presented first, we converted the values of Column 3 to equivalent sigma values and plotted the data in Figure 5.3. A straight line was fitted to these eight points and the *DLs* were graphically determined, as before. We see that the negative time error has shifted the curve upward for these trials with a resultant decrease in the upper *DL* and an increase in the lower *DL*, as compared with determinations made from Figure 5.2. Another assessment of the effect of the negative time error has been made by determining what comparison value would yield a sigma value of zero. This zero value on the sigma scale corresponds to a set of "longer" responses on 50 per cent of the trials. A comparison stimulus would yield a fifty-fifty split between longer and shorter judgments, we would expect, if it were subjectively equal in stimulus value to the standard. With the standard losing apparent magnitude on these trials due to the negative time error, we see that this *point of subjective equality*, or *PSE*, falls at 1.9500 in. on the scale of stimulus values. The difference between this *PSE* and the point of physically equal magnitude, at 2 in., is a measure of the magnitude of the negative time error, −0.0500 in.

Suppose we were to convert the data of Column 4 of Table 5.7 to sigma values and then construct a graph similar to Figure 5.3. We would find that for these trials, with the standard stimulus presented second, the *DLs* and the *PSE* are affected by the time error in a way opposite to that portrayed in Figure 5.3. As compared with our earlier treatment of the entire set of psychophysical data, the upper *DL* would now be increased and the lower *DL* decreased in magnitude. For this fraction of the data the *PSE* would correspond to a comparison value greater than 2 in. in length, but a negative time error would still be indicated by this.

THE SPACE ERROR. In determining *DLs* in the visual modality, for example, *DLs* for brightness, we need not encounter any risk of a time error since we can present two stimuli simultaneously for the required comparison on each trial. We need to consider a somewhat analogous problem, however, known as a *space error*. Our judgments of two stimulus magnitudes may be biased by their positions in space. If two illuminated areas are side by side, for example, the one on the left may appear extra bright because of some retinal or environmental factor enhancing it. Like time errors, space errors can be neutralized by counterbalancing and measured by fractionation of the psychophysical data.

Space errors and time errors are considered as forms of *constant error* in psychophysics since they tend to influence the calculated values in particular directions on particular sorts of trials, like "standard first" trials or "standard on the left" trials. As we have seen, their effects can be caused to cancel out with counterbalancing of stimulus pairings. Referring to these temporal or spatial effects as "errors" is misleading in some degree since they represent phenomena of considerable interest to some investigators.

SCALING SENSATION AND PERCEPTION

We have seen how various psychophysical methods may be used to determine *RLs* and *DLs* for various dimensions of sensation and perception. In applying these measurement techniques, we vary the physical stimuli but the subjects respond in terms of the magnitude of their own sensory or perceptual experience. The *RL* may thus be considered an endpoint, and the *DL* an increment, on a psychological scale. A number of approaches have been taken to develop such scales quite completely. We shall see that this work is sometimes based on the methods we have already examined and we shall discuss additional methods used in scaling sensation and perception.

DL or *JND* Scales

One of the techniques for scaling sensation is quite directly based on the basic constructs in psychophysical work, the *RL* and the *JND* or *DL*. By considering the *JND* or the *DL* as the unit of the sensory scale, we might start down at the *RL* and determine the magnitude of successive *DLs*. These could then be piled one on the other to create a sensory scale—an extremely laborious technique. Theoretically, it leads to a scale of sensation on which we can specify any point by stating how many *JNDs* it is above the threshold. This clearly indicates the adoption of the *JND* (or *DL*) as the unit of sensory measurement. Of course, our psychophysical work in constructing such a psychological scale would reveal the physical stimulus value which corresponded to each sensation value. Thus, physical values could be used to designate successive discriminable points on the psychological continuum.

THE WEBER-FECHNER FORMULATION. We have already seen how early psychophysical studies led Weber to assert that the just noticeable increment to any stimulus value is a constant proportion of that particular value. If we were to assume the Weber formula, $\Delta R/R = K$, to be valid, we could create a ΔR scale (essentially a *DL* or *JND* scale) of sensory magnitudes without the time-consuming determination of successive *DLs* all the way up the scale. We would merely need to gather psychophysical data to determine ΔR values at a few points. From these we would calculate a value for *K*. Using this constant of proportionality, *K*, we could step off a sensory scale along the physical dimension beginning at the *RL* and carrying it as far as we wished. We know today, of course, that Weber's law is not valid over the entire range of any stimulus dimension. Therefore the hypothetical method we have discussed would not be considered appropriate.

Fechner, who did a great deal to codify some of the early psychophysical methods, accepted the Weber formulation, $\Delta R/R = K$. By integration over the series of *R*s which makes up the sensory dimension, he transformed the equation to $S = k \log R$, where *S* is the sensory magnitude (actually the cumulative number of ΔRs above threshold), R is the physical stimulus value expressed as a multiple of the absolute threshold value, R_0, and k is a constant determined by the particular sensory dimension and modality. This Weber-Fechner law is, of course, no more valid than the Weber formula on which it is based. However, the Weber formula does seem to hold over a restricted range of stimulus values, those of moderate magnitude. For this middle range of intensities, then, the Weber-Fechner formula also has a measure of validity. The essential idea which it expresses is that linear increases in sensory magnitude will be aroused by logarithmic increases in the physical stimulus value. It suggests, for example, that a twofold increase in brightness will result from a hundredfold increase in light intensity, provided this physical change is measured in relation to the absolute threshold for vision.

The Fechnerian approach to scaling sensation via the *JND* has long been criticized on logical and mathematical grounds. A modern constructive criticism is set forth by Luce and Edwards (1958) who offer a mathematically complex functional-equation solution to the scaling problem to replace the solution in which Fechner employed the integration technique. These authors do not recommend the practical use of their equations, stating that a graphic method of placing *JND*s one upon the other will yield a scale more simply.

The entire concept of the *JND* scale has been questioned by Stevens (1957). He objects to the indirectness of the Fechnerian approach in which an index of confusion, the *DL* or *JND*, is taken as the unit of a sensory scale. The logarithmic relationship between sensation and physical stimulus energy is questioned by Stevens who indicates that a modern reorientation of psychophysics reveals that for many stimulus dimensions a power function relates sensation level to stimulus intensity. In this formulation for scaling sensory experience a basic principle is that equal sensation ratios tend to be aroused by equal stimulus ratios. This is revealed empirically by the relatively direct ratio scaling methods which we shall consider next.

Ratio Scales

Techniques for ratio scaling of sensation share the essential feature of requiring subjects to make quantitative estimates of subjective events. Methods of *ratio estimation, ratio production,* and *magnitude estimation* are among those listed by Stevens (1957, p. 163). In ratio estimation two stimuli are presented to the subject and he must state the ratio of the sensory experiences which they arouse, for example, he might state that one of two luminances aroused a brightness sensation of ten times that which the other aroused—a 10:1 ratio estimate for the two sensations. Turning to ratio production, we find that *fractionation* is a common procedure. Given a tone of a particular loudness, for example, an observer should be able to indicate a tone half as loud as this standard by adjusting an attenuator which controls the energy level of a comparison tone. By such a process of bisection, which may vary widely as to procedural details, experimental subjects reveal a great deal about the scale of sensory magnitudes as they experience them. The technique of magnitude estimation approaches ratio scaling by having subjects assign numbers to different stimuli as they are presented, with the understanding that these numerical responses are proportional to the sensation levels aroused. A particular value may be initially assigned to one stimulus by the experimenter, but this is not always a part of this method.

Stevens (1957, p. 166) has listed a number of sensory and perceptual dimensions which have been subjected to ratio scaling. Among these are loudness, brightness, visual distance, visual length, visual area, taste, and heaviness (of lifted weight). For these continua, and several others, the functional relationship between subjective sensory or perceptual magnitudes and the physical dimension being manipulated appears to approximate a power function. The general formula for such a relationship is presented by Stevens (1957, p. 162) as

$$\psi = kS^n$$

where ψ = the sensation magnitude.

S = the physical stimulus intensity.

k and n = parameters characteristic of the kind of experience being scaled.

When the equation is converted to logarithmic form, expressing log ψ as a function of log S, the power function can be graphically represented by a straight line with n as its slope. A number of such linear plots on log-log coordinates are presented by Stevens and Galanter (1957, p. 387) in order to compare the outcomes of several experiments which attempted to scale the sensation of heaviness aroused when subjects lift weights. Two studies will serve to illustrate for us the ratio scaling that may be accomplished by fractionation and by magnitude estimation.

A RATIO SCALE OF HEAVINESS; FRACTIONATION METHOD. An experiment by Harper and Stevens (1948) indicates how a fractionation technique yields a ratio scale of subjective magnitudes. The physical dimension that was varied in the study was the weight of stimulus objects, the

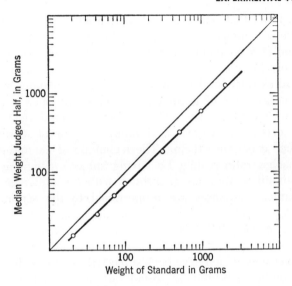

Fig. 5.4. The median weight judged half as heavy as the standard weight plotted as a function of the standard weight. Each plotted point represents the median of 36 judgments given by 12 observers, each giving 3 judgments. Values are scaled logarithmically on both coordinates. (After Harper and Stevens, 1948.)

aim being to construct a psychological scale for the sensory experience of heaviness when weights are lifted.

Each trial in this investigation consisted of presenting a standard weight, 100 grams, and a series of comparison weights: 70, 75, 80, 85, 90 and 95 grams. These comparison values were found in a preliminary study to cover a satisfactory range. The subject's task was to lift the standard and the different comparison weights (which were unmarked and all of identical size with the standard) until he could indicate which of the comparison weights he judged to be half as heavy as the standard. The scaling study thus employed a procedure somewhat analogous to that of the method of constant stimulus differences in order to obtain bisections on the subjective weight dimension. Here, of course, the comparison stimulus values bracketed the expected point of bisection rather than bracketing the physical value as in the search for the *DL*.

In the experiment we are describing, 12 subjects (designated *Os* for "observers") were given 3 trials each in selecting a bisection point from among the comparison stimuli. The median of the 36 values thus selected was taken as the bisection point for scaling purposes.

Such a median bisection point was determined for each of eight standard weights: 20, 40, 70, 100, 300, 500, 1000, and 2000 grams. The eight median bisection points that were obtained are plotted as a function of the standard weight values in Figure 5.4, with a straight line fitted by inspection. From this function we may determine, for example, that a weight of about 72 grams would be judged half as heavy as the 100-gram standard.

From the empirical data and the fitted function of Figure 5.4, Harper and Stevens derived a scale of subjective weight. They began by assigning a subjective value of 1.0 to the perceived weight that corresponds to the lifting of the 100-gram weight. Since a 72-gram weight is judged half as heavy as the 100-gram weight, it is assigned a value of 0.5 unit on the subjective scale. From the graphic plot they determined that a 100-gram weight would be judged half as heavy as a 140-gram weight. Since 100-grams has a sensory unit value of 1.0, then the subjective sensation aroused by 140 grams was given a sensation value of 2.0. Starting with the arbitrary assumption of unit sensation value as being aroused by 100 grams on the physical scale, the experimenters thus used the bisection data to assign sensation values to every other physical value.

Proceeding as we have described, Harper and Stevens plotted sensation values for lifted weights as a function of physical values. Instead of presenting the curve which they obtained, we shall examine a more representative power function derived by Stevens and

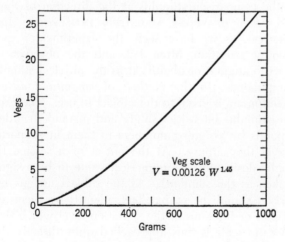

Fig. 5.5. Veg scale of subjective weight. (After Stevens and Galanter, 1957.)

Galanter (1957, pp. 386–390) from the results of this and other studies. The name *veg*, from an old Norse verb for "lift," is given to the unit of experienced heaviness. In Figure 5.5 we see that the sensed magnitude of lifted weight is a power function of the physical weight The equation for this idealized curve worked out by Stevens and Galanter is

$$V = 0.00126 \ W^{1.45}$$

where V = number of vegs.
             W = physical stimulus weight, in grams.
   0.00126 = the parameter k.
      1.45 = the parameter n.

This power function is an empirical example of the general equation which we examined earlier (p. 127).

VARIANTS OF THE FRACTIONATION METHOD. Different procedural techniques can be used within the broad category of fractionation. A constant stimulus method was used by Harper and Stevens (1948) in the experiment to obtain a veg scale for the sensation of lifted weight. MacLeod (1952) used a similar method to scale the sweetness of sucrose and glucose solutions. Stevens and Poulton (1956) used an adjustment technique in a study of loudness fractionation, permitting each observer to manipulate a control so as to set a comparison tone to half the loudness of a standard tone. A modified adjustment method was employed by Hanes (1949) in scaling subjective brightness. Here the experimenter manipulated the intensity control for the comparison stimulus at the direction of the observer.

A RATIO SCALE OF HEAVINESS; MAGNITUDE ESTIMATION. In the fractionation method, as we have seen, the experimenter specifies the desired ratio of sensation, often 1:2, and the observer or subject then attempts to attain it or identify it as the physical stimulus dimension is manipulated. In the *method of magnitude estimation* the numerical continuum is given to the subject to use. The experimenter presents the stimulus intensities singly and in random order and the subject responds by assigning numbers to them in proportion to the sensation level they arouse. At the outset of a session the experimenter usually designates one numerical value to be assigned to one stimulus, taken as the standard. As the subject assigns numbers to the comparison stimuli he is, in effect, identifying them as arousing either multiples or fractions of the sensation level which the standard arouses. A ratio scale is thus approached quite directly through the magnitude estimations that are made.

Stevens and Galanter (1957, p. 387) describe how this method was applied to the ratio scaling of heaviness by three members of the Harvard Laboratory: Stevens, Nachmias, and Pertschonok. Keeping the standard weight always available for comparison, these experimenters required subjects to make magnitude estimates of the comparison weights. The weights used ranged from 19 to 193 grams. In different parts of the study, subjects were told that the 19-gram weight was to be defined as having a value of 1, that the 92-gram weight was to be designated as 100, or that the 193-gram stimulus was to be called 100. The method permits this flexibility in the one numerical value which the experimenter assigns in different phases of the same scaling effort. Using the one numerical referent given to him, the subject must assign numbers proportional to the experienced heaviness of the comparison weights. Upon examining the median values assigned to each comparison stimulus the experimenters found them to yield a power function of actual physical weight, in general agreement with the fractionation results of Harper and Stevens (1948).

The Harvard Laboratory studies employed certain procedural variations which illustrate the administrative flexibility of the method of magnitude estimation. In one part of the research the standard was presented only prior to every three comparison weights. In still other variations no standard value was designated at all. In the latter case the individual estimates were pooled only after a transformation to bring to 100 the value assigned to the 98-gram stimulus. These procedural variations appear not to interfere with the attainment of a scale for subjective weight. Such details of method have been discussed by Stevens (1956) in connection with the psychophysical scaling of loudness. In this article several suggestions are made for the most effective employment of the method of magnitude estimation. Among the rules offered are the following, paraphrased from the original list:

1. Use a standard stimulus which impresses the observers as being moderate in sensation level.
2. Assign to the standard a number that is readily multiplied and divided, like 10.
3. Present additional stimuli for estimation that are both above and below the standard.
4. Use more than one standard, but only in separate scaling sessions.
5. Modify the random order of presentation to avoid very extreme values on early trials before subjects gain experience.
6. Keep the experimental sessions brief enough to avoid fatigue.
7. Let the subject present stimuli to himself, using self-pacing.
8. Use enough subjects or observers to obtain stable medians of the

estimations, this statistic being less sensitive than the mean to
the extreme values which some will give.

By using just one standard stimulus and its assigned numerical value
in any particular phase of a magnitude estimation study, the experimenter gives the subject freedom to indicate ratios of sensation as
he assigns values to the other stimuli. A true ratio scale can thus
result. If, however, the experimenter were to fix numerical values for
two different stimuli of the series, a ratio would be forced on the
subjects and their further rating of sensory magnitudes could only
indicate the intervals or categories into which they would put the
sensory experiences aroused by the additional stimuli presented.
Such category scaling has been attempted, with a variety of methods,
for numerous sensory and perceptual dimensions. This type of exploration of the domain of experience occupies our attention next.

Category Scales

In using one of the category scaling techniques we may construct
an interval scale of sensation level. Such scales have been shown by
Stevens and Galanter (1957) to relate to ratio scales of the same
continuum in a curvilinear fashion in many instances. As was the
case for ratio scaling, category scaling may be attempted by a number of related approaches. These variations of technique bear such
names as the methods of *single stimuli, absolute judgment,* or *equal
intervals.* The method of *rating,* to be discussed at some length in
Chapter 6, is another technique for category scaling. The essence of
this kind of scaling is that the observer has to react to stimuli presented
singly by assigning each to some category along the sensory continuum. Usually the subject is given some information about the
upper and lower points of stimulation to be used, so that his task
becomes that of partitioning the range into intervals to which he
assigns the individual stimuli as each one is experienced. Our acquaintance with scaling efforts will be furthered by reviewing an
attempt to scale loudness, using the method of absolute judgment.
Later we shall briefly consider some of the independent variables
which may affect the determination of category scale values.

AN EQUAL DISCRIMINABILITY SCALE OF LOUDNESS. The method of
absolute judgment is considered to yield a scale of sensation in which
equal scale distances represent equal tendencies to judge two stimuli
as being in the same category. The units of the scale thus represent
units of equal discriminability. We shall see how such a scale was
established for loudness in a study by Garner (1952).

In this experiment a 1000-cycle tone of 1 sec duration was presented every 6 sec with intensity varied from 5 to 100 db in 5 db steps (reference level: 0.0002 dyne/cm²). These 20 intensities were presented in irregular order until each had been given 100 times to each of 10 subjects. In other parts of the experiment Garner used reduced stimulus ranges and uneven spacing of intensities on the decibel scale, but these parts of the study will not concern us.

As they listened to each presentation of the tone in this experiment, subjects were required to respond by writing down a numerical loudness rating from 0 to 20, where 0 indicated the tone was inaudible and 20 was to be used for the loudest tone in the series. (Inaudible presentations could be inferred by the subject since every stimulus presentation was preceded by a signal light.) Intermediate numerical values were to be used, of course, for loudness falling between the two defined extremes. Before data were taken, each subject listened to random presentations of the intensities until he felt familiar with the range of loudnesses he would hear. He was never informed as to how many different intensities were used. The absolute threshold for a 1000-cycle tone was at about 5 db re 0.0002 dyne/cm², equivalent to the tone of lowest intensity in the series.

An equal discriminability scale was constructed by taking as the scale value for each stimulus intensity the median response value assigned to that intensity. This was done separately for each subject. The scale values for each intensity were then obtained for the group by pooling their sets of scale values. By way of examining the E.D. (equal discriminability) scale constructed in this experiment, Garner compared the scale values with the tone intensities expressed in decibels. Between 30 and 80 db, the relationship was essentially linear. Since the E.D. scale is one of sensation and the decibel scale is a logarithmic one of physical intensities, this finding is in accord with the Weber-Fechner formulation in this range of values. No simple relationship was found between the E.D. scale of loudness and a ratio scale of loudness based on a unit derived from fractionation data, the *sone*. This is a particular instance of the point mentioned earlier—that category scales relate in a curvilinear fashion to ratio scale values (Stevens and Galanter, 1957).

INDEPENDENT VARIABLES IN CATEGORY SCALING. Although space does not permit us to review a number of other category scaling studies, we can indicate task dimensions which have been investigated. Using size of paper squares as the stimulus dimension, Eriksen and Hake (1955) varied the range of stimuli given, the number of different size values extending over each range, and the number of response categories which the observers or subjects were permitted to use. A report by Parducci (1956) describes experiments employing as stimulus dimensions the size of square cards and the frequency of pure tones, with an attempt made to determine how judgments change when the stimulus range is shifted after differing amounts of judging experience with an initial range of values. In an experiment by Johnson (1949) subjects were permitted to respond either "low" or "high" as tones of different frequencies were presented, with the range and the distribution of frequencies found to affect the indifference point for judged pitch. The common demonstration of these studies is that category scaling efforts are particularly sensitive to procedural details of the experimentation, especially to the range and spacing of physical stimulus values.

USING PSYCHOPHYSICAL METHODS IN RESEARCH

Psychophysics was very prominent in the work of early psychology laboratories. There was great interest in developing these quantitative methods and in applying them as techniques for exploring sensation. Although relatively less important now, due to the proliferation of paths of inquiry in modern psychology, the psychophysical methods are primary tools for the laboratory study of perceptual and sensory processes. Among the different standard procedures the investigator will usually find one quite suited to his purposes. Further, the methods are flexible so that modifications may be devised if a study will not permit the use of a conventional technique in its entirety.

Wide Applicability

In organizing our discussion of the psychophysical methods, we saw how they have been used to explore sensory boundaries in measuring RLs, to measure discrimination through determining DLs, and to scale sensation. Modern use of psychophysics is often directed toward complex perceptions. The methods prove themselves useful in quantifying perceptual processes like distance perception, for example, which was studied by Purdy and Gibson (1955) using a fractionation technique. The perception of brief time intervals was investigated by Gregg (1951) with subjects performing fractionation by successive adjustments of a comparison stimulus. A modified method of limits was used by Vanderplas (1953) to determine the recognition thresholds for paralogs (nonsense words) presented tachistoscopically, that is, with very brief exposures.

Special Suitability for Different Problems

It should always be kept in mind that a particular problem will probably be best studied by means of a particular psychophysical method. For example, if we are trying to determine olfactory *DLs* we might find the method of constant stimulus differences to be about the only one we could use. The method of adjustment could hardly be used because of the technical difficulties of gradually varying the strength of olfactory stimulus and because of rapid adaptation in the sense of smell. Our search to find the right method for a study should be conducted with deliberation. Our plan may involve details which preclude the use of the most conventional approach to the problem under investigation. A different psychophysical method may be better suited to our purpose. Of course, we should not expect that different methods will yield the same values for such constructs as the *DL*. Such computed values naturally depend upon the procedures through which they were obtained.

Flexibility in Use

We tend to speak of different psychophysical methods by conventional names and to describe the procedures in accord with certain stereotypes. Our complete appreciation of these techniques is demonstrated, however, in our willingness to modify them where the research demands it. For example, we may use only ascending series of trials in seeking the threshold during dark adaptation. Descending series would require supraliminal stimuli which might destroy the adaptation process we were trying to plot.

There are few problems which can be investigated by only one psychophysical method. Some studies have actually applied different procedures to the same basic problem in a sort of comparative psychophysics. An example is an investigation of simultaneous brightness contrast by Diamond, Scheible, Schwartz, and Young (1955) in which several methods were used. Besides illustrating the comparing of different techniques, this study gives evidence of the suitability of the methods to modification for special purposes. Throughout the investigation, for example, the standard test field was presented to one eye while the comparison match field was presented to the other.

Precautions in Psychophysical Studies

As a complicated, indirect measurement of inner experience, research in psychophysics is very demanding of experimental rigor.

All the guides to conducting psychological research which we considered in Chapter 2 must be observed in psychophysical studies. In addition to respecting general procedural rules, we must often take special precautions in working with the stimuli and the responses they elicit if our measurements are to be valid.

GENERAL PROCEDURES. Preliminary studies can be very useful before undertaking a major psychophysical investigation. Such pilot experiments may be needed to establish an appropriate series of physical stimulus values for use in the later study. They may help to train both the experimenter and subjects for the complex performances required of them in some psychophysical procedures.

Detailed advance planning is required for good psychophysical research. The sequence of stimulus presentations should be prepared on the data record sheets if methods like limits or constant stimuli are to be used. Even for the method of adjustment we need to plan in advance the sequence of starting points to be used for the variable stimulus.

Precise quantitative control over stimuli is of paramount importance in psychophysics. Controlling the particular physical stimulus dimension that is being varied is a prime consideration, of course. Other physical dimensions of the stimulus cannot be ignored; they are usually held constant at values dictated by the general purpose of the investigation. Temporal dimensions of stimulation are important, too. There is evidence of many kinds that the duration of stimulus presentation and the interstimulus interval will affect psychophysical data. In addition to providing for adequate control over the stimuli being used, an experimenter must occlude unwanted stimulation while conducting a psychophysical study.

Many psychophysical investigations employ trained subjects since volunteer subjects, casually recruited, cannot perform the required task satisfactorily. A trained subject is familiar with the dimension of sensation being investigated. He can respond, for example, to changes in hue without being unduly influenced by differences in saturation. A trained subject will avoid making the "stimulus error." That is, he will not respond to what he knows to be the fact about the physical stimulus, but will respond on the basis of his sensation only. Besides his knowledge of how a subject ought to perform the assigned task, a person well-suited as a subject will bring the proper motivational level to psychophysical research. He will realize that his careful attention must be given each time he is called upon to make a response. He will also understand that a great number of data are required in most psychophysical work if the desired statistical values are to be computed reliably.

While a study in psychophysics is under way, the experimenter must be careful that unwanted processes like fatigue do not exert an effect on the data. In speaking of fatigue we refer actually to numerous possible processes that might reduce the validity of the results of the study. For example, boredom might set in during a long session, making the subject inattentive and careless in responding. By properly motivating our subjects, of course, we tend to prevent the development of boredom. We might find actual muscular fatigue, perhaps in visual accommodation, in some studies. To prevent fatigue from becoming an unwanted source of variance in a study, we might resort to the general rule of providing rest periods at reasonable intervals.

Another process that might distort psychophysical data is learning. One form of learning that might occur in a study of discrimination would be that of making judgments on the basis of cues other than the stimulus dimension being studied. If, in trying to vary saturation, the experimenter varied the intensity of visual stimuli, subjects might learn to respond to brightness cues while paying less attention to the dimension of saturation which was really the object of the investigation. A somewhat different form of learning might take place if a subject began to form impressions of the correctness of his responses. If such impressions were groundless, it is difficult to say what effect they might have had on the data. However, if the experimenter in some way was providing information that certain responses were right or wrong, the subject or observer might gradually improve his performance as he gained familiarity with the stimuli being employed. An experimenter must guard against giving any sign of approval or disapproval of responses made to stimuli.

STIMULUS VALUES. The choice of stimulus values to be used is important in any experiment, but in psychophysics it is a primary problem. What considerations would guide our choice of comparison stimuli to be used in determining the DL for lifted weights by the method of constant stimulus differences? We would conventionally choose three or four comparison stimuli on either side of the standard in order to yield a psychophysical function that would permit both a lower and an upper DL to be determined. For some of the more involved calculational procedures, the heavier and the lighter series of weights would have to be evenly spaced on the physical continuum. We would not want to use any comparison weights that were so different from the standard that they were judged heavier or lighter 100 per cent of the time. Such data would not contribute much to our plotting of the psychophysical function. Our selection of stimulus values would usually be guided by previous findings or by some exploratory testing.

There has been much discussion of how the range of stimuli used might influence psychophysical scaling. A striking example was provided by Garner (1954) in a study of loudness scaling by a bisection technique based on the method of constant stimuli. Various comparison tones were paired with a standard tone of 90 db (0.0002 microbar being the reference sound pressure level), with observers having to indicate whether the comparison tone was more or less than half as loud as the standard. The 90 db standard was employed for all three groups of subjects, but each group had a different series of comparison tones. These series ranged in intensity from 55 to 65 db, from 65 to 75 db, and from 75 to 85 db. We should not expect that each of these ranges of comparison stimuli would contain a value half as loud as the standard. Nevertheless, almost all the subjects in Garner's experiment accepted the particular comparison series they heard, and proceeded to call some of the stimuli louder, and some softer, than the half-loudness point as they estimated it. Thus, each group yielded a different bisection point on a loudness scale, indicating the dependence of such a value on the range of comparison stimuli employed.

This potential influence on sensory and perceptual processes of the values of the particular stimuli presented is widely recognized in psychophysics. One result of this context effect is that the middle portion of a range of stimulus values tends to take on a neutral value on a sensation scale as the stimuli are repeatedly presented. Helson (1947) has formulated a concept of *adaptation level* to account for such phenomena. The studies by Garner (1954) and Johnson (1949), cited earlier, provide examples of how the scaling of sensory magnitudes might be distorted by such an adaptation effect. The mechanisms involved may have more subtle effects on psychophysical data, too. After reviewing a number of investigations which revealed complex stimulus effects on observers' judgments, Harris (1948) reached the conclusion that even where a standard stimulus is presented on every trial, there may be influences from earlier stimulus presentations that affect the subjective experience. The subject may respond to a combination of the presented standard and temporally "remote" standards gradually developed in his experience on preceding trials. One suggestion that Harris offered after empirical study of the method of constant stimulus differences is that the fixed standard be replaced by a random series of standard values ranging very closely around the value that would normally be the standard. This proposal is further evidence of the fact that different aspects of psychophysical methods, in this case, the choice of stimulus values, may be considered as problems requiring carefully considered and tested solutions rather than as procedural rules dictated by convention.

CONTROL CHARACTERISTICS. Another precaution that must be taken in psychophysical research is to avoid having any bias introduced into the data by the characteristics of any control on the apparatus which must be operated by the subject. Suppose, for example, that in testing for the absolute threshold we required the subject to move a switch to the right if he detected a stimulus, to the left if not. If that switch were constructed so that it could be moved easily to the left but with considerable difficulty to the right, we might find that a subject resolved any doubt about detecting the stimulus by moving the switch left, indicating he had not detected anything. The per cent of "No" responses might thus be artificially increased, with a resultant "raising" of the threshold we determined. Although our example might be somewhat exaggerated, it may serve to illustrate our need to consider the subject's task in every detail in planning a psychophysical study.

The method of adjustment typically calls for apparatus manipulation on the subject's part. In a study of loudness fractionation, Stevens and Poulton (1956) provided two different attenuation control knobs for the subjects to use. The amount of rotation of one control knob was related on a decibel scale to the intensity of the tone it controlled. Each 3° of rotation provided 1 db of attenuation of the test tone. The other control knob was arranged to relate proportionally in its rotation to the sone scale of psychological loudness instead of to the physical decibel scale. The results of the study indicated a definite influence of the differently connected control knobs on the estimation of half loudness, even though stimulus intensity was the primary determinant of the responses made.

SUMMARY

A number of psychophysical methods have been devised to explore boundaries of sensation, to measure sensory and perceptual discrimination, and to scale the magnitudes of sensory experience aroused by stimuli of known physical values. Such techniques as the method of limits, the method of adjustment, and the method of constant stimuli are all useful for such research. Along with other methods for ratio and category scaling, these procedures are flexible enough to permit their use for many experimental purposes.

Besides a fairly complex statistical treatment of the data, the psychophysical methods demand many precautions as the data are being gathered. We saw, for example, how errors of anticipation or habituation might affect results if proper safeguards are not taken. Time error and space error are other possible sources of bias in data which must be considered as we design a psychophysical study.

Besides learning experimental, statistical, and graphical procedures in psychophysics, we gave our attention to certain concepts like the *RL*, the *DL*, the *JND*, and the *JUD*. We noted, too, the futile attempt to summarize the data on differential sensitivities by means of Weber's law. The Weber-Fechner formulation, of historical importance in psychophysical scaling, was reviewed with some modern criticisms noted.

Ratio scales may be constructed by using such methods as ratio estimation, ratio production, and magnitude estimation. Fractionation is a common form of the ratio production method. Numerous sensory and perceptual dimensions have been subjected to ratio scaling. An approximation to a power function, $\psi = kS^n$, has generally been obtained as the relationship between subjective magnitudes and physical values. Two studies which sought to scale the heaviness of lifted weights were reviewed. One investigation used a fractionation method; the other employed magnitude estimation. General rules for this technique of ratio scaling were reviewed.

Category scales are established by using the methods of single stimuli, absolute judgment, equal intervals, or rating. Constructing an equal discriminability scale of loudness served as an example of applying the method of absolute judgment. Other research into category scaling involved such stimulus dimensions as size of geometric forms and frequency of tones.

Our study of the psychophysical methods was illustrated by reference to several experiments which might be done in the student laboratory. The research that was cited gave evidence of the wide applicability of these methods. They can be used for basic studies and applied investigations in both sensation and perception. Their flexibility, however, does not mean that they can be employed carelessly. Many procedural precautions are required for valid work with the psychophysical methods. The choice of subjects and of stimulus values are two primary problems. The task demanded of the subject, especially if he must operate any control device, is also a potential source of error. In psychophysical work, as in all psychological research, we realize that the behavior under study is dependent on surrounding conditions in a complex way.

REFERENCES

Diamond, A. L., Scheible, H., Schwartz, E., & Young, R. A comparison of psychophysical methods in the investigation of foveal simultaneous brightness contrast. *J. exp. Psychol.*, 1955, 50, 171–174.

Eriksen, C. W., & Hake, H. W. Absolute judgments as a function of stimulus range and number of stimulus and response categories. *J. exp. Psychol.*, 1955, 49, 323–332.

Garner, W. R. An equal discriminability scale for loudness judgments. *J. exp. Psychol.*, 1952, 43, 232–238.

Garner, W. R. Context effects and the validity of loudness scales. *J. exp. Psychol.*, 1954, 48, 218–224.

Gregg, L. W. Fractionation of temporal intervals. *J. exp. Psychol.*, 1951, 42, 307–312.

Guilford, J. P. *Psychometric methods.* (2nd ed.) New York: McGraw-Hill, 1954.

Hanes, R. M. A subjective scale of brightness. *J. exp. Psychol.*, 1949, 39, 438–452.

Harper, R. S., & Stevens, S. S. A psychological scale of weight and a formula for its derivation. *Amer. J. Psychol.*, 1948, 61, 343–351.

Harris, J. D. Discrimination of pitch: suggestions toward method and procedure. *Amer. J. Psychol.*, 1948, 61, 309–322.

Helson, H. Adaptation-level as a frame of reference for prediction of psychophysical data. *Amer. J. Psychol.*, 1947, 60, 1–29.

Johannsen, Dorothea E. *The principles of psychophysics with laboratory exercises.* The author: Saratoga Springs, 1941.

Johnson, D. M. Generalization of a reference scale for judging pitch. *J. exp. Psychol.*, 1949, 39, 316–321.

Luce, R. D., & Edwards, W. The derivation of subjective scales from just noticeable differences. *Psychol. Rev.*, 1958, 65, 222–237.

MacLeod, S. A construction and attempted validation of sensory sweetness scales. *J. exp. Psychol.*, 1952, 44, 316–323.

Mote, F. A., Briggs, G. E., & Michels, K. M. The reliability of measurements of human dark adaptation. *J. exp. Psychol.*, 1954, 48, 69–74.

Newhall, S. M. An interpolation procedure for calculating thresholds. *Psychol. Rev.*, 1928, 35, 46–66.

Parducci, A. Direction of shift in the judgment of single stimuli. *J. exp. Psychol.*, 1956, 51, 169–178.

Purdy, Jean, & Gibson, Eleanor J. Distance judgment by the method of fractionation. *J. exp. Psychol.*, 1955, 50, 374–380.

Stevens, S. S. The direct estimation of sensory magnitudes—loudness. *Amer. J. Psychol.*, 1956, 69, 1–25.

Stevens, S. S.   On the psychophysical law.   *Psychol. Rev.*, 1957, 64, 153–181.
Stevens, S. S., & Galanter, E. H.   Ratio scales and category scales for a dozen perceptual continua.   *J. exp. Psychol.*, 1957, 54, 377–411.
Stevens, S. S., & Poulton, E. C.   The estimation of loudness by unpracticed observers.   *J. exp. Psychol.*, 1956, 51, 71–78.
Vanderplas, J. M.   Frequency of experience versus organization as determinants of visual thresholds.   *Amer. J. Psychol.*, 1953, 66, 574–583.

ADDITIONAL READINGS

Bergmann, G., & Spence, K. W.   The logic of psychophysical measurement.   *Psychol. Rev.*, 1944, 51, 1–24.
Graham, C. H.   Behavior, perception and the psychophysical methods.   *Psychol. Rev.*, 1950, 57, 108–120.
Karlin, L.   The time-error in the comparison of visual size.   *Amer. J. Psychol.*, 1953, 66, 564–573.
Parducci, A.   Learning variables in the judgment of single stimuli.   *J. exp. Psychol.*, 1954, 48, 24–30.
Stevens, S. S.   Problems and methods of psychophysics.   *Psychol. Bull.*, 1958, 55, 177–196.
Verplanck, W. S., Cotton, J. W., & Collier, G. H.   Previous training as a determinant of response dependency at the threshold.   *J. exp. Psychol.*, 1953, 46, 10–14.

Psychological Scaling

Experience can be quantified along many dimensions even when there is no specified physical stimulus attribute arousing it. In contrast to the psychophysical methods, which employ physical measurements as an indirect way of scaling experience, psychological scaling is accomplished in units that have no physical referent. The scales that are achieved reflect the quantitative aspects of judgmental responses like, "This picture is more pleasing in composition than that one." It might be possible to scale the pleasingness of pictorial composition by means of certain physical measurements in complex combination, but we take a psychological approach when we ask subjects or observers to give us their comparative judgments of several pictures. By having them attend particularly to the artistic composition we obtain data which permit us to locate the stimulus pictures on an ordinal or interval scale of this characteristic.

As is the case with the psychophysical methods, the psychological scaling techniques which we shall study in this chapter represent the summarizing of many data obtained by fairly conventional methods. We will not be seeking absolute or differential thresholds but will be establishing scales. Sometimes the scales are set up for general use in further research or practical application. More commonly in psychological experimentation, a particular group of stimulus items are quantified with respect to some attribute. This might be done, for example, to determine how the scale values obtained are affected by some experimental treatment. Our study of psychological scaling will require us to become familiar with the procedures for obtaining the judgmental data and for converting them statistically into scale values.

In the *method of rating*, subjects are asked to give some sort of quantitative description to the stimuli that are considered singly.

The responses given may be descriptive in a verbal way, or numerically, or even graphically. The *method of ranking* requires each observer to put all the stimulus items in order with respect to the attribute being scaled. In the *method of pair comparisons,* a subject must compare every stimulus with every other one. For each pair he must state which has the greater degree of the attribute being scaled. Most studies use many subjects, with statistical manipulations of the raw data being required to attain scale values.

RESEARCH APPLICATIONS

Before we turn to the methods of psychological scaling we shall survey the numerous uses they have. Not only are they techniques of value in laboratory research but they are among the foremost of psychological tools with respect to their general utility. They are used in clinical, industrial, and social psychology. Even beyond their employment by psychologists, they are used in government and business for many purposes. For example, personnel evaluation and opinion polling are two activities which have a psychological scaling aspect. As interesting as these varied uses are, we shall have to limit the applications we discuss, concentrating on the psychological scaling methods themselves as research instruments. As techniques for quantifying judgmental behavior they serve well in the search for quantified relationships in psychology. We find them used in scaling stimuli, in quantifying complex behavior, and in the investigation of the judgmental processes themselves.

Scaling Stimuli

A primary use of the psychological scaling methods is to assign values to stimuli with reference to dimensions that are not scalable in physical units. Such intangibles as the beauty of a painting, the palatability of a cup of coffee, the friendliness of a smile, or the funniness of a cartoon can all be rated or ranked or otherwise quantified by these methods. In the psychological scaling of such stimuli we employ the human yardstick, the judgments of persons, since it is human appreciation toward which these qualities are directed. Having selected an appropriate group of subjects, observers, or judges, as they may be variously called, we accept their responses to the stimuli as the raw data from which our scale is constructed. Being aware of certain tendencies in judgmental behavior, we may instruct the observers and collect and treat their observations in such a way as to minimize distortion of the scale values by any extraneous process.

ESTHETIC STIMULI. Considerable pioneer work on the psychological scaling methods was directed toward quantifying the degree of pleasure or approval aroused by different stimuli. What proportion of width to length makes for the most pleasing rectangle? The answer to this question would seem to be important to artists and architects. When it was sought experimentally by presenting rectangles of different proportions, no definitive result was obtained. As they were presented, without context or meaning, several different rectangles were judged most pleasing by different viewers. This result need not be disturbing since esthetic judgments made by different observers are based on divergent past experiences and should hardly be expected to coincide perfectly. In the type of study described, lack of agreement is almost invited by assigning no potential application to the rectangles being judged.

PERSONALITY TRAITS. Although theories differ widely as to the direct observability of the key aspects of personality, they tend to agree that some observable traits may be important indicators of personality structure. This suggests the desirability of quantifying the degree to which certain traits, such as sociability, are present in a person. The psychological scaling of manifest aspects of personality can be useful in both clinical practice and research. As observers for the scaling of personality traits, one research design may demand trained judges such as clinical psychologists, whereas another investigation may require that the traits be rated by observers who spend considerable time in everyday situations with the person being rated.

ADVERTISING AND CONSUMER PRODUCTS. Applied psychologists find techniques like rating and ranking very useful in areas like market research. They may pretest advertising copy by having it rated for its effectiveness by potential customers. In a different study they may have sample telephones ranked by color preference so that their manufacture can be concentrated on a few hues which have wide appeal. Psychological scaling is applied also to product names before they are adopted and used in expensive promotional campaigns.

VALUES. It is commonplace to state that different groups of persons have different standards of value. Psychological scaling is one way to describe value systems which exist for such diverse realms as ethics, social attitudes, sense of humor, fashions in clothes, and food preferences. Different investigators have attempted scaling in all these domains, quantifying the judged severity of different crimes, preferences for different nationality groups, funniness of cartoons, appeal of necktie patterns, and choices among vegetables. In athletics we find scaling methods used in judging the diving at swimming meets and in voting the Most Valuable Player awards in baseball.

SUBJECTIVE STATES. Considerable use has been made of psychological scaling methods in quantifying the affective arousal accomplished by various stimuli. Colors, odors, and tonal combinations have been scaled for their pleasantness or unpleasantness. Although we may refer to the stimuli as being pleasant or unpleasant, judges are actually scaling the quality and intensity of their own feelings as they attend to them.

A quantified description of a subject's current mood state is the aim of the adjective check list employed by Nowlis and Nowlis (1956). Given a list of about a hundred mood-descriptive adjectives like "drowsy" or "amused," the subject must rate each one on the degree to which it is applicable to him at that moment. This rating is quickly done by marking the check list opposite each adjective. Different code marks are used to indicate different points on a scale of applicability of the adjective to the rater's current mood.

Quantifying Behavior

Even though psychological scaling offers promise of quantifying subjective experiences like perceiving, valuing, and enjoying, it has its uses in the investigation of more overt behavior as well. Examples of such employment may be found in applied psychology as well as in research.

MERIT RATING. Supervisors in industry are sometimes asked to rate workers on their performance. Such ratings are particularly useful in evaluating for advancement those workers whose duties do not provide other performance indices such as number of items assembled. Ratings by supervisors sometimes provide the criterion measures for evaluating the validity of aptitude test scores. No matter what their purpose, merit ratings need to be based on competent instruction in the task of rating.

BEHAVIOR RESEARCH. Scaling methods have potential application wherever behavior in an experimental situation is too complex to permit its quantification in some more direct way. For example, we might use ratings by judges to quantify the degree of aggression exhibited by subjects in a study to test the hypothesis that frustration leads to aggression.

OPINION-ATTITUDE ASSESSMENT. Surveys or polls of opinions or attitude may be considered to represent psychological scaling in at least three ways. We may have respondents rate themselves on the extent of their agreement with some statement, from "strongly disagree" to "strongly agree." In a more elaborate scaling effort we may assign a scale value to an individual indicating his position on some attitude continuum, like his attitude toward women in politics. His scale value will be based on his endorsing or rejecting numerous statements on this topic. Finally, psychological scaling is demonstrated in describing group opinion, as when we say that 73 per cent of a sample of voters stated that they would vote for a woman as governor of their state. Whether attitude assessment is aimed at subjective states or at behavior may be debated. Here we have made the assumption that attitude expression is a form of verbal behavior that is quantified by psychological scaling methods.

Investigating Judgmental Processes

We have seen that psychological scaling methods may be used to quantify stimuli or behavior. In either of these applications we tend to take the ratings or rankings of the judges at face value. We realize, however, that the judgment that we require them to make is itself composed of complex psychological processes. Sometimes research which employs these scaling techniques is aimed at elucidating these judgmental processes, with no primary interest in the stimuli.

IDIOSYNCRASIES IN RATING. Persons doing rating sometimes reveal particular persistent tendencies as they go about their task. Some judges, for example, tend to be unduly lenient in rating traits of others. Another idiosyncrasy that is sometimes observed is the tendency to avoid using either of the end points of the rating scale that is provided. A judge exhibiting this tendency will have a restricted variability in the ratings he assigns. The distortions in data that stem from these personal habits of rating may sometimes be offset in statistical treatment of the ratings. Preferably, judges will be selected and trained to prevent any such distortions in the scaling.

INFLUENCES ON JUDGMENT. A general problem in the study of judging is to identify the numerous factors which may influence judgments. From past research on psychological scaling we may draw a few examples. Studies of many sorts have revealed that influences of a social nature can seriously affect judging behavior. If an individual knows the ratings that others are assigning, he may be swayed so that his ratings tend to correspond more closely to theirs than would otherwise be the case. The practice of having ratings given independently is a recognition of such a social influence, of course.

A judge may also be influenced by previous ratings that he himself has given to the same person or object being rated. In merit rating, for instance, if a supervisor rates an employee very high on "productivity," he may also give a high rating on "good will toward the company" even though evidence on which to base the latter rating is meager. It is as though the earlier rating provides a halo for the person being evaluated so that he is perceived thereafter as a superior being; the term *halo effect* has therefore been applied to this sort of influence of a readily made judgment on those less easy to determine. Although the terminology seems to imply positive bias, you can see that the same sort of interdependence of judgments might have an adverse effect in which a strongly negative response on the part of the rater would influence some of his other ratings in the negative direction.

Research on the processes of judgment is a source of aid in the improvement of psychological scaling techniques. As they are refined, these techniques will serve us better in many sorts of psychological investigations.

THE METHOD OF RATING

Under the method of rating the type of rating scale which a rater has to apply to the stimuli being judged may vary greatly. Verbal, numerical, or graphic scales have all been used. By locating stimuli at some point on such a device, the judges provide data which are used to establish a scale value for each of the stimuli. Sometimes called the method of successive categories or the method of graded dichotomies, the fundamental rating method is amenable to several variations in data analysis, as Guilford points out (1954, Chapter 10).

Criteria for Using Rating

There are a few considerations which favor the use of the rating method for psychological scaling as opposed to the method of ranking or of pair comparisons. When the use of these other two methods is precluded because the stimuli cannot be presented together for comparative judgments, some rating technique must be employed. Rating is to be preferred also for its economy of time when a large number of stimuli are to be judged. Comparing them pair by pair would be very time consuming.

The rating task, involving some kind of scale provided for the judges, is not overly simple; we must be confident of the judges' ability to use the scale properly before we turn to rating for psychological scaling. The method does have the advantage of letting the judge indicate the distance separating different stimuli on the continuum. In the other methods, only comparative judgments are given.

Devising Rating Scales

A rating scale serves to aid judges in making a set of judgments and communicating them. Lacking such a device, it would be difficult to judge a series of items and to describe the judgments meaningfully. We shall examine some of the types of rating scales to see how they facilitate judgmental behavior and quantify it at the same time.

NUMERICAL AND VERBAL SCALES. Quantitative concepts are so much a part of our thinking that judgments may be expressed readily by the use of a numerical scale. Although most people find them easy to use, there are a few precautions to take in the establishment of such a scale. One rule is to provide a number of scale points or intervals appropriate to the needs of the rater. A three-point scale, for example, may not permit enough categories to which a judge may assign the items. On the other hand, a fifteen-point scale might imply finer differences than it would be possible to use in doing the rating. Since raters tend to avoid using the end points of a rating scale, it is useful to provide more points than would seem desirable for the ratings themselves to cover. Thus, a nine-point scale might yield a set of ratings that are largely confined to seven points.

Besides trying to fit the number of rating points or categories to the problem facing the raters, we need to think about an odd number of points vs. an even number for a rating scale. An odd number permits the center point to be used as a neutral index if that seems appropriate. Such a neutral point may be a zero, with positive and negative numbers arranged to represent degrees of judgment of desirable and undesirable traits or attributes. In the interest of simplicity, however, negative numbers are often avoided in setting up a scale. One of the series of positive numbers may then be verbally indicated as an indifference point if desired. Where such a neutral point is not considered appropriate, an even number of scale points may be provided to force judgments in one direction or the other.

It is common practice to give a verbal description of every point on a numerical rating scale. For example, consider the following scale for esthetic appeal:

9   Extremely appealing
8   Very appealing
7   Moderately appealing
6   Slightly appealing
5   Neither appealing nor unappealing
4   Slightly unappealing
3   Moderately unappealing
2   Very unappealing
1   Extremely unappealing

The scale points are identified by the graded series of adverbs— "slightly, moderately, very, and extremely"—which are assigned to the adjective "appealing" to form one part of the scale and to its opposite "unappealing" to form another part. At "5" on the scale the descriptive phrase indicates an indifference point. In a different numerical schema this point might have been considered "0," with the other values ranging up to "4" and down to "−4." For scaling in other value systems we might employ the same set of adverbs with pairs of adjectives like pleasant–unpleasant, or desirable–undesirable.

Numerical rating scales may be employed where the complexity of the material being judged would preclude simple verbal description. In a study of group behavior, for example, a judge might rate each observed group on the extent to which their morale level and their efficiency in communicating would lead him to predict success for them in cooperatively solving a difficult problem. In such an experiment in social psychology, the ratings might thus be applied to predicted behavior instead of observed behavior.

The rating scale that ranged from "extremely appealing" to "extremely unappealing" had every point verbally indicated so that these descriptions actually form a verbal scale. The numbers, convenient in recording judgments, might be discarded if we wished. It is common practice to use verbal statements like "agree" or "strongly disagree" when we scale a subject's degree of agreement with each of a series of attitude-indicating statements. In other types of psychological measurement a test may require a person to indicate by meaningful symbols, +, −, or ?, whether given statements are applicable or not to that which is being judged. Although not strictly verbal themselves, such symbols might be considered equivalent to terms like "applicable," "inapplicable," and "cannot say."

GRAPHIC SCALES. In the graphic method of rating, judges are asked to indicate on a physical continuum—a straight line segment—the location which they feel represents the place of the item being rated on some psychological continuum or dimension. By placing a mark near one end of the line, for example, a rater may indicate his judgment that a painting has a great esthetic appeal. Various points along the line may be indicated by verbal statements as indicated below:

Very high esthetic appeal	Moderate esthetic appeal	Very low esthetic appeal

Our sample graphic rating scale illustrates a number of principles that are felt to represent good practice. The line is a continuous one so that the rater may locate his mark at any point along it. This continuity imposes no restraints on the rater or on the numerical scoring that is done later. The verbal statements near the ends of the line are not so extreme as to cause raters to cluster their indicating marks near the center. It is considered better to have the "good" end of the scale at the left. A graphic rating scale may be a vertical line, too, permitting verbal statements to be readily placed alongside it at several points.

Graphic scales are interesting to use. They free the rater from some of the influences that might arise if he had to give numerical judgments repeatedly. They are readily scored with a scoring stencil or template which can, in some research uses, be adapted to the ratings that have been given. For example, if raters are found to have avoided the ends of the scale, the scoring divisions of the template can be adjusted so that a reasonable spread of numerical values results anyway. Another value of the graphic method is its extension into a series of scales which yields a profile representation of the multidimensional scaling of any item.

SPECIAL SCALES. A number of variants of rating scale methods may lend themselves to application in research. One of these is the *standard scale* in which points along the continuum are designated by providing graded samples for the rater to use as he judges each item. For example, if we wanted ratings on the skill exhibited by different subjects in drawing a picture of a person, we would provide between six and twelve sample pictures of varying degrees of excellence.

Judges could compare each subject's work with these standards in order to arrive at a rating.

A *sorting-tray* technique may be employed conveniently if verbal items are being judged. By printing the items on 3 × 5 cards we may require them to be sorted into a long tray containing perhaps 9 compartments. Having designated a numerical value and a verbal label for each compartment, we obtain ratings for the sorted items. With this technique it is feasible to allow subjects to relocate some items as the sorting proceeds. The scale can be evaluated continuously by the subject as he proceeds with his task. In this way, the ratings given to the earlier items do not distort the rating scale by exerting an anchoring effect, to be discussed later in this chapter.

A *check-list* procedure permits scale values to be developed in a cumulative process involving numerous judgments. Textbooks, for example, might be rated by checking the applicable items from a long list of descriptive words or phrases like "sturdy binding" and "useful index." The ultimate rating is based on the sum of all the values applied to the checked items for any particular book being judged. Different items may carry different weights, if desired, and negative weights may also be used.

Administrative Procedures

Having begun our use of a rating method by selecting an appropriate rating scale, we would continue by setting up proper conditions surrounding the collecting of the ratings. Primary problems confronting us would include the instructing or training of the judges and the presenting of the stimulus materials to them.

INSTRUCTIONS TO RATERS. In experiments requiring that ratings be given by subjects or judges, the requirement that they be motivated to do their best is important, as in nearly all psychological research. In addition to arousing their interest, instructions to subjects should give them considerable information about how to perform their task. A prime requirement is that the dimension or attribute on which the ratings are to be given must be clearly defined. The validity of ratings might be ruined before they were even collected if judges misunderstand what they are to rate about the stimulus objects or persons presented to them. It is especially important to specify carefully the trait to be judged if it is a characteristic that is not too prominent in the total stimulus pattern. We must proceed carefully, however, in order not to define a stimulus dimension in such a way that we force some bias into the ratings given to the different stimuli. For example, it would be unwise to say, "You are to rate these paintings on their excellence in color harmony, as in a balanced presentation of deep purples, light tans, and fiery reds." The mention of particular hues might cause observers to give special attention to any painting that contained the three that were mentioned. The best instructions avoid any source of influence on the ratings (unless this is an experimental aim) while defining the attribute clearly enough to eliminate any misunderstanding on the part of the raters.

Besides making sure they know what they are rating, we must be sure that judges employ the rating scale properly. We saw that the proper devising of any type of rating scale can do much to insure its proper use. We may wish to direct the judges to use the full extent of the scale, counteracting any tendency to avoid extreme values. Sometimes instructions are worded to suggest or even to dictate what proportion of the cases should be given each rating. This procedure might be used, for example, to assure a normal distribution for the assigned ratings. Such instructions should be given to judges only if the restraints are felt to impose no great difficulty on their performance of the rating task.

If there is any question about the adequacy of instructions for a rating task, they should be pretested on a group of persons similar to those who will be judges in the experiment. Such a preliminary tryout may reveal points of confusion which can be eliminated by clarifying the wording of the directions for judging. Some research may deal with perceptual judgments that are so difficult to make that some training of the observers must precede the actual collecting of the ratings. Such prior practice is often appropriate, but it should be remembered that the final scale values that are achieved are not the same as might have been obtained with untrained observers.

PRESENTATION OF STIMULUS ITEMS. Perceptual processes are so complex that many factors may affect the ratings which observers give to stimulus items. In the judging of paintings, for example, ratings related to color characteristics might be distorted if illumination were inadequate or too strong. Viewing distance also may seriously affect a judge's reaction to a picture. Which would be the sounder procedure, to keep viewing distance a constant or to let it vary at the desire of those who are rating a series of pictures? In a different judging task, what problems would you foresee in presenting musical selections to be rated?

One advantage of rating over some other methods of psychological scaling is that items to be judged can be presented successively rather than simultaneously. However, there are difficulties with an experimental design which presents stimuli singly, one after the other, for rating. As the judges rate the first few items they may employ a certain part of the rating scale. These early judgments may exert an *anchoring effect* for any similar stimuli judged later in the series. Such an anchoring effect may distort the assigned ratings from what they might have been if a different, and perhaps more representative, set of items had been experienced early in the task. To avoid introducing distortion, it is often good practice to give judges a preliminary acquaintance with the stimuli to be judged. Sometimes all the stimuli are presented in advance of actual judging; sometimes the judges are shown a sample of stimuli which is assumed to include representatives from all parts of the continuum that will be encountered in the actual rating. Either technique tends to offset the development of an anchoring effect.

Treatment of Rating Data

The data analysis which follows the collecting of ratings may range from a simple determination of central tendency to an elaborate series of calculations leading to the establishment of interval scale values. Our discussion will center on the simpler treatments of the data with a brief sample of more elaborate scaling techniques.

DISTRIBUTION OF THE RATINGS. Although it is feasible to proceed immediately to the computation of measures of central tendency and variability when rating data have been collected, it is often well to make frequency distributions of the ratings assigned to each stimulus item first. Consider, for example, the contrasting sets of ratings on artistic merit given to hypothetical paintings A and B in the following frequency distributions:

	Rating							
	1	2	3	4	5	6	7	
Frequency distribution, Painting A:	0	2	4	12	19	3	1	$N = 41$
Frequency distribution, Painting B:	8	7	2	1	5	8	10	$N = 41$

We could compute the mean or median rating for each picture and the standard deviation of the ratings. These statistics would not reveal the entire difference, however, between the two sets of judgments. If we inspect the frequency distributions, we find that the distribution of the 41 ratings for Painting B is bimodal. Judges rated it either fairly high or else quite low. This aspect of the distribution adds to the information we would get from the computed statistics. In fact, it indicates any measure of central tendency to be somewhat misleading. The bimodality of ratings is the salient fact about

Painting *B* requiring explanation. We might infer, for example, that there is some characteristic of this work of art which elicits strong approval from some viewers but evokes censure from others.

CENTRAL TENDENCIES OF THE RATINGS. Often the use of ratings will not be oriented toward the determination of interval scale values, and a simple form of data analysis will be appropriate. As a measure of central tendency, the mean rating given to each stimulus item may be determined, to be statistically compared with the means for other items. In many studies there may be reasons for regarding the median as a more appropriate measure. If a number of judges particularly disliked a certain item, they might give extremely low ratings to it as "votes against" it. This would lower the mean rating unduly, but the median rating would not differ from the value it would have had if their dislike of the item had been expressed in moderation.

In other instances, extreme ratings may accurately reflect great approval or disapproval of an item. If a great number of ratings fall at one end point on the rating scale, we might infer that many of the judges would have rated even more extremely if this had been possible. In such a case a mean rating would not reflect the true central tendency of the judgments. A median would still do so, provided the median did not actually fall in this end category.

VARIABILITY OF THE RATINGS. The mean or median ratings given by a group of judges may be far less important in indicating their reactions to some stimulus items than a measure of variability of the ratings. If variability is extremely low, indicating very strong agreement among the judges in rating a stimulus item, this fact is likely to be noteworthy. If variability is great, the widespread disagreement indicated is a fact also requiring attention. In this case we would need to ask whether the lack of agreement stemmed from the nature of the stimulus item, from the composition of the group of judges, or from some sort of ambiguity in defining the rating task for them. By calculating the standard deviation, we may seek information about the experimental rating procedures as well as about the stimulus items.

DETERMINING INTERVAL SCALE VALUES. Computational procedures described by Guilford (1954, pp. 223–244) permit us to obtain interval scale values from rating data. The treatment of the rating data from a large number of judges represents a correction for the probable occurrence of inequalities in the intervals represented in the rating scale as it was employed. The assumption is made that ratings of each stimulus item would hypothetically be normally distributed. Wherever the distribution of ratings is empirically skewed, the application of this assumption of normal distribution represents a determination of either (1) the limits of the successive rating categories or (2) representative scale values. The latter approach to interval scale values is the one which Guilford recommends. Although many studies employing ratings may be carried out with simpler treatments of the data, it is well to be aware that there are procedures for more ambitious efforts at psychological scaling.

Precautions in Using the Method of Rating

In discussing administrative procedures we noted some rules concerning the instructing of raters and the presentation of stimulus items to them. Earlier, we discussed the care that must be taken in setting up rating scales. All these precautions represented our recognition of the complexity of the judgmental behavior situation. We may now consider a few additional precepts which deserve consideration if we are to use rating methods in research.

If each stimulus item is to be rated on a number of dimensions, it is desirable to consider one dimension at a time, rating all the stimuli on this factor. This is preferable to completing all ratings on a particular item at one time. The latter procedure tends to invite the operation of the halo effect which we discussed earlier.

By way of augmenting a good definition of the trait or dimension to be rated, it is desirable to select with care the verbal cues which identify points or regions on the rating scale. The wording employed in these cues should be clear, brief, and relevant to the dimension being rated. They should leave no doubt as to the degree of the trait which each of them implies. In brief, the labels attached to a rating scale should aid the rater rather than make his task difficult.

A Sample Experiment Using Ratings

The usefulness of the rating method in studying a psychological phenomenon is illustrated by an experiment conducted by a group of students in one of the writer's classes.* The investigation employed ratings in two ways, once in a preliminary way and once in two different tests of the hypothesis.

THE PROBLEM. The problem was to determine if ratings given to paintings and to musical selections would be raised by attributing the work to a well-known artist or composer. The hypothesis was that "prestige suggestion" would improve the group mean ratings.

* A report written by Louis Miller, then a graduate student in the experimental psychology course at the University of Rochester, was used in writing this summary of the study.

THE METHOD. Ratings were first employed in this study to determine which artists and composers could be considered well-known and which could be regarded as obscure. The names of 25 artists and 25 composers were rated on a nine-point numerical rating scale by the 36 college students who were to be subjects later in the main part of the study. In this preliminary rating task, the following instructions were given:

> Please rate the following artists (or composers) according to your *personal* opinion of their excellence. Beside the name of each one, place a number from 1 to 9, using the higher numbers to show a high regard, the lower numbers to indicate a poor rating. If you have never heard of a particular artist (or composer), place a question mark beside his name.

Half the subjects rated the artists first, then the composers; the other subjects rated the two classes of men in the reverse of this order. This counterbalancing served to prevent boredom from influencing unduly the ratings of either category. The lists presented to raters had previously been randomized as to sequence of names.

On the basis of the per cent of judges recognizing their names and the mean ratings given them, two groups of artists and two groups of composers were selected. In each category, the high prestige group consisted of five men having a high degree of familiarity and also a high mean rating. Five low prestige names in each category were those who were infrequently recognized and who were given low ratings. The resulting lists of artists and composers are presented in Table 6.1.

A week later the same subjects participated in the main part of the study, being required to rate ten paintings and ten musical selections attributed to persons of either high or low prestige. Half the subjects, in Group I, rated the paintings first, and then the musical excerpts. The others, Group II, rated the music first and then the pictures, projected by colored slides. Besides counterbalancing for possible boredom in giving ratings, this grouping and task sequence permitted another very important control to be exerted. Any picture that was attributed to an artist of high prestige when it was shown to Group I was attributed to an artist of low prestige when shown to Group II, and vice versa. The same plan was followed in naming the composers who were credited with the musical excerpts that were played on a tape recorder. This aspect of experimental design meant that every one of the ten paintings or musical selections was represented in the data for both the high and low prestige conditions. Each item was thus rated by 18 subjects under a high prestige sug-

TABLE 6.1

Per Cent of Judges Recognizing and Mean Ratings Assigned to Artists and
Composers in the High and Low Prestige Groups

	Artist	Per Cent Recognized	Mean Rating	Composer	Per Cent Recognized	Mean Rating
High prestige groups	Michelangelo	100	8.0	Strauss	87	6.8
	Da Vinci	95	7.9	Stravinsky	76	6.3
	Rembrandt	100	7.7	Sibelius	58	6.0
	Raphael	92	7.3	Bloch	53	5.9
	Rubens	71	6.2	Shostakovitch	55	5.8
Low prestige groups	Venenziano	8	4.7	Fauré	18	5.0
	Verrochio	13	4.6	Villa-Lobos	8	5.0
	Lorenzetti	10	4.3	Walton	32	4.9
	Mantegna	5	4.0	Holst	5	4.5
	Carracci	8	3.0	Scriabin	10	4.5

gestion and by 18 subjects under the low prestige suggestion. These
suggestions were accomplished by identifying each item, just before
presenting it, as the work of one of the men listed in Table 6.1. In
no case had the work actually been created by the artist to whom it
was attributed although each item was matched in general style to
the work of the man to whom it was credited.

REASONS FOR USING THE RATING METHOD. Before seeing the results
of this investigation we might ask why rating was the preferred technique for the psychological scaling. In the preliminary part of the
study, rating was a good technique to use since the subjects could
rate only those men whom they felt to be at least slightly familiar
to them. The omission of those whom they did not know did not
interfere with the psychological scaling of the familiar artists or
composers. In the methods of ranking or pair comparisons, as we
shall see, it would not be feasible to omit items from the judging in
this way.

In the judging of the musical excerpts the method of rating was
advantageous because it permits the successive presentation of the
stimuli with no demand for their comparison with each other. In
the case of the paintings, subjects did not have to view each one
repeatedly as they would with some other methods. A different
reason for using rating in this part of the study was that the subjects

had become familiar with this method, including the nine-point scale, in the preliminary scaling task.

THE RESULTS. The data obtained in this experiment confirmed the hypothesis that prestige suggestion can influence the ratings given to artistic works. The mean ratings given under the two conditions of suggestion are presented in Table 6.2, together with standard devia-

TABLE 6.2

Means and Standard Deviations of Ratings Given to Paintings and Musical Excerpts under High and Low Prestige Suggestion. $N = 36$

	Paintings		Musical Excerpts	
	Mean	SD	Mean	SD
High prestige	6.6	2.1	6.2	1.8
Low prestige	5.8	1.4	5.7	1.6

tions. Since each subject rated five items under the high prestige suggestion and five under the low prestige condition, the paired measures treatment of the data could be used. The t test indicated the mean difference for the rating of paintings to be significant at the 1 per cent level; the difference for the musical excerpts was significant at the 5 per cent level. Both sets of data thus contribute to our confidence that ratings of this sort are influenced by "knowledge" of the artist involved.

THE METHOD OF RANKING

The *method of rank order,* sometimes called the *order of merit method,* is a simple technique for psychological scaling in which the items are merely placed in order with reference to the dimension being judged. The data that are so obtained may be treated quite simply or may be subjected to elaborate transformations aimed at establishing a scale of some refinement.

Criteria for Using Ranking

Ranking is a useful technique in the judging of stimuli that may be moved around physically. If a collection of cartoons is spread out on top of a table, for example, it is convenient for a judge to arrange them in order of their excellence of humor. Ranking is not confined to situations where the stimuli are movable or even physically present. Subjects can assign ranks to famous authors, for example, or to makes of automobiles. The method is readily used when the number of stimuli is fairly small; it is not as convenient as rating when very many items must be judged.

An advantage in the use of ranking is that it forces every judge to use all parts of the scale that might hypothetically be considered as being applied. The highest ranks must be assigned to some of the stimulus items and the lowest must be given to others. Judges thus have no way of committing the error of central tendency that may occur in rating if they avoid using the extremes. Another advantage of ranking over rating is that it forces a decision among stimuli that may be hard to judge as different from each other. In rating, a judge might evade this difficulty by assigning the same rating to these items, often a legitimate thing to do in using rating scales. Ranking, however, demands decisions which, in effect, differentiate every item from every other one according to the judgments of the observer.

Administrative Procedures

With no rating scale requiring construction, an investigator finds himself with fewer preliminary problems if he decides to use the method of rank order. Its simplicity, however, does not mean that the method can be used carelessly with any prospect of getting valid results.

INSTRUCTIONS TO JUDGES. The initial instructions to judges in a ranking task may be considered even more important than in the rating method since cues that a rating scale provides are lacking in the method of rank order. This lack of cues requires special emphasis on the dimension with respect to which the ranking is to be done. This dimension must be especially carefully defined if it pertains to attributes of the stimulus items other than their major ones. Suppose, for example, we ask judges to rank popular singers on their enunciation of the lyrics in rendering their songs. As the ranking task is undertaken, our judges may slip unthinkingly into ranking these well-known singers according to their general appeal rather than on the specific dimension we indicated. The attribute to be scaled must be stated with emphasis at the beginning of the ranking task. These initial instructions may well be augmented by a printed reminder prominently displayed.

Another important point to cover in instructing judges is the indicating of which rank is considered most meritorious. Conventionally, of course, a rank of 1 symbolizes the best, with higher rank numbers designating inferior positions on the dimension being judged. It may be especially important to stress this to judges who might be inclined to think in terms of numerical ratings being assigned to the stimulus items.

PRESENTATION OF STIMULUS ITEMS. For ranking purposes the stimuli all have to be available at once for comparison, whether physically present or symbolically represented. Thus, no problem as to sequence of presentation arises. If stimuli are physically arranged by each subject in order of merit, however, we must be sure that the arrangement is not permitted to influence the ranking done by the next subject. The items need to be randomly mixed between presentations to judges.

Treatment of Data

Where a hundred or more judges have engaged in ranking the stimulus items, we might wish to use elaborate computational procedures for scaling which are described by Guilford (1954, pp. 183–188). For many research purposes simpler treatments of rank data will suffice and we shall discuss them here.

DISTRIBUTION OF THE RANKS. For each stimulus item we might make a frequency distribution showing how many times it was ranked in each position. The series of such frequency distributions covering all the stimuli could be combined into one matrix for convenient summary of the ranking. A sample of such a matrix is found in Guilford's Table 8.2 (1954, p. 180).

Examination of the distribution of the ranks assigned to each stimulus may reveal any stimuli which were ranked with good agreement or with great disagreement among the judges.

CENTRAL TENDENCIES IN THE RANKS. Since the assignment of ranks represents only ordinal scaling, it is not proper to compute mean ranks for the stimuli as if the ranks were interval scale values. The median rank assigned each item thus becomes a preferred descriptive statistic. The whole rank number where the median falls may be taken as an index of central tendency. Refining such a median by interpolation may not be sound in view of uncertainty about the scale widths of the different ranks.

VARIABILITY OF THE RANKS. Inspection of the frequency distribution matrix of ranks assigned to stimulus items will indicate the degree of agreement among judges. If a descriptive statistic is desired, the semi-interquartile range is appropriate to use. Without being permitted to calculate a mean rank we cannot obtain the SD as a measure of variability.

TRANSFORMATION TO C SCALE VALUES. One way to refine ranking is to apply the assumption that the trait or attribute that was judged was one that was normally distributed in the sample of items presented for judging. Under such an assumption we consider that the end-most ranks represent a fairly wide separation of interval scale values. The middlemost ranks would be assumed to represent scale values that were closer to each other than those represented by the ranks at either end of the set of ranks. By applying mathematical relationships represented in the normal distribution it is possible to transform ranks into centiles. After describing such a transformation, Guilford (1954, p. 182) suggests another convenient transformation, to his C scale values. This C scale is based on the normalizing transformation of the ranks with the additional convenience that a mean C value of 5.0 and a standard deviation of 2.0 are utilized. The transformation of ranks to normalized C values is readily accomplished by use of Table 6.3, adopted from Guilford (1954).

TABLE 6.3

Ranks Corresponding to C Scale Values for Different Numbers of Items Ranked (After Guilford, 1954)

Number Ranked	C Scale Values								
	1	2	3	4	5	6	7	8	9
10	. . .	10	9	7–8	5–6	3–4	2	1	. . .
11	. . .	11	9–10	8	5–7	4	2–3	1	. . .
12	. . .	12	10–11	8–9	6–7	4–5	2–3	1	. . .
13	13	. . .	11–12	9–10	6–8	4–5	2–3	. . .	1
14	14	. . .	12–13	9–11	7–8	4–6	2–3	. . .	1
15	15	14	13	10–12	7–9	4–6	3	2	1
16	16	15	13–14	11–12	7–10	5–6	3–4	2	1
17	17	16	14–15	11–13	8–10	5–7	3–4	2	1
18	18	17	15–16	12–14	8–11	5–7	3–4	2	1
19	19	18	16–17	12–15	9–11	5–8	3–4	2	1
20	20	19	16–18	13–15	9–12	6–8	3–5	2	1
21	21	20	17–19	14–16	9–13	6–8	3–5	2	1
22	22	21	18–20	14–17	10–13	6–9	3–5	2	1
23	23	22	19–21	15–18	10–14	6–9	3–5	2	1
24	24	22–23	20–21	15–19	11–14	6–10	4–5	2–3	1

Since the normalized C values are considered to be interval scale values, we can find mean C values for each stimulus item as a way of refining our psychological scaling. This transformation to C values does not demand the large number of judges that are required in some of the more elaborate scaling procedures. A point to keep in mind, however, is that we assume the normal distribution of the attribute over the sample of items being judged. Such an assumption may be valid for samples of handwriting from 20 second graders, selected at random. It is probably not a valid assumption to make about the distribution of humor in 20 cartoons from *The New Yorker*.

Precautions in Using the Method of Ranking

In discussing the rank ordering of stimuli in psychological research we noted the care which must be taken in instructing the judges, in presenting the stimuli, and in treating the data. A general rule which may be added is to use ranking only when the number of stimulus items is reasonably small. To demand that very many items be placed in rank order is to invite frustration on the part of the judges with subsequent unreliability of rank data. Where many stimuli must be judged it is better to provide a good rating scale.

THE METHOD OF PAIR COMPARISONS

In using scaling methods like ranking or rating we ask a judge to assign a numerical value, directly or by implication, each time he considers a stimulus item. In the method of pair comparisons judgments are in themselves less quantitative than in these other methods. Stimuli are paired and compared with each other instead of with any numerical rating scale or set of ranks. Judges merely say which member of each pair is preferred or possesses more of the quality being scaled. This comparative judgment of the various pairings of stimuli gives the method its name. From the expressed preferences we obtain scale values by a series of computational steps.

Criteria for Using Pair Comparisons

This method may be used when it is desired to obtain an interval scaling of some psychological dimension. If we merely desired a rough ordinal scale, we would employ ranking or rating with a minimum of elaboration on the raw data. We would further restrict our choice of pair comparisons to a scaling task where the stimulus items to be judged are not too numerous. As the number of stimuli to be compared rises, the number of pairings increases much more rapidly. Thus, it takes 10 trials to present 5 stimuli in all possible pairs whereas

45 trials would be needed for 10 stimuli. If there are 15 stimuli, it takes 105 trials to present all possible pairs. It taxes the motivation of observers to be asked to make even this many comparative judgments. It would be practically impossible, in most studies, to require such pair judging when stimuli are more than 15 in number. It should be noted, though, that the method does not actually require all possible pairs to be judged. A reduced number of pairings may yield good results if there is some knowledge of approximate rank order, perhaps gained in preliminary research.

Administrative Procedures

Many of the general rules for obtaining opinions from judges or observers apply to the method of pair comparisons as well as to the other methods we have discussed. A clear definition of the dimension or trait on which judgments are to be based is the essential initial step in all psychological scaling. Judges must be motivated, too. To these general requirements we add the special techniques that typify the pair comparison method.

PRESENTATION OF STIMULUS ITEMS. It is in the pairing of the stimuli as they are presented for judgment that this method is unique. For ranking, we make them all available for the judges to place them in order of merit. For rating we present them singly, but usually only after a wide sample has been given to the raters to acquaint them with the range covered. In contrast, the method of pair comparisons minimizes the impact of the entire group of stimuli on the judges. The stimulus items are to be considered just two at a time. Ideally, a choice is made between these two without reference to any of the other stimuli, whether previously experienced or anticipated. This comparative judgment within a pair can be encouraged by isolating the pairs from each other as they are presented, perhaps by spacing the presentations in time. Some applications of this method, it is true, present lists of paired words or names to be judged so that all the stimuli are before the observers at once. Such a technique would seem to invite a tacit rank ordering of the stimuli as a guide to the judging of the various pairs. While this might enhance the consistency of the preferences within pairs, it is not required by the rationale for the method of pair comparisons. As long as the stimuli are to be judged in pairs it would seem appropriate to present them that way, rather than instructing the judges to give their attention to just a pair at a time when all pairs are in front of them during the judging.

Another procedural rule is to present each stimulus as often on the right as on the left, to keep a space error from distorting the data. If stimuli are paired successively in time instead of contiguously in space, then of course a similar counterbalancing of first and second presentations would be used; in this case to control for possible time error.

INSTRUCTIONS TO JUDGES. If we strive to keep judgments confined to within-pair evaluations by the way we present the stimuli, we would do well to augment this procedure by instructions. Judges must be told to take each pair as a new problem. Preference must be expressed at the time of presentation with no specific effort made to recall previous stimuli.

Judges must make a choice from every pair in this method of pair comparisons. There is no provision in the computational techniques for any failure to select one stimulus of each paired presentation as the superior one on the quality being scaled. Even if a judge feels it impossible to make a choice in any instance, he must be instructed to express one anyway.

Assumptions—the Law of Comparative Judgment

Since each judgment in the method of pair comparisons is not a quantitative value, we do not arrive at psychological scale values for the stimuli by any simple statistical process. Instead, we use the relative frequencies with which each stimulus is preferred in its comparisons with every other stimulus. The proportions of times that each is chosen provide us with data from which interval scale values may be derived. Before we consider the computational processes, we shall briefly examine the rationale that underlies the treatment of the data.

Thurstone (1927) formulated a *law of comparative judgment* which describes how preference data arise from judgmental processes that are assumed to operate when two stimuli are compared. A fundamental assumption is that the judgmental responses made to any stimulus vary in a normally distributed fashion around a central response value which characterizes the judgments of that particular stimulus. The variations in judging a stimulus are assumed to arise from a large number of internal and external factors whose random fluctuations contribute small increments or decrements to the judgment being made. On most occasions the increments and decrements will nearly cancel each other so that the given judgment will not deviate far from the "true" judgmental response. Less frequently, most of the factors will contribute increments so that the judgment that is made will be somewhat higher than usual. Equally rarely, it is assumed, will there be a piling up of decremental factors so that an unusually low judgment results. By assuming the contributory factors to be uncorrelated in their positive or negative effects from moment to moment, we find it possible to assume further that the distribution of resulting judgments is normally distributed around some central value. Such a distribution is termed a *discriminal dispersion* in discussions of comparative judgment.

Thurstone's law of comparative judgment consists of a series of assumptions which relate hypothetical response value separations and their discriminal dispersions to the proportion of judgment favoring either of two stimuli which are repeatedly compared. The assumptions differ in particular cases subsumed under the general law. We may assume that individual differences may be taken as one factor contributing to discriminal dispersions. Thus, we often treat judgmental data gathered from many observers in the same manner as we would treat data based on repeated judgments made by a single observer.

The method of pair comparisons uses the law of comparative judgment as its basis for psychological scaling. As different stimulus items are considered in pairs, the proportion of times that one is preferred over another is an indicant of the scale separation of the items. For example, if Stimulus G is preferred over Stimulus R on just 520 comparisons out of a thousand, this indicates the scale values of these two items to be quite close. In contrast, if Stimulus W is preferred over Stimulus J in 831 out of 1000 judgments, then W is indicated to be much higher on the scale than J. The different proportions obtained from the comparison of all possible pairs of stimuli can be converted to estimates of the different scale separations of the judgmental responses to the stimuli. By pooling these estimates we arrive at scale values. Guilford (1954, pp. 154–177) provides discussion of the law of comparative judgment and computational guidance for the investigator who wishes to use pair comparisons to accomplish interval scaling for some psychological dimension.

Precautions in Using the Method of Pair Comparisons

The method of pair comparisons should be avoided if the stimuli are so numerous as to make the judgmental task very long and tedious. It may be noted in this regard that a reduction can be made in the number of pairings employed if the scaling effort is planned to provide for such a modification in procedure (Guilford, 1954, pp. 168–169).

To insure that judgments are made within each pair of stimuli as presented, it is good practice to keep the other stimuli out of the subject's field of attention. One advantage of this method over ranking is that it demands the consideration of only two stimuli at a time. This advantage might be lost, however, if judges have access to other stimuli while a particular pair is supposedly under comparison.

For the most exacting applications of the pair comparison method we would have to determine which assumptions under the law of comparative judgment could properly be applied.

A commonly observed precaution in treating pair comparison data is to omit from consideration any preference proportion value more extreme than .977 and .023. Such extreme proportions are likely to introduce unreliability into the estimates of scale separation. Where such values are disregarded, we may take scale separation estimates from each of the more moderate preference proportions. These scale distances may then be averaged to obtain the final scale.

PSYCHOLOGICAL SCALING METHODS EVALUATED

Having completed our survey of various procedures for psychological scaling, we may conclude our discussion with a general evaluation. Our attention will range across the major methods of rating, ranking, and pair comparisons.

Choice of Method

In choosing a method for psychological scaling we would be guided by the stimulus dimension to be studied and by the persons available as judges. We would also consider the purpose of our research, whether it aimed toward establishing an interval scale or required only ordinal scale values. The number of stimuli to be judged and their availability for simultaneous or successive presentation would also bear upon our choice of method.

Rating scale techniques are preferred when there is so large a number of stimuli to be judged that other methods would be prohibitively time consuming. By proper selection or construction of a rating scale, we may do much to assure that the judgmental data we collect will actually serve the purposes of our investigation. Ratings may be obtained even when stimuli are not all available at once, a condition usually required by the other methods.

Ranking has the advantage of forcing judges to exhibit a maximum number of discriminations among the stimuli. It can be accomplished quickly for a small number of stimuli, particularly if these can be moved around physically. It requires the consideration of all the stimuli for comparative purposes.

The pair comparison method is a good one if accurate and dependable scaling is desired for a small number of stimuli. It becomes too time consuming if the number of items is much beyond a dozen, unless a technique reducing the number of pairings is adopted.

Scales Achieved

The methods of rating, ranking, and pair comparison can all yield ordinal scale values. Ordinal scaling is represented directly in the rank order method. In rating, too, an ordering occurs although several stimuli may be given the same value. The complete treatment of pair comparison data yields an interval scale with ordinal sequence as one of its properties, even though complete ordinal consistency may be lacking in the judgments of individual judges. Interval scales can also be achieved by appropriate treatment of the data obtained by rating and ranking. Such scaling should be attempted only when a large number of judgments has been made. In dealing with ranks we may employ the normalizing process to get interval scale values or we may first obtain from the rankings a pair comparison set of proportions of preference. This set then becomes the basis for determining interval scale values as in the pair comparison method.

General Precautions in Psychological Scaling

Perhaps the best guide to using psychological scaling in research is the general formulation that behavior is a function of the person, with his past experience, and the environmental situation in all its aspects. Judgmental behavior will depend on our choice of judges, the instructions, and the training we give them. It will depend on the particular set of stimuli we give them to rate or to compare. Finally, the scale values we obtain will depend on all the operations involved in the scaling. These operations include our definition of the dimension to be scaled and the treatment we give to the data that are collected.

COUNTERACTING THE STIMULUS ERROR. The *stimulus error* is said to occur whenever a judge's knowledge of the stimulus is permitted to alter the judgment he would make solely on the basis of perception of the stimulus dimension being scaled. For example, if a series of weights to be judged was constructed by varying the size of stimulus objects, the size cue would be a source of information that might strongly influence the judgments of the weights as they were lifted.

Any extraneous source of information about the stimuli is a potential contributor of stimulus error. To counteract this error, then, we must prevent judges from knowing anything about the stimuli except what is gained through perceptions of the dimension to be scaled.

AVOIDING ANCHORING EFFECTS. Anchoring effects need to be remembered as we plan stimulus presentation for almost any psychological scaling. Where these arise from sampling a restricted range of stimuli early in the judging, they may be precluded by presenting all stimuli first, before judging actually begins. We must also avoid setting up anchoring effects by revealing our own evaluations of stimuli during the course of the investigation.

GUARDING AGAINST DISTORTING PROCESSES. Some of the behavior processes which can occur in many situations are potential sources of error in psychological scaling. Learning, for example, might give a spurious consistency to the data if we asked a judge to rate or rank the same set of stimuli over and over again. Fatigue might introduce a careless attitude in a prolonged pair comparison session. Another possible mechanism for the introduction of error would be the suggestions regarding stimulus values that might come from the experimenter if he were to talk informally to judges about the stimulus items.

SUMMARY

Methods like rating, ranking, or pair comparison can be used in scaling experience aroused by stimulus dimensions which may lack a physical referent. By applying the conventional procedures and calculations we may arrive at ordinal or interval scale values for esthetic qualities, personality traits, mood states, or other evaluative judgments.

The psychological scaling methods have numerous applied uses as well as utility in research. In laboratory studies they may be employed to measure stimulus attributes, to evaluate certain aspects of behavior, or to investigate judgmental processes.

Verbal, numerical, or graphic scales may be used in the method of rating. These devices must be carefully constructed and administered. The method is particularly appropriate when many stimulus items are to be evaluated. Special techniques like the standard scale, the sorting-tray, and the check list illustrate the variety of formats in which rating may be utilized. Instructions to raters must indicate clearly the dimension to be scaled and the proper use of the rating scale. The presentation of stimulus items must be planned to avoid any distorting influences like the halo effect or the anchoring effect. Simple treatment of rating data will yield ordinal scale values, whereas interval scaling may be accomplished by more elaborate computations. A student experiment using the rating method demonstrated that raters may be influenced by prestige suggestion.

Ranking may be employed conveniently for stimulus items numbering up to about twenty. It requires each judge to discriminate among all the items. Like other methods, it requires care in instructing the judges and presenting the stimuli. Ranking data can be simply treated to yield an ordinal scale. Transformation to C scale values provides an interval scale.

The method of pair comparisons is somewhat time consuming, but it yields interval scale values that may be regarded as quite accurate, assuming adequacy of procedure. Practical only for small numbers of stimuli, this scaling technique is based on various assumptions of the law of comparative judgment. Basic pair comparison data are proportions of times that each stimulus in various pairs is chosen or preferred. From these proportions, scale separations of each stimulus from the other stimuli can be estimated.

The judges to be used and the stimuli to be scaled would be among the first factors to consider in choosing a psychological scaling method. Among special considerations, we find that ratings may be given even when stimuli cannot be brought together for comparative purposes. Ranking of a small number of stimuli is usually accomplished with facility, especially if the stimuli can be moved around physically. Pair comparison is generally reserved for more elaborate efforts at psychological scale construction. All the methods can be made to yield interval scales as well as ordinal scales. Psychological scaling certainly requires complex behavior and therefore demands as careful attention to detail as does any other laboratory research. Among the special precautions are safeguards against stimulus error, anchoring effects, and distorting processes.

REFERENCES

Guilford, J. P. *Psychometric methods.* (2nd ed.) New York: McGraw-Hill, 1954.

Nowlis, V., & Nowlis, Helen H. The description and analysis of mood. In Techniques for the study of behavioral effects of drugs. *Ann. N. Y. Acad. Sci.,* 1956, 65, 345–355.

Thurstone, L. L. A law of comparative judgment. *Psychol. Rev.,* 1927, 18, 289–293.

ADDITIONAL READINGS

Edwards, A. L. *Techniques of attitude scale construction.* New York: Appleton-Century-Crofts, 1957.

Thurstone, L. L. *The measurement of values.* Chicago: Univer. Chicago Press, 1959.

Torgerson, W. S. *Theory and methods of scaling.* New York: Wiley, 1958.

West, Evelyn M., & Bendig, A. W. Esthetic fatigue in ranking. *Amer. J. Psychol.,* 1956, 69, 285–287.

CHAPTER 7

Writing
Research
Reports

A scientific research project may be considered to be complete only when it has been reported. By using scientific journals or widely circulated technical reports to describe his investigations, each scientist contributes to the success of further research efforts undertaken by others. Contributions to this advancement of the scientific enterprise are made by scientists in government and university laboratories, and in industry. Reports of industrial research may sometimes be given limited circulation when related to a company's operations. Contrasting with this private circulation of laboratory findings is the public dissemination of knowledge that characterizes most modern science as a cooperative effort.

As a prominent aspect of human culture, written communication has many purposes and takes on many forms. Scientific writing, having its own purposes to fulfill, has evolved forms that contrast, for example, with the style of a lyric poem or a political speech. It is our purpose to examine the conventional ways of reporting research. Conventions that are followed are often appropriate for student reports as well as for articles prepared for journal publication.

COMMUNICATION IN SCIENCE

The observations that a scientist makes are essentially a part of his private experience. They become a part of scientific knowledge only as they are communicated to other scientists. Successful description of what the observations were and the conditions under which they were made puts research findings in their place in theory. A well-written research report also provides a basis for judging the reliability of the findings and for conducting further experiments to verify them.

Types of Scientific Communication

Although we are concentrating on the research report because it is the form of scientific writing which is needed to bring laboratory work to completion, we need to be aware of other types of writing which are important adjuncts to laboratory investigations. We find that *review articles* offer great economy in surveying the past work that has been done in a particular problem area. *Theoretical papers* stimulate research by suggesting hypotheses to be tested in attempting to test the theory. *Research reports* of individual studies describe procedures and findings which modify theory and provide guidance for the planning of further work.

REVIEW ARTICLES. The cooperative nature of science is illustrated in review articles where authors bring together a summary of the work that has been done on some topic. Such articles may take the form of bibliographies or lists of references, often organized according to some categorization of the subject matter. Some review articles offer comments on previous work that are sometimes evaluative or critical. A review should be regarded only as a starting point for a search of the literature. We should go back to the most relevant of the original studies wherever possible since these reports contain details which are omitted in the review.

THEORETICAL PAPERS. Expositions of theory are a form of scientific writing that is less circumscribed by convention than the review article or the research report. Theoretical papers may differ along a number of dimensions including the breadth or inclusiveness of the theoretical formulation and the degree of formality with which the presentation is made. Rather than dealing with the determinants of behavior in general, most theories in psychology treat special aspects of behavior. Some theoretical papers are characterized by evaluations of past research, by expositions of the logic used in constructing the theory, and by statements of hypotheses for testing in suggested research. Other articles may be much narrower in scope, dealing with a single hypothesis or treating one or two constructs.

RESEARCH REPORTS. Several different matters are treated in a single research report. One or more reasons are usually cited for undertaking the study. The findings may be interpreted, with implications drawn for the modification of theory or for the conducting of further investigations. The core of an experimental report, however, consists of information about how the research was carried out and what the results were. Details of procedure and the presentation of the data that were obtained are facts with which the reader of the report must reckon no matter what the author's interpretation of the study. It is the responsibility of the report writer to give these facts as clearly and completely as possible.

Purposes of the Reader

Our discussion of the writing of research reports will be aided if we first consider the aims of a reader of such a report. A description of an investigation that has been conducted may serve a number of purposes for different readers. By considering different aims that a reader may have in looking at a report, we may gain some insight into the criteria a report must meet to be judged satisfactory.

REPEAT THE STUDY. One reason for getting the facts about a research effort is to guide a repetition of the investigation. The repetition of a study may be undertaken as an instructive exercise, perhaps to become acquainted with a particular research method. Another reason for repeating a study may be to resolve any doubts that one might have about the outcome of the original investigation. Successful repetition adds confirmatory strength to the tested hypothesis.

DEVISE NEW RESEARCH. More common than the repetition of a study is the planning and conducting of new research that may be related to work that has been reported. Reports of earlier experiments can be helpful in numerous ways. They may suggest new hypotheses to be tested. They may report findings which require extension by means of using additional values of the independent variable or by utilizing new variables together with those from the earlier work. Research reports may also describe experimental techniques which are applicable to other investigations of other problems, possibly quite different from those explored in the original research. A reported experiment that supports a particular theory may stimulate additional work that will relate the empirical results to the theory more completely. In contrast to this, a study that is supportive of one theoretical position may be the instigation for an experiment that offers countering strength to a rival theory.

MAKE PRACTICAL APPLICATIONS. The reader of a research report may not have any scientific utilization in view. He may wish to incorporate the experimental findings in some practical application. For example, an industrial psychologist might wish to employ findings on the performance of physical work as he formulates recommendations for machine design. Like the person devising further research, he must be concerned not only with the data reported but also with the methods by which they were obtained. To ignore the procedural details of the experiment would be to risk misapplication of the results.

The Key Aim: to Inform

In the research report the writer's chief responsibility is to inform the reader completely and accurately about the conducting of the investigation and its outcome. The reader of a review or a theoretical article may have recourse to other papers to clarify his understanding of matters that are discussed, but a report of research often is the sole source of information about procedures that were followed or results that were obtained. If these are not presented clearly, much of the value of doing the study may be lost. The prime importance of giving the reader precise and complete information is a reflection of the aims of the reader in seeking out the research report. Whether he wants to repeat or extend the research, to use it in theory construction or practical application, he must be told without ambiguity or omission how the experiment was carried out and what observations or measurements were made.

Scientific reports are read by busy people. This suggests a need for brevity in writing. Brief research reports are desirable also on the basis of publication costs which are borne by the writers and readers of scientific articles. A number of conventions in report-writing have been adopted in the interests of saving time and money. Standard abbreviations, for example, conserve space on the printed page without any sacrifice of meaning. Since informing the reader is its cardinal goal, the writing of research reports calls for the economy of brevity only insofar as clarity of communication can be maintained. With the constraints of brevity on the one hand and clarity on the other, the writing of good reports of experiments is almost as much a challenge to skill in composition as is literary writing.

Conventions in Report Writing

With its informative purpose so paramount and with economy of time and money so pressing, it is easy to understand why certain conventions in the writing of research reports have evolved. The evolution of style and content of experimental reports in psychology is evident in the published journals of recent decades. In the interests of keeping the articles brief, the trend has been toward omitting many details of experiments that were formerly cataloged completely. Fortunately, other means of shortening reports with no loss of communication have been developed. These include abbreviations and brief phrases that are descriptive of commonly employed procedures. Some of these practices have been adopted informally and some have been made the subject of rules or suggestions adopted by the editors of psychology journals.

GUIDES TO WRITING CONVENTIONS. A primary guide for the preparation of research reports in psychology is the *Publication Manual of the American Psychological Association: 1957 Revision*. This booklet contains much information about the publications and editorial policies of the association. It discusses the preparation of manuscripts in great detail, treating such topics as organization, headings, punctuation, abbreviations, tables, figures, and references.* In preparing his first manuscript for publication, the research psychologist may find it troublesome to have to adhere to so many rules. Once the conventional ways of writing a report are learned, the job is actually expedited by using the methods that have been agreed upon. The real benefit for scientific communication comes from the combination of brevity and clarity that is achieved.

Although you will probably not be writing manuscripts for journal publication, you will want some guidance in the preparation of reports of the experiments you perform as part of your work in experimental psychology. Rather than setting up some arbitrary rules we shall follow the conventions set forth in the *Publication Manual* as we discuss the sections of the research report and present a model for your consideration.

A MODEL RESEARCH REPORT

Your reports of experiments you perform are not likely to be as long as journal articles on research. Your introduction and your discussion of the results may be fairly brief. The design of a study which you carry out will probably be simpler than many that are reported in the journals, permitting a shorter description of the experimental method employed. To supplement your study of technical journals, then, you may wish to study carefully a model report such as might be prepared by a student in experimental psychology. The

---

* The rules for the listing and citing of references were changed in 1958 amendments of Section 4.7 and Paragraph 8.25. These amendments concerning references are incorporated in the discussion and illustrations which are given in this chapter.

following report of a reaction time study is only intended as a guide, of course. Your instructor may have particular rules for you to follow in preparing certain reports, just as the editors impose certain requirements on those who submit articles to the psychology journals.

SIMPLE REACTION TIME AS A FUNCTION OF VISUAL VS. AUDITORY MODALITY STIMULATED AND PREFERRED VS. NONPREFERRED HAND USED IN RESPONDING

JOHN X. DOE

Studies of reaction time were very prominent among the investigations conducted in the first laboratories of psychology. RT experiments provide a good example of the formulation which states that a response depends on both the nature of the stimulus and the structure or state of the responding organism. This will be illustrated in the present experiment.

According to Woodworth and Schlosberg (1954, p. 16) the finding that RT to a visual stimulus is longer than to an auditory stimulus goes back to early investigations by Hirsch. A study by Seashore and Seashore (1941) yielded no significant difference between the mean RTs for the right and left hand.

The modality stimulated and the effector employed were both varied in the present study. The problem was to determine if a significant difference exists between the mean RTs for (1) auditory and visual stimulation and (2) preferred and nonpreferred hands.

METHOD

Subjects. The Ss were 22 students enrolled in the experimental psychology class at Alaska State University.

Apparatus. The RT apparatus was of the conventional type with a telegraph key to be released by S as soon as possible after the presentation of the stimulus. The release of the key stopped a Standard Electric timer which had been started when the switch was operated to present the stimulus. The timer permitted the determination of RT to the nearest hundredth of a second. The visual stimulus was a green-jeweled pilot lamp with a neon bulb used to eliminate filament lag. The auditory stimulus was a doorbell-type buzzer. Both stimulus devices were mounted on a plywood panel which separated S from E. A silent mercury switch was used by E in presenting the stimuli to avoid an auditory cue when the light was presented.

Procedure. All Ss were given 10 practice trials with each of the stimuli to acquaint them with the operation of the apparatus. They were instructed to react as quickly as possible on every trial. With the preferred hand used in responding, every S was then given 30 trials with each of the stimuli. A particular stimulus was presented for a block of 5 consecutive trials. The blocks of 5 trials were counterbalanced for the two stimuli, half of the Ss getting their first trials with the light, half with the buzzer.

In the second part of the experiment, only the buzzer was used as a stimulus. The preferred and nonpreferred hands were used in responding in counterbalanced blocks of 5 trials, as had been used earlier for the two stimuli.

Every stimulus presentation was preceded by E's calling "ready." A foreperiod that varied from 1 to 3 sec intervened between this warning and the stimulus. On approximately 1 trial out of 10 no stimulus was given following the ready signal. If S responded on such a "catch test," the data for that entire block of 5 trials were discarded, to be replaced by data taken in an extra block of trials given later.

RESULTS

The means and SDs of RTs to the auditory and visual stimuli are presented in Table 1.

TABLE 1

Means and SDs of RTs to Auditory and Visual Stimuli.
(N = 22, each S given 30 trials with each stimulus)

	Auditory Stimulus	Visual Stimulus
Mean RT	158.3 msec	198.7 msec
SD	29.4	32.3

A test of significance of the difference between the means presented in Table 1 yielded a value of $t = 8.59$ which for 21 degrees of freedom is significant at beyond the 1 per cent level of confidence.

For reactions to the auditory stimulus the preferred and nonpreferred hands yielded the mean and SD values for RT that are given in Table 2.

Inspection of the mean and SD values of the RTs for preferred and non-preferred hands indicated that the means did not differ significantly.

Raw data and computations are given in Appendix A.

TABLE 2

Means and SDs of RTs to an Auditory Stimulus by the Preferred and
Nonpreferred Hands

(N = 22, each S given 30 trials in responding with each hand)

	Preferred Hand	Nonpreferred Hand
Mean RT	156.2 msec	157.1 msec
SD	29.1	29.8

DISCUSSION

It was concluded that auditory RT is significantly shorter than RT to visual stimuli, when both types of stimulus are presented at values well above threshold. This finding is in agreement with data given by Woodworth and Schlosberg (1954, pp. 16, 26). The values obtained in the present experiment were somewhat greater than those cited in the literature. Among factors which might have accounted for this are ages of Ss in the samples used in different experiments, lack of training for Ss in the present study, or distractions occurring in the laboratory while the experiment was in progress.

It was concluded that there is no significant difference between RTs to an auditory stimulus by the preferred and nonpreferred hands. The finding of no difference for the two hands agrees with the results obtained by Seashore and Seashore (1941). Again, the values were somewhat greater for the present study, possibly for one or more of the reasons cited above. The apparent equality of performance of the two hands in such a simple reaction would probably not extend to tasks requiring dexterity, in which the preferred hand might show superiority.

SUMMARY

Simple RTs of college students to visual and auditory stimuli were compared, with the preferred hand used in responding. The generally obtained finding of shorter RTs to an auditory stimulus was confirmed.

RT to an auditory stimulus was found not to differ significantly for the preferred and nonpreferred hands, again in agreement with previously obtained results.

REFERENCES

Seashore, R. H., & Seashore, S. H. Individual differences in simple auditory reaction times of hands, feet and jaws. J. exp. Psychol., 1941, 29, 346–349.

Woodworth, R. S., & Schlosberg, H. Experimental psychology. (Rev. ed.) New York: Holt, 1954.

APPENDIX A

1. Data for individual trials of S No. 13, with computation of mean RT for each experimental condition. Data in 1/100 sec.

	Part I			Part II	
	Auditory RTs	Visual RTs		Preferred Hand	Nonpreferred Hand
	14	19		15	15
	15	19		15	14
	.	.		.	.
	.	.		.	.
	.	.		.	.
	14	18		14	13
Σ:	459	564		447	438
M:	15.3	18.8		14.9	14.6

2. Individual S means for each condition, with computation of group means for each condition. Data in milliseconds.

	Part I		Part II	
S	Auditory RTs	Visual RTs	Preferred Hand	Nonpreferred Hand
1	143	178	142	146
2	161	188	158	154
.	.	.	.	.
.	.	.	.	.
.	.	.	.	.
21	153	181	149	151
22	160	174	161	163
Σ:	3483	4371	3436	3456
M:	158.3	198.7	156.2	157.1
SD:	29.4	32.3	29.1	29.8

3. $\underline{t}$ test of significance of difference between group means for auditory and visual $\underline{RT}$:

$$t = \frac{D_M}{SE_{D_M}} \qquad \text{(Equivalent of Formula 4.3, p. 85)}$$

$$D_M = M_V - M_A = 198.7 - 158.3 = 40.4$$

$$SE_{D_M} = \frac{1}{N}\sqrt{\frac{N\Sigma D^2 - (\Sigma D)^2}{N-1}} \qquad \text{(Formula 4.7, p. 90)}$$

$\Sigma D = 888$	$(\Sigma D)^2 = 788{,}544$
$\Sigma D^2 = 46{,}128$	$N = 22$

$$
\begin{aligned}
N\Sigma D^2 &= 1{,}014{,}816 \\
-(\Sigma D)^2 &= -788{,}544 \\
\hline
&226{,}272
\end{aligned}
$$

$$\sqrt{\frac{226{,}272}{21}} = \sqrt{10{,}774.85} = 103.8$$

$$SE_{D_M} = 103.8 \div 22 = 4.7$$

$$t = \frac{40.4}{4.7} = 8.59 \qquad \text{Significant for } df = 21$$

SECTIONS OF THE RESEARCH REPORT

Our model report on the RT experiment has already illustrated the various sections of a research report and their organization. The format that we have suggested should be appropriate to any studies you may conduct and it conforms to the rules that govern publication in psychology journals. Another good way to get some help in preparing research reports is to browse through the psychology journals in which reports of investigations are given. Not all these journals adhere to the rules cited in the manual to which we have referred, because not all are published by the American Psychological Association. You will find, however, that the presentations of experimental studies are fairly similar in their broad outlines. Beyond acquainting you with some of the standard rules for the structure and content of reports, a survey of journal articles will familiarize you with some of the ways in which a writing style is slanted to achieve clarity of communication. You will see that a great deal of information about an experiment can be packed into an article of five or ten pages. We now need to consider a research report section by section, sometimes commenting on the model report and sometimes making points that are not covered in the model.

Title

A comparison of the titles of psychological experiments and of popular novels will quickly convince you that there are vast differences, and for good reason. The titles of research reports might seem to be unnecessarily long and detailed, but the purpose underlying this is an important one for communication in science. When we search the literature for background material before we begin an experimental study we find that well-written titles in the cited references are a great aid to deciding which articles may be pertinent to our study and which probably are not.

Current practice is to give titles to reports of research with both the dependent variable and the independent variables indicated. With the major outline of the study revealed in its title, anyone searching the literature may establish his own criteria for looking up the report itself. If he is writing a critical review of studies in a certain problem area, he will go to more of the actual reports than if he is merely looking for a passing acquaintance with how research in that area is conducted. You may find it interesting to see how much you can guess about the way an experiment was carried out by merely reading its title.

To indicate both the phenomenon under investigation and the factors or conditions that were varied, many titles of research reports take one of two forms:

$$Y \text{ as a function of } X$$
$$\text{The effect of } X \text{ upon } Y$$

In both cases Y refers to the dependent variable or the behavior being studied and X refers to the independent variable(s) manipulated. Some authors introduce verbal variations within these formats and a few writers avoid such a standardized way of creating a title. Despite the stereotypy they introduce into tables of contents in research journals, these forms are good guides to follow. If key words are fitted into them carefully, they insure a title that will convey as much information to a reader as may be expected.

Introduction

The word "Introduction" did not appear as a heading in the model report, but the section between the title and the METHOD section was precisely that. A heading is customarily omitted from this introductory part for reasons of appearance, considering that the title and author's name are already placed above the body of the report. The introductory section usually indicates the problem toward which the experiment was directed, so sometimes these paragraphs are considered as the "problem" part of the research article. Many introductions present background material first and then lead up to a statement of the problem or the hypothesis to be tested.

An introduction should answer the question "Why was this experiment carried out?" "To fulfill requirements and help me pass the course" is the sophomoric answer that repeatedly delights the hearts of instructors. There are several more tolerable answers to the question, too. One or more of these should be cited in the opening paragraphs of a research report. Very often an experiment is conducted to extend previous work. In such a case the prior studies are mentioned and cited as references and the relation of the current investigation to the past work is explained. Studies are often undertaken to test hypotheses that are derived from theory. The introductory portion of the report indicates the theoretical background and the derivation of the hypothesis, paving the way for the reader to understand how the study actually tests the hypothesis and, indirectly, the theory. Another reason for doing research is to obtain answers that may be applied in the solution of a practical problem. Here an appropriate introduction may be to outline this problem and then to indicate what information must be sought experimentally that may help in solving it.

CITATION OF REFERENCES. You have probably seen references cited in technical books by footnotes. In a number of psychology journals a different convention is followed, as illustrated in the model report. The two references in that report were presented in a list alphabetized by authors' names. The dates of publication were used parenthetically in the citations in the introductory section of the model report together with the authors' names. Where citations are made of sources of some length, like the book by Woodworth and Schlosberg, it is customary to add page numbers to the parenthetical citation to help the reader find the part cited. Where the citation is of a major finding of an experiment, the research report is usually mentioned without any page number, as in the citing of the paper by Seashore and Sea-shore in the model report. Citation data are usually placed right after the authors' names. In many instances authors' names and publication dates are given parenthetically instead of in the text. This is done particularly when several references are cited together or when the writers of a report make reference to their own previous work. Example: "Recent experiments (Jones. 1958, Jones & Smith, 1959) have shown . . ."

If material is quoted from any source, the parenthetical citation should include the author, year of publication, and the page number where the portion quoted may be found. The parentheses enclosing the citation data are placed right after the closing quotation mark.

Method

This section of a research report is sometimes headed *Procedure* although this term appears more commonly as a subheading, as in the model report. Other subsections that appear quite regularly are those that deal with the subjects used in a study and with the ap-paratus employed. The apparatus subsection is often expanded to cover apparatus and materials, where the selection of particular stimu-lus items, for example, forms an important part of the experimental method in the study. Like other major section headings of a research report, METHOD should be capitalized and centered on the page.

Under the procedure subsection the writer of a research report must indicate the design of the experiment and must describe the treatment given to the subjects under the various conditions. In simpler experiments the design may be presented implicitly as the administering of the different conditions to the subjects is described. In more complex research, the design of the experiment may some-times be outlined in a subsection of its own plus the clarifying aid of a table which shows the different conditions with perhaps the sequence of their administration to different groups of subjects. In describing the running of subjects it is well to indicate key aspects of instructions that were given to them. Where instructions might play an important role it is customary to quote from them in the *Procedure* subsection of the report. In the case of student reports it is often desirable to have a verbatim copy of the instructions as one appendix.

It is not easy to state categorically how detailed a description of the method of a study is needed. An experimenter should certainly describe every aspect of the investigation which is relevant to the hypothesis being tested or to the results that were obtained. If space permits, he may go further and give factual details that were only indirectly involved in the experimental test. Ideally, a research report should be complete enough to permit the study to be repeated in all its essential characteristics. In the technical journals, an economy is effected in describing experimental method if reference can be made to an earlier published description of the techniques used. Changes in procedure may be briefly described when these are variations in a standard method that has been described before. In student reports it is sometimes permissible to refer to a laboratory work sheet to indicate the procedures employed. If this is done, it is especially important to note in the METHOD section any departures from the techniques described in the guide to the laboratory work.

Results

Our major tasks in writing the RESULTS section of an experimental report are (1) to present descriptive statistics on the outcome of the study and (2) to indicate the statistical tests that were applied in evaluating the data. The model report indicates how this may be done sequentially, the presentation of means and SDs from each part of the study being followed by description of the analysis to which the data were subjected.

The reader of a report can save time if the results are summarized in concise tables and figures. In order to tie them together in proper sequence they should never be presented without referring to them in the text of the report. This requirement is especially pertinent where complex experiments involve a number of measures of behavior which must be analyzed.

TABLES. Organization and labeling of tables must be properly done if they are really going to aid communication. A complete title is demanded because a reader may turn directly to a table without reading the textual material dealing with experimental results. The title should identify the statistics that are being presented, the response measures from which they were derived, and the conditions under which these measurements were taken. You can see how this has been done in the titles of tables in the model report. Such information is included even though some of it is repeated in the headings of the rows and columns. Our sample titles include additional information concerning the data that have been collected and reduced to the statistics that are given. In many cases the N for different groups or conditions might be provided in the body of the table. We have identified the unit of measurement, milliseconds, in the body of the tables; this is sometimes done as an adjunct to the title. Sometimes data on the statistical tests of significance are also presented in tabular form, either together with descriptive statistics or separately. It will pay you to study numerous examples of tables in experimental journals to see how a well-planned table summarizes the results of an investigation. Tables are numbered consecutively through a research report.

FIGURES. The term *figure* is applied to a variety of graphic presentations which includes photographs and diagrams of apparatus, and graphs showing the results of a study. Figures are numbered through the report in a separate series of arabic numerals, so that the text of the report might state, for example, that "Figure 1 shows a schematic diagram of the apparatus . . ." and "Figure 2 presents the performance curves for the two groups . . ." We do not refer to "Diagram No. 1" or to "the first graph."

Figures that portray the results of an experiment may be of a number of different types: histograms or bar graphs, line graphs connecting plotted points, or smooth curves fitted by inspection or by mathematical methods to the plotted data. The type of graph to be employed should be determined by the information that is to be portrayed. For example, a bar graph seems most appropriate for representing separate statistics derived from discrete experimental conditions. This type of figure might be drawn, then, to indicate the values of the means in Table 1 of the model report since those values were derived from distinctly different stimulus conditions in the *RT* study. The same type of figure would be used for showing the means of Table 2 since they stemmed from the use of different effectors in making the response. If, however, we wished to picture a practice effect in the *RT* data—assuming that one had been observed to occur—we might use a line graph with straight line segments connecting the mean *RT* values for successive blocks of trials under a particular condition. The connecting of the segments would serve to portray the continuity of the process that might be assumed to underlie the gradual decrease in *RT* values. Instead of connecting all the points we might choose a smooth curve which would pass among them, representing the abstract process underlying the empirical measurements that were taken.

A graph showing experimental results should be planned and executed with great care. The scale for the dependent variable generally ranges upward along the ordinate whereas the values of the independent variable, or the designations for the different conditions, are placed along the abscissa. The scale markings should be located along each coordinate so as to take advantage of the available space for the figure. To avoid compressing the performance measures unduly, the values plotted on the ordinate are often just those which will include the set of obtained values. The ordinate axis is then "broken" to indicate that the scale does not range upward from zero. The points and lines plotted in the graph are coded in different ways, with this coding indexed by a key that is located within the graph.

Below every figure is a figure number and a legend that aids in understanding the graphic portrayal and gives pertinent facts. These legends vary in length. Where several sentences are given, the first is usually a title for the graph with the others adding information about conditions under which the portrayed data were gathered. The values of N, the number of subjects in different groups or conditions, are sometimes included in the legend, sometimes in the key of a figure. Amplify your understanding of graphic presentations by studying carefully the figures in this textbook and in other sources of research reports.

Discussion

This section of the report is essentially a consideration of the results obtained in the experiment as they bear upon the problem which was stated in introducing the report. This discussion of the outcome of the study must be guided by the statistical analyses of the data that were reported in the RESULTS section. The report writer states what conclusions have been reached as a result of the experiment, or indicates whether the hypothesis being tested is considered tenable or is rejected. Agreement or disagreement with previous findings is often mentioned. If the study was formulated to test some theoretical question, the implications of the results for the theory are discussed.

If unexpected results have been obtained, it is sometimes permissible in this part of the report to refer to the way in which the experiment was conducted and to suggest possible reasons for the outcome. This is a game that ought to be played with restraint. It should never be assumed that verbal explanations of an unwanted result automatically reverse the finding. Nor is fluency in listing the flaws in an experiment any substitute for carefully designing and executing the study in the first place. The value in discussing a result that was not anticipated lies in the suggestions it may generate for new ways of experimenting further with the problem.

Summary

The SUMMARY section in research reports is another aid to scientific communication. It provides a saving of time for the reader who wishes quickly to acquaint himself with the investigation. For one who has read the entire article, the summary provides a useful review of the salient facts. Although kept very brief, this section should reflect something from each preceding part of the report, at least by implication. The reason for undertaking the research should be indicated, the chief aspects of method should be mentioned, and the major results should be stated together with some notion of the discussion that was given to them.

References

When a report is being prepared, the entire list of references should be alphabetized by authors' names. The forms to be used in presenting two common types of reference, book and journal article, are illustrated in the model report. You should study these very carefully so that you will be able to list references with complete accuracy of form. Pay close attention to what is included in each reference, the sequence of items, the capitalization, and the punctuation. Examine the references given in this book to obtain further information on matters like the abbreviation and capitalization of journal titles. The number which follows the year of publication is the volume number of the journal. It is important to include this because some journals are issued in more than one volume per year. You may wish to refer to a chapter that appears in an edited book. The form for such a reference is as follows: Hovland, C. I. Human learning and retention. In S. S. Stevens (Ed.), Handbook of experimental psychology. New York: Wiley, 1951. Pp. 613–689. The book and journal titles which you are asked to underline would appear in italics in print; thus any italicized parts of references that you see in books or journals should be underlined when you prepare a report or a manuscript. In listing a chapter which appears in an edited book the inclusive page numbers are given; this is the only time that page numbers from a *book* should appear in a listing of references. You may recall from the model report that a specific page in a book may be cited parenthetically in the text of a report. Inclusive page numbers of *journal articles* are always given in a list of references, and a particular page may occasionally need to be cited in a report. A page citation must definitely accompany quoted material.

Appendices

An appendix is never found in the usual journal report of an experiment, although one or more may be included with a long monograph. However, in student reports there is often a definite need for appendices. If a laboratory work sheet guided you in carrying out an experiment, it may be advisable to use it as Appendix A to the report you write. Your instructor may permit you to refer to this Appendix A in writing the METHOD section of your report. Even if this is not the case, the reader of reports may be helped if work sheets are appended to them. A verbatim copy of the *Instructions to Subjects* is also a useful appendix. Another appendix in your report, like Appendix A in our model report, might present the raw data of the experiment and the calculations you performed in treating the results. Part of the data, as in our example, might have been collected on an individual subject whom you have run. It is best if you submit the actual work sheet on which you took down the response measures in the laboratory. This will tend to show how carefully you have carried out the research and will avoid errors that might occur in transcribing data.

Important General Considerations

We have considered the report of an experiment section by section, from the title to the appendices. There remain a few points about report-writing that apply to the report generally rather than to any particular part. These should provide guidance that will help you to write good reports on your early attempts rather than by learning through the painful correction of your errors. We repeat, too, that close examination of a publication like the *Journal of Experimental Psychology* will teach you techniques of report-writing that our space limitations would never permit us to treat. Do not become discouraged if you find that some research reports are difficult to understand. The more of them that you read, the more comprehension you will gain for their further study.

ORGANIZATION. A great degree of organization is imposed on a report when the different prescribed sections are used. You should be careful not to violate the intended structure by putting material into the wrong parts. You may find it a real challenge to your writing skill to say the right thing in the right place. It is all too easy to begin describing the experimental method while you are still writing the introduction. Sometimes it is actually difficult to avoid it. There may be great temptation, too, for you to begin discussing the results while you are still presenting them. And when you finally do get to the discussion section you may slip into repeating results unnecessarily. Discipline yourself to structure your writing with the conventional section headings as your blueprint.

Organization of another sort is desirable in reporting experiments of complicated design. Our model report is a simple example of this. You will recall that we were testing two hypotheses in that *RT* study, one dealing with the modality of stimulation and one with the hand used in responding. If you will review the report you will find that in the introduction, in the RESULTS, in describing the procedure, and in the DISCUSSION, we treated these two aspects of the research in the same sequence. We thus attained a regular structure within sections that contributed to the unity of the report.

REDUNDANCY. While organization is something to be desired in reports, redundancy, or repetition, is something that should be avoided in the interest of brevity. Study the *Procedure* subsection of the model report and note how various phrases are used to tell the story of the design of the experiment and the running of the subjects. Without too much repetition, this is accomplished in eleven sentences. If anything, this report may err in leaving out important details.

We did note a couple of places where redundancy in an experimental report is desirable. One is the titles of tables and the legends of figures where some indication of conditions under which the data were collected is given even though this information is contained in the body of the report. This is done as a convenience to a reader who wishes to peruse the results of the study quickly. Repetition is also needed, of course, in the summary. We should repeat major points very briefly, avoiding the tendency to write the report all over again in the summary. Anyone who wishes details can read the appropriate parts of the report.

STYLE. Even the style of writing research reports has been conventionalized to some degree. The demand for conciseness naturally rules out long, flowery phrasing. It is customary to write impersonally. Omitting personal pronouns leads to very common use of the passive voice. Instead of saying, "I presented the stimulus light," we say, "The stimulus light was presented." Again, you can learn about these conventions of style by reading some of the psychology journals.

The past tense is widely used in reporting studies since the experiments are completed at the time the report is read. Since the data have already been analyzed when the report is prepared, we refer to the outcome of the analysis in the past tense also. We do use the present tense when we state that "means and *SD*s of *RT*s . . . are presented in Table 1" because here we are making a statement about the report, which is present, and not about the experiment or its analysis, which are past. If the problem of which tense to employ ever causes you concern, referring to the model report should answer your questions.

AVOIDING ERRORS. Students writing their first reports of experiments are likely to make several sorts of errors. It is impossible to anticipate what difficulty you may encounter personally, but a general indication of some of the pitfalls might be of some assistance. Vague statements and factual errors sometimes creep into student reports. Omission of important details is a common error. Irrelevant discussion is occasionally introduced, as if in response to some nonexistent rule like: *Discuss, and discuss, but always discuss.* More serious from a scientific point of view is a tendency to overgeneralize from the results of a study. For example, the data from the model report might be overgeneralized to the point where a student would state as a conclusion that "Responses to auditory stimuli are 40.4 msec faster than reactions to visual stimuli." This conclusion is a totally unjustified generality even though the value cited is based on the data of the experiment. Still more alarming to read is discussion by some students of unexpected findings. Often they are explained away, so that the writer may go on to reach the conclusions which were his firm belief even before he conducted the experiment. In writing your first reports you will avoid making mistakes of some sort only if you edit your first draft very carefully. Report-writing, of any kind, is work. It becomes relatively effortless only after considerable practice.

SURVEYING THE PSYCHOLOGICAL LITERATURE

Most research grows out of past investigations. In planning an experiment a research worker needs to know what previous work has been done on the same problem. This knowledge can serve him in a number of ways, like suggesting experimental techniques, giving performance data, and providing hypotheses to test. If you should undertake an original experiment on some problem, you will want to look up anything you can find that pertains to the investigation you propose to conduct. Where would you look? We shall list some of the types of sources to which you might turn for information.

Books

The experimental journal literature on any major topic in psychology is voluminous. It would fill volumes, and it does. Fortunately much of this literature has been brought together, in summary form, in textbooks, handbooks, and books that deal with certain broad topics.   Many of these special books are listed among the references and readings given at the end of chapters in this textbook.   You are referred to these lists for books, for example, on color vision or human learning.   Besides these topical books, there are a few books that give a compendious coverage to broad segments of the research literature in psychology.   Listed at the end of this chapter, they are the textbooks by Woodworth (1938), Osgood (1953), and Woodworth and Schlosberg (1954) and the *Handbook of Experimental Psychology* edited by Stevens (1951).

Reviews and Bibliographies

Review articles and annotated bibliographies, commonly found in the *Psychological Bulletin,* bring together numerous references on a topic, usually including research reports from a period of years. Enough information is usually given about each one to help you decide which of the cited articles you need to look up to obtain more information.   The review of simple RT studies by Teichner, which is cited in Chapter 14, is an example of this type of bibliographic aid. We shall describe later how to locate these reviews by using *Psychological Abstracts.*

Another sort of research review is found in the *Annual Review of Psychology.*   With a new volume issued annually, this periodical is cited in reference lists like a journal, that is, by year and volume number.   Instead of coming out in separate issues, however, it is published in a single bound volume for each year.   Each volume contains almost twenty chapters, each dealing with some broad topic in psychology.   For each of these topics, the chapter author cites and comments upon the publications that have come out in the previous year, thus providing a useful key to recent research.

Psychological Abstracts

To locate all that may be found upon a fairly narrow research topic, the periodical *Psychological Abstracts* is a very likely source of help.   In this journal are printed brief abstracts of articles gleaned from recent issues of approximately 500 periodicals in psychology and related fields, including numerous foreign language works published in all parts of the world.   Besides locating individual reports of recent experiments you may find the *Abstracts* helpful in finding review articles and bibliographies on particular topics.   The *Abstracts* for 1956, Volume 30, contained, for example, about 8500 entries of which about 360 were bibliographies or reviews covering special problem areas.

It is not necessary to wade through several hundred entries in each volume of *Psychological Abstracts* to try to locate a few references that may be relevant to your needs. A subject index is most thoughtfully provided in the last issue of each annual volume. Under numerous headings, subheadings, and sub-subheadings you should be able to locate the topic in which you are interested. One or more index numbers will be given there. These are the numbers of the abstracts which you should look up in that particular annual volume of *Abstracts*. The consecutive numbering of abstracts as they are printed begins all over again each year. When you have read the abstracts which you have located you may then be able to decide whether to seek out the original articles to read.

Locating a good review article is a good way to cover several years of research with an economy of effort. Reviews and bibliographies on all topics are brought together in the subject index of *Psychological Abstracts* under the heading "Bibliographies" with subheadings alphabetized according to the subject matter covered in the articles. Relying on review articles always entails the risk that the reviewer may have omitted some references that would be especially useful to you. You should estimate this risk as it relates to your scholarly needs. If it seems advisable, you may lessen the risk by extensive cross-checking of lists of references and by searching the *Abstracts* diligently yourself.

An author index also appears annually in *Psychological Abstracts*. If you know that a scholar has been particularly active in an area of research that interests you, it might prove helpful to look up his name in each volume and review the abstracts of his published reports. This may help to locate articles relevant to your needs which might have been overlooked if you relied solely on finding their listing in the subject index.

SUMMARY

Reporting an experiment and its outcome is the final step that completes a particular piece of research. Scientific advance thrives on good communication among scientists. Psychological studies, like research in other disciplines, are reported in fairly standardized ways that represent the current stage in the evolution of report-writing. Good reports provide the information needed to generate new research and to modify existing theory.

The aims of psychological science are fostered by several types of communication: reviews, theoretical articles, and reports of investigations. All these represent starting points for further study. A reader of an experimental report, for example, may wish to extend the test of the hypothesis to a wider set of values of the independent variable. Making practical application of findings may be another purpose of a reader.

The key aim of a scientific communication is to inform. Clarity and completeness of writing are therefore very much desired in research reports. A reader must be told exactly what was done in an experiment and precisely what was found. While meeting these goals, the report writer must strive for brevity to avoid consuming his reader's time unduly. Clarity and brevity may be sought through consistently following the conventional rules that have been developed for reporting psychological investigations. The same rules established for reporting in psychology journals are excellent guides for the writing of student reports. A model research report illustrates how they are applied.

Every section of the experimental report, from the title through the references, should give full and accurate information to the reader. He should be told exactly how the experiment was conducted and what results were obtained. The outcome of statistical analysis of the data should also be stated. Discussion should be guided by previous work cited in introducing the study and by the findings as analyzed statistically. Evaluation of a research effort should never wander far from the facts. In student reports, appendices provide a means of conveying additional details about the performing of the experiment.

Your efforts in writing reports will be rewarded if you strive for good organization and adopt a style that resembles the writing in psychology journals which report on experiments. You should avoid redundancy in your writing except where it is purposely introduced, as in titles of tables and legends of figures, to aid the reader to grasp the essentials of the research quickly.

You have a vast literature at your disposal as you plan and report experiments in psychology. Textbooks and handbooks organize a great amount of information for you on particular problem areas. Review articles and bibliographies introduce you to reports from which you may select a few for further study. The *Annual Review of Psychology* helps to identify trends in research on a number of broad topics. The original research literature is open to you if you learn how to use *Psychological Abstracts* to track down the information you need. Both a topical index and an author index are provided in each annual volume of the *Abstracts* to aid you in locating the particular abstracts which may interest you. You may then go on to read the most promising of the references in their original sources.

REFERENCES

American Psychological Association, Council of Editors. *Publication Manual of the American Psychological Association: 1957 Revision.* Washington: The American Psychological Association, 1957.

Osgood, C. E. *Method and theory in experimental psychology.* New York: Oxford Univer. Press, 1953.

Stevens, S. S. (Ed.) *Handbook of experimental psychology.* New York: Wiley, 1951.

Woodworth, R. S. *Experimental psychology.* New York: Holt, 1938.

Woodworth, R. S. & Schlosberg, H. *Experimental psychology.* (Rev. ed.) New York: Holt, 1954.

ADDITIONAL READING

Nelson, J. R. *Writing the technical report.* (3rd ed.) New York: McGraw-Hill, 1952.

CHAPTER 8

Theory
and
Research

The task of the scientist is to observe and describe the regular relationships which occur among natural events, including relationships between environmental events and behavioral events in the case of psychological science. His observations, often made under controlled conditions, are the heart of his research. His descriptions of what he observes are incorporated into a constantly changing body of hypotheses and laws which we call theory. In this chapter we are going to deal with theory at some length and expand our consideration of research. We shall also see how these relate intimately to each other. Our point of departure is an examination of the place which research and theory occupy in the scientific enterprise.

The Nature of Science

The so-called natural laws which are expressed in the events of nature do not write themselves down for us. The interrelated character of these events is known only through careful observations. Such observations then guide the formulation of descriptions of the relationships which the scientist has witnessed, often quite indirectly. These formulations often involve creations or constructs which the scientist distills out of his experiences. The laws of science are thus seen to be somewhat removed from the natural events which they purport to mirror.

The correspondence of the events of nature, the observations of the scientist, and the hypotheses and laws he formulates may be better understood if we represent these three elements of science in a simple graphic way. In Figure 8.1 we see three triangles, each representing a different part of the schema we are considering. The triangle on

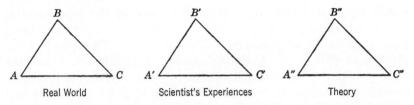

Fig. 8.1. Schema representing three aspects of the scientific enterprise.

the left, *ABC*, represents the interrelationships of three aspects of the real world. If we draw an example from the realm of behavior, *A* might represent the intensity of a stimulus presented to a subject, *B* might represent the fact that this subject had been given 150 mg of caffeine 20 min earlier, and *C* might represent the mean reaction time of this subject for a group of 40 simple repeated responses. We are aware, of course, that stimulus intensity and caffeine intake are only two of the many factors which would affect the response latency of an experimental subject. Our illustration will serve to indicate that the interrelationships of events going on in the natural world (of which a psychology laboratory is definitely a part) include both behavioral events and events which affect behavior. In other words, reality includes aspects corresponding to both the dependent and independent variables of our research formulations. The triangle, *ABC*, represents the dependence of reaction time, *C*, on the intensity of the stimulus, *A*, and the state of the human subject as represented in the administration of the caffeine, *B*. Despite our assumption that the regular relationship of Triangle *ABC* exists in the real world, it is known to us only through the observations of an investigator. We turn next, then, to a consideration of the second triangle.

In the center of Figure 8.1 Triangle *A'B'C'* represents the cognitions and perceptions of the experimenter who is conducting the research on caffeine and reaction time. In performing the experiment he sees to it that the stimulus intensity is set at the proper value for the particular condition being administered, that the caffeine is administered in the proper amount, and that the proper time elapses before testing. These experiences in conducting the research are represented as *A'* and *B'* in the Triangle *A'B'C'*. Numerous other procedural details are also subject to administration and surveillance by the behavior scientist. The manipulations of the independent variables are his way of putting his question to the natural world concerning the hypothesis he is testing. His readings of the timer or chronoscope and his averaging of the data to obtain a mean *RT* value are represented by C' in Figure 8.1. What happened in the experiment is known only through the experimenter's cognitions of what he did and his perceptions of what occurred in the situation. The record of the experiment will be his testimony about his experiences. We take this conservative view rather than claiming that the scientist is dealing directly and errorlessly with the natural world as he formulates and tests his hypotheses. Triangle $A'B'C'$ represents the mediational role played by observation in science.

At the right of Figure 8.1 we see Triangle $A''B''C''$ which represents a statement of the relationships which hold among three constructs or variables. Two of these, A'' and B'', are the independent variables of our study, defined with reference to the operations which the investigator performed in setting up the experimental conditions. C'' is the value obtained for the dependent variable, RT, according to prescribed techniques of measurement and statistical representation. Insofar as A'' and B'' have also been quantified, Triangle $A''B''C''$ represents a functional relationship describing quantitatively the dependence of RT on stimulus intensity and caffeine intake. This mathematical function might actually be based on the testing of numerous subjects, with additional statistical description of variability included to delineate individual differences.

In examining the entire schema representing the scientific enterprise in Figure 8.1, our purpose may be served best if we emphasize Triangles $A'B'C'$ and $A''B''C''$ and the relationships between them. Triangle $A'B'C'$ represents the experiences of the scientist as he conducts his investigations. It is research in action, in all of its aspects. Triangle $A''B''C''$ is the conceptualized outcome of this research, a symbolic representation of interrelationships as experienced by the investigator. We might say, then, that $A''B''C''$ stems from $A'B'C'$, that it is the empirical result of experimentation, even a set of empirical laws. There is some validity to this view, but it does not completely account for the interrelationships of these two triangles. Triangle $A''B''C''$ may not only depend on $A'B'C'$, but it may conversely be a determinant of it. Triangle $A''B''C''$ represents hypotheses as well as laws. These hypotheses may be formulated symbolically, using various techniques of logic and inference, and may then be used as guides to the making of experimental observations, $A'B'C'$.

We see, then, that Triangle $A''B''C''$ has a dual relationship to Triangle $A'B'C'$ stemming from its dual nature. Triangle $A''B''C''$ represents both a body of laws and a set of hypotheses. The empirical laws stem from past research and the hypotheses guide future research. An interrelated set of laws and hypotheses pertaining to a particular realm of observation may be termed a *theory*. In other words, the place occupied by Triangle $A''B''C''$ in our schema of science is the place reserved for theory, a set of symbolic abstractions from experience. In considering both hypotheses and empirical laws to be a part of theory we recognize that these are essentially one sort of relationship, differing in the degree to which they have been supported by observations.

THEORY

Having noted the place occupied by theory in science—it is the symbolic abstraction of scientists' experiences of natural phenomena—we may proceed with a closer examination of this structure. Many things considered later in this chapter should help to delineate the nature of theory. Initial orientation may stem from an attempt at verbal definition, offered in an effort to insure a proper framework for the remainder of our discussion. One way of defining theory is as follows:

> *Theory is an ever-changing structure of interrelationships— hypotheses and laws—among abstract concepts which are founded on observations.*

Among the elements included in this definition are indications that theory is (1) dynamically complex, (2) heterogeneous in composition, (3) symbolic, and (4) related to the empirical aspect of science. These different facets of theory will all receive attention in our continuing discussion.

It is commonplace to use phrases like "Hull's theory" or "according to the theory" in referring to particular sets of hypotheses. Our use of the word theory has a broader connotation, indicating *all* of the laws and hypotheses pertaining to a realm of investigation. Specific formulations offered by different theorists are all encompassed by our usage. As we shall employ it the term will also cover stated relationships observed by even those research workers who profess no interest—even protest their disinterest—in theorizing. With such inclusiveness, we might even ignore the boundaries of different scientific disciplines and let a unified conception of theory reflect the empirical interrelated aspect of modern science. Our interests in a particular part of theory would then be dictated by practical criteria like the problem area of our research.

Adopting a broad definition of theory means that we are dealing with an entity of numerous facets or dimensions. In subsequent discussion we shall try to point to some of these. We are dealing also with a dynamic entity. Theory changes every time an hypothesis is formulated, and every time an experimental outcome leads to the acceptance or rejection of a postulated relationship. Theory is unfinished business. It demands extension into areas not already covered and revision in places previously explored.

The Construction of Theory

What is the form taken by this complicated thing we are calling theory, which changes a little bit every time an experiment is performed? Despite its essential modifiability we shall find that theory is constructed in a fashion which will permit us to discuss it systematically and even to give it a graphic representation in schematic form.

OPERATIONAL DEFINITION. The terms which a scientist uses in describing his work are given essential meaning by the operations involved in the research he conducts. Such operational definition takes precedence over any verbal definitions in our understanding of the nature of theory. Suppose two investigators measure reaction time in identical procedures, obtaining with accuracy the interval from the onset of stimulus presentation to the initial phase of a simple motor response. The complete description of the measurement process is the valid representation of RT in scientific theory, regardless of any verbal definitions offered. One research worker might write "RT is the latent period of behavior occupied with the encoding and decoding of informational cues." The other might state that "RT is the sum total of chemical, neural, and muscular process times which are required before voluntary action can occur." Neither of these verbal statements affects the place that RT occupies in theory. That place is determined by the experimental operations by which RT was determined. It is the full description of such operations that permits anyone to test any hypotheses involving RT.

Suppose our two experimenters had used somewhat different techniques as each attempted to measure RT, a more likely occurrence in today's behavioral science. In this instance, the differing procedures followed would place RT at two different points in the structure of behavior theory. We might find it necessary to identify different "brands" of RT with numerical subscripts, RT_1 and RT_2, as one technique for keeping them separate.

LEVELS OF ABSTRACTION. In an experiment as it is being conducted RT might seem to be "a reading on the face of a chronoscope," but as a part of theory *RT* is an abstraction defined by *all* that was done in translating behavior into a numerical value. Its complete operational definition would include reference to the calibration of the chronoscope and its placement in the electrical circuit of the *RT* apparatus, the instructions given to motivate the subject, the warning signal, the stimulus energy, and the characteristics of the motor response required. *RT* is seen to be an abstract concept, defined in terms of other abstract concepts.

Abstractions may vary in how directly they are related to actual observations made by the scientist. A definition of the acidity of a chemical solution might refer to its taste. Although crude, this definition would be quite directly related to the scientist's observation, in this case his tasting of the solution. Some refinement in operational definition might be gained by referring to a test for acidity using litmus paper, which changes from blue to red when dipped into acid. The basic sensory experience defining acidity is now visual. The definition is less direct since it involves the proposition that the litmus paper does undergo such a change in hue when brought into contact with acid. For many purposes a more refined definition of acidity would be desired, perhaps one yielding a quantitative value. Such refinement would be gained by placing more degrees of abstraction, involving more chemical laws, between the direct sensory observations of the investigator and the definition of the solution as acid.

In psychology, as in chemistry and other branches of science, operational definitions which link any concept to the experience of the scientist may vary in directness or complexity. Strength of a subject's grip, which might need to be measured, that is, defined, for a study of motor performance, could be ascertained by a simple test with a hand dynamometer. The observation defining strength of grip would be the investigator's reading of the kilogram scale under a few specified conditions. Contrastingly, if an experiment required that the IQ of subjects be known, it would be necessary to administer some standardized intelligence test. The IQ determined for each subject would thus be very abstractly defined, depending not only on the numerous steps in giving the test but on the earlier steps which had been taken in standardizing the test so that scores would be meaningful with respect to some particular population. The observations of those who devised the test are thus pooled with the experiences of the test administrator in providing the measurement of intelligence, an abstract concept indeed.

Our notions about levels of abstraction of various operational definitions may be enhanced if we formalize them somewhat. We may think of four different levels of abstraction: (1) fundamental observational level, (2) basic construct level, (3) abstract construct level, and (4) theoretical construct level, listing them in ascending order of abstraction. Each higher level is built upon those below it. The fundamental observational level refers to the sensory experiences of the scientist as he sets up experimental conditions and notes the occurrence of events. In a study of RT, for example, the visual pattern of the chronoscope hand on the clock face is the sensory referent of the operational definition of the construct, RT. At the basic construct level we have such conventional dimensions as space, time, and numerosity. In the RT experiment we are taking as an example, the measurement of elapsed time, a basic construct, is built upon the fundamental observation of the chronoscope. In turn, this measurement provides the basis for defining RT when the conditions surrounding the temporal measurement are stated. RT may be considered to be operationally defined at the abstract concept level.

An example of a construct at the theoretical level, even more abstract, may be taken from the history of RT research. Early investigators noted that discriminative RT to two or more stimuli was greater than simple RT to a single stimulus. They ascribed this difference to the requirement in discriminative RT measurement that the subject make his response only to one stimulus and not to any other. They felt that the observed time difference from simple RT was occupied in judging the stimuli. For such a process they defined the theoretical construct "discrimination time" as the difference between discriminative RT and simple RT. Although this subtractive approach to the duration of mental processes was later found to be unsatisfactory, discrimination time can serve our purposes as an example of defining theoretical constructs in terms of abstract constructs. We saw that the abstract construct RT was defined in terms of basic constructs and therefore indirectly in terms of fundamental observations. Valid operational definitions, however great their degree of abstraction, always permit us in principle to trace down to the observations required of the scientist. Any construct in a theory has such a subjectively founded definition. By clearly specifying the subjective observations which are required, the scientist provides a way by which the subjective experiences of other observers can corroborate his own findings. It is this intersubjective verification which is the essence of so-called scientific objectivity.

In actual practice we do not find it necessary to state a full operational definition for every term used in a theoretical formulation or in a report of an experiment. We do not have to go all the way down to the fundamental observational level for most of the terms we employ. The reason for this is that many constructs at the abstract or basic levels have standard operational definitions. We tacitly rely on these in scientific communication. For example, if we say that strength of grip was measured in kilograms using a hand dynamometer, it is generally not necessary to say any more about the unit of measurement or the instrument used. We may need to enlarge our operational definition by telling about the number and spacing of trials used in taking the measurements. In other words, we need to give special attention to showing just how our operational definitions have been built up from standard operations plus our own special techniques of observation or measurement. If ever we employ techniques or formulations that are novel to a considerable extent, we must present our operational definitions quite fully. From our descriptions of the steps taken, another investigator should be able to duplicate our work.

HYPOTHETICAL CONSTRUCTS AND INTERVENING VARIABLES. According to the usage of terms which some scientists employ, the highest degree of abstraction in theory construction, which we have called a theoretical construct, may be termed either an *intervening variable* or an *hypothetical construct*. The term intervening variable is used to describe a quantified construct defined mathematically in terms of constructs measured at lower levels of abstraction. The values of intervening variables sometimes play the role of substitute values, replacing several other measures as further theory construction is undertaken. A set of intervening variables thus serves as a simplifying device for calculations and further definitions. A hypothetical construct may be defined in essentially the same way as an intervening variable, in terms of less abstract constructs. The complete operational definition of an hypothetical construct is usually quite complex, requiring the description of all the operations for the lower level constructs to be included. What distinguishes this from the intervening variable is the postulation that a more direct operational definition is theoretically possible for the hypothetical construct. That is, the construct being measured so indirectly is assumed to be measurable more directly, in principle. For example, we might define "fatigue" in terms of work curve measurements, an indirect formulation. To regard the concept as a hypothetical construct would imply hope that a more direct assessment technique might be found, perhaps a bloodstream measure of muscular waste products. Some psychologists try to maintain the distinction between intervening variable and hypothetical construct while others do not employ it, preferring to let each operational definition speak for itself.

Some intervening variables may be indirectly defined in terms of others. This may be illustrated by reference to a central part of the theorizing done by Hull (1943, 1951, 1952). Corresponding to any habitual response made by an organism is a habit strength, H, which is operationally defined in terms of the number of prior reinforcements, or rewards, which have followed the making of the response in a particular stimulus situation. Another intervening variable, D, is defined as the drive strength indicated by such operations as the feeding schedule of experimental animals or certain psychological test scores attained by human subjects. Having devised equations for anchoring quantitative values of H and D to experimental manipulations or observations, the theorist postulated that another intervening variable, E, representing the excitatory potential for the making of the response, was jointly dependent on them. E is defined by an equation which shows it to be a function of the product, $H \times D$. We see that E has not been defined by its own set of operations but by those which define H and D, plus the equation indicating the computation of E from their values. In the entire behavioral theory, various dimensions of the response—such as its latency—are postulated to be functions of E. These relationships of E to behavior measures are postulated to hold no matter what combination of H and D values may have contributed to a particular E value. The concept of excitatory potential, E, thus serves as a useful reference point in studying how behavior depends on the state of an organism. Hull's theoretical formulations are more complex than we have indicated here, but the quantitative definition of some intervening variables in terms of others is typical.

COORDINATING LINKAGES. Two constructs at the abstract or theoretical level may have been built up through different operational definitions and still may possess an essential equivalence in the way they relate to other constructs. A statement of this functional equivalence may be termed a *coordinating linkage*. An example would be a statement that IQ as determined with the Stanford-Binet test might be assumed, for certain practical purposes of theory construction, to be the same as IQ obtained with the Wechsler Intelligence Scale. By using such a linkage a theorist might bring into conjunction two different sets of research findings which had been based on the two different measuring instruments. A coordinating linkage does not assert the identity of the constructs involved. Their different operational definitions actually give them different identities. The linkage simply asserts a working equivalence. With respect to our IQ example, a coordinating linkage might permit us to state that IQ_{SB} was related to certain other specified constructs in the same way that IQ_W had been found to relate to them. Such a statement is actually an hypothesis for potential testing. The tentative assumption based on the coordinating linkage helps to give a temporary filling-in of the theoretical picture.

SCIENTIFIC SIGNIFICANCE. We have already seen that a construct must have an unambiguous operational definition if it is to be a useful part of science. Even a complete and precise operational definition, however, does not guarantee much utility for a construct. To be useful in theory construction a construct should also have *scientific significance*. This may be described as empirically determinable relationships to *other* constructs. In other words, a significant construct is one which enters into the formulation of hypotheses and laws. We may note in passing that scientific significance is only distantly related to statistical significance.

The futility of complete operational definition without any scientific significance has been aptly demonstrated to the classes of Professor Bergmann of the State University of Iowa. Students are asked to copy from the blackboard the formula for the Bergmann Index, one of its forms being as follows:

$$B = \frac{W_B - L_T}{N_H}$$

where B = the Bergmann Index for any person.
  W_B = his body weight, in kilograms.
  L_T = the length of his great toe, in centimeters.
  N_H = the number of hairs on his head.

Students are most impressed when they see the formula in its symbolic form. As they hear each term described they must admit that the definition is operational. By following the formula we can compute the value of the index for any individual, a somewhat laborious task when we encounter the denominator, N_H. Despite its beautiful operational definition, the Bergmann Index is a construct which has found no place in biological or social science. It lacks scientific significance, any relationship to other constructs. It is found in no behavior laws in psychology, nor even in the multitude of hypotheses which candidates for advanced degrees have formulated in great profusion. The obviously patient care with which Professor Bergmann constructed his index goes for naught, if naught be found to correlate with it or to depend mathematically upon it. At this point, many students helpfully suggest that the index *might* correlate with something after all. Perhaps the index increases with chronological age. Devised merely for pedagogical purposes, this construct may turn up in an M. A. thesis yet.

There is a dilemma in the requirement that a construct must have both operational definition and scientific significance in order to be of use in theory construction. How much effort can we expend in devising a complete operational definition when we risk the discovery that the construct is not related to others as we might have hypothesized? On the other hand, if no relationship is empirically found between two constructs, to what extent might this be due to a failure to invest heavily enough in an operational definition which demanded elaborate control over conditions? Or might a lack of relationship be attributable to narrowly missing the necessary operational definition of one of the constructs involved? These questions indicate the close interdependence of operational definition and scientific significance.

The solution to the dilemma seems to lie in a stepwise approach to theory construction. Constructs are given operational definitions which are judged sound enough to reveal any relationships which may exist among these constructs or among any constructs which might be defined by similar operations. If no hint of relationship is found, the definitions of one or more constructs may be changed quite drastically, or some concepts may be abandoned. If some degree of relationship is found empirically, the scientist may attempt to refine this part of theory by making moderate changes in one or more constructs or by adding more relevant constructs to the hypothesis before testing it again. Operational definition, making hypotheses, and empirical testing thus succeed each other in an endless spiral which is a basic process in theory construction. When an operational definition is achieved which reveals considerable scientific significance for a particular construct, that definition may be maintained for some time as more extensive relationships are sought for that construct. We should be somewhat conservative about abandoning constructs for which there are numerous empirical relationships.

A Schematic Representation of Theory Construction

We may be aided in understanding theory construction by a graphic portrayal of the processes involved and the structure which results from them. The schematic representation of Figure 8.2 incorporates most of the aspects of theory building which we have just been

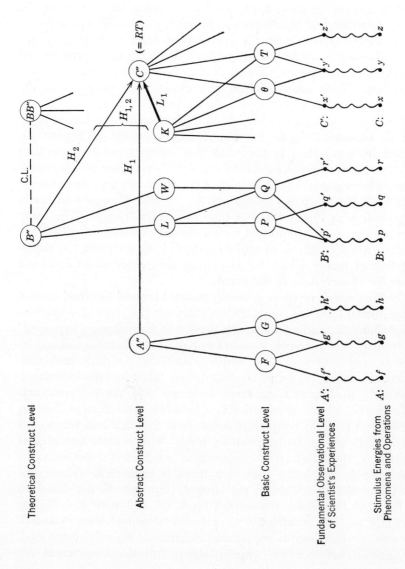

Fig. 8.2. Schematic representation of theory construction as explained in the text.

Theoretical Construct Level

Abstract Construct Level

Basic Construct Level

Fundamental Observational Level of Scientist's Experiences

Stimulus Energies from Phenomena and Operations

discussing. In addition we find that it incorporates elements from the general plan of science which was presented in Figure 8.1. We shall be reviewing these matters as we examine the details of the figure, beginning at the bottom and working generally upward.

The elements shown at the very lowest level in Figure 8.2 are physical energies arising from experimental operations and the natural phenomena accompanying them. These are events in the real world of nature. They are organized into clusters for purposes of the definitional use to which they will be put. At this level of real existence the cluster units have been designated by the letters A, B, and C, corresponding to the use of these symbols in Figure 8.1. Linked by wavy lines to these stimulus energies are the scientist's sensory and perceptual experiences which they arouse at the fundamental observational level. As part of the observer's experiences these have been clustered and labeled as A', B', and C'—again in correspondence with Figure 8.1, this time the center triangle. The wavy lines are supposed to represent such a close dependence of experience on the natural events in carefully conducted research that the superstructure of theory which we erect may be considered to represent either the observations or the events.

The lines which progress generally upward beyond the fundamental observational level are considered to represent the steps of operationally defining the various constructs needed to formulate an hypothesis for testing. For example, F and G as basic constructs are defined by various combinations of f', g', and h'. Similarly, the other basic constructs are defined in terms of observations taken in varied combinations. At the abstract construct level we find several constructs including C'' which represents RT, a behavior measurement, here as in Figure 8.1. This temporal measurement is defined in terms of θ and T, both at the basic construct level. θ represents the angular position of the hand on a chronoscope, whereas T represents the time scale in which the face of a timer is calibrated. These two constructs, along with others not labeled, contribute to the definition of RT. At the abstract construct level we also note K. This is evidently another construct with a temporal aspect since θ and T are seen to enter into its operational definition. K is the foreperiod, the interval between the warning signal and the stimulus in RT experimentation.

Also at the abstract construct level we see A'', L, and W. We shall find that A'' is part of Triangle $A''B''C''$ of the earlier schema of Figure 8.1. L and W are abstract constructs which combine to define B'' at the theoretical construct level. B'' was also seen before in

Triangle $A''B''C''$. This triangle is virtually formed for us here by the lines H_1 and H_2. These lines represent hypotheses that A'' and B'' are both independent variables which are lawful determinants of the value of C''. At the convergence of H_1 and H_2 we have applied the label $H_{1,2}$ to indicate the more complex hypothesis which states how A'' and B'' interact in determining the RT which C'' represents. We have thus chosen in our example to present Triangle $A''B''C''$ as a set of hypotheses to be tested rather than as a set of laws already having strong empirical confirmation.

In one part of Figure 8.2 we do have an empirical law represented by L_1 which represents the dependence of C'' (RT) upon K (the fore-period). This is but one of many laws which must be considered in setting up tests of hypotheses about RT. At the top of the figure we see one more aspect of theory construction portrayed. The dotted line connecting B'' and BB'' is designated C.L. to represent a coordinating linkage. This means that B''—as operationally defined from p', q', and r' via P, Q, L, and W—is tentatively considered to be equivalent to BB'', a construct which might have been defined in quite different ways. This linkage indicates that the theorist feels that any confirmation of the $A''B''C''$ relationships should be tentatively regarded as indicating a relationship involving BB'' with A'' and C'' also. Later it would be necessary to test this hypothesis empirically, by building BB'' instead of B'' into an experiment.

Figure 8.2 may do justice to portraying the stratified nature of the theoretical structure and to indicating some of its components. It comes nowhere near representing the enormous complexity of theory. Operational definitions have many more components than the figure indicates and more constructs enter into the formulation of almost any hypothesis or law. We must add complexity as we view the figure in an attempt to visualize the nature of theory. We must also add the dimension of change as we view Figure 8.2, a facet of theory building for the portrayal of which a motion picture would be needed. Theory changes as new constructs are defined and new hypotheses are formulated. This extends the area covered and fills in gaps. Theory also changes as research confirms hypotheses and these take on the status of empirical laws.

Dimensions of Theory

A scientific theory is a multidimensional structure. Some of its more prominent dimensions have already been revealed in our prior discussion and our schematic portrayal of theory. After mentioning these again briefly we shall list several other dimensions of theory, or of particular theories. Our list may serve as a set of categories for the examination of the offerings of particular theorists in behavior science whose formulations we may encounter in our reading in the psychological literature.

LEVELS OF ABSTRACTION EMPLOYED. We need to be flexible in thinking about the levels of abstraction which we have considered. Instead of a few distinct levels it might be more faithful to the facts of theory building to think of innumerable degrees of abstraction. These may be considered to be stratified, one upon the other, with major groups of strata designated by names such as we have applied: basic construct level, abstract construct level, and theoretical construct level. One reason for keeping such levels in mind is that different theories vary greatly in the degree of abstraction represented in the constructs they employ. Some formulations may involve relationships in the lower regions of the abstract construct level. The dependence of RT on the foreperiod, which we designated as L_1 in Figure 8.2, is an example. At such low levels of abstraction, hypotheses can usually be put to fairly direct empirical test, which then may give them the status of laws in the system. Most of the relationships which research psychologists have verified experimentally are at the lower levels of abstraction. More indirectly defined constructs, at higher levels, enter into hypotheses which require somewhat indirect testing. These remain hypotheses for a longer time, requiring more extensive experimentation before they can be considered as behavioral laws.

DEGREE OF CONFIRMATION OF RELATIONSHIPS. Hypotheses and laws have been repeatedly mentioned as two major types of relationship existing among constructs in theory. As we found necessary in discussing levels of abstraction, we need to repeat that these are not distinct kinds of relationship. The two terms are employed to emphasize different degrees of confirmation. When a relationship between constructs has been merely postulated, prior to any experimental testing, we term it an hypothesis. Repeated validation in research may establish it as a law. A single validation of an hypothesis may strengthen its tenability without warranting our calling it a law. At higher levels of abstraction a law may be established when numerous hypotheses, logically derived from it, are found to be tenable at the lower levels of abstraction which permit ready empirical testing.

A convenient way to think of degree of confirmation is in terms of probability. A relationship is a law if there is very high probability that it will prove sound in further direct testing or if there is a high probability that propositions carefully derived from it will be found to be valid. A relationship is only an hypothesis if only low or moderately high probability exists for its continued validation. The concept of probability offers a quantified model for thinking of the continuum of tenability of the many postulated relationships which go to make up a theory.

SCOPE. When we speak of theory construction as a unified enterprise in which all the scientific disciplines contribute to a picture of the nature of the universe and its inhabitants, we are dealing with an effort of practically limitless scope. The dimension of scope, or inclusiveness, becomes meaningful only as we examine particular theories or sets of hypotheses and laws which cohesively form a limited system. Various systems which different theorists in psychology have offered are characterized by great differences in the breadth of phenomena for which the system attempts to account. A few theories try to achieve a general accounting for behavior, utilizing principles of wide applicability to animal and human activity. Such formulations necessarily include many areas which require filling in with details. Other theories are *miniature systems* which deal with a very circumscribed area of behavior such as rote memorization or the resolution of conflicting response tendencies. These more modest attempts to treat a part of the vast realm of behavior are usually characterized by a more detailed set of hypotheses and an attempt to include most of the relevant variables.

In working with any theoretical system it is advisable to be aware of the scope of coverage intended by the theorist. It is particularly important to respect the limits which may have been set for the application of the theory, avoiding any testing in areas where the formulation is not intended to apply. This does not preclude attempts to extend a theory, but it suggests that these efforts be clearly identified as such. If an attempted extension should fail, this does not necessarily weaken the system in its area of intended applicability.

DEGREE OF FORMALIZATION. We have suggested that research workers are continually modifying theory as they formulate hypotheses and test them. Such changes frequently do not constitute theory construction as a deliberate undertaking. When we turn to the work of those who have consciously tried to treat some area of behavior in a systematic fashion, we find wide divergence in the degree of formalization of statements defining constructs and hypothesizing relationships. Theorists have also differed in the extent to which they have arrived at hypotheses by applying logic as opposed to using a more intuitive approach.

It is not in any verbal elegance that the merit of a formally stated system lies, but in the precision with which terms are used and hypotheses are stated. Such precision generally lends itself to experimental testing of the formulations. Less formally stated hypotheses are sometimes characterized by a vagueness which discourages rigorous attempts at validation.

We must remember, of course, that even the most formal of verbal definitions must be in agreement with the operational definitions of the research supporting a theory if the formal statements are to be given due weight. Another caution regarding formalization is that it may be carried further in the direction of making specific, quantitative predictions than is warranted by the status of the system. Degree of formalization, like degree of confirmation of relationships, is a dimension of theory which should be expected to develop as theory construction proceeds. The pace of theory building depends largely on success in identifying potential relationships among variables and in testing them experimentally; this pace cannot be accelerated by resorting to devices that are merely verbal.

SIZE OF UNITS OF DESCRIPTION. In choosing the constructs to be used in formulating hypotheses, a theorist generally makes a choice among possible units of description for the events to be studied. Psychologists have employed descriptive units in great variety, with size of unit forming a sort of dimension. Depending on research purposes, an investigator might report that a subject scored in the upper quartile in problem solving, that he solved 10 out of 12 problems of a specific test battery, or that he made 3 errors in solving Problem No. 11. The nature of Problem No. 11 would have to be part of the operational definition of some particular construct before such detailed attention to its solution would be warranted. In a relative sense, different size units of description are termed *molar* or *molecular*. Molar refers more typically to the activity of the entire organism during a fairly protracted period of time. Molecular generally indicates a more restricted segment of behavior covering a brief time span and sometimes involving responses that represent only a fraction of ongoing behavior. The molar-molecular continuum is always present in behavior. A particular choice of size of unit for describing behavior represents a strategic decision in research and theory construction. Although the terms molar and molecular have been employed with other meanings than these, the foregoing viewpoint seems to be the most useful for us to adopt.

REDUCTIONISM. In theory construction *reductionism* refers to the use of constructs and laws from one scientific discipline to explain the relationships found in another realm of investigation. In psychology a theory may be considered reductionistic if, in addition to describing behavioral events, it employs constructs from physiology. For example, a theorist might wish to go beyond the delineating of empirical laws surrounding a motor performance like repetitive tapping. Having quantified rate of tapping and its decline with continued performance, he might seek to describe the neural, the muscular, and the metabolic events which constitute a different aspect of the behavior. These relatively more molecular events would naturally have to be approached by quite different techniques or operational definitions. Laws from both the behavioral and the physiological levels of inquiry would all be part of the theory, all being descriptive of regular relationships existing in nature under specified conditions. The description of intramuscular events, however, might be considered as explanatory of the events of overt motor performance. *Explanation* can be seen here to consist of *description* at a more molecular level.

Many psychological theorists do not employ reductionism in expanding their theories. They accomplish a more complete understanding of behavioral events by formulating and verifying more and more hypotheses at the behavioral level. The structure of theory is strengthened by increasing the number of constructs and interrelationships among them which are taken into account. By using operational definition properly, these theorists provide just as strong a foundation at the fundamental observational level for their constructs as may be obtained for physiological constructs. Thus theoretical advances in the behavioral sciences can be made without reductionism. On the other hand, since the boundaries between levels of inquiry represent mere classificatory conveniences, the complete development of theory in unified science must involve the use of investigative techniques of all disciplines. Laws which describe natural events of all kinds must ultimately be tied together, with reductionism necessarily involved. In this joining of different realms of theory, coordinating linkages will be needed to identify equivalent constructs which have been established by different operational definitions.

THEORETICAL MODELS. In formulating new hypotheses a theorist may sometimes be guided by a *model*—a set of interrelationships borrowed from somewhere besides the realm of natural events which he is investigating. Models of various sorts have been employed in behavioral theory development. They are adopted as guides to the creative thinking of the theorist when some aspects of the model appear to be congruent with certain aspects of the psychological events. Having noted these parallel interrelationships, the theorist borrows further relationships from the known model to be used as predictions of relationships which will be sought among the constructs with which he is working. Another use of a model may be to guide the operational definition of a new construct which appears necessary in the theory to complete its resemblance to the model.

In our discussion of theory building prior to this point, we did not find it necessary to consider the use of a model. In our brief treatment of how models are used we have just seen that they are guides to thinking, adjuncts to theory construction which never become part of the theory itself. They are analogies or analogues of the interrelated events which a theory describes. Thinking by means of an analogy can be a creative process, suggesting good hypotheses for testing. It can be misleading as well, indicating relationships that do not prove to be verifiable. However, this latter aspect can do little harm as long as experimental checks continue to be applied as a theory develops. The danger in using models is that the laws observed in the models will be considered to indicate laws in the theory itself when this is not justified. A further restriction on the employment of a model is that it may prove deceptively simple, having variables enough to resemble some aspects of the events under study but not reflecting their total complexity.

Almost all theorists who attempt to formulate quantified relationships make some use of limited mathematical models. When an experimental outcome yields data to which a curve is fitted, the mathematical form of the fitted function is used as a model for the relationship which is postulated as part of the theory. It remains for further empirical research to determine whether the function selected and the parameters determined by curve-fitting can be retained as descriptive of the relationship holding among the constructs of the theory. New data may require finding a new function as the model for the relationship. This limited use of mathematics is usually not considered as an employment of a model. A model generally involves a more complex set of interrelationships borrowed from mathematics, from electronics, or elsewhere.

RESEARCH

Discussion of research is found in all chapters of this book, with varied emphases ranging from details of specific methods to illustrative experimental findings. Here we shall consider in general the aims of research and the various types of research endeavor which are found in the science of behavior.

Aim of Research

In Chapter 1 we suggested that the formulating and testing of hypotheses were the aim of experimentation. We need not abandon that position at this juncture, but we can strengthen it by using our discussion of theory as an anchor point.

MODIFICATION OF THEORY. We have seen that theory is a structure composed of hypotheses in varied degrees of confirmation which interrelate constructs that have been operationally defined. If research is the formulating and testing of hypotheses, as we have said, then it is a most essential part of theory construction. Research activity begins with the operational defining of constructs involved in theorizing. It is the enterprise which places the different constructs in their positions in the theoretical structure and strengthens these placements by empirical validation. Besides strengthening existing parts of theory, research extends theory by providing new constructs to fill in gaps.

Research may weaken as well as strengthen and extend parts of theory. It reveals certain hypotheses to be untenable in the light of certain experimental results. Besides leading to the rejection of specific hypotheses, negative outcomes of studies may cast doubt on the general scientific significance of particular constructs. In this way research forces the theorist to modify operational definitions or to define new constructs.

Types of Research

There is no homogeneity of appearance in the activities which are all a legitimate part of scientific research. Despite the general aim which we have claimed for it all, specific investigators give different directions and degrees of impetus to their studies. We shall try to improve our orientation in behavioral research by noting a few major types of experimentation.

BASIC AND APPLIED STUDIES. If an investigator seeks facts or relationships which he may apply in the solution of some practical problem, his studies are often labeled applied science. If relationships are sought by testing hypotheses without regard for their applicability, the investigations are often termed a part of basic or pure research. A prime quality of some basic research is its generating of new constructs. These may open vast territories of the theoretical domain for further exploration. Often the constructs involved in basic science may be operationally defined at a higher level of abstraction than those which figure in applied research. Despite this distinction and others which may be made with a modicum of validity, it is rightly pointed out that so-called basic and applied research have fundamental similarity which results in an overlap of their consequences. This is illustrated by the fact that applied research cannot help but explore relationships which can be profitably strengthened in the theoretical structure. A more dramatic illustration is found when basic research, undertaken as a pure exploration of natural phenomena, proves to have practical applicability of great importance.

ABSTRACT AND REPRESENTATIVE EXPERIMENTS. Another dimension along which behavioral studies may vary is the degree to which they resemble real life situations. Some investigators prefer to manipulate independent variables over ranges which reflect the values which a person might encounter in actuality. It might be further desired to utilize sets of these variables in combinations which similarly mirrored real experience. These are among the aspects of *representative experiments,* designed to reveal behavior as it actually functions. The utility of this approach in applied research is fairly apparent since it should yield useful findings. It is maintained by some behavior scientists that these realistic guidelines for experimental design should be followed even in basic research.

Abstract experiments, or *systematic studies,* have more typically been employed in laboratory experimentation. This approach to ferreting out relationships among constructs is typified in many of the studies which we encounter as illustrations in this book. It involves using an isolated, controlled situation in which just one variable is permitted to vary so that its effect on behavior may be noted. This effect is a real one even though it could not be observed outside the restricted situation established in the study. Such a univariate design is replaced in much recent research by multivariate studies which still represent severe abstraction from everyday behavioral situations. Such systematic research reveals relationships and dependencies among variables which might be obscured in the complexity of an experiment which represented real life more accurately.

"CRUCIAL" AND FUNCTIONAL EXPERIMENTS. Occasionally an experimenter attempts a "crucial" test of some theoretical formulation, perhaps some hypothesis that is a part of a miniature system. A plan for such an experiment is often an ingenious creation, designed to reveal once and for all if the hypothesis is tenable. Unfortunately, the study rarely seems so decisive when the data have been collected. Even if the one hypothesis be rejected, a substitute takes its place, slightly different but tenable even in view of the new findings. Then it is time for another "crucial" experiment. Not infrequently, a theorist may debate the right of an experimenter to reach a particular negative conclusion in a research report on the grounds that the research worker did not adhere to certain requirements of the theoretical system as he set up the experimental operations.

As an alternative to the usually futile attempts at "crucial" experimentation, we may note the merit of the more plodding search for functional relationships. There is value in strengthening a miniature system by adding to the scientific significance of its constructs. It may be useful also to revise some of its operational definitions. These positive attempts to improve one theoretical system are the best way to insure its competition with other systems.

METHODOLOGICAL RESEARCH. Some experimentation in psychology is directed at devising and refining techniques, especially methods of quantifying behavior. The outcome of such efforts is perhaps most broadly portrayed in the psychophysical methods and the techniques for psychological scaling. Individual psychological tests of many kinds also represent instruments of considerable potential in the further search for behavior laws. The proper development of such tests is a research effort of great magnitude. One more type of methodological research which may be cited is the delineation of various aspects of stimulus materials, ranging from the meaning of words to the mathematical properties of various polygons and other forms useful in perceptual research.

Although methodological research is preliminary to investigations aimed more directly at theory construction, it is to be hoped that it will prosper. Sound methods, once devised, can be incorporated in operational definitions so as to provide a good foundation for constructs at various levels of abstraction. Too often in psychology experimenters have adopted makeshift methods, resulting in unique operational definitions. Standardized techniques can provide standard definitions of terms with the result that theory should mature more rapidly due to a greater interlocking of empirical findings.

PROGRAMMATIC RESEARCH. A research worker, or a team of investigators, will often carry out a consecutive program of studies which has certain advantages over conducting individual experiments unrelated to each other. The familiarity that arises from repeated excursions into some problem realm is a primary benefit. Another advantage is found when a preliminary strategy is mapped out for a series of studies. In planning the sequence it is possible to insure progression from one relevant variable to another instead of frantically trying to cram everything into one experiment which might be grandiose in design but minuscule in yield. Serially conducted studies typically contain an element of repetition which may add confirmation to earlier results when later findings are examined. Programmatic research repeats the use of particular operational definitions and therefore leads to networks of relationships instead of isolated outcomes.

The preplanning of a group of experiments should not prevent investigators from turning aside to pursue some unexpected aspect of behavior which may occur. The pursuit of such fortuitous leads represents some of the most exciting and rewarding moments in the history of science. By executing a succession of studies in the same problem area we increase our chances of recognizing anything unusual. We should keep our research planning flexible enough to exploit such an opportunity.

ANIMAL RESEARCH. In this textbook our discussion of experimental techniques and findings is limited to research employing human subjects. The number of topics which are treated is a testimony to the vastness of this part of psychological science. We recognize that a similarly vast endeavor is represented in behavioral research that utilizes animals as subjects of study. It would require volumes even to sample adequately this realm of investigation. We must limit ourselves here to taking passing note of the assumptions involved in research on animal behavior and the advantages of such experimentation.

We are familiar with the assumptions made by research physiologists that cats and dogs, rabbits and guinea pigs have digestive, circulatory, and neural processes which resemble those of the human. Laws which are verified through research on these animals have proved applicable to human beings with but little change. Where physiological differences among species are found, these become the content of comparative physiology. In the realm of behavior, psychologists have also noted similarities and differences between the reactions of animals and those of human subjects. As in physiology we can delineate the differences in a comparative psychology and we can utilize the similarities in putting certain hypotheses to experimental test.

This use of animal research in extending and refining behavior theory must always be done with great care. Species differences place severe limitations on the generalizability of principles of behavior discovered with animal subjects, but the fortunate fact is that theory building can be aided by animal research even while recognizing these limits. Human behavior often involves interrelationships among variables which are not even represented at the animal level, as in the case of verbal processes. On the other hand, many factors of importance in governing animal behavior are also present among the determinants of responses made by humans. This latter fact is the source of utility of animal studies in constructing general behavior theory.

Experimentation on the behavior of animals affords certain advantages which need be noted only briefly. The entire life histories of animal subjects can be known to the experimentalist who rears them in his laboratory. He can subject them to conditions like 24 hours of food deprivation to which few human subjects would voluntarily submit. Animals are readily accessible for repeated or prolonged treatments or observations not feasible for studying human subjects who permit only limited encroachments on their time. This tribute to the role of animals in behavioral research may well be concluded by noting that they are the pioneers whose reactions to the conditions of space travel were first studied.

RELATIONSHIPS BETWEEN THEORY AND RESEARCH

Close relationships between theory and research are indicated in the definition of theory considered earlier in this chapter. We suggested that theory is a structure composed of hypotheses and laws. It is research which gives us these laws by confirming hypotheses in empirical test. We shall discuss two major classes of relationship between theory and research. First we shall note several ways in which research modifies theory and then we shall see how theory provides hypotheses for experimental testing.

Research Modifies Theory

As we have broadly defined theory, any carefully conducted research contributes to it. Even though the investigator is not a theorist nor intends to test a particular theory, his work does represent a test of some hypothesis. His results are findings which probably bear indirectly on a dozen hypotheses already a part of the structure of theory. Some of these may gain strength whereas others may lose it as a result of the data he has obtained. In the case of a research worker who deliberately seeks to influence theory through empirical research, the impact of experimental results is likely to be greater. We shall see that research modifies theory in several different ways.

RESEARCH STRENGTHENS TENABILITY OF HYPOTHESES. If a particular hypothesis is set up, postulating a relationship among operationally defined constructs, the experiment will be planned to yield data which reveal the dependence of one variable on others. Some technique of statistical inference will be applied to determine if the hypothesis should be considered tenable. If this proves to be the case, then this segment of theory is strengthened. After an hypothesis has won such support in several tests, it may even be considered to be a law. In this event, it would be retained as part of theory unless strong evidence was found in further research for judging it to be not valid.

Hypothesized relationships may often be tested indirectly, especially when they are postulated to hold among variables at the theoretical level. The actual test in such an instance will often be conducted at a lower level of abstraction. If the specific hypothesis tested is judged tenable, the relationships at both levels are strengthened, one by direct exeriment and one by the logical extension that is involved when definitions are carried to a higher level of abstraction. At the higher levels, coordinating linkages may add strength to relationships among certain constructs even when their particular operational definitions are not involved in the experimental procedures.

RESEARCH EXTENDS AREA OF THEORY. If a behavioral hypothesis has been given considerable confirmation, a common step taken by investigators is to begin manipulating other variables which may be of relevance. A gradually growing list of relevant independent variables determining some behavior measurement is one way in which the area covered by theory is expanded. As the network of relationships grows, the dependent variable gains scientific significance. The mathematical curve relating one independent variable to the behavior measure is replaced by a family of such curves. Each curve may be of the same general form but they differ individually as some other independent variable takes on a succession of values. Another extension of theory may be accomplished when quantitative relationships are filled out by empirical interpolation and extrapolation. The curve obtained in earlier research guides the selection of values for an independent variable that is to be used again. A choice of intermediate or larger values can fill out the mathematical function that describes the relationship under study.

RESEARCH LINKS DIFFERENT PARTS OF THEORY. Many programs of research have developed theoretical systems treating different realms of behavior. As these isolated systems gain strength and bid for a permanent place in theory, there arises a need to tie them together. New research may accomplish this connecting of systematically structured areas. This may be done by choosing some variables from one established system and some from the other. If it is found that an hypothesis involving these variables can be considered tenable in new experimentation, the linking of the systems is under way.

The coalescence of different systems is not as easy as it may sound, especially if the systems be those of different theorists. The difficulty may be that the operational definitions required for one theorist's constructs may not fit into the same experiment with the operations demanded by the other theorist. Another barrier to joining the work of different theorists may be that neither one has provided complete and unequivocal operational definitions for his constructs. Each may have a system that is not rigidly fixed in the theoretical structure we have described. Some constructs may have been defined only verbally. Others may have only partial specification of the defining operations. Under these conditions a system may have been developed as a flexible edifice, shifting dynamically to meet the stress of each new empirical test. This condition does not lend itself to linking one such structure to another.

Theory Provides Hypotheses for Research

Even when a particular experiment is not intended to be a test of a particular theory or hypothesis, it is planned on the basis of known facts and relationships which are a part of theory as we have broadly defined it. The specific hypothesis being investigated may of course be an extension or extrapolation from what has previously been affirmed through research, but its points of departure are still parts of the theoretical structure. As a representation of past research, theory is a ready source of new hypotheses to be tested.

We saw that there were several different ways in which research modifies theory. If we re-examine each of these points we shall see that each one suggests a particular way in which theory stimulates further research. We stated that research strengthens the tenability of hypotheses. We may now note that it is by indicating the amount of confirmation that a particular hypothesis has received that theory invites further testing of the same hypothesis with a view toward strengthening it into a law. We considered earlier that experimentation extends the area covered by theory. Looking at this fact from our present point of view, we can see that it is the role of theory to point out gaps in our knowledge so that this type of research is undertaken. Similarly, research aimed at linking different parts of theory is stimulated by the thoughtful examination of theory which helps an investigator to perceive just where a bridge of experimentation can be advantageously built.

It is unlikely that we can stress too much these interrelationships between theory and research. The danger may be that by describing them analytically we may make them seem too formal. We may make it appear that every research worker has at his elbow a volume filled with theory which he scans to pick out the next problem to investigate. The usual situation, of course, is far less formally structured than this. Most hypotheses are selected for testing even as the prior research is being reported. This intimate serial linking of research efforts is precisely what we have described in a systematic way as an interaction between theory and research. The findings of previous research are exactly what we mean by theory as it influences further investigation. The fact that some investigators do not label their findings as theory does not invalidate our analysis of how the descriptions of scientists' observations—their contribution to theory— and their laboratory activities are mutually supporting as the scientific enterprise moves forward.

SUMMARY

We saw the nature of science to be understandable on the basis of a three-part schema representing the interrelationships of natural events, the interrelationships among different aspects of scientists' observations, and the linkages among the constructs they utilize in describing their observations and the conditions under which the data were collected. The latter structure of linked constructs we termed theory. Various relationships among the constructs were called hypotheses or laws, depending on their degree of confirmation in empirical research.

Operational definition was described as a basic process in theory construction. It was seen to give meaning to the concepts employed, spanning the gap between raw observation and the theory language of science. Since constructs may be defined by operations of varying degrees of complexity, we found that theory is a structure with several levels of abstraction representing these different degrees of construction upward from simple observations. As a convenience we indicated that such levels might be labeled as a fundamental observational level or as one of the levels where constructs are encountered, these being arbitrarily tagged as basic, abstract, or theoretical. At the theoretical construct level we discussed two kinds, the hypothetical construct and the intervening variable.

Besides the constructs which are the stuff of which theory is made, we noted structural members in the form of coordinating linkages, hypotheses, and laws. We noted that it is in these relationships to other parts of the theoretical system that a construct takes on scientific significance. We considered the dilemma which faces a scientist who tries to attain a good operational definition for a construct while at the same time trying to see if the construct actually relates to anything. The Bergmann Index was used to show that operational definition does not guarantee scientific significance. A second schema helped us to visualize the nature of theory as it stems from research efforts.

Our general appreciation of how theory arises formed a background for our looking at several of its dimensions. We saw that theories may differ in the levels of abstraction of the constructs they utilize. We noted that different parts of theory may differ in the degree of confirmation of the relationships they involve. Different theories vary in scope, some being very general in their nature and others being miniature systems. Another aspect in which theories differ is their degree of formalization. Next on our list was a consideration of their units of description, whether molar or molecular. We then dealt with the extent to which particular theories involve reductionism and the use they may make of theoretical models.

Turning to research, we saw the modification of theory as one way to describe its primary aim. We then devoted our attention to several different kinds of research, beginning with a view of its basic and applied aspects. Then came a discussion of abstract and representative experiments, followed by a comparison of "crucial" and functional studies. We next discussed methodological and programmatic research, concluding our survey by noting certain characteristics of animal research.

Having treated the nature of theory and having rounded out our acquaintance with behavioral research, we concluded by considering the relationships between theory and research. They are closely related, we found, with research modifying theory and theory suggesting hypotheses for future experimental exploration. Research strengthens hypotheses that are already a part of theory and it extends theory into new areas, linking earlier findings. Theory, in turn, stimulates these research efforts by helping the investigator to see where his efforts may make a useful contribution to knowledge.

REFERENCES

Hull, C. L. *Principles of behavior.* New York: Appleton-Century, 1943.
Hull, C. L. *Essentials of behavior.* New Haven: Yale Univer. Press, 1951.
Hull, C. L. *A behavior system.* New Haven: Yale Univer. Press, 1952.

ADDITIONAL READINGS

Bergmann, G. *Philosophy of science.* Madison: Univer. Wisconsin Press, 1957.

Boring, E. G. The role of theory in experimental psychology. *Amer. J. Psychol.,* 1953, 66, 169–184.

Dallenbach, K. M. The place of theory in science. *Psychol. Rev.,* 1953, 60, 33–39.

Good, C. V. & Scates, D. E. *Methods of research: educational, psychological, sociological.* New York: Appleton-Century-Crofts, 1954.

Marx, M. H. (Ed.) *Psychological theory: contemporary readings.* New York: Macmillan, 1951.

Osgood, C. E. *Method and theory in experimental psychology.* New York: Oxford Univer. Press, 1953.

Pratt, C. C. *The logic of modern psychology.* New York: Macmillan, 1939.

PART 2

Selected
Areas
of
Investigation

CHAPTER 9

Visual
Processes

Vision and other sensory processes were being investigated scientifically even before psychology emerged as a formal discipline. The interest of physicists in the nature of light and of physiologists in the functioning of sensory nerves and their accessory structures, such as the eye, led to the discovery of many problems that were psychological in nature. The research workers followed wherever the problems led, regardless of the field in which they had been formally trained. Today, problems of visual sensation and perception elicit keen interest from psychologists engaged in laboratory studies of many kinds. The experiments being done have many practical applications as well as theoretical implications. We deal with visual perceptions in Chapter 10, concentrating here on the sensory processes that may be said to underlie them.

We experience visual phenomena in rich variety. Such variety has two sources, the diversity of our physical surroundings and the complexity of the eyes and the neural tracts associated with them. Although there are generally few light sources in any environment, the absorption, reflection, diffusion, and transmission of the light, with respect to numerous objects and surfaces, create a complex visual field for the viewer. When the light enters the eye, all of these physical processes continue within the receptor itself, together with the optical refraction which results in the focusing of the retinal image. The photochemical and neural activity of the retina itself plays a primary role in visual experience. Seeing has motor aspects, too, involving the muscular control of pupillary diameter and the positioning of the eyes. The anatomy and physiology of the neural optic tract also contribute to the phenomena that we sense visually. It should be apparent that a science of seeing is being developed only through the cooperative efforts of many specialists. The technical subtleties of the information they have already amassed are forbidding to anyone but the experts themselves. We shall therefore set as our goal a closer approach to the facts and methods of visual science, with full realization that its finer intricacies could not possibly be grasped with the limited effort we can make.

BACKGROUND FACTS ON VISION

One mark of the expert is the great number of facts and concepts at his command as he thinks about a problem or reads reports of research. Even though it is not our aim to become specialists in visual investigation, we do aspire to some understanding of research that has been conducted. We shall need at least a few facts as we review some studies in the psychology of seeing. We need facts about light, about the eye, and about some of the visual mechanisms that may be operative in almost any experiment. Since many of the facts are quantitatively expressed, we require some acquaintance with units and techniques of measurement.

The Physical Stimulus

There are two specifications that must be given to designate the light that stimulates visual sensation. These are the amount of luminous energy and its distribution among the wavelengths of electromagnetic radiation that fall within the visible spectrum. In many experiments on vision we need also to specify the size and location of the visual stimulus in order to indicate the retinal area upon which its image falls.

ASPECTS OF LIGHT ENERGY. There are a number of terms now conventionally used to describe light energy in various aspects. We refer to the energy level of the light generated at a source as the *luminance* of that source. If the energy is emitted from a point source, we speak of the *luminous intensity* of the point source. As the light energy radiates out in all directions we refer to it as the *luminous flux*. When it falls upon a surface we speak of the *illuminance* of the surface by the light energy. Most surfaces will absorb part of the light and reflect part of it, the latter part of the energy being called the *luminous reflectance*. If light falls on a surface that has some degree of transparency, the energy which passes through is termed the *luminous transmittance*.

You may notice that we have not referred to the "brightness" of a light source or the "brightness" of an illuminated surface. After years of ambiguity in the use of this term, scientists dealing with light and vision have agreed to reserve it for the psychological experience aroused through the activation of the visual receptors by light. When we view a light source we experience its *illuminant brightness*, that is, its potential for illuminating. When we look at an illuminated surface, its luminous reflectance arouses the visual experience called *surface brightness*. Our impression of surface brightness, which is psychological, depends partly upon the *retinal illuminance* that enters the eye through the pupil. Retinal illuminance alone does not determine the value of the brightness sensation we experience; much depends on factors like the state of the retina as determined by its recent or concurrent activity.

PHOTOMETRIC MEASUREMENT. Light energy is photometrically measurable at many points in its pathway from its source to the retina of the eye, with different units of measurement conventionally used for its different aspects. Figure 9.1 indicates how some of the commonly used units of light measurement are defined, their abbreviations, where they are appropriately used, and the symbols employed to represent certain aspects of light. The International Candle is the standard unit for specifying the luminous intensity, I, of a point source of light. The source of light in the figure is represented as a candle to indicate that it is considered a point source of one *candle* of luminous intensity. An extended source of light, as opposed to a point source, has its luminance, L, specified in *candles per square meter* of its surface. By definition, the *lumen* is the amount of luminous flux, F, that emanates from a point source of one candle intensity and radiates out in a cone equivalent in size to a unit solid angle, a term taken from solid geometry. By geometrical definition, light passing through a unit solid angle will illuminate 1 sq ft of area at a distance of 1 ft from the point source and 1 sq meter of area at a distance of 1 meter from the source.

The illuminance, E, falling on a surface that is 1 ft distant from a point source of one candle is 1 *foot-candle*. Since at this distance from a one candle source, a lumen of luminous flux covers a sq ft of surface, the resultant illuminance may also be considered as 1 *lumen per square foot*. This is the illuminance falling on Surface X in Figure 9.1.

By the time a lumen of flux has traveled a meter from the point source, it is spread out over an area of 1 sq meter. It is this geometrical spreading out of the energy from a light source that gives rise to the inverse square law, that the illuminance falling on a surface is inversely proportional to the square of the distance from the source to the surface. The illuminance of Surface Y in the figure is 1 lumen

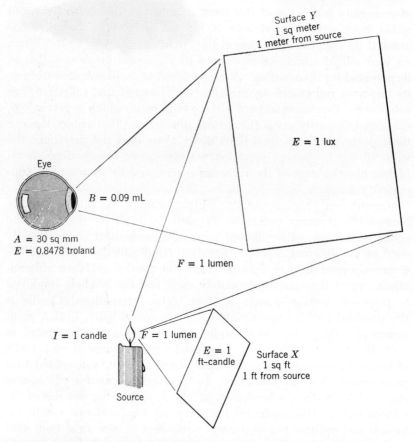

Fig. 9.1. Some of the fundamentals of photometric measurement as described in the text.

per square meter or 1 *lux*, which is by definition the amount of illuminance reaching a surface 1 meter distant from a point source of one candle. By the inverse square law, Surface Y is receiving about one-tenth of the illuminance that is falling on Surface X, a fact that is shown in the relative values of the foot-candle and the lux, 1 lux being equal to 0.093 foot-candle.

Surface Y in Figure 9.1 is receiving a lumen per square meter or 0.0001 lumen per square centimeter. If it were perfectly reflecting, the surface would give off 0.0001 lumen per square centimeter which equals 0.0001 *lambert* or 0.1 mL. The millilambert is a common measure of luminous reflectance and luminous transmittance. Also used as a measure of luminance from extended sources, the millilambert equals 0.314 candle per square meter.

Assuming that Surface Y actually has a reflectance value of just 90 per cent and is perfectly diffusing, that is, reflecting evenly in all directions, the eye represented in the figure is receiving a luminous reflectance of 0.09 mL or 0.02826 candle per square meter. The retinal illuminance, E, is computed in *trolands* by multiplying the pupillary area, A, expressed in square millimeters by the luminous reflectance, B, expressed in candles per square meter. Assuming $A = 30$ sq mm, the calculation for the situation in Figure 9.1 yields a retinal illuminance of 0.8478 troland.

SPECTRAL DISTRIBUTION OF LIGHT ENERGY. We have been discussing the measurement of light energy at various points in its journey from its origin in candle flame or incandescent filament to the retina. We stated, however, that a complete description of the physical characteristics of any light requires specification of the distribution of its energy among the wavelengths of radiation that comprise the visible spectrum. Light that reaches the eye directly from a source or reflected from a surface is always a mixture of many different wavelengths. The bright October sunlight streaming down on the football stadium contains all the visible wavelengths in about equal proportions. Its reflection from the stars and six of the stripes of the American flag is also about equally distributed among them. In the reflection from the other seven stripes, however, the longer and shorter wavelengths are more heavily represented, those of medium wavelengths having been absorbed more completely by the dye in the material. A different dye, in the rectangular field surrounding the flag's stars, absorbs most of the longer and medium wavelengths so that the light it reflects is predominantly composed of shorter wavelengths. Thus the spectral distribution of most light that reaches our eyes varies according to the selective absorption and reflection of the different wavelengths by the objects and surfaces from which it has been reflected.

You may have noted that in describing the energies reflected from the American flag we made no mention of any color. That is because color is a psychophysical concept and we are still limiting ourselves to describing the physical stimulus for vision. Strictly speaking, we should not be referring to light, either, but merely to radiant electromagnetic energy. It is perfectly possible to describe the flag in purely physical terms. We can even portray these attributes of the flag without requiring our printer to use anything but his regular ink. This portrayal is included in Figure 9.2.

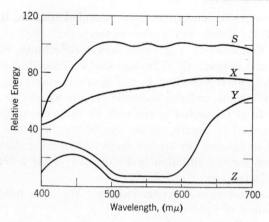

Fig. 9.2. Spectral distribution curves for the luminous energy of sunlight, Curve S, and the luminous reflectance from different parts of the American flag, Curves X, Y, and Z. (Curve S after Evans, 1948.)

SPECTRAL DISTRIBUTION CURVES. Each of the four curves in Figure 9.2 is a spectral distribution curve. Along the abscissa of the graph are the visible wavelengths, ranging from about 400 to about 700 millimicrons (mμ). Scaled upward along the ordinate are the relative energy levels of the illuminant or reflected light. Each curve shows the proportion of the energy that occurs in different wavelengths. Thus, the illuminance reaching the flag from the sun is pictured by the top curve, arbitrarily called distribution S. It indicates that wavelengths from about 475 to 700 mμ are found in about equal proportions in the sunlight with progressively less energy present as the wavelengths below 475 mμ are considered. Distribution X, as we have called the next curve, represents the reflectance from the stars and six of the stripes. From these portions of the flag the reflected energy is still more evenly distributed among the wavelengths than in the illuminant. Light reflected from the other seven stripes is pictured in the third curve, designated Y. Since these stripes have absorbed most of the medium wavelengths from the illuminant, the reflected light is composed chiefly of wavelengths of more than 600 mμ and less than 500 mμ. Contrasting with this is the lowest curve which shows the spectral distribution of the rectangular field on which the stars appear, distribution Z. The curve indicates that the energy reaching our eyes is chiefly of shorter wavelengths with a peak concentration around 450 mμ. The familiar red, white, and blue have become the Y, X, and Z in our arbitrary designations for these curves.

The fact that distributions X, Y, and Z are represented by curves placed much lower on the graph than distribution S indicates that the reflected energy is weaker in all wavelengths than the illuminant energy. In other words, every portion of the flag absorbed considerable energy of every wavelength. In each part, however, there was some relative selectivity of absorption so that the reflected spectral distribution in no case duplicated that of the incident light.

The Receptor

The morphology or structure of the eye is probably somewhat familiar to you. Light entering the eye passes through four transparent media before reaching the retina. Both the cornea and the crystalline lens, by virtue of their shape, contribute to the refraction of the light and the formation of an image on the retina. This image is usually resolved or focused by the reflex action of the ciliary body or muscle whose contraction and relaxation change the thickness and curvature of the lens for viewing near and distant points, the lens becoming thicker and more curved for near vision. This focusing adjustment for any distance is called *accommodation*.

THE PUPILLARY RESPONSE. Another aspect of ocular structure and function that must often be considered in conducting visual research is the pupil and its reflex response to light. As you know, the pupil constricts in bright light and dilates in dim illumination, its size ranging from about 2 mm diameter when fully constricted to about 8 mm diameter when completely dilated. Keep in mind that the amount of light entering the eye is proportional to pupillary area and not diameter. The extremes in pupil size thus represent a ratio of 16 to 1, the square of the diameter ratio, in the amount of retinal illuminance. The change in the amount of light reaching the retina due to pupillary action sometimes poses a problem in experimentation that may be met by having subjects look through a small aperture called an artificial pupil whose constant diameter simplifies the computing of retinal illuminance.

THE FOVEA. It is useful to consider the location in the retina of the foveal pit or *fovea*. The fovea lies in the optical axis of the eye; it is aligned, that is, with the center of the cornea and the lens. The image that falls on the fovea thus corresponds to whatever point in space the eye is *fixating*, looking at directly. This fact makes the fovea a convenient reference point for mapping points on the retina that are subject to stimulation. These retinal stimulation points are controlled in some experiments by providing a *fixation point* for the subject to look at. While this fixation is maintained by the subject, the experimenter may present stimuli at some predetermined angular displacement in the visual field, thus assuring the stimulation of a point in the retina of similar angular displacement from the fovea.

SUBTENDED VISUAL ANGLE.   Since angular measurements are used to designate the size of retinal images as well as the location of specific points of stimulation, it is well to note how these values are calculated, using simple trigonometry.   Figure 9.3 shows the geometrical relationships in the formation on the retina of the image of a printed arrow 7.34 in. long, viewed at a distance of about 12 in. and fixated at the center of its length.   The length of the arrow would typically be specified for visual research purposes by stating the size of the angle, θ, that it subtends.   This would be calculated as follows: the half-length of the arrow, 3.67 in., is divided by the viewing distance, 12 in., yielding a value for the tangent of the half-angle of 0.3058.   This indicates the half-angle to be 17°.   The angle, θ, subtended by the entire arrow is twice this amount, or 34°.   The arrow, then, is said to subtend a *visual angle* of 34° and this value refers to both the portion of the visual field occupied by the arrow and the portion of the retina occupied by the image of the arrow.   In citing any measurements of visual angle we should be sure to state whether viewing distance was calculated from the *nodal point* just behind the lens as

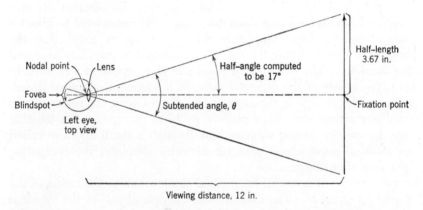

Fig. 9.3.   Diagram indicating the geometrical relationships used in calculating the visual angle, θ, subtended by a stimulus object.   By using the half-length of the arrow being viewed and the viewing distance in the formula for the tangent, the half-angle was found to be 17°.   The complete angle, θ, is thus 34° as subtended by the object in the visual field and also as subtended by the retinal image.   The location of the blindspot is incidentally revealed as 17° from the fovea.

in Figure 9.3, or whether it was measured from the front surface of the cornea as is sometimes done. This latter measurement requires a slight adjustment if we are to calculate the size of the retinal image precisely.

LOCATION OF THE BLINDSPOT. The *blindspot,* sometimes called the *optic disk,* is a small area about 3 mm from the fovea on the nasal side of each retina. Here there are no retinal rods or cones since nerve fibers leave the eye at this point to become the optic nerve.

Since Figure 9.3 is a cross-sectional view of the left eye as seen from the top, we may note that it gives us additional information about a retinal measurement. It may be seen that the head of the arrow falls about on the blindspot. The diagram thus shows the blindspot to be located in the nasal side of the retina about 17° from the fovea. For the image of a point like the arrowhead to fall on the nasal side of the retina, the point must be located in the temporal half of the visual field. Keep in mind that Figure 9.3 is a top view so that the arrow is portrayed as horizontal in visual space. The blindspot actually falls slightly below the horizontal retinal meridian.

Any point in the visual field that throws an image on the nasal retina of one eye forms an image on the temporal side of the other retina. It is impossible, therefore, for any point to throw its image on both blindspots simultaneously. When we engage in monocular viewing, of course, there is a tiny portion of the visual field that corresponds to the blindspot and might be expected to appear as an empty space in our visual pattern. There seems to be a perceptual filling-in, though, so that it is usually necessary to seek out the effect of this gap in the retinal mosaic in order to be aware of it.

RETINAL STRUCTURE. Although we do not intend to study the retina in great detail, either as to its complex cellular structure or its photochemical and neural functioning, we do need to review a few basic facts to complete our foundation for the understanding of some of the visual mechanisms. The light-sensitive elements of the retina are the rods and the cones, each named for its cellular shape. These cells are located toward the back of the retina, their tips pointing toward the choroid coat. The light that reaches them travels first through a microscopic layer of nerve fibers and connecting cells. For almost every cone there is connection, through a bipolar cell, to an individual fiber of the optic nerve. In contrast to this, several rods are connected with a single bipolar cell and thence to an optic nerve fiber. The difference in their connective patterns suggests that the cones, especially at the fovea, afford finer resolution of the retinal image.

In addition to differing in their neural connections, the rods and cones differ markedly in their distribution over the retina. Centered on the fovea is a 3° area composed exclusively of cones, the fovea itself comprising the midmost 1.5° of this area. Outside this central portion of the retina the density of cones is greatly reduced. As the cones become less numerous, rods are found more and more frequently as we move out from the fovea, reaching a peak density about 20° out from the center and then gradually becoming less frequent as the periphery is approached.

Visual Mechanisms

As additional background for reviewing research reports of visual studies and conducting experiments of our own, we need to discuss some of the facts about the visual process that might play a role in almost any investigation. These facts were themselves determined by research, of course, and the phenomena we cite are the topic for current study as visual scientists seek even greater refinement of knowledge.

SPECTRAL SENSITIVITY CURVES. A fact of great importance in vision is that the eye is not equally sensitive to all wavelengths of light There is much greater sensitivity to wavelengths around 540 mμ than to the longer and shorter wavelengths. In addition it has been found that the distribution of sensitivities is shifted slightly toward the shorter wavelengths for the rods as contrasted with the cones These facts were obtained by applying psychophysical methods, our topic in Chapter 5, to the determination of thresholds or limits of vision for different wavelengths. The *spectral sensitivity curves* are shown in Figure 9.4. As plotted, these functions may be better termed threshold curves since they indicate the minimal radiant flux at any wavelength that is needed to arouse *rod vision* or *cone vision*. For rods, the lowest threshold occurs at about 510 mμ, whereas for cones the threshold is lowest at 555 mμ. If these curves were inverted to become direct representations of sensitivity, then these values would represent peak sensitivity. Both rod and cone reactivities are much lower for wavelengths at a distance from their peak sensitivities, with much greater amounts of radiant flux needed to reach threshold and excite a sensation.

The threshold data for cone vision forming the *photopic visibility curve* of Figure 9.4 were obtained by applying a test stimulus to the rod-free area at the fovea. This had to be done, of course, to avoid arousing sensation in the more sensitive rods, thus making it virtually impossible to determine at what intensity value the cones would become

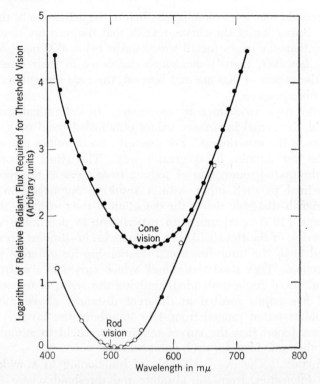

Fig. 9.4. The absolute threshold curves for rod vision and for cone vision as a function of wavelength of the test stimulus. The photopic visibility curve (cone vision) differs from the scotopic visibility curve (rod vision) in general level of radiant energy required to arouse sensation, in point of lowest threshold or peak sensitivity, and in extent of responsiveness to longer wavelengths. (After Chapanis, 1949.)

functional. The data for rod thresholds forming the *scotopic visibility curve* were taken at some distance from the fovea. The presence of cones at that locus was no problem since the testing values were well below cone threshold as the curves indicate. What would a subject's sensation be if we presented him with a spot of light of 500 mμ wavelength directed 10° from the fovea, and gradually increased it from well below threshold value? Since both rods and cones are present in that area of the retina, we see from Figure 9.4 that the rods would be activated first, this wavelength actually being very near their peak sensitivity. The figure also shows that the intensity of the test light would have to be increased by about two log units, a hundredfold increase in luminance, before the activation of the cones began. Inspection of the curves reveals that the rods are much more sensitive than the cones for all wavelengths below 600 mμ. At about 650 mμ, however, there is not much difference in their sensitivities, and in the region of 700 mμ and beyond, the rods are generally considered unresponsive.

EXAMPLE OF A THRESHOLD DETERMINANT. In determinations of the threshold, the actual luminance values obtained depend on a number of factors in the experiment. For example, lower values are obtained when the test stimulus has a greater area. This effect is considered due to the spatial summation of activity from areas of the retina that are proximal to each other with a resulting augmentation of the neural signals that give rise to the detection of the test light. Riopelle and Chow (1953) performed an experiment to determine whether this lowering of the threshold with an increase in stimulus area would be found to be the same functional relationship for different portions of the retina. They used test stimuli which varied in size from 7 to 57 min of visual angle subtended, applying this series of ten stimuli to each of five points located at different distances above the fovea. These points tested ranged from 4 to 48° above the fovea. The investigators found that the curves relating threshold to stimulus area were of the same form for each point tested.

ADAPTATION. The eye is capable of functioning in a wide range of light intensities, from the absolute rod threshold where it is responsive to an intensity of less than a millionth of a millilambert to the upper limit of tolerance for very bright light at about 16,000 mL. The increase from threshold to upper limit, then, is more than a ten billionfold change in intensity. The eye has to adapt to the illuminance impinging on it in order to function over so great a range. The constriction or dilation of the pupil can change retinal illuminance by a factor of sixteen. The remainder of the adaptive process takes place in the cones and the rods.

The retinal adaptive processes, either light adaptation or dark adaptation, require some time to bring the eye to an optimal functioning point. It is the temporal course of adaptation, particularly to darkness, that has been studied extensively. Adaptation to light appears to take place in just a minute or so after the eye encounters a higher intensity value. Dark adaptation, which is actually a decline in threshold or an increase in sensitivity as the eye remains in darkness, requires about 20 min to approach completion and often shows a slow change even beyond that interval.

Figure 9.5 shows a family of dark adaptation curves. The experi-

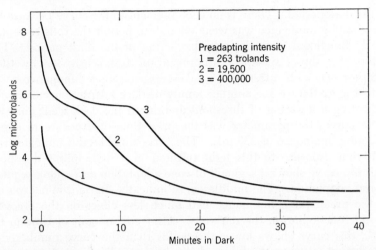

Fig. 9.5. Dark adaptation curves showing declining absolute visual threshold as a function of time in the dark, with intensity of the 2 min of preadapting light as the parameter differentiating the three curves. (After Hecht, Haig, and Chase, 1937.)

mental parameter which differentiated the curves was the intensity of the preadapting light to which the eye was exposed for 2 min just prior to beginning the period in the dark. Absolute threshold determinations were made after different intervals in the dark in order to obtain these curves. We see that the preadapting intensity had a great effect on the level of the absolute threshold during the whole period of dark adaptation. The curve numbered 3 shows that after the most intense prior stimulation, the threshold was at a high point. The first segment of this curve indicates that the cones increased in sensitivity from the very first moment of darkness, leveling off at the absolute cone threshold after about 10 min in the dark. After about 12 min of dark adaptation the rods recovered enough from their previous impairment of responsiveness by the preadapting light to continue the lowering of the threshold for a long period of time. The middle curve of the figure shows cone adaptation first and then rod adaptation beginning after about 5 or 6 min in the dark. This threshold curve numbered 2 indicates greater sensitivity or lower threshold throughout the plotted course of dark adaptation when compared with the curve numbered 3. The lesser preadapting intensity permitted speedier recovery of sensitivity. The lowest curve in the figure indicates a sensitivity of the rods from the very beginning of the dark period. There is no cone segment to the curve because the preadapting luminance was weak enough to permit the rods to remain partly functional from the very beginning of the dark period. This curve also shows speediest attainment of full sensitivity by these receptor elements after the weakest preadapting luminance.

In Figure 9.6 we see another family of dark adaptation curves also indicating a lowering of threshold as time in the dark went on. For these curves the parameter was the prior time of exposure to a preadapting luminance of 333 mL. The curve numbered 3 indicates that a 10-min exposure to this light resulted in a high initial threshold. This top curve shows a segment of cone adaptation and a long segment of rod adaptation. The middle curve indicates that a 2-min exposure to the preadapting luminance had much less effect on the recovery of rod functioning in the darkness. After any amount of time in the dark, this curve shows lower thresholds than the curve numbered 3. The lowest curve in the figure shows how rapidly the rods recovered their sensitivity when the preadapting exposure to light had been brief, only 10 sec. Absolute rod threshold is seen in the curve numbered 1 to be approached in less than 10 min following this short exposure to the light.

The phenomenon of dark adaptation is difficult to describe in words, so our resorting to the plotting of curves like those in Figures 9.5 and 9.6 would seem to be an excellent way of describing the course of

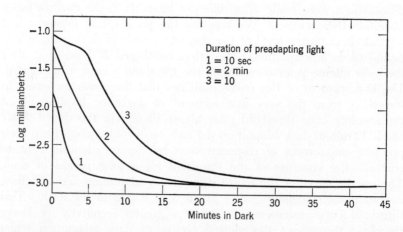

Fig. 9.6. Dark adaptation curves showing declining absolute visual threshold as a function of time in the dark with duration of exposure to a 333 mL preadapting light as the parameter differentiating the three curves. (After Wald and Clark, 1937.)

the process in time. Such curves may be said to define the temporal change in threshold, however, only when they are augmented by a description of the way in which the data were gathered. The operational definition of the process, in other words, requires specification of numerous facts about the experimental conditions.

The need for stating how the plotted values were obtained is highlighted by the fact that the shape of dark adaptations curves can be materially affected by changes in the locus and size of the retinal area tested, and the intensity and duration of the preadapting light. If the test light were limited to a 3° area located at the fovea, we would obtain only the first portion of the dark adaptation curve since there are no rods in that locus to carry the threshold lower than the cone threshold. As to size of the test stimulus, it is found that both portions of the dark adaptation curve drop more sharply and to lower values if the test stimulus is increased in size from about 3 to about 20° or more of subtended visual angle. If the preadapting light field is very weak, then the cone adaptation, represented in the first segment of the curves numbered 2 and 3 in Figure 9.5, does not appear. The rod adaptation curve, now assuming we are stimulating a retinal area where rods as well as cones are present, drops more steeply than it does after strong preadapting intensities, as the curve numbered 1 in the same figure shows. This sharper drop in the dark adaptation curve also occurs if briefer exposure to the preadapting field has taken place, as we saw in Figure 9.6. The principle represented in the families of curves we examined is that rod recovery is faster if the impairment of rod function has been made minimal by either a low intensity or brief exposure of the preadapting illuminance.

INTERSENSORY EFFECTS AND DARK ADAPTATION. Some interesting experiments on dark adaptation were performed by Chapanis, Rouse, and Schachter (1949) to check claims that had been made to the effect that various kinds of nonvisual stimulation could affect the course of dark adaptation and even lower the threshold values ultimately attained. In one experiment subjects listened to a tone, or smelled oil of wintergreen, or took light exercise during the course of dark adaptation, measurements of their thresholds being taken repeatedly over the course of 40 min in the dark. These different forms of stimulation were found to have no demonstrable effect on the course of dark adaptation or the level of sensitivity attained. An experiment with negative results is by no means to be thought of as a valueless one. The findings in these carefully conducted studies raise serious questions about the earlier claims for intersensory effects on dark adaptation. Where contradictory findings are reported we must depend on further research to resolve the issues.

Visual Research Techniques

A primary technical problem in experimentation on vision is the exercise of strict control over stimulation. At this point, we shall cite some of the general ways of controlling various important dimensions of visual stimuli, including retinal illuminance, size of stimulus, retinal locus of stimulation, duration of stimulation, and retinal state induced by prior illumination.

CONTROLLING LUMINANCE. If we are engaged in psychophysical research aimed at the determination of brightness thresholds, then control over the luminance of the test stimulus is obviously of paramount importance. Even in attacking other problems, however, with luminances well above threshold, it is important to specify and control light intensity. Techniques for the control of luminosity naturally vary in their suitability for attacking different problems. Some of those we mention are cited for their ease of employment even though they contain flaws which preclude their use in serious work demanding great rigor in the specification and control of the light stimulus.

One way to control the luminous intensity of an incandescent source is to vary the applied voltage with a resultant variation in light intensity; one drawback of this method is that it alters the spectral distribution of the light produced. Another convenient method for varying the illuminance of a test surface or the luminance transmittance of a translucent test stimulus is to utilize the inverse square law by moving the light source toward and away from the surface being viewed. A difficulty here is that the law may not strictly apply because of reflectance from nearby surfaces and also that the lamp which may be used will not be the point source that is theoretically required.

Another class of techniques for controlling light intensity calls for interposing something in the light path between the source and the eye, usually between the source and a transilluminated surface of high diffusing quality like flashed opal glass. One method is to interpose a sectored disk rotating at high speed in the light beam. Openings in the disk allow the light to pass through intermittently. At a high rate of intermittence, the effect is one of a steady light of lessened intensity. Another way of reducing the intensity of a light beam is to insert into it one or more neutral density filters. The per cent of light transmitted by these is specified so that their use in combination can often achieve a desired value. They are termed neutral to indicate that their transmission characteristics do not alter the spectral composition of the light passing through. A circular filter of regularly graded density is called an *optical wedge*. By rotating it in the path of a light beam we can obtain a continuous range of luminous transmittance. The optical wedge is often used in conjunction with one or more neutral density filters to provide desired light intensity.

The luminance of a source or test stimulus is often not so important as the retinal illuminance. Since pupillary dilation serves to let more light in when intensity is low, retinal illuminance in such a circumstance is controlled by providing an artificial pupil, a viewing aperture with a small fixed diameter. In addition to retinal illuminance, the adaptive state of the rods and cones needs to be considered. This is often controlled by letting the eye become completely dark adapted before testing or else specifying the intensity and duration of a preadapting field which is viewed prior to the presentation of the test stimulus.

SPECIFYING STIMULUS SIZE. The size of a test stimulus employed in visual research is usually specified in terms of the visual angle it subtends. It is often useful to state the viewing distance and whether it was measured from the corneal surface or elsewhere. An important reason for specifying size of stimulus is that brightness varies with the size of small stimuli. That is, larger stimuli appear brighter even for the same retinal illuminance. The effect is considered due to a spatial summation deriving from the neural interconnections in the retina. Hanes (1951) investigated this relationship of brightness to stimulus size for stimuli ranging from 9 to 144 min of visual angle and for luminances ranging from 0.1 to 100 mL. For 0.1 and 1.0 mL, brightness increased as size increased. For 10 mL the functional relationship differed somewhat, with brightness decreasing as size increased from 9 to 50 min and then increasing as stimulus size increased to greater values. This finding suggests caution in generalizing about visual functional relationships and emphasizes the need to explore them empirically with careful manipulation of relevant variables over a wide range.

SPECIFYING RETINAL LOCATION. Specifying the retinal location of a point of stimulation is necessary in view of what we know of the distribution of rods and cones over the retinal surface. The specification is usually made in terms of visual angle from the center of the fovea, often measured along the horizontal nasal or temporal meridians or perhaps up or down on a vertical meridian passing through the fovea. The fovea is a convenient reference because the image of any point fixated falls upon it. Thus, the visual angle on the retina from fovea to image point is the same in size as the angle formed in space by the fixation point, the eye and the test stimulus. The angular direction is reversed, of course, by the inverting of the image optically. Thus, points in the upper half of the visual field impinge on the lower part of the retina and vice versa. Points in the temporal portion of the field fall on the nasal half of the retina and vice versa. It is obviously important to use terms like "nasal" and "temporal" with careful reference to either visual field or to the retina.

DURATION OF STIMULATION. When visual capacities are explored by means of very brief test flashes of light, the duration of such stimulation is an important determiner of indices of visual performance such as the absolute threshold. The threshold will not be found as low in luminance value if the test flash is extremely brief. The effective brightness of a test flash at threshold levels is a product of its luminance and its duration, these two factors being reciprocally contributory to the sensory effect as indicated in the formulation that a constant threshold effect, K, is achieved by the product of retinal illuminance, I, and duration of flash, t. $K = I \times t$, known as the Bunsen-Roscoe law, is considered to hold for small test areas, less than $1°$, and for flashes briefer than 50 msec at threshold intensity.

PREADAPTATION. No matter how carefully we control the presentation of a test stimulus we have not exerted adequate precautions unless we have also controlled the recent history of the retina being stimulated. Exposure to light alters the chemical state of the retina, the modification being dependent on the intensity of the light and its duration. This alteration then affects the responsiveness of the retina to subsequent illumination. These facts were illustrated by the dark adaptation curves of Figures 9.5 and 9.6.

VISUAL ACUITY

The ability to detect fine spatial detail in the visual field is termed *visual acuity*. Various acuity targets like letters of the alphabet or broken circles are presented in different sizes and at different distances, the subject's task being to detect a small critical detail like the break in the circle. The visual acuity rating is the reciprocal of the visual angle in minutes of arc subtended by this just detectable detail. If the break in the circle, for example, subtended 2 min of arc, the acuity rating would be 0.5, the reciprocal of 2.0. An acuity rating of 1.0, corresponding to the detection of a detail subtending 1 min of arc, is considered to be "normal," but a number of factors need to be specified before this becomes particularly meaningful.

Acuity Targets

Among the types of acuity targets that have been employed are fine wires viewed against an illuminated background, gratings through which light is directed at the eye, and pairs of parallel bars or rectangles. Samples of the latter type of acuity target are shown in Figure 9.7 together with the Landolt ring, as the broken circle is usually called. The bars are shown in two different contrasts, white on black as well as black on white, since it has been found that this is a determinant of the detectability of the separation between them which is the detail actually used in measuring acuity. For the Landolt ring it is conventional to have the break or separation equal to one-fifth the outside diameter of the ring. Most geometrical types of acuity targets may be considered superior to the alphabet letters used, for example, on the Snellen eye chart. The letters are perceptible or distinguishable on the basis of several different cues rather than a single detail as is desirable for a good operational definition of acuity.

Although the acuity rating is defined in terms of subtended visual angle and should therefore be independent of viewing distance, it has been found to differ with the distance from eye to target for some individuals. Individual differences in accommodation for near viewing are thought to account for this. At distances beyond 20 ft

Fig. 9.7. Geometrical targets for measuring visual acuity. The critical details to be detected are the space between the parallel rectangles and the break in the Landolt ring. By detecting the detail a subject can state the orientation of the bars, horizontal or vertical, or of the ring. His acuity rating is computed as described in the text.

this should pose no problem. For experimental work at nearer distances it is well to specify all dimensions of the viewing situation.

FLICKER AND FUSION

Some facts of both theoretical and practical importance are found in the visual phenomena that arise when the eye is intermittently stimulated by light. Such stimulation may be presented by means of the flashing of a stroboscopic light, by the interruption of a beam of light by a rotating sectored disk of alternate open and opaque sectors (such a disk being termed an *episcotister*), or by reflecting light from alternate black and white sectors of a rotating disk.

Critical Flicker Frequency

How an intermittent light appears to the eye depends primarily on the *rate* of intermittence, that is, the rate at which the light stimulation and the dark periods alternate. At low rates of intermittence the light and dark phases will be experienced separately, the stimulus being seen as flickering. The apparent rate of flicker does not necessarily correspond to the external rate of intermittence, however; any departure from correspondence is believed due to response characteristics of the visual system.

As the rate of stimulus intermittence is increased, a point will be reached at which the two phases of stimulation fuse to yield a sensation of steady light, of lower brightness than that of the light phase of the stimulus. This particular frequency of light-dark alternations per second is called the *critical flicker frequency*, often abbreviated *cff* or *CFF*. This abbreviation is sometimes interpreted to mean "critical fusion frequency" or "critical flicker fusion." No matter what the verbal phrase, the phenomenon that identifies this particular frequency is the dividing point between experienced flicker and experienced fusion into a steady state.

There are a number of determinants of the cff. Among them are luminance of the light phase and its contrast with the dark phase, the area of the test stimulus, and the part of the retina that is stimulated. The central part of the retina yields fusion at a lower rate of intermittence than the peripheral retina when the test stimulus area is large; when a small test stimulus is used, the fovea requires higher rates for fusion than does the periphery. Another factor in determining the cff is the ratio of the duration of the light phase to the length of the total cycle in the intermittent stimulation. The dependence of cff on light-dark ratio, abbreviated LDR, is a complex one. Here we may merely note that in most experiments on flicker and fusion the LDR is set at .50, that is, with the light period comprising exactly half the total cycle and the dark period the other half.

The Talbot-Plateau Law

At any rate of intermittence above the cff the effective luminance of the steady-appearing stimulus is found to be equivalent to a weighted average of the luminances of the light and dark phases of the stimulus. If the LDR is .50, the weights of the light and dark phases are equal and the effective luminance would be the average of the two luminances. If the dark phase is actually an interruption of the light and the LDR is .50, the average luminance for the intermittent stimulus is exactly half that of the light phase. This effect would be produced by interrupting the light by rotating in its path an episcotister disk whose open sectors were equal in angular size to its opaque sectors. The formula we are applying here is known as the Talbot-Plateau law, after two early investigators who independently worked it out.

CONTROLLING LUMINANCE WITH THE TALBOT-PLATEAU LAW. Suppose that photometric measurement has revealed that a light source has a luminance of 15 mL and that we wish to have a value of precisely 10 mL for experimental purposes. The Talbot-Plateau law tells us that we will achieve the desired resultant luminance if we average the 15 mL value with a zero value, weighting them 2 to 1, respectively. We multiply each luminance value by its weight and then divide by the number of weights to get the average: $\dfrac{2 \cdot 15 + 1 \cdot 0}{3} = 10$. Since the weights indicate the relative durations of the light and dark phases of the intermittent stimulation, we see that we need a light phase that is twice as long as the dark phase. We can achieve this by constructing an episcotister disk with open sectors totaling 240° and opaque sectors totaling 120°. When this disk is rotated above cff in the optical pathway between the 15 mL stimulus and the eye, the LDR of .67 will reduce the effective luminance to 10 mL. You can see that an episcotister disk constructed with sectors that are adjustable is a useful device for obtaining any luminance desired by proper manipulation of the light-dark ratio from some source of greater luminous intensity.

EFFECTIVE LUMINOUS REFLECTANCE. If we rotate a black and white sectored disk at a rate above the cff, we may calculate the effective luminous reflectance of the resulting gray by applying the Talbot-

Plateau formula. In this application we need to consider the reflectance value of the black sector since it does not represent a perfectly dark phase in the intermittent stimulation. The luminances of the black and the white sectors must each be weighted by their respective angular sizes since these are equivalent to the durations of the light and dark phases that reach the eye from any portion of the rapidly spinning disk. As an example consider a disk with a 90° black sector and a 270° white sector, giving the LDR of .75. Suppose that the white sector has a reflectance of 94 mL and that the black has reflectant value of 6 mL; the formula works out as follows:

$$\frac{3 \cdot 94 + 1 \cdot 6}{4} = 72 \text{ mL for the effective luminous reflectance.}$$

FUNDAMENTALS OF COLOR VISION

Although we have neglected it to this point we need to turn our attention to the sensing of hue and the manipulation of the spectral composition of light in research on vision. We previously identified energy level and the distribution of wavelengths as important specifications of light. We may now pair these with the quantitative and qualitative aspects of visual sensation to which they contribute. Table 9.1 indicates the correspondence of visual sensory attributes

TABLE 9.1

Relationships between Characteristics of Light and Basic Attributes of Visual Sensation

Characteristics of Light	Basic Attributes of Visual Sensation
1. Luminous energy level	1. Brightness
(a) Luminance	
(b) Illuminance	
(c) Luminous reflectance	
(d) Luminous transmittance	
2. Dominant wavelength	2. Hue
3. Purity of spectral composition	3. Saturation

to the characteristics of the light which is usually associated with their arousal. We have mentioned brightness before as the quantitative sensing of the light energy level or luminance value. We saw of course that the sensation aroused is greatly dependent upon the state of adaptation of the eye as well as on the impinging energy value. The table indicates that hue and saturation depend on the spectral composition of the light.

Chromatic and Achromatic Colors

Hue and *saturation* which are attributes of *chromatic* visual sensation need to be discussed in their relation to the spectral composition of light. By chromatic vision we mean the sensing of colors like blue and red as opposed to white and gray. It is now customary to think of all vision as color vision, the term "color" having been broadened to take in whites and grays. A distinction is still maintained by applying the term chromatic vision to the sensing of hues like green and yellow and using an opposed term, achromatic vision, to apply to the sensing of gray and white. Notice that the word hue is the generic term now applied to what are commonly called colors. Saturation is the qualitative intensity of a hue, the redness of a red or the greenness of a green. A so-called deep red is a highly saturated red; a pink is a desaturated red.

Brightness is an aspect of both chromatic and achromatic sensation. We can have blues and reds of different brightnesses, essentially independent of their saturation. We can also have grays of greater or lesser brightness, commonly called lighter or darker grays. Being achromatic or hueless, whites and grays do not differ qualitatively but only in their brightness value. As a sensation, brightness depends on the level of retinal illuminance among other things.

Modes of Appearance of Colors

A group of perceptions that are closely related to sensations are the modes of appearance that colors may have. Most of our color experience comes from light that has been reflected from surfaces and we perceive the hues as being an inherent part of those surfaces; such percepts are known as *surface colors*. When we look at the sky, however, we do not see a blue surface; the space we are regarding seems to be permeated with the color, and this type of percept is called a *field color*. In some laboratory experiments we may be asked to fixate an aperture in a screen while some light source is located beyond the screen, perhaps with colored filters as part of a stimulus system. The hue produced may seem to fill the aperture that we are viewing, the color seemingly located in the same plane as the screen. Such a percept is called an *aperture color*. We see, then, that in addition to the usual sensory aspects of color—brightness, hue, and saturation—we may have perceptual aspects as well, with an interpretive quality about them.

Sensations Mediated by Rods and Cones

In very dim illumination, below the threshold for activating the cones, only white, gray, and black images are experienced. The mediators of this scotopic vision, the rods, do not give rise to any sensations of hue even though they are differentially sensitive to wavelength as their spectral sensitivity curve in Figure 9.4 showed. Only cone vision is chromatic, giving rise to sensations of hue; rod vision is achromatic, yielding hueless visual experience. We can now give a more complete answer to our question (p. 237) regarding a person's sensations if a light of 500 mμ wavelength impinging 10° from the fovea were gradually increased in intensity from below threshold. After its luminosity was equal to the rod threshold it would be seen as a white light, becoming gradually brighter as luminosity increased but evidencing no hue at first. Only after the cone threshold was reached would the subject begin to experience the green hue associated in cone functioning, or photopic vision, with that wavelength of light. The difference in luminosity values between the rod threshold and the cone threshold is known as the *photochromatic interval*. The area between the scotopic and the photopic sensitivity curves in Figure 9.4 is thus a representation of the changing values of the photochromatic interval as we proceed along the spectrum. You can see that the interval is greatest for the shorter wavelengths. The different sensitivity curves for the two types of receptor elements are apparently determined by the two kinds of photosensitive materials they contain, rhodopsin in the rods and iodopsin in the cones.

Chromatic Sensation

Hue and saturation correspond to the spectral composition of the light that reaches the eye. Because of the selective transmittance of a filter or the selective reflectance of a surface, the energy reaching the eye may be unevenly distributed among the various wavelengths with a particular band of values predominant. It is usually the predominant wavelength in the mixture that determines the hue that is experienced. If you will look again at Figure 9.2, you will see that the spectral distributions represented for certain parts of the flag are peaked at certain wavelengths. The peak at the longest visible wavelengths arouses the sensation of red, whereas the peak at about

450 mµ gives rise to blue. The colors of the spectrum thus correspond to particular bands of wavelengths. The hues of the familiar listing, red, orange, yellow, green, blue, and violet, are arranged in order from the longest to the shortest wavelengths.

The Color Circle

If we space these hues appropriately around the perimeter of a circle we may obtain an arrangement known as a *color circle,* a convenient schema for describing certain facts about color. Figure 9.8 shows a color circle representing all the spectral hues plus a commonly experienced nonspectral hue, purple. Also in the nonspectral region is the red usually considered psychologically "pure." The greatest saturation of any hue may be considered to lie on the circumference of the circle. As we move in along any radius we continually encounter the same hue but in ever-decreasing saturation. This is illustrated by the locations of deep pink and pale pink inside the circle. When the center of the circle is reached, the desaturation is complete so that only an achromatic gray or white is represented

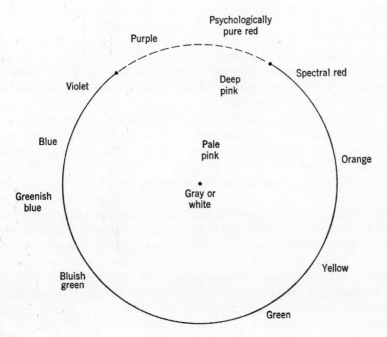

Fig. 9.8. The color circle—a schematic representation of certain facts about colors.

there. A color circle includes all the hues at all degrees of saturation, but it is conventionally considered to represent only one level of brightness. To incorporate all of color experience in our schema we need only to consider that a great number of color circles are stacked one on the other, ranging upward from the lowest to the greatest brightness.

Additive Color Mixture Principles

The color circle is a convenience in remembering the principles of additive color mixture and the principle of complementaries. The mixture principle is that the addition of any two hues will result in a hue that is intermediate in its position on the circle and of lesser saturation than the hues employed in the mixture. The additive mixture of blue and green, for example, results in a blue-green or aqua, whereas a mixture of red and green gives yellow. We are speaking here of the *additive* mixing of light of different predominant wavelengths and not of the mixing of paints or pigments which is called *subtractive* mixture. The principle of complementaries states that a mixture of hues that are diametrically opposite on the color circle will result in white or gray. The hues complement each other so perfectly that they yield an achromatic sensation. If two hues are mixed that are almost complementary, the mixture will be greatly desaturated but will not actually be achromatic.

COMPLEMENTARIES. Although our usual sensation of white is aroused by light containing about equal proportions of all the wavelengths in the spectrum, the principle of complementaries must be understood to mean that a similar experience is stimulated by a mixture of just two complementary wavelengths in proper proportions. Such pairs of wavelengths include 671 and 493 mμ, which would appear red and blue-green, respectively, when viewed separately. Blue and yellow, represented by wavelengths of 477 and 579 mμ, respectively, are also complementaries. Wavelengths up to 492 mμ have their complementaries beyond 568 mμ in the visible spectrum. Wavelengths between 492 and 568 mμ do not have any complementary wavelength. These hues, the greens, have as their complementaries various purple hues which are attained only by mixing two spectral hues, a red and a blue. In passing we may note that a hue that has a fundamental red appearance, one of the so-called psychological primaries, is actually a nonspectral hue attained by adding a little violet to a spectral red. The spectral red alone is too yellowish to be judged a real red. The other psychological primaries, blue, green and yellow, correspond to wavelengths of about 470, 500, and 570 mμ, respectively.

TRISTIMULUS MIXTURE. Besides the principles of two-color additive mixture which we have been discussing, there is an important principle of tristimulus mixture. It is that white may be achieved by the additive mixture, in proper proportions of luminance, of any three wavelengths provided that one is selected from the violet-blue region of the spectrum, one from the green region, and one from the red region. Attaining white by the tristimulus method may be conceptualized in terms of the mixture of complementary hues. For example, if we are given a particular wavelength in the red region, we mix the blue and the green to obtain the blue-green hue that is the complementary of the given red. The tristimulus mixture thus appears to reduce to a mixing of just two hues. However, the principle of tristimulus mixture does not impose the rigid specification upon the particular wavelengths employed that we mentioned as a requirement in the principle of complementaries.

An additional feature of tristimulus mixture, besides its ability to yield white, is that any hue whatsoever may be attained by mixing in required proportion just three wavelengths, each one chosen from one of the three regions of the spectrum. These regions of the spectrum thus provide us with physical primaries, one that is violet or blue, one that is green, and one that is a red with a yellowish tinge to it. It is important to note that none of these primaries is defined with reference to a specific wavelength. Various sets of primaries might be selected that would demonstrate the principle of tristimulus mixture.

COLOR SPECIFICATION

Color science finds in the tristimulus mixture principle more than just an interesting phenomenon. With every possible hue and saturation specifiable in terms of the proportionate mixture of three primaries, you can see how conveniently a color may be described by stating the proportions of the three primaries in a mixture that matches the particular color. A particular blue-green, for example, might be specified by the equation, $BG = .06R + .31G + .63B$, where R, G, and B represent specified primaries and their coefficients indicate the proportion of each one required in the mixture to match the blue-green. Such primaries were specified by the International Commission on Illumination in order to permit a conventional method for giving color specifications. With reference to these I.C.I. primaries it is possible to write an equation for any color: $X = xR + yG + zB$. The equation we used to specify the blue-green in our example was of this precise form, with particular coefficients specified for the proportions of the primaries in the mixture. Since the coefficients in the three terms of the equation always sum to unity, the specification of any color is actually complete when the first two terms are given. Our sample blue-green is adequately identified by the equation $BG = .06R + .31G$. The coefficient indicating the proportion of the blue primary in the mixture, .63, is determined by the relationship, $x + y + z = 1$, and therefore need not be stated.

The I.C.I. Chromaticity Diagram

Since any hue, together with an indication of its purity, may be described by two coefficients, x and y, of the I.C.I. red and green primaries mixed with the I.C.I. blue to match the given hue, a single point on a two-dimensional plot can give a graphic representation of the color. Such a graph, called the *I.C.I. chromaticity diagram*, is shown in Figure 9.9. Along the abscissa is scaled the coefficient, x, indicating the proportion of the red component in any matching mixture. The scale for the green coefficient, y, forms the ordinate of the graph. The solid curved line in the diagram represents the locus of points representing the colors of the spectrum. The violet end of the visible spectrum is at the lower left of the diagram where the wavelength 400 mμ is shown. The spectral greens occupy the top portion of the curve, whereas the red end of the spectrum is represented at the right of the chromaticity diagram as indicated by the notation, 700 mμ, at the long wavelength end of the visible spectrum. The straight line connecting this point to the other end point of the spectral curve at 400 mμ is the locus of points representing the nonspectral reds and purples. This straight line and the spectral curve above it may be considered to form a sort of distorted color circle since all of the hues are arranged in order around the perimeter. The roughly triangular area bounded by these lines includes all the points which represent the characteristics—the hue and the purity—of any color that can be achieved with spectral stimuli. The I.C.I. chromaticity diagram thus represents a convenient way of representing the chromatic aspects of any color likely to be used as a stimulus in an experiment.

THE I.C.I. STANDARD OBSERVER. The chromaticity diagram of Figure 9.9 may be considered to be a "portrait" of the I.C.I. *standard observer*.

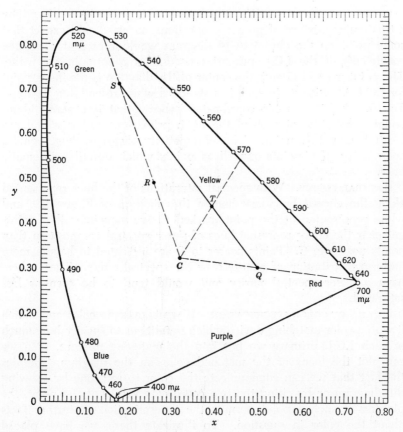

Fig. 9.9. The I.C.I. chromaticity diagram, used in specifying illuminants and colors and in predicting the results of additive color mixtures. (After Judd, 1951.)

This construct, the standard observer, represents international agreement on particular empirical data on color-mixing obtained with representative subjects and specified primaries. The chromaticity diagram assumes these primaries as the ones being mixed and indicates the proportions of the primaries needed by the standard observer, actually a particular set of experimental subjects, to match the different spectral hues and the purples. Once the primaries had been agreed upon and the locus of these basic hues had been plotted, the diagram became the reference for further indexing of hues by other research workers. The earlier psychophysical work had been used to forge a very useful tool for subsequent investigations.

WHITE ILLUMINANTS. We stated that white may be achieved by a tristimulus mixture of proper proportions, so we should expect that some point on the chromaticity diagram would represent the three coefficients of the I.C.I. primaries needed in a formula for white. The point marked C near the center of the diagram is the index point for I.C.I. *Illuminant C* which is a standard white resembling daylight. You see that its graphic coordinates indicate that it contains about equal proportions of each of the I.C.I. primaries. Other whites are located near this point. The chromaticity diagram thus includes achromatic color points as well as points which describe chromatic hues.

SPECTRAL PURITY. With spectral saturations of the hues represented along the curved boundary line in the diagram of Figure 9.9, and white represented at the point marked C, we may infer that points out near the curve represent hues of purer spectral composition than points nearer to C. Points nearer to C are indicated to have a more uniform distribution of energy over the spectral range. These, then, have a lesser spectral purity and would tend to be seen as less saturated.

DETAILS OF COLOR SPECIFICATION. If we take some color and match it with a color-matching device which permits us to specify how much of each I.C.I. primary we put into the matching mixture, then we can plot the locus of the matched color on the diagram. Besides the fact that we can communicate the color to someone by showing the diagram or by citing the two coordinate values of the point, the plotting of such a point permits the determination of further facts about the color in question. To illustrate these, we have placed the points marked Q, R, and S in the diagram of Figure 9.9. These points represent three different colors for which the I.C.I. primary proportions have been determined. We see that color Q was matched by proportions .50, .30, and .20 of the I.C.I. red, green, and blue, respectively. For color R the corresponding coefficients were .26, .49, and .25, whereas for color S they were .18, .71, and .11. The straight dotted line drawn from Illuminant C through the point representing any color intersects the boundary curve at a point that represents the dominant wavelength of the color being described. To indicate the purity of the color in question we determine how far its index point is from white and then express this distance as a per cent of the total distance from white to the dominant wavelength of the color. For example, we note that the dotted line that passes from C through Q intersects the boundary at 670 mμ, indicating the dominant wavelength in color Q to be a spectral red. Q is located over four-tenths of the way out from C along this dotted line and it is calculated to have a spectral purity of about 45 per cent. Looking at points R and S we see that they fall on the same straight line drawn from C to the perimeter and therefore they have the same dominant wavelength, 528 mμ, corresponding to a green. R and S differ in their purity, however, with R having a value of 33 per cent and S 75 per cent. Thus, S would appear to be a more saturated green than R would seem to be.

SPECIFYING PURPLES. Recalling that the heavy straight line boundary at the bottom of the enclosed space represents the purples, we may note that if a color point were located below C in the diagram a dotted line from C drawn through that point would be likely to indicate the dominant hue to be a purple with no direct spectral wavelength specified. The convention in such a case is to extend the dotted line upward until it intersects the spectral boundary at some point. By determining the wavelength of this spectral green and writing it with a c after it to stand for "complementary," we have indicated that the dominant hue is the complementary of a particular spectral wavelength. This determination, incidentally, illustrates another fact about the chromaticity diagram—that complementary hues lie at the opposite poles of straight lines drawn through the point representing white.

PREDICTING ADDITIVE MIXTURES. One more illustration of the usefulness of a standard chromaticity diagram is also given in Figure 9.9. It can be employed to predict the result of the additive mixing of any two colors. The prediction is based on an extremely simple graphic procedure. Suppose we want to predict the outcome of mixing Q and S in certain proportions. We simply connect those two points in the diagram with a straight line segment. All colors resulting from a mixture of these two will fall somewhere on this line, depending on the proportions of Q and S that went into the mixture. If we want to predict the outcome of mixing with two parts of Q with one part of S, we would locate the mixture point nearer to the preponderant constituent, Q. In fact, it would be located one-third of the distance from Q to S, as indicated at T in the diagram. The rule for predicting the result of a two-color mix in any proportion, then, is to locate a point on the connecting line whose distance from each of the constituent points is inversely proportional to their proportions in the mixture. This rule locates the mixture point nearer to the greater contributing color in the diagram. Once the mixture has been located, we may use the diagram to determine its dominant wavelength and its purity by drawing a line, as shown in Figure 9.9, from the locus of the illuminant, C, through the mixture point, T. In our example, this leads to the prediction of a dominant wavelength of 572 mμ, indicating a yellow resultant when Q and S are mixed in the indicated proportions. The proportionate distance of T from C along this radial line gives us a prediction of the purity of the yellow, about 52 per cent in our example.

COLOR VISION PHENOMENA

Despite the fact that the realm of color is a highly subjective one, a number of laboratory approaches have revealed some solid facts about it. We have already cited the principles of color mixture and indicated the progress that has been made in standardizing color specifications. These mixture principles, and a number of other color phenomena, provide topics for student investigation that give us an excellent means for getting better acquainted with visual research.

Color Mixture Techniques

We have indicated that the principles of color mixture that we have discussed are those which apply to the additive mixing of different wavelengths. To experiment with additive mixture, then, we need to obtain samples of light composed of different dominant wavelengths and to mix these samples as they stimulate the eye. A direct approach to our problem is to obtain two light sources, like slide projectors, and two filters of different colors, like a red and a green Wratten filter. By aiming the two projectors at the same white screen and putting one filter in the beam of each, we are effectively mixing the two different wavelength bands which these filters transmit. As we view the screen, our eye is stimulated by the mixed light. The resultant hue that we experience may be anywhere between a red and a green in the spectral series, depending upon the relative amounts of light reaching the screen through each filter. This can be controlled for each projector beam separately, using any of the techniques we suggested for the control of luminance. However, our warning against varying lamp voltage to change luminous intensity is particularly to be stressed here since a variation in the color of either light source would affect the color mixture. In the demonstrations we are discussing, another feasible method of controlling the screen illuminance from each projector, and hence the relative proportions of the colors being mixed, is to put an adjustable camera aperture in each beam of light as it emerges from the projector. The stop settings of such a camera diaphragm provide a means of specifying the relative proportion of the constituent colors used.

With three projectors and red, blue, and green filters it is possible to demonstrate tristimulus mixture by projecting three overlapping circles of light on the screen, one coming through each filter. If some sort of luminance control is included in each of the three optical systems, it should be possible to show that white can be achieved by mixing three primaries in proper proportions. When white is perceived in the center of the cloverleaf of overlapping circles, it will be found that the mixture of each possible pair of colors has been adjusted to yield the complementary of the third color. In the outer portion of the pattern, where the circles of color overlap in pairs, we find that the mixture of each pair yields an intermediate hue that is the complementary of the third color. There will be a blue-green complementary of the red, a purple complementary of the green, and a yellow complementary of the blue.

THE COLOR WHEEL. Another way of verifying the principles of color mixture is to place different colored papers on a disk or *color wheel*. The overlapping sectors of different colors can be adjusted so that their angular proportions represent the proportional contribution that each color will make to the mixture. The mixture is achieved by spinning the disk at a high rate of speed with a motor. The spectral distribution of wavelengths reflected from each colored paper do not actually mix as the light travels from the disk to the eye. Light striking any portion of the retina on which the image of the disk falls is actually coming alternately from the two colored sectors of the disk, assuming just a two-color mixture. The retinal excitation resulting from light from one colored paper does not cease instantaneously when that sector of the disk gives way to the other colored sector. Instead, it persists and combines with the excitation aroused by the second color. As the disk whirls, the result of this process is a fusion of the two colors that is functionally equivalent to mixing the light reflected from the surface of each and sending the mixture steadily into the eye. The spinning disk of the color mixer will thus appear to have a surface of uniform color, the resultant of the mixture. By adjusting the angular proportions of the two colored sectors on the disk we can explore the range of intermediate hues attainable. We might also attempt to match some paper of "unknown" color to determine the proportions of its constituent hues. With most models of the color mixer it is necessary to stop the disk to adjust the colored papers that form the sectors. On more elaborate forms of the device this adjustment can be done while the disk is spinning, permitting greater facility in color matching.

Contrast

A visual phenomenon in which a portion of the visual field is changed in appearance as a result of stimulation in another part of the field is known as *contrast*. Laboratory studies have revealed a number of principles which are operative as this phenomenon is experienced. We shall mention a few of these which you may wish to verify for yourself.

A procedure which may be regarded as an operational definition of achromatic contrast is to place small samples of a medium gray paper upon backgrounds of white, light gray, dark gray, and black. The contrast effect will be experienced in the different surface brightnesses that the sample gray assumes when viewed against these different backgrounds. Against the white background the test patch of gray will appear darkest and it will also appear darker when seen against the light gray. Against the dark gray background the medium gray patch will appear lighter than "usual" and on the black it will appear lightest of all. The contrast principle seems to be that the background brightness induces an opposite or contrasting brightness in the test patch. For this reason, contrast effects are said to occur through *induction,* a term which is applied also to a somewhat different phenomenon associated with the blindspot.

Chromatic contrast may be studied by a procedure similar to the one just described for achromatic contrast. We may take samples of the same neutral gray and place them on red, blue, green, or yellow backgrounds of fairly high saturation. The achromatic gray test patch will now be seen as having a chromatic tinge to it which will be a hue that is complementary to the background. Viewed against red, the gray will be seen to have a blue-green tinge. Against blue it will appear slightly yellowish and against yellow it will seem to be a blue of very low purity, that is, having an appearance of extremely low saturation.

The phenomena we have described, both achromatic and chromatic, are examples of *simultaneous* contrast, the term indicating that different parts of the retina are simultaneously being stimulated by different illuminances or different chromaticities. This type of contrast effect is differentiated from *successive* contrast experienced when stimulation by some color has been preceded by the impingement of a different color on the same part of the retina, an afterimage effect which we shall discuss later.

When colored papers are used to demonstrate simultaneous contrast, the effect may be enhanced by placing a thin tissue paper over the test patch and background. Another way is to hold the stimulus papers so near to the eye that the edges of the test patch cannot be clearly perceived. Both these techniques weaken the objective perception of the test patch; such objective viewing seems to reduce simultaneous contrast. An additional principle of contrast is that it is best when the test area is small and the surrounding background is large. It has also been found that simultaneous chromatic contrast is greater when the background is of high purity. When the test patch is fairly large, the induced contrast effect is greatest near its edges.

Peripheral Hue Sensitivity

Peripheral portions of the retina vary with respect to their sensitivity to different wavelengths of the spectrum. We find that chromatic sensation is absent in the most peripheral portions of the visual field, presumably due to the reduced density of cones in the outer retina although the data on cone frequency do not correspond perfectly to findings on peripheral hue sensitivity. Exploration of the portion of the retina where chromatic sensitivity is present reveals that certain hues are sensed more peripherally than others. Blue and yellow, for example, are sensed farther from the fixation point than are red and green. These different areas of differential hue sensitivity are sometimes called the *color zones* of the retina.

The extent of the different hue-sensitive zones along any meridian of the retina is determined by exploring the corresponding meridian of the visual field with a stimulus patch of particular dominant wavelength. This is conveniently done by using a *retinal perimeter,* a device with a semicircular arc along which the test patch may be moved. At the center of the arc is a fixation point which the subject fixates steadily during the perimetry. He reports the hue of the test patch as soon as he senses it while the experimenter moves it slowly in along the arc toward the fixation point. With the arc calibrated in degrees from the fixation point, a direct indication of the outer limit of sensitivity for that hue is obtained, expressed in degrees from the fovea. It is commonly found that some hues are rather regularly misidentified as the test patch is moved inward, the correct hue being named only after the patch is moved farther in toward the fixation point.

The actual locus of correct hue identification along any meridian of the retina depends on a number of factors in the test situation. Besides the hue itself, other determinants of the identification point include the purity of the test patch, its luminance, and its degree of contrast with the background. If the test stimulus is only momentarily presented, its exposure time will also determine how peripherally the hue will be correctly sensed. Below a certain value, the area of the test patch also is a determinant of peripheral hue sensitivity measurements.

Binocular Rivalry and Fusion

Some interesting experiments can be done by using a stereoscope to present stimulus fields of different hues to the two eyes. A typical stimulus card might have a blue field to be viewed by one eye, with a green field for the other. If the two hues are this similar in dominant wavelength, the result will be *fusion*, a term applied to such binocular color mixing which yields a sensation that is intermediate in hue to the separate constituents—a blue-green resultant in our example.

If the hues presented separately to the two eyes are quite different in their dominant wavelength, the effect is chiefly one of *rivalry*, the sensing first of one of the hues and then the other. The alternate sensing of the two hues in rivalry may be interrupted occasionally by fleeting sensation of the hue that color mixing of the two separate hues would yield, that is, by a momentary fusion. For example, red and green would generally lead to rivalry, but with occasional fusion into yellow.

Where binocular rivalry of two hues is experienced, it is possible to chart the temporal course of the alternate sensations by having a subject press a key as long as he is sensing one of the hues and releasing the key while he is experiencing the other. The key may be wired to a magnetic marker which traces the alternations of the two phases of the rivalry on a kymograph tape. The key might operate a clock if it were desired merely to total the time occupied by one of the hue sensations during a given period of observation.

If red and green were placed in rivalry and it was found that the red dominated the rivalry by being sensed most of the time, it would be possible to increase the proportion of time that green was sensed by marking the green half of the stereoscope card with a penciled fixation point. Such a fixation point seems to lend potency in the hue rivalry to the eye for which it is provided.

Hue Adaptation

With chromatic sensation arising from essentially the same sort of physiological processes as vision in general, we might expect to find that the phenomenon of adaptation might occur for hue as well as for brightness. A rather unique experiment by Hochberg, Triebel, and Seaman (1951) was undertaken to see if complete adaptation to a chromatic stimulus could be achieved so that only achromatic experience would remain after adaptation to a continuous colored light. Eyecaps made from halves of table tennis balls were taped over the eyes of the subjects. These were then flooded with either red or green light obtained by passing the beam of a projector through an appropriate filter. Under continuing red illuminance five out of six subjects reported within 3 min that the initial red sensation had given way to a total disappearance of hue. Under the steady green light all subjects attained an achromatic state in 6 min or less. Since the subjects did not know the nature of the study, most of them were confident that the experimenter had been changing the illumination during the test session. Trying some of the numerous possibilities for varying spectral composition of the stimulus, for presenting the light intermittently and for treating each eye in a different fashion, the investigators have shown that the method of flooding the total visual field with uniform illumination may be a technique of considerable potential for exploring color vision.

AFTERIMAGES

With the stress that we place on vision as a psychophysical process one might suppose that we are interested in the functioning of the visual system only while it is undergoing physical stimulation. We can easily show, however, that visual experience outlasts the stimulation that initiates it. To various sensations that occur after the termination of the physical stimulus we give the name *afterimages*. A study of afterimages, both achromatic and chromatic, may yield additional information about the visual sense.

Achromatic Afterimages

Like other visual phenomena we have discussed, afterimages are capable of demonstration in achromatic experience. Later, we shall mention chromatic effects.

POSITIVE AFTERIMAGES. Essential for the production of most after-images is some pattern of the relative illuminances in the visual field that provides the stimulus for the aftersensation. If this aftersensation has the same pattern of relative brightnesses as was being experienced when the eye was still stimulated, we refer to a *positive afterimage*. The term is analogous to our reference to a snapshot as a positive print, one that maintains the light-dark relations of the original scene. You have probably experienced a positive afterimage after viewing an intense source of light, perhaps the sun. As you averted your eyes because of the discomfort, you are likely to have seen a persistent bright spot which remained in your visual experience for a few seconds even if you closed your eyes. This was a positive afterimage. They are seen most often after a brief exposure to a very strong light.

NEGATIVE AFTERIMAGES. At much lower luminance levels than are needed for positive afterimages it is possible to generate a *negative afterimage*, one which has its light-dark relationships reversed from their appearance in the original scene, as in a photographic negative. The particular requirement for producing a good negative afterimage is to fixate a particular point in the visual field or on a test pattern for about 30 to 60 sec and then to turn the eyes toward a uniform field against which the afterimage may be seen. To demonstrate the phenomenon to yourself, if you are not already familiar with it, you might stare at the center point of a black triangle located on a white background. After the greater part of a minute has elapsed while you hold this fixation, you need merely to shift your gaze to some-thing like a gray piece of cardboard. Seemingly superimposed on this surface you will see a light gray triangle surrounded by a darker gray field. This negative image may persist for a few seconds, fade from sensory experience, and then reappear again. Such waxing and waning are typical of the afterimage experience. The vividness of a negative afterimage depends on such factors as the luminance con-trast in the original stimulus pattern, the length of the original fixa-tion, and the luminance of the background upon which the afterimage is "projected."

Chromatic Afterimages

If a stimulus target has a dominant wavelength so that it appears as having a particular hue, it will be found that its afterimage viewed against an achromatic surface has a complementary hue. A red target arouses a blue-green afterimage and a blue target a yellow afterimage. A fairly simple explanation may be offered for this hue reversal. If a blue target is viewed, a certain amount of adaptation to this hue takes place in the cones that are responding to it. They gradually become less responsive to it. This localized retinal effect is probably quite similar to the hue adaptation of the total field which we discussed earlier. As the blue target is fixated, in fact, it is likely to appear to lose saturation due to adaptation. When a white or gray background is then viewed, its reflected light finds the target portion of the retina to be somewhat less responsive to the wavelengths in the blue region of the spectrum. Since responsiveness is still normal in the green, yellow, and red regions of the spectrum, the retinal activity approximates that which would be aroused by such a distribution of incoming light energy. The yellow afterimage that is sensed is the normal accompaniment of such a pattern of retinal activity. We see, then, that an afterimage is the joint product of the ongoing physical stimulation at the time of its perception and the state of the retina created by the prior patterned stimulation.

BINOCULAR AND MONOCULAR AFTERIMAGES. The fact that an afterimage has its primary source in the state of the retina of the stimulated eye does not mean that differences may not exist between afterimages that follow binocular stimulation and those which result from monocular stimulation. The neural inputs from two retinas may interact in some way to result in such differences. This effect might be in the quality of the afterimage experience such as a change in its perceived hue or it might be in some quantitative aspect of the phenomenon. Misiak and Lozito (1951) determined the latency and the duration of the negative afterimage that followed chromatic stimulation, comparing these values for monocular and binocular viewing. After a dark adaptation period of 10 min, subjects fixated either a red or a green cross for 30 sec, the stimulus having an intensity of 5 foot-candles. They then looked at a white afterfield of 15 foot-candles. Simultaneously with the cessation of the test pattern and the illumination of the afterfield, a chronoscope was started. As soon as the subject saw the complementary-hued afterimage he depressed a key which stopped this latency clock and started a second one. As soon as the afterimage cross faded and lost its shape the key was released to stop the second clock, which thus provided a measure of the duration of the afterimage. It was found that binocular stimulation gave 15 per cent shorter latency and 24 per cent longer duration of afterimage, both differences being statistically significant. These results indicate an enhancement of the afterimage experience resulting from binocular stimulation, possibly arising from a central neural facilitation.

SUMMARY

Scientists interested in vision have investigated visual processes from several different aspects—physical, psychophysical, and physiological. Our background for the understanding and conducting of research on this complex topic begins with the study of light, and the terms and units of measurement used in specifying visual stimuli. Luminance, in various aspects, and spectral composition are two major dimensions of light. The structure and functioning of the eye constitute a second factual area which must be mastered as part of a foundation for the study of research in vision. A knowledge of the retina is particularly useful in understanding visual phenomena.

Certain visual facts, arising from basic research, must be kept in mind when pursuing further investigations. The facts about photopic and scotopic vision, represented in the spectral sensitivity curves, need to be kept in mind when working near threshold values of luminance. In many studies the state of adaptation of the eye must be carefully controlled when measurements of vision are attempted.

Numerous experimental studies of vision provide evidence of the need for careful research techniques, especially in control of the physical stimulus. The luminance of the stimulus may be controlled in a number of ways. The size of stimuli and the retinal location at which they impinge need to be specified if research is to extend our knowledge. Another physical dimension, duration of stimulation, must also be considered in many experiments.

Problems of visual acuity, of considerable interest in vision testing, need to be explored more fully in basic research. A prime consideration in such work is the nature of the acuity target used.

Studies of visual flicker and fusion under intermittent stimulation offer special means of investigating visual functioning. The Talbot-Plateau law, stating the effective luminance of stimuli that are interrupted at rates higher than the cff, offers guidance to controlling stimulus intensity by means of an episcotister in some visual experiments.

Our understanding of color vision begins with our knowledge of how chromatic and achromatic sensations depend on the distribution of spectral wavelengths in the stimulating light. Two fundamental aspects of chromatic sensation are hue and saturation. The activity of the retinal cones mediates chromatic sensation, whereas rod functioning yields only achromatic experience.

The color circle provides a convenient schema for summarizing facts about color mixture and complementaries. Principles of tristimulus mixture may also be described with reference to three points on the color circle. For more precise specification of color, we utilize the I.C.I. chromaticity diagram with its rectangular coordinates. Stating the coordinate values of any point in the diagram is a way of indicating a tristimulus mixture of the I.C.I. primaries that we would need to match the color we are describing. The chromaticity diagram permits the graphic determination of the results of additive color mixture, with the dominant wavelength and the spectral purity of the mixture being determinable. The I.C.I. chromaticity diagram, based on psychophysical research which defines the "standard observer," may also be used to locate various white illuminants.

The color wheel, or other mixing apparatus, can be used to explore the rules of additive color mixture. Other visual phenomena with which we may experiment include contrast, peripheral hue sensitivity, binocular rivalry and fusion, and color adaptation.

Afterimages, both achromatic and chromatic, are other visual phenomena which can be easily experienced. Besides mere demonstration, some afterimage phenomena are amenable to quantification in carefully conducted experiments.

REFERENCES

Chapanis, A. How we see: A summary of basic principles. In National Research Council, Committee on Undersea Warfare, Panel on Psychology and Physiology. *Human factors in undersea warfare.* Washington: National Research Council, 1949. Pp. 3–60.

Chapanis, A., Rouse, R. O., & Schachter, S. The effect of intersensory stimulation on dark adaptation and night vision. *J. exp. Psychol.,* 1949, 39, 425–437.

Evans, R. M. *An introduction to color.* New York: Wiley, 1948.

Hanes, R. M. Suprathreshold area brightness relationships. *J. opt. Soc. Amer.,* 1951, 41, 28–31.

Hecht, S., Haig, C., & Chase, A. M. The influence of light adaptation on subsequent dark adaptation of the eye. *J. gen. Physiol.,* 1937, 20, 831–850.

Hochberg, J. E., Triebel, W., & Seaman, G. Color adaptation under conditions of homogeneous visual stimulation (Ganzfeld). *J. exp. Psychol.,* 1951, 41, 153–159.

Judd, D. B. Basic correlates of the visual stimulus. In S. S. Stevens (Ed.), *Handbook of experimental psychology.* New York: Wiley, 1951. Pp. 811–867.

Misiak, H., & Lozito, C. C. Latency and duration of monocular and binocular after-images. *J. exp. Psychol.,* 1951, 42, 247–249.

Riopelle, A. J., & Chow, K. L. Scotopic area-intensity relations at various retinal locations. *J. exp. Psychol.,* 1953, 46, 314–318.

Wald, G., & Clark, Anna-Betty. Visual adaptation and chemistry of the rods. *J. gen. Physiol.*, 1937, 21, 93–105.

ADDITIONAL READINGS

Erlick, D., & Landis, C. The effect of intensity, light-dark ratio, and age on the flicker-fusion threshold. *Amer. J. Psychol.*, 1952, 65, 375–388.

Geldard, F. A. *The human senses.* New York: Wiley, 1953.

Judd, D. B. *Color in business, science, and industry.* New York: Wiley, 1952.

CHAPTER 10

Visual
Perception

Investigations of perception account for a considerable portion of modern experimental psychology. This fact may be verified by even a casual perusal of psychological journals carrying reports of research and those which present theoretical articles. Such a survey would attest also to the variety of perceptual phenomena being studied, even within a single sense modality like vision. With a few experiments on auditory perception considered in Chapter 11, we shall limit ourselves in this chapter to visual perceptual processes. Our concentration on visual perception parallels the major attention that this sense has been given by investigators and theorists interested in perception.

Perceptual processes, like attention, discrimination, recognition, and interpretation, usually intervene between sensation and response. Our perceptions are so closely dependent upon the sensations that we are experiencing that perceptual processes are often conceptualized as extensions of sensory processes. On the other hand, our perceptions loom so large as the determinants of the responses that we make in any situation that perception may be characterized as readiness to respond. Both viewpoints offer useful guidance for research on perceptual phenomena.

SOME DEFINING CONSIDERATIONS

Having noted that perceptual processes occur between stimulation and the behavior that it elicits, we may try to portray their general nature more fully by identifying their place in a psychological schema. Perceptions, as experienced, are generally considered to be functions of the environmental energies impinging upon an organism and of the state of that organism which may have resulted from numerous factors including past experience. They become part of psychological science only as inferences are drawn from the behavior which they generate in conjunction with the person's motives and habits.

Relation to Sensation

Most of the statements we have just been making about perceptions would apply as well to sensations—they depend on the environment and the state of the person, and they are private experiences to be inferred from the responses made to them. Perceptions often seem to be either a synthesis or an analysis of sensations, sometimes incorporating sensory cues from several modalities. We perceive a blazing hearth when we simultaneously see the flames in the fireplace, hear the twigs crackling, and smell the smoke from the green wood. Even "seeing" the flames is a perception resulting from the synthesis of the hues, and the spatial and temporal patterns of the incandescence. Perception of an analytic sort occurs when we search through a sea of visual sensations until we locate something, perhaps a familiar face, to which we can respond.

What are the sensory elements out of which percepts are constructed in our experience? Reasoning from the facts of optical image formation and the retinal mosaic of rods and cones, early workers argued that a multitude of points of color, varied as to brightness, hue, and saturation, were the building stones from which our visual perception of the environment was constructed. These pioneer elementarists, knowing that visual stimulation was a pinpoint process at the retina, introspected mightily to see these points of color in their percepts. In contrast to this view, Gibson (1950) has suggested that our perception of an object, for example, can be reduced only to our sensation of its edges and surfaces, these being the irreducible elements in our visual experience of the world around us.

Relation to Response

It may be appropriate, for some purposes, to define a perception as a tendency to respond. If we place a slide in a projector and gradually turn up the projection lamp voltage from zero, a subject who has been instructed to report what he sees may say, "I see *something* now . . . it's a *circle* . . . it's a *bicycle wheel*." We may infer that he experienced three successive perceptions. We might go further and say that a perception *is* a tendency to make a particular response. A tendency to respond is still part of private experience which may be inhibited or which may be changed before an overt response occurs. Therefore, in accepting a response-tendency definition of perception, we do not commit ourselves to accepting any response as a direct indication of the perception aroused by the stimulus situation.

Relation to Learning

The view that perceptual processes are strongly influenced by experience or learning is widely held, being supported by much experimental evidence. Unfortunately, by the time a person is old enough to participate as a subject in research, the experience that contributes to basic perceptual processes is long since past. The effects of experience which immediately precedes perception are easier to investigate. Such experience may establish a perceptual *set*, a readiness to make responses of a particular type.

Past learning may also fortify a particular perception by providing an associative filling-in for any cues that may be missing. In our earlier example, for instance, it is not necessary to draw every spoke to obtain a perception of a bicycle wheel. In the case of an ambiguous stimulus, past experience may even be the principal source of any perception that occurs. This fact underlies the use of projective tests in psychology, of course.

Relation to Motivation

One area of research on perception has centered on the influence of the motives, needs, and values of the perceiver. Like learned habits, motives may be presumed to affect the relative strengths of various response tendencies, and therefore the likelihood of certain perceptions. A kind of study that has exemplified the relation of perception to motivation involves presenting ambiguous stimuli to subjects who have not had anything to eat for various periods of time. For longer periods of food deprivation a greater tendency to perceive food-related objects has been observed.

TECHNIQUES OF STUDY

We may further our understanding of what perceptual processes are by considering some of the methods that are used for their study. Having conceptualized them as intervening between stimulus and response, we see that the manipulation of the stimulus situation is one approach to their study. As private experiences, perceptions may be studied by an introspective or phenomenological technique, the scientist reporting on his own percepts. A more behavioristic approach is to manipulate stimulation experimentally, with instructions to subjects designed to elicit observable responses that indicate the underlying perceptions.

Phenomenological

The study of psychological phenomena by directly experiencing them is the *phenomenological* method. Reflecting upon their visual experiences, phenomenologists were able to formulate principles that appeared to operate in their perceptions. Men of the gestalt school, particularly, worked out rules that governed the perceiving of stimulus configurations, or *Gestalts*. Other investigators worked with stimulus materials like geometrical figures, creating perceptual illusions like apparent curvature in a physically straight line. Besides using oneself as subject, it is possible to extend the phenomenological study of perception by getting reports from others on how they perceive stimulus material.

Functional Relationships

In contrast to those experiments which seek to *demonstrate* the existence of certain perceptual phenomena are studies which *seek functional relationships* between the determinants of the perceptions and the responses to which the perceptions give rise. The gestalt principles that are often demonstrated by means of illustrative examples are amenable, along with many other perceptual processes, to this quantitative approach. Besides the commonly used manipulations of physical stimulus dimensions, we may mention a few special techniques that are useful for the study of a variety of perceptual problems.

STIMULUS IMPOVERISHMENT. One way to study the interrelated effects of environmental and other factors on perception is to reduce the external stimulation in some important respect. We can reduce the duration of presenting a stimulus word to subjects, for example, to determine the limiting length of presentation which still permits the word to be perceived correctly by the majority of persons. We would thus be determining a sort of absolute threshold for word recognition. In addition to exploring limits of perception, various impoverishment techniques may be used to reduce the stimulus contribution to perceptual processes in order to permit other factors like the past learning or the motivation of the subjects to reveal their impact upon the perception.

There are a number of ways of impoverishing visual stimulation. Devices of various kinds which limit stimulus exposure to very brief durations are called *tachistoscopes*. In the *fall* tachistoscope the stimulus is momentarily revealed by having a cutout window pass in front of it as an opaque screen falls. In the *Dodge* tachistoscope a subject looks at a semitransparent mirror, with the stimulus shown briefly by a quick change in illumination on the two sides of the mirror. Tachistoscopic stimulation can be given to a large group of subjects at one time by using a projector whose beam is briefly permitted to pass through a sector disk or a camera shutter. Besides using tachistoscopic exposure, we may impoverish stimuli by reducing the brightness contrast in projected stimuli by cutting down the projection lamp intensity or by increasing the room illumination. Blurring the focus of a projected image will also reduce its perceptibility. A graded impoverishment of typewritten stimulus material can be achieved by using the faint carbon copies that are in the neighborhood of the legibility threshold.

TRAINING OR ESTABLISHING A SET. Besides looking for the effect on perception of whatever a person's past experience may have been, a more direct study of the relationship of learning to perception may be undertaken by administering training to experimental subjects and noting how it affects their perceptual processes. Gibson (1953) has reviewed the results of a large number of experiments employing this general method. Somewhat akin to giving perceptual training, in that it manipulates the subject's experience, is the use of instructions or some other means to establish a *set*, a particular response tendency.

PSYCHOPHYSICAL METHODS. How round is a circle? Most views we get of circular objects are from an angle so that the retinal image in most cases is actually elliptical, yet we perceive the object as round. Our objective knowledge of the probable situation is a potent determiner of our perceptions in such cases. Without the benefit of such actual knowledge, how much elliptical distortion could a circle be given while still being perceived as perfectly round? We are asking here about the differential threshold for circularity. This might be determined by applying the method of constant stimuli, described in Chapter 5, with a number of almost circular ellipses used as comparison stimuli. Ellipses and circles might be presented at various angles of regard, the subjects being asked to state whether the stimulus object was circular.

PERCEPTION OF FORM

Vision is the modality through which we gain a very great part of our information about the spatial characteristics of our environment. A classic perceptual problem has been how we perceive depth, distance from ourselves in three-dimensional space, when the retinal image is a two-dimensional representation of our surroundings. Some of the answers to this question were worked out to a considerable extent over two centuries ago. You are probably familiar with the lists of monocular and binocular cues to depth perception. There are also space perception problems of the extent and the form of stimuli located in a flat surface that is perpendicular to the line of sight. How the areas and shapes of certain stimulus configurations are perceived is also a question for research.

Gestalt Principles

The objects and surfaces in our environment tend to be patterned in certain physical shapes so that the stimuli from them form visual patterns that are similar to the objects or are geometrically different from them in certain regular ways. For example, a circular ashtray may appear perfectly circular if viewed from a particular set of points; more commonly it will be viewed from an angle that will give it an elliptical appearance. The patterns of our visual perceptions, then, tend to be generated by the patterns that exist in the physical world around us. However, we shall see that the experiencing of patterns may involve factors beyond those in the immediate physical environment.

There seem to be a number of principles that govern how we perceive patterns or configurations in the incoming stimulation. These are called gestalt principles because the German word for configuration, *Gestalt*, was employed in the early research on these perceptual phenomena. The gestalt psychologists have enumerated a number of principles which can be readily demonstrated to be operative in perception. Although they are hypothetically amenable to quantification, and have been approached with quantitative methods in some cases, they are chiefly presented as phenomena which are experienced by almost everyone. The fundamental gestalt principles thus had a phenomenological foundation historically, although beginnings have been made on an experimental superstructure.

GROUPING. In Figure 10.1 you see illustrated the gestalt principle of perceptual grouping on the basis of physical proximity. You perceive most readily a group of three dots and a group of four. Try to see a group of five and a group of two in Figure 10.1. Draw a light pencil line enclosing the group of two that you have perceived. You have probably encircled two dots that are fairly near to each other. The distance between them is probably less than the median interdot

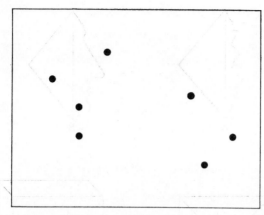

Fig. 10.1. Perceptual grouping—a demonstration figure explained in the text.

distance for all possible pairs among the seven dots. If this be the case, we see that the principle of grouping based on proximity is a perceptual process that holds even when the most commonly seen three-four grouping is eliminated by adopting, in this case, a two-five set.

FIGURAL GOODNESS. Perceptual acceptance is given more readily to those stimulus patterns that are "good" in some respect. This "goodness" which enhances perception is sometimes apparently a symmetry of design, sometimes a thinglike aspect. The right side of Figure 10.2A is a better figure than is the left side because of its symmetry and its triangularity. The same pattern seems less potent in perception when it is seen as the right side of Figure 10.2B where it is exceeded in goodness by the left side of this pattern which is readily perceived to be a human profile. Figure 10.2C is readily perceived as a square with its diagonals, a symmetrical geometrical design in two-dimensional space. Figure 10.2D, although also printed on the two-dimensional page, is not a symmetrical design. Further, its proportions and angles strongly suggest a three-dimensional figure, a cube. It is a "good" cube but a "bad" two-dimensional pattern. It tends, therefore, to be perceived as a cube, the good figure.

There are a number of patterns which may be perceived either as cubes or as bidimensional designs. Four of these, called *Kopfermann cubes* after one investigator who employed them, are shown in Figure 10.3. The hexagonal pattern Z in this group has greater bidimensional symmetry than W, for example. This greater symmetry as a plane figure would make Z less often perceived as a cube because its good

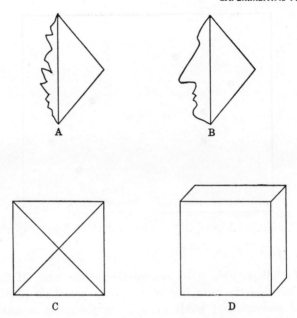

Fig. 10.2. Demonstrations of figural goodness discussed in the text.

form in two dimensions would favor a two-dimensional perception. Kopfermann (1930) developed this hypothesis from the gestalt principle of figural goodness and confirmed it in reports from observers of the patterns. Hochberg and McAlister (1953) performed an experiment to test the assumption that figural goodness can be given a better objective description than may stem from reference to symmetry alone. They noted that designs Y and Z have fewer line segments, angles, and points of intersection than do designs W and X. This economy in number of parts, they felt, was a key to the figural goodness of these designs for bidimensional perception. The fewer the parts, the better the figure. Since the proportions and angles of the designs all corresponded to a cube, it was assumed that tridimensional goodness was equal for all the designs.

If Y and Z have greater amounts of bidimensional goodness than W and X, they should be seen as plane figures to a greater extent. Hochberg and McAlister tested each design to see if it was seen predominantly as bidimensional or as a cube. Subjects viewed each design for 100 sec, with a signal tone sounding at irregular intervals during the observation period. Whenever the tone sounded, each subject marked a response sheet to indicate whether he had

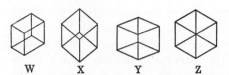

W   X   Y   Z

Fig. 10.3. The Kopfermann cubes employed in a study of figural goodness. (After Hochberg and McAlister, 1953.)

just been perceiving the bidimensional design or the cube. Y and Z were indicated to yield bidimensional perceptions about half the time, whereas bidimensional responses were made to W and X only about 1 per cent of the time. The hypothesis was thus confirmed that having fewer lines, angles, and intersections contributed to bidimensional figural goodness.

Geometrical Illusions

Perceptions are of paramount importance in developing our cognitions, our items of information, about the world around us. Early students of perception showed, however, that discrepancies might exist between our perceptions and the objective facts. Visual deviations from reality were particularly demonstrable in specially prepared geometrical figures. Distortions could be created in the apparent length of line segments, in the straightness of a line, or in the parallel relation of two lines. Several of these phenomenal illusions are presented in Figure 10.4. In the Sander parallelogram the di-

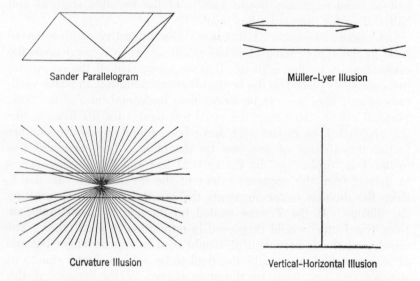

Sander Parallelogram

Müller–Lyer Illusion

Curvature Illusion

Vertical–Horizontal Illusion

Fig. 10.4. Some geometrical illusions useful in demonstrating and quantifying certain perceptual principles.

agonals are actually equal in length, as are the horizontal segments of the Müller-Lyer illusion. The apparent inequality of these lines is an effect induced by the other lines in the drawings. A somewhat different effect is induced in the curvature illusion which is an example of configurations in which straight lines seem curved. The vertical-horizontal illusion involves a somewhat different perceptual principle in which the orientation of lines in the visual field affects their apparent length. Although there was a tendency in early research to regard these various illusions as perceptual curiosities to be given some special explanation, the modern view is that they stand with "normal" perceptions as phenomena to be incorporated in any comprehensive theory.

THE MÜLLER-LYER ILLUSION. Named for one of the pioneer investigators who worked with it, this is one of the illusions of length that lends itself to quantification. The two line segments may be placed end to end, one terminating in arrowheads and the other in lines resembling an arrow's feathers. By making the length of one segment adjustable we may determine the point of subjective equality, the *PSE*, using a method of limits or a method of adjustment. (These psychophysical methods are described in Chapter 5.) When a setting represents the *PSE*, the ratio of the physical lengths of the segments will be an index of the magnitude of the illusion. In designing such an experiment we would probably plan to give a number of trials, half of them requiring inward motion of the movable segment and half calling for outward adjustment.

THE VERTICAL-HORIZONTAL ILLUSION. Our subjective or phenomenal scale in the experiencing of visual extent seems to depend upon the orientation of the line segments that we view. This is the interpretation commonly placed on the vertical-horizontal illusion, in which vertically placed lines seem to be longer than horizontal lines of the same physical extent. However, the usual test figures for the illusion, like the inverted *T* in Figure 10.4, have been found to involve another factor, the division of one line by the other. The horizontal line in the *T* is "broken up" by the vertical line and this division seems to detract from the apparent extent of the divided line. In the *T*, then, the *division factor* augments the *orientation factor* in creating the illusion. If the *T* were turned on its side by a 90° rotation, these two factors would be placed in opposition to each other. The crossbar of the *T*, now vertical, would tend to appear longer because of its orientation, but would also tend to be seen as shorter due to its division into two parts by the stem portion of the figure. If this division factor is potent enough, it may even overcome the orientation factor so that the vertical-horizontal illusion—the enhancement of apparent length of vertically oriented lines—does not appear.

Künnapas (1955) conducted an experiment to quantify the contribution of the two factors we have mentioned to the apparent length of line segments, one vertical and one horizontal, in configurations resembling either a *T* or an *L* in one of four possible orientations. By presenting figures that had been drawn on cardboard, he used the method of constant stimuli to determine the point of subjective equality for the two line segments for each figure in each orientation. (This psychophysical method is discussed in Chapter 5, p. 103.)

Analysis of the data indicated that the orientation factor made a contribution that could be considered as a constant, an enhancement of the apparent length of the vertical line of about 3 per cent. The division factor, on the other hand, seemed to be a variable factor which made its strongest contribution when the dividing point was the midpoint of the intersected line. This equal division of the intersected line, as in the letter *T*, contributed an apparent difference that was computed to be almost 10 per cent, favoring the dividing line over the line which it bisected. When one line was not bisected, but was divided unevenly, the division factor was less potent in its effect on the apparent lengths. In the *L*, the segments met at their terminal points so that there was no intersecting and therefore no division factor operating.

The values calculated for the orientation factor and the division factor indicate that when a *T* constructed of equal segments is presented on its side, the division factor, contributing a 10 per cent difference that favors the horizontal segment, will overcome the orientation factor that contributes a lesser enhancement to the crossbar, now seen vertically. If the intersection point of the *T* is changed so that the figure begins to resemble an *L*, the division factor loses potency and the orientation factor may become the greater contributor, with the net result that the vertical-horizontal illusion again appears to be operative. Of course, when a *T* is presented in normal orientation, or is inverted, both the division and the orientation factors favor the perceptual shortening of the crossbar. Künnapas' findings indicate, somewhat ironically, that the usual inverted *T* used in demonstrating the vertical-horizontal illusion is affected in its apparent lengths of segments less by its orientation than by the division factor.

Experimental Studies of Form Perception

It seems of little use to adopt phenomenological description as a technique for the study of form perception. It might yield only such obvious information as the fact that a circle appears more rounded and less angular than a square. Instead of asking subjects to *describe* their perceptions, most experimenters seem to bring perceptual processes to an observable state by requiring subjects to make discriminatory responses as various stimulus shapes are presented.

DISCRIMINATION STUDIES. The discriminability of a number of common forms, like triangle, ellipse, and cross, has been studied in two experiments which present an instructive contrast in methods employed. Casperson (1950) prepared stimulus cards using six such familiar geometrical shapes, with variants of each shape created by altering its dimensions. For example, the rectangular form was varied from an actual square to a slim rectangle that was six times as long as it was wide. All these different figures were made in seven different absolute sizes, too, so that a threshold of discriminability could be determined for each one by having the forms viewed at a fixed distance with a fixed illuminance. The measure of perceptual behavior was the number of correct identifications of the forms. The data indicated that the cross and triangle were more readily identified than the other forms in the study, with the ellipse and diamond being more difficult to discriminate.

A very different measure of form discriminability was used in a study by Sleight (1952). Twenty-one different forms cut out of black paper were mounted on small plastic squares. Six identical copies of each form were used, and the resulting 126 pieces of plastic were spread randomly in different orientations on top of a circular board which was surrounded by small compartments into which the forms had to be sorted. The particular kind of form to be located and sorted out on any trial was designated by the experimenter. On the critical trials when sorting time was measured to provide a score, each set of forms was replaced after a particular sorting so that the next sorting had to be made from among all 126 pieces of plastic. It was found that forms like the swastika, circle, crescent, cross, and star were sorted most quickly. The shapes that were sorted most slowly included the hexagon, heptagon, and octagon. The outcome of an experiment of this type appears to be strongly influenced by the different forms among which the subject must discriminate.

STIMULUS MATERIALS. When particular forms, like geometrical shapes, are used in perceptual studies, the question arises as to how widely the results may be generalized. It must be assumed that the subjects' familiarity with the forms has some effect on the measures of performance that are obtained. The problem becomes particularly acute when the experimenter wishes to manipulate the amount of experience which the subjects have with different ones of the forms. This calls for the use of forms that are essentially unfamiliar, but where do we get such forms?

Various experimenters have devised techniques for creating forms whose shapes are determined in part by numerical values drawn from a table of random numbers. Such random sampling was used by Fitts, Weinstein, Rappaport, Anderson, and Leonard (1956) in filling in the squares of a matrix to form a figure with an irregular upper contour like that of a histogram. Variants of this type of figure were used in a study in which a subject had to locate one figure in each of the six rows that matched the given test figure. The time taken to locate the six matching figures from among 48 similar forms was the score for each trial. One finding was that recognition time depended on specific characteristics of the form and its orientation. A sample of one of these metric figures is shown in Figure 10.5A.

A random-numbers technique was also employed in creating the other forms shown in the figure. Arnoult (1956) used nonsense

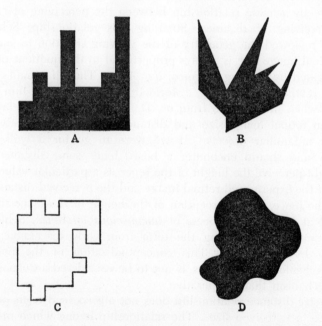

Fig. 10.5. Stimulus materials used in different studies of form perception in an effort to keep initial familiarity at a low value. Form *A* is one type employed by Fitts et al. (1956). Form *B* resembles those devised by Arnoult (1956). Form *C* is one used by Hake and Eriksen (1956). Form *D* is similar to another series devised by Arnoult (1954).

shapes like those in Figure 10.5B in an experiment where he found a curvilinear relationship between the number of times a shape was displayed and the rating of familiarity later assigned by the subjects to that shape. By way of further demonstration of the variety of figures that may be useful in perceptual research, we have included, in Figure 10.5C, a sample nonsense form devised by Hake and Eriksen (1956). These researchers used aerial photos and geometric forms in a study of how practice in labeling different forms may contribute to their later recognition. Figure 10.5D shows still another type of nonsense shape, employed in a different study by Arnoult (1954) in which the discrimination of forms was shown to depend on the relationships of the angular orientations of the two forms to be compared.

PERCEPTION OF SIZE AND DISTANCE

Much of the research on size perception indicates, either more or less directly, a close relationship between the perceiving of size and the perceiving of distance. Stressing this relationship, Schlosberg (1950) reviewed the geometry of the viewing situation to show that the retinal image size is always proportional to the quotient of object size divided by viewing distance: $a = A/D$. Thus, if a man's height, A, is 6 ft, the retinal image, a, formed when we look at him will be halved when his distance from us, D, is doubled. This relationship between retinal image size and distance is useful in perceiving the size of unfamiliar objects. If we were to go for a walk in the country and should encounter a board fence some distance away, we might perceive the height of the fence as a particular value on the basis of the experienced retinal image and the perceived distance from us to the fence. Our perception of the height of the fence might be arrived at by a swift process of *unconscious inference,* Schlosberg's paper suggests, borrowing the term from early discussion of perception by Helmholtz. This conceptualization of the perceptual process, Schlosberg indicates, is not to be considered an exposition of the mechanism that is operative.

The size-distance relationship does not always lead from perceived distance to perceived size. The relationship is one which may serve in the perception of either size or distance, depending on what is observed and upon the viewing conditions. As we shall see, a perception of the size of an object may lead to a perception of its distance from the viewer.

Demonstration of Size-Distance Relationship

If there is a psychological relationship between our perceptions of size and distance, we should be able to demonstrate it by presenting objects of different sizes and getting estimates of their distance from the perceiving subject. In such an experiment we would try to remove all cues to distance except the size of the object displayed. A simple way to study the size-distance phenomenon is provided by one of the Ames demonstrations in perception, described by Ittelson (1952). In a darkened room the subject views monocularly three vertical lines of light of different lengths. When asked to describe the distance of each line from him, the subject will usually say that the tallest line is nearest to him, the shortest one is farthest, and the line of intermediate height is at an intermediate distance. Actually, all three lines are at the same distance, being created by slits in the same opaque mask, illuminated from behind. So strong is the size-distance relationship in perception that when all distance cues except size are eliminated, size becomes the determining factor in the perception of distance. In this demonstration, then, the shortest line is perceived as most distant, the longest one as closest.

Size Constancy

Although perceptual processes are intricate, usually dependent upon a number of simultaneously occurring sensations, the percepts to which they give rise are often very stable. The stabilities that are exhibited by several kinds of percepts are called perceptual *constancies*. For example, *shape constancy* is demonstrated by the fact that a rectangular table top appears rectangular even though the sheaf of light rays reflected from its surface takes on various trapezoidal shapes as we view the table from different angles. We *perceive* the rectangle from many viewpoints even though we *see* the rectangle only from one vantage point, located directly above the center of the table.

The perception of size also involves mechanisms which lead to a constancy effect. As we drive along the highway, a billboard always appears to be billboard-sized no matter what changes occur in the retinal angle that it subtends. We shall see how this *size constancy* phenomenon may be demonstrated and quantified in laboratory studies.

QUANTIFYING SIZE CONSTANCY. It is possible to quantify the size constancy phenomenon to see if the size-distance relationship operates reliably in the perception of various sized objects viewed at different distances. An experiment performed by Smith (1953) will serve to introduce us to the general method that may be employed for such a purpose. On a particular trial the subject would view with both eyes a wooden test cube located at some distance from him. While viewing the distant cube, the subject was presented with a graded series of comparison cubes, seen one at a time about 2 ft from the eyes. His task was to indicate which of the comparison series he judged to be of identical physical size with the test cube. The experimenter, you can see, was using the psychophysical method of limits to determine the *point of subjective equality* for perceived size. (This psychophysical method is discussed in Chapter 5, p. 99.) Should this *PSE* turn out to be equal to the physical size of the test cube at all viewing distances, then the operation of size constancy would have been confirmed. This measuring technique, then, or others like it, constitutes an operational definition of *size constancy* insofar as perceivers actually exhibit it.

The design of Smith's investigation had a 2-in. test cube and a 4-in. test cube, viewed on different trials at distances of either 16, 80, or 320 ft. The comparison cubes varied from ½ in. to 6 in. in quarter-inch steps, a limited portion of this series being used on any one trial in either an ascending or a descending order. As a further method of generalizing the approach to size constancy, the test cube was presented under a second experimental condition at the 2-ft distance with the comparison cubes being shown in turn at one of the three specified viewing distances.

The mean size of the matching cube selected from the comparison series by the subjects is the statistic that indicates the validity of the size constancy principle as a description of size-distance perception. If these values are the same at all viewing distances as the physical size of the test cubes, then constancy will be demonstrated to be completely operative under these conditions. Smith found mean error to be under 10 per cent for the 2-in. cube and under 5 per cent for the 4-in. cube when these were viewed at the two shorter distances. Error was somewhat greater for the longest viewing distance, indicating a tendency for the size of objects viewed at 320 ft to be overestimated. This departure from size constancy at longer viewing distances had also been found in earlier experiments, sometimes being attributed to possible experimental error. Smith suggests that this deviation from constancy may be due to an overestimation of the longer distances. With a longer viewing distance being estimated, a given retinal image will be perceived as arising from a larger object. There is no way of knowing from this type of experiment whether an overestimation of distance is indeed occurring. Perhaps it is best to consider the process as one of combined size-distance perception.

PERCEPTION OF THE VERTICAL

Our usual surroundings contain many vertical and horizontal lines which provide an orientation of the visual field. Our body orientation, sensed by means of a variety of proprioceptive stimuli, also gives us cues for the perception of the gravitational vertical. Most of the time the visual cues and the body cues are in agreement. If the head is tilted, the lines that are known to be vertical in the visual field provide a referent for the perception of verticality. But what if the visual environment has been experimentally tilted? How accurately can a subject perceive the gravitational vertical under such circumstances? We shall review two studies aimed at answering this question.

Varying the Visual Field

A series of experiments was performed by Asch and Witkin (1948) to determine the extent to which visual cues from a tilted environment influence the perception of the vertical. They constructed a small room with a table and a chair located against the back wall. A book was placed on the table and a picture hung on the wall above it. The objects were secured so that they would not move when the room was tilted 22° before permitting subjects to look into it. Also located on the back wall of the room was a rod that could be rotated about its center point and thus adjusted to any angle with respect to the vertical. Under the first viewing condition the subject looked into the room from 6 ft away through an 8-in. tube which permitted him to see only the lower part of the back wall of the room, the objects we have mentioned, and adjacent parts of the floor and sidewalls. After 4 min of looking into the room through the tube, with his attention called to the picture to occupy the time while the room cues were impinging upon him, the subject was asked to guide the setting of the adjustable rod to a true vertical or horizontal. The experimenter turned the rod slowly from outside the room and the subject stated when it was perceived to be vertical or horizontal, these cardinal directions being required to be perceived on alternate trials until three settings of each had been accomplished.

Under the second condition the subject was required to look into the tilted room from a position much closer to it, his view being unrestricted by the viewing tube this time. After inspecting the interior of the room for 1 min he was again given three trials in indicating his perception of each of the two major directions. For the third situation the subject was again placed about 6 ft back from the open side of the tilted room. His unrestricted view now included details of the laboratory room as well as the smaller tilted room within it. With this expanded frame of reference, which included several horizontal and vertical lines of the normal room, he was again required to guide the settings of the rod mounted on the back wall of the tilted room.

Under the first two conditions, with the visual field confined to the interior of the tilted room, not one of the 76 subjects was able to establish a true horizontal or vertical setting of the indicator rod. Every setting was in error in the same direction as the tilt of the room. For both these viewing situations and for both the vertical and horizontal directions, the mean error was about 15°. The 22° tilt of the room seemed to have influenced the judgments of vertical and horizontal to a considerable extent. Under the third viewing condition, with details of the upright laboratory also visible, errors in adjusting the indicator rod located in the tilted room were still very predominantly in the same direction. The mean error was about 9°, significantly less than under the other viewing conditions, but still reflecting a strong effect of the tilted-line cues that surround the indicator rod.

We have reviewed Experiment I from the report by Asch and Witkin (1948). The same article describes further experiments with the 22° tilt of the room and with the subject placed in a chair tilted similarly or in the opposite direction. With the subject himself tilted in either of these directions, the influence of the tilted room cues was even more potent, the mean error being about 20° in the same direction that the room was tilted.

Varying the Amount of Tilt

In a tilted-room, tilted-chair experiment by Mann (1952) two different amounts of tilt, 10° and 30°, were used for the room and for the subject. Under some conditions the tilt of the subject's chair was in the same direction as the tilt of the room and under others it was in the opposite direction. A perfectly upright position of room or chair was also included in the permutations that constituted the experimental conditions.

When the tilting room was actually upright, the errors made in adjusting the target-rod to vertical did not differ significantly from zero. Whenever the room was tilted, subjects showed a constant error in the same direction, greater when the room-tilt was 30° than when it was 10°. The error tended to be accentuated when the subject was tilted 30° in the chair in either the same or opposite direction as the room. When compared with the experiments by Asch and Witkin (1948) this study adds the information that the error in perceiving the vertical tends to be proportional to the amount of tilt in the visual field provided.

DYNAMIC VISUAL PERCEPTIONS

Perception tends to be a constructive process. A complex combination of sensory cues is the basis of most perceptions, but when some of these are missing the percept may still occur when the remaining cues maintain the proper relations to each other. The perceptual process fills in for the missing elements. We shall try to illustrate this principle by referring to two kinds of dynamic perception—that is, perception of motion. In one case, when stimulus conditions are properly arranged, motion is perceived even though there are no moving elements in the physical environment. In the second case, three-dimensional motion is perceived when the stimulus motion is only two-dimensional.

Apparent Movement

When we maintain a particular eye fixation, an object moving in our physical environment forms an image that is successively located on different parts of the retina, there being particular time-space relationships in the retinal stimulation for different rates of movement. The experimental work that led to the development of motion pictures was aimed at creating the illusion of motion by presenting a series of discrete stationary images, each in a slightly different position. For the laboratory study of motion perception one of the pioneer gestalt psychologists, Wertheimer, simplified the situation to just two stimuli successively presented at different points in space. If the interval between the presentations of the two stimulus lines is extremely short, they will be perceived as occurring simultaneously side by side. If the time interval is quite long, the two lines are seen successively, each in its own position. However, there are intermediate time intervals which lead to the perception of movement of a line from one position to the other. This phenomenon is called *apparent movement*, a perception of motion created by successive stationary images. It is the same principle that the developers of motion pictures incorporated in their inventions.

The time interval between presentations of successive stationary images is a key variable in the apparent movement demonstration. A series of perceptal experiences takes place as the time interval between the two stimuli is increased. First comes simultaneity, and then optimal perception of apparent movement. With longer intervals movement becomes partial, each stimulus seen as moving somewhat but without the perception of a single object in one continuous motion. When the interval is still longer, a phenomenon called *pure movement* is said to be experienced. This is a perception of motion alone, divorced from any sense of an object that is moving. Another term given to this particular form of apparent motion is the *phi phenomenon*. Finally, when the time interval becomes great enough, there is no perception of motion but only of successive stimuli.

Primary experimental interest in apparent movement has centered, according to the account by Boring (1942, pp. 595–602), in discovering the determinants of optimal movement. Investigations by Korte sought to determine the dependence of perceived optimal movement on three variables: the time interval between the two stimuli, their intensity, and the distance separating them. It was found that for a given time interval at which optimal movement was perceived, the best distance of separation varied directly with the intensity of the stimuli. If the separation distance was increased, the stimulus intensity had to be increased to maintain the perception of apparent movement in its optimal form. With spatial separation of stimuli constant, the intensity for optimal perception was found to vary inversely with the time interval. If the time interval was reduced, the intensity would have to be increased. With intensity held constant, the time interval for optimal motion increased proportionately with the distance separating the stimuli. If the distance was made greater, the time had to be increased. Besides these physical aspects of stimulation—space, time, and intensity—optimal perception of apparent movement has been found to depend on subjective factors like the attitude of the subject. Too analytic an attitude, bolstered by knowledge that nothing in the situation is really moving, makes it difficult to experience apparent movement. A passive, accepting attitude is best, as witnessed by the fact that we perceive the motion in animated outdoor advertising even though some aspects of the physical stimuli may not be perfect for inducing the perception.

Kinetic Depth Effect

A number of different experiments are reported in an article by Wallach and O'Connell (1953) on the *kinetic depth effect,* which is the perception of three-dimensional form aroused by two-dimensional stimulation that is moving and changing in form. Their Experiment 2 will serve as our example of the laboratory approach to this phenomenon. They constructed a wire form in the shape of a parallelogram divided into two triangles by its short diagonal. The form was bent so that these two triangles occupied different planes which met at an angle of 110° along the line of the diagonal. This wire form was rotated back and forth through an angle of 42° at the rate of one cycle per 1.5 sec. The subject did not see the form itself but observed its shadow on a translucent screen for trial periods of 10 sec each. The subject was asked for a report on his perception after each trial period, with some reports also being given during observation. In this part of the experiment all fifty subjects reported perceiving a three-dimensional form turning back and forth, much like the wire form and its motion. This perception was aroused by the motion and the shortening and lengthening of the line segments seen on the translucent screen. When several different *stationary* projections of the form were shown to another group of subjects, no three-dimensional perceptions occurred. The impression of a third dimension was apparently built up by the succession of shadow projections that were seen by the experimental group as the wire form oscillated. The perception seems to depend not so much on present sensory stimulation as on immediate past sensory input. The kinetic depth effect, the authors note, is a perceptual process which has an important temporal dimension.

ATTENTION

Paying attention is a perceptual process which seems to have a strong mentalistic flavor. Perhaps this is because the introspectionists approached the topic of attention by stressing the clarity of consciousness that it produced. At any rate, behaviorally oriented investigators seem not to have explored the problem of attention from as many different starting points as might prove profitable. From among those experimental studies that have been performed we shall select a small sample for review, first mentioning one or two kinds of investigation to which we can give no extended consideration.

What sorts of visual stimulation capture our attention? Experience tells us that a change in the visual field, often conspicuous because of its motion, will usually cause us to attend to it. If a shadow falls across the page we are reading, our attention is diverted from the book to whatever or whoever caused the shadow. Having investigated, we return our attention to our reading; this return indicates the directing of attention by motivational factors. Some research has been done on the capturing of attention by stimuli. Sometimes the stimuli are near threshold and the performance measure is the per cent of them that are noticed. In other studies the stimuli are intended to be distractors of attention and the measure of their effectiveness is the decrement of performance in the assigned task.

An index of visual attention is fixation. When something attracts our attention, we look directly at it, thereby gaining the benefit of clear foveal vision. Another experimental approach to attention therefore is to plot the fixations that a subject makes in exploring any visual field by photographing his eyes and later identifying the different parts of the field he was fixating. This has been done, for example, to see what parts of advertisements get most attention. In another application of the technique, experimenters have photographed a pilot's eye movements as he landed a plane, their purpose being to determine those dials on the instrument panel which required most attention in this performance.

A question inherited by psychologists from the philosophers was one which asked how many items could occupy the attention simultaneously. Speculative answers suggested that there was some fixed *span of attention,* a limit of perhaps five or six items to which a person could attend at once. Out of this question there grew a technique of tachistoscopically presenting several items, like dots projected on a screen, to determine if a subject could correctly apprehend their number. It was hoped that a particular limiting number might be identified as the span of attention. A similar approach was taken to determine the span of attention for printed material like numerals. letters of the alphabet, and words.

Span of Apprehension

When material is tachistoscopically presented to subjects, it is not so much their range of attention that is being tested as it is the amount of material that they can actually grasp with stimulation being very brief. They may attend broadly but grasp little. Such studies, then, are aimed at determining the *span of apprehension,* the limits of the subject's perceptual grasp. We no longer consider that there is a fixed limit to this span. Rather we consider performance to depend on a variety of variables, some physical and some psychological, as our review of illustrative experiments will show.

LUMINOUS INTENSITY AND EXPOSURE TIME. An experiment by Hunter and Sigler (1940) sought to determine the number of dots that could be perceived under different values of two independent variables: exposure time and luminous intensity of the field on which the black dots were located. The *span of discrimination,* a term analogous to span of apprehension, was defined as that point at which subjects were correct 50 per cent of the time in identifying the number of dots that were briefly exposed. This definition of the span indicates that it is conceptualized like a differential threshold to be sought in a psychophysical experiment. The investigators were seeking a functional relationship between psychological performance, the discrimination of the correct number of dots, and two physical variables, time and intensity. The results of the study are shown in Figure 10.6 where the ordinate is a scale of the dependent variable, the number of dots correctly identified half of the time. In other words, the ordinate is a scale of the span of discrimination or apprehension. The abscissa is the scale of one of the physical variables, the luminance of the stimulus field expressed in log units. Each curve in the figure is plotted for a separate value of the other independent variable, exposure time,

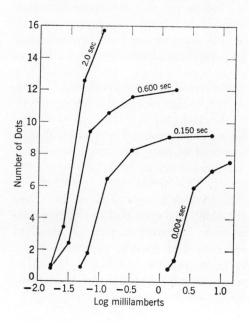

Fig. 10.6. Span of discrimination curves showing the number of dots correctly perceived as a function of luminous intensity of the background field. Duration of exposure was the parameter which differentiates the four curves shown. (After Hunter and Sigler, 1940.)

expressed in seconds. The curve at the extreme right, for example, gives the results obtained with the briefest exposure time, 0.004 sec. The plotted data indicate that with such a brief exposure subjects could perceive only about seven dots with 50 per cent accuracy, and this was accomplished only when the visual field was illuminated to 1.0 log mL. A reduction of luminance to 0.5 log mL is shown by the curve to have reduced the span to six dots, and further reduction in luminance cut the span very drastically when exposure time was so short.

If we look at the curve in Figure 10.6 that represents performance under an exposure time of 0.600 sec, we find a much different picture. The span is seen to be much higher, with as many as twelve dots being perceived on half the trials when luminance exceeded a millilambert. This curve also shows that cutting down on the luminance resulted in a lower span of discrimination. The span decreased gradually as luminance was reduced to about −1.0 log mL and then dropped very sharply when luminance was further decreased. The family of curves in Figure 10.6 indicates, then, that span of apprehension for dots is a function of both the intensity of visual field and exposure time.

RT AS A MEASURE OF SPAN. We have seen that there is no fixed answer to the old philosophical problem of how many things can be attended to at one time. The concept of span of apprehension has to be given some arbitrary definition, like the number of objects perceived 50 per cent of the time, before we can determine the span under any particular viewing conditions. However, the per cent of correct response under tachistoscopic exposure need not be considered the only behavioral index to the perception of numerosity of stimulus objects.

Saltzman and Garner (1948) performed an experiment which demonstrates the feasibility of using RT as an index of the perception of number. They also employed the tachistoscopic method with the same stimulus materials and viewing conditions, but we shall look only at the RT part of the study. Instead of dots, the stimuli were concentric circles projected on a translucent screen of 2.0 effective foot-candles of luminous transmittance. The largest circle projected was always 3 ft in diameter, subtending a visual angle of about 14° when viewed from a distance of 12 ft. Each trial consisted of the presentation of between two and ten of these concentric circles. A Standard Electric timer was started at the instant of stimulus presentation and was stopped when the subject called out the number of circles he perceived. The vocal response was picked up by a throat microphone which activated a relay to stop the clock.

It was found that RT provides a sensitive measure for the perception of numerosity. It took only about three-fourths of a second to respond when two or three circles were presented, for example, but over 3 sec to respond when the number of circles was nine or ten, these RT values being the approximate group means for the first ten trials. A practice effect was noted, especially for the stimulus patterns with the larger number of circles, so that RT for nine or ten circles was reduced to about 2 sec by the tenth group of ten trials. The experimenters suggest that the RT method for studying span of apprehension leads to a reliable measurement in fewer trials than are needed when the per cent of correct responses is used as the behavioral index of the perceptual process.

SPAN FOR WORDS AS A FUNCTION OF FREQUENCY OF USAGE. When the tachistoscopic method is used in measuring the span of apprehension, the procedure is essentially a determination of a threshold. We try to determine what value of stimulus duration is needed to elicit a correct response, usually on a certain per cent of trials. Howes and Solomon (1951) employed the method to ascertain the duration thresholds for the recognition of words. Their study was an exploration of the dependence of perception on past experience, since the stimulus words were chosen to represent a wide range of frequencies of occurrence in the written English language. From the list of 60 words used in their Experiment I, an example of a commonly occurring word is *GOVERNMENT*, whereas one that is encountered very rarely (if at all!) is *PERCIPIENCE*.

The duration threshold for each word was found by gradually increasing the length of successive tachistoscopic exposure of the word until it was correctly recognized, an ascending series in the method of limits. (This psychophysical method is discussed in Chapter 5, p. 99.) The words were presented in different orders to different subjects to minimize distortion of the group means by practice effects. Subsequent data analysis supported the wisdom of this procedure since practice effects proved to be very strong, subjects showing rapid improvement in recognizing tachistoscopically presented words. The hypothesis that duration thresholds would be inversely related to frequency of occurrence of words was confirmed. A correlation of −.73 was obtained between the log mean frequency of occurrence in two standard word counts and the mean duration of exposure needed for recognition.

CONTROLLED FREQUENCY OF WORD USAGE BY THE INDIVIDUAL. In the experiment by Howes and Solomon (1951) the index of frequency of usage was based on compilations by Thorndike and Lorge (1944) of how frequently words occur in magazines, encyclopedias, and other English language sources. Although a substantial relationship was found between duration threshold and word frequency, the results leave open the question of how a person's recognition thresholds relate to the amount of past usage of a word which he has personally experienced. Estimates of word frequencies in various printed sources may be only a crude approximation to the number of times a particular individual has encountered a given word. Experimental control over the experience that subjects have had with certain words is needed in order to delineate further the dependence of recognition thresholds on this experience.

An article by Solomon and Postman (1952) describes experiments in which the number of times a subject encountered a particular word was controlled before his being tested for his apprehension of the words under tachistoscopic exposure. Each subject was given a pack of cards with a seven-letter nonsense word printed on each card. The pack contained ten core-words that were later to be used in the perceptual threshold determination. Two of these were repeated in the pack twenty-five times each. Two were repeated ten times, two five times, two twice, and two appeared on just one card each. These different repetition values applied to different ones of the nonsense words for different subjects so that the threshold data to be gathered later would not be biased by peculiarities of particular words. The subject had to go through the pack of cards, which also contained fourteen single filler words of the same type, and pronounce each nonsense word as though it were an English word. He thus received five different levels of experience with the ten core-words. The next part of Experiment I was a determination of recognition thresholds for these ten nonsense words plus ten others which had not been seen before by the subjects. An ascending method of limits was used to determine the tachistoscopic exposure needed to elicit a correct response. The average threshold duration was found to be a decreasing negatively accelerated function of the number of times the subject had previously encountered the words. Those never before seen required an average exposure of about 1 sec. The words that had been seen and pronounced just once before were recognized at an average exposure of 0.40 sec, whereas those encountered twice before gave 0.27 sec as the mean threshold value. The words that had been seen five, ten, and twenty-five times before were perceived at mean exposure values of 0.26, 0.20, and 0.12 sec, respectively.

Visual Search

Experiments which demand visual searching by subjects may be considered to be investigations of the process of attention in one of its most active forms. What are the dimensions of a visual searching task? One is spatial—we must specify the area that has to be searched. Another pertains to numerosity—we must indicate how many figures requiring examination there are on the background to be searched. Still another factor is temporal—we need to state what time limits, if any, are placed on the search. The two investigations we shall review differed markedly in the treatment of the temporal factor. The first one made search time the measure of performance; a trial ended only when a subject had completed the search, his time for the task being recorded. The second study placed a time limit on each trial; the measure of performance was the number of trials on which the search was successfully completed within this imposed limit. Both studies had the size of the display and the number of objects it contained as variables. In addition to differing in their treatment of the time variable, they differed in countless procedural details.

SEARCH TIME AS A MEASURE OF PERFORMANCE. In an experiment conducted by Eriksen (1955) the subject stood before a vertically mounted display area, a square divided into many small cells by vertical and horizontal lines. Ten of the cells, distributed through the matrix in one of a number of irregular patterns, each contained a triangular target cut out of gray cardboard. Nontarget figures, cardboard squares and diamonds, were placed irregularly in some of the other cells. At the bottom edge of each cell was an electrode, a small metal contact plate. When the display was revealed by the dropping of a sliding panel to begin a trial, the task of the subject was to search the matrix to locate the triangles. With a metal stylus he had to touch the electrode in each cell that contained a target figure until he had located all ten, thereby stopping the clock which had been started at the drop of the panel. The time scores indicated the efficiency of visual search under the different experimental conditions that were imposed.

The design of this study involved three independent variables: the size of the display area, the number of cells into which it was divided, and the number of figures scattered through this matrix of cells. The display area was either an 18-in. square, a 24-in. square, or a 32-in. square, a different group of twelve subjects being given each size. The display was divided into a 9×9, a 13×13, or a 16×16 matrix of cells for different trials. For a given trial, either 20, 40, 60, or 80 of the cells were occupied by geometrical figures, 10 of these being the target triangles. This variable of the number of cells in the matrix that were occupied was referred to as the *saturation* of the display. Every subject was tested with the four degrees of saturation and the three different matrices. A different arrangement of the figures in the matrix was used for each of the twelve trials that a subject received.

Eriksen found, as was expected, that search time increased as a monotonic function of two variables, saturation of the display and the number of cells of the matrix. The mean search time for finding the 10 target figures located among 20 in the 9×9 matrix was about 10 sec, rising to about 20 sec when a total of eighty figures were located in the 16×16 matrix. Analysis of the data indicated that the effect on performance of both of these variables was statistically significant.

Search time was also found to be significantly related to the size of the display, but the functional relationship of performance to display size was not a monotonic one. The smallest and largest displays required about the same search time to locate the ten targets, but the 24-in. display required longer to search. Eriksen points to the perceptual-motor methods of performing the task as probably accounting for this finding. For the two smaller displays, the stylus was held essentially stationary while the eyes scanned the display. The subject reached out and touched the electrode with the stylus as each target was located. It presumably took longer to scan the larger of these two displays, so that recorded times were longer for the 24-in. display. In the case of the 32-in. display subjects seemed to prefer using another method; they moved the stylus along the rows of cells as they scanned the figures visually. Whenever a target was seen, the touching of the electrode with the stylus occupied a very brief time with this technique. The search times for this group were thus brought down to about the same level as was achieved with the 18-in. display using the other method of working with the stylus. This analysis of the results emphasizes the fact that a particular research problem in psychology must be approached with a broad understanding of the numerous factors that may affect measurements of human behavior.

SEARCH TIME AS AN INDEPENDENT VARIABLE. An experiment by Boynton and Bush (1956) affords an interesting contrast in method with the study by Eriksen, although both investigations were directed toward a better understanding of visual search performance. Search time was an independent variable in the study by Boynton and Bush, with a subject being given either 3, 6, 12, or 24 sec to locate the critical target form, if any, in a random array that contained a total of either 16, 32, or 64 forms. The dependent variable in this experiment was the per cent of correct identifications of the target for those trials on which a target was present in the array of forms. Another independent variable, besides viewing time and number of forms in the array, was the viewing distance. This was varied over five values ranging from 20 to 68 ft, with resultant variation in the visual angle subtended by the display and the forms which comprised it. At the longest viewing distance the array of figures subtended a visual angle of 2.23° and an individual form subtended an angle of about 5′ of arc.

Critical targets in this study were selected from among six classes of rectilinear figures: triangles, quadrangles, pentagons, crosses, Y-shapes, and nothingons. A *nothingon* was a multipointed figure which resembled the type of nonsense shape seen in Figure 10.5B. Another coined term, *struniform*, was applied to the irregular curvilinear figures which were used as the confusion forms in each array. These resembled the nonsense shapes used by Arnoult (1954), shown in Figure 10.5D. All the forms used in the experiment had been selected for their discriminability on the basis of preliminary study. The particular number of opaque struniforms required for any experimental session were cemented to a circular glass plate which could be rotated to any one of 30 positions to change the general appearance of the array from trial to trial. For half the trials there was no critical target in the array. On other trials, a single one of the rectilinear forms was substituted for one of the struniforms. The subject's task on each trial was to search the array and indicate which of the critical target shapes, *if any*, was present. The opaque forms on the transparent plate were viewed against a diffuse white background sheet that was transilluminated to a level of about 75 mL.

The results of this experiment indicated that the per cent of correct recognitions of critical targets was related in approximately linear fashion to viewing distance and to exposure times up to 12 sec. No difference in performance level was observed when exposure time was increased from 12 to 24 sec, the subjects indicating that in the shorter time they could accomplish all the searching which seemed necessary. The per cent of correct responses was also found to be a decreasing function of the number of forms in the array to be searched, a result that is in agreement with the finding made by Eriksen using very different experimental procedures.

Analysis of the data revealed a number of significant interaction effects of the variables, of which we may mention the one between the number of figures in the array and the exposure time. It was found that for the 3-sec exposure, the number of figures in the array was a more potent determiner of performance than it was when the exposure was 6 sec. When the exposure was 12 or 24 sec, the numerousness of the forms was still less strong in its effect on the per cent of correct recognitions.

FIGURAL AFTEREFFECTS

Most of the perceptual phenomena we have considered have involved some dependence on present visual stimulation. A perceptual effect with an important temporal dimension is the *figural aftereffect*. This effect is a displacement of points or lines in the visual field as a result of *previous* exposure to stimulation occurring in adjacent parts of the field. We may briefly consider the general procedure for demonstrating or investigating the effect before we examine specific research which will further clarify the nature of the phe-- nomenon. The effect is initiated by presenting an *inspection figure*, or *I*-figure, usually containing heavily printed lines or geometric forms, with instructions to fixate a specified point for a period of one to two minutes. A *test figure*, or *T*-figure, is then presented immediately with instructions to fixate a particular point. This fixation point and the one in the *I*-figure have been selected so that one portion of the *T*-figure is seen at a point in the visual field that is close to the position just previously occupied by one or more elements of the *I*-figure. This part of the *T*-figure appears, by comparison with another part of the *T*-figure, to be displaced slightly. This figural aftereffect is readily demonstrated, and the amount of displacement in the *T*-figure can be measured, as our sample study will show.

The figural aftereffect should not be confused with the negative afterimage. The phenomenon we are discussing requires that a particular sort of test pattern be fixated in order to reveal the aftereffect, whereas the afterimage, you will recall, is observed while viewing a blank background. The afterimage mechanism is readily shown to be based on residual retinal activity since monocular stimulation permits the afterimage to be seen only with that eye. The figural aftereffect, on the other hand, can be shown to depend on central neural processes by a similar test. Monocular fixation of the

I-figure can result in a displacement in the *T*-figure when it is subsequently viewed with the other eye.

Measuring Test Figure Displacement by Adjustment Method

We can learn some of the details of creating and measuring a figural aftereffect if we review an experiment conducted by Hammer (1949). Figure 10.7 shows two forms of the *I*-figure, the *T*-figure as presented, and the *T*-figure as it appears when the figural aftereffect is operative. In each case, the dot represents the fixation point. Looking first at the *T*-figure in Figure 10.7C, we note that there are an upper and a lower line, with the lower one located so as to be adjacent to the point in the visual field where either inspection line had been. It is this lower line that is laterally displaced in the figural aftereffect. The upper line in the *T*-figure is placed there as a reference mark for measuring the displacement of the lower line. Of the two different *I*-figures that were used in this study, you see that the one in Figure 10.7A is positioned to the left of where the test line will fall in the visual field and the inspection figure in Figure 10.7B is located to the right of where the test figure will occur. The figural aftereffect is a displacement of the test line *away from* the position of a line in the *I*-figure. The first *I*-figure then, being located on the left, will displace the lower line in the *T*-figure to the right. The second *I*-figure, being to the right of where the test line will be seen, will displace the test line to the left. This direction of displacement is indicated in the hypothetical diagram of Figure 10.7D, which shows how the *T*-figure appears after the inspection figure of Figure 10.7B has been previously fixated.

In this experiment subjects could adjust the physical location of the lower line of the *T*-figure until it *appeared* to be aligned with

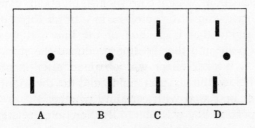

Fig. 10.7. Two forms of the *I*-figure (A and B) and the *T*-figure (C) employed by Hammer (1949). The dot in each case is the fixation point. D represents the appearance of the test figure exemplifying the figural aftereffect which follows prolonged inspection of the *I*-figure in B.

the upper line. This physical adjustment, compensating for the figural aftereffect being experienced, provided a measure of the magnitude of the effect. With this method of adjustment providing the dependent variable, the experimenter studied the effect of certain temporal variables on the magnitude of the figural aftereffect. In Experiment 1 reported by Hammer (1949) the displacement effect was measured every 15 sec to determine how its magnitude changed as a function of the time that had elapsed since the completion of the inspection period. In Experiment 2, aimed at answering the same question, a measurement was taken just once after each inspection. The separate measures were taken after different amounts of time had elapsed so as to reveal the same functional dependence of the effect on time, but without the possible complications that might arise from adjustments made in rapid succession as were required in Experiment 1. Both these experiments showed that the magnitude of the displacement effect decays in time as a negatively accelerated function that begins its decline at the moment that fixation is changed from the *I*-figure to the *T*-figure.

Experiment 3 reported by Hammer (1949) had the duration of the viewing of the *I*-figure as the independent variable. After each inspection, fixation was immediately switched to the test figure for a measurement of the displacement effect. The amount of immediate displacement was found to be a negatively accelerated increasing function of the previous inspection time, with times up to about 75 secs showing an increase in the strength of the effect that was fairly marked. With inspection times beyond this value, only very slight increases in displacement were indicated.

It should be emphasized that the spatial displacement effects observed in the figural aftereffect are not of great magnitude. For instance, the largest group mean displacement obtained by Hammer (1949) was 0.20 mm, which corresponds to about 2 min of visual angle with the viewing distance of 14 in. In all three of the experiments it was found that inspection of the line that was on the left of the fixation point and the test line produced the stronger displacement effect. A weaker effect was obtained after inspection of the line directly below the fixation point and to the right of the test line. It cannot be stated with certainty whether the greater potency of the left inspection line was due to its directional relationship to the test line and the fixation point or to its greater distance from the fixation point. Hammer notes that there is some evidence that figural aftereffects tend to be greater with inspection and testing done peripherally. No matter what explanation is offered, it would appear that this measurement technique might offer a means of studying the functioning of central visual mechanisms as they relate to different portions of the visual field.

SUMMARY

Perceptual processes like attention, discrimination, and recognition intervene between sensation and response. Sometimes they may be considered to be processes of synthesis, sometimes of analysis. Although closely related to sensory processes, perceptions show marked dependence on past experience and on motivation. They loom so large as determinants of behavior that percepts may be considered as tendencies to respond.

The study of perception may be undertaken phenomenologically, with description of experience as the product of the investigation. Many problems have been studied with more conventional experimental methods used in seeking functional relationships between manipulated variables and responses that reveal perception. Among the techniques that have been used are the psychophysical methods for scaling perceptions, stimulus impoverishment for determining limiting factors, and special training for exploring the dependence of perception on past experience.

The perception of form constitutes a vast problem area for the study of perceptual processes. Gestalt principles are readily demonstrated. They may be subjected to quantified investigation as well. Geometrical illusions, once considered as perceptual curiosities, may be analytically studied to obtain data that bear upon normal perceptual functioning. The perception of form can be approached by requiring discriminative performances from subjects.

Size-distance perception is another important problem area. Like other perceptual processes, many of its phenomena are amenable to phenomenological description and to quantification. These different approaches have been used in the study, for example, of size constancy.

The potency of cues from the stimulus configuration is shown in experiments on perception of the vertical. When the environment is seen as tilted, a gravitational referent for the vertical cannot be maintained. The visual cues exercise a measurable effect on subjects' responses in experiments.

Dynamic visual processes are illustrated in the apparent movement phenomenon and the kinetic depth effect. Amenable also to either a phenomenal or an experimental approach, these illustrate the importance of considering the temporal dimension as an important one in perception.

Even though early discussions of attention were very mentalistic in flavor, this perceptual process can be studied with various revealing techniques. The classical span of apprehension studies find counterparts in modern research using dots, circles, and words. These studies aim at refining our quantitative description of the factors that influence the span of apprehension. Visual search experiments represent another mode of attack on attention as an active perceptual process.

Figural aftereffects are a class of phenomena that represent perceptual dynamics with important time-space dimensions. They offer one means of exploring the effects of the organism's structure and functioning on perception. Besides being demonstrable phenomenally, they can be quantified.

REFERENCES

Arnoult, M. D. Shape discrimination as a function of the angular orientation of the stimuli. *J. exp. Psychol.*, 1954, 47, 323–328.

Arnoult, M. D. Familiarity and recognition of nonsense shapes. *J. exp. Psychol.*, 1956, 51, 269–276.

Asch, S. E., & Witkin, H. A. Studies in space orientation: I. Perception of the upright with displaced visual fields. *J. exp. Psychol.*, 1948, 38, 325–337.

Boring, E. G. *Sensation and perception in the history of experimental psychology.* New York: Appleton-Century-Crofts, 1942.

Boynton, R. M., & Bush, W. R. Recognition of forms against a complex background. *J. opt. Soc. Amer.*, 1956, 46, 758–764.

Casperson, R. C. The visual discrimination of geometric forms. *J. exp. Psychol.*, 1950, 40, 668–681.

Eriksen, C. W. Partitioning and saturation of visual displays and efficiency of visual search. *J. appl. Psychol.*, 1955, 39, 73–77.

Fitts, P. M., Weinstein, M., Rappaport, M., Anderson, Nancy, & Leonard, J. A. Stimulus correlates of visual pattern recognition: a probability approach. *J. exp. Psychol.*, 1956, 51, 1–11.

Gibson, Eleanor J. Improvement in perceptual judgments as a function of controlled practice or training. *Psychol. Bull.*, 1953, 50, 401–431.

Gibson, J. J. *The perception of the visual world.* Boston: Houghton Mifflin, 1950.

Hake, H. W., & Eriksen, C. W. Role of response variables in recognition and identification of complex visual forms. *J. exp. Psychol.*, 1956, 52, 235–243.

Hammer, Elaine R. Temporal factors in figural after-effects. *Amer. J. Psychol.*, 1949, 62, 337–354.

Hochberg, J., & McAlister, E. A quantitative approach to figural "goodness." *J. exp. Psychol.*, 1953, 46, 361–364.

Howes, D. H., & Solomon, R. L. Visual duration threshold as a function of word-probability. *J. exp. Psychol.*, 1951, 41, 401–410.

Hunter, W. S., & Sigler, M. The span of visual discrimination as a function of time and intensity of stimulation. *J. exp. Psychol.*, 1940, 26, 160–179.

Ittelson, W. H. *The Ames demonstrations in perception.* Princeton: Princeton Univer. Press, 1952.

Kopfermann, H. Psychologische Untersuchungen über die Wirkung zweidimensionaler Darstellungen körperlicher Gebilde. *Psychol. Forsch.*, 1930, 13, 293–364.

Künnapas, T. M. An analysis of the "vertical-horizontal illusion." *J. exp. Psychol.*, 1955, 49, 134–140.

Mann, C. W. Visual factors in the perception of verticality. *J. exp. Psychol.*, 1952, 44, 460–464.

Saltzman, I. J., & Garner, W. R. Reaction time as a measure of the span of attention. *J. Psychol.*, 1948, 25, 227–241.

Schlosberg, H. A note on depth perception, size constancy, and related topics. *Psychol. Rev.*, 1950, 57, 314–317.

Sleight, R. B. The relative discriminability of several geometric forms. *J. exp. Psychol.*, 1952, 43, 324–328.

Smith, W. M. A methodological study of size-distance perception. *J. Psychol.*, 1953, 35, 143–153.

Solomon, R. L., & Postman, L. Frequency of usage as a determinant of recognition thresholds for words. *J. exp. Psychol.*, 1952, 43, 195–201.

Thorndike, E. L., & Lorge, I. *The teacher's word book of 30,000 words.* New York: Teachers College, Columbia Univer., 1944.

Wallach, H., & O'Connell, D. N. The kinetic depth effect. *J. exp. Psychol.*, 1953, 45, 205–217.

ADDITIONAL READINGS

Anderson, Nancy S., & Leonard, J. A. The recognition, naming, and reconstruction of visual figures as a function of contour redundancy. *J. exp. Psychol.*, 1958, 56, 262–270.

Bevan, W., & Dukes, W. F. Color as a variable in the judgment of size. *Amer. J. Psychol.*, 1953, 66, 283–288.

Boring, E. G. Visual perception as invariance. *Psychol. Rev.*, 1952, 59, 141–148.

Chalmers, E. L., Jr. Monocular and binocular cues in the perception of size and distance. *Amer. J. Psychol.*, 1952, 65, 415–423.

Gibson, J. J. What is a form? *Psychol. Rev.*, 1951, 58, 403–412.

Gibson, J. J. The relation between visual and postural determinants of the phenomenal vertical. *Psychol. Rev.*, 1952, 59, 370–375.

Green, B. F., & Anderson, Lois K. Color coding in a visual search task. *J. exp. Psychol.*, 1956, 51, 19–24.

Heinemann, E. G., & Marill, T. Tilt adaptation and figural after-effects. *J. exp. Psychol.*, 1954, 48, 468–472.

Ittelson, W. H. The constancies in perceptual theory. *Psychol. Rev.*, 1951, 58, 285–294.

Mountjoy, P. T. Effects of exposure time and intertrial interval upon decrement to the Müller-Lyer illusion. *J. exp. Psychol.*, 1958, 56, 97–102.

Onley, Judith W., & Volkmann, J. The visual perception of perpendicularity. *Amer. J. Psychol.*, 1958, 71, 504–516.

Taylor, Janet A. Meaning, frequency, and visual duration threshold. *J. exp. Psychol.*, 1958, 55, 329–334.

CHAPTER 11

Auditory
Processes

Language communication and the enjoyment of music are two outstanding characteristics of our day-to-day life. Our understanding of speech and the pleasure we derive from listening to music both depend, of course, on our sense of hearing. This auditory sense stands with vision in posing a multitude of problems for the experimental psychologist. Our interest will center in research on human hearing, conducted largely by means of the psychophysical methods which are discussed in Chapter 5. Since the experience of hearing normally begins with the impingement of physical energy on the auditory receptors, we shall begin our discussion of audition by considering the physical stimulus. We shall then review the auditory structures, going on to describe basic processes. Finally, we shall study some experimental investigations of auditory perceptual processes like localization of sound sources, discrimination of pitch, perception of speech, and estimation of time intervals.

BACKGROUND FACTS ON HEARING

As a link with our surroundings, hearing originates with energy changes in the environment. To understand auditory research we must know something of how experimenters generate, transmit, and measure the sound energies they use as controlled stimuli in their laboratory studies of hearing. We need to know the major facts about the response of the ear to such physical stimulation, including phenomena that need to be considered in planning almost any investigation into auditory processes.

The Physical Stimulus

Sounds originate in the mechanical vibration of objects like violin strings, vocal cords, or diaphragms in telephone receivers or loud-speakers. These vibrations set up disturbances in the adjacent air that are propagated through this medium as waves of alternate compression and rarefaction. These waves of pressure, or sound waves, are transmitted in the mechanical action of the air molecules until they beat repetitively upon the eardrum to initiate the receptor activities that result in hearing.

THE VIBRATING SOUND SOURCE. Musical instruments and tuning forks produce sound that has a *tonal* quality. Other sources of sound, like a hissing radiator or a phonograph record clattering to the floor, yield noise that is *atonal* in quality. Tonal quality is generated by regularly repeated vibrations of a sound source, whereas noise comes from irregular and heterogeneous mechanical action. Simple harmonic motion of a vibrating body such as a tuning fork yields pure tones. Musical notes result from mechanical disturbance patterns of greater complexity than this when different parts of the vibrating instrument make their own regular contributions to the pressure exerted on nearby air molecules. Speech contains both tonal and atonal qualities.

Besides the distinctiveness of their vibratory patterns, two musical instruments, like the violin and the clarinet, may both produce a great variety of vibrations that differ in two other major respects—their frequency and their force. These physical dimensions of the vibration depend on how the instrument is constructed and how it is played. All the physical characteristics of the sound source, its vibratory pattern, its frequency, and its force per unit area, are represented in the sound waves that travel through the transmitting medium.

TRANSMISSION THROUGH A MEDIUM. Sound waves can travel through any medium that has some degree of elasticity, like air, water, metal, or bone. We shall concentrate our discussion on the propagation of sound waves in air. A vibrating object alternately compresses and rarefies the air that is immediately adjacent to it. As the air molecules are struck and pushed together, they strike other molecules that are adjacent to them, and so on. The region of compression in the air thus moves out from the sound source in a traveling wave even though the air molecules themselves merely vibrate back and forth over a very short distance in replication of the vibrations of the sound source. One direction of motion of a physical object compresses nearby air and the other direction rarefies it, causing a slight partial vacuum. This partial vacuum draws air molecules from somewhat farther away to fill it, and this leads to rarefaction farther on, and so on. A complete sound wave traveling out from a source consists, then, of one or more regions of relative compression and one or more regions of relative rarefaction of the air. As the source continues to vibrate many times per second it generates wave upon wave traveling out through the propagating medium.

Figure 11.1 presents a schematic representation of several sound sources with the waves they send out through the air. The molecules of air are represented by the dots, close together to represent a region of compression and far apart to represent rarefaction. A complete sound wave, generated by each complete vibration of the source, extends from any point in the patterns of compressions and rarefactions to the corresponding point in the adjacent pattern. In Figure 11.1A, the point w designates a location where compression is maximal and point x designates an identical location in the adjacent pattern. The distance from w to x thus encompasses one complete sound wave. A complete sound wave is also designated by the distance from y to z in Figure 11.1B, the terminal points in this instance having been arbitrarily chosen at corresponding regions of rarefaction. Having indicated the terminal points of two sound waves, it might seem natural to go on to specify their wavelengths. Every sound wave has a wavelength that depends on the frequency of the vibrations of the sound source and on the medium through which the wave is passing. Sound travels about four times as fast through water as through air, with wavelengths that are correspondingly four times as great for the same frequency of vibration. Rate of propagation and wavelength also vary for air transmission with temperature and barometric pressure. Due to these variations, it is not customary to refer to the wavelength of sound waves but only to their frequency, the number that pass a given point in a second. This corresponds, of course, to the frequency of vibration of the source.

The tuning fork in Figure 11.1A is vibrating at 512 cycles per second. (A symbol often used to indicate *cycles per second* is ~. Another abbreviation for the term is *cps*.) Our diagram indicates that the tuning fork in Figure 11.1B is generating sound waves at only half the rate that they are initiated by the tuning fork A. Thus the frequency for B is 256 ~, corresponding to the frequency of middle C on the piano. The tuning fork in Figure 11.1C also has a vibration rate of 256 ~, but since it was struck about a millisecond later than tuning fork B, its waves are out of correspondence with those from B by a quarter of a cycle. Correspondence in waves is referred to as *phase*, so we say that the waves from B and C are *out of phase*. Our

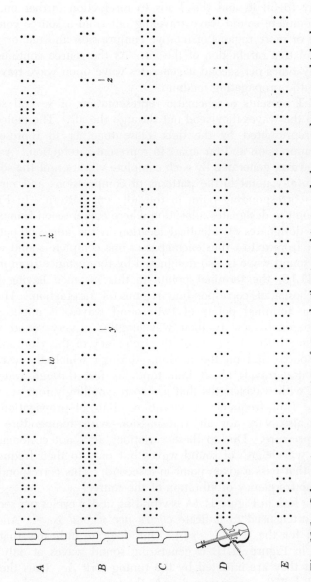

Fig. 11.1. Schematic representation of several vibrating objects and the sound waves which they produce in the air.

schematic representation of the air molecules in the sound waves indicates another difference in the waves from tuning forks B and C. In the waves from C the molecules, represented by dots in the figures, are less densely concentrated in the regions of compression and are more numerous in the regions of rarefaction. These regions thus depart less markedly from the even distribution of molecules in undisturbed air than do the regions of compression and rarefaction generated by tuning fork B. We might infer that tuning fork C is not vibrating as vigorously as B, possibly because it was struck less sharply to set it in motion. Its rate of vibration is the same, due to its identical dimensions, but the force it exerts on nearby air depends on the force applied in setting it vibrating.

The violin string represented in Figure 11.1D is represented as also generating sound waves of 256 $\sim$, but the distribution of regions of compression and rarefaction within each wave is more complex. Although a wave from the tuning fork contains just one region of compression and one of rarefaction, a wave from the violin string contains several alternations of pressure higher and lower than normal for the undisturbed air represented in Figure 11.1E. Such complexity results from the vibration of the string as a whole and by separate parts. Special patterns of vibration are characteristic of different musical instruments and of the human voice in producing particular sounds. The patterns differ from the simple sound waves produced by tuning forks which are designed to produce *pure tones.*

REPRESENTATION OF SOUND WAVES. Figure 11.1 employs dots to represent air molecules in an arrangement which they assume at any instant when sound waves are radiating out from a vibrating object. Although this schema has the merit of close analogy with the actual momentary positioning of molecules when sound waves are being transmitted, it does not permit us to perceive readily the dimensional details of the waves. To do this, another method of representation is preferred. Such a graphic portrayal is shown in Figure 11.2 which represents in the conventional way all the waves which we saw in Figure 11.1. The height of any of the four curves represents, in arbitrary units, the momentary pressure at any point in the waves. The light horizontal line in each part of the figure represents the normal air pressure. Points on the curves that are above this line therefore represent various degrees of compression whereas portions of the curves below the line represent rarefaction in different amounts. All the features of the different waves that could be determined by inspection of Figure 11.1 can be seen even more readily in Figure 11.2. We can see that tuning fork A is producing sound waves at twice the rate that B and C are vibrating. We can see that B and C are out of phase, and also that the regions of pressure and rarefaction produced by C are not as far from normal air pressure as those produced by tuning fork B. It can be seen very clearly, too, that the violin string is producing a wave of some complexity every 1/256th of a second.

The pressure curves of Figure 11.2 may be interpreted in two different ways insofar as their horizontal dimension is concerned. The horizontal axis may be considered to represent the space through which the different pressure distributions are extended at any given instant in time. This interpretation makes these graphs correspond closely to the schematic diagrams of Figure 11.1. Instead of representing space, the abscissa may be considered to represent time with the waveform curve indicating the moment-to-moment change in pressure that occurs at any particular point in space near the vibrating object. If the abscissa is taken as representing space, then the distance from w to x in either of the figures represents the wavelength of waves propagated through air from a tuning fork vibrating at 512 $\sim$, just under 28 in. There are so many factors that affect wavelength that it is more conventional to use time as an abscissa in plotting waveforms. If the abscissa represents time, then the distance from w to x in each figure is 1/512th of a second. This value is called the *period* of the sound wave; it is defined as the interval during which the wave goes through a complete cycle at any point in space. Since the period of the wave is the reciprocal of the vibration frequency, we know that the period represented in Figures 11.1 and 11.2 by the distance y to z on the abscissa for tuning fork B is 1/256th of a second.

With the conventional way of representing sound waves that is shown in Figure 11.2 we speak of the maximum deviation of the curve from the baseline as the *amplitude* of the wave. For each tone represented in the figure this maximum amplitude has been indicated by the vertical dimension line marked A. With A representing the maximum height of the curve, the lower case a may be used to designate an amplitude at any other point on the curve. Considering the waveforms of Figure 11.2 as a time analysis of the auditory stimulus, we have suggested that any amplitude may be considered to represent the pressure of the air at a given place and time.

STIMULI IN AUDITORY RESEARCH. Experimenters studying audition occasionally use complex stimulation such as musical selections or speech sounds. More typically they employ simpler stimuli like pure tones or clicks of very short duration so that the response of auditory mechanisms may be described in relation to these controlled inputs. Sometimes a tone of intermediate complexity will be created by com-

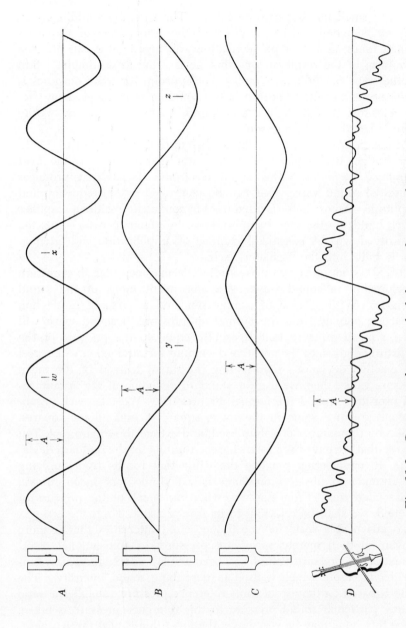

Fig. 11.2. Conventional portrayal of the sound waves of Figure 11.1.

bining a small number of pure tones. These combine additively so that by knowing the amplitudes and the frequencies of the component tones, and their phase relations, an investigator can plot the waveform of the resultant tone that he is using as a stimulus. Still another type of auditory stimulus that is useful for some purposes is *white noise,* so-called because it is a random mixture of many frequencies just as white light is a mixture of many wavelengths. White noise is heard as a hissing sound.

Although pure tones were obtained from tuning forks in early auditory studies, the common tone generator in use today is the *beat frequency oscillator.* This is an electronic device that produces sinusoidal sound waves that can be controlled as to frequency and amplitude. An oscillator is often used in conjunction with an amplifier which builds up the sound amplitude or an attenuator which cuts the intensity down. A considerable range of amplification and attenuation is built into the oscillator itself.

THE MEASURE OF SOUND INTENSITY. We may consider the pressure developed in a sound wave as a convenient index of the sound intensity. With an area of compression and an area of rarefaction departing equally from the normal air pressure, a sound wave will have a mean pressure that is exactly equal to the pressure of the undisturbed air since the negative deviations for rarefaction will cancel the positive deviations representing pressure. Instead of the mean pressure value, then, we use the standard deviation of the instantaneous pressures around the normal air pressure. We take each instantaneous pressure value in the wave, square it, add all the squares, divide by the number of values used, and extract the square root. You can see that we have been following the formula for the standard deviation. In engineering practice the value that results from applying this formula to physical measures is called the *root mean square,* abbreviated rms. From now on, when we speak of the pressure of a sound, we shall be referring to its rms pressure.

To arrive at a scale for specifying sound intensities that is more convenient than merely specifying pressures, a conventional transformation of pressure values has been widely adopted. This yields the *decibel scale* which is used in describing sound intensity. The scale is based on the use of some reference pressure value. The ratio of any particular sound pressure to this reference pressure is taken. Since this value may be very large, the logarithm is next taken. Next, multiplying by a factor of 2 we arrive at a value in *bels.* (The factor of 2 essentially converts the ratio of pressures to one of energies.) To convert to decibels we multiply by 10. Of course, these two multiplication steps are usually combined so that we use 20 as the multiplier of the logarithm of the pressure ratio to obtain sound intensity in decibels, abbreviated db.

Using a reference pressure of 1 dyne per square centimeter, a unitary physical value, let us calculate the intensity in decibels of a sound whose pressure is 100 dynes per square centimeter. First we take the ratio of this sound pressure to the reference pressure: 100/1 or simply 100. The logarithm of 100 is next taken, giving a value of 2. This value is multiplied by the factor 20 to obtain 40 db as the intensity of the sound. It is very important to note that this value of 40 db is a scale value based on a particular reference pressure. As we have described the calculational steps, the formula for N, the number of decibels, is:

$$N = 20 \log \frac{p_1}{p_0}$$

where $p_1 =$ the pressure of the sound being measured and p_0 is the reference level pressure.

Wherever sound intensities are expressed in decibels, the reference level should be given. Decibel values mean nothing unless the reference pressure is known or can be confidently assumed. A commonly used reference pressure is 0.0002 dyne per square centimeter, which is the approximate value of the threshold of hearing for a 1000 $\sim$ tone. If we recompute the sound intensity that corresponds to 100 dynes per square centimeter, we find that it is 114 db when this conventional reference level is used. This reference pressure is one that is used in setting up the scale on some sound level meters with sound intensity readings given directly in decibels, without the need for any computation.

The Receptor

Since hearing is a psychological experience that depends on the functioning of the auditory sense organs as well as on the physical stimulus, we must turn our attention to some of the details of structure of the ear. The different parts of the ear serve to gather in the sound waves and to transmit their patterns inward to the auditory nerve endings which must be activated if we are to hear.

THE OUTER EAR AND TYMPANIC MEMBRANE. The part of the ear that is external to the head is the *pinna,* which serves to help in localizing sound sources. Sound waves entering the outer ear pass through the canal termed the *auditory meatus* until they impose their temporal patterns of pressure upon the eardrum or *tympanic membrane.*

THE MIDDLE EAR. Behind the tympanic membrane lies an air-filled chamber of about 2 cc volume, called the *middle ear.* Suspended by ligaments in the middle ear are the auditory *ossicles,* three small bones called the *malleus, incus,* and *stapes,* or hammer, anvil, and stirrup, respectively. Their principal purpose is to amplify the pressures that impinge upon the eardrum in transmitting them to the fluid-filled inner ear. A part of the malleus rests on the inner side of the tympanic membrane so that vibration of the membrane causes the malleus to "hammer" on the incus, with which it interlocks. The motion is imparted from the incus to the stapes, the footplate of which presses on the *oval window* which leads into the inner ear.

THE INNER EAR. Labyrinthine fluid-filled cavities in the skull comprise the inner ear. Two portions, the *vestibule* and the *semicircular canals,* function in our sensing of head position and motion, whereas a third part, the *cochlea,* contains the sensitive receptors for hearing. Coiled in its bony cavity that is shaped like a spiral snail shell is the *cochlear duct,* which would measure about 35 mm in length if straight. The cochlea or the cochlear duct is divided into three channels by the *basilar membrane* and the *vestibular membrane* which extend the length of the spiral. The foot of one channel is the oval window where the stapes imparts pressure to the cochlear fluid, called *perilymph.* At the foot of another channel is the *round window,* covered with a membrane which can bulge slightly into the middle ear cavity when the perilymph transmits pressure which has been received at the oval window.

The basilar membrane and associated structures are the parts of the inner ear which function to transform the mechanical energies that have been transmitted from the external world into the neural energies of the *auditory nerve.* The basilar membrane is about 0.04 mm wide at the stapes, broadening to about 0.5 mm as it spirals inward. Several thousand *hair cells* rest on the basilar membrane. Collectively comprising the *organ of Corti,* these cells are connected to the fibers of the auditory nerve. It is their stimulation that is therefore believed to be the final step in the functioning of the inner ear.

Dimensions of Hearing

As a sensory experience hearing has certain dimensions which correspond to different aspects of the physical stimulus, sound waves. Some of the attributes of hearing correspond quite closely to particular aspects of sound waves, whereas others seem more dependent upon interactions of different physical characteristics of the stimulus.

CORRELATES OF INTENSITY, FREQUENCY, AND WAVEFORM. These physical dimensions of sound tend to give rise to particular attributes of auditory experience, although we shall see that the simple relating of one psychological dimension to one physical characteristic is not possible. We shall begin, however, by reviewing the relationship of each aspect of hearing to its *principal* physical determinant.

Loudness is a psychological attribute of every kind of experienced sound, whether pure tone, musical note, speech, or noise. Its principal determinant is the physical intensity or sound pressure level of the stimulus. It is mediated by the amount of physical displacement of the moving portions of the ear. The greater this physical action, the more fibers of the auditory nerve that are activated. The vigor of the action initiated by sound waves is also represented in the rate at which the nerve fibers initiate neural impulses.

Pitch is the sensory aspect of tonal sounds which is determined principally by the frequency of the sound waves. Low pitched tones result from low frequency stimulation and high pitch is experienced when vibration frequency is high. The mediation of low pitch is generally believed to occur through the firing of volleys of nerve impulses in synchrony with the frequency of physical stimulation. For high pitch the mechanism is thought to be the occurrence of maximum stimulation at particular points along the length of the basilar membrane, each region corresponding to particular degrees of pitch.

A qualitative dimension of auditory sensation is *timbre,* that characteristic by which we distinguish the voice from a violin, and perhaps one violin from another, even though each one is sounding a note of the same intensity and frequency. Timbre, sometimes termed *quality,* is dependent on the waveform of the sound waves.

INTERACTION OF INTENSITY AND FREQUENCY. Although we were quite correct in identifying intensity as the principal determinant of loudness, and frequency as the chief determinant of pitch, careful scaling of these two attributes of sensory experience shows that they are dependent on an interaction of the two physical characteristics of sound. When an 8000 ∼ pure tone is raised about 40 db in intensity, for example, it will be heard as becoming considerably higher in pitch. The change in this sensory attribute is so great as to require a decrease of about 14 per cent in frequency if the tone is to seem of the same pitch when it is so intensified. Pure tones that are low in pitch seem to become lower when they are intensified. Tones between 2000 and 3000 ∼ do not change much in pitch when they become louder due to an increase in physical energy level.

Loudness, principally dependent on sound intensity, changes quite markedly with changes in frequency. Tones between 1000 and 5000 ~ may be considered as sounding loudest for a given physical intensity level. An intensity level that makes a 100 ~ tone barely audible, for example, will be about 40 db above threshold for a 2000 ~ tone.

OTHER AUDITORY ATTRIBUTES. Auditory phenomenology has a long history of naming tonal attributes in addition to loudness and pitch. Two such aspects of hearing which survived the test of psychophysical investigation are *volume* and *density*. Volume, as a technical term in audition, should not be confused with intensity or loudness to which we refer when we speak of the "volume control" on a radio. As a dimension of auditory experience, volume is defined as the bigness or space-filling quality of a tone. Density is the experienced degree of concentration of a tone. Both of these dimensions of auditory experience were found by Stevens (1934) to depend strongly on interaction between intensity and frequency of the test tones. In comparison with a standard tone, if a test tone of the same intensity was increased in frequency, its volume was lessened while its density was increased. Intensity and frequency contribute more equally to these qualities of hearing than they do to loudness—primarily dependent on intensity—and to pitch—primarily dependent on frequency.

Limits of Hearing

Not all disturbances of the air which would seem to qualify as sound waves actually arouse tonal experience. Both major dimensions of vibration, intensity and frequency, have absolute thresholds in hearing. As in other senses, too, there are differential thresholds. In audition there are limits to our discriminatory abilities for both loudness and pitch.

ABSOLUTE THRESHOLDS. One absolute threshold or *limen* is reached when intensity level or sound pressure level becomes too weak to activate the receptor sufficiently to arouse any sensation. An important fact about the intensitive threshold is that it varies with the frequency of the test stimulus. From about 1000 to about 3000 ~ the threshold is at or near a minimum physical intensity which may be conveniently considered to be a sound pressure level of 0.0002 dyne per square centimeter. The dependence of the threshold on frequency is illustrated by the fact that with a test tone of 10,000 ~, the absolute threshold is found to be around 15 db higher than the reference level of 0.0002 dyne per square centimeter. For a tone of 100 ~, the threshold is almost 40 db higher than this reference value. A plot of the absolute intensitive threshold as a function of frequency, then, yields a U-shaped curve that is higher at the low frequency end than at the high frequency end, with minimal values reached around 2000 ~.

Frequency of vibration also affects hearing limits. When frequency drops below about 15 or 20 ~, tonality disappears from auditory experience, giving way to a variety of repetitive auditory sensations instead of a single sound. When frequency exceeds 18,000 or 20,000 ~ a tone is also no longer heard, the ear being effectively unresponsive to such high rates of vibration.

An upper auditory threshold is considered to exist at the point where sound intensity becomes so great that audition gives way to a variety of tactile sensations in the ear, usually somewhat unpleasant. This limit, not varying as much as the absolute limen with vibration frequency, is reached at from 120 to 150 db above the reference pressure level of 0.0002 dyne per square centimeter.

DIFFERENTIAL THRESHOLDS. We have seen that there are absolute limits of audibility that depend on both the intensity and the frequency of the test tone. There are also limits on the ability of the ear to discriminate between tones that differ only slightly in intensity or frequency. Psychophysical studies have shown that discrimination of loudness, like absolute sensitivity to tones, is best from frequencies between 1000 and 3000 ~. Tones in this frequency range are distinguishable if they differ by 1 or 2 db, provided their absolute intensity is 20 db or more above threshold. If they are only about 5 db above the absolute limen, a difference of about 3 db is needed to discriminate loudnesses in this frequency range. For tones of higher or lower frequency, intensity differences have to be somewhat greater to be detectable. Differential thresholds, like absolute thresholds for intensity, thus depend on the frequency of the test tone.

The differential threshold or limen for the discrimination of pitch also varies with intensity and with the frequency of the standard tone used in testing. Pitch discrimination is best for tones below 1000 ~. For these lower tones a difference of about 5 ~ is usually detectable when intensity is fairly low and at higher intensities, the just noticeable difference drops to about 3 ~. For tones above 2000 ~, the just noticeable difference tends to be a roughly constant proportion of the standard frequency used in the test. At about 10 db above threshold, a frequency difference of about a half of 1 per cent is required for discrimination. With intensity raised to 40 db above threshold, a frequency difference of about a fourth of 1 per cent is detectable when the frequencies being compared are above 2000 ~.

Auditory Phenomena

A phenomenological description of hearing includes many auditory experiences beyond the mere sensing of tones with simple attributes like pitch, loudness, and timbre. We must next consider some of these phenomena and suggest some of the mechanisms that underlie them.

AUDITORY FATIGUE. Analogous to adaptation effects in vision, the ear loses sensitivity as it undergoes stimulation and regains it during a period of no stimulation. The loss in sensitivity, termed *auditory fatigue,* is shown by a raising of the threshold just after the ear has been exposed to stimulation. An experiment by Caussé and Chavasse (1947) showed that the amount of auditory fatigue increases with both the intensity and the duration of the fatiguing tone. Harris, Rawnsley, and Kelsey (1951) similarly found the fatigue effect to increase with the sensation level of the fatiguing tone. Amount of fatigue was less for tones in the frequency range of about 1000 to 4000 ∼ than for tones of lower or higher frequency. Recovery of sensitivity following exposure to a fatiguing tone of short duration takes place in a fraction of a second.

COMBINATION TONES. When two pure tones of different frequencies are sounded together, other auditory phenomena arise on the basis of the response characteristics of the ear. It is the nonlinearity of response, failure to follow the stimulus pattern with complete accuracy, that gives rise to *combination tones.* The frequency of various combination tones derives from the addition and subtraction of the frequencies of the two stimulus tones.

Let us suppose that two intense pure tones are sounded, one of 800 ∼ and one of 100 ∼. We find that in listening to this combination we may be able to hear a *summation tone,* so-called because its frequency, 900 ∼, is the sum of the frequencies of the two tones. A second-order summation tone would have a frequency of 1000 ∼, stemming from a summation of the 800 ∼ frequency and twice the frequency of the 100 ∼ tone. There are also summation tones like 1700 ∼ and 1800 ∼, involving twice the frequency of the 800 ∼ tone plus some multiple of the 100 ∼ tone. Although some of the summation tones are detectable by a listener, the existence of others can be demonstrated only by special experimental techniques.

Analogous to the creating of summation tones by summing various combinations of the stimulus frequencies is the creation of *difference tones* whose frequencies may be calculated by subtraction. For example, the 800 ∼ and the 100 ∼ stimulus tones would give a difference tone of 700 ~. To compute the frequencies of other difference tones we might double the frequency of either component before subtracting. This would lead to 1500 and 600 ~ as second-order difference tones. Again, some difference tones may be heard and others may be detected by special means.

BEATS. The simultaneous sounding of two intense pure tones that are not far apart in frequency results in *beats*. Beats are heard as alternate waxing and waning of loudness. For example, if a 256 ~ tone and a 258 ~ tone are presented together, they will arouse an auditory sensation that will be alternately louder and softer twice each second. The periodicity of this loudness cycle is calculated by subtracting one of the component frequencies from the other. Tones of 1004 ~ and 1000 ~ would thus yield 4 beats per second if sounded together. With small frequency differences giving rise to beats and large ones creating difference tones, some intermediate values of frequency difference yield a rough intermittent quality of sound.

MASKING. If two pure tones of different frequencies are presented to the same ear and they differ widely in intensity, they may not produce combination tones or beats. Instead, the *masking* of the less intense tone by the more intense one may occur. Masking of a tone means rendering it inaudible, or raising the threshold for its detection. If masking is the raising of the threshold for the weaker tone, then the intensity value to which this tone must be raised in order to be heard provides a measure of the masking effect of the more intense tone, the masking tone.

The masking effect is an increasing function of the intensity of the masking tone, as we might expect—the louder the masking tone, the greater the increase in the weaker tone needed to render it audible. The amount of masking that occurs also depends greatly on the frequencies of the two tones employed. Any loud pure tone is generally effective in masking tones that are of a greater frequency than its own. It is less potent in masking tones of lesser frequency. Translating to sensory attributes, the finding is that a tone masks other tones of higher pitch more effectively than it masks tones of lower pitch. Another functional relationship in masking is that a tone is most effective in masking tones of somewhat similar frequency.

AUDITORY LOCALIZATION

Although the spatial aspects of our environment are primarily explored by means of vision, we find that sound sources can be localized in space by means of auditory cues. Among the sound localization problems which have been studied experimentally are the aspects of stimulation which provide the information used in localizing and the size of errors of localization in different planes and directions.

Monotic, Diotic, and Dichotic Stimulation

In everyday life the same sounds impinge on both ears so that localization of sources is based on binaural reception. Laboratory study of auditory localization sometimes requires special manipulation of sound presentation. If a sound is delivered to just one ear, we speak of *monotic* stimulation. Presenting the same stimulus to both ears is *diotic* stimulation. The stimulation is termed *dichotic* when stimuli that differ in one or more respects are applied separately to the two ears.

Physical Bases for Sound Localization

With normal diotic stimulation from a sound source that is to one side or the other of the median plane of the head, the cues to localization are differences in the sound that reaches each ear. If a sound source is to the left of the listener, the sound reaching the left ear is slightly more intense than that reaching the right ear. This difference in intensity is due to the partial blocking of sound waves by the head. The intensity difference serves as a cue chiefly for high frequency tones since these are more effectively blocked by the head. Another difference with diotic stimulation is temporal; tones reach the left ear first, in our example. If a tone is continuous there is generally a phase difference in its reception by the left and right ears. The results of research indicate that these temporal cues are important for tones below about 2000 $\sim$. In the case of complex sounds there are higher frequency overtones so that intensive and temporal differences in diotic stimulation both serve as cues for localization. Complex tones, and clicks or brief pulses as well, have been found to be more accurately localizable in space than pure tones. With diotic differences serving as the cues to localization we might expect —and it can be demonstrated—that monotic stimulation leads to markedly inferior localization.

Discrimination of Points in Auditory Space

Although left-right localization can be quite readily achieved on the basis of diotic differences in the intensive or temporal dimensions of the sound that is heard, such cues are not available for discriminating the elevation of sound sources. Discrimination of different locations is particularly poor when the sound source is in the median plane of the head, equidistant from both ears. If the sound is a familiar one it may be localized as coming from in front of us or from in back on the basis of its intensity, the pinnas acting to reduce slightly the loudness of sounds originating in back of our heads. In laboratory studies, with somewhat unfamiliar sounds presented, we sometimes find confusion of the front-back direction when the source is in the median plane. In everyday life we would rarely make such localization errors because of the extra cues that our surroundings give us. When we are seated at our desk studying, the familiar voice of a friend is more likely to be perceived as coming from the doorway behind us than from the wall in front of us.

Fusion and Precedence

Think for a moment about the auditory cues for localization when an experiment is conducted in the usual laboratory room. In addition to a sound wave's traveling directly from its source to the two ears, there are numerous pathways taken as the sound is reflected from surfaces in the room. The variety of such indirect pathways should serve to complicate the diotic cues for localization, both as to intensity and temporal relationships. We might expect to hear a succession of echoes from even a simple click, yet we hear but one sound. The first stimulation, reaching the ears by direct pathways, seems to dominate, whereas the later stimulation combines with it in a phenomenon called *fusion*.

If the echoed sounds all contributed to cues for localization, we might expect that the localization would depend greatly upon the location and nature of reflecting surfaces in the room. It might seem that by placing good sound reflectors on the right or left of the subject we might alter the apparent location of the sound source. However, it has been found that localization for sources to the right or left is quite good, no matter what the acoustical properties of the room. A *precedence* effect gives a greater potency for localization to the sound waves that reach the ear first, those arriving over the direct pathways. The echoed sounds, arriving slightly later, do not seem to function as cues for locating the sound source.

An experiment carried out by Wallach, and described by Wallach, Newman, and Rosenzweig (1949), indicates that fusion and the precedence effect may be experienced when the same sounds are presented from two sources, loudspeakers placed in front of the subject and 30° on either side of the median plane. With the two speakers equidistant from the subject, a series of clicks produced in both of them simultaneously was heard as coming from a single source near the head or sometimes in the median plane between the two speakers. This illustrates that fusion was operative in this situation. The precedence effect was found to operate also when moving one speaker somewhat closer to the subject seemed to make it the single source of clicks or music. The same sounds coming from the farther speaker seemed to yield to the precedence of those from the near speaker. Both time and intensity differences in the sounds from the two speakers might seem to account for the precedence of the nearer one as the apparent source of the auditory stimulation. A further experiment, involving intensity reduction of the clicks from the nearer speaker, still left this speaker as the apparent sound source. This suggests that the temporal arrival is probably the key to the precedence effect, although the results with music tended to suggest the opposite conclusion—that the more intense source will be the dominant one in determining apparent localization.

Wallach, Newman, and Rosenzweig (1949) also used temporal disparity in dichotic stimulation to study the precedence effect. A pair of clicks was presented in one of their experiments with a temporal disparity for the first click that simulated one locus for the sound source and a disparity for the second click that simulated a different locus. With the two clicks presented in such close succession that they fused into one, the disparity of the first click determined the apparent locus of the source. When the disparity in the dichotic presentation of the second click was made greater, however, the apparent locus was shifted slightly in the direction of the locus that this disparity would have yielded if presented alone.

PITCH DISCRIMINATION

The discrimination of pitch enters importantly into the appreciation of music as well as its production by instrumentalists and vocalists. We have seen that pitch discrimination is best for frequencies below 1000 ~, corresponding to the greater part of the range of most musical instruments and singers. Investigations into pitch discrimination have sometimes used musical instruments to produce the test tones and have often employed trained musicians as subjects.

Besides its importance in music, pitch discrimination is an auditory process which demands study for the information it can yield on how the ear functions. An illustrative study will show how the interval between two test tones was systematically explored as a variable that affects pitch discrimination. Then we shall compare two investigations of a pitch discrimination ability that is of interest in music, *absolute pitch*.

Pitch Discrimination as a Function of Interstimulus Interval

If two successively presented tones are to be discriminated as to their pitch, there must obviously be some neural representation of the first tone at the time the second one is experienced in order that the discrimination can be attempted. It might be hypothesized that the neural representation of the first tone might become less precise as time passed. This should result in an increasing differential threshold as the time separating the two tones to be compared is increased. Harris (1952) systematically investigated the effects on pitch discrimination of interstimulus intervals ranging up to 25 sec.

In one experiment Harris presented the same standard tone of 1000 ~ repeatedly with a comparison tone following it each time after an interval of 3, 7, 15, or 25 sec, these interstimulus intervals being randomly mixed in the long series of trials. On each trial the subject had to say whether the comparison tone was higher or lower than the standard. The differential thresholds were found to be 3.9 and 4.1 ~ when the interstimulus intervals were 3 and 7 sec, respectively. It rose to 4.7 ~ when the interval was 15 sec and to 6.9 ~ when 25 sec separated the tones from the two sine-wave oscillators.

With the standard tone frequency being presented repeatedly it is likely that subjects develop a perception of the standard pitch that helps them in judging each comparison tone as higher or lower. To relate pitch discrimination more definitely to the presentation of the standard tone, Harris also used a roving standard which varied from 950 to 1050 ~. The comparison tone on each trial thus had to be related to the pitch that had just been experienced. Without the opportunity to develop a subjective standard based on many presentations of the same standard, it was found that the differential threshold was greater and that it increased more rapidly as the interstimulus interval increased. For the three interstimulus values that had been used in the fixed-standard procedure, 3, 7, and 15 sec, it was found that differential thresholds were 5.1, 5.4, and 7.9 ~, respectively. The different relationships between threshold and interstimulus interval found with the two different procedures are another illustration of the dependence of experimental results on the design of the experiment. In the present case, both sets of data would need to be considered in any complete theory of auditory perception.

Studies of Absolute Pitch

A discriminatory skill of considerable interest among musicians is *absolute pitch*, the ability to name tones from the range of musical notes. This skill involves more than differentiating two frequencies since it demands the differentiation of a single frequency that is presented from a great number of possible frequencies that are not sounded. Brammer (1951) has presented a number of facts about absolute pitch that are supported by the research literature. After reviewing these we shall compare his experiment with that of Van Krevelen (1951). Although both investigations used trained musicians as subjects and both involved active adjustment of tones as well as passive listening and identification, the details of the studies form an instructive contrast in method.

Brammer notes that absolute pitch has been variously defined with accuracy limits that range from 0.01 to 1 semitone. Despite this diversity in the allowable error, there are conventional tests for selecting persons with this ability. Absolute pitch is an acquired ability rather than an innate skill, with the accuracy of unmusical observers being amenable to improvement through systematic training. Conversely, the ability declines over periods that afford no practice opportunity. Timbre and other qualitative cues are mentioned as helpful by those who demonstrate this skill. Absolute pitch is most easily exercised for notes in the middle of the piano range. Outside this range there is a tendency to judge high tones lower and low tones higher.

JUDGING AND ADJUSTING INSTRUMENTAL TONES. Forty-two violinists were subjects in the study by Brammer (1951), fourteen of them claiming to have absolute pitch. In one session the experimenter sounded notes on a violin and on a clarinet while the blindfolded subject gave directions to change the tuning or playing until the note A-440 was judged to be reached. Five such judgments were taken for each of the instruments. In a second session the subject was required five times to tune a violin A-string to A-440, being permitted to adjust the other strings if desired.

In directing the tuning of the violin by the experimenter, the fourteen subjects who claimed absolute pitch had a group median error of less than 10 cents, a *cent* being 0.01 semitone. For the twenty-eight subjects who did not claim absolute pitch the group median error was over 50 cents, only four of these subjects performing as well as the median of the absolute pitch group. When directing the sounding of the clarinet the violinists not claiming absolute pitch did less well than in directing the violin tuning, with the group median error exceeding 100 cents or a semitone. The group claiming absolute pitch again showed a median error of about 10 cents. In adjusting the violin themselves the two groups showed median errors of about 10 and 60 cents, the absolute pitch group again being superior. In all the pitch-judging tasks there was no complete dichotomy of performance between the two groups of subjects. Some of those not claiming absolute pitch did as well as some who did claim this skill. The nonabsolute pitch subjects indicated more frequently that they used additional cues like other reference tones, auditory imagery, and kinesthetic cues in performing the tasks.

RECOGNIZING AND PRODUCING OSCILLATOR TONES. The study by Van Krevelen (1951) sought a quantitative description of absolute pitch performance under laboratory conditions. Subjects with absolute pitch were selected by means of two screening tests, the first one involving all 88 piano notes and the second employing pure tones from an oscillator. Forty music students who had evidenced absolute pitch were reduced to a group of seventeen subjects by this intensive selection procedure.

In Experiment I a randomly ordered series of pure tones 40 db above threshold were presented for 1 sec each. There were 39 of these, ranging in frequency from 404 to 478 ~, each presented ten times. The subjects had to identify each one as musical notes or as deviations, sharp or flat, from notes like G#, A, or A#, the three notes that fall in this frequency range. The analysis of the data centered on the 2300 responses that indicated a presented tone to be judged on pitch for G#, A, or A#. This number of on-pitch judgments was made although the total number of presentations of these three notes was only about 500 for the entire study. Many of the presented tones were only a few cycles different from one of these three notes, of course. Of the 500 on-pitch presentations, just under 50 per cent were named as on pitch, the others being called sharp or flat. The group mean frequencies of tones judged as on pitch for the three musical notes are presented in Table 11.1 together with the standard frequency values for these notes. It will be seen that judgments of G# tended to be given for tones that averaged about 6 ~ higher than this note, a group mean constant error of about 24 cents. For judgments of A the average frequency of on-pitch reports was too high for about half the subjects and too low for about half. As the table indicates, the group mean for these judgments was very close to the standard A of 440 ~, the mean constant error being smaller than 2 cents. For the higher note, A#, on-pitch judgments averaged about 6 ~ too low in frequency, a group mean constant error of about −24 cents. Of the tones reported "on pitch" by individual subjects, the SD values indicating a person's variability around his own mean frequency value for on-pitch judgments ranged from under 5 ∼ or 20 cents to over 10 ∼ or 40 cents. The group mean of these individual SDs was just over 7 ∼ or about 28 cents.

In Experiment II the same selected subjects were asked to adjust the frequency dial of the oscillator so as to produce either G♯, A, or A♯, called for 100 times each in random order. The adjustment required was a decrease in frequency on half the trials and an increase on half the trials, the amount of change required being varied from trial to trial.

TABLE 11.1

Group Mean Frequencies of Tones Judged as On Pitch in the Recognition Method of Experiment I and Tones Produced in the Production Method of Experiment II (After Van Krevelen, 1951)

| Method | Tone Reported in the Recognition Method or Attempted in the Production Method | | |
	G♯ (415.30 ∼)	A (440.00 ∼)	A♯ (466.16 ∼)
Recognition	421.08 ∼	440.43 ∼	460.30 ∼
Production	415.67 ∼	438.73 ∼	460.21 ∼

The group means for the oscillator settings are also shown in Table 11.1. Accuracy was greatest for G♯ in terms of group mean constant error. Attempts at producing A♯ gave the greatest group mean constant error. The SD for an individual's settings tended to be slightly smaller than those computed for the on-pitch judgments in Experiment I.

PERCEPTION OF SPEECH

Besides serving us esthetically as we listen to music, our sense of hearing functions as the receiver in speech communication. Although most of our use of speech involves the speaker and the hearer in a face-to-face situation, important segments of our use of spoken words involve devices like public address systems, telephones, television, and radio—as used in general broadcasting and in special communication networks. Engineers concerned with the design and operation of such equipment have long been concerned with the intelligibility of speech as it is affected by the reduction of fidelity and the introduction of noise in communication systems.

Psychologists interested in problems of hearing have followed the lead of research workers in the communication field in taking the perception of speech as a major problem area. From the communication scientists they have borrowed the *articulation test,* a practical technique designed for evaluating speech transmission, and have employed it as a framework for systematic investigation.

The Articulation Test

An *articulation test* assesses the effectiveness of a speech communication system by measuring the intelligibility of the spoken messages that are transmitted. The people who do the talking and listening, as well as the electrical and mechanical devices, are considered as factors in experimental work. The articulation score is the per cent of the spoken material that is correctly reported by the listener. A great number of variables can affect scores attained in such a situation.

The person who speaks may be considered to be a source of variables in an articulation test, and the material he is required to deliver is a contributing factor of several dimensions also. The equipment used in the speech transmission can influence the sound patterns of the message in numerous ways. The listeners, too, may vary in their speech perception abilities.

Speakers and listeners selected for articulation tests might simply be persons who were free from defects of speech and hearing. Poor qualities of voice, aside from outright defects, might be sufficient reason for not using some speakers. Auditory tests might be employed to screen listeners. The selection and training of personnel for their tasks are obviously part of such research requiring careful consideration.

The material comprising the "messages" in speech communication research can importantly affect test results. If the listener hears parts of words he may reconstruct the message that was transmitted. If we merely use the digits from one to nine, we find that most of them can be distinguished on the basis of the vowel sound alone. Thus, hearers might frequently miss the consonant sounds but still make high scores. Nonsense syllables are sometimes the material of choice because each *phoneme,* each vowel or consonant sound, must be heard if the item is to be correctly recorded.

Speech Perception under Distortion and Noise

As sound, speech is characterized by great complexity. Physical analysis of even elementary units like phonemes reveals a succession of changes in sound pressure patterns. The sound changes that rapidly succeed each other as we speak involve different amplitudes, frequencies, timbres, and durations. This complexity does not make speech perception more difficult but makes it easier instead. The fundamental dimensions of pure tones, amplitude and frequency, do not play major roles in making speech intelligible. They can greatly be interfered with while articulation scores remain high.

Three ways of interfering with speech are amplitude peak-clipping, interruption, and masking with noise. The hearing of speech has been found quite resistant to masking by noise. The noise level must be raised quite high to reduce articulation scores. In other words, the signal-to-noise ratio, abbreviated S/N, may fall quite low before intelligibility is greatly reduced. Speech is also resistant to the effects of periodic or aperiodic interruption. As much as 50 per cent of a message can be "chopped out" without reducing the transmission of the message by more than 10 per cent, provided the intermittency of sound and silence is at a high rate like ten times per second.

Many devices distort speech by clipping its amplitude peaks, since the power is not available for faithful following of the sound waves through these peaks. Later in the system amplification may boost power again but, of course, the sound wave will have had its form changed in the peak-clipping part of the system. Research has shown that peak clipping can be quite severe without materially reducing speech intelligibility.

Articulation Test Materials

The importance of the kind of spoken material used in articulation tests is illustrated in the data from an experiment by Miller, Heise, and Lichten (1951). A microphone-amplifier-earphones system was used to deliver the test messages from speaker to listener at an intensity of about 90 db re 0.0002 dyne/cm^2. Also introduced into the earphones was a variable level of noise. By using the intensity of the message signals as a reference, the various values of the S/N were expressed in decibels, ranging from -18 with noise at the maximum value employed to $+18$ with noise at the minimal level used in the study. With type of material as a parameter, functional relationships between the per cent of items correctly recorded and the S/N were determined. These curves, for digits, words in sentences, and nonsense syllables, are shown in Figure 11.3. In looking at the figure, remember that it is the S/N that is plotted on the abscissa. With the message signal intensity held constant, the noise level decreases as we proceed from left to right along this scale. As expected, the per cent of items recorded goes up as this decrease in noise occurs. We see that the three plotted functions in Figure 11.3 differ markedly, indicating that the intelligibility of speech in the presence of masking noise varies with the different types of material used in the articulation test.

In pursuing further their analysis of the message in articulation tests, Miller, Heise, and Lichten (1951) point out that the difficulty of the auditory discrimination that is demanded depends very much on the number of alternatives which might be used as items in the test. The per cent of correct identifications will be high if only "boom" and "soup" are the items which may be transmitted. If the list of potential items includes "boom," "boon," "boot," "dupe," "doom," "dune," "soon," "soup," and "zoom," then the articulation scores are likely to be lower. This hypothesis was tested by establishing pools of test monosyllables ranging in number from 2 to 256. The experiment with S/N as a variable was repeated with these different degrees of message restriction. As expected, the per cent of correct responses was higher at any noise level for the more restricted pools of possible test items.

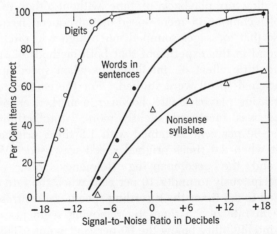

Fig. 11.3. Per cent of items correctly identified in articulation tests as a function of signal-to-noise ratio with type of test material as the parameter differentiating the curves. (After Miller, Heise, and Lichten, 1951.)

Speeded Speech

We noted that a spoken message can be interrupted several times a second with brief periods of silence equal in length to those of speech transmission with only slight reduction in intelligibility. Research has also shown that speech may be speeded up considerably and still be understood. Experiments have been performed with tape-recorded speech played back at rates up to 1.4 times the normal speed before great reduction of articulation scores occurred. This technique raises the pitch of the sound, and this distortion is probably the reason for intelligibility loss when higher playback rates are used. Another method involves having talkers read at extra high rates, but this, too, invites additional distortion in timing and enunciation.

Garvey (1953) experimented with the speeding of speech without introducing the frequency shift that comes when tape recordings are played back at supernormal rates. His technique is based on the work which showed that up to 50 per cent of a message could be replaced by silence without very great loss of intelligibility. In that work the silent periods had been "left in" so that total time for transmitting a message was not changed. What Garvey did was to chop out segments of tape which might be considered as silent periods. Then the tape was spliced together to present the remaining speech segments successively, without silent spaces between them. The cut-and-spliced tape was played at the normal rate. He equated the shorter message times thus achieved with times obtained by merely speeding up playback of tape without other manipulation. This control technique of mere speed-up introduced frequency shift, of course, so that messages sounded much higher in pitch.

It was found in this experiment that both methods of speeding the message had little effect on intelligibility when speed-ups of up to 1.8 times original speed were studied. For the control technique of merely increasing playback rate, however, a marked change occurred when speed was increased slightly more. Intelligibility dropped from around 90 per cent, obtained with 1.8 times original speed, to 65 per cent when 2.0 times original speed was used. With further speed-up, and the accompanying frequency shift, intelligibility dropped precipitously to under 10 per cent when the rate of playback was increased to 2.5 times the recording speed. In contrast, obtaining an increase in rate of 2.5 times by removing segments of tape did not reduce intelligibility below the 90 per cent point. This technique could be used to speed message transmission by 3.5 times and still sustain intelligibility at almost 60 per cent. When the speed-up achieved by cutting and splicing the tape gave message transmission at 4.0 times the normal rate, intelligibility dropped to 40 per cent. The experiment shows that recorded speech may be greatly speeded by removing portions of it and compressing the remaining parts with only a gradual loss of intelligibility as the deletions become more drastic.

TIME PERCEPTION

Auditory stimulation is patterned in time. The temporal dimension is an important one in the analysis of individual sounds and in the description of rhythmic grouping of tones. Discrimination of tonal durations is one of the abilities measured by the Seashore Measures of Musical Talents. Even aside from its implications for musical performance and appreciation, our perceiving of the passage of time is a psychological process that has attracted much experimental study. Some standard techniques of investigation have been devised and conclusions have been reached which describe some facets of time perception. Regarding some details about time estimation, however, there is wide disagreement among the findings. Undoubtedly many of the discrepancies can properly be ascribed to differences in experimental methods. Instead of citing selected results, then, we shall concentrate our discussion of time perception on methods of study and on key independent variables.

Methods of Study

Our experiencing of the passage of time is a private psychological process. It is made accessible for objective study by devising time-judging tasks to be performed by experimental subjects. The standard methods of investigation differ in their requirements so that we do not expect perfect agreement in the measurements they yield. On the other hand, it is to be hoped that experimental techniques will be refined and further standardized, so that a body of reliable facts may emerge from research.

DISCRIMINATION. As in the study of other types of perception, the measurement of discriminatory abilities is one technique for investigating the time sense. Two intervals are successively presented to the subject who must state if the second is longer or shorter than the first. Each interval may be denoted by a stimulus continuously presented during the interval, or the beginning and end of each interval may be signaled by a brief stimulus like a click. An interval so delimited is referred to as an *empty interval.* Empty intervals were used in a study by Blakely that is summarized by Woodrow (1951, p. 1224). For intervals of 0.2 to 1.5 sec a difference of less than 10 per cent could be detected on three-fourths of the trials. This relative difference value, detectable on three trials out of four, rose to 16 per cent when the intervals were about 2 or 4 sec. With even longer intervals, up to 30 sec, this performance level was attained only when the two intervals differed by 20 to 30 per cent. For the comparison of longer intervals, a subject has to retain his perception of the first interval until the second one is terminated. This disadvantage may account for the seemingly less keen discrimination of these longer values. For shorter intervals, it might be appropriate to present them with a compensatory increase in the time separating them so that the retention demand placed on the subject would be comparable to that imposed by the giving of two long intervals for comparison.

ESTIMATION. Quite different from the discrimination method is the presentation of a single interval with the requirement that its duration be estimated by the subject in conventional units like seconds or minutes. The subject's grasp of these temporal units, as well as his perception of the elapsed interval, may affect the reported values. Great variability may appear in the data if subjects are quite unfamiliar with using these temporal measures. If the ability to use these units of time is the focus of study, this is no problem. If, however, we are investigating the effect of different treatments or conditions on the perceived passage of time, then inability to give reports with some consistency may preclude finding reliable differences. In this kind of study, preliminary training in reporting elapsed time might be permissible. The elimination from the experiment of subjects who perform very poorly might also be justified if the effect of different conditions on time perception is the chief problem being studied.

PRODUCTION. This method is the converse of estimation. The subject is required to produce, by manipulating a switch of some kind, an interval or a duration stated by the experimenter. A subject's conceptualization of units like seconds and minutes is likely to be strongly reflected in this performance also. The method is therefore another direct approach to the ability to use standard temporal units in guiding performance. As in the estimation method we would generally consider techniques like counting to be undesirable. The method of production would not be satisfactory for very short intervals unless we could be sure that the motor actions required of the subject are not contributing some bias to the data. It would be undesirable, for example, to make the subject throw a switch that was difficult to operate. For longer intervals, the data might be little affected by the time consumed in the switching action.

REPRODUCTION. In the method of reproduction, the experimenter delimits a time interval by operating a switch, either manually or by means of some timing device, and the subject has to reproduce the interval by throwing a switch on and off. This task demands much less familiarity with units of temporal measurement. Again, counting would not be generally regarded as acceptable. As in the method of production, too, the motor actions required would have to be such as not to distort the data.

Describing Results

The variety of methods for studying time perception is accompanied by a variety of ways of describing results. Bindra and Waksberg (1956) have summarized the terms which have been used in describing the outcome of time estimation studies. They point out, for example, that when the subject's judgment is greater than the standard set by the experimenter, this would be an underestimation of elapsed time in the method of production but an overestimation of elapsed time in the verbal estimation method. This is because the passage of time is part of the subject's response in the production method, with the experimenter having presented merely a numerical value as the standard. In the verbal estimation method the standard interval presented by the experimenter involves the passage of time while the subject merely gives a numerical estimate of the duration involved. The possibility of describing overestimation or underestimation of elapsed time does not arise in the method of reproduction since the passage of time occurs in both the stimulus presentation and the subject's response.

Independent Variables

It is generally agreed that our perception of time intervals is affected by the activity that fills them. Research workers have varied the sensory stimulation of subjects and the activity in which they engaged as they performed time estimations. Besides overt activity, a period of time may be filled by thought processes which are more difficult to control experimentally. A degree of control over this factor may be afforded by careful choice of a task that the subject must perform. Doing mental arithmetic, for example, leaves little time for day-dreaming if one's performance is being watched in terms of answers successively obtained.

The length of interval to be judged is obviously a variable of considerable importance. Studies of the discrimination of shorter intervals have concentrated on control of stimulation, whereas longer periods of time have been used when the behavior in which subjects engage has been the focus of interest. A recurrent problem has been to identify tendencies to overestimate or underestimate periods of various lengths. Improvement of time estimation with practice has been the object of some studies. Still another area of great potential importance has been the effect on the time sense of different physiological states such as those induced by fatigue and by certain drugs. A number of the different experiments attacking all of these problems have been reviewed by Gilliland, Hofeld, and Eckstrand (1946). Rather than duplicating this summary of studies, we shall discuss some of the classes of independent variable that must be employed in further work to establish facts about time perception.

SENSORY CHANNEL. The sensory modality used to delimit presented time intervals was found by Goodfellow (1934) to be an important determiner of time perception, with auditory stimuli leading to superior performance when compared with visual and tactual stimulation. Important for short intervals, the sensory cue is less important for longer durations when the ongoing activity of the subject plays a more important part. For durations of about a second or more, intervals signaled by clicks or by continuous tones or lights have yielded similar data on discriminability (Woodrow, 1951, p. 1225).

ONGOING ACTIVITY. In identifying time perception as a process of mind, philosophers related it closely to ongoing conscious processes. Time was a dimension of these mental activities; they had duration which was perceptible although perceived time might not correspond accurately to real external time. The perception seemed to depend a great deal on the content with which the mind was engaged. When experimental psychologists undertook the study of the time sense, they tried to objectify the relation between time perception and ongoing activity by assigning tasks to be performed by their subjects.

One kind of study in this area is a comparison of time judgment when the interval is filled with some activity and when it is unfilled with any assigned task. Results of such experiments are not in agreement, a considerable part of the difficulty probably stemming from lack of control over the covert behavior of subjects during an unfilled interval. They may actually fill the interval with pleasant day-dreaming, with impatient emotion, or with counting aimed at improving their time estimation. It certainly seems likely that there are types of activity that would affect a person's perceiving of the passage of time. Such activities might vary along dimensions of pleasantness, of demand upon attention, and of required intellectual involvement, for example. It might be best to compare various tasks for their effect on time judgment, omitting the dubious control condition with the "unfilled" interval.

LENGTH OF INTERVALS. An early generalization regarding time perception was that short intervals tend to be overestimated and long intervals tend to be underestimated. From our discussion on the describing of results we know that overestimation and underestimation are terms that depend for their meaning on procedures that have been used. We know that a careful interpretation of reported results would be necessary to see if the generalization is upheld in any experiment.

If long intervals are experienced as shorter than they really are, and short intervals seem longer than their objective duration, then there must be some temporal value that would tend to be judged with accuracy. This would be a duration not short enough to be overestimated and not long enough to be underestimated. It is termed the *indifference interval*.

The determination of the indifference interval has been attempted in numerous investigations, with resultant values about equally as numerous. This elusive point on the time-perception scale has usually been found to be a major fraction of a second. The disagreement of experimental outcomes may merely reflect the sampling error that arises when individual differences are great. Further, since time estimates are generally regarded as very dependent on the stimulus presented as well as on details of experimental method, the indifference point obtained should also reflect these factors. Finally, there is evidence (Woodrow, 1951, p. 1227) that the indifference interval may shift with repeated trials toward the mean or median value being employed in testing. It would appear that instead of isolated studies aimed at a determination of the indifference interval we need a broad empirical attack upon time perception. Such a program of study would certainly cover a range of time intervals and would give careful consideration to stimuli employed, to ongoing activity of subjects, and to details of experimental method.

SUMMARY

Although physiological research is needed to provide a complete picture of auditory processes, many facts about the sense of hearing and related perceptual activities can be determined through psychophysical experiments. The external stimuli for hearing are sound waves. Their pressure levels, frequencies, and waveforms give rise to key aspects of auditory experience: loudness, pitch, and timbre. A partial understanding of how this occurs is to be found in a study of the ear, particularly the tympanic membrane, the ossicles of the middle ear, and the basilar membrane with associated cochlear structures. Auditory functioning is studied by means of a variety of stimuli: pure tones, clicks, complex tones, and noise.

The amplitude or intensity of a sound is measured by comparing its pressure level with that of some reference pressure level, often 0.0002 dyne/cm². Since such pressure ratios may become very great, a logarithmic scale of bels or decibels is employed.

Although loudness is primarily dependent upon intensity or sound pressure level, it depends to a lesser degree on frequency. Pitch, dependent primarily on frequency, is also affected by the sound intensity. Psychophysical studies have shown the existence of two other attributes of auditory sensation, volume and density.

There are absolute limits to hearing, found at both high and low extremes of intensity and at high and low frequencies of sound vibration. Sensation disappears when intensity is too low or frequency becomes very high. When intensity gets very great, hearing gives way to painful sensations in the ear. When frequency gets too low, tonality disappears. Besides these absolute thresholds, hearing has its differential thresholds, quite thoroughly investigated for loudness and pitch. Difference limens for these two attributes vary with both frequency and intensity.

A number of auditory phenomena must be taken into account in planning experiments on hearing. Among those which have been studied quantitatively are auditory fatigue, combination tones, beats, and masking. Sometimes these processes pose problems for designing simple investigations. On the other hand, they may be used as tools for exploring the domain of hearing.

A problem in audition which has been examined with varied experimental techniques is sound localization. The auditory cues that normally permit our localizing of a sound source are binaural. In research, however, diotic stimulation has been augmented by monotic and dichotic stimulation to aid in delineating the localization process. In dichotic stimulation the binaural differences in intensity and phase are sometimes simulated to elicit a localization response. In monotic stimulation, binaural differences are absent; the resultant deterioration of localization indicates the importance of these differences in normal localizing. Localization in a room that has not been soundproofed against echoes is possible because of the fusion and precedence effects, which themselves have been studied experimentally.

Research in pitch discrimination revealed that the differential threshold increases as the interval separating the tones lengthens. This functional relationship varies somewhat as the psychophysical method used in the study is modified. In the form of absolute pitch, a special musical ability, the discrimination of frequencies was studied with a number of experimental techniques in two different investigations. Such research offers an interesting contrast in procedures.

The perception of speech involves many problems in audition which have led to research. Stemming from applied work, the articulation test is a tool of wide utility. Such a test may be used to measure the resistance of speech perception to distortion, noise, and speeded transmission. The materials used in articulation tests have themselves been made the focus of study.

Time perception relates importantly to audition since the temporal dimension is so important in this modality. How accurately we perceive the passage of time has been investigated by numerous techniques. Methods of discrimination, estimation, production, and reproduction have been employed. Time perception has been shown in different studies to depend upon the sensory channel involved, on current activity of the subject, and on the length of intervals used.

REFERENCES

Bindra, D., & Waksberg, Hélène. Methods and terminology in studies of time estimation. *Psychol. Bull.*, 1956, 53, 155–159.

Brammer, L. M. Sensory cues in pitch judgment. *J. exp. Psychol.*, 1951, 41, 336–340.

Caussé, R., & Chavasse, P. Études sur la fatigue auditive. *Année psychol.*, 1947, 43–44, 265–298.

Garvey, W. D. The intelligibility of speeded speech. *J. exp. Psychol.*, 1953, 45, 102–108.

Gilliland, A. R., Hofeld, J., & Eckstrand, G. Studies in time perception. *Psychol. Bull.*, 1946, 43, 162–176.

Goodfellow, L. D. An empirical comparison of audition, vision, and touch in the discrimination of short intervals of time. *Amer. J. Psychol.*, 1934, 46, 243–258.

Harris, J. D. The decline of pitch discrimination with time. *J. exp. Psychol.*, 1952, 43, 96–99.

Harris, J. D., Rawnsley, Anita I., & Kelsey, Patricia.   Studies in short-duration auditory fatigue: I. Frequency differences as a function of intensity. *J. exp. Psychol.*, 1951, 42, 430–436.

Miller, G. A., Heise, G. A., & Lichten, W.   The intelligibility of speech as a function of the context of test materials. *J. exp. Psychol.*, 1951, 41, 329–335.

Stevens, S. S.   The volume and intensity of tones. *Amer. J. Psychol.*, 1934, 46, 397–408.

Van Krevelen, Alice.   The ability to make absolute judgments of pitch. *J. exp. Psychol.*, 1951, 42, 207–215.

Wallach, H., Newman, E. B., & Rosenzweig, M. R.   The precedence effect in sound localization. *Amer. J. Psychol.*, 1949, 62, 315–336.

Woodrow, H.   Time perception. In S. S. Stevens (Ed.), *Handbook of experimental psychology*. New York: Wiley, 1951. Pp. 1224–1236.

ADDITIONAL READINGS

Corso, J. F.   Absolute thresholds for tones of low frequency. *Amer. J. Psychol.*, 1958, 71, 367–374.

Hirsh, I. J.   *The measurement of hearing.* New York: McGraw-Hill, 1952.

Stevens, J. C., & Tulving, E.   Estimations of loudness by a group of untrained observers. *Amer. J. Psychol.*, 1957, 70, 600–605.

CHAPTER 12

Word
Association
and
Meaning

Verbal behavior is an outstanding characteristic of human culture. Language, in spoken and written forms, has long been of interest to specialists outside of psychology—anthropologists, communications engineers, cryptanalysts, and philologists, to name a few. Although the particular emphases with which these various disciplines study language have many psychological implications, we must keep our present discussion somewhat restricted in scope.

Our language habits represent learning of long standing. Although maturation played an important part in our early development of language, it is perhaps reasonable to assume that my verbal behavior today differs from yours largely because of our different patterns of past experience. At the same time, our verbal responses under certain conditions would probably coincide, this time offering evidence of similar past learning. Both the divergence and the coincidence of past language experience may be of interest as subjects perform verbally in our experiments. In studies of meaning and word association we shall be interested in discovering relationships among certain variables. These findings will often reflect learning that took place years before the experiment began, even though studying the learning process is not our aim in the research.

A Key Concept: Association

We may use the term *association* as an intervening variable relating verbal units to each other and to other forms of stimulation and response. It is the value or strength of such associations that is increased through learning. The strength of an association may be inferred from the speed with which a verbal response is given in a certain stimulus situation or from the frequency with which it is given in a group of subjects in particular circumstances.

Association, or associative strength, is a useful concept because it helps us to think about verbal behavior in a number of natural contexts as well as in some of the standard experimental situations. As an intervening variable, association may be considered to be the probability that a particular response will occur in a given stimulus situation. In word association research we study the strength of association that exists between a stimulus word which the experimenter gives and the response word offered by each subject as "the first word that comes to mind." In the measurement of meaning we often find an index of associative strength or the number of associations given used as an indicant in quantifying the semantic aspects of different words. In these two types of research we usually investigate the strengths of association that have developed in the past verbal experience of our subjects.

WORD ASSOCIATION

Philosophers and introspectionists in the early days of psychology noted a structuring of their thought processes, with successive ideas being related by their association in past experience or their logical connection or opposition. One pioneer investigator, Galton, used words as stimuli, noting the nature and the speed of responses that they evoked when he encountered them some time after having written them on slips of paper. We follow his lead today when we use single words as stimuli and record the verbal responses which they elicit from our subjects.

Classification of Methods

As in most other areas of psychological experimentation, there are basic methods in word association study with numerous variations possible to meet research requirements.

DISCRETE VS. CONTINUOUS ASSOCIATION. In *discrete* association we require the subject to respond with the first word that occurs to him when he hears or sees the stimulus word. By asking for a single response we reveal our interest in determining the strongest of all the possible associations between the stimulus word and the others in the subject's vocabulary.

Continuous association is demanded when we ask subjects to produce a list of words as rapidly as they come to mind upon hearing the
stimulus word. Sometimes the stimulus for continuous association is
the naming of some category, like "names of famous men," within
which responses are to be produced in as rapid succession as possible.

FREE VS. CONTROLLED ASSOCIATION. In *free* association, as the term
implies, subjects are free to produce any response words that first
occur to them. In *controlled* association, responses are restricted to
some announced category like "opposite in meaning" which might
be required for discrete responses to adjectives as stimuli. Our
"famous men" category represents a type of control for continuous
association.

EMPLOYMENT OF THE METHODS IN RESEARCH. Either a free or a
controlled condition may be imposed on either discrete or continuous association, giving four possible combinations. Our prior
discussion has briefly indicated how the free-discrete, controlled-
discrete, and controlled-continuous combinations might be used. The
free-continuous type of association might be initiated by merely
requesting a subject to "say words as they come to mind." In using
controlled association, we might employ different restrictive categories that would impose varied degrees of limitation on the responses
that could be made. Contrast, for example, the restriction imposed
by "famous men" with "famous scientists" as a designation of the
category for controlled association.

The word association test has been used to examine individual
persons and to determine empirical response probabilities in large
samples of subjects representing some population. In these uses,
some conventional form of the basic methods has been employed in
a fairly straightforward manner. As a tool for experimentation today
the fundamental aspects of word association can be supplemented by
a variety of technical procedures to explore more dynamic aspects
of verbal behavior.

Indices of Associative Strength

The stimulus-response behavior which is studied in word association
is generally supposed to reveal the strength of association existing
between the stimulus word and the response word that is given.
Some of the frequency measures that are taken are indices that
represent general associative tendencies in the group being studied,
whereas other measures refer more specifically to the verbal habits of
the individual being tested.

FREQUENCY OF INDIVIDUAL RESPONSE WORDS. It is generally found that a group of subjects of similar general background will tend to give one of a fairly small number of response words to a particular stimulus item in a free-discrete association test. By preparing a frequency distribution of the responses that are given we may scale the more frequently given responses as being the stronger in associative strength for this group of persons.

FREQUENCIES WITHIN RESPONSE CATEGORIES. The diversity of individual response words that may be given to a particular stimulus word has led investigators to devise categories for the description of responses. A fourfold classification presented in Woodworth and Schlosberg (1954, p. 52) serves to illustrate such an attempt. It is given here with slight changes in class labels and different examples:

Class 1. Definition. This class would include synonyms, supraordinates, and probably subordinates.

Examples: To the stimulus AFRAID, a synonym response might be SCARED.

To TABLE, a supraordinate response might be FURNITURE.

To FISH, a subordinate response might be FIN.

Class 2. Completion or predication. Many associations in this class might be of the adjective-noun or the noun-verb sort, expressive of a descriptive or a functional association.

Examples: WHITE—SNOW
TABLE—EAT
AFRAID—DARK

Class 3. Coordinates and opposites. Similar or contrasting responses are classed together because they have been found to go together in the responses made by particular subjects to a large number of stimulus words. If many coordinates are given by a subject, many opposites are usually given also; if one of these types of response is scarce, the other is likely to be infrequent as well.

Examples: TABLE—CHAIR
WHITE—BLACK
AFRAID—BRAVE

Class 4. Unique responses. These are less often governed by semantic relations between stimulus and response. Many types of unique response may occur. The associations may stem from the personal experience of the person responding. The responses may be evaluative in relation to the stimulus. Another variety is the so-called *clang* association, with the response tending to echo part of the stimulus sound.

Examples: TABLE—CELERY
WHITE—ALMOST
AFRAID—ROCKS

The preceding system of classification, like others which have been suggested, is not without its difficulty of application in some instances. We shall see later, however, that categorization is useful in describing some word association phenomena.

REACTION TIME. The response latency between stimulus and response has been considered an index of associative strength just as *RT* has been taken as a measure of reaction potential in other research. This temporal measurement of the interval from the giving of the stimulus word to the making of the response word in discrete association can be obtained through the use of voice-activated electrical switches, termed *voice keys*. These are operated as experimenter and subject say the stimulus and response word, respectively. Voice-key reaction times may be affected by extraneous verbalization on the part of a subject, as when he says "uh . . ." before giving the response word itself. This difficulty may be overcome by having the experimenter do all timing with a stop watch. This method, too, has possibilities for error but is satisfactory for some purposes.

RATE OF RESPONSE PRODUCTION. In the method of continuous association, the number of items produced in each successive interval is one measure of performance. If oral responses are tape-recorded, such counting of responses may be done when the tape is played back, dividing the verbal production into segments of any desired duration. If subjects are required to write their continuous associations, they may be asked at regular intervals to draw a line under the word just written in order to designate the passage of time. With time intervals indicated throughout the verbal production we can plot the response rate for various parts of the task.

CLUSTERING. If free-continuous association is a subject's task, we are likely to observe *clusters* of words in sequence at various points in the performance. Such clusters have to be identified on the basis of independent information about associative values or semantic scaling of the words. Once these facts have been determined, the description of verbal behavior in free association is enhanced by cluster analysis.

Clustering may occur within a continuous controlled sequence of associations. Within the category assigned for the task there may be subcategories. These may give rise to special clusters in the sequence of word production. Thus, if asked to name scientists, a subject might tend to cluster the names he produced by scientific specialty or by nationality of scientist.

Background Facts and Findings

The fundamental free-discrete association experiment involves giving a stimulus word and recording the verbal response to it, often measuring the response latency. Before we turn to studies which elaborate on the basic procedure, we will discuss some of the facts encountered in the simpler stimulus-response situation.

FREQUENCY DISTRIBUTIONS OF RESPONSES. Rosanoff (1927) has reported on the responses given orally by individuals to 100 stimulus words presented orally by an examiner in an individual testing situation. The stimulus words of this Kent-Rosanoff list, often used in subsequent research, are presented in Table 12.1. The frequencies with which various discrete responses were made in free association by the Kent-Rosanoff sample of 1000 people are presented on page 345 for three of these stimulus words, TABLE, WHITE, and AFRAID.

TABLE 12.1

The 100 Stimulus Words of the Kent-Rosanoff List (After Rosanoff, 1927)

TABLE	SWEET	HIGH	MEMORY	BUTTER
DARK	WHISTLE	WORKING	SHEEP	DOCTOR
MUSIC	WOMAN	SOUR	BATH	LOUD
SICKNESS	COLD	EARTH	COTTAGE	THIEF
MAN	SLOW	TROUBLE	SWIFT	LION
DEEP	WISH	SOLDIER	BLUE	JOY
SOFT	RIVER	CABBAGE	HUNGRY	BED
EATING	WHITE	HARD	PRIEST	HEAVY
MOUNTAIN	BEAUTIFUL	EAGLE	OCEAN	TOBACCO
HOUSE	WINDOW	STOMACH	HEAD	BABY
BLACK	ROUGH	STEM	STOVE	MOON
MUTTON	CITIZEN	LAMP	LONG	SCISSORS
COMFORT	FOOT	DREAM	RELIGION	QUIET
HAND	SPIDER	YELLOW	WHISKEY	GREEN
SHORT	NEEDLE	BREAD	CHILD	SALT
FRUIT	RED	JUSTICE	BITTER	STREET
BUTTERFLY	SLEEP	BOY	HAMMER	KING
SMOOTH	ANGER	LIGHT	THIRSTY	CHEESE
COMMAND	CARPET	HEALTH	CITY	BLOSSOM
CHAIR	GIRL	BIBLE	SQUARE	AFRAID

to TABLE:		*to* WHITE:		*to* AFRAID:	
267	chair	308	black	197	fear
76	wood	170	color	114	dark
75	furniture	91	snow	106	scared
63	eat	51	light	55	nervous
57	cloth	35	dark	55	timid
40	dishes	34	dress	53	coward
36	stand	20	pure	48	frightened
34	eating	19	purity	18	brave
29	food	17	cloth	16	darkness
26	dinner	17	paper	15	danger
17	cover	11	colorless	12	night
14	board	10	clean	11	courage
13	leg	9	blue	9	fright
11	desk	9	milk	9	terror
10	legs	7	red	8	child
10	round	7	yellow	8	fearful
9	bench	6	green	8	fearless
9	hard	6	sheet	7	dread
9	square	6	wall	5	courageous
8	article	5	paint	5	cowardice
7	book	4	bright	5	lonesome
7	chairs	4	cloud	5	nothing
7	floor	4	house	5	uneasy
6	meal	4	tablecloth	4	ghost
6	spoon	1, 2, or 3 of 111		4	go
6	writing		others, including:	4	nervousness
5	books		almost	4	run
5	dish		bird	1, 2, or 3 of 161	
5	flat		Broadway		others, including:
4	dining		cherries		accidents
4	large		colored		animals
4	meals		daylight		bears
4	plate		face		careful
1, 2, or 3 of 90			good		dare
	others, including:		innocence		dogs
	accommodation		lovely		happy
	celery		nearly		hurt
	eatables		pleasing		lonely
	ink		rightness		mouse
	Mabel		silvery		police
	old		soul		rocks
	room		tent		shy
	soup		wedding		suffering
	tea				timidity
	whist				worry

Several facts stand out in these sample frequency distributions of responses:

1. Certain response words are given by substantial proportions of the group tested. "Chair" was given as the verbal response to TABLE by almost 27 per cent of those tested. The stimulus WHITE elicited "black" from over 30 per cent of the subjects. Several other responses were found to be made commonly to each of these stimuli.

2. In contrast to the communality of some responses were the large number of individual responses given. The majority of the words presented at the end of each of the response lists were given by only one person.

3. Almost all the response words are seen to have a semantic relation to the stimulus word. Word association offers promise for the study of meaning, an aspect of verbal behavior to which we shall pay special attention later in this chapter.

4. The different responses appear to reflect an experiential contiguity with their stimulus word. This may have occurred in past verbal behavior as in commonly used phrases like "afraid of the dark" or it may have been part of more overt behavior patterns like sitting at the dining table to eat.

5. Some responses are found that reflect each category or class in the classification system which we reviewed earlier. For example, look at the following tabulation:

| | Response Category | | | |
Stimulus	Definition	Completion	Coordinate	Unique
TABLE	furniture	eat	chair	whist
WHITE	color	snow	blue	pleasing
AFRAID	scared	dark	brave	rocks

Although the frequency values indicating communality of response to a stimulus like TABLE drop off very rapidly after we pass the most frequent two or three, by making certain semantic combinations we can identify some very common associations which find expression through a number of response words. For example, we find that *eating* is reflected in over 200 responses to TABLE if we consider that this concept is represented in these responses from the Rosanoff tabulation: *dining, dinner, dish, dishes, eat, eating, food, meal, meals, plate, spoon.* Such a grouping of responses may heighten the usefulness of the frequency index of communality in word association research. We might conduct an experiment, for example, to see if responses related to *eating* occur more commonly just before meal times or just after meals when the stimulus word for discrete free association is TABLE.

COMMUNALITY DIFFERENCES BETWEEN SUBJECT GROUPS. The establishing of normative frequency data, as in the Kent-Rosanoff investigation, is obviously desirable as a basis for studies aimed at determining the antecedents of word association and exploring its mechanisms. We face the serious question, however, of what group is to be considered appropriate as the source of such norms. It has been pointed out that the frequency distribution of responses is likely to vary with the cultural background, the age, and the intelligence of those tested.

Our culture itself has changed in the half-century since the Kent-Rosanoff data were collected. This would call into question the present-day validity of the frequencies they obtained for responses to at least some of their stimulus words. The difficulty in drawing a large random sample of persons from the general population has precluded any attempt to keep the normative data current. It may be that psychologists can organize a cooperative effort to obtain such data in all parts of the country. If such a study were undertaken, the careful selection of the stimulus words to be used would contribute greatly to its value. Which words from Table 12.1 would you include in the investigation, and what other words would you suggest for the stimulus list?

College students have been found to give the same responses most frequently as had been given by the 1000 men and women in the Kent-Rosanoff study several decades earlier. However, a considerably larger per cent of Brown University students responded with the most popular response than was the case in the Kent-Rosanoff group or in a group of students at the University of Minnesota. Woodworth and Schlosberg (1954, pp. 55–56) present these comparative data with the suggestion that the set for speed, which was induced by the reaction time measurement in the procedure at Brown, may have led these subjects to give predominantly superficial responses, opposites and other coordinates, with resultant concentration of the responses which occur most popularly.

ADDITIONAL FACTS ON RESPONSE COMMUNALITY. What is the strength of the associative connection between the concepts *man* and *citizen?* Perhaps you will agree that these two notions tend to be moderately associated with one another. By using one of them as a stimulus word we might use the response frequency of the other one as an index of associative strength. We find, however, that our choice of which one to use as the stimulus would greatly affect our finding.

TABLE 12.2

Responses Given, with Frequencies Indicated, to the Stimulus Words MAN and CITIZEN by 1000 Adult Subjects (After Rosanoff, 1927)

to MAN:	*to* CITIZEN:
394 woman	278 man
99 male	35 American
44 boy	27 city
32 strength	26 good
30 person	25 native
22 human	23 inhabitant
19 being	19 foreigner
15 father	17 country
12 animal	14 alien
12 tall	11 law
11 large	
10 child	
10 good	

Also, a sample of responses occurring fewer than 10 times: adult, animate, appearance, baby, bad, beard, beast, biped, blond, body, cane, certain, Charles, children, devil, doctor, dress, educator, female, form, fraud, Fred, friend, gentle, gentleman, girl, husband, individual, insane, janitor, Joe, labor, laborer, lord, love, machine, maiden, mammal, manhood, mankind, manliness, manly, marriage, married, masculine, misery, money, monkey, passion, people, pleasure, policeman, self, sex, shirt, shoes, short, sweetheart, thought, trousers, wedding, whiskers, wife, wise, works, worker, working, young

Also, a sample of responses occurring fewer than 10 times: America, Americans, army, Brooklyn, brother, business, civics, civilian, civilized, clothes, club, commander, constitution, cosmopolitan, democrat, duties, duty, dweller, emigrant, emigration, faithful, farm, farmer, fellow, fellowship, gentleman, German, government, green, helper, home, honest, honor, honorable, human, I, immigrant, independence, legislature, Lincoln, little, live, lives, loyal, male, manhood, mayor, nationality, natural, naturalization, nonsense, obedient, obey, occupant, paper, papers, patrician, patriot, president, proud, relative, republic, statesman, stationed, straight, subject, village, voting, Washington

As Table 12.2 shows, the Kent-Rosanoff study showed no one responding with "citizen" when MAN was the stimulus. When CITIZEN was the stimulus, though, almost 28 per cent of the subjects said "man" in response. The word MAN suggests many coordinates and supraordinates including *animal, being, boy, father, human, person,* and *woman.* These take up many of the response frequencies, competing successfully with any tendency there might be for "citizen" to occur as a response. The response "woman" was given to the stimulus MAN by almost 40 per cent of the Kent-Rosanoff subjects, for example. In the absence of such a prominent coordinate response, CITIZEN tends to elicit "man" as a defining-type of response. The monosyllabic "man" would also lend itself to the requirement for a quick response.

With dozens of different responses being given to any particular stimulus word in the Kent-Rosanoff study, we need to discover why substantial numbers of them are concentrated in particular response words. Our examination of the frequency tables suggests a major determinant of the popular responses—semantic or experiential relationships. Data have been presented by Johnson (1956) to suggest another factor that may contribute to the particular response words that are given in word association tests. He found that the most commonly given responses in the Kent-Rosanoff study are those which appear most frequently in printed English according to a word count by Thorndike and Lorge (1944). The Kent-Rosanoff stimuli are themselves words of very frequent occurrence for the most part. It might be well, in compiling stimulus lists, to use a few words of rare occurrence to see if the common responses still tend to be words frequently employed in the written language.

RELATION OF REACTION TIME TO COMMUNALITY. If communality and reaction time are two measures of associative strength in discrete free association, then we might expect them to be correlated. Associations that appear with prime frequency in a group of subjects ought to be so well developed in the individuals that they occur with short latency. We suggested earlier that adopting a set for quick response seemed to increase the proportion of college students who gave the most popular response.

The relationship between communality and associative reaction time was investigated by Schlosberg and Heineman (1950). Using just the monosyllabic Kent-Rosanoff stimuli and having the experimenter operate a 0.01 sec timer when the stimulus and response were given, they tested 204 college students. Skewness in the RT data was eliminated by a logarithmic transformation. The median log RT was then determined for each degree of communality represented in the response frequency data. From the paired measures, degree of communality in per cent and median log RT, a correlation coefficient of $-.80$ was computed. The negative value indicates, of course, that shorter RTs were found for the more frequently given responses. This general relationship has been known as Marbe's law, after one of its early investigators.

REACTION TIME OF FREE VS. CONTROLLED ASSOCIATIONS. One question that might be asked about the four response categories presented earlier is whether they relate closely to the performance of subjects in word association or whether they are merely classes of word relationships useful for the experimenter's purposes of organizing frequency data. Evidence that this classifying of responses is a meaningful way of dealing with word association is found in a study of associative reaction times.

Baker and Elliott (1948) measured association-times for common responses to stimulus words under two experimental conditions. Under one condition subjects were instructed to give opposites as their responses to certain adjectives and to give part-whole reactions to selected nouns. These instructions resulted, for example, in their saying "down" in response to UP and "fish" in response to FIN. These were the common responses which occurred most frequently under the other condition with no special instructions as to any class of response desired. If the coordinate category of opposites and the completion category of the part-whole relationship are actually related to the organizing of verbal behavior, we should expect the instructions to make a certain class of response to be facilitating in the selection and making of the response under this condition. Association-times, or associative reaction times, should be shorter with such facilitation under this controlled association condition.

Comparing mean reaction times of different groups for the occurrences of the most commonly made response only, Baker and Elliott (1948) found that in all instances shorter *RT*s were found under the controlled condition than under the free association condition. Several of the differences were statistically significant. It appears that instructions to respond with words of a certain class of relation to the stimulus words result in a facilitating set, or response readiness.

Illustrative Experiments in Word Association

Now that we are acquainted with some of the basic facts about word association and its measurement, we may examine a small sample of studies which elaborate on the fundamental procedures. These deal with methodology, with special experimental manipulations, and with certain aspects of continuous association.

A METHODOLOGICAL STUDY ON MODE OF PRESENTATION. An investigation of several procedural variations in free-discrete association was made by Buchwald (1957). We shall here discuss only Experiment I which compared the auditory with the visual mode of presentation of stimulus words, the responses being written by the subjects who were run in groups. The effect of this procedural difference on the frequency distribution was sought for ten stimuli from the Kent-Rosanoff list: AFRAID, BED, BOY, COMFORT, DARK, EAGLE, HEAVY, TABLE, THIRSTY, and WISH.

The distributions of responses showed no significant differences for seven of the stimulus words. For AFRAID, EAGLE, and HEAVY, however, significant differences were found. This effect of how the stimulus words were presented is certainly strong enough to demand attention in comparing studies in word association. Frequencies of different responses under different conditions should be compared only if the mode of stimulus presentation was the same.

MANIPULATION OF CONTEXT STIMULI. The verbal stimuli to which we respond when we read or when we hear someone speak are rarely experienced as single isolated words. More often they reach us in a sequential context of surrounding words. Two studies which attempted to work with this dimension of verbal stimulation may be cited. They form an interesting contrast in experimental procedure and findings.

Cofer and Ford (1957) created a preceding-word context by having subjects alternately read and give word associations to stimulus words presented individually in a series. The words read were either a synonym of the stimulus word which followed or else were unrelated to it. It was hypothesized that reading a context word of similar meaning would establish a facilitating set for the associative response to the stimulus word presented next in the list. This was expected to lead to shorter reaction times than would a context word of unrelated meaning. It was found, however, that associative reaction times under these two different context conditions were not significantly different. This was the finding despite the fact that the context words were experienced both as stimuli and as overt responses occurring when the subjects read them from the list.

Howes and Osgood (1954) provided a verbal context by speaking four successive words to the subject, having instructed him to give a discrete free association to the fourth one. The first three words were either related or unrelated in meaning to the fourth one in different combinations which formed the experimental conditions. The pattern of response frequencies to the fourth word was found to change, in one experiment, to an extent that depended on whether one, two, or three of the preceding context words had been chosen for their semantic relation to this stimulus. With a greater number of them suggesting a certain meaning for the stimulus word, a greater influence on the response frequencies was found. For example, when *devil, fearful, sinister* were the semantically related context words which preceded the stimulus word, *dark*, a greater frequency of response words fell in the associative cluster, *bad, evil, fear, fright,* etc., than when the context words were *devil, eat, basic.*

In another experiment reported by Howes and Osgood (1954), three different context words were varied in sequence as they were presented just before the stimulus word. Each context word was semantically related to the stimulus in a different way. It was found that the context word which was presented most proximally to the stimulus word, that is, in the third position in the series of four words, exerted most influence on the responses which were made by the different subjects.

ASSOCIATIVE STRENGTH IN RECALL. High associative strength between "table" and "chair" is indicated by the high frequency with which this pair occurs in group data on word association and by the short associative *RT* with which one of these is given as a response to the other. If this associative strength is to be a really useful intervening variable it should be reflected in verbal behavior even outside the word association experiment where the concept had its major development. We shall next examine two studies in which intraverbal associations manifested themselves in the verbal behavior exhibited in a memory task.

In a study by Jenkins and Russell (1952) 24 of the Kent-Rosanoff stimulus words and the 24 corresponding responses of greatest frequency of occurrences were put in a random order to form a list. This list was read to experimental subjects who were then given several minutes to write down all the words they could recall, without any concern for sequence of presentation. The hypothesis was that the associative bonds found in word association would reveal themselves in this recall task by the coming together of stimulus-response pairs as subjects wrote out their responses. It was found that these pairs did occur together in the word lists produced by the subjects. The mean number of words recalled was about 24 out of the 48. The predicted pairings were far more frequent than the occurrence of arbitrarily designated word pairs which provided control data. It was also found, as predicted, that the associated pairs were given by subjects more frequently in the stimulus-response order than in the response-stimulus order. This associative clustering of word pairs is evidence that such associations as *table-chair* and *man-woman* are functional in verbal behavior more generally than in just word association tests.

In a somewhat similar investigation, Bousfield and Cohen (1955) created two 60-word lists, each composed of 15 words from each of the following categories: animals, masculine names, professions, vegetables. One list consisted of items frequently used, whereas the other contained words from the same four categories but of much lower frequency of usage. These two lists were presented to separate groups by projecting them in a random order on a screen at the rate of about 20 per minute. A 10-min recall period was given following this single presentation of the 60 words. Subjects wrote down all the words they could remember. It was found that words from each of the four categories—A, N, P, or V—tended to cluster together in these recall lists. The list of words of higher frequency of usage led to better recall and a greater tendency to clustering than the list of less frequently used words.

CHARACTERISTICS OF CONTINUOUS CONTROLLED ASSOCIATION. In listing measurements of word association, we noted that rate of occurrence would be an appropriate behavioral measure for continuous association. Bousfield and Sedgewick (1944) have described some quantified analyses of continuous controlled association. They had subjects write down all the words they could think of within certain categories like "U. S. cities" or "birds." As the subject listed their responses as rapidly as possible, they were instructed after every 2 min to draw a line below the last word written and to continue writing. The experimenters thus obtained data on the number of word associations occurring in successive 2-min intervals.

The group means of cumulative number of responses were plotted as a function of elapsed writing time. The curves which were obtained depicted performance of this continuous controlled association task. Two such functional relationships are presented in Figure 12.1 where the points represent the empirical group statistics for two tasks. Task A was the continuous naming of fellow college students, whereas Task B was the writing of names of animals of two or more syllables. The curves represent the equation fitted to these two sets of data. It was found that this type of verbal performance can be represented by the following equation:

$$n = c(1 - e^{-mt})$$

where n = the cumulative number of responses given.

t = elapsed time devoted to the task.

e = the base of common logarithms, 10.

c = a constant representing the numerical limit of available associations.

m = a constant representing the negatively accelerated rate of approach to this limit, c.

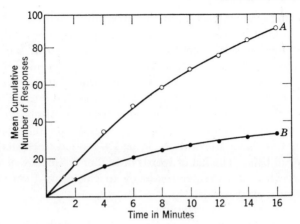

Fig. 12.1. Group mean cumulative numbers of responses given in two continuous controlled association tasks. *Task A:* naming fellow college students. *Task B:* naming animals. (After Bousfield and Sedgewick, 1944.)

When this general equation was fitted to the empirical data for Task A, represented in Figure 12.1, it was calculated that $c = 128$ and $m = 0.0775$ for producing the names of fellow students. This value for c suggests that 128 names would be the average production by this sample of subjects if they were given unlimited time. The interpretation of the value of m is best achieved by reference to the plotted curves. The curve for Task B has a c value of 37.3 and an m value of 0.1427. Task B is thus seen to have a lower limit to theoretical total production but a faster rate of approach to that limit. This faster rate, represented by the greater m value for Task B, is identifiable in the plotted curves.

A different quantitative analysis was applied to the verbal behavior occurring in continuous controlled association in a study by Bousfield and Barclay (1950). They tested the hypothesis that the responses given more commonly by the group of subjects would also be those which occurred earlier in the lists of words produced by individuals in the group. We noted earlier that group frequency data are considered to reflect associative strengths. This hypothesis suggests a correlation between such frequency data and the order in which words are produced. Ordinal position in continuous association is thus offered as another index of the associative strength linking a particular response to the key word with which the experimenter designates the category of words to be produced. The lower the ordinal rank, that is, the earlier a response word is given, the higher the strength of association or habit that is indicated.

In one part of this study 100 subjects were given preliminary instructions and then asked to "list the names of as many birds as you can." On the average, subjects listed about 36 names of birds in the 18 min allowed. To test the experimental hypothesis, the words that had been produced were classified according to their frequency of occurrence in the group's lists. For each frequency interval—1–5, 6–10, . . . , 96–100—the mean ordinal rank was computed, based on the ordinal position of each word in the individual lists. It was found that the mean ordinal rank decreased as the frequency of occurrence increased, thus confirming the hypothesis. The word ROBIN, for example, was listed by 99 of the subjects and its mean ordinal rank in their lists was 5.4, the lowest attained by any word. Words which occurred in the group's production with a frequency of 5 or less had a mean rank of 29.0, the highest for any frequency class. In this type of performance, subjects first produce their strongest associations and later bring in responses that occur less readily. Associative strength is reflected in how early a word is produced and how many persons give it when the group is composed of individuals of similar general background.

The finding that early occurring responses tend to indicate high associative strength should encourage investigators to use a minute or so of continuous association in place of discrete association as a way of studying verbal behavior. An analysis of the first five responses given to a stimulus word in such a procedure should reveal more about the semantic relations of the stimulus word than merely tallying the first response word given by the subjects. Where such an analysis is attempted, of course, we must be aware that responses given early in the sequence may serve as stimuli themselves, either in conjunction with the original stimulus or relatively independently.

MODIFICATION OF CONTINUOUS ASSOCIATION. We have seen that response frequency in word association tests appears to depend in part upon pre-experiment frequency of experiencing the associations. Another factor which may alter the frequency of occurrence of words of a particular class is the effect which follows when a subject gives any response from this class in continuous free association. If a subject's saying an adverb, for example, is followed by the experimenter's saying, "good," then the tendency to say adverbs will increase as performance continues. Experiments of this kind offer support, in verbal behavior in continuous free association, for the *law of effect*, a learning principle which states that responses which have a satisfying effect will tend to be repeated. In the studies we are considering, it is a class or category of responses that is reinforced to obtain an increased probability of occurrence for other members of the response class.

An investigation which illustrates certain aspects of the modification of continuous association by reinforcement was conducted by Wilson and Verplanck (1956). The instructions given to the subjects were: "This is a study of the vocabulary of college students. Say words. Do not repeat. Do not count. Do not say sentences." Each subject was kept at the task until he had said a total of 800 words. One means of reinforcement used was to have the experimenter casually say "mmm-hmm" or "good" whenever a certain type of response was given. A different way of reinforcing other subjects was to write down, or appear to write down, those words that were given in a certain category. The pattern of offering either type of reinforcement as the session proceeded may be indicated as follows:

	First 100 Responses	Responses 101–400	Responses 401–500	Responses 501–800
Group I:	No reinforcement	Plural nouns reinforced	No reinforcement	Adverbs reinforced
Group II:	No reinforcement	Adverbs reinforced	No reinforcement	Plural nouns reinforced

The two groups were employed to counterbalance the sequence of introducing the two categories of response that were reinforced, either plural nouns or adverbs. It was found that the rate of giving responses in either reinforced class increased greatly in most of the individual subjects when the reinforcement for that category of word was in effect. When the no reinforcement condition was introduced after the 400th response of the session, the rate of giving the previously reinforced category of response went down for most of the subjects. Almost all the subjects were aware of the experimenter's preference for words of a certain class during some parts of the session.

In a second experiment of this study Wilson and Verplanck (1956) found it possible to use "mmm-hmm" or "good" as reinforcement to increase the occurrence of two other categories of word. This time the categories were semantic instead of grammatical. The subjects were reinforced for producing "travel-words" or "living-thing-words." Again most subjects were aware of the reinforcement and about half could give a general identification of the category of word which had led to the reinforcement effect.

The modification of verbal behavior by the use of reinforcement was carried out by Cohen, Kalish, Thurston, and Cohen (1954) in a situation somewhat more complex than continuous word production. On each of 80 3 × 5 cards the experimenters had printed a different verb in the past tense. Below this verb, in some random order on each card, they had printed the pronouns: I, We, He, They, She, and You. The set of cards was shown, one at a time, to a subject who was asked to make up a sentence using the verb and any one of the pronouns. The experimenter wrote down the sentences which were given. A different sequence of presentation for each subject was obtained by shuffling the cards.

In this Experiment I, subjects were randomly assigned to either an experimental or a control group, with 20 men in each. Both groups were treated identically as the first 20 cards were presented, with the experimenter merely recording sentences given. Beginning with the twenty-first card and continuing through the eightieth, the men in the experimental group were reinforced whenever they offered a sentence beginning with two of the pronouns, I or We. This was done by having the experimenter say "good" in a neutral tone following the use of either of these pronouns. For the control group, sentences were merely recorded throughout the session. The results of this first experiment of the study are presented in Figure 12.2. The mean number of responses employing I or We as the pronoun is plotted as a function of successive blocks of 20 card presentations. For the first block of 20 presentations, the two groups show about the same frequency of use of these key pronouns. However, the frequency curves diverge significantly as the reinforcement is introduced for the experimental group. This group uses I or We increasingly as the reinforced occurrences continue, whereas the control group seems to drop slightly in its employment of these words.

The results pictured in Figure 12.2 are strong evidence that verbal behavior of some complexity can be influenced by manipulating reinforcement. A notable finding of this study was that none of the subjects reported an awareness of how the experimenter's verbal behavior had related to their choice of pronouns. The contrast, on this point, with the findings of Wilson and Verplanck (1956) might be attributable to one or more factors. Sophistication of subjects in the two studies as to the aim of the experiment might have differed. Cohen et al. used hospital patients as subjects and Wilson and Verplanck used college students, with one exception. The complexity of the sentence construction task may have obscured the relationship of the spoken reinforcement to the pronoun employed, whereas in the

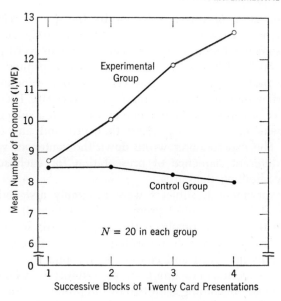

Fig. 12.2. Mean number of sentences beginning with "I" or "We" as a function of successive blocks of card presentations. Ss in the experimental group were reinforced beginning with the twenty-first card for using these two pronouns. Ss in the control group were given no selective reinforcement. (After Cohen, Kalish, Thurston, and Cohen, 1954.)

word production the corresponding relationship was more direct and more temporally proximal.

In Experiment II of this study, Cohen et al. (1954) found that omitting the reinforcing "good" after 80 reinforced trials did not seem to reduce the mean frequency with which I and We were employed. However, this frequency did drop in a different group of subjects when the experimenter now reinforced a different pair of pronouns, He and They.

MEANING

In our discussion of word association we saw that most of the responses that subjects give are related semantically—that is, by virtue of meaning—to the stimulus word or the instructions. By *meaning*, we shall refer to a number of aspects of words that are revealed in behavioral operations. The aspects of verbal material that come under this rubric of meaning will be indicated by the techniques that have been devised to explore them. We shall find that meaning is described and measured by associational procedures, by psychological scaling, by statistical treatment of language, and by certain combination methods.

Meaning is a dimension, or set of dimensions, of verbal material. It represents important stimulus properties of such material and it offers a way of interpreting verbal responses. By conceptualizing meaning in the context of verbal stimulus-response behavior, we purposely neglect some of the approaches to meaning that have been taken by philosophers and linguists. We shall limit ourselves to examining how psychologists have dealt with the description and measurement of meaning. Their studies have generally been oriented toward utilizing the meaning concept in other research on verbal behavior. For example, we see in Chapter 13 how meaning has been used as a dimension of the verbal material employed in some experiments on rote memorization.

The Qualitative and Quantitative Description of Meaning

As we attempt to describe the psychological properties of a word we find that our description has both qualitative and quantitative aspects. The qualitative description of a word takes place when we indicate items that are associated with it. We may point to the objects or events to which a word refers; this indicates its *denotative* meaning. More frequently our qualitative description of meaning will involve exploring other words which any given word connotes, synonyms and related words; this reveals its *connotative* meaning. The word association technique tends to portray the connotative meaning of a word as it yields other words that are associated with the stimulus. The list of response words represents a qualitative description of the stimulus word as it functions in behavior.

The quantitative aspect of meaning is brought out by statistical analysis of language behavior or by psychological scaling. The first of these approaches is illustrated by the frequency distribution we obtain for word association responses—the higher the frequency, the stronger the association between stimulus and response. This is a quantitative approach to connotative meaning. A similar approach to denotative meaning has been to use pictures or even objects as stimuli for eliciting verbal associations. Additional quantitative description of verbal material, as we shall see, may stem from other sorts of statistical analysis of language. Psychological scaling employs judges to obtain quantified descriptions of meaning. Some descriptions of meaning combine a qualitative and a quantitative approach as we shall see.

Associative Techniques

The nonsense syllable was invented to reduce the variance which would be introduced into rote memory experiments by words of varied familiarity and meaning. However, it was found that nonsense syllables themselves differed in connotative meaning as revealed by the extent to which they suggested associated words. Accordingly, associative techniques were used to classify numerous syllables with respect to the number of associations they elicited. Classified lists based on the studies of several different experimenters—Glaze, Hull, Krueger, and Witmer—have been presented by Hilgard (1951, pp. 540–546). These lists have provided a ready source of material for research in verbal processes. We should rely on such association values cautiously, however. For example, the per-cent figures cited as association values for the Glaze lists are based on how many subjects out of 15 offered associations to each syllable. The response, or failure to respond, of just one person thus represents a 7 per cent change in association value. The unreliability of the values has led most investigators to utilize widely spaced values in designing experiments. A second reason for caution in relying on associative descriptions of this sort is that certain syllables may rise or fall in apparent meaning as the verbal environment changes over the years.

The associative technique for describing meaning has been extended to real words by Noble (1952) with one notable change from the Glaze method of quantifying. Instead of deriving an association value from the number of persons responding, Noble based his index on the number of continued associations given in a certain time. *Meaningfulness*, m, was defined as the mean number of acceptable written responses given to a word in one minute. This index was obtained for 96 two-syllable nouns and paralogs, the latter being pronounceable letter combinations without real meaning—MIBEM or SAVUL, for example. The standardization was based on 119 subjects with a coefficient of reliability for m of .975 based on subgroups. Some examples which represent differing m values are the following:

High m	Medium m	Low m
KITCHEN	SEQUENCE	MEARDON
ARMY	PALLOR	NEGLAN
MONEY	TANKARD	GOJEY

Scaling Techniques

Psychological scaling techniques were used by Haagen (1949) to achieve a quantitative description of 480 common adjectives. These words were rated for their familiarity, F, by 40 undergraduate students who served as judges for this part of the study. In the other parts of the investigation, adjectives were presented in pairs to be rated by different groups of 80 undergraduates on three other dimensions: similarity of meaning, M; closeness of associative connection, A; and vividness of connotation, V. The pairs, presented by projection on a screen, were formed from 80 different groups of words with 6 similar adjectives in each. In each group of 6 adjectives one was designated a standard. The other 5 were each paired with this standard so that the 80 groups of adjectives gave 400 pairings to be judged on each factor.

For dimensions M, A, and V a seven-point rating scale was used with possible ratings of adjective pairs ranging from 0.5 to 6.5, with the *lower* ratings representing the *higher* degrees of each factor. The familiarity factor, F, was rated for each separate adjective on a five-point rating scale, with values from 0.5 to 4.5 possible. Again the *lower* values represent *greater* familiarity. The median values assigned to the different adjectives paired with ABSURD as a standard are represented here.

Adjectives Being Rated		Median Rating			
Standard:	ABSURD	*M*	*A*	*V*	*F*
Other adjectives:	FOOLISH	2.1	1.6	3.7	0.5
	INSANE	2.9	3.3	3.4	2.1
	SENSELESS	2.2	1.8	3.7	0.6
	SILLY	1.8	1.5	3.5	0.6
	STUPID	3.0	2.3	3.4	0.5

The median ratings for M, A, and V were based on the pairing of each of the related adjectives with ABSURD. The pairs based on this group of words were temporally spaced in the judging sequences, with adjective pairs from the other 79 groups interspersed. Although pairs of adjectives were definitely required for the M and A ratings, Haagen (1949) notes that the vividness rating, V, might preferably be based on adjectives presented individually instead of paired with the standard for each group. Familiarity, F, was rated for single adjectives.

It was found that the median M and A ratings were highly correlated with each other for the 400 word pairs. Since the M ratings were
judgments of similarity of meaning and A represented closeness of
associative connection, we find in the high correlation, $r_{MA} = .90$, a
confirmation of our earlier observation that association tends to reflect
the meaning relationship. This correlation is found for adjectives
that are synonyms or near-synonyms, of course. We have seen in our
examination of word association that a noun and an adjective like
MOUNTAIN and HIGH, for example, may be closely associated
while being far from synonymous.

The Semantic Differential Technique

Osgood (1952) has discussed meaning and its measurement at considerable length, offering the *semantic differential* technique for the
quantified description of meaning. This method combines the associative and the psychological scaling techniques. A series of seven-point
rating scales are identified by pairs of adjectival opposites like
ANGULAR-ROUNDED, WEAK-STRONG, and ROUGH-SMOOTH.
The seven steps of the scale for such a semantic dimension as WEAK-
STRONG, for example, would range as follows:

WEAK ____: ____: ____: ____: ____: ____: ____: STRONG
         (1)   (2)   (3)   (4)   (5)   (6)   (7)

where (1) is "very closely related to WEAK."
      (2) is "quite closely related to WEAK."
      (3) is "only slightly related to WEAK."
      (4) is "equally related to WEAK and STRONG."
          or "completely irrelevant."
      (5) is "slightly related to STRONG."
      (6) is "quite closely related to STRONG."
      (7) is "very closely related to STRONG."

In its employment, this scale would not show the numerical values
that we have placed in parentheses. It would be a graphic scale with
7 intervals provided for checking. A number of such scales, perhaps
10, would appear under each other. The word or concept to be
differentiated semantically would be printed on top of the page.
Figure 12.3 shows such a page with the rating check marks of an
experimental subject or judge filled in to show his reactions to the
word POLITE. Looking at the third scale, we see that this judge has
rated POLITE as very closely related to SMOOTH. This illustrates

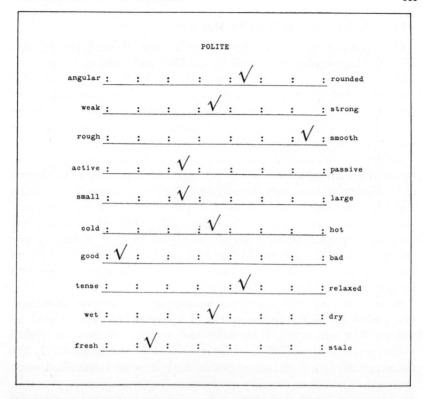

Fig. 12.3. Sample page in administering a semantic differential scaling of "POLITE" with check marks of an hypothetical judge indicated. (After Osgood, 1952.)

the associative aspect of the semantic differential technique. The profile which we would obtain by connecting the check marks in Figure 12.3 would tend to describe the meaning of POLITE as it is perceived by this subject. Similar sorts of profiles may be based on median group ratings.

The semantic differential technique yields a picture of the connotative meaning of a word with respect to whatever associative dimensions are represented in the adjectival scales which an investigator chooses to employ. Osgood has pointed out that both SIMON LEGREE and WAR might yield similar profiles on some scales even though their denotative meanings are poles apart. If it suited our research purposes we might obtain different connotative profiles for two such concepts by utilizing other descriptive scales.

Statistical Indices Related to Meaning

One approach to the meaning of words comes through the description of a language as it is used in speaking and writing. Spoken or written language is a product of verbal behavior, so we are still employing behavior measures when we compute statistics that are descriptive of certain samples of language. This statistical approach to the meaningfulness of words and word sequences may be seen in two contrasting examples.

FREQUENCY OF WORD USAGE. One aspect of word meaning is the familiarity with which a word is perceived by a person. The degree of familiarity, in turn, may depend upon the frequency with which the word has previously been used or encountered. For research purposes we may wish to know how frequent, relatively speaking, has been the experiencing of different words in the past history of our subjects. A partial answer to this problem is offered by the data on frequency of usage of 30,000 words in English writing, a compilation by Thorndike and Lorge (1944).

DEGREE OF APPROXIMATION TO MEANINGFUL LANGUAGE SEQUENCE. Our discussion of the measurement of meaning has concentrated on indices that are applied to individual words. Studies of verbal behavior have shown that context is a key determinant of the meaning attributed to some words and it would therefore seem appropriate to try to measure meaning in longer sequences of words. In a string of words that forms a sentence the individual words lend meaning to each other. A string of words that is not structured is not so meaningful.

Our English language has a structured character to it that is represented in the different relative frequencies with which particular words succeed each other in speech or writing. For example, the word "blue" may be followed fairly often by "sky" or "mood" but very rarely, if at all, by "if" or "say" even though these words are frequent in their general occurrence. The probability of a particular word's being used in a sequence is governed even more by a preceding string of words. Would "sky" or "mood" have the greater probability of coming next after the phrase "reflecting a blue . . ."? Would the probabilities change if the contextual phrase were given more fully as "mournful song reflecting a blue . . ."?

Sequences of words which vary over several different degrees in their approximation to the statistical structure of the English language may be constructed by using a technique described by Miller and Selfridge (1950). A second-order approximation to English prose was achieved by creating word sequences in the following manner. A person was asked to use a common word like "book" in a sentence. "The book was on the shelf" might be the response. Whatever word followed "book"—in this case "was"—served as the word to be employed by the next person, who knew nothing of the previous word or sentence. This second person might use "was" in the sentence "It was raining hard yesterday." This makes "raining" the word to be given to the next person, who might say "I noticed it was raining out so I decided not to go." The next person might say "She ran out of flour." Next we might get "Of course I'll try to be there." The sentences that are offered indicate what word has a fairly high probability of following, in English speech, each cue word that we use. Our example has generated the sequence "book was raining out of course." Although this bears little resemblance to normal meaningful language, the two-word sequences have a fairly high probability of occurrence as evidenced in the way they were obtained. This sequence is termed a second-order approximation to English.

If we use *two* words as the cue in requesting a sentence to be formed, we can generate a third-order approximation to English by noting the third word added by our subjects. The two words to be presented to each successive subject are selected by dropping the first word of the three-word sequence from the previous person's sentence. If we started with the cue words "to the," we might get the following sentences from seven persons in the succession:

> I went to the store to get some bread.
> The store manager inventoried the stock.
> A store manager has a tough job.
> The manager has three good infielders.
> The French flag has three colors.
> Three colors make a car look funny.
> The selection of colors make some paintings look real.

We thus obtain "to the store manager has three colors make some." This is a third-order approximation to English as defined by our method of generating it.

Fourth, fifth, and seventh orders were also obtained by Miller and Selfridge (1950) by giving three, four, and six words, respectively, to be incorporated as a sequence into a sentence. Samples of these orders which they obtained include:

> *Fourth order:* went to the movies with a man I used to go toward Harvard Square in Cambridge is mad fun for
> *Fifth order:* road in the country was insane especially in dreary rooms where they have some books to buy for studying Greek

Seventh order: easy if you know how to crochet you can make a simple scarf if they knew the color that it

To extend the continuum of language material represented by these second to seventh orders of approximation to English, the experimenters created a zero order and a first-order approximation. They also obtained samples of actual prose text from which they extracted sequences of the desired length. The first order was obtained by scrambling the words in some of the higher order sequences. The zero order was created by random selection from the 30,000 commonest words listed by Thorndike and Lorge (1944). Samples of these additional three levels of approximation to the statistical structure of English, given by Miller and Selfridge (1950), are:

Zero order: betwixt trumpeter pebbly complication vigorous tipple careen obscure attractive consequence expedition pane unpunished prominence chest sweetly basin awoke photographer ungrateful

First order: tea realizing most so the together home and for were wanted to concert I posted he her it the walked

Text: more attention has been paid to diet but mostly in relation to disease and to the growth of young children

The zero order of approximation, because of the way it was created, tends to lack the commonly used prepositions, pronouns, and articles that appear frequently in the higher orders. It might be possible to generate a zero order by randomly selecting words used by the undergraduate subjects in unrelated sentences.

Miller and Selfridge (1950) used such sequences as those we have presented in a study of rote memorization. The higher orders of approximation to the structure of English sentences were found to yield better learning. A similar finding was obtained in an experiment by Marks and Jack (1952) who employed somewhat different procedures. These studies indicate that sequential structuring is an aspect of meaning that relates importantly to verbal performance, exemplified in the memory tasks of these experiments.

Measures of Meaning in Verbal Research

The measurement of meaning of words constitutes empirical behavior research in itself since word meanings are a product of social usage. In addition, we find that meaning as a verbal dimension relates to research in word association, which we surveyed earlier in this chapter, and in rote memorization, considered in Chapter 13.

INTERRELATIONS OF DESCRIPTIONS OF MEANING. If different ways of measuring meaning are approaching the same aspect of verbal behavior, we should expect them to show some relationship. We noted that ratings obtained by Haagen (1949) correlated quite highly for the degree of synonymity and the judged associative strength of word pairs. We might expect also that such ratings might relate to other descriptions of meaning. We might find that words that are rated as very vivid are those which yield semantic differentials with the end points on the several scales very frequently used. Another example might be found if judged association value of a word pair proved to be related to the communality with which one of the two words occurs as a word association response when the other is the stimulus word. As each measurement technique is refined, it needs to be related to other descriptions of meaning.

RELATION OF MEANING TO WORD ASSOCIATION RESEARCH. We have already noted that rated degree of association may be reflected in word association communalities. Another connection between these two realms of research lies in the possibility of using what we know of word meanings to combine the responses in word association into meaningful categories. This grouping would increase the frequency of responses falling into particular classes. In turn, the statistical comparison of different response frequency distributions would be aided.

The description of the meanings of a wide variety of words should encourage their use in word association tests. It is quite possible that our knowledge of verbal behavior would be gained more rapidly if we replaced the 100 common words of the Kent-Rosanoff list with alternate forms of 50-word lists that had been selected for their representation of several aspects of meaning.

SUMMARY

The key concept of association has been prominent in much psychological research on verbal behavior. Word association has been studied by a variety of methods, with the required production of responses being either discrete or continuous, and free or controlled. Indices of associative strength include (1) frequencies of occurrence, of individual response words or words within categories, (2) reaction time, (3) rate of response production, and (4) clustering.

Among the background facts available to investigators are frequency of response data obtained from large groups of subjects. Response communalities are often high in such normative data, but they tend to vary with the group tested. The relationship of communality to reaction time suggests that each is an index of associative strength between stimulus word and response word. There is some evidence that reaction time is shorter for controlled associations than for free associations.

Illustrative experiments which were cited show great variety among factors which influence associative strength as it is revealed in verbal behavior. Stimulus variables which have been manipulated include mode of presentation and context words. Research which we reviewed included the study of clustering in recall of words previously studied and the description of quantitative trends in continuous association, including the effects of reinforcement.

Meaning has been quantified through associative methods, scaling procedures, and the semantic differential technique. Statistical analyses of language have also contributed to research on meaning. The further study of meaning promises to be of use in investigating word association and rote memorization.

REFERENCES

Baker, L. M., & Elliott, D. N. Controlled and free association-times with identical stimulus- and response-words. *Amer. J. Psychol.*, 1948, 61, 535–539.

Bousfield, W. A., & Barclay, W. D. The relationship between order and frequency of occurrence of restricted associative responses. *J. exp. Psychol.*, 1950, 40, 643–647.

Bousfield, W. A., & Cohen, B. H. The occurrence of clustering in the recall of randomly arranged words of different frequencies-of-usage. *J. gen. Psychol.*, 1955, 52, 83–95.

Bousfield, W. A., & Sedgewick, C. H. W. An analysis of sequences of restricted associative responses. *J. gen. Psychol.*, 1944, 30, 149–165.

Buchwald, A. M. The generality of the norms of word associations. *Amer. J. Psychol.*, 1957, 70, 233–237.

Cofer, C. N., & Ford, T. J. Verbal context and free association-time. *Amer. J. Psychol.*, 1957, 70, 606–610.

Cohen, B. D., Kalish, H. I., Thurston, J. R., & Cohen, E. Experimental manipulation of verbal behavior. *J. exp. Psychol.*, 1954, 47, 106–110.

Haagen, C. H. Synonymity, vividness, familiarity, and association value ratings of 400 pairs of common adjectives. *J. Psychol.*, 1949, 27, 453–463.

Hilgard, E. R. Methods and procedures in the study of learning. In S. S. Stevens (Ed.), *Handbook of experimental psychology.* New York: Wiley, 1951. Pp. 517–567.

Howes, D., & Osgood, C. E. On the combination of associative probabilities in linguistic contexts. *Amer. J. Psychol.*, 1954, 67, 241–258.

Jenkins, J. J., & Russell, W. A. Associative clustering during recall. *J. abn. soc. Psychol.*, 1952, 47, 818–821.

Johnson, D. M. Word-association and word-frequency. *Amer. J. Psychol.*, 1956, 69, 125–127.

Marks, M. R., & Jack, O.   Verbal context and memory span for meaningful material.   *Amer. J. Psychol.*, 1952, 65, 298–300.

Miller, G. A., & Selfridge, Jennifer A.   Verbal context and the recall of meaningful material.   *Amer. J. Psychol.*, 1950, 63, 176–185.

Noble, C. E.   An analysis of meaning.   *Psychol. Rev.*, 1952, 59, 421–430.

Osgood, C. E.   The nature and measurement of meaning.   *Psychol. Bull.*, 1952, 49, 197–237.

Rosanoff, A. J.   (Ed.)   *Free association test (Kent-Rosanoff)*.   New York: Wiley, 1927.

Schlosberg, H., & Heineman, C.   The relationship between two measures of response strength.   *J. exp. Psychol.*, 1950, 40, 235–247.

Thorndike, E. L.. & Lorge, I.   *The teacher's word book of 30,000 words*.   New York: Bureau of Publications, Teachers College, Columbia Univer., 1944.

Wilson, W. C., & Verplanck, W. S.   Some observations on the reinforcement of verbal operants.   *Amer. J. Psychol.*, 1956, 69, 448–451.

Woodworth, R. S., & Schlosberg, H.   *Experimental psychology* (Rev. ed.)   New York: Holt, 1954.

ADDITIONAL READINGS

Brown, R.   *Words and things*.   Glencoe, Ill.: Free Press, 1958.

Cofer, C. N., & Shevitz, R.   Word-association as a function of word-frequency.   *Amer. J. Psychol.*, 1952, 65, 75–79.

Jenkins, J. J., Russell, W. A., & Suci, G. J.   An atlas of semantic profiles for 360 words.   *Amer. J. Psychol.*, 1958, 71, 688–699.

Maltzman, I., Bogartz, W., & Breger, L.   A procedure for increasing word association originality and its transfer effects.   *J. exp. Psychol.*, 1958, 56, 392–398.

Rosen, E., & Russell, W. A.   Frequency-characteristics of successive word-association.   *Amer. J. Psychol.*, 1957, 70, 120–122.

CHAPTER 13

Rote
Memorization

In the word association technique we study associations already developed through past experience. An important alternative is to design experiments which provide for the development or strengthening of verbal associations in the subjects as the laboratory procedures are administered. By requiring rote memorization to take place under our close surveillance we achieve important control over the conditions surrounding the learning process. Besides being able to manipulate relevant variables, we provide for adequate measures of the increasing strengths of association when we bring learning into the laboratory.

METHODS OF STUDY

The materials to be memorized and the mode of presenting them to subjects offer an experimenter many choices as he plans procedural details of research on memorizing. Measuring the acquisition of the new associations may also be accomplished in several ways. We shall consider such methodological matters before examining a few illustrative studies.

Materials

In rote memorization studies, the verbal materials that are employed are an important factor since they may possess associations already strengthened in subjects' previous experience. A variety of symbolic material has been used in different investigations, with evidence that among the various aspects of the learning process there are some which depend heavily on what is being memorized and others that are independent of such a factor.

WORDS IN LISTS OR MEANINGFUL PASSAGES. It might seem that studying verbal behavior would demand that words be the material to be memorized, but we shall see later that this is not always the case. However, words are often used in experiments as stimuli and responses. They are required in many cases where dimensions like meaningfulness or degree of synonymity are among the variables under study.

Although experimenters have occasionally presented passages of prose or poetry to be memorized, the possible familiarity of this type of material and its varied contextual associations have made it unpopular for most research. Laboratory studies of verbal learning have more often presented words in lists or in pairs, often limiting them to particular parts of speech like adjectives or nouns.

NONSENSE SYLLABLES AND PARALOGS. The pioneer investigator of rote memory, Ebbinghaus, fearing the effect of already existent associations among words, used mechanical rules to create *nonsense syllables*. Working in the German language, with more consonant and vowel symbols than we have in English, he created thousands of consonant-vowel-consonant combinations. By assembling these syllables into lists he provided the material for his memory research in which he served as his own subject.

Research workers have used the consonant-vowel-consonant rule to create many "English" nonsense syllables, many of these having been scaled for their association values, as noted in Chapter 12, p. 360. The early scaling efforts are open to some criticism and furthermore have suffered from language changes over the decades. Striking shifts in association value undoubtedly resulted when certain nonsense syllables were usurped by the makers of soaps and detergents as names for their products.

The resemblance of many of the usual nonsense syllables—GUL, KIL, TYP, or WAV—to meaningful words led to other attempts to provide materials with less potential associative strength. One such effort is the *paralog*. Paralogs may take the form, for example, of two-syllable nonsense combinations of letters that are pronounceable but may bear little resemblance to words—BAMEP, DUKAG, LIPOB, or RONID. Although they seem to provide advantages over nonsense syllables or meaningful words as units for memory experiments, such paralogs do not seem to have found favor with investigators.

Because nonsense syllables might offer pronunciation difficulties as well as being heterogeneous in their resemblances to words, the *consonant syllable* has sometimes been used. Intended for spelling by subjects, such a syllable is a combination of three consonants—BJL, ZQW, or FBJ. In suggesting people's initials or designations of government agencies, these also risk some heterogeneity of associative value.

As we noted in discussing meaning, Hilgard (1951, pp. 540–546) has brought together lists of nonsense syllables which have been graded according to their association values.

NUMBERS AND SYMBOLS. If we adopt the broad definition of verbal behavior that Skinner (1957, pp. 2, 14) has offered, we may consider numbers and various other symbols as appropriate materials for use in experiments. The symbols might be very familiar ones like a plus sign or a question mark. They might also be specially contrived ones, requiring some perceptual discrimination as well as associative learning. The availability of names, like "triangle" or "star," which could be readily used as substitutes for certain symbols in forming associations would be a factor in a learning situation.

Modes of Presentation

Choosing a particular way to present items for rote memorization offers certain advantages. It permits control in some studies over the time spent in studying each portion of the material. Some presentation techniques allow the introduction of particular independent variables, as we shall see.

SERIAL LISTS. By presenting a list of items to be learned sequentially, we call for the forming of a chain of associations. Each item in the sequence is both a response, to be associated with the previous item, and a stimulus, the cue for the next item. Careful control over the time allowed for the study of each item may be achieved by using some sort of exposure device. This might be as simple as a cardboard mask with a slit cut in it to permit the subject, perhaps moving the mask himself, to view one item on a printed list at a time. Successive exposures might be signaled by a timing device or by the experimenter. Another simple technique is to print the words on a strip of heavy paper and draw it up or down through appropriate slots in a masking screen, with the subject seeing only one word at a time. Also used are motor-driven drums with a list printed on paper tape and disks with items in a radial arrangement printed on them or on cards held in slots. Such devices expose one item at a time through a small window in a masking screen, with exposure time automatically controlled by the mechanism which advances the drum or disk a step at a time. The item presentation time is kept brief in an attempt to prevent undue silent rehearsal.

PAIRED ASSOCIATES. We sometimes wish to use certain verbal items as stimuli and others as responses, instead of letting each one serve in both capacities. This is accomplished by the *paired associates* technique where items are arranged in pairs. Each pair consists of a stimulus item and a response item. The subject is to learn to give the response whenever the stimulus is presented. The pairs should not be given repeatedly in the same sequence since this may permit the responses to be memorized serially without reference to the stimulus items. Paired associate material can be presented mechanically, with first the stimulus and then the stimulus-response pair appearing in the exposure window. Different orders of printed lists are used to avoid serial learning.

Subjects are typically run one at a time in paired associate learning studies, being required to say the appropriate response word, if they can, when the stimulus word is presented. The appearance of the pair of items then serves to reinforce the response or to prompt the subject if he has not yet mastered the pair.

WHOLE PRESENTATION. Contrasting with the item-by-item exposure of material for serial or paired associate learning is the method of *whole presentation*. In this procedure an entire passage of poetry or prose might be given to subjects for study. After the study period they are tested for their mastery of the selection. Whole presentation is not confined to connected passages but may be applied to lists or sets of pairs of items as well. Although this technique permits subjects to concentrate on more difficult parts of the task, it has the advantage over other types of presentation of simulating actual study conditions. This may make it especially useful in educational research in contrast to those studies which require a closer look at the memorizing process itself.

MATRIX PRESENTATION. Anderson and Ross (1955) have reported an experiment in which material was presented in a matrix of 25 cells consisting of 5 rows and 5 columns. In different phases of the investigation, the matrices contained sets of 2-digit numbers, 3-letter words, symbols, or geometric figures. After a 1 min study period, the subject attempted to fill in a blank matrix with as much of the material as he could recall in 1 min. The learning session consisted of a series of such brief study and recall periods with 30 sec intervening between each recall attempt and the next study session. This rest interval was increased to 2 min whenever a new type of material was to be introduced.

This method would lend itself well to a looseleaf notebook format where printed study pages would be alternated with blank matrix test pages. It is found that the matrix arrangement asserts its influence no matter what type of material is studied, with some positions being learned more readily than others. A variant of this method might be to present successively several different partially filled matrices, each identified by a code letter, before giving the test blanks. This would tend to simulate certain study situations which demand that complex material be learned in some organized fashion.

Measurement of Rote Memorization

The progress that subjects make in learning a list of nonsense syllables or a meaningful paragraph may be measured in a number of ways. The different ways of assessing memorizing may yield slightly different pictures of the process. Furthermore, the taking of some indices may affect the course of the learning itself. We choose our measurement technique to give us data that bear upon the hypothesis that we are testing.

Each performance index that we take probably reflects the strengthening of associations and the retention of these increments of strength as well. Our data are, in a sense, measures of immediate or short-term retention. When we study "Retention" in Chapter 16 we shall find that similar measurements, taken at longer intervals after learning, serve as data which reveal the operation of memory and forgetting.

ANTICIPATION. The *anticipation* method of assessing strength of association is interrelated with the memorizing process itself. As a serial list or a set of paired associates is being presented item by item, the subject tries to anticipate the next response item before it is shown. His score for any trial is the number of correct anticipations he makes, a trial being defined as one run-through of the list or set of pairs. If a subject correctly gives a particular response, the appearance of that item in the window of the apparatus serves as a reinforcement for the response. If he fails to make a correct anticipation, then the item's appearance prompts him as to what he should have said. As trials continue, then, a subject is both learning the material and being tested for his memorization of it at the same time. On the first trial, with the material being seen for the first time, we naturally expect no anticipations. This is frequently not counted as a trial when data are tabulated.

In administering this anticipation method the experimenter follows along with a check sheet, tallying the correct responses on each trial. He may also jot down any incorrect responses that are given. These are termed *intrusions*. Often we find that intrusions are actually response items from another part of the material that is being memorized. In the case of paired associates, a stimulus item may also intrude as an erroneous response. In some cases the source of an intrusion may be learning that was done earlier in the experiment. Occasionally it may be a subject's own verbal behavior history that gives rise to an intrusion. Although they may occur rarely, intrusions can be quite important as indices of the existence of verbal associations of some strength.

RECALL. Instead of mixing testing and training as in the anticipation technique, we may choose to defer our measuring of the acquired associations until a trial has been completed. We present the list or set of items and then we ask the subject to recite or write down those which he can recall. This *recall* technique is a commonly used method of measuring retention when an interval of time has elapsed since learning. However, when it is used after each trial it may be considered an index of the memorizing process itself. In paired associate learning we would present a list of the stimulus items to serve as appropriate cues in the recall test. In serial learning no such cue would be given. The number of responses correctly recalled would constitute a subject's score in either case, with proper sequence of the items being demanded before serial learning was considered complete.

When the material to be memorized is a passage of poetry or prose, the recall technique is slightly more complicated. The problem is that the material is not a fixed number of items as in a list or set of paired associates. The usual way to meet this problem has been to divide the passage into "ideas" to be used as the unit of scoring. A study by Levitt (1956) has shown that different experimenters tend to divide a passage into different segments for recall measurement, with resultant differences in the scores which subjects make. The measurement of learning thus poses a methodological problem when passages of verbal material are memorized.

RECOGNITION. Another technique, generally used for measuring retention, may also be used to assess learning as it progresses. This is the *recognition* method in which the material being learned is intermingled with extra material to provide a test. Subjects have to indicate which items they recognize as belonging to the items which they have been studying. This method does not lend itself to serial learning, but it may be used to check on the mastery of material in which sequence of items is not a factor.

The recognition method is at the heart of a technique which permits entire classroom groups to be run simultaneously on a paired associates task. In this method, suggested by Schmidt and Bunch (1951), we might first present the entire set of pairs by projecting them on the screen. Then we would project the different stimulus items along with about five alternative responses including the correct one. Sub-

jects would indicate their choice by marking an answer sheet. This
testing would be followed by other presentations and testings for a
given number of trials. The progress in learning which is evidenced
in this method will obviously depend in part upon the multiple-
choice alternatives used in testing as well as on the nature of the
stimulus-response pairs themselves.

Treatment of Verbal Learning Data

The general problem in treating results in verbal learning studies
is to portray the progress of subjects in mastering the material, that is,
forming the required associations. We shall here note two techniques
for describing this memorization process. Our illustrative data may
be assumed to have come from the serial learning of a ten-word list,
with six subjects performing by the anticipation method. Ways of
dealing with more specialized aspects of verbal learning will be considered as we describe particular experiments later.

MEAN NUMBER CORRECT. Our hypothetical group of subjects would
be making more and more correct anticipations as trials continued.
A common measure of such a group's progress is the mean number
of correct responses as a function of trials. Such a series of means
is presented along the bottom of Table 13.1 to represent the central
tendencies of the columns of data. In calculating these means, it
was assumed that once a subject had reached the criterion of ten
correct anticipations he would continue to perform at that level if
trials were continued. The data of this table are represented graphically in Figure 13.1, a curve of rote memorization.

The data of Table 13.1 are characterized by considerable variability in the number of trials required by different subjects to reach

TABLE 13.1

Number of Words Correctly Anticipated on Successive Trials

S No.	Trials											
	1	2	3	4	5	6	7	8	9	10	11	12
1	0	2	2	4	6	5	6	8	9	10		
2	0	1	2	3	3	4	7	8	8	10		
3	0	1	2	5	6	9	9	10				
4	0	0	1	2	4	5	4	5	7	8	8	10
5	0	2	4	7	8	9	10					
6	0	1	3	6	7	8	8	10				
Mean No. of Words:	0	1.2	2.3	4.5	5.7	6.7	7.4	8.5	9.0	9.7	9.7	10.0

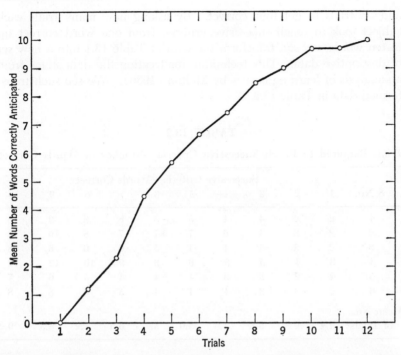

Fig. 13.1. Illustrative empirical rote memorization curve showing the mean number of words correctly anticipated as a function of trials. The hypothetical data represent the learning of a ten-word list by six subjects, as presented in Table 13.1.

the criterion of ten correct anticipations. As a result, it is the performance data for the slower learners which contribute strongly to the shape of the final portion of the curve in Figure 13.1. The curve reaches the mean of ten correct anticipations at the twelfth trial because that is how long the slowest subject, No. 4, took to learn the list. The curve might have been either shortened or lengthened by a trial or two had this subject performed somewhat differently.

MEAN TRIALS TO SUCCESSIVE CRITERIA. As we examine the performance of our serial learning task we might ask a different question about the progress that subjects have evidenced. Instead of asking, "How many words did S No. 2 get correct on Trial 2 or Trial 4?" we might ask, "How many trials did S No. 2 require to get two words correct, three words correct, four words?" We can examine Table 13.1 for the answers. We find that S No. 2 required three trials to reach two correct anticipations, four trials to anticipate three words correctly, and six trials to get four correct. By asking how many trials each subject took to reach successive criteria, from one word correct up to ten words, we can transform the data of Table 13.1 into a new set of descriptive data. This technique for treating the data stems from an analysis of learning curves by Melton (1936). We see such transformed data in Table 13.2.

TABLE 13.2

Trials Required to Reach Successive Criteria—Number of Words Correct

	Successive Criteria—Words Correct									
S No.	1	2	3	4	5	6	7	8	9	10
1	2	2	4	4	5	5	8	8	9	10
2	2	3	4	6	7	7	7	8	10	10
3	2	3	4	4	4	5	6	6	6	8
4	3	4	5	5	6	9	9	10	12	12
5	2	2	3	3	4	4	4	5	6	7
6	2	3	3	4	4	4	5	6	8	8
Mean No. of Trials:	2.2	2.8	3.8	4.3	5.0	5.7	6.5	7.2	8.5	9.2

If we look at the successive scores reported in Table 13.1 for S No. 1 we can see how they were transformed in filling in Table 13.2. This S No. 1 had two correct anticipations on his second trial. For the criterion of two correct in Table 13.2 (the column headed "2") we have shown an entry of 2 for this subject, indicating it took him this number of trials to reach this performance level. Actually, he also reached and surpassed the criterion of one correct on that same trial, so we have shown the same entry of 2 in the column headed "1." This subject did not reach the criterion of three correct until the fourth trial when he actually anticipated four words correctly. We have therefore made the entry of 4 to indicate the trial on which these two criteria were reached or surpassed. By the next trial, the fifth, he had reached the criteria of five and six correct so a 5 is entered in the table for those two columns. S No. 1 did not reach seven correct until the eighth trial when he also reached the level of eight correct. This fact is indicated by the entry of 8 in the two columns for the seventh and eighth criteria. The criterion of nine correct was reached on the ninth trial and ten correct was achieved on the tenth trial, so these trial numbers become the final entries for S No. 1. Looking back at his performance record in Table 13.1, we see that his slipping back on Trial 6 to only five words correct is not reflected in the transformed data.

The transformed data indicate the earliest trial number when a particular criterion of words correct was reached or surpassed. By following this rule you should be able to see how every entry in Table 13.2 was obtained from some entry in Table 13.1. The numbers in the two tables are not the same, of course, since one set of data refers to words recited and the other to trials experienced. The data naturally do not correspond by columns in the tables since twelve columns were required in Table 13.1 to accommodate data for S No. 4, whereas Table 13.2 has just ten columns to represent the successive criteria at which we chose to examine the progress of the learners. The correspondence of these two tables simply stems from the application of our transformation rule.

At the bottom of Table 13.2 we have presented the mean number of trials required by the subjects to attain the successive criteria of mastery of the list. Every subject has contributed to each of these means. These values also permit the plotting of a performance curve, shown in Figure 13.2. As is conventional in functions representing behavioral data, the ordinate represents the units of performance, the successive criteria of mastery of the material being memorized. The abscissa resembles conventional learning curves in representing the succession of trials experienced by the subjects. The function simply departs from conventional graphs in that we have plotted a group mean to the right of each value on the ordinate instead of plotting a group mean above each value on the abscissa.

INTERPRETING GROUP LEARNING CURVES. We noted that the curve of Figure 13.1 reached a mean of ten words correct at the twelfth trial, this fact being dependent on the performance data of S No. 4. Since this mean represents an errorless performance which was not indicated in any earlier portion of the group curve, we might be tempted to conclude that twelve trials were required, on the average, to master the ten-word list. But we know this conclusion would not be valid, because most of the subjects achieved a perfect trial earlier. Once they had made ten correct anticipations we subsequently credited them with that level of attainment in computing the group means. Even though additional trials would have led to a greater degree of mastery, to overlearning, we used a score of ten in our calculations. This is another way of pointing up the later part of this function as chiefly dependent on the slower learners.

The means of Table 13.2, plotted in Figure 13.2, are more representative measures of central tendency. Consider, for example, the mean

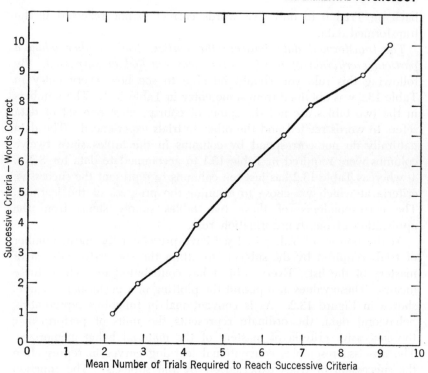

Fig. 13.2. Illustrative empirical rote memorization curve plotting the mean number of trials required to reach successive criteria of mastery of a ten-word list. The hypothetical data which yield this function are presented in Table 13.2.

number of trials required to attain ten correct anticipations. To the mean, each subject has contributed an empirical datum. In its calculation we did not use any value which really reflected a different stage of the memorization process, as was partly the case when we computed the means of Table 13.1 and Figure 13.1. From these considerations it would seem that the functional relationship of Figure 13.2 is a better reflection of the group's performance.

Either of the curves we have been discussing has a weakness in reflecting the learning process. Certain empirical facts, evident in the data of individual subjects, tend to be suppressed when group means are taken. This is true whether we consider the mean number of words correct or the transformed data, mean trials required to reach successive criteria. The empirical facts obscured are the occurrences of either plateaus or sudden increases in the performance data of some subjects. If we regard these parts of the records as mere chance deviations from a smooth learning curve which characterizes the learning of the hypothetical ideal individual, then our averaging is merely an aid to recapturing a valid representation of memorizing. If, however, these aspects of individual data represent subprocesses which are parts of the learning process, then they deserve our attention. Until we can identify the factors leading to these characteristics of individual data we cannot definitely distinguish them from chance occurrences and we are willing to allow them to be hidden in the group curves. To discover how such group functions reflect the influence of different independent variables is a major aim as we study verbal behavior. We must keep the statistical nature of the group learning curves squarely in mind, however. Describing the phenomena which occur in the performance of the individual subject may be important too.

INDEPENDENT VARIABLES AFFECTING
ROTE MEMORIZATION

Investigators have not lacked for relevant variables to manipulate as they studied rote memorization. It would be impossible to review, or even to represent by systematic sampling, all the experiments of interest and importance. We must limit ourselves to illustrating how researchers have found the memorizing process to be affected by different variables in a triple classification—learner, material, and conditions of presentation.

Warm-Up and General Practice

One important fact about the learner in a rote memory task is his past experience at such a task. It has long been known that such memorization is facilitated by prior learning under similar conditions. Sometimes the facilitation, occurring as successive lists are learned within a session, has been ascribed to a warm-up effect. Where the improvement has shown itself in widely spaced memorization efforts, a general practice effect or a learning-to-learn has been postulated. It is important to know all we can about warm-up and general practice effects in verbal learning since these might bear importantly on our design of experiments on this task of rote memorization.

Thune (1951) conducted a study which affords us considerable empirical information on both of the processes we are discussing. He required 60 undergraduate subjects to learn three sets of paired associates in a single session on each of five days. Improvement from one set to the next within a daily session would be evidence for warm-up, whereas improvement from day to day would reveal a general practice effect. Both of these phenomena appeared in the data obtained in this study.

The gain in rate of learning as subjects proceeded from the first to the second and then to the third set of associates was quite impressive. On the fifth day, this warm-up effect was just about as potent as it had been on the first and the intervening days.

A general practice effect was also statistically significant, with subjects doing slightly better each day. These day-to-day gains, found in each of the three successive learning efforts which constituted a day's performance, were not as great as the gains within any day which were ascribed to warm-up. The curves presented by Thune indicate that memorizing skill is acquired as a negatively accelerated function of tasks within a day and of successive days of practice. The gains attributable to either factor are apparently so potent as to demand that experiments on rote memorization include preliminary practice, strict counterbalancing, or other form of experimental control whenever subjects are required to learn successive lists under different conditions which are being compared.

Implicit Verbal Chaining

Subjects who participate in rote memorization studies come to the experiments with long histories of verbal behavior. It has been proposed by a number of theorists that the forming of new verbal associations is facilitated by a mediational role played by associations established earlier in the learner's history. Again we see that the state of the learner is considered important, this time as a result of experience antedating the memorizing session by many years.

As an example of the mediational role which associations may play, consider the requirement to memorize these two paired associates: TREE-DISGUISE and KNIFE-MAP. A person may be aided in linking TREE and DISGUISE by the existence of several mediate word associations, specifically TREE-SURGEON, SURGEON-MASK, and MASK-DISGUISE. The bond between KNIFE and MAP may be aided by the existence of KNIFE-FORK, FORK-ROAD, and ROAD-MAP in the verbal habit structure of an experimental subject. Rather than discuss these illustrative examples, let us turn to an actual experiment designed to test the possible verbal mediation mechanism.

In paired associate learning, mediate associations may form an implicit verbal chain which connects the two members of a pair in such a way as to aid the memorizing. Russell and Storms (1955) identified such verbal chains as OCEAN-WATER-DRINK by an examination of word association data which indicated WATER as the most common response to OCEAN and DRINK as the commonest response to WATER. Following the mediation hypothesis, they postulated that if OCEAN were linked with a nonsense syllable like ZIL in a paired associates task, it should subsequently prove easier to connect that same nonsense syllable to the word DRINK than to some other word like DOCTOR. Restating this in general symbols, we label the word association chain B-C-D, the nonsense syllable A, and the neutral or control word X. The hypothesis is, then, that A-B learning will facilitate subsequent A-D learning when the latter is compared with the A-X type of paired associate.

These experimenters presented an A-B set of ten paired associates to a group of women students. After this task had been mastered, each subject was given a test list employing the same ten nonsense syllables as stimuli. The response words were chosen so that five items were A-D pairs and five were A-X pairs. These two groups of pairings were counterbalanced through the use of two subgroups of subjects. Examples of the verbal materials used by Russell and Storms are the following:

Original Paired Associates		Implicit Mediator	Alternatives for Test List Response	
A	B	C	D	X
CEF	STEM	FLOWER	SMELL	JOY
YOV	SOLDIER	ARMY	NAVY	CHEESE
JID	THIEF	STEAL	TAKE	SLEEP
ZIL	OCEAN	WATER	DRINK	DOCTOR

In a comparison of A-D memorizing with A-X memorizing, each subject served as her own control. It was found that the A-D pairs were memorized somewhat more readily than the A-X pairs, thus offering support to the hypothesis that implicit verbal chaining can play a mediational role in the forming of new associations. A different group of students constituted a control group who learned the A-D and A-X pairs without the prior A-B learning. Their performance served to show that A-D pairs were not inherently easier to master than A-X pairs.

Meaningfulness and Familiarity

A number of studies have shown that real words are easier to learn than are nonsense syllables or paralogs. This may be due to the fact that the words are more meaningful or more familiar, or both. Two experiments by Noble (1952*b*, 1955) show how each of these verbal dimensions is related to rote memorization.

Noble (1952*b*) constructed three different lists of two-syllable nouns and paralogs. The twelve items that comprised each list were selected to yield a high, medium, or low *m* value for that list. This *m* value was an index of meaningfulness defined as the mean number of associations which had been given to an item in one minute in a separate study (Noble, 1952*a*). It was found that high meaningfulness led to faster memorization, whereas low meaningfulness retarded the serial learning. The meaningfulness of the items used in this experiment was found to correlate highly with their rated familiarity. The learning data may also be interpreted, therefore, as showing a relationship between rate of learning and judged familiarity.

A six-item serial learning task was employed in another study by Noble (1955) with familiarity of items being manipulated by varying number of exposures of various items in a familiarization phase of the experiment. Items of low *m* value were exposed to be pronounced by subjects either 0, 1, 2, 3, 4, 5, 10, or 20 times in this initial phase. This manipulation of familiarity contrasts with the judged familiarity mentioned in the earlier study (Noble, 1952*b*) which presumably reflected the earlier verbal history of the undergraduate judges.

For determining how familiarity affected rate of memorization, lists of six items were constructed to represent the different degrees of prior familiarization. Subjects were required to learn these by the method of anticipation. It was found that the mean number of trials required to reach successive criteria of mastery was quite different for items which had previously been seen and pronounced 0, 10, or 20 times. Previous experience of 1 to 5 times tended to give performance curves that interlaced, generally falling between those for 0 and 10 preliminary exposures. Statistical analysis supported the inference that rate of learning depends on familiarity of material.

Serial Position

A phenomenon that has been repeatedly observed in the rote memorization of serial lists has been that items at the beginning and end of the list have been learned more readily, with those near the

middle taking longer. Describing this *serial position effect* somewhat
differently, we find that more errors are made in attempting to anticipate the items near the middle of the list than are made in mastering
the first few and the last few items. This functional relationship
between mean number of errors and serial position of the items in
the list is illustrated by the solid curve in Figure 13.3, adopted from
a research report by Deese and Kresse (1952).

As the figure indicates, the mean number of total errors yielded
the bow-shaped curve that is usually obtained, even to the typical
asymmetry. The asymmetrical nature of the curve reflects easier
learning of the first items than the last, with both markedly easier
than items at the center. The central portion of the function also
reveals the asymmetry, with items just past the midpoint of the list
showing more errors than items just before the midpoint.

Deese and Kresse (1952) categorized the errors in their serial
learning experiment into three classes: failure to respond, intrusions
from other parts of the list, and overt intrusions not identifiable as
other items in the list. The intralist intrusions were found in Experiment I to bear a functional relationship to serial position that was
fairly symmetrical. This is shown by the dotted curve in the lower
portion of Figure 13.3. Overt intrusions showed no regular relation-

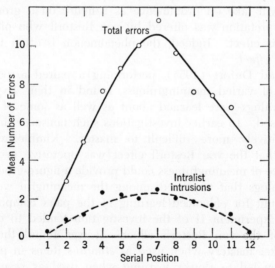

Fig. 13.3. Mean number of total errors and intralist intrusions as a function of the serial position of the nonsense syllables in the twelve-item list.
(After Deese and Kresse, 1952.)

ship to serial position. It would appear, then, that the asymmetry or skewing of the serial position curve is due to the distribution of failures to respond.

With failures to respond identified as the contributor of asymmetry to the serial position function, Deese and Kresse (1952) explored the phenomenon further in their Experiments II and III. Assuming that failure to respond in the allotted time might often result from conflict of response tendencies which could not be resolved in time, they introduced a change in procedure from Experiment I. In Experiments II and III, the subject himself determined the rate at which he proceeded through the list. In these two experiments, using different types of nonsense syllables, it was found that errors of not responding were still more numerous in the latter half of the list even when no time pressure was applied. The usual serial position curve is thus found to derive its skewness principally from response failure. Intrusion errors do not appear to contribute to the asymmetry of the function even though they add their bit to the bow shape by virtue of their greater occurrence nearer the center of the list.

Stimulus Isolation

It has been found that an item which differs from the others in a rote memorization task tends to be learned more readily. A proper name in a list otherwise composed of adjectives will be isolated from them and will take on prominence as a figure on a ground. This gestalt interpretation was offered by von Restorff who pioneered in studying this effect. Indeed, the phenomenon is often termed the *von Restorff effect*.

Kimble and Dufort (1955), performing a paired associate study with items of varied meaningfulness, found in their Experiment I that the paralogs were learned about as well as some of the words that were used. In earlier investigations such nonsense material had proved relatively more difficult to master. Kimble and Dufort postulated that the von Restorff effect was operative in a situation where degree of meaningfulness could provide a figure-ground pattern for the paralogs that appeared among the meaningful words. This would account for enhanced learning of the pairs composed of the paralogs. Experiment II of the investigation tended to confirm the operation of the von Restorff effect. It was found that paralogs led to quicker mastery when used as *stimulus* items in paired associates. They led to slower learning when used as *response* items. This evidence is congruent with the assumption that the effect is essentially a perceptual phenomenon which would operate when isolated material was employed in the stimulus role in paired associate learning.

Rate of Presentation

The rate at which items were presented was one major variable in a study by Underwood and Archer (1955). This experiment employed a somewhat different form of verbal learning than we have discussed before. Consonant syllables were presented in pairs, but instead of trying to associate the two items, the subject had to spell out the one which was "correct." Getting about half right on the first trial (chance expectancy), subjects gradually learned to identify all the syllables that had been designated as "correct." Each pair of syllables was presented in the window of a memory drum for a timed exposure, followed by the member of the pair which had been randomly designated as "correct." The sequence of pairs and the positioning of the pair members were varied from trial to trial to prevent serial or positional learning. The learning of a practice list preceded the experimental learning by one day.

High intralist similarity characterized the lists used in studying how rate of presentation would affect learning. Only nine different consonants were used in constructing the fourteen pairs of consonant syllables that comprised a list. Each of these consonants appeared between eight and ten times in the list.

These hard-to-discriminate items were presented to different subject groups at either a 2-sec or a 1.5-sec rate. Either of these designated exposure times would apply to the presentation of a pair of items in the drum window and to the subsequent presenting of the correct item alone. With separate groups being given one of the two rates, the expected result was found—the faster rate of presentation made subjects take more trials to reach the criterion of one perfect trial with the list. A similar effect of different presentation rates has been found for serial and paired associate learning.

Distribution of Trials

Besides rate of presentation of items, the distribution of trials is another temporal variable in rote memorization. Riley (1952) chose 8 sec and 2 min as values for this independent variable, the intertrial interval. Most of the 2-min interval was filled with color-naming by the subjects. The verbal task involved both verbal-discrimination and paired associate learning. This complexity was due to the fact that the correct response member of each pair had to be selected from among alternatives under some conditions. Early performance required discovery of the correct nonsense syllable, which then had to be associated with the symbol used as stimulus. The stimulus item was presented for 2 sec, followed by the response possibilities for the same length of time.

For the two degrees of distribution of trials that were investigated, it was found that the more distributed condition led to better performance. This was true for the regular paired associate learning as well as for the more complex situations involving multiple response possibilities within pairs.

Motivation

The role that motivation plays in verbal learning and performance has been discussed at some length by Farber (1955). An important point which he makes is that motivational states may have both a general energizing or drive factor and an associative factor arising from their stimulus or cue properties. When experiments are conducted to investigate the effect of the drive factor upon verbal learning, it is important to consider what effects associative factors may have. If motivation is raised by giving electric shock, subjects may indulge in the associated verbal behavior of swearing under their breath—or aloud. If we motivate them by arousing their fear of failing, we may set them to talking reassuringly or reproachfully to themselves. It should be clear that any such verbal responses to manipulations in motivation may complicate the verbal processes that are the focus of study. By careful choice of materials and procedures, however, we should be able to arrive at inferences concerning the functioning of the drive factor itself in verbal learning.

Besides manipulating motivation-producing conditions, we may design experiments on the basis of different levels of drive which subjects bring to the study. An example of this approach is represented in the work of Taylor (1951) who hypothesized that different drive levels existed in subjects who scored high or low on an inventory scale of manifest anxiety, now termed the A scale. When combined with postulated relationships between drive level and different learning situations, this hypothesis yields deductions about the learning of the two groups of subjects which can be tested experimentally.

The use of this A scale in differentiating subject groups is illustrated in a verbal learning study by Spence, Farber, and McFann (1956). In both of the experiments of this investigation, subjects were college students who scored in either the upper or lower 20% on the A scale. These high-anxious and low-anxious groups represented high drive and low drive, respectively. Groups of both types performed in each experiment.

These two experiments differed in the degree of response competition that was represented in the required paired associate learning. In Experiment I competition among the responses was minimized by using two synonyms to form each pair and by avoiding either meaningful or formal similarities between words in different pairs. In Experiment II a high degree of response competition was achieved by using four pairs of words from the list of Experiment I and adding eight more synonyms to the stimulus items, two of these being synonymous with each of the four stimuli borrowed from Experiment I. With these eight new stimuli, nonassociated response words were paired. The competition stemming from the use of four triads of synonyms as stimulus items offered the likelihood of much response competition in Experiment II. By contrast, Experiment I promised almost no response competition in learning the different pairs in which the stimulus and response items were synonymous only with each other and not with other words in the list.

Somewhat different performances were expected from high-anxious and low-anxious subjects in learning the noncompetitive list of Experiment I and the competitive test list of Experiment II. Because of the general energizing value of a high drive level, the high-anxious group was expected to do better in learning the noncompetitive list of Experiment I where the pairs of words were already linked by strong associative values which would be intensified by the higher drive level of these subjects. This expectation was confirmed when the high-anxious group mastered the list more rapidly and with fewer errors. In Experiment II the higher drive level of the anxious subject group was expected to intensify the response competition generated by the use of synonyms among the stimulus items. Confirming this expectation, the high-anxious subjects took longer to reach the criterion of mastery in Experiment II.

SUMMARY

Experiments on rote memorization have permitted the learning process to be studied under carefully controlled conditions. Subjects have been required to develop associations among symbols of various sorts: words, nonsense syllables, paralogs, and numbers. Such items have been presented in serial lists, in pairs, in matrix arrangements, or in meaningful passages. With repeated presentations, the developing strengths of associations are assessed by several techniques such as the anticipation method, the savings method, and tests of recall and recognition. The data obtained in a verbal learning study may be summarized as mean number of items correct or mean trials to successive criteria. Either method of treating the data can yield a learning curve.

Having decided on some combination of conventional or specially devised methods, an experimenter finds many relevant variables which need to be considered as he designs a study. Our review of research included investigations of warm-up and practice effects, of verbal chaining, and of the roles played by meaningfulness and familiarity of items being memorized. Other experiments explored serial position effects and stimulus isolation. Still further evidence of the variety of factors operative in rote memorizing were studies dealing with motivation and with temporal dimensions of stimulus presentation.

REFERENCES

Anderson, Scarvia B., & Ross, S. Memory for items in a matrix. *Amer. J. Psychol.*, 1955, 68, 595–604.

Deese, J., & Kresse, F. H. An experimental analysis of the errors in rote serial learning. *J. exp. Psychol.*, 1952, 44, 199–202.

Farber, I. E. The role of motivation in verbal learning and performance. *Psychol. Bull.*, 1955, 52, 311–327.

Hilgard, E. R. Methods and procedures in the study of learning. In S. S. Stevens (Ed.), *Handbook of experimental psychology.* New York: Wiley, 1951. Pp. 517–567.

Kimble, G. A., & Dufort, R. H. Meaningfulness and isolation as factors in verbal learning. *J. exp. Psychol.*, 1955, 50, 361–368.

Levitt, E. E. A methodological study of the preparation of connected verbal stimuli for quantitative memory experiments. *J. exp. Psychol.*, 1956, 52, 33–38.

Melton, A. W. The end-spurt in memorization curves as an artifact of the averaging of individual curves. *Psychol. Monogr.*, 1936, 47, No. 2 (Whole No. 212), 119–134.

Noble, C. E. An analysis of meaning. *Psychol. Rev.*, 1952, 59, 421–430. (a)

Noble, C. E. The role of stimulus meaning (m) in serial verbal learning. *J. exp. Psychol.*, 1952, 43, 437–446. (b)

Noble, C. E. The effect of familiarization upon serial verbal learning. *J. exp. Psychol.*, 1955, 49, 333–338.

Riley, D. A. Rote learning as a function of distribution of practice and the complexity of the situation. *J. exp. Psychol.*, 1952, 43, 88–95.

Russell, W. A., & Storms, L. H. Implicit verbal chaining in paired-associate learning. *J. exp. Psychol.*, 1955, 49, 287–293.

Schmidt, W. H., & Bunch, M. E. Group methods of studying paired associates and maze learning. *Amer. J. Psychol.*, 1951, 64, 106–108.

Skinner, B. F. *Verbal behavior.* New York: Appleton-Century-Crofts, 1957.

Spence, K. W., Farber, I. E., & McFann, H. H. The relation of anxiety (drive) level to performance in competitional and non-competitional paired-associates learning. *J. exp. Psychol.*, 1956, 52, 296–305.

Taylor, Janet A. The relationship of anxiety to the conditioned eyelid response. *J. exp. Psychol.*, 1951, 41, 81–92.

Thune, L. E. Warm-up effect as a function of level of practice in verbal learning. *J. exp. Psychol.*, 1951, 42, 250–256.

Underwood, B. J., & Archer, E. J. Studies of distributed practice: XIV. Intra-list similarity and presentation rate in verbal-discrimination learning of consonant syllables. *J. exp. Psychol.*, 1955, 50, 120–124.

ADDITIONAL READINGS

Astin, Helen S., & Ross, S. Learning of numbers in differentially shaped and positioned matrices. *Amer. J. Psychol.*, 1958, 71, 764–765.

Hayes, K. J., & Pereboom, A. C. Artifacts in criterion-reference learning curves. *Psychol. Rev.*, 1959, 66, 23–26.

Wishner, J., Shipley, T. E., & Hurvich, M. S. The serial-position curve as a function of organization. *Amer. J. Psychol.*, 1957, 70, 258–262.

CHAPTER **14**

Perceptual-
Motor
Behavior

Perceptual-motor behavior is a term we use to describe coordinated activity usually involving the use of arms, hands, and fingers in performing a variety of tasks. Although the phrase is often shortened to "motor behavior" or "motor performance" in emphasis of the motion involved, the designation "perceptual-motor" gives proper recognition to the perceptual guidance of the movements that we make. Visual perception guides much of our motor activity, but always in conjunction with another important sense—kinesthesis. Our actions are so dependent on this sense of motion that some investigations of motor performance are interpreted as studies of kinesthetic perception.

A few examples will remind us that perceptual-motor behavior deserves considerable study in a science of behavior. When we sign our name, drive a car, or tap to the rhythm of our favorite melody, we are engaging in perceptual-motor behavior. The quarterback flipping a short pass, the marksman steadying the rifle, the surgeon wielding the scalpel—these, too, are performing motor tasks guided by their perceptions. Of course we do not necessarily go to the football field, the rifle range, or the operating room for scientific studies of motor behavior, although psychologists have performed experiments in the first two of these situations. Conventionally, we use one of a number of standard tasks to be performed by experimental subjects in the laboratory. The study of their achievement under different conditions is the way we attempt to clarify the principles of perceptual-motor behavior.

PERCEPTUAL-MOTOR TASKS

There are a number of laboratory tasks which may be used to study such aspects of perceptual-motor behavior as speed, accuracy, steadiness, and manipulative dexterity. They are designed for fairly standardized administration and they require about the same work methods from all subjects. The scores that they yield are therefore usually good indices of skill or of the effects of the experimental conditions on performance.

Static Motor Performance

One kind of motor behavior is actually aimed at minimizing motion. We have already mentioned the rifle marksman who maintains an essentially motionless posture as he prepares to fire a round. We may think, too, of the diver poised on the high board, immobile just before he springs into the air. Despite their lack of motion, these performances are characterized by a high degree of muscular coordination. Such static motor performance, then, is a proper topic for our study.

We may wish to investigate the static motor performance involved in posture. The measurement of such behavior often involves the making of a graphic record of body sway. By fitting a subject with a headband and linking this by threads and pulleys to recording styluses, we can make a continuous record of his postural sway on a kymograph drum or tape. Later this record may be analyzed to determine such things as the amplitudes and the periodicity or frequency of his motion.

Most of us have noticed that our hand shakes slightly when we extend it and attempt to hold it motionless. A simple apparatus devised for testing hand steadiness provides a convenient task for investigating the effect of any independent variables that an experimenter might select. The apparatus consists of a stylus and a metal plate in which there are nine holes of graded diameters. The stylus, a metal rod with a wooden handle, and the plate are usually wired in series with a counter which is activated whenever the subject accidentally touches the metal plate as he attempts to insert the stylus in one of the holes without touching the side of the hole. In the standard procedure for measuring steadiness, the subject would be required to begin with the largest hole, inserting the stylus to the required depth and then withdrawing it without touching the metal plate. He would then proceed to the next smaller hole, and so on, until he touched the plate while attempting to insert or withdraw the stylus. His steadiness score would be determined by how far down through the series of holes he had proceeded successfully before touching the metal plate. The counter is not necessarily used to record the number of contacts but serves to indicate clearly that the stylus has touched the metal plate.

Discrete Motor Responses

Discrete responses like pushing a button, releasing a telegraph key, or snapping a switch are among the simplest motor behaviors. Even such elementary reactions have posed problems for psychological research.

SIMPLE REACTION TIME. A key fact in perceptual-motor behavior is that there is a time lag or latency period between a stimulus and the response that it elicits. This response latency is called *reaction time* in the laboratory situation created to study the independent variables that affect it. The term *simple* reaction time refers to tests in which a single response is made as quickly as possible to a single stimulus, both clearly identified in the instructions to the subject. In a typical experiment the subject is required to release a telegraph key as soon as he perceives the onset of a light located on a panel in front of him. A warning signal usually precedes the stimulus light by a second or so. Simultaneously with the onset of the stimulus light a chronoscope is started, to be terminated by the release of the subject's key. By starting the clock by means of the same switch that presents the stimulus and stopping it the instant the reaction occurs, the reaction time is measured accurately. The chronoscope is calibrated in milliseconds or else in hundredths of a second.

The laboratory situation for the measurement of reaction time, or *RT*, is designed to minimize the response latency. The stimulus light is placed in full view of the subject, who is instructed to fixate it— that is, to look directly at it. In case *RT* to an auditory stimulus is being studied, the buzzer or tone employed as the stimulus is clearly audible. Even though the stimulus, light or tone, is readily perceptible to the subject, its presentation is preceded by a warning signal. This signal, a different light or tone or simply the spoken word, *Ready?*, is used to bring the subject's attentiveness to a peak just before the stimulus itself is given. On the response side, the probability that the measured *RT* will be very brief is enhanced by requiring the simplest possible motor reaction, the release of a key that has been held depressed. The motion involved is thus less than that which would be needed to push down on a telegraph key to close a circuit.

Several conditions in the standard *RT* experiment are typically utilized in an effort to minimize the values obtained. Past research has indicated how varying some of these conditions can affect *RT* (Teichner, 1954). We select a stimulus that is fairly intense because it has been found that decreasing stimulus intensity increases *RT*. The subject is instructed to use his right hand on the key since the left hand has sometimes been found to yield slightly longer *RT* values. For simple visual *RT* the subject is instructed to fixate the light since peripheral stimulation leads to longer *RT*s than does foveal stimulation. In studying the effect of any one of these independent variables it is customary to arrange for optimal values of the others, unless an interaction effect is being sought.

With all values chosen to provide optimal conditions, the standard *RT* experiment has afforded some interesting findings, as reviewed by Teichner (1954). It has generally been found that *RT* to an auditory stimulus is shorter than to a visual stimulus. Teichner (1954, p. 129) has pointed out that our inability to equate intensities of auditory and visual stimuli raises a question for the interpretation of this common finding. With respect to the variable of subjects' ages the standard *RT* procedure has indicated that *RT* grows shorter as chronological age increases from about four to possibly thirty years of age and lengthens slowly thereafter as the upper age limit of subjects tested is approached. It has been found that men show faster reactions in the *RT* experiment than do women.

DISJUNCTIVE REACTION TIME. There are separate, or disjoined, reaction possibilities when two stimuli are presented in a reaction time experiment. The subject may be instructed to respond to one stimulus and to refrain from responding to the other or he may be given two response keys and told to use one whenever one stimulus occurs and use the other for responding to the alternate stimulus. Both these situations are considered to call for *disjunctive reaction,* sometimes referred to as discrimination or choice reaction. On the sensory side, the subject must discriminate between the stimuli. On the motor side he must select between responding and not responding or between left key and right key in reacting. With this greater complexity of task, disjunctive *RT* exceeds simple *RT* by up to a fifth of a second.

Disjunctive *RT* is undoubtedly dependent upon many of the variables that we mentioned as determinants of simple *RT*. For the study of such independent variables as stimulus intensity or age of subjects, simple RT was the procedure chosen since using a disjunctive task would unnecessarily complicate the experiment. The nature of the disjunctive task, however, has naturally given rise to the investigation of two variables which were not found in the simple RT task. In studies which employed anywhere from two to ten alternative stimulus-response pairs, it has been found that RT increases as the number of alternatives increases (Hyman, 1953; Woodworth, 1938, p. 332). With just two stimuli to be discriminated, it has been found that RT is longer when the simultaneously presented stimuli are more similar in some physical respect. Thus, Henmon is reported by Woodworth (1938, p. 333) to have found that when two lines were presented side by side and the subject was to respond with the key on the side of the longer line, the RT obtained was a decreasing function of the difference in length of the lines—the greater the difference, the lower the RT.

Positioning Reactions

In the operation of many sorts of equipment controls there is required a kind of perceptual-motor response that is characterized by a demand for some precision in positioning the control at a given setting. Such positioning reactions are called for in tuning a radio, focusing a projector, or operating airplane controls like the throttle controlling engine speed or the rudder pedals for banking the plane. This type of response may be guided by visual or auditory cues, or such positioning reactions may need to be made on the basis of kinesthetic cues alone, with considerable reliance placed on past experience or habit. Positioning reactions have been studied in laboratory investigations aimed at establishing functional relationships between the response measures and the independent variables manipulated in the experiment.

LINEAR POSITIONING. An experiment by Brown and Slater-Hammel (1949) indicates one method of investigating the performance of linear positioning tasks, those demanding motion in a straight line. These investigators varied the direction and the distance that subjects had to move a sliding pointer in a horizontal plane along a line parallel to the frontal plane of the body. Positioning accuracy was demanded by requiring that the pointer be stopped opposite a marker that was located at a distance of either 2.5, 10, or 40 cm from the starting point, either to its right or left. A graphic record of the motion was made so that primary-movement time and secondary-movement time could be determined for each reaction. These temporal measures were defined as the time taken for the initial movement to the vicinity of the terminal marker and for the settling movement for final positioning, respectively. It was found that primary-movement time increased with the distance to be moved, but the increases in time were not proportional to the changes in distance. Secondary-movement time was found to increase as the required distance of movement was changed from 2.5 cm to either of the longer distances, but for the 10 and 40 cm distances there was no significant difference in this index of performance.

In contrast to the experimental method of Brown and Slater-Hammel, which used temporal performance measures while demanding precision, is the technique employed by Weiss (1954) in which the error of the positioning reaction was measured. Weiss allowed the subject 2.5 sec for moving the airplane-type control stick either forward or back, requiring that this positioning reaction be made on the basis of kinesthesis after the visual cue for the required amplitude of motion had been removed. He recorded the amount by which each response was an overshooting or an undershooting of the absolutely accurate position. With one variable in this experiment also being the distance that had to be moved, a significant tendency to overshoot was observed in relative error size on those trials where the shortest movements were required.

ROTARY POSITIONING. The adjusting of control knobs calls for rotary positioning reactions which may be guided by visual, auditory, or kinesthetic cues. A rotary positioning task was visually guided in a study conducted by Jenkins and Connor (1949). Subjects had to move a pointer to a designated point along a linear scale by turning a knob. The experimenters measured travel time, required to get to the vicinity of the indicated terminal point, and adjust time, occupied in the final adjustment of the pointer at the required location. As one independent variable the amount of pointer movement accomplished by one revolution of the knob was varied from 0.22 to 33.6 in., these values representing the fine and the coarse ends of a range of movement ratios provided in the mechanical linkage of knob to pointer. In an experimental session a subject had to make about 120 settings, each involving pointer travel that varied from 0.187 to 5.5 in. It was found that travel time declined as the movement ratio became coarser, whereas adjust time increased with the coarser ratio. These two functional relationships were represented by curves which intersected at the ratio of 1.18 in. of pointer movement per revolution of the knob. This point is approximately at the fine end of a region along the ratio scale in which the total time for making a setting, that is, travel time plus adjust time, is minimal for this task. Inspection of the data suggests that 2 in. of pointer motion per revolution of the knob might be considered as a representative value for this range of optimal ratio values. Much finer ratios require excessive travel time, whereas much coarser ratios make the final adjustment difficult and time consuming.

A different type of investigation of rotary positioning performance was carried out by Spragg and Devoe (1956). These investigators required blindfolded subjects to turn a knob through an angle that was delimited by metal pins. After turning through the angle once in each direction the subject had to turn once more, trying to bisect the angle he had sampled. One independent variable was the size of the angle presented for bisection, ranging from 20 to 160°. The accuracy of the final knob setting on each trial was dependent on the kinesthetic cues provided by the samplings of the angle. It was found that the constant error (algebraic mean), when expressed as a per cent of the angle to be bisected, was greater for the smaller angles than for the larger.

Repetitive Motor Performance

In contrast to the single response which is the unit of study in *RT* experiments and studies of positioning reactions, perceptual-motor behavior can be investigated by means of a variety of tasks in which an action is repeatedly performed. In these tasks the subject works as quickly as possible, his score usually being the number of units accomplished in a fixed amount of time. Each trial or session is short enough so that scores are not unduly affected by fatigue. A number of these procedures have been borrowed by experimental psychologists from the batteries of psychomotor aptitude tests devised for the selection of military or industrial personnel. In some research these may be administered in about the same way as originally employed. In other investigations the test materials, apparatus, or procedures must be modified to seek the effects of particular independent variables.

TAPPING. One of the simplest of repetitive performances employed in the study of motor behavior is tapping. A simple motion of limited amplitude, involving wrist, hand, and fingers, is repeated as fast as possible. Despite its simplicity this kind of activity can be approached by means of several different techniques which differ in their task dimensions. One method for the study of tapping is to have the subject repeatedly tap a telegraph key that is connected to a counter to record the number of taps during a fixed interval so that the rate of tapping may be computed. Even with this simple arrangement there are several physical dimensions of the task which might affect performance scores. The force that is required to depress the key would be a determinant of tapping speed, as would the distance that the key actually had to be moved. This distance would enter into the performance *if* the key were required to make a contact at the top as well as at the bottom of its movement. If such full key movement were not demanded, then the subject might keep the key near the bottom contact point to tap out a higher score than if he had to let up on the key each time. With only the bottom contact to be made, the counter readings might reflect a manual vibration rate rather than a tapping rate.

To eliminate some of the mechanical influences on performance that are introduced by the telegraph key, tapping is frequently studied by providing a metal stylus that the subject uses to tap on a metal plate. Each contact of stylus and plate completes an electrical circuit and advances the counter one unit. A weakness in this technique, as with the key, is that the subject may vibrate the stylus in contact with the plate so that the counter score evidences rate of voluntary tremor instead of tapping rate. This difficulty is avoided in a different version of the task by providing two metal plates which have to be struck alternately by the stylus. Such a two-plate tapping board not only prevents the vibratory response, but introduces two physical task dimensions which may be varied to determine their effect upon the rate of response. These dimensions are the separation of the plates, which determines the travel of the hand and arm in performing, and the size of the plates, which influences the accuracy with which the response must be terminated at each end of the oscillatory motion. The location of the tapping board in relation to the subject constitutes another physical variable that will affect tapping rate.

To eliminate some of the variability that may be introduced by the use of the stylus, Finan and Malmo (1944) have devised a two-plate tapping board in which the plates are simply struck alternately by the fingers. The plates are mounted over sensitive microswitches which operate a counter each time a plate is depressed by the slight tap. This version of the apparatus has the extra advantage that, with the board placed on the floor, the subject can be required to tap with his toe, thus extending the measurement of motor performance that can be made.

Tapping performance may be studied by means of a technique quite different from those we have been discussing. A paper and pencil task may be provided in which the subject has to place three dots in each of the small circles printed on the page. The score is the number of dots so placed in one or more trials of fixed duration. The size and spacing of the printed circles are task dimensions which influence the performance measure obtained. Another task dimension can be manipulated by requiring that some other number of dots be put in each of the circles.

MINNESOTA RATE OF MANIPULATION TEST. This standard aptitude test provides a repetitive motor task in which the repeated action is a manipulatory one, considerably more complex than tapping (Ziegler, 1933). In addition to requiring quite different manual involvement from tapping, this task also requires much more visual guidance. The test apparatus consists of 60 cylindrical blocks and a 60-hole board. Two different speed tasks may be administered. In the first, the subject is timed as he places the blocks in the holes. For the second task, all the blocks are initially in the holes and the subject must pick up one at a time with one hand, transfer them to the other hand, and replace them inverted in the same hole. The scores earned, of course, depend on the time taken to place or turn the cylinders. One could modify some of the dimensions or procedures of this test to study effects on performance in laboratory experiments, but even with apparatus dimensions retained in standard form, the test can be a useful research tool for studying the influence of variables like age and sex and of environmental conditions such as lighting and temperature.

PEGBOARD TASKS. Another type of performance test that can be used in laboratory studies of perceptual-motor performance is one which calls for eye-hand coordination and fingertip manipulation of small objects. This kind of task is represented by a variety of pegboard tests in which subjects have to pick up small pegs or metal pins and place them as rapidly as possible in the holes arranged in rows on the pegboard. The motion pattern required is thus a repetitive one, although it is obviously more complex than tapping because of the manipulative requirement. Among the physical dimensions of such tasks that we would expect to influence the scores attained would be size of pins and size and spacing of holes in the pegboard. Two methods have been used in scoring performance on these tasks. In the work limit method, subjects must perform a stated amount of work—that is, fill a set number of holes, usually one hundred. The score for this method is the time, often expressed in seconds, that was taken to accomplish this amount of work. In the time limit method, the subject is allowed a fixed amount of time—perhaps 4 min. Here the score is the number of holes filled within the time limit. Note that in the work limit method, the score made is a time score; in the time limit method, the score is the amount of work done. We should incorporate in our operational definition of the behavior whichever scoring method is judged to be more appropriate for the particular investigation planned. Our decision should be guided by earlier related research and by considerations like the reliability of the measurement and its susceptibility to influence by end spurt and fatigue.

Serial Motor Performance

In everyday life, in industrial and clerical work, in playing a musical instrument or in participating in athletics, perceptual-motor performance is not so often strictly repetitive as it is serial in nature. That is, actions occur sequentially, in a series that may repeat itself but in which each repetition involves a segment of behavior that contains two or more distinct activities. As we observe such performance we may note that one response leads to another, usually with a considerable amount of perceptual guidance quite evident. Psychological research has been carried out on such serial motor performances as typewriting or playing the piano, as well as a great number of industrial tasks like machine operation, light assembly, or packaging. For more controllable study of the determinants of serial performance a number of laboratory tasks have been devised.

CARD-SORTING. In the usual card-sorting task subjects are given a pack of numbered cards, thoroughly shuffled, to be sorted into a sorting tray divided into bins, each bin identified by a number which appears repeatedly in the set of cards. The tray might contain from 16 to 30 bins, and the pack of cards might contain from about 60 to 120 cards with each number included from four to eight times. The bin numbers are generally arranged randomly in the tray so that some searching is required on early trials to locate the bin into which a card must be tossed. As you can see, this card-sorting task is one that is likely to exhibit a strong practice effect as subjects become familiar with the bin locations. The performance measure for this task is the time taken to sort the entire pack of numbered cards.

There are a number of procedural details which should be observed to contribute to success in experiments using a card-sorting task. As we mention them we may note that each rule implies some determinant of performance. As a first aspect of technique it may be suggested that the experimenter be sure of the perceptibility of the numbers, both on the cards and on the bins. This requirement calls for attention to the size and contrast of the printed numbers, the room illumination and the subject's angle of regard in viewing the bin numbers. It is desirable to use only two-digit numbers to reduce the variation in perceptibility that using some one-digit numbers would introduce. Very important is the requirement that the cards be shuffled thoroughly between trials, since they are taken in sorted groups from the bins. It is much sounder research if improvement in scores from trial to trial can be interpreted as a practice effect in the subject's sorting rather than as a fatigue effect in the experimenter's shuffling. To avoid another source of distortion of apparent practice effect it is well to cover the sorting tray immediately on the completion of a trial so that the subject may not study the bin locations during the intertrial interval.

INVERTED-ALPHABET PRINTING. Another serial motor task quite suitable for laboratory studies is inverted-alphabet printing. In this paper and pencil task, subjects begin at the right side of a page and work toward the left, printing the letters of the alphabet upside down and in sequence so that if the page were rotated 180° the alphabet would appear as normal. Trials are set at some convenient length; 30 sec have been used, for example. On each successive trial the subject is required to begin with the next letter after the one with which he ended the previous trial. When Z is reached, the subject continues from A again. The score for each trial is the number of letters printed in the correct inverted fashion.

Although there are not too many task dimensions which may be manipulated as independent variables, inverted-alphabet printing has been used in several studies investigating the influence of the work-rest ratio on performance and determining the effect of introducing a long rest period after several minutes of massed practice (Archer & Bourne, 1956; Kimble, 1949; Kientzle, 1946). By *work-rest ratio* we mean the ratio of duration of work, or of the trial during which the work is performed, to the duration of the rest interval given between trials. Thus, a 30-sec trial followed by a 10-sec rest would constitute a work-rest ratio of 3:1, whereas the same rest period alternated with 40-sec trials would yield a 4:1 ratio. By *massed* practice we refer to continuous work trials with no rest periods interspersed. Of course, the experimenter can divide a session of massed practice into as many "trials" as he wishes for scoring purposes. When fairly long rest periods are given between trials, the condition is often referred to as *distributed* practice. Kimble (1949) found that distributed practice, 30 sec of work and 30 sec of rest, led to greater improvement in inverted-alphabet printing in a forty-trial experiment than did massed practice, 20 min of continuous performance. He also found that giving a 10-min rest after varying amounts of massed practice led to an immediate improvement but that scores gradually dropped again as massed practice was resumed.

MOTION ANALYSIS TASKS. In defining serial motor performance we stated that it involved different actions performed in sequence. Professor K. U. Smith devised techniques for obtaining separate measures of the component behaviors in sequential tasks. Assisted by his students at the University of Wisconsin, Smith measured the time occupied by different aspects of performance in tasks of varying complexity. In one experiment Davis, Wehrkamp, & Smith (1951) gave subjects sixteen rotary switches arranged on a control panel in a four by four matrix. The task was to manipulate the switches in regular sequence by giving each one a clockwise rotation. Under four different conditions a subject was required to work across the four rows from left to right, or from right to left, or else to work up the four columns of switches, or down the columns. Electrical scoring circuits were arranged so that total manipulation time was accumulated on one clock and total travel time was accumulated on another. It was found that manipulation time was not affected by the pattern of travel from switch to switch. Travel time was not different for the left-right and right-left patterns of travel. However, it was found that travel time was significantly shorter when the subject moved downward from switch to switch than when he had to move upward through each column of switches.

In a similar experiment, Harris and Smith (1953) studied the effects of a number of task variables on different components of performance. A series of such investigations constitutes a dimensional analysis of motion as it occurs in serial manipulatory operations. In addition to studying the direction of travel as in the earlier study, the plane of hand travel, either vertical or horizontal, was also investigated. The direction of rotary manipulation was varied, the requirement being sometimes for clockwise rotation, sometimes for counter-clockwise, and sometimes for each of these to be used alternately in proceeding from switch to switch. This latter requirement was one way to introduce complexity of manipulatory pattern into such a task.

Continuous Adjustive Performance

There is a kind of perceptual-motor performance in which a repetitive action is not demanded of the subject, nor is he required to perform any prescribed sequence of actions. The task assigned is rather for the subject to manipulate a control in such a way as to keep at a minimum the positional discrepancy between two elements that he is watching. A general term applied to many specific examples of this type of performance is *tracking*. The term is borrowed from antiaircraft gunnery where a soldier was required to "track" a plane by means of a gunsight or optical instrument—that is, to keep the moving plane aligned as much as possible with the cross-hair or other reticle of the sight. This was usually accomplished by rotating cranks that moved the sight and the gun.

Tracking is a designation for many tasks besides that performed by the gunner. It applies to the task performed by some radar operators as they seek to keep a marker positioned over the blip on the face of the radar scope that represents a moving plane or submarine. A sort of tracking task is accomplished by the planesman on a submarine as he watches the depth indicators in adjusting bow or stern planes in diving the sub to a prescribed depth. But tracking is not limited to military situations. The term may be applied to the task performed by any pilot as he performs a visually guided landing on an airport runway. And as we drive a car down a winding road we are engaged in continuous adjustive behavior which might be called tracking. We are tracking the roadway as we steer the car. Although research on tracking has often had applied aims, usually of relevance to military applications, we can see that as a type of perceptual-motor performance it cannot be overlooked if we are to explore human behavior systematically. Indeed, tracking tasks have been used in experiments directed at behavior problems of a most general sort such as transfer of training, for example. It is their use as tools for psychological research that prompts us to consider tracking tasks here.

Two types of tracking task are generally distinguished. *Compensatory* tracking requires a subject to manipulate a control so as to keep a moving target aligned, as much as possible, with a stationary reference mark. He must employ the control, which is linked to the representation of the target, to compensate for any drift of the target away from the designated null point. The visual display on which are represented the moving target and the null point may be any one of a number of types as may the control that the subject moves to keep the target nulled. In different laboratory studies of tracking, displays viewed by the subject have incorporated as targets such things as metal disks moved around mechanically, pointers on dial indicators of different kinds, and spots on the face of a cathode ray oscilloscope. Controls have been employed in great diversity, too, including cranks, knobs, and levers.

A second type of tracking is called *following* or *pursuit* tracking.

Here there are two moving elements in the display, the target, over which the subject exerts no control in this type of tracking, and the follower which is an indicator, perhaps a pointer or a ring, which must be kept aligned with the moving target as much as possible. Continuous adjustive performance is called for in following tracking just as in compensatory tracking.

For both types of tracking the research apparatus includes some type of target programmer or target course generator by means of which the path taken by the moving target is directed. This pathway is generally not observed in compensatory tracking since the subject's control is also connected to the target, and target motion is therefore a resultant of both the movement generated by the target course program and the compensatory movements made by the subject. In following tracking, on the other hand, the target motion that is governed by the apparatus programmer is perceptible to the subject since his control motions do not affect it but move only the follower.

As in other parts of this chapter, we can consider only a sample of a particular sort of perceptual-motor performance. We shall look at rotary pursuit performance, the laboratory tracking task that probably has been most widely studied. We shall deal again with tracking in Chapter 15 and Chapter 17.

ROTARY PURSUIT PERFORMANCE. In this tracking task the target is a small metal disk set in the surface of a turntable which rotates at a constant speed, usually sixty revolutions per minute. The subject tries to keep the tip of a metal stylus in contact with the target as it travels its circular pathway. The pursuit rotor, as the apparatus is usually called, thus requires following tracking. The linkage between stylus handle and tip which are the control and target follower, respectively, is a direct one in the rotary pursuit task. In most other tracking tasks this linkage between control and target follower is indirectly accomplished by mechanical or electrical means. The measure of performance for the rotary pursuit task, as for many other tracking tasks, is time on target, usually measured in milliminutes, seconds, or hundredths of a second. The clock accumulating the subject's score is operated by current passing through the stylus and the metal target, so that it runs only when the subject is on target.

The operational definition of the rotary pursuit task naturally begins with the specification of physical dimensions of the apparatus on which the subject is asked to perform. The definition would proceed to statements about the illumination provided, the ambient (environmental) temperature, and the lengths of trials and rest intervals. As to the apparatus characteristics, Ammons (1955) has eloquently argued the desirability of standardization from one laboratory to another. This would introduce a great measure of agreement into operational definitions of the task as it is employed in different experiments. Unfortunately, as Ammons goes on to demonstrate, various models of the rotary pursuit apparatus differ widely in important respects even though all are descendants of the original apparatus devised by Koerth (1922). Experiments have differed in the size of target used and the speed of turntable rotation, both of which were shown by Helmick (1951) to affect the scores attained. With these and other task dimensions differing from study to study, it is naturally difficult to profit from previous research in planning experiments. The problem is made more acute by the lack of information in many reports about apparatus specifications.

SOME DETERMINANTS OF PERCEPTUAL-MOTOR PERFORMANCE

We want next to consider a few of the determinants of performance that have been manipulated as independent variables. With the behavior measures and the experimental treatments both in mind we shall grasp some idea of the vast domain of laws of perceptual-motor performance that has been only barely explored in studies already conducted. We can include only a fragmentary sample of the independent variables that investigators have employed.

If we ask any intelligent person what will determine the score to be expected when a subject performs a motor task, among the answers that may be offered will be the assertion that his past experience in performing that task or anything similar to it will be a major determinant of how well he will do. We recognize the truth of this statement and, in fact, we regard the past learning of skill as such an important factor that we shall devote a part of Chapter 15 to a discussion of perceptual-motor learning. Likewise, the problem of how performance is affected by past experience with *similar* tasks will occupy our attention in Chapter 17 which deals with transfer of training. Because learning and transfer are to be treated extensively later, we shall not list them among the determinants of performance here.

Physical Dimensions of the Task

Since most perceptual-motor behavior involves the manipulation of objects or the operation of equipment, the physical dimensions of the task are important variables determining performance. We might note, in passing, that it is these man-machine interdependencies that make the principles of human performance a useful guide to the designer of equipment. The formulating of such applicable principles of behavior is one of the aims of research in engineering psychology.

PLANE, DIRECTION, AND EXTENT OF MOVEMENT. The plane, vertical or horizontal, in which a motion must be performed can affect performance of several sorts. Brown, Knauft, and Rosenbaum (1948) studied linear positioning reactions in the horizontal and vertical planes, finding that downward responses in the vertical plane tended to be overshot even for the longer movements, an effect which did not hold for upward movements or for movement in the horizontal plane. They suggested that the overshooting might be attributable to a gravitational effect, although an opposing negative effect was not found for upward adjustive movements. In an investigation of the repetitive motor task of crank turning Reed (1949) found higher speed was attained when the plane of rotation was vertical than when it was horizontal.

The direction of motion does not appear to affect the accuracy of linear positioning reactions very strongly. Weiss found no significant difference in the accuracy of positioning of push and pull responses in two studies (1954, 1955). Brown, Knauft, and Rosenbaum (1948) found that very short adjustive motions away from the body were more accurate than motions toward the body. For the very short distances, too, the motions away from the body were less variable than movements toward the body. At the longest distance studied, 40 cm, an opposite finding was obtained, with the movements away from the body being more variable than movements toward it.

Directions of rotation of switches on a panel were studied by Harris and Smith (1954). They found practically no difference in manipulation time for clockwise vs. counterclockwise rotation. The sole exception was for the greatest arc of rotation tested, 120°, on the seventh day of practice when a statistically significant difference of about 1 sec in the turning time for 25 switches was found, favoring the clockwise direction.

Reed (1949) studied the effect of rotational direction on the speed that could be attained in crank turning. It was found that direction of rotation made no significant difference in the speed of cranking that could be attained. This general conclusion was drawn from tests based on three crank orientations, two levels of friction, and the use of both right and left hand.

Even though the direction of motion may not strongly affect the speed or accuracy of response in simple tasks, the directional relationships between control motions and the effects they produce on displays that subjects are watching in complex tasks like tracking may be very important in determining level of performance. These display-control directional relationships will be given some attention in Chapter 17.

In studies of the accuracy of linear positioning reactions as a function of the extent of motion required Brown, Knauft, and Rosenbaum (1948) and Weiss (1954) found that shorter distances tended to be overshot, whereas undershooting occurred in the longer movements. This tendency has been noted in studies of sensation as well as motor performance and has been designated as the *range effect*. It is presumed due to a subject's becoming accustomed to a particular range of stimuli and responding to the middle portion of that range as well as to the stimulus presented when he reacts on any given trial. In a later study Weiss (1955) demonstrated that the range effect, which was quite evident when stimuli and responses occurred in series of randomly mixed amplitudes, could be greatly reduced by presenting the same stimulus and calling for the same response amplitude numerous times in succession. With the latter procedure there was far less tendency to overshoot and to undershoot than had been observed with the mixed series.

Bahrick, Bennett, and Fitts (1955) varied the extent of movement required of subjects who had to position, in the horizontal plane, an arm control that pivoted about a point under the subject's elbow. Disregarding overshooting and undershooting, which were minimized by the procedure employed, and averaging the amplitude of error without regard to its sign, they found that the average error increased as the motion increased over the three values tested, 17.5°, 35°, and 70°. Error did not increase, however, in proportion to the distance moved.

FORCE DEMAND. Another physical task dimension is the force demand that is made upon the operator of a piece of equipment as he moves the controls. Bilodeau and Bilodeau (1954) demonstrated that the rate of rotating a crank is inversely related to the load imposed on the crank. Reed (1949) also found that cranking was faster as torque demand was lower, when cranks of very small radius were used. With larger cranks, permitting adequate leverage to meet the torque demand, the difference in rate due to the torque became smaller, reaching zero difference at about a 7 cm radius when the greatest torque used in the study was 5000 gm-cm.

Resistance to motion offered by a control cannot be considered completely undesirable. Where adjustive motions are kinesthetically guided, there is the possibility that resistance in the control being moved will provide cues to the kinesthetic sense that will be useful in guiding the motor response. Evidence to this effect is found in the study by Bahrick, Bennett, and Fitts (1955) who found that the accuracy in positioning a control was better when there was a torque resistance provided by torsion rods or springs than when no such resistance to movement was offered. They found also that for two of the three extents of movement studied, positioning accuracy improved as the relative torque change represented by one degree of movement at the terminal position increased.

Having seen that resistance in a control is sometimes beneficial, we must note that this should not be regarded as a general principle applicable in all perceptual-motor performance. Indeed, it is not always found to hold for spring-type resistance to positioning reaction. In two different studies by Weiss (1954, 1955) it was found that adding different amounts of spring-loading to the control stick did not increase positioning accuracy. The difference between the findings of Weiss and those of Bahrick, Bennett, and Fitts is no cause for doubting the adequacy of either investigation. It is such seeming discrepancies in research results that are the stimulus for many investigations. Actually there were enough differences in the motor reactions required and in the training and testing procedures of these experiments to account for the different outcomes.

RATE DEMAND. In tasks where reactions have to be made repetitively, the rate of response that is demanded can be an important determinant of performance. In a crank turning task where the subjects were asked to maintain a designated rate of rotation, Lincoln (1954) found that the size of the lag error and the frequency of oscillatory errors both increased as higher rates of cranking were required. For a quite different task, rotary pursuit performance, Helmick (1951) found that time on target scores became lower as turntable speeds ranged upward from 50 to 80 rpm.

PRECISION DEMAND. In the study just cited Helmick also found that when greater precision was demanded by making the target smaller, scores also dropped. In a somewhat more complex task, following tracking performed by operating two control cranks, Green (1955) similarly found much lower scores when the target was smaller.

Stimulus Dimensions of the Task

Just as the dimensions of motion are determinants of perceptual-motor performance, the stimulus aspects of tasks play a role in providing cues for the perceptual guidance of the responses. We shall examine a few studies very briefly to see the techniques used in regulating the cues provided for the subjects.

AVAILABILITY OF STIMULI. A common way to study the part which cues play in governing motor reactions is to render certain stimuli unavailable and to look for resultant deterioration of performance. Riopelle and Stritch (1952) reduced available cues by having one group of subjects wear special goggles that were modified to permit vision with the right eye only. They administered a pegboard task to this experimental group and to a control group that was permitted normal binocular vision. Poorer scores were made by the experimental group, deprived of the extra cues for spatial perception that binocular vision affords.

Edwards (1949a) used a very different technique for reducing the perceptual guidance available for the control of a simple motor task. He required subjects to glance to the side as they attempted to hold a steering wheel motionless. The involuntary movement of the wheel was found to be greater for those conditions that called for a shift of attention to the side as compared to the control condition, permitting fixation of a point directly ahead.

PERCEPTIBILITY OF STIMULI. In addition to rendering cues unavailable, an experimenter may render them less perceptible to subjects to determine how motor performance will be affected. Chocholle (1948) found that simple auditory RT was lengthened as the intensity of the stimulus tone was decreased. Similar results have been found for the visual modality. In vision, another way of making the stimulus less perceptible is to present it from a peripheral point in the field of view. Woodworth (1938, p. 328) indicates that Poffenberger found that simple RT was increased by about two hundredths of a second by presenting the visual stimulus 45° from the fixation point. A number of related studies of simple RT have been reviewed by Teichner (1954).

DISCRIMINABILITY OF STIMULI. In an early study cited by Woodworth (1938, pp. 333–334) Henmon used one subject in testing the hypothesis that when stimuli were more physically similar disjunctive RT would be longer. The hypothesis was confirmed with several types of stimuli: colors, tones of different frequency, and lines of different length. Shorter disjunctive RT results when stimuli are made more discriminable.

Conditions of Testing

All the variables which affect perceptual-motor performance are not stimulus or motor dimensions of the task. Environmental conditions or the state of the person being tested have also been investigated in laboratory studies. In some cases, it should be noted, the interest of the investigator actually centers upon the condition that is being manipulated; the perceptual-motor task may have been selected as a convenient index of the effect of this factor on human performance.

TEMPERATURE. Teichner and Wehrkamp (1954) studied the effect of ambient (environmental) temperature on rotary pursuit performance. Subjects were tested at a room temperature of 55, 70, 85 or 100° Fahrenheit on five successive days. Analysis of scores indicated that performance is optimal at about 70° with significant detrimental effects resulting from either higher or lower temperatures.

In his review of research on simple RT, Teichner (1954) indicates that an effect of temperature on RT has not been demonstrated. He suggests that the lack of such a demonstration may be due to technical difficulties in the studies in which temperature was varied.

ANOXIA. The advent of high altitude flight generated an interest in the effects of anoxia, a lessened amount of available oxygen, on physiological and psychological processes. McFarland (1932) found that simple RT was lengthened under conditions of anoxia, the effect reaching statistical significance when the oxygen lack corresponded to an altitude of 20,000 ft.

Malmo and Finan (1944) studied the effect of anoxia on two other simple motor performances, hand steadiness and tapping. They found that steadiness was impaired when anoxia was equivalent to that encountered at an altitude of 12,000 ft, and that it deteriorated even more when conditions simulated 18,000 ft. Tapping rate was slower at 18,000 ft but not at 12,000 ft or 15,000 ft. It was suggested that tapping rate may have been sustained by an extra motivational factor arising from the subject's sense of failure at the steadiness task which immediately preceded the tapping test in each session.

ROTATION. As an example of the effect on motor behavior of a treatment administered to the subject rather than an environmental factor we may consider the effect of rotating the subject prior to testing him. Edwards (1949b) placed subjects on a rotating platform in either an upright or prone position and revolved them for six revolutions. They were then given standard tests for body sway and finger tremor. It was found that body sway was increased greatly by rotation but that finger tremor, measured with the subject seated extending his arm, showed only a slight increase that was not statistically significant despite the use of a large number of subjects. Rotation affects postural coordination through its action on the vestibular sense organs of the inner ear.

Characteristics of Subjects

Other determinants of perceptual-motor performance besides those we have briefly suggested may be sought in the characteristics of the person performing. Individual differences in age, sex, intelligence, physique, handedness, and visual acuity might be mentioned as possible contributors to scores made at different tasks. We shall limit our attention here to examples of performance found to depend on the age or sex of the subjects.

SEX. Using college students as subjects in an inverted-alphabet printing task, Archer and Bourne (1956) found that women were significantly faster in performing this task than were men. A detailed analysis of the component parts of the performance showed that the superiority of the women was based on their shorter travel times from letter to letter rather than on printing time itself, in which the sexes did not differ significantly.

Testing boys and girls from the third through the twelfth grades of school on a rotary pursuit task, Ammons, Alprin, and Ammons (1955) found that the boys made superior scores at all grade levels. The superiority of the boys' scores was greater for the older subjects. The difference between the boys' scores and those of the girls was also found to be greater following a 5-min rest given after the first 3 min of continuous practice.

AGE. In the rotary pursuit experiment by Ammons, Alprin and Ammons it was found that scores made by boys were increasingly greater for higher school grades, the skill exhibited thus seeming to be parallel to chronological age or physical development. For the girls there was a similar rise in scores from the third through the ninth grade levels, but scores were lower in the eleventh grade group than for the ninth grade pupils and lower still for those in the twelfth grade.

Welford (1951) has summarized a number of studies of perceptual-motor performance with subjects whose age range extended into the seventies. He and his colleagues devised several different kinds of task with emphasis on obtaining several different measures of performance so as to reveal particular aspects of the activity in which differences among the age groups might be found. This analytic approach proved profitable in that some of the error and time scores showed no differences as a function of age, whereas others were significantly different, helping to pinpoint the reasons for differences in over-all performance. In a complex task on grid-position matching, for example, the older subjects tended to make many fewer small errors because their work method was more deliberate. The younger subjects willingly made many more small errors, with the result that their trial-and-error approach to the task enabled them to complete more units of work in the time available.

SOME PERCEPTUAL-MOTOR STUDIES

We can complete our survey of research on perceptual-motor behavior by examining a few additional experiments. These will illustrate some of the techniques that are characteristic of studies in this area of psychology.

Simple Visual Reaction Time as a Function of Foreperiod

In introducing this experiment Klemmer (1956) makes the interesting point that in simple *RT* tests the subject has no uncertainty about what the stimulus will be or how he is to react to it; he is uncertain only as to when the stimulus will occur. This highlights the foreperiod as a variable of primary importance, and Klemmer goes on to show that it is not only the length of the foreperiod but its variability over a series of trials that will contribute to determining the *RT*. The *foreperiod*, we may recall, is the interval between a warning signal and the stimulus to which the subject is to respond. In this investigation different mean values and different ranges of the foreperiod were used.

An auditory click was used as the warning signal, the stimulus was provided by a neon bulb clearly visible in a darkened room, and the response was the operation of a telegraph key. For some of the series of trials, the foreperiod was held constant at either 0.25, 4.25, or 8.25 sec. For other series of tests the foreperiods were of mixed lengths presented at random from one of the following ranges of values: 0.25 to 2.25, 3.25 to 5.25, 6.25 to 8.25 or 0.25 to 8.25, all values expressed in seconds.

For those series in which there was no variation in the foreperiod, the mean *RT* found for the shortest foreperiod, 0.25 sec, was 209 msec increasing to 252 and 269 msec for the foreperiods of 4.25 and 8.25 sec, respectively. To discourage subjects from responding prematurely, Klemmer repeated any run in which a response occurred before the stimulus light flashed on.

On the basis of the invariant foreperiod series of tests just cited, it would appear that *RT* is an increasing function of length of foreperiod. The function is very much dependent on the invariability of the foreperiods within a series, however, as Klemmer's results for the series with a range of foreperiods show. When there was a 2-sec range of foreperiods, no difference was found between the mean *RT* values found for the series with mean foreperiod values of 1.25 and 4.25 sec. There did appear to be a slightly longer mean *RT* when the foreperiods were varied from 6.25 to 8.25 sec with a mean fore-period at 7.25 sec. When the foreperiod was varied even more extensively from 0.25 to 8.25 sec a still greater mean *RT* was obtained. It appears, then, that *RT* increases with an increase in range of fore-period employed or with an increase in the mean value of a set of varied foreperiods. The rise in *RT* under these two conditions, how-ever, is by no means as steep as its rise as a function of the value of a foreperiod that is never varied within a series of trials. The varia-bility of foreperiods employed must therefore be given careful con-sideration whenever a functional relationship between *RT* and fore-period is sought. Another conclusion that Klemmer reaches is that the particular foreperiod value on a trial is not as potent a determiner of the *RT* on that trial as is the group of foreperiod values employed in the preceding series of trials, especially insofar as these may be invariant or greatly varied.

Pegboard Performance as a Function of Angle of Regard

In addition to having subjects use either monocular or binocular vision in performing a pegboard task, Riopelle and Stritch (1952) also systematically varied the angle of regard or viewing angle at which the subjects looked at the pegboard. They did this by elevating the board to the eye level of the seated subject for a viewing angle of zero degrees and lowering it to a point 400 mm directly below his eyes for a 90° angle of regard. Separate groups of subjects were run with the board in these two extreme positions and with the intermediate positions located at the same distance from the eyes, with viewing angles of 5, 10, 30, 45, 60, and 80° below horizontal. Subjects worked for twelve 30-sec trials with a 30-sec rest between trials. In the intertrial interval a subject rested his hand on the near edge of the board. It was found that the mean number of peg placements per trial was an increasing function of the angle of regard for both the monocular and binocular conditions. Performance was particularly poor for the low angles of regard with monocular vision.

The pegboard was chosen for this study because the placing of pegs is a task which permits the subject to reach a performance limit in a relatively few trials. We see, then, that the experimenters took practice effect into account when designing the experiment. A possible fatigue effect was also considered, as shown by the fact that liberal rest intervals were given. Performance data for the individual trials are not given, so we cannot tell from the report what the course of achievement over trials may have been. The plotted functions are evidently based on all trials combined. The question of a possible effect of fatigue on performance arises particularly because the work-surface height was varied to change the angle of regard. Subjects who worked at the low angles of regard had to reach up to about eye level to place the pegs. They also had to rest their hand on the board at this level between trials. It may have been that greater arm fatigue developed over the 12-min session for the groups given the higher placement of the pegboard to provide the lower angles of regard. It is probably not possible to vary the perceptual factor of viewing angle without making some change in the physical place-ment of the pegboard in relation to the subject's body but other means of perceptual variation should probably be tried. One way might be to maintain the work-surface height comfortably low while tilting the pegboard to provide different angles of regard. Although this technique would alter a physical task dimension, it might still be a useful way of estimating the potency of the perceptual factor.

Inverted-Alphabet Printing as a Function of Sex and Intertrial Interval

The study by Archer and Bourne (1956), in which it was found that women performed faster at the inverted-alphabet printing task, is instructive for the way in which many procedural details were arranged by the investigators. We shall review some of these, noting the purpose they served in the study.

Only right-handed subjects were accepted as volunteer participants. This made it possible to set up a certain direction for doing the print-ing without the risk that this would be harder for left handers so that their scores would add to the variability of the data. Another pro-cedural attempt to reduce variability was the calling to the subject's attention that the letters H, I, N, O, S, X, and Z looked the same whether inverted or not. Unless told this, a subject might have discovered it only gradually, thus retarding mastery of the task.

Innovations in the administration of this task included running the subjects individually and recording separate time scores for the act of printing and the travel from letter to letter. This recording was accomplished by having a 6-volt relay activated while the lead pencil, wired into the circuit, was in contact with the aluminum plate on which the printing was done. These separate scores permitted the discovery that it was in travel time, and not in printing time, that the women were superior to the men.

Since they were studying the effect of intertrial interval on performance, the investigators naturally required subjects to perform several trials. Twenty trials of 30-sec duration were given, then a 5-min rest, then six more trials. Two groups, one of men and one of women, were given no rest during the first twenty trials. Two other groups were given a 30-sec rest after each trial in that part of the experiment, and two more groups were permitted intertrial intervals of 60 sec. After the 5-min rest all six groups were given the 30-sec intertrial interval in the final six trials. For the different intertrial intervals the slopes of the pre-rest and post-rest performance curves were found to differ significantly. Over the first twenty trials the groups given the 60-sec intertrial interval tended to improve most rapidly, whereas the groups given no rest between trials made the slowest improvement. After the 5-min rest some groups improved rapidly, whereas others tended to slump somewhat so that the slopes of the performance curves were different.

Multiple trials were called for in the design of this experiment for studying the effect on performance of the intertrial interval. They proved to be a boon in discovering the difference in performance between men and women, too. If, for some reason, only one trial had been given, this difference would not have come to light. Analysis of the data for the first trial alone indicated no significant difference in scores attributable to sex. In planning any experiment it is well to consider whether trials, or even treatments, can be added after the needed trials have been completed, with the possibility that the study will yield an extra dividend of information about the behavior being investigated.

Rotary Pursuit Performance as a Function of Prolonged Low Temperature

The experiment we shall consider next illustrates how research is generated from the results of previous studies. You may recall that Teichner and Wehrkamp (1954) had found that excessively high or low temperatures resulted in lower scores for rotary pursuit than did the 70° temperature. All groups showed improvement over the five daily sessions, but the groups performing under the high or low temperatures never reached the level of performance attained by the 70° group. Would they ever reach it? In other words, might they have become accustomed to working in the heat or the cold and gradually reached the same final level of skill as those who had practiced more comfortably? Or do extremes of temperature set lower ceilings on performance no matter how much opportunity is afforded for getting used to the environmental condition? To answer this question as it applied to low temperature, Teichner and Kobrick (1955) put five soldiers clad in socks, shorts, and T-shirts in a room kept at 55° Fahrenheit. Kept there for twelve days, these men had plenty of opportunity to develop skill at the rotary pursuit task.

The experiment actually began with a baseline period of sixteen days during which the room temperature was kept at 75°. Then the mercury plunged to 55° for the twelve-day cold period, followed by a thirteen-day recovery period with the temperature again at 75°. Fifteen trials on the pursuit rotor were given on each day of the experiment. To show the day-to-day improvement function only the scores for the middle five trials from each day were plotted. The first five were discarded to eliminate the warmup effect and the last five were omitted to get rid of the end spurt phenomenon.

It was found that the curve fitted to the middle five trial scores for the first sixteen days could be extended to pass through the points that represented scores made during the recovery period. In other words, when the temperature was restored to 75°, performance rose to the level that might be expected as a result of the intervening twelve days of practice. However, scores made during that twelve-day cold snap were by no means continuous with those of the baseline and recovery period. When the temperature dropped on the seventeenth day of the experiment, the score dropped too. The performance level for that first day of the cold period was about the same as for the first day of the baseline period. The rate of improvement in the cold period was about as fast as it had been in the baseline period too, although curves fitted to the two sets of data were not found to correspond completely when a statistical analysis was made.

The question as to whether the men could acclimatize to the cold to the point where their final level of performance would reveal no detrimental effect was not answered unequivocally in this study. A considerable adaptation to the cold was revealed in the improvement made. The fact that learning was continuing during the cold period was revealed by the continuation of the baseline function when the 75° temperature was restored. Although performance improved over the cold period, the curve fitted to the data was negatively accelerated. The experimenters concluded that such a low ambient temperature affects the final limit of performance so that they would not predict complete recovery from its detrimental effects even with a more extended period for acclimatization.

SUMMARY

An important segment of human behavior, perceptual-motor performance, is studied in the psychology laboratory by requiring subjects to perform one of a variety of tasks. Static motor performance is studied by measuring body sway or hand steadiness. Latency of response is investigated in experiments on simple or disjunctive RT. Other simple performances that have been required in research are linear and rotary positioning reactions and repetitive tapping. Serial motor activity is represented in psychomotor tests and laboratory tasks such as performing with pegboards, card-sorting, inverted-alphabet printing, and manipulation of switches. Continuous adjustive reactions are studied in compensatory and following tracking tasks, including rotary pursuit performance.

The variables which affect perceptual-motor performance are very numerous. Physical task dimensions, either of a motor or sensory sort, are among those which have been manipulated in many investigations. Factors in the environment and prior treatments of subjects are likely to affect performance scores. Skill levels have also been found to depend upon characteristics of the subjects, like sex and age.

Reviews of several different experiments illustrate how many different considerations of experimental procedure are demanded in research on even the simplest sorts of perceptual-motor performance. The tasks involved in the different studies cited were simple RT, pegboard performance, inverted-alphabet printing, and rotary pursuit performance.

REFERENCES

Ammons, R. B. Rotary pursuit apparatus: I. Survey of variables. *Psychol. Bull.,* 1955, 52, 69–76.

Ammons, R. B., Alprin, S. I., & Ammons, Carol H. Rotary pursuit performance as related to sex and age of pre-adult subjects. *J. exp. Psychol.,* 1955, 49, 127–133.

Archer, E. J., & Bourne, L. E., Jr. Inverted-alphabet printing as a function of intertrial rest and sex. *J. exp. Psychol.,* 1956, 52, 322–328.

Bahrick, H. P., Bennett, W. F., & Fitts, P. M. Accuracy of positioning responses as a function of spring loading in a control. *J. exp. Psychol.,* 1955, 49, 437–444.

Bilodeau, Ina McD., & Bilodeau, E. A. Some effects of work loading in a repetitive motor task. *J. exp. Psychol.,* 1954, 48, 455–467.

Brown, J. S., Knauft, E. B., & Rosenbaum, G. The accuracy of positioning reactions as a function of their direction and extent. *Amer. J. Psychol.*, 1948, 61, 167–182.

Brown, J. S., & Slater-Hammel, A. T. Discrete movements in the horizontal plane as a function of their length and direction. *J. exp. Psychol.*, 1949, 39, 84–95.

Chocholle, R. Quelques remarques sur les variations et la variabilité des temps de réaction auditifs. *J. Psychol. norm. path.*, 1948, 41, 345–358.

Davis, R., Wehrkamp, R., & Smith, K. U. Dimensional analysis of motion: I. Effects of laterality and movement direction. *J. appl. Psychol.*, 1951, 35, 363–366.

Edwards, A. S. Attention and involuntary movement. *J. appl. Psychol.*, 1949, 33, 503–509. (*a*)

Edwards, A. S. The effect of bodily rotation upon involuntary sway and finger tremor. *Amer. J. Psychol.*, 1949, 62, 590–591. (*b*)

Finan, J. L., & Malmo, R. B. New tapping board and steadiness box. *Amer. J. Psychol.*, 1944, 57, 260–263.

Green, R. F. Transfer of skill on a following tracking task as a function of task difficulty (target size). *J. Psychol.*, 1955, 39, 355–370.

Harris, S. J., & Smith, K. U. Dimensional analysis of motion: V. An analytic test of psychomotor ability. *J. appl. Psychol.*, 1953, 37, 136–141.

Harris, S. J., & Smith, K. U. Dimensional analysis of motion: VII. Extent and direction of manipulative movements as factors in defining motions. *J. appl. Psychol.*, 1954, 38, 126–130.

Helmick, J. S. Pursuit learning as affected by size of target and speed of rotation. *J. exp. Psychol.*, 1951, 41, 126–138.

Hyman, R. Stimulus information as a determinant of reaction time. *J. exp. Psychol.*, 1953, 45, 188–196.

Jenkins, W. L., & Connor, Minna B. Some design factors in making settings on a linear scale. *J. appl. Psychol.*, 1949, 33, 395–409.

Kientzle, Mary J. Properties of learning curves under varied distributions of practice. *J. exp. Psychol.*, 1946, 36, 187–211.

Kimble, G. A. Performance and reminiscence in motor learning as a function of the degree of distribution of practice. *J. exp. Psychol.*, 1949, 39, 500–510.

Klemmer, E. T. Time uncertainty in simple reaction time. *J. exp. Psychol.*, 1956, 51, 179–184.

Koerth, W. A pursuit apparatus: eye-hand coordination. *Psychol. Monogr.*, 1922, 31, No. 1 (Whole No. 140), 288–292.

Lincoln, R. S. Rate accuracy in handwheel cranking. *J. appl. Psychol.*, 1954, 38, 195–201.

McFarland, R. A. The psychological effects of oxygen deprivation (anoxemia) on human behavior. *Arch. Psychol.*, 1932, No. 145, 1–135.

Malmo, R. B., & Finan, J. L. A comparative study of eight tests in the decompression chamber. *Amer. J. Psychol.*, 1944, 57, 389–405.

Reed, J. D. Factors influencing rotary performance. *J. Psychol.*, 1949, 28, 65–92.

Riopelle, A. J., & Stritch, T. M. Placing precision and angle of regard. *J. exp. Psychol.*, 1952, 44, 407–409.

Spragg, S. D. S., & Devoe, D. B. The accuracy of control knob settings as a function of size of angle to be bisected, and type of end-point cue. *Percept. mot. Skills*, 1956, 6, 25–28.

Teichner, W. H. Recent studies of simple reaction time. *Psychol. Bull.*, 1954, 51, 128–149.

Teichner, W. H., & Kobrick, J. L.   Effects of prolonged exposure to low temperature on visual-motor performance. *J. exp. Psychol.*, 1955, 49, 122–126.

Teichner, W. H., & Wehrkamp, R. F.   Visual-motor performance as a function of short-duration ambient temperature. *J. exp. Psychol.*, 1954, 47, 447–450.

Weiss, B.   The role of proprioceptive feedback in positioning reactions. *J. exp. Psychol.*, 1954, 47, 215–224.

Weiss, B.   Movement error, pressure variation, and the range effect. *J. exp. Psychol.*, 1955, 50, 191–196.

Welford, A. T.   *Skill and age: an experimental approach.*   London: Oxford Univer. Press, 1951.

Woodworth, R. S.   *Experimental psychology.*   New York: Holt, 1938.

Ziegler, W. A.   *Minnesota Rate of Manipulation Test.*   Minneapolis: Educational Test Bureau, Inc., 1933.

ADDITIONAL READINGS

Bartlett, N. R., & Bartlett, Susan C.   Synchronization of a motor response with an anticipated sensory event. *Psychol. Rev.*, 1959, 66, 203–218.

Fleishman, E. A.   Dimensional analysis of psychomotor abilities. *J. exp. Psychol.*, 1954, 48, 437–454.

CHAPTER 15

Perceptual-Motor Learning and Fatigue

Almost any perceptual-motor performance exhibits measurable changes as it is practiced repetitively. Such changes may reveal increments in level of skill or they may indicate decrements in quality of the performance. The incremental process we might call *learning* and the decremental process we might term *fatigue*. Either sort of process is an inference which we draw from the performance curves we obtain as practice continues under prescribed conditions. We may also infer that both learning and fatigue are operating simultaneously if our data warrant such a conclusion.

In Chapter 14 we described many sorts of perceptual-motor behavior represented in laboratory tasks like hand steadiness, simple or disjunctive *RT*, linear or rotary positioning, tapping, placing pegs in a pegboard, card-sorting, inverted-alphabet printing, and tracking. We saw how the performance of various types of task might be affected by physical or motor dimensions of the task, by its stimulus aspects, by the conditions of testing, and by the subjects employed in the studies. In this chapter we go on to examine one very important condition affecting performance measures—the practice which the subject has had prior to the moment of the measurement of response. The common approach to such study is to measure performance as repeated trials are given. We thus determine the empirical function relating performance to practice. Such a performance curve—or a set of them—is the basis for our inferring incremental or decremental processes. In many cases just one type of process is considered to be the major determinant of performance change, and the empirical curve is called either a learning curve or a fatigue curve. In other instances the rate of improvement is considered to reflect a decremental process going on concurrently with an incremental one. The problem in such a case is to infer properly how much of a contribution each of the opposing forces, learning and fatigue, is contributing to the data. We shall see that the inference needs to be based on measurements obtained under several experimental conditions if it is to be more than a mere guess.

Besides learning and fatigue two other processes which may affect performance are *warm-up* and *end spurt*. Warm-up is the improvement that occurs early in a performance session as the subject settles down to the task at hand. As we conceptualize it, warm-up is not the same as learning although the initial effects of the two processes may be practically indistinguishable in a task about which the subject has something to learn. In a task which may be considered very well learned, like tapping, we would consider any improvement in rate over the first minute or two as attributable to warm-up. The muscular warm-up familiar to us from athletics would be a likely part of the warm-up effect observed in motor performance, but the phenomenon is thought to consist of other factors as well. We find that the warm-up effect is observable in mental activity like doing arithmetic problems. If we are looking for the effect of an experimental condition on general performance and not just on the warm-up phenomenon, we would do well to design studies with performance of sufficient length to meet our requirements.

End spurt refers to the improved performance that is noted sometimes when a subject knows he is nearing the end of an experimental session or a performance interval. Anticipating the termination of the session, or at least the occurrence of a rest period, he makes an especially strong effort at the task for a period of time. End spurt is most likely to affect the data, of course, when performance has slumped or has proceeded along a plateau due to fatigue or boredom. If it is considered undesirable, end spurt can be eliminated in some experimental designs by the simple expedient of not letting the subject know what the length of the session will be. If there are repeated trials of the same length, though, a subject is likely to learn to anticipate the end of a trial. End spurt may not really be an undesirable phenomenon in an experiment. It represents a lift in a motivational state that may have dropped a bit as the session wore on. Because it gives information about what a person *can* do under certain conditions, it may even be desirable in some studies to induce an end spurt by telling subjects, as they begin the final portion of performance, to do their best since the trial or session is drawing to a close.

All the tasks discussed in Chapter 14 might be used in studies of perceptual-motor learning or fatigue. We would find that the variables which we cited as affecting performance level might also affect the rate of performance change, whether incremental or decremental. This implies, of course, a vast potential program of empirical study. Such a program has partially been realized in scores of experiments conducted by psychologists. Rather than attempting to review their findings, we shall limit our discussion to a few tasks and variables here.

LEARNING

We begin our study of perceptual-motor learning by examining a special laboratory task—*maze learning* by human subjects. Several different forms of the maze-learning task are found in the repertory of the experimental psychologist. In surveying this research area we shall give special attention to the condition termed *knowledge of results* as it affects maze learning and the learning of other perceptual-motor skills.

Elements of Maze Learning

Most studies of maze learning have used animal subjects, particularly the albino rat. Our attention will focus, however, on the use of the maze in research on human learning.

TYPES OF TASK—SENSORY CUES AND MOTOR RESPONSES. If we first consider the kinds of motor responses required of human subjects in maze learning we find that there are just two major types. Either the subject engages in locomotion through a large maze—a task comparable to that of the rat experiments—or he is required to trace a smaller maze manually. This latter task lends itself more readily to the dimensions of most laboratories. We shall limit our subsequent discussion to mazes requiring manual performance.

The sensory cues given to subjects provide the principal source of variation for maze tasks. Such tasks may be classified by the amount of visual guidance a subject may employ as he traces the maze pattern. Some procedures allow no vision, forcing the subject to use only tactual-kinesthetic guidance by blindfolding him or otherwise preventing him from seeing the maze as he traces it with his finger or a stylus. In a finger maze the pathways are grooves or elevated lines which trace out the blind alleys and the path to the goal. Such a maze may be constructed, for example, of wire or string mounted on cardboard. In a stylus maze the paths are grooves cut into wood or

metal.   Without looking at the maze, the subject has to trace his way
through it by moving the tip of the stylus through the pathways.

Some experimental procedures permit a limited amount of vision
in maze learning.   In a punchboard maze the subject sees a series of
holes arranged in a matrix of rows and columns.   By inserting a pencil
into successive holes he tries to find his way through the maze without
error.   An error is signaled, for example, when the pencil punches
through the underlying paper.   The method thus gives a record of
errors.   Another way of giving limited vision is to have a subject
look at a large printed maze through a viewing tube which permits
him to see only a small portion of the maze at any time.   As the subject
progresses through the maze with the viewing tube, the experimenter
traces his progress on a record sheet for each trial.   One more procedure allowing a restricted use of vision is a stylus maze in which
the pathways are all visible to the subject but in which there are
hidden stops which prevent the passage of the stylus, thus creating
blind alleys in different parts of the pattern.

Complete use of vision is permitted in some types of maze.   Task
difficulty is imposed by using maze patterns of sufficient complexity to
impose considerable perceptual demand on subjects.   A printed maze
devised and described by Porteus (1950) has been used widely as a
psychological test.   The printed lines of the Porteus maze outline
various pathways and blind alleys in different patterns.   Careful visual
inspection is required as a person traces with a pencil the path leading
from the starting point to the goal.   A different perceptual-motor task
is required in a letter maze.   Letters of the alphabet are scattered in
a seemingly random pattern on a printed page and subjects have to
use a pencil to connect the letters in some specified sequence.

MAZE PATTERNS.   The spatial arrangements of research mazes tend
to fall into one of three classes, each variable in its extent and complexity.   These are illustrated in Figure 15.1.   One class of maze
pattern is *nonsystematic* with varied orientations of the true pathway
and the blind alleys.   The segments of pathways are of varied lengths
and the turns occur irregularly in such a maze.   *Multiple-unit* mazes
are more regular in their patterning, with similar elements being repeated in sequence.   This type includes multiple-*T*, multiple-*U*, and
multiple-*Y* arrangements.   *Alternate pathway* patterns form the
third class, with more than one route from starting point to goal being
available.   Such an arrangement is particularly useful for studying
any stereotypy of behavior on successive trials with the maze.

THE MEASUREMENT OF MAZE LEARNING.   With repeated trials maze
performance typically shows improvement which can be measured by

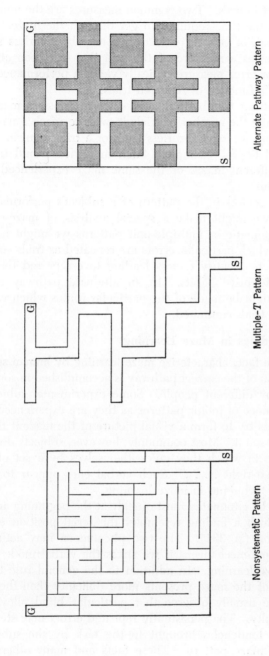

Fig. 15.1. Maze patterns of several different classes. The multiple-*T* pattern is one form of the multiple-unit type.

Nonsystematic Pattern

Multiple-*T* Pattern

Alternate Pathway Pattern

means of different indices. Two common measures are the number of errors made and the time required to get through the maze. If full vision is permitted, of course, performance may be errorless so that only time remains as a measure of the skill that has been attained. Either the time or error measure typically yields a performance curve that decreases as a function of repeated trials.

Instead of plotting trial-by-trial curves we may assess maze performance by noting the number of trials it takes to reach a particular criterion, like two successive errorless trials or a trial requiring under 20 sec to complete, for example. Such an index would then be compared for different mazes or the same maze experienced under different conditions.

If our interest centers in the pattern of a subject's performance on repeated trials, we might make a special analysis of maze-running data. In nonsystematic or multiple-unit patterns we might note the frequency with which particular errors are repeated as trials continue. This might help to identify factors leading to errors and their persistence as nonadaptive habits. In an alternate pathway maze a detailed count might be made of the particular routes which were repeatedly used as trials continued.

Empirical Findings in Maze Learning

Several general facts characterize maze learning by human subjects. The memorization of the correct pathway is accomplished in somewhat different ways by different people. Some experimental subjects attend to the sequence of motor patterns as they are experienced kinesthetically. Others try to form a visual picture of the maze if they are not permitted to see it. Most commonly, however, subjects develop a verbal technique in which they guide themselves by a set of directions like "left-left-right . . . ." Such verbal cues appear to be the most facilitative technique in maze learning.

Errors tend to be eliminated most quickly at the beginning and ends of the maze. Such a finding resembles the serial position effect in rote memorization (p. 384). The two phenomena may actually be based on the same mechanisms if we stress the verbal mode of self-guidance in maze learning. In addition to the general rule that the middle portion of the maze presents more difficulty than the beginning or end, we usually observe that particular blind alleys cause particular difficulty. The persistently repeated errors may stem from strong response tendencies brought to the task by the subjects or induced by the maze pattern. These facts and many others based on research in human maze learning are presented in an excellent review by Woodworth and Schlosberg (1954, pp. 646–654).

RESPONSE TENDENCIES IN THE STYLUS MAZE. Let us consider the general observation that strong response tendencies cause subjects to make some errors repeatedly. We naturally want to know the reason for this in each study where we observe it. Often, however, the complexity of maze patterns employed would permit numerous interpretations as to why a particular error was persistent while others were eliminated more readily. What is needed is a more analytic approach to maze behavior, one that will delineate specific influences on response tendencies. Such an approach is illustrated in a study by Thompson (1952) who arranged a simple test of how previous turns in a stylus maze might influence the subject's response at a subsequent choice point. Three different maze patterns were constructed in which a single choice point was preceded by either one, two, or three right-angle turns in a clockwise direction. The turns are called clockwise in direction instead of right or left since each maze was placed on the table in four different orientations. It was postulated that the more frequently the clockwise turn was experienced on the single trial given, the greater the proportion of subjects who would turn in the counterclockwise direction when the choice point was reached. This hypothesis was found to be supported by the greater number of subjects who turned counterclockwise after two or three clockwise turns as compared with those who had experienced only one clockwise turn. The results were interpreted as reflecting an increasing reactive inhibition as clockwise turns were repeated. This factor would lead to an avoidance of clockwise turning when the choice point was encountered. It may be that directional orientation was also a factor, with subjects realizing that repeated turns in the same direction were leading them nowhere, so to speak. Many analytic studies of this sort, especially in an actual learning situation with repeated trials, are needed to reveal completely the factors which enter into human maze performance.

RESPONSE TENDENCIES IN THE LETTER MAZE. The increasing tendency to make the identical choice among alternate pathways in a letter maze has been studied by Andreas and Miller (1960). Over successive trials the acquisition of response tendencies reflects itself in improved performance scores, such as number of letters connected in a standard trial period. The growth of habit as a function of repeated trials can be seen in a more molecular analysis of the behavior as well. These investigators chose several points in the maze of letters where each subject had to go in tracing out a sentence. Touching these particular letters was a necessity since they appeared only once on the page which comprised a trial. From these unique points a subject might move to any one of several locations where the next required letter was found. Assuming a particular one of these responses to have been made, what is the probability that it will be repeated on the next trial? What is the probability that a response will be repeated after it has occurred two times before? Three times? This probability of occurrence as a function of the number of previous experiences was sought empirically. Relative frequency of repetition among the opportunities for such repetition was the definition adopted for the probability value.

The data of this investigation yielded negatively accelerated curves for the increase of probability of repetition as a function of number of previous occurrences. As an example, consider the p values of the following table:

	Number of Previous Occurrences of Any Specific Response								
	1	2	3	4	5	6	7	8	9
p for repetition of the specific response:	.57	.80	.85	.91	.95	.92	1.00	1.00	1.00

These data show that the proportion of subjects repeating a particular T-H response in spelling the required sentence while tracing the maze was .57 when the response had occurred just once before. After two previous occurrences, the p for repetition rose to .80 on the next trial. Smaller increases in the probability of repetition occurred as trials continued. After six repetitions there is seen to be a slight drop in the tabled value. This is probably attributable to the unreliability of proportions based on the relatively few cases represented in the right half of the table. After seven or more previous occurrences we see that the probability of repetition was 1.00; all subjects who had made a particular T-H response at least seven times in tracing the maze continued to make that same response on all subsequent trials.

Knowledge of Results in Perceptual-Motor Performance

We noted earlier that numerous independent variables affect the scores made on perceptual-motor tasks and that these same variables also determine the increments of skill or habit that are acquired as practice continues. Since it is impossible to catalog all these variables we shall concentrate now on one factor that is closely related to the learning process—*knowledge of results.* It is found widely that giving a subject knowledge of the results he is achieving is beneficial to his mastery of the task being practiced.

DUAL FUNCTION—INFORM AND MOTIVATE. The knowledge that a person has about his performance as he engages in a task may serve him in two ways. It may be such that it tells him what he may be doing wrong, and thus how he may improve. Such information may take the form of knowing that a constant error is being made repeatedly, perhaps some kind of overshooting. Being informed in this specific way, a subject may correct his error during continuing practice. Some studies have shown that more specific information about error leads to better improvement than does general information.

Besides informing him, knowledge of performance may motivate a person who is practicing a complex task. Knowing how he is doing from trial to trial, he may adjust his level of aspiration or enter into competition with himself. Knowledge of results is both a motivation insofar as it goads a person to greater effort and an incentive to be attained insofar as a better score or a lesser error is perceived as a goal. With knowledge of good performance serving as a goal, we find that such information may also be considered a reward or reinforcement for correct responses.

SOURCES—INTRINSIC OR EXTRINSIC. A person will almost always have some idea of the results he is getting as he performs a task. Thus, knowledge of results tends to be partly intrinsic. In research and in practical situations we can almost always add to the amount of knowledge provided by the task. We may provide some special cue which is given to the subject whenever he makes a correct response. This would be a form of *psychological feedback* that would emphasize the informational aspect of knowledge of results. If we put a visible scoring record on the equipment being operated, the operator would receive psychological feedback that was primarily of the incentive-motive type. Such techniques are manipulations of the intrinsic knowledge of results which a task may provide.

Extrinsic knowledge of results occurs when a person is informed of his performance after a trial or work period is completed. This often represents a delayed knowledge of performance which is regarded as less efficient in guiding improvement than is immediate knowledge. On the credit side, extrinsic knowledge may add precision to what a subject learns from the intrinsic sources which the task happens to provide. In research, both intrinsic and extrinsic sources of knowledge of results may be experimentally manipulated to a considerable extent.

KNOWLEDGE OF RESULTS IN MAZE LEARNING. An attempt was made to influence stylus maze learning in a study by Crafts and Gilbert (1935), who told each subject what the average student had accomplished and then gave him reports, trial by trial, on his own accumulated errors and elapsed time. The hypothesis was that a stated goal and the trial-by-trial knowledge of results would both serve to motivate better performance. It was found, however, that this experimental group did no better than a control group given no information.

A number of suggestions are given by the experimenters as possible explanations for the failure of knowledge of results to show any effect. One possibility offered was that the motivation and knowledge of results that are inherent in the maze performance itself were sufficient to sustain the efforts of the subjects. Thus the control subjects were at no loss when compared with the experimental group to whom the information offered may have been superfluous. A quite different suggestion is that the knowledge of results may have introduced disturbing emotion in the experimental subjects. We may note also that the knowledge of results given in this experiment carries little information about the specific performance of the task, errors being announced only at the end of a trial and not as they occurred. Even the motivating data provided for the experimental subjects were averages for complete task mastery instead of trial-by-trial averages which would have offered more incentive as learning progressed. Despite its negative findings, this study of maze learning calls to our attention a number of aspects of knowledge of results which may play important roles in motivating and guiding the learning process.

KNOWLEDGE OF RESULTS IN OTHER PERCEPTUAL-MOTOR TASKS. Numerous tasks besides maze performance have been used in research exploring the motivational and informational functioning of knowledge of results. A few experiments may be briefly mentioned to illustrate the diversity of experimental manipulations and the nature of some of the findings. Some of the reports cited, together with numerous others, have been employed by Ammons (1956) in an attempt to formulate some general principles summarizing the role of knowledge of performance in mastering various tasks.

In a repetitive block-turning task performed by several groups of subjects, Helmstadter and Ellis (1952) found that simply giving knowledge of results after each trial was as effective in sustaining steady improvement as were more complicated motivational techniques. The latter involved the establishment of goals for the successive trials undertaken by the subjects. A control group given no statement about achievement might reveal how much motivational and informational value is inherent in the mere performance of such a simple repetitive task.

Rotary pursuit performance was required of different groups of subjects by Reynolds and Adams (1953). They gave experimental subjects a type of knowledge of results in the form of a loud click each time that a continuous period of on-target performance occurred. The required on-target period varied from 0.1 to 2.0 sec in different groups. A control group received no click during performance. It was found that the repeated clicks led to better performance in the experimental groups when compared to the control subjects. The data indicated that an optimal effect of the click was obtained when it was presented after each 0.5 sec of continuous time on target. This optimal on-target value may depend on task difficulty.

The informative function of knowledge of results tends to be prominent whenever a positioning task is required to be performed with little or no visual guidance. Macpherson, Dees, and Grindley (1948–49) found that mastery of a lever positioning task was better accomplished when the intertrial interval was brief. This seemed to permit the better utilization of the kinesthetic cues in conjunction with the knowledge of results provided after each setting.

With intertrial interval kept constant at 30 sec Greenspoon and Foreman (1956) studied the manual positioning task represented in attempting to draw 3-in. lines. They found that a greater degree of improvement accompanied a lesser delay in giving knowledge of results to the subject after each attempt. The relationship between the knowledge imparted by the experimenter and the kinesthetic cues obtained by the subject would seem to be crucial here also, even though the temporal dimension was different from that which was manipulated by Macpherson, Dees, and Grindley (1948–49).

Knowledge of results was varied quite differently by Bilodeau and Bilodeau (1958) in a study of the acquisition of a lever-positioning skill. One group of subjects was informed after every trial as to the magnitude and direction of their error. Other groups were given such information only after every third, fourth, or tenth trial. These different groups were given differing numbers of trials, but in each case a total of ten knowledge of results experiences were administered according to the fixed ratio cited. It was found that the improvement in performance was similar from group to group as a function of the number of administrations of knowledge of results rather than as a function of the absolute number of trials. This suggests that knowledge of results is a key contributor to the learning process for such tasks.

FATIGUE

For many perceptual-motor tasks which we might study in the psychology laboratory, we might find that any fatigue decrement in performance as practice continued was completely hidden by increments due to the acquisition of skill as trials continued. It is possible, through proper experimental design, to arrive at inferences concerning both decremental and incremental processes that are going on simultaneously. Later in this chapter we shall examine this type of experiment. First, we turn our attention to research where the assigned tasks were chosen for their minimal reflection of learning so that decremental processes could be studied more directly.

Fatigue Decrement in a Motor Task—Manual Cranking

A study of repetitive crank-turning conducted by Bilodeau (1952) will illustrate for us the direct approach to fatigue decrement in motor performance with continued practice. In his research report the author points out that the task was selected as one which would minimize the learning factor, or incremental process. This permitted the direct investigation of the motor performance as it was affected by the force requirements imposed on the subjects. Two different crank loadings were used, one demanding about three times the horsepower output of the other. In both cases the output increased with faster crank rotation and, conversely, lessened as cranking became slower.

A partial review of the findings of this experiment reveals different decremental curves for two groups which performed continuously for 5 min, each turning the crank against one of the two loads. During the first minute of work the crank-turning rate decreased more rapidly for the group performing with the heavier load. During this first minute this group decreased from about 80 to about 55 revolutions completed in a 20-sec period, whereas the group performing against the lighter load dropped from about 80 to about 65 revolutions per 20 sec in the same period. In the subsequent 4 min of work, both groups declined at about the same rate, somewhat more gradually than in the early decline of output. The group turning against the heavy load tended to level off at about 50 revolutions per 20 sec, whereas the group given the easier task showed a nearly asymptotic performance at about 60 revolutions per 20 sec. When a 40-sec rest interval was given at the end of 5 min of continuous work, both groups showed a partial recovery of their earlier output rate. In about 1 min of the resumed continuous performance, work output had again dropped to the asymptotic values we have cited.

Decrement in Perceptual Tasks—Vigilance and Discrimination

Decrements over long periods of performance may occur for tasks which involve very little motor effort but which demand sustained perceptual effort. In common parlance we might speak of fatigue or boredom in accounting for a person's decreasing effectiveness in a prolonged task demanding his attention. No technical term for such a process seems to have been adopted, so we may follow the lead of investigators who refer to decrements in vigilance, or vigilant behavior, or decrements in discrimination.

DECREMENT IN VIGILANCE. An experiment performed by Adams (1956) will illustrate how the detection of irregularly intermittent stimuli provides a task suitable for the study of decrement in vigilant behavior over a prolonged period. A dimly illuminated spot appearing for 1 or 2 sec on a screen was the stimulus whose detection the experimental subjects had to signal by pressing a toggle switch. Sitting alone in a small experimental room, each subject watched the screen for a continuous period of 110 min. Each 10-min period was considered to be a trial, with the signal presented ten times at intervals ranging from 0.25 to 2.00 min. After this long session of continuous observation, each subject was permitted to relax for 10 min, and then was given a final 10-min trial. The measure of vigilance was the number of stimuli detected during each 10-min "trial" with ten detections representing perfect performance. Four different groups of subjects were run in a factorial design involving two levels of stimulus luminance, both very low, and two stimulus durations, either 1 or 2 sec.

Every experimental group showed a decrement in vigilance over the 110 min of continuous observation. The number of detections was greater for the two groups given the 2-sec duration of stimulus. After the 10-min rest period, recovery from decrement was observed in the detection scores of the final trial.

DECREMENT IN DISCRIMINATION. In the usual test of prolonged vigilance, subjects are required to detect stimuli which are presented at irregular intervals. The usual decline in successful detections might be interpreted as a decline in discrimination between the stimulus and the no-stimulus conditions. Presenting this sort of rationale for his investigation, Bakan (1955) repeatedly determined brightness discrimination thresholds over two 1.5-hr sessions, a day apart. The threshold was determined by a modified method of limits. (This psychophysical method is discussed in Chapter 5, p. 99.) Incorporated in a series of standard light flashes, at the rate of one per second, were threshold trials in which every fifth flash was a member of an ascending series of brighter-than-standard flashes. When the subject signaled that he had detected a flash brighter than usual, the trial ended with this determination of the discrimination threshold. The series of standard intensity flashes continued at the regular rate.

It was found on both days that discrimination became worse, the differential brightness threshold generally increasing from one 15-min period to the next, although a plateau was obtained in the performance curve on each day. When the data were fractionated to separate the better from the poorer subjects in terms of general level of discrimination ability exhibited, it was found that the better subjects had been able to arrest the decline in their performance about halfway through the daily sessions. Their thresholds had increased over the first 45 min and had then been reduced again to a level that had characterized the discriminations of the second 15-min period. The poorer subjects showed a decline in the discrimination performance that continued through the entire daily sessions.

PERFORMANCE REVEALING LEARNING AND FATIGUE

We have noted a common tendency for perceptual-motor performance to improve with practice, and we have seen also that decremental processes may occur in both the perceptual and the motor realms. We therefore realize that some scores may at the same time reflect both learning and retardation of measured improvement due to negative factors like fatigue or lessened discrimination. We shall see how the positive and negative factors are detected in experimental data. Rotary pursuit tracking performance will first be examined since this task has been a favorite one for such studies. Later, we shall examine illustrative experiments which employed other perceptual-motor performances.

Incremental and Decremental Processes in Rotary Pursuit Performance

Numerous investigations have presented evidence that a decremental process is operative even when subjects are acquiring skill on a task and thus making increasingly good scores as practice continues. This evidence is primarily reflected in a comparison of the performance curves of different groups, some given *massed practice* and some given *distributed practice*. By massed practice we mean performance of the task that is continuous (or nearly so) for an extended period. By distributed or spaced practice we mean performance during discrete trials separated by rest periods of relatively substantial duration.

An experiment by Kimble and Shatel (1952) indicates how spaced practice and massed practice on the pursuit rotor were administered to two different groups of subjects to study incremental and decremental processes. The spaced practice group received 50-sec trials separated by 70-sec rest pauses. The massed practice group was given 50-sec trials with just 10 sec between trials. Both groups received 15 trials per day for ten days.

Each of these groups showed improvement over the course of the 150 trials. The performance curve for the massed practice group rose less steeply, however. This apparent retardation in the acquisition of proficiency is the basic fact from which we infer that a decremental process is occurring. Such a process is variously termed *reactive inhibition* or *work decrement* in different theoretical formulations. Such a decremental factor, built up during a work period or trial, is considered to dissipate during an extended rest interval. This dissipation of the work decrement is the reason that performance data obtained on well-distributed trials yield a steeper curve for the acquisition of proficiency. The less steep curves obtained under massed practice are attributed to the development of reactive inhibition which cannot dissipate completely during continuous performance or during very brief intertrial intervals. As such a decremental factor accumulates, it opposes the demonstrated gain in skill more and more. This opposition is responsible for the less steep performance curves obtained under massed practice.

Even greater extremes of massing and distribution of practice are represented in a pursuit rotor experiment conducted by Ammons and Willig (1956). The massed practice was represented in continuous 10-min periods of practice. These periods of continuous practice were separated by 20-min rest intervals. Distributed practice was represented in 1-min trials separated by 2-min rest pauses. In this study, the accumulation of temporary work decrement was so great during the continuous 10-min performance periods that the trend in scores during those minutes was actually downward. However, successive periods of performance, separated by the 20-min rest periods, showed an upward trend in scores. This indicates that an incremental process of skill acquisition was taking place even though it was masked by the work decrement within any period of continuous practice.

Other Studies Involving Incremental and Decremental Factors

Early in this chapter we noted that all the perceptual-motor tasks mentioned in Chapter 14 might require investigation of incremental and decremental processes during continued practice. We next consider a few such studies that will illustrate the variety of research possibilities in this area.

MASSING AND DISTRIBUTION OF TRIALS IN INVERTED-ALPHABET PRINTING. In reviewing pursuit rotor experiments we saw that different work and rest intervals and different work-rest ratios of intervals may be taken as representing distributed or massed practice. The degree of massing or distribution of practice, then, is a relative matter. It should be possible to show that the forms taken by perceptual-motor performance curves depend on the degree to which rest intervals are provided for the dissipation of work decrement.

Archer (1954) used inverted-alphabet printing as a task for which different groups of subjects were given different degrees of spacing of trials. All groups were given 20 trials of 30-sec duration. In one group a 30-sec rest interval was given after each trial, providing the greatest degree of distributed practice in this study. Another group received an intermediate degree of spacing of trials with 15-sec rest after each trial. A third group was given massed practice in which the "trials" were strung together with no rest interval at all, thus demanding 10 min of continuous performance from these subjects.

That these three degrees of distribution of practice led to different patterns of performance is clearly shown in the empirical curves of Figure 15.2. These curves represent just a portion of the findings presented by Archer since we are centering our attention on how spacing of practice affects the performance of perceptual-motor tasks as trials continue. The introduction of different rest intervals, 15 sec and 30 sec, is clearly facilitating with respect to scores subjects can make in inverted-alphabet printing. Further, the amount of facilitation is related to the amount of rest given, although this relationship is not necessarily a linear one.

REST PAUSE BEHAVIOR AS A FUNCTION OF TASK EFFORT. In most of the perceptual-motor studies we have mentioned, the approach to work decrement has been an indirect one. The fact that a decremental factor had been piling up during performance was inferred from the superior scores made when rest intervals were provided for the assumed dissipation of the negative factor. A somewhat more direct approach to work decrement is to vary the work demand of the task itself. You will recall that this was the method employed by Bilodeau

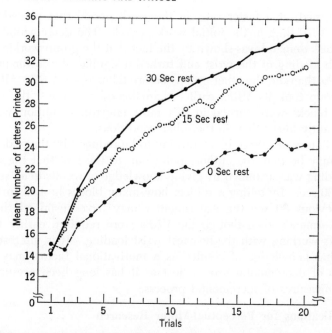

Fig. 15.2. Performance curves for inverted-alphabet printing under three different degrees of distribution of practice. (After Archer, 1954.)

(p. 432) in the cranking study. A manipulation of task effort in the block-turning task of the Minnesota Rate of Manipulation Test was accomplished by Boldt and Ellis (1954). They varied the amount of physical demand on the subjects by applying weighted cuffs to their wrists. As a subject sat before the task board he might be required to support a 3-lb lead weight as he stretched out his hands to turn the blocks over. Besides this highest degree of work demand, there were lesser weights of 0.5 and 1.0 lb employed as well as a condition in which the cloth wrist cuffs were not weighted at all.

Instead of specifying the work interval as is usually done in studies of decremental processes, these experimenters instructed subjects to continue working until they felt like taking a voluntary rest pause (*VRP*) of 1-min duration. The rate of responding and the number of responses made in the period prior to the first and second *VRP* provided the data which would reflect the work decrement under the different conditions of effort.

The results of this experiment indicated that both incremental and decremental behavior processes were occurring simultaneously. The increment in proficiency was revealed by the fact that more blocks were turned, at a faster rate, in the work period that preceded the second *VRP* than in the initial work period. The decremental effect of the task demand was shown by the fact that the group working with the 3-lb loading of the wrist cuff turned a significantly lower number of blocks than did the other groups before taking each *VRP*. Although this group took its *VRPs* earlier than the other groups, the rate at which blocks were turned in this most effortful condition was not significantly lower than in the other conditions.

The failure of rate of block turning to be reduced by the added task effort may be due, the authors point out, to the fact that the rate of responding was sustained by giving knowledge of results to all subjects every 30 sec. By telling a subject how many blocks he had turned in the previous 30 sec the experimenter may have sustained the rate of performance even though the *VRPs* were required earlier by the subjects working with the heaviest wrist loading. It is interesting to note that knowledge of results, as a motivational factor, may affect indices of decremental process just as it has long been presumed to affect measures of incremental process.

Implications for Perceptual-Motor Research

The close relationship between incremental and decremental processes as a perceptual-motor task is practiced has important implications for research in this area of behavior. Facts already revealed in past studies serve to warn us that neither type of process, incremental or decremental, can be investigated without reckoning with the other. On the other hand, we should be encouraged that proper experimental designs can help us to determine the contribution of both types of factor to performance data. Studies of processes like learning and fatigue offer considerable guidance for applied research to determine the proper spacing of work and rest periods for the almost infinite variety of tasks performed in business and industry.

Besides relating to further studies of continuing performance, our knowledge of incremental and decremental behavior processes must guide us in designing other experiments. Even if we are not concerned with plotting the course of such processes, we must take them into account as we investigate how other variables affect performance scores. Wherever we choose to run the same subjects sequentially under two or more different conditions, we must be sure that processes like learning and fatigue are considered. Techniques like extensive preliminary training, wide spacing of practice sessions, or counterbalancing may need to be employed to try to rule out any biasing of results by such behavior processes.

SUMMARY

As a task is performed repeatedly over a series of trials, a trend toward higher or lower scores is often evident. From such performance data we may draw inferences about processes like learning or fatigue. The problem of arriving at correct inferences is complicated by the fact that incremental and decremental effects are often intermixed, with numerous variables contributing to their development.

One task in which human subjects demonstrate learning is in the goal-seeking behavior demanded by maze learning. Mazes of different sorts have been used in research, with knowledge of results as one experimental variable. Subjects tend to develop certain work methods and to exhibit particular response tendencies as they learn a maze.

Knowledge of results has been found to contribute importantly to the development of many perceptual-motor skills. It serves both to inform the subject of the effect of his actions and to motivate him to continue trying to improve. This factor was manipulated in several studies we reviewed briefly, with subjects being required to perform tasks like a stylus maze, block-turning, rotary pursuit tracking, or linear positioning.

Decrements in performance have been observed when subjects were assigned either a motor task like repetitive cranking or perceptual tasks like vigilance and discrimination. Other studies that we reviewed gave evidence of both incremental and decremental processes. The massing or distribution of practice trials provided one approach to the description of these processes. Tasks studied in this way included rotary pursuit tracking, and inverted-alphabet printing. A different approach to decremental trends was to study voluntary rest pauses as subjects engaged in block-turning. Such experiments are not only important in themselves but they bear implications for the designing and conducting of perceptual-motor research in which other variables may command primary attention.

REFERENCES

Adams, J. A. Vigilance in the detection of low-intensity visual stimuli. *J. exp. Psychol.*, 1956, 52, 204–208.

Ammons, R. B. Effects of knowledge of performance: a survey and tentative theoretical formulation. *J. gen. Psychol.*, 1956, 54, 279–299.

Ammons, R. B., & Willig, L. Acquisition of motor skill: IV. Effects of repeated periods of massed practice. *J. exp. Psychol.*, 1956, 51, 118–126.

Andreas, B. G., & Miller, L. Probability of response repetition in serial motor performance as a function of number of previous occurrences. 1960, (Unpublished manuscript).

Archer, E. J. Postrest performance in motor learning as a function of prerest degree of distribution of practice. *J. exp. Psychol.*, 1954, 47, 47–51.

Bakan, P. Discrimination decrement as a function of time in a prolonged vigil. *J. exp. Psychol.*, 1955, 50, 387–390.

Bilodeau, E. A. Decrements and recovery from decrements in a simple work task with variation in force requirements at different stages in practice. *J. exp. Psychol.*, 1952, 44, 108–113.

Bilodeau, E. A., & Bilodeau, Ina McD. Variable frequency of knowledge of results and the learning of a simple skill. *J. exp. Psychol.*, 1958, 55, 379–383.

Boldt, R. F., & Ellis, D. S. Voluntary rest pause behavior in a block-turning task as a function of wrist-cuff weight. *J. exp. Psychol.*, 1954, 47, 84–88.

Crafts, L. W., & Gilbert, R. W. The effect of knowledge of results on maze learning and retention. *J. educ. Psychol.*, 1935, 26, 177–187.

Greenspoon, J., & Foreman, Sally. Effect of delay of knowledge of results on learning a motor task. *J. exp. Psychol.*, 1956, 51, 226–228.

Helmstadter, G. C., & Ellis, D. S. Rate of manipulative learning as a function of goal-setting techniques. *J. exp. Psychol.*, 1952, 43, 125–129.

Kimble, G. A., & Shatel, R. B. The relationship between two kinds of inhibition and the amount of practice. *J. exp. Psychol.*, 1952, 44, 355–359.

Macpherson, S. J., Dees, Valerie, & Grindley, G. C. The effect of knowledge of results on learning and performance: II. Some characteristics of very simple skills. *Quart. J. exp. Psychol.*, 1948–49, 1, 68–78.

Porteus, S. D. *The Porteus maze test and intelligence.* Palo Alto: California Pacific Books, 1950.

Reynolds, B., & Adams, J. A. Motor performance as a function of click reinforcement. *J. exp. Psychol.*, 1953, 45, 315–320.

Thompson, M. E. Reactive inhibition as a factor in maze learning: III. Effects in the human stylus maze. *J. exp. Psychol.*, 1952, 43, 130–133.

Woodworth, R. S., & Schlosberg, H. *Experimental psychology.* (Rev. ed.) New York: Holt, 1954.

ADDITIONAL READINGS

Bilodeau, E. A. Speed of acquiring a simple motor response as a function of the systematic transformation of knowledge of results. *Amer. J. Psychol.*, 1953, 66, 409–420.

Hamilton, C. E., & Mola, W. R. Warm-up effect in human maze learning. *J. exp. Psychol.*, 1953, 45, 437–441.

CHAPTER 16

Retention

The learning process, which we have considered in dealing with both verbal and perceptual-motor performance, is a strong contributor to behavior because what is learned is often retained for a long time. Yet retention, or memory, is not perfect. It is better regarded as a process than as a constant state, since verbal material or skills are retained less and less completely as time goes on, assuming no practice or rehearsal. This lessening effectiveness of retention is commonly called forgetting. The functional relationships which this process has with elapsed time may thus be described as either curves of retention or curves of forgetting.

The retentive process is operative as learning itself takes place. Improvement in performance occurs from trial to trial as new increments of response tendency are added to what has been retained from previous trials. If there were no retention, the cumulative incremental effect of repeated trials could not occur. We generally combine the retentive and incremental processes under the topic of learning whenever trials are repeated at regular intervals, sometimes with spacing up to 24 hr, although generally with much closer spacing. In contrast a retention experiment typically involves one or more fairly long intervals of no practice which follows an effort at rote memorization or acquisition of some perceptual-motor skill.

Psychological research has provided considerable evidence that the mere passage of time does not account in itself for forgetting. It appears, rather, that the activity in which a person engages during the retention interval is a factor which strongly contributes to the gradual reduction in the amount retained. The process by which ongoing activity interferes with retention is called *retroactive inhibition,* the term suggesting that the effect is retroactive with respect to the original learning of the material being retained. With retroactive inhibition being assumed to occur when certain activity intervenes between original learning and some test of retention, we shall see that experiments are often directed at determining what factors are responsible for the potency of the interfering effect.

When a group of experimental subjects is tested after a short lapse of time following practice, it is sometimes found that their performance is actually better than at the end of practice. This improvement over a period of no practice is given the technical name, *reminiscence*. We mention this gain, in contrast to the loss which retentive decline would lead us to expect, since reminiscence is a phenomenon that may be encountered as empirical data on retention are sought.

AIMS AND METHODS OF RESEARCH ON RETENTION

Our fundamental assumption of behavioral lawfulness is brought to bear on retention when we seek to measure and describe this process in carefully controlled experiments. Techniques for measuring and describing retention will occupy our attention in a major part of this chapter as will the design of experiments for its investigation. Later we shall review some illustrative studies of the retention of verbal material and of perceptual-motor proficiency. Before we take up either methods or findings, however, we shall first try to get a clearer understanding of the aims of such investigations.

Some Relationships Sought in Retention Studies

Attempts to find functional relationships and attempts to test certain hypotheses both characterize research on the retention process. The early systematic studies of Ebbinghaus generated curves of forgetting as a function of time elapsed since original learning. Such forgetting curves or retention curves, as they may equally well be termed, are still sought in retention experiments which may involve a variety of independent variables as parameters of the functions. Besides looking at the retention of any particular type of learned activity, experimenters often try to contrast different types of activity with respect to retention. We shall see, for example, that there is interest in the question of whether verbal or perceptual-motor habits are better retained. Another type of study is aimed at measuring how much retroactive inhibition is evidenced as resulting from the activity of an experimental group during a retention interval when their scores are compared with those of a control group.

RETENTION OF VERBAL AND PERCEPTUAL-MOTOR SKILL. Memorizing verbal material and learning a manual skill are both such common behavioral phenomena that the question as to which acquisition is followed by better retention is a natural one. There is both anecdotal and experimental evidence that both verbal and perceptual-motor habits are quite resistant to forgetting. As to which shows superior retention there is some controversy. Worse yet, there is serious question about trying to put the issue to experimental test. Problems of equating verbal with motor tasks as to level of complexity, degree of organization, and familiarity to subjects are among the obstacles to incisive research. Despite difficulties, an attempt at direct comparison has strong appeal.

Van Dusen and Schlosberg (1948) used a panel containing 16 switches, arranged in two concentric circles, to provide a motor task for their subjects. A subject had to learn which of the outer switches had to be operated with each of the switches in the inner circle. Only one outer switch could be tried each time that an inner switch was turned on. A trial consisted of one circuit around the inner circle of switches with attempts to match an outer switch with each one. Subjects took an average of 30.67 trials to reach the prescribed criterion of three successive errorless trials.

By having each switch on the panel labeled with a nonsense syllable, these experimenters had their subjects learning a verbal paired associate task at the same time they were learning the perceptual-motor task of parallel format. This congruence of task requirement, plus the fact that any subject received the same number of trials at each task, comprised the way in which verbal and motor training were made equivalent in this study. Subjects had been instructed that they would be tested separately at the completion of learning for their knowledge of the pairs of switches and the pairs of nonsense syllables. With half of the subjects taking these tests in each order, verbal-motor or motor-verbal, it was found that the average subject got 4.61 of the syllables correct and 6.41 of the switches correct. This difference, indicating better learning of the pairs of switches, was statistically significant.

Retention of verbal and motor performance was studied by dividing the group into three subgroups, tested separately on the syllables and switches after 1, 7, or 28 days. Scores made after these retention intervals were compared to those made immediately after learning. These scores indicated the amount retained for either type of habit to be a negatively accelerated decreasing function of elapsed time. The exception to these two trends was a gain in score when the retention of the syllables was tested in the 1-day retention subgroup. Although not statistically significant, this gain was suggestive of reminiscence. The retention curves for the two types of performance are shown in

Figure 16.1. Despite the apparent superiority of retention for the pairs of switches, the scores represented in this upper curve are not statistically significantly superior to the scores for the syllables, except at the preretention test for which scores are indicated on the ordinate. These results would seem to call for the conclusion that verbal and motor habits are retained about equally well. However, the scores made on each performance immediately after learning suggested that the syllable pairs had not been learned as well. The comparison of verbal and motor retention would seem to require further research, perhaps based on the promising approach taken by Van Dusen and Schlosberg (1948).

CURVES OF RETENTION AND FORGETTING. The curves of Figure 16.1 which portrayed the outcome of the study we reviewed also serve to illustrate the functional relationship of performance to elapsed time that many studies seek. It is typically found, as in the experiment we discussed, that amount retained is a negatively accelerated decreasing function of the time between original learning and testing. We may note also that a test given immediately after learning is logically on the time continuum with later retention tests. Normally, every point on a retention curve will be contributed by a different group of subjects, since repeatedly giving tests to the same persons

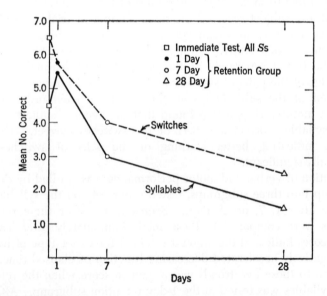

Fig. 16.1. Verbal and motor retention curves as represented by performance on paired syllables and paired switches. (After Van Dusen and Schlosberg, 1948.)

would constitute a renewal of learning to some extent. In the Van Dusen and Schlosberg (1948) study, the immediate test was considered to be a preretention measurement rather than an initial point on the retention curve itself. Figure 16.1 also shows us that reminiscence may be revealed by the same essential operations as are used in studying retention. It is demonstrated whenever a delayed test of recall yields performance that is significantly superior to immediate recall. We noted that the rise in the retention curve for syllables at the 1-day interval was not a significant one when analyzed statistically; therefore Figure 16.1 should not be misinterpreted as demonstrating reminiscence for the verbal material at the 1-day interval. The reminiscence phenomenon is generally considered to appear very much sooner after the cessation of the original practice.

RETROACTIVE INHIBITION. Certain abbreviations are often used in describing experiments on retroactive inhibition, with RI designating the process being studied. Three other abbreviations, OL, IL, RL, designate the three successive phases of performance required of the experimental subjects: original learning, interpolated learning of different material, and relearning the original task. Most studies involve a control condition in which IL is replaced by simply a lapse of time or some activity quite unrelated to OL, with RI in such an instance presumed to be negligible. Comparisons of RL data between the control group and the experimental group provide an indication of the potency of the interfering RI effect of IL on the retention of OL. We shall review the findings of illustrative RI studies later in this chapter.

The Measurement of Retention

Just as many different performance measures may be used in studying learning, the retention process may also be examined with behavior measurements of various sorts. These different methods of measurement may well yield slightly different functional relationships. In a sense, different operations performed by the experimenter, with somewhat different performances required of subjects, are operational definitions of different "retentions." From what we learn about any specific empirical retention function, we may ascribe characteristics to a more abstract concept of retention, but the latter has validity only insofar as it remains linked to our observations of behavior.

RECALL. When a subject has previously learned a serial list of verbal items, we may require him to demonstrate his retention of the material by recalling as much of it as possible. We may score his responses, given orally or written, with respect to serial order or we may ignore this and merely count the correct items. We may or may not include a penalty for erroneous intrusions in the list he gives. In contrast to free recall, the anticipation method, using serially presented cards or a memory drum, requires the subject to give the next item in the list as each one is presented. There are, then, a variety of possibilities for administering and scoring a recall test, but the essential aspect of this method is that the subject is given a specific opportunity to recall whatever he can of the previously learned material.

RECOGNITION. In a recognition test a subject is given a different type of opportunity to demonstrate what he has retained. The items that he has previously learned are all presented to him again, but they are interspersed among numerous other items of a similar nature. In a recognition test, then, the subject must recognize previously seen material, discriminating it from material which has not been studied. This is a somewhat easier task than free recall. The recognition score depends in part, of course, on the degree of similarity between the items that are correct and those that are provided as foils. In setting up such a study it would seem advisable to draw the items to be learned randomly from a larger pool of items, with those not chosen for the learning task being retained as foil items in the recognition test. The difficulty level of such a test would probably then depend on the degree of similarity or heterogeneity of the items in the original pool.

RECONSTRUCTION. A less frequently employed way of measuring retention is to present all the correct items in a mixed order or arrangement, requiring the subject to reconstruct the original sequence or pattern of items. This tests for the retention of the relationships among the items instead of assessing memory for the items themselves.

SAVINGS. The savings method of measuring retention is one in which each subject relearns the material he has learned earlier. The per cent of time or trials saved in this relearning effort, when compared with original learning, is the measure of retention. If original learning to a specified criterion took 15 trials, for example, and relearning after 1 day takes only 5 trials, we find that the 10-trial difference represents a saving of 67 per cent, the index of retention after this interval. If a different group of subjects took 15 trials to learn the list and 9 trials to relearn it after 1 week, the 6-trial difference would indicate a 40 per cent saving as the measure of retention at this point on the retention curve.

A special advantage of using the savings method for measuring retention is that the first of the relearning trials may provide a recall index of the amount remembered. Suppose, for example, that we are using cards to present a list of nonsense syllables for serial rote memorization by the anticipation method. On the first trial of the relearning session we might find that subjects had correctly anticipated 7 out of 20 syllables. This would be the recall score for this retention interval and we would proceed normally with the relearning trials until we had reached the designated criterion. Then we could compute the savings score for the same list at the same retention interval. Obtaining both a recall and a savings score at the same interval after original learning represents a potential bonus of information about the retention process.

HYPOTHETICAL THRESHOLDS IN RETENTION. The well-established fact that recognition scores are better than recall scores after any given interval may be conceptualized in terms of a hypothetical memory trace for each previously learned item. A given memory trace may not be strong enough to lead to active recall of the item, but its strength may be sufficient to make this item discriminable from others on a recognition test. We can schematize this relationship with a graphic representation. On this graph we use arbitrary units for a scale of the strength of the memory trace. On the same scale we represent the demands of recall and recognition as hypothetical thresholds, the value of which must be exceeded by memory trace strength before that type of retention performance can occur. In

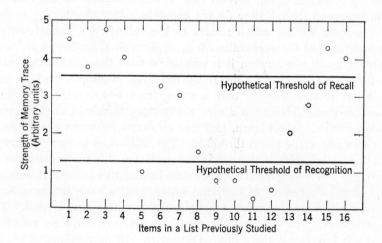

Fig. 16.2. Illustrative representation of the strengths of memory traces of several previously studied items in relationship to hypothetical thresholds of recall and recognition.

Figure 16.2, where this schema is presented, you see that we have placed the threshold of recall higher on the scale, indicating that this task requires a stronger trace than does recognition which is shown at the lower threshold. Some items are below even the recognition threshold. Among these, there are differences in the strength of the memory trace. These differences would be revealed by a savings method test of retention. The items of lower strength would require more trials to relearn, that is, to strengthen them up to the threshold of recognition or, more typically, of recall.

The utility of such a schema as Figure 16.2 may be illustrated by noting how it corresponds to certain facts revealed in an experiment by Postman, Jenkins, and Postman (1948). Forty-eight nonsense syllables were spelled out orally for subjects, going through the list in a different order six times. Then subjects were given a recall and a recognition test, each test being given to half the subjects first. Given immediately following the reading of the syllables, these two tests constituted the measurement of immediate memory or short-term retention. The group of subjects tested first on recognition than on recall had 27.66 and 9.09 syllables correct on the two tests, respectively. The other group scored 7.20 syllables correct on recall and then 24.23 correct on recognition. The great superiority of scores made on recognition testing suggests that many syllables had a strength of the hypothetical memory trace which would fall between the recognition and recall thresholds of the schema of Figure 16.2. All that can be recalled can also be recognized, but several can be discriminated on the recognition test even though they do not occur in active recall.

A second finding which relates to the schema we have been examining is that the recognition test, if given first, facilitates the subsequent recall score when it is compared with the recall score made in the group which took the recall test first. Postman, Jenkins, and Postman (1948) suggest that a recognition test is actually a final learning trial. The items above recognition threshold are rehearsed as the subject checks them, and this rehearsal serves to elevate some of them above the recall threshold. The difference in recall scores of about two syllables is the gain attributable to this temporal order of testing. The recognition scores made by the two groups of subjects also showed an effect of temporal order; in this case, it was a detrimental effect on the group taking the recognition test second. The experimenters suggest that the recall process can have no effect on traces below recall threshold. During the 10 min occupied by the recall test, the strengths of some of these would decline to points below recognition threshold. This may account for the difference of more than two syllables in recognition score, favoring the group which was given the recognition test first, immediately after the sixth presentation of all the syllables.

MEASURING RETENTION OF PERCEPTUAL-MOTOR SKILL. Recall and recognition scores are most applicable in testing memory for verbal material. To assess the retention of perceptual-motor habits, we typically ask subjects to perform the task so that we may obtain any conventional performance measure. By comparing this score, made after the elapsed retention interval, with the score obtained at the end of original practice, we get an index of the degree of retention. It is probably a good principle to carry such a performance test of retention over a number of trials of moderate length. The data may then reveal the extent to which a warm-up phenomenon occurred when the retention test was begun. Any tendency for the test administration to lead to additional skill acquisition might also be indicated. The score indicative of retention level might have to be selected according to rules which minimize bias from either warm-up or continued learning. Such rules cannot be specified in any inclusive fashion; they must be formulated in accordance with facts about processes operating in perceptual-motor performance. This illustrates the interlocking nature of empirical facts at this point in the development of many areas of psychological inquiry.

The Description of Retention

The measurement of amount of retention permits us to describe functional relationships, especially curves of retention as a function of time. Memory is considered to have qualitative attributes also. These may be studied in psychological research of a different sort.

THE NATURE OF QUALITATIVE CHANGE. Attempts to determine the qualitative changes that occur during retention have relied very much on visually perceived geometric forms as stimulus material. This choice of item to be retained by experimental subjects reflects the attempt to extend gestalt principles of form perception to the memory process. For example, the law of Prägnanz—that a slightly asymmetrical figure will be perceived as a "good" symmetrical figure—is considered to operate during retention to make previously perceived figures progressively "better." Terms like leveling or normalization have been applied to such memory processes. A contrasting process, accentuation of some feature of the perceived figure, has been called sharpening. Factors determining whether leveling or sharpening will occur in a given instance do not seem to have been clearly identified, but the assumption is made that the effect of either tendency becomes stronger as time goes on. We shall see that methods for describing and measuring changes in a memory trace pose a number of problems.

Before turning to procedures of study we need to note another process of memory change, termed *assimilation*. Here, the memory trace is influenced by factors other than the visual stimulus itself. For example, verbal labels have been shown to have some effect on the memory for visual forms, the memory trace assimilating certain features from the verbal label. Assimilative changes should probably not be thought of as constituting a type of process distinct from the seemingly more autonomous change since even the latter may be considered to reveal assimilation from the subject's past experience.

THE MEASUREMENT OF MEMORY CHANGES. A variety of methods have been employed in studying memory dynamics. Some of the procedures have been criticized for introducing distortions into the process supposedly being examined. We shall point out such criticism as we review the different methods of investigation.

There are two ways of getting at the memory trace which a subject has retained from an earlier perceptual experience. In the *method of reproduction,* we ask him to draw the geometric figure he was shown, the assumption being that in the absence of the stimulus pattern his drawing is guided by the memory trace of the percept rather than by the percept itself. Alternative ways of reproducing geometric figures may include some technique of adjusting mechanically presented lines. Such an adjustment procedure approaches the other major method, involving comparison reports by subjects. In the *method of comparison* we show the subject a new figure after the retention time has elapsed. We ask him to compare it with the standard figure that he saw earlier. Again, of course, we assume that the memory trace of the earlier percept is utilized. The comparison he states will thus permit an inference about this trace. For example, if he says that a comparison line is more curved than the standard line he saw earlier, when both lines are actually identical in curvature, we may infer that the memory trace of the line first seen has become less curved than it was at the time of its direct perception. A single comparison like this does not give us a direct indication of the amount of change that has taken place in memory, as does the method of reproduction. The comparison method is sometimes extended toward quantification by presenting several comparison stimuli and asking that the subject point out the one which matches the standard stimulus he saw originally. The one selected is presumed, of course, to be a quantitative representation of the memory trace at the time of comparison.

Besides choosing either the reproduction method or the comparison method, an experimenter who is investigating progressive changes in memory trace will have another methodological decision to make. He will have to decide whether to test the same subjects successively at the different intervals being studied, or whether to test different groups of subjects after each interval has elapsed since the original stimulus presentation. Either of these possibilities may be combined with the reproduction or the comparison techniques. Thus we have the *method of successive reproduction* or the *method of single reproduction*, with the same alternatives applying to comparison.

The successive testing of the same subjects at different intervals cannot be recommended. We have noted it because it has been used quite extensively. It has been criticized on the fundamental ground that the attempt at measurement actually interferes with the process being measured. If we are trying to plot the course of memory change, it is a mistake to stimulate the subjects repeatedly, either with comparison stimuli or with their own attempts at reproducing the original figure. A similar danger may exist in the modified method of single comparison in which several comparison stimuli must be viewed at a single point on the continuum of elapsed time.

Even if the single testing of any subject is employed, both the reproduction and the comparison methods have some drawbacks as attempts to reveal the nature of the memory trace of a previous percept. The data from the reproducing of geometric figures may suffer from the subjects' weaknesses in drawing. It must be admitted, however, that this should not pose too great a problem if the required drawing is simple, instructions are adequate, and the research design stresses comparison of drawings made by similar subject groups at different intervals rather than comparison with the standard itself. The method of single comparison has the inherent danger of altering the memory trace at the time when the subject is presented the comparison stimulus.

A STUDY OF MEMORY FOR FORM. An experiment conducted by Hanawalt (1952) will illustrate points of procedure which need to be considered when memory change is investigated. The method of single comparison was used so that the memory traces of a subject would not be affected by repeated perception of the same stimuli. Six different designs were shown to subjects by projecting each design on a screen for 5 sec. The designs included a circle with a gap in it, an acute angle, and a squarelike figure composed of four dots. The retention test consisted of eleven questions such as "Is the gap in the circle wider or narrower?" Such questions accompanied the presentation of identical figures after different retention intervals; subjects were led to believe that these test figures differed slightly from those which they had seen originally. Any subject was tested after just one of the retention intervals: 3 min, 10 min, or 7 days.

The data in this study were the per cents of subjects at each retention interval who gave a particular one of the alternative answers to a question about the test figure. For example, if the gestalt principle of closure were operative in the memory trace of the broken circle, the gap in the test circle, objectively identical, would be judged to be wider by many subjects. If closure constituted a progressive change in the trace, then this per cent of "wider" judgments would increase as a function of the retention interval.

To cite a part of the findings, the per cent "wider" judgments at the three retention intervals were, in order, 47, 57, and 44 per cent. These obviously do not form a progression and none of these per cents is significantly different from 50 per cent. Consequently, it cannot be concluded that any progressing tendency to closure in the memory trace of the broken circle was demonstrated. Neither do the data support any hypothesis of an opposite trend, progressive accentuation of the gap in the memory trace.

Significant departures from chance expectancy in the subjects' judgments were found consistently for just one of the figures employed, a "dipper" consisting of a straight line "handle" and a curved segment "cup." When inspecting the test figure, subjects consistently reported the straight line segment to be "shorter." This indicated that this part of the memory trace was longer, although the effect did not change progressively with the retention interval. The curvature of the arc in the test figure was seen by most subjects as "greater," with a lesser curvature being indicated in the memory trace. This effect seemed to diminish as the time since inspecting the original figure became greater.

Taken as a whole, the results of this investigation offer little support to the hypothesis that memory traces undergo progressive changes consistent with gestalt principles. The research report emphasizes the use of the single test method as freeing the data from influences which may have been operative in earlier studies where each subject was tested repeatedly.

AN EXPERIMENT ON ASSIMILATION IN FIGURE REPRODUCTION. Perceptual assimilation may occur in ambiguous configurations due to the influence of verbal labels applied. This hypothesis is demonstrated in a study by Bruner, Busiek, and Minturn (1952). The method used required subjects to draw a figure immediately after it had been briefly projected on a screen. Immediate memory rather than long-term retention was thus the target of the investigation. The principal experimental manipulation was to attach different verbal labels to each of the four figures just before exposure. For example, a curved closed figure was labeled either a "lima bean" or a "canoe" for two different experimental groups. Two control groups were also run, one receiving no verbal label prior to seeing and reproducing the figures, and one being given both labels. According to the assimilation hypothesis the reproductions drawn by those in the experimental groups should depart from the originally presented ambiguous figure in the direction of whichever verbal label had been given. The control groups' drawings revealed any tendency for changes in the form to occur in the absence of special induction of assimilation.

All the figures that subjects had drawn were submitted to judges who had to rate each one on the direction and degree of its departure from a direct copy of the original ambiguous form. A strong resemblance to a lima bean would be given a +3 rating, for example, whereas a slight deviation toward a likeness of a canoe would be rated −1, with 0 serving to indicate no judged distortion in either direction. Judges were unaware as to the group from which any drawing had been taken.

The assimilation hypothesis was widely supported in the data for the different ambiguous figures as reproduced by the two different experimental groups. The results further showed that assimilation occurred, in some instances, more readily in one direction than in the other. Since reproduction of the forms took place immediately after the brief stimulus exposure, the investigators identify their study as dealing with assimilation in perception rather than in memory.

Mnemonic Devices and Memory Principles

In the practical art of remembering, many people rely on *mnemonic devices*, special techniques which aid the memory. "Thirty days hath September . . ." goes the bit of verse used to recall how many days there are in each month. Rote memorization is still required to learn "April, June, and November" instead of "April, May, and November" as the key line. In Rochester and vicinity some children learn how to spell "geography" by using the mnemonic sentence "George Eastman's old grandmother rode a pig home yesterday".*

* Personal communication from Cheryl Lynn Andreas.

Rote memorizing of the sentence may be easier than memorizing the sequence of letters for several reasons: the associative interdependencies among the words in the meaningful sentence, the interesting picture conveyed by the sentence, and the motivational appeal of knowing such a delightful tidbit of gossip.

A different mnemonic device has been used by the author in giving a classroom demonstration of immediate memory. After proceeding around the room having students each name an object, it is then possible to recite the list back in correct order. This is paired associate learning, with each object being associated with one of the cardinal numbers in sequence. To do this by rote memory in just one hearing is not easy, but a mnemonic device makes it possible. The "memory expert" has prememorized a series of associations like "1–bun, 2–shoe, 3–tree, 4–door . . ." With these objects firmly in mind, I need only to associate each named object with the prememorized object. This is done by bringing them together in a visual image, the more bizarre the better. For example, if the fourth student says "pen," I imagine this student pinned to a "door" (No. 4) by a huge fountain pen. Twenty such visualizations are easier to retain than an equal number of pairs associated by rote.

Since mnemonic devices are demonstrably beneficial in certain retention tasks, they must embody certain principles of memory. An examination of these techniques should therefore be a good source of hypotheses about memory for experimental testing. Another line of research might be to determine the advantage of using a mnemonic device over simple rote memorization. After matching two groups of subjects, one could be trained in the use of a mnemonic device. Then each group could be assigned one or more memory tasks with performance appropriately measured.

Design of Experiments on Retention

In our discussion of the aims and methods of research on memory we have occasionally noted problems of experimental design. The design of retention studies is illustrated in each experiment cited in this chapter. Several special points may be noted here in order to assure their consideration in any experiment we might undertake.

NECESSITY FOR INDEPENDENT EQUIVALENT GROUPS. If we are attempting to plot a curve of retention, we should use separate groups of subjects to obtain each point on the curve. If we were to overlook this rule and test the same subjects repeatedly at different intervals, we would be interfering with the very retention process we were trying to measure. With separate groups required for each memory interval, the next demand is that these be equivalent groups. Equivalence may be sought in matching the subjects on a relevant performance. To establish groups on some other basis, such as the willingness of some of the volunteers to be scheduled for a test 6 hr later, is to risk a bias in the data collected. Subjects from whom a special degree of cooperation is required are likely to possess a special degree of motivation in performing the task.

AMOUNT OF TRAINING AND STAGE OF PRACTICE. The amount of original learning accomplished by subjects is an important determinant of their retention of the material. Some experiments would seem to call for giving a fixed number of training trials. In other studies it may be better to carry each subject to a designated criterion of original learning. This again is one of those problems for which a universal solution does not exist.

If groups of subjects are presented with the material during original learning, it would seem advisable for each such training group to contain some subjects who will ultimately be in each different retention interval test. This rule will assure us that any bias introduced during the training will be reflected in each retention group rather than in just one. The latter situation might arise if groups selected for different retention intervals were each trained as a unit.

Rote memorization experiments have revealed a practice effect reflected in the quicker learning of successive lists as subjects become acquainted with performing such a task. This effect must be considered in designing verbal learning studies. A study was conducted by Greenberg and Underwood (1950) to see if a similar practice effect might be found in retention when subjects were given training on a list of words and then a retention test on it, continuing this over four different lists. When recall scores were examined, a decrement in scores as a function of stage of practice was found when the retention interval was either 5 hr or 48 hr. That is, subjects actually did progressively less well at recall as they learned and were tested successively on four different lists. There was evidence that proactive inhibition from the earlier lists was affecting recall scores for the later ones. Such a finding must be considered in any study requiring that the same subject serve repeatedly in a memorization and recall situation. In this same study subjects went on from each recall test to relearn the list they had learned earlier. These relearning scores did *not* reflect a negative practice effect as had the scores on the recall test.

INFORMATION GIVEN TO SUBJECTS. A point for careful consideration in the designing of a retention study is the information given to a subject concerning the retention interval over which his memory is to be tested. A subject told that he will be tested 5 days later will probably behave differently from one told that the retention test will take place in 2 hr. In some studies it may be desirable to conceal the fact that retention is to be tested at all. Here, of course, we are not dealing with any experiment where the subjects' expectations of subsequent testing are purposely being varied.

MATERIAL TO BE RETAINED. An investigator wishing to study retention may choose from a great number of perceptual-motor and verbal tasks for his subjects to learn and retain. Within the verbal realm any of the materials we cited in Chapter 13 might be selected, from paralogs to poetry. The experimenter must be aware, however, that his choice is likely to affect the retention curve he obtains. Memory for different kinds of material may even interact with the type of retention test employed.

ACTIVITY DURING RETENTION INTERVAL. The operation of retroactive inhibition during any retention interval needs to be considered in designing studies. This is patently true when the experiment deals with RI itself, but it applies in principle to all investigations of retention. Since RI research indicates that a person's activity can influence his retention of earlier learned material, an experimenter must be sure that different retention intervals he employs are not characterized by vastly different sorts of activity on the part of his subjects.

STUDIES OF VERBAL RETENTION

Verbal materials have been widely chosen for experiments on retention, just as they have been favored in studying human learning. Many of the variables which are postulated, and often demonstrated, to have an effect on rote verbal learning have also been tested for their influence on the retention process. Despite a close relationship between learning and retention, it cannot be assumed that factors affecting one will affect the other in a similar fashion. Consequently, a program of empirical study of considerable scope is demanded in order to discover all the functional relationships which involve the retention process.

It is impossible for us to take a representative sample of verbal retention studies for review. As selected illustrations of research in this area we shall first examine two studies in which meaningfulness of material to be retained was an independent variable. Then we shall consider two investigations of retroactive inhibition, since RI remains a key concept in explaining forgetting. Finally, we shall turn to a study in which verbal labels were employed as an aid to retention prior to recall and recognition of objects after a 1-week interval.

Meaningfulness and Retention

Some interesting comparisons in experimental method may be found in two studies of the effect of meaningfulness on retention. Both investigations made use of more than one technique for measuring retention. Underwood and Richardson (1956) selected nonsense syllables of high and low association values as the material to be learned, and tested retention after 24 hrs. Dowling and Braun (1957) tested at this 1-day interval and also at 7 days, using words scaled for meaningfulness by Noble (1952).

HIGH AND LOW ASSOCIATION VALUE. Besides varying association value of syllables based on association scaling, Underwood and Richardson (1956) studied the effects of intralist similarity and serial position on retention as well. Our review of the study will emphasize their findings related to meaningfulness. It will be noted that this variable interacted with intralist similarity in affecting some measures of retention.

These experimenters point out that variables which affect rate of learning do not necessarily influence recall. The finding that meaningfulness affects learning rate, which we noted in Chapter 13, does not preclude a need to test the action of this verbal dimension on recall.

Four lists of ten nonsense syllables were prepared, two with high intralist similarity and two with low similarity. For each level of similarity one list contained items of 93 per cent or 100 per cent association values from the Glaze scaling. The other contained low association value syllables, 0 to 20 per cent. These lists were learned by different groups of subjects to a criterion of one perfect trial using the serial anticipation method, with syllables being spelled. Twenty-four hours later, the list given to each subject was relearned, with performance during the first trial yielding a recall score. Both these recall scores and the number of trials required for relearning were analyzed for effects of the independent variables.

The original learning data confirmed earlier findings in showing that the two degrees of meaningfulness or association value led to different rates of mastery of the lists, those of high association value being memorized more readily. When recall scores were examined, meaningfulness proved to be not significant in its effect. The other major variable, intralist similarity, was not significant either, but it did interact with meaningfulness. In the interaction, the two lists of low meaningfulness revealed that high intralist similarity was detrimental to recall, whereas this did not occur when meaningfulness was high. A special analysis of recall data, based on the estimated probable number of words correct had there been another learning trial, also showed meaningfulness not to have a significant effect. The same interaction was found and similarity itself was found to be significant in this analysis.

When relearning scores were examined, meaningfulness did show a significant effect, as did intralist similarity. These scores reflect the original learning scores very closely, the authors note. If we compute a conventional index of retention, per cent savings at relearning, by comparing mean number of trials to learn and to relearn the same list to the same criterion, we find that the savings score for each list is close to 81 per cent. It appears that this savings score agrees with the recall score in showing that meaningfulness does not affect retention.

As we consider a major finding of this investigation—that meaningfulness did not affect recall scores nor savings scores—we must keep in mind that the materials learned were all nonsense syllables. Different lists varied widely in Glaze association values, but they were still composed of nonsense syllables, with high meaningfulness represented by such letter combinations as BES, LIB, DOZ, and HIN. Any general conclusion about the effect of meaningfulness on retention should probably be based on additional experiments, considered with this one, in order to include a broader sampling of the dimension of meaning.

HIGH, MEDIUM, AND LOW M VALUE. The scale values assigned to nouns and paralogs in a study by Noble (1952) provided the three levels of meaningfulness, m, for the three 12-item lists used by Dowling and Braun (1957). These lists were learned by different groups of subjects by a pronunciation-anticipation method to a criterion of two successive errorless trials. Separate groups were then tested at two different retention intervals, 1 day and 7 days, using various measures of retention. At each interval one group was tested with a method of unaided recall, requiring a subject to write down as many of the 12 items as he remembered in any order. For other subjects a reconstruction test was used; the stimulus items were printed separately on 3 × 5 cards and these had to be placed in proper serial order. Two different measures of retention were obtained on the other groups of subjects. They were required to relearn the lists so that a savings score could be computed and, in addition, their scores on the first relearning trial constituted a measure of aided recall.

The data obtained by the different methods of measuring retention were treated in two different ways by these experimenters. One, they were analyzed in the form of raw retention scores: unaided recall, reconstruction, savings in relearning, and aided recall. Two, the retention scores were coded or adjusted on the basis of what each subject had accomplished during original learning. The findings relating retention to meaningfulness and to retention interval depended greatly on the method of measuring retention and on whether scores were used in raw or coded form.

Considering raw scores first, it was found that retention interval was a significant factor no matter what measure of retention was used. At the 7-day interval, performance was poorer than after just 1 day. Meaningfulness, however, affected raw scores significantly only when retention was measured by per cent savings in relearning. For this method of measurement, meaningfulness interacted significantly with retention interval. At both retention intervals, however, the data agree in showing retention for the medium m list to be worse than that for the list of low m value as well as that of high m value. This finding in the raw scores shows that savings scores are not related to meaningfulness in monotonic fashion. Instead, the function seems first to decrease and then to increase.

When coded scores—adjusted for rate of original learning—were analyzed, both meaningfulness and retention interval were found to have a statistically significant effect only for the aided recall and unaided recall methods of measurement. In both these instances, a monotonic relationship between meaningfulness and retention was indicated, with retention being poorer for lists of lower meaningfulness.

Besides its empirical findings, this experiment is instructive for its illustration of the principle that experimental findings may depend heavily on the methods of measurement, or operational definition, of the dependent variable. In the case of retention it may be hoped that different findings based on different techniques of assessment will not lead to confusion but will eventually help to reveal the nature of the retention process.

Retroactive Inhibition

Two studies of RI which we shall review are similar in that materials are selected for the two learning tasks, OL and IL, which will lead to considerable RI when RL is scored. (RI = retroactive inhibition,

OL = original learning of a list, IL = interpolated learning of a different list, and RL = relearning of the original list.) The studies differ in that the first stresses quantitative manipulation of two variables, whereas the second involves qualitative changes in conditions surrounding the different learning phases.

DEGREE OF ORIGINAL AND INTERPOLATED LEARNING. Two factors which can be manipulated quantitatively in the RI paradigm of OL-IL-RL are the amount of practice devoted to the OL task and the amount of practice given over to the IL task. The greater the degree of OL that is accomplished, the less interference from IL that is reflected in RL scores. When amount of IL is varied, the functional relationship to RL is slightly more complex. RI increases as IL practice increases up to a point, so that RL scores become worse. But a degree of IL training is reached where RI levels off or even begins a slight decrease as IL training is increased even further. Noting that studies varying the amount of OL have held IL practice at a constant value, and vice versa, Briggs (1957) undertook a study of RI in which he employed a design that involved both these factors as variables.

Five groups of subjects were used in this study, each group being assigned a particular amount of IL training, 0, 2, 5, 10, or 20 trials. On each experimental day a subject would be given some number of trials, 2, 5, 10, or 20, at learning an OL list of paired associates. A subject received one of these Trials OL values on each day of experimental participation, following an initial day of introduction to paired associate learning. He then received the amount of IL training each day which was indicated for members of his group. The IL lists were created to contribute to RI by having new response adjectives paired with the same stimulus adjectives as had been used in the OL list for that day. The next step in each daily session was a modified free recall (MFR) test in which the set of stimulus words was presented with instructions to give the first response word which came to mind. This was followed by five RL trials which yielded an index of RI. The response words for RL were, of course, those of the OL list. A final daily step was to give practice on other lists to four of the groups to bring their stint at the memory drum up to that of the group given 20 trials of IL. The group given no IL trials constituted the traditional control group of a study of RI.

The effects of varied amounts of OL and IL on RI were sought in a traditional recall measure, the mean number of OL responses correctly anticipated on the first RL trial. Such an index is inversely related to RI, of course. When the transformed data were subjected to analysis of variance, the classical effects of the main variables were found: RI was inversely related to amount of OL and directly related to the amount of IL. There was no evidence of a downward turning in the latter function although the anticipated asymptote was indicated. For every level of OL, that is, some amounts of IL practice were found which yielded about the same amount of RI. The special contribution of the multivariate design of this experiment was to reveal a significant interaction between Trials OL and Trials IL as the independent variables. For example, it was found that after 10 or 20 OL trials, most of the different IL groups yielded different scores on the first RL trial, whereas after 5 OL trials, the groups having from 2 to 20 IL trials did not differ significantly among themselves but only differed from the control group.

Additional analyses of the data of this experiment gave further insight into the RI process. Although we cannot consider them fully, we can note the nature of these findings. The functional relationship between amount of IL and the RL scores was found to disappear rapidly as RL trials were continued beyond the first. This was interpreted as a dissipation of RI, an effect which had been noted in earlier studies. The modified free recall (MFR) test gave data which showed the greater tendency to give IL responses in the groups which had received more IL trials. This analysis, plus an examination of intrusion errors on the first RL trials, helped to elucidate the role of response competition as it contributes to RI.

STIMULUS CONDITIONS SURROUNDING OL, IL, AND RL. A large number of studies of RI have manipulated the different materials to be learned under OL and IL, with stimulus conditions surrounding the practice periods kept constant. A different way of exploring the nature of the RI process is to vary these stimulus context conditions while keeping the items to be learned the same for all groups. Finding conflicting results in earlier research, Greenspoon and Ranyard (1957) performed an experiment to see how the amount of RI developing in the conventional OL-IL-RL sequence would vary with changes in the stimulus situation in which the different stages of learning took place. The basic hypothesis was that IL would be less interfering or would lead to less RI if it occurred in a different environmental context than OL. Underlying this hypothesis is the assumption that when material is learned, the items are associated with cues from the room and from the method of presentation as well as with each other. If IL takes place under the same conditions as OL, these associations with surrounding cues intensify the competition between OL and IL responses when RL is undertaken. If IL occurs under different conditions than OL, however, then the two sets of learned responses are not associated with the same external stimuli and therefore they compete much less at the RL stage of the experiment.

All groups of subjects were given the conventional OL-IL-RL sequence in this investigation, learning one serial list of ten nonsense syllables for OL and RL, and a similar list during the IL phase. The experimental variations that differentiated the four groups were the conditions under which different learning phases took place. These conditions differed in two fundamental ways, the mode of presentation of the items and the room where the learning occurred. In the Card Room, presentation of the serial list was accomplished by means of cards, each bearing one syllable, which were presented serially by the experimenter. The brightly lighted room was cluttered with old furniture and experimental apparatus, and the departmental animal colony could be seen in an adjoining room. In the darkened Drum Room, a memory drum was used to present the items with the experimenter out of sight in an adjoining room.

The design of the experiment involved different patterns of employing the Card Room and the Drum Room for the different phases of a subject's participation. Letting A stand for either room and B for the other, the sequential treatments of the four groups are indicated by AAA, AAB, ABA, and ABB. Group AAA was given all three phases, OL-IL-RL, in one room, the Card Room being used for half the subjects, the Drum Room for the others. Group AAB received OL and IL in one room and RL in the other. Group ABA had its IL experience in a different room, with its unique conditions, from that in which OL and RL took place. For Group ABB, the only change in rooms took place after OL had been accomplished. Within this design, the experimenters counterbalanced for the list used as the first of the two to be learned and for the room given the A designation.

It was found that neither the particular list nor the particular room affected OL significantly, so the various subgroups were pooled for the subsequent analyses into the major groups we have noted, AAA, AAB, ABA, and ABB. The effect of these different combinations of surrounding stimulus conditions on the amount of RI was sought. The hypothesis that different OL-IL conditions would lessen RI was tested in two different performance measures at the RL stage: number of OL syllables correctly anticipated on the first RL trial, and number of trials of RL to reach a criterion of two successive errorless trials.

Both of the RL performance measures supported the hypothesis. RI was found to be least in amount in Group ABA in which IL had taken place under surrounding conditions quite different from those of OL and RL. Poorest recall and relearning, indicating greatest RI, were found in Group *AAB* which had experienced OL and IL under similar environmental conditions, making for greatest response competition through association with the same cues and for least environmental support at relearning. Groups *AAA* and *ABB* gave RL performances that were intermediate in comparison with the best and worst groups we have mentioned. They did not differ significantly from each other on either measure.

Verbalization as a Memory Aid

The realm of verbal behavior is heavily represented in retention research by studies in which verbal material had to be memorized and retained. A different role of verbal items was investigated in a study we shall examine next. Kurtz and Hovland (1953) studied the one-week retention of school children for objects they had seen. They studied how memory was affected by applying the familiar verbal label to each object at the time it was originally viewed. The hypothesis was that such verbalization, using the names of the objects seen, would enhance retention when it was tested by a recognition or a recall method.

Considerable care had to be exercised in designing this experiment to avoid introducing bias which would favor verbalization and give spurious support to the hypothesis. There would be danger of bias from degree of participation in the task, for example, if one group of subjects actively verbalized the names of the objects as they viewed them while the control group merely viewed the items passively, making no response to them. This problem was obviated by requiring control subjects to circle the picture of each object on a photograph during viewing just as the experimental subjects had to circle the name of each item on a check sheet in the first session. At the recognition test a week later, a procedural bias might have occurred if the items were all presented in verbal form to the two groups. The experimenters avoided this source of distortion by using a photographic recognition test for checking on the retention of half the items and a verbal recognition test for the remaining items.

Our discussion of the experimental design has revealed some of the details of this experiment. In the first session subjects individually were permitted to view 16 common objects: toys, miniature animals, small household articles, etc. While viewing the 4 × 4 array, the fifth-, sixth-, or seventh-graders in the verbalization group had to circle the name of each object on a typewritten sheet and to pronounce it aloud. This was done as the experimenter pointed to different objects in random sequence. Comparable subjects of the visualization group had to circle the picture of each item on a photograph, thus attending actively to each one in a similar random order. No mention of giving names of the objects was included in the instructions of this visualization group. Neither group of subjects was told that a retention test would be given.

One week later some of the subjects from each group took a recognition test. This test was composed of two halves, with one half requiring recognition of the names of objects, the other half demanding recognition of pictures of objects. Among the correct items were interspersed an equal number of similar items that were incorrect. Other subjects from each group had their retention tested after the same interval by taking a written recall test, listing all the objects they could remember. On the recall test and on the recognition tests of either the verbal or visual sort the number of correct responses and the number of errors provided two separate, though correlated, measures of retention.

Although differing in some details, the pattern of results for this study definitely supported the principal hypothesis that verbalization aids retention. A subsidiary hypothesis was that the method of testing for retention—verbal or photographic—would interact with the verbalization or visualization method of initial study. This hypothesis also received support in the data collected.

STUDIES OF PERCEPTUAL-MOTOR RETENTION

Earlier in this chapter we reviewed an experiment which compared the retention of perceptual-motor habits with memory for a set of equivalent verbal associations. Important as that type of comparative investigation may be, there is need for a thorough empirical study of retention in either the verbal or the motor realm taken singly. Turning next to perceptual-motor performance, we shall examine two retention studies which both have the merit of investigating the same phenomenon in more than one sort of task.

Distribution of Practice During Acquisition

Reynolds and Bilodeau (1952) studied 10-week retention of skill for three different tasks, giving spaced or massed trials to different groups during the period of skill acquisition. Equating the amount of original practice presented a problem. It might seem sufficient merely to give an equal number of minutes of practice to each group. These experimenters point out, however, that a distributed practice group will make more correct responses in a given time while performing some tasks than will a massed practice group. In this study they equated amount of original acquisition practice in terms of number of correct responses made or designated amount of successful performance in the case of two of the tasks. The more conventional duration of trials was used to equate groups practicing the other task.

Three different experiments are actually reported in this study, each one studying the acquisition and retention of skill on a different task as a function of distribution of acquisition trials. We shall briefly review each study in turn, concentrating on its retention aspect. In each experiment retention was examined by giving a series of relearning trials 10 weeks after original learning.

RUDDER CONTROL EXPERIMENT. Subjects were required to position a small rotating cockpit by pushing on rudder pedals to keep it aligned with a small target. Time on target provided the performance measure. Two groups were run, one given 12 massed trials of 30 secs each, and the other given the same number and length of trials with a 30-sec rest following each trial. The group which had been given distributed original practice, and which had been scoring higher at the end of the acquisition training, did better on the first retention trial. On the very next trial, however, the group trained under massed practice did as well, and the two groups continued to perform similarly during the remainder of the retention test. For this task, then, we see evidence that distributed practice yields briefly superior performance after a long interval of retention. However, even this transient difference seems largely due to the better performing which the distributed group had been doing at the end of acquisition.

COMPLEX COORDINATION EXPERIMENT. This test required subjects to match panel lightings by moving both a stick and rudder pedals. For this experiment a trial was defined as a block of 10 such matches or settings of the controlled lights. A massed practice group and three groups performing with 12-, 60-, or 120-sec rest intervals were each given 8 trials. Original practice was equated for number of responses because of the definition of a trial which had been adopted. Besides original training, all groups were given test trials which followed the end of training by 10 and 15 min. On the 10-week retention test the group which had been trained with trials most distributed was superior to the others. Again, however, this superiority had been preceded by superior performance in training and testing.

Again, too, it did not persist beyond the first retention trial. The results of this study thus paralleled those of the rudder control experiment.

ROTARY PURSUIT EXPERIMENT. Looking toward equating practice in all groups, the experimenters defined a rotary pursuit trial as 6 sec of keeping the stylus on the target as the turntable revolved. Rest intervals were the same as in the Complex Coordination experiment, as were the introduction of test trials a few minutes after training. In this study the groups differed significantly in how long they took to accumulate 6 sec on target, with the more distributed practice leading to greater proficiency. At the 10-week retention test, however, there were no significant differences between groups.

In general, it would appear that scoring differences at the end of original training may be reflected temporarily when retention testing is begun. This seemed to have been the case in the Rudder Control and Complex Coordination experiments. In the Rotary Pursuit study this retention score difference did not appear, even though group scores were most divergent at the end of training. The different types of perceptual-motor task would seem to involve factors which preclude the description of a phenomenon like retention with complete generality.

Long-Term Retention of Skills

Ammons, Farr, Bloch, Neumann, Dey, Marion, and Ammons (1958) used two different complex tasks in a study of retention over intervals ranging from 1 min to 2 yr. In order to increase the information gained from the investigation, two different amounts of original practice were given. Guided by the research report, we shall consider the separate experiments which were similar in design but different in the task which subjects learned and retained.

A PROCEDURAL TASK. A sequential performance was required of subjects in a procedural task consisting of several controls like switches, handles, and pushbuttons which had to be operated in a particular order. The different controls were mounted on a panel together with a chart which indicated the correct sequence of operation. A signal light was also provided which lighted whenever an error in sequence was made. The subject had to correct the error and extinguish this light before proceeding. Each completion of the entire sequence constituted a trial, with 1-min rest being given between trials. Half the subjects had 5 trials and half had 30 trials of original learning. Time to perform and number of errors made were recorded for each trial. The time scores were emphasized in the analysis of the data since errors occurred quite infrequently after the first few training trials. Time scores made on the first trial of original learning were used in obtaining 12 matched groups, comprising a 2 × 6 factorial design. There were 2 levels of original learning, either 5 or 30 trials, and 6 retention intervals: 1 min, 24 hr, 1 month, 6 months, 1 yr, and 2 yr.

During original learning the time scores per trial fell rapidly, from group means of about 1.75 min on the first trial to about 0.39 min on the fifth trial where training was terminated for 6 of the groups. In the other 6 groups, continued practice yielded a decrease in time scores which was gradual beyond about the fifth trial, with group means on the thirtieth trial being about 0.20 min.

Retention was measured after the appropriate interval by administering 10 retraining trials. The different retention interval groups differed most widely on the first retraining trial, with loss of skill being greater over the longer intervals as we would expect. These intergroup differences were quickly lessened by the rapid relearning in the groups where the loss of skill had been great. However, some trace of differences in scores as a function of retention interval persisted even at the tenth trial of retraining.

A COMPENSATORY PURSUIT TASK. A continuous adjustive performance, the moving of an airplane-type stick and rudder pedals, was needed to keep a model plane in proper "on target" orientation in the second experiment. A cam and pulley arrangement kept the small plane banking and turning so as to demand coordinated corrective movements from the subject. Time "on target" during each 1-min trial was the subject's score. The two degrees of original training involved either 1 hr or 8 hr of practice, with 10-sec rest between trials and a 5-min rest after each 30 min of practice. Retention intervals ranged from 1 day to 2 yr.

At the beginning of retraining it was found that considerable losses of skill had taken place over the longer retention intervals. In just a few minutes of retraining a major part of such losses had been overcome. The initial losses as per cents were about the same for the two degrees of original training, according to an analysis of scores made on the first 15 min of retraining.

SUMMARY

Retention is shown to be functionally related to learning by the fact that well-learned behavior patterns are often retained over a long period of time. Further, the cumulative effects of learning are based upon retention from trial to trial of some part of the activity in which a person is engaged. Empirical studies of retention, and its converse, forgetting, have led to the postulation of processes like retroactive inhibition and reminiscence.

Some studies seek functional relationships between performance measures and elapsed time since last practice. Other experiments aim at comparing this retention function, or curve of retention, for different kinds of activity such as memorizing or performing a perceptual-motor task. Investigations of retroactive inhibition typically employ a standard experimental sequence, OL-IL-RL.

When planning a retention study we may use one of several ways of measuring the amount retained. These include the recall, recognition, reconstruction, and savings methods. The scores which subjects make as these different techniques are applied may help to delineate the nature of the retentive process, with hypothetical thresholds as one concept we may employ.

One descriptive approach to retention centers upon the qualitative changes which may occur in the representation of the material in memory. Processes like leveling, sharpening, and assimilation have been postulated. Techniques like the methods of reproduction and comparison permit them to be investigated, with a single performance by each subject being preferable to several successive testings. Illustrative experiments show how memory for geometric figures and simple line drawings is measured. Mnemonic devices are another aspect of the retention process which might be explored by research.

In designing experiments on retention, we should keep in mind the need for independent equivalent groups of subjects. The amount of training and the stage of practice of subjects are among the key variables which cannot be ignored, no matter what the specific aim of a retention experiment. Other important variables are the information given to subjects concerning the memory task, the material selected for retention, and the activity of subjects during the interval of retention.

Verbal retention has been prominent in memory research. Two studies which we reviewed were based on the uniquely verbal independent variable of meaningfulness. Two experiments on retroactive inhibition also occupied our attention. A special relation of verbal behavior to retention was studied in research which required verbalization by some subjects as they sought to remember a number of objects.

When the behavior to be retained is a perceptual-motor skill, the index of retention is typically one or more performance measures as subjects undertake the task after a period without practice. This was demonstrated in two illustrative experiments where several different tasks were used.

REFERENCES

Ammons, R. B., Farr, R. G., Bloch, Edith, Neumann, Eva, Dey, M., Marion, R., & Ammons, C. H. Long-term retention of perceptual-motor skills. *J. exp. Psychol.*, 1958, 55, 318–328.

Briggs, G. E. Retroactive inhibition as a function of the degree of original and interpolated learning. *J. exp. Psychol.*, 1957, 53, 60–67.

Bruner, J. S., Busiek, R. D., & Minturn, A. L. Assimilation in the immediate reproduction of visually perceived figures. *J. exp. Psychol.*, 1952, 44, 151–155.

Dowling, R. M., & Braun, H. W. Retention and meaningfulness of material. *J. exp. Psychol.*, 1957, 54, 213–217.

Greenberg, Ruth, & Underwood, B. J. Retention as a function of stage of practice. *J. exp. Psychol.*, 1950, 40, 452–457.

Greenspoon, J., & Ranyard, R. Stimulus conditions and retroactive inhibition. *J. exp. Psychol.*, 1957, 53, 55–59.

Hanawalt, N. G. The method of comparison applied to the problem of memory change. *J. exp. Psychol.*, 1952, 43, 37–42.

Kurtz, K. H., & Hovland, C. I. The effect of verbalization during observation of stimulus objects upon accuracy of recognition and recall. *J. exp. Psychol.*, 1953, 45, 157–164.

Noble, C. E. An analysis of meaning. *Psychol. Rev.*, 1952, 59, 421–430.

Postman, L., Jenkins, W. O., & Postman, Dorothy L. An experimental comparison of active recall and recognition. *Amer. J. Psychol.*, 1948, 61, 511–519.

Reynolds, B., & Bilodeau, Ina McD. Acquisition and retention of three psychomotor tests as a function of distribution of practice during acquisition. *J. exp. Psychol.*, 1952, 44, 19–26.

Underwood, B. J., & Richardson, J. The influence of meaningfulness, intralist similarity, and serial position on retention. *J. exp. Psychol.*, 1956, 52, 119–126.

Van Dusen, Frances, & Schlosberg, H. Further study of the retention of verbal and motor skills. *J. exp. Psychol.*, 1948, 38, 526–534.

ADDITIONAL READINGS

Bousfield, W. A., Cohen, B. H., & Silva, Joan G. The extension of Marbe's law to the recall of stimulus-words. *Amer. J. Psychol.*, 1956, 69, 429–433.

Lovibond, S. H. A further test of the hypothesis of autonomous memory trace change. *J. exp. Psychol.*, 1958, 55, 412–415.

Miller, G. A. Free recall of redundant strings of letters. *J. exp. Psychol.*, 1958, 56, 485–491.

Postman, L. Learned principles of reorganization in memory. *Psychol. Monogr.*, 1954, 68, No. 3 (Whole No. 374).

Underwood, B. J. Interference and forgetting. *Psychol. Rev.*, 1957, 64, 49–60.

CHAPTER 17

Transfer
of
Training

A transfer of training effect is the action that practicing one activity or task has upon the subsequent performance of another task. A transfer effect will usually be either *positive*, that is, beneficial or facilitating, with respect to the second task, or *negative*, that is, detrimental or interfering. For example, the steering practice one gets in riding a tricycle might facilitate learning to ride a bicycle, a positive transfer effect. However, a negative transfer effect might be experienced in trying to stop a bicycle equipped with hand brakes when one has been trained on a bicycle with a pedal-operated brake. In transfer research we also encounter *zero* transfer effects, where the first task has no measurable effect on the second. *Transfer* is the term applied to the process underlying *transfer effects*, and often "transfer" is used to refer to the effect instead of the process.

Relationships to Learning, Retention, and Retroactive Inhibition

If we consider the learning process to be reflected in the incremental effect that practice of an activity has upon the subsequent performance of the *same* activity, we see that it parallels the transfer process quite closely. Retention may be similarly defined in this framework with stress placed upon the interval separating original practice and subsequent performance. If we emphasize the fact that learning or retention trials are never absolutely identical with earlier practice, we may conclude logically that these are not different in essence from transfer. In behavior studies we differentiate transfer from these other processes by pointing to the deliberate task differences between original practice and testing for transfer effects.

Transfer effects bear a resemblance to retroactive inhibition which is the interference of one activity on the *retention* of a previously practiced task. Retroactive inhibition acts upon present traces of past activity, whereas transfer is the action of traces of present activity revealed when a later task is attempted, a proactive process. Since retroactive inhibition is not revealed until a subsequent test of performance, it is not logically distinguishable from a transfer effect to that performance. Again, however, it is the design of the study that distinguishes retroactive inhibition experiments from transfer research.

Kinds of Behavior Investigated

The definition of a transfer effect places no limitation on the kinds of activity in which the transfer process may be studied. Any sort of behavior may be a potential source of transfer or may reveal transfer effects from prior activity. The operation of transfer in everyday life, particularly as we go through the developmental and educational years, may be considered as common as the learning process. In psychological research we necessarily select certain laboratory tasks as tools for studying transfer of training. Our consideration of different studies will show that these include a variety of verbal and perceptual-motor tasks. Transfer processes are often too complex to permit casual observational analysis. We need the controls that the psychological laboratory offers if we are to discover how the mechanisms of transfer work.

Hypotheses Concerning Transfer Mechanisms

We should not expect to find transfer effects between any two tasks that were merely selected at random. The mechanisms of transfer are usually sought in tasks that are related to each other in some particular way. We shall briefly survey some of the relationships to which transfer effects have been credited. The experimental approach to the precise identification of such factors operating in transfer involves systematic varying of the content and the practice conditions for the two tasks.

IDENTICAL ELEMENTS. When we examine many instances of positive transfer we find that there are elements in the second task which were found also in the first. The acquisition of these elements as the first task is practiced permits their use when the second task is undertaken. The identical elements which subserve transfer may be specific habits, methods of work, or principles which can be applied in the second activity.

SIMILARITY AND GENERALIZATION. Performance on a second task may be benefited by an earlier activity even when there are no mutual identical elements. Facilitation may occur when similar stimuli and responses are involved. Sometimes positive transfer effects may stem from a combination of identity and similarity of elements in the two tasks concerned.

Explanation of transfer effects involving similarity of stimuli or responses is usually based on a process termed *generalization.* This is observed to occur in experiments on learning or conditioning when a response associated with one stimulus is found to be elicited by similar stimuli. This is called *stimulus* generalization. Quantitative studies show that the response tendency aroused by a generalized, that is, similar, stimulus is greater when the test stimulus is more similar to the training stimulus. This functional relationship is termed a *gradient of generalization. Response* generalization is a tendency for similar responses to be strengthened when a particular response is learned. A gradient of generalization may be noted here as well as in stimulus generalization.

Generalized response tendencies, based on either stimulus or response generalization or both, are considered to develop in practice on any task. If a second task then involves similar elements, these generalized tendencies operate to facilitate its learning and performance. Similarity of tasks thus resembles identical elements as a basis for transfer except that generalized tendencies instead of identical tendencies are involved.

STIMULUS-RESPONSE RELATIONSHIPS. In our foregoing discussion of transfer based on identical elements or on generalization, positive transfer was assumed to result from similar or identical stimulus-response associations in the two tasks. Patterns of stimulus-response relationships between two tasks that tend to yield positive transfer include the following:

> Identical stimuli elicit identical responses.
> Similar stimuli elicit identical responses.
> Identical stimuli elicit similar responses.
> Similar stimuli elicit similar responses.

When stimulus-response associations are markedly different in the two tasks, identical or similar elements can lead to negative transfer effects. An especially potent source of interference occurs with reversal of these associations which demands that opposite responses be made when the second task is undertaken. With reversed associations encountered, identical elements may contribute strongly to negative transfer instead of positive. We may list two conditions contributing to negative transfer:

Identical stimuli elicit different or opposite responses.

Similar stimuli elicit different or opposite responses.

MEDIATION. Besides the overt behavior involved in a study of transfer, there may be covert symbolic behavior which serves as a mechanism contributing to transfer effects. This mediation of transfer might occur, for example, when practice on the first task leads subjects to formulate a rule which they then apply to the second activity when they encounter it. Such self-guidance would usually involve verbalization that would not be observable in task performance but which might be reported later by subjects or might be inferred from data taken under special conditions. Verbal mediation of transfer might sometimes be a mechanism that is not established until the second activity is begun. If a subject encounters a task demand for opposite responses, for example, he might say to himself, "The controls must now be moved in opposite directions from the way I practiced earlier." In this case we see that mediation is employed in an effort to reduce the negative transfer effect that normally accompanies reversal of response requirements.

Mediated generalization is another form in which mediation may be found in transfer studies. In setting up two paired associate tasks, for example, an experimenter might retain the same response words while changing the stimulus words to synonyms when drawing up the second lists. In its fundamental definition stimulus generalization is based on stimulus similarity with respect to some physical stimulus dimension. In the use of synonyms the nonphysical dimension of meaning would be involved and generalization would have to be mediated by the verbal habits which subjects would be assumed to have.

DESIGN OF TRANSFER EXPERIMENTS

As is the case with numerous areas of scientific study, transfer of training research has developed designs for experiments which provide a framework for planning specific studies. Murdock (1957) has presented an evaluative review of numerous designs used in transfer experiments. We shall consider a few variations of the designs which have been principally employed. In outlining the plan of any transfer study, it will usually be convenient to use Task A as a label for the task *from which* transfer effects are considered to arise, and Task B as the designation of the task *to which* transfer is accomplished. The fundamental investigation of transfer from Task A to

Task *B* involves the comparison of Task *B* performance in a group who had previously been trained on Task *A* with the performance on Task *B* in a group without the prior practice on Task *A*. The former group is the transfer group, or experimental group, whereas the latter is the control group.

Randomly Assigned Groups

Quite commonly subjects are assigned at random to an experimental and a control group in a study of the transfer from Task *A* to Task *B* in a basic design:

> Experimental: Task *A* then Task *B*
> Control: Activity *X* then Task *B*

In this paradigm we have used Activity *X* to represent anything that control group subjects might have been doing before engaging in, or learning, Task *B*. Such activity might be assigned by the experimenter, who selects a task for control subjects which is assumed to have no transfer effect to Task *B*. An alternative possibility is that nothing specific is required of control subjects before undertaking Task *B*.

The design represented in the foregoing paradigm should yield information about the empirical transfer effect from Task *A* to Task *B* when the second task performance of the two groups is compared. Both the direction and amount of transfer are represented in the Task *B* scores of the groups. The effect as measured may represent transfer of several sorts, general and specific, and it may be confounded with warm-up effect as well. In order to determine the transfer effects that are based specifically on relationships of Task *A* to Task *B*, a molecular analysis requiring more groups may be required. We shall see later how more extensive designs permit such analysis to help identify warm-up effects and general positive transfer effects like learning how to learn.

Only the transfer from Task *A* to Task *B* is represented in the schema we have examined. It may often be desired to determine transfer from Task *B* to Task *A* as well. We depart from the rule that Task *A* is the source and Task *B* is the recipient of transfer, and map out the following:

> Group I: Task *A* then Task *B*
> Group II: Task *B* then Task *A*

Still using only two randomly assigned groups of subjects we can now examine transfer effects bidirectionally, from Task *B* to Task *A* as well as from Task *A* to Task *B*. In the fundamental comparison to examine empirical transfer effects from Task A to Task B, we would use the performance of Group II on Task B, initially practiced, to provide control data. To find transfer from Task B to Task A we use Group I as a control, comparing its Task A performance with that of the transfer group, II, on Task A. In this bidirectional assessment of transfer effects, then, each randomly constituted group contributes control data from its first performance and experimental data from its second task. If differences are found between the two directions of transfer, these may permit us to draw some cautious inferences about the mechanisms of transfer. Whether differences are found or not, this design provides the same information we might get from the first design we listed, plus the dividend of a second assessment of transfer. This is accomplished at minimal extra cost by merely having subjects who begin with Task B go on to take practice on Task A. Any desired Activity X may be inserted in the plan of the study prior to first task practice for both groups.

Matched Groups

A more precise experiment may result if we employ matched experimental and control groups instead of setting up two groups by random assignment. Especially useful if the number of available subjects is small, matching is often based on data from some pretest. A common design is represented in the following schema:

Experimental: Pretest B'—Task A then Task B
Control: Pretest B'—Activity X then Task B

Of course, the two groups are not actually established until the pretest scores are available for use in matching.

THE MATCHING FACTOR. We have used the designation B' for the pretesting in the matched group design since this matching factor may often resemble Task B quite closely. Not infrequently, the pretest may actually consist of a few trials on Task B. If this task is not itself employed in pretesting, the matching factor should at least correlate with Task B performance or else it is of no value for matching the two groups. The whole purpose in matching is to equate the groups so that differences in their performance on Task B may be attributed to their prior activity, either Task A or Activity X. Although we have referred to pretesting as a part of the experimental procedure, it is also possible that the matching factor may not be a performance score which the experimenter obtains but may be something like IQs or aptitude scores that are available for the subjects who are to be used. The B' symbol is still appropriate for the paradigm since some correlation with Task B scores must exist if the use of the matching factor is to be justified.

AMOUNT OF PRETESTING. If the matching factor is to be a score on a few trials of Task B or something closely resembling it, the amount of such pretesting becomes an important characteristic in the experimental design. We would naturally want pretesting to be extensive enough to yield reliable scores. However, if very much learning of Task B takes place in the pretesting stage, the study becomes one which deals to a considerable degree with the effect of Task A on the retention of Task B rather than on its learning. With extensive training on Task B, or B', in the first part of the experiment, the design becomes identical with that for retroactive inhibition, discussed in Chapter 16. Ideally, an investigation of transfer from Task A to Task B would seek only a proactive effect, without any involvement of memory traces from prior practice on Task B. Since pretesting on Task B represents a compromise with this ideal, it should probably be kept to a minimum even when employed to obtain matched groups of subjects.

Second Task Varied

The transfer of training designs we have considered up to this point have involved comparison of performances on an identical task after some prior learning which differentiated between the groups. A contrasting way to explore mechanisms of transfer is to keep first task training the same for each group and to vary the second task, to which transfer occurs. This design is represented in the following paradigm:

Experimental Group I: Task A then Task B
Experimental Group II: Task A then Task B''

If we compare the Task B performance of Experimental Group I with the Task B'' performance of Experimental Group II, we might feel that we were measuring their differential profiting from transfer from Task A. The design does not warrant such a conclusion, however. Any difference in scores on Tasks B and B'' might simply be due to differences in difficulty between these two similar tasks. Another possibility is that Task B and B'' might differ in the transfer benefits they derive, not from Task A but from other prior experiences shared by both groups of subjects. To complete this design, then, we might add two control groups:

Control Group I: Activity X then Task B
Control Group II: Activity X then Task B''

Here we have used "Activity X" to designate any prior experience of the subjects which might affect their performance on Task B or B''. Such a factor would be assumed to be equivalent for randomly selected groups. If we now were to compare the differences between experimental groups with that between control groups, we would gain some idea of how Tasks B and B'' were affected by practice on Task A.

If we rearrange the four groups we now consider to be necessary to make this design workable, we can obtain the following pairs:

Experimental Group I: Task A then Task B
Control Group I: Activity X then Task B

Experimental Group II: Task A then Task B''
Control Group II: Activity X then Task B''

This alignment proves to be a double transfer experiment of the design which we examined first in this chapter. One part of the study would reveal the transfer from Task A to Task B and the other part the transfer from Task A to Task B''. It is in comparing these two parts, then, that we would find the answer to the question of whether Task B or B'' benefits more from prior practice on Task A.

We began with a design in which the second task was varied. Murdock (1957) has cited numerous studies (p. 315) involving this design. He has indicated also (p. 317) that the design is not valid without appropriate controls. We have seen that the addition of control groups changes the study into two transfer experiments with the initial activity varied, the second task identical in each case. The design which we found to be necessary in such a study emphasizes the fact that psychological laws are to be found by varying antecedent conditions and measuring behavioral consequences.

Molecular Analysis of Transfer

We have considered a number of designs for transfer of training experiments. In the elementary form in which we reviewed them, most of them featured a single comparison; a single difference between groups was sought which might be attributed to differential prior treatment. The full development of the final design we discussed yielded two possible differences, with these differences then to be compared. This sort of elaboration of the basic transfer design is what is needed for a full elucidation of transfer mechanisms. Extensions of the basic design often involve several variations of Task A or Task B in the same study, with numerous groups of subjects being run.

One reason why a single molar comparison of data tells us little about transfer is that there may be many factors that contribute to an empirical transfer effect between Task A and Task B. Transfer based on specific perceptual-motor habits may be confounded with transfer stemming from general work methods and with warm-up effects. The molecular analysis to separate these different sources of influence involves running several groups of subjects under different conditions. For example, to separate warm-up effect from positive transfer based on identical elements or on stimulus generalization, we might vary the interval between Task A and Task B in several different groups so that the warm-up effect from Task A would have a chance to dissipate over the longer intervals. The residual benefits appearing in Task B, with warm-up assumed to have dissipated, might be attributed to learned elements which were more persistent over time.

Where several different kinds of habit are presumed to underlie a transfer effect, several different variations of Task A may be used to delineate the contribution of several factors. Another approach to this problem is to vary the amount of training given to different groups on Task A. This would prove useful when different Task A habits were acquired at different rates or reached asymptotic strengths after different amounts of practice. A different way of studying transfer in detail is to employ several different measures of Task B performance. These may provide different bits of information about the transfer process.

MEASUREMENT OF TRANSFER EFFECTS

In treating the data obtained in a transfer of training experiment, as in most research, we have a dual problem—to compute statistics which describe the transfer that occurred and to test appropriate differences for statistical significance. Although descriptive statistics generally pose no great difficulty, we shall see that the description of transfer involves multiple comparisons which must be made properly. A further goal of the data analysis is sometimes to describe the transfer effects in relative terms so that different experiments may be compared without reference to specific units of performance measurement.

Two General Principles

Before we examine several ways of measuring and describing transfer effects we should note two general rules which apply to the treatment of transfer data. First, each different performance measure taken on Task B may yield information on the transfer process and therefore each measure may warrant separate analysis. For example, in a paired associate learning study we may obtain the number of responses correct on each trial and the number of intrusion errors as well. Data analysis may be performed on each of these indices of Task B performance, comparing the experimental and control conditions. It is entirely possible that two such measures may not agree perfectly in the picture of transfer effects which they present. There may also, of course, be close agreement. Where there are divergent indications of the transfer that has occurred, these may help to delineate the process itself by suggesting some of its mechanisms.

A second principle about transfer measurement is that the experimental and control groups should often be compared at more than one point on their Task B performance curves. As practice continues on Task B, an initial transfer effect may change or disappear. Since almost all performance curves ultimately approach an asymptote, it is particularly likely that transfer effects will finally approach zero magnitude as experimental and control subjects carry on their practice of Task B. This means that our description of any transfer effect will often involve stating its initial magnitude and direction and telling how long it persisted into the repeated trials of Task B. Information about the persistence of a transfer effect is an important reason for providing several trials of Task B practice.

Combining these two rules for the description of transfer effects we may say that a separate index for the sign and magnitude of a transfer effect may be separately computed for each performance measure at each stage of practice on Task B.

Comparison with Control Groups

Most of the transfer designs that we have considered require us to compare an experimental group's performance on Task B, following practice on Task A, with that of a control group whose initial performance on Task B was not preceded by Task A. This investigates transfer from Task A to Task B in comparison to performing on Task B with no special prior training. Another way to assess the transfer effects accruing from Task A is to compare them with the results obtained in a control group in which equal time is devoted to prior practice on Task B itself. We shall examine each way of assessing transfer, using illustrative data.

COMPARISON WITH INITIAL CONTROL PERFORMANCE. A study was carried out by Andreas, Green, and Spragg (1954a) to determine the transfer effects between a compensatory and a following tracking task. (These two types of tracking task are described in Chapter 14, p. 404.) We shall examine the data from two of the groups to see how transfer between the tasks in each direction was examined. Group III was given 8 trials on the following tracking task and then 8 trials on the compensatory tracking task. Group IV performed first on compensatory and then on following tracking, also changing after Trial 8. The mean and SD of the time on target scores for each group over their 16 trials are given in Table 17.1.

TABLE 17.1

Mean Time on Target and Standard Deviation in Milliminutes for Groups III and IV on Each of the Sixteen One-Minute Trials. $N = 23$ in Each Group (After Andreas, Green, and Spragg, 1954a)

Trial	Group III		Group IV	
	Mean	SD	Mean	SD
1	240	142	542	188
2	336	140	616	183
3	442	136	621	167
4	372	148	645	178
5	492	190	683	175
6	482	156	693	171
7	545	163	727	170
8	548	183	752	170
Change in Task				
9	758	143	294	170
10	812	86	355	166
11	837	107	389	154
12	831	122	412	191
13	858	94	421	196
14	836	116	475	139
15	878	113	509	187
16	852	97	505	199

These two groups from the investigation comprise a transfer design of the type—Task A then Task B, Task B then Task A. This permits us to determine separately the transfer effects from each task to the other. To see if Group III performed better on the compensatory tracking as a result of prior practice on following tracking, we may compare scores made by this group on Trials 9 to 16 with scores made by Group IV on Trials 1 to 8 which involved initial performance on the same task. The research report indicates that a *t* test of the grand means for these blocks of trials indicated Group III to have performed significantly better than did Group IV in the control condition. This indicated positive transfer from the following tracking task to the compensatory task in this experiment. If there were any doubt about the persistence of this transfer effect, a trial-by-trial comparison could be performed on these data. However, inspection of the data shows that the difference between groups continued in this study over all 8 trials.

When the transfer data from Group IV, Trials 9 to 16, were compared with the initial control data of Group III, Trials 1 to 8, it was found that no facilitation on the following tracking task had resulted from compensatory tracking practice. This failure of the intertask facilitation to be reciprocal may be ascribed to similarities and differences between the two tasks. It would require further experimentation to pinpoint reasons for the unidirectional nature of the transfer effect that was noted.

COMPARISON WITH EXTENDED CONTROL PERFORMANCE. The data of Table 17.1 are plotted as empirical points in the open and closed circles of Figure 17.1. To the empirical data we have added hypothetical mean scores which might have been obtained by a Group IV*e* (*e* for extended practice) which continued to perform on the compensatory tracking task for the entire 16 trials of the experiment. The triangular points represent the assumed empirical data of this hypothetical Group IV*e* for Trials 9 to 16. (For Trials 1 to 8 we may assume that these subjects performed identically with those of Group IV.) In this extended performance curve, the triangular points show us the level of performance found, hypothetically, for compensatory tracking beyond 8 trials. This empirical extension of the performance curve, had it been obtained in the study, would have permitted a further statement to be made about the transfer effect from following tracking which Group III exhibited. Examination of Figure 17.1 tells us that the transfer performance of Group III on Trials 9 to 16 would not be found significantly below that of Group IV*e* on those trials. This means that the positive benefits from practice on the following tracking task were complete, equivalent to a similar amount of practice on the compensatory task itself. If the actual transfer performance curve of Group III were somewhat lower, statistical analysis might have revealed a transfer effect that was significantly positive but not complete.

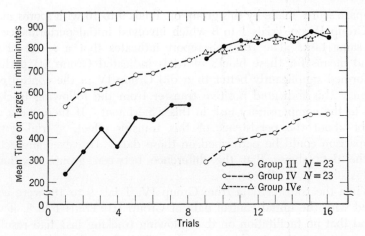

Fig. 17.1. Performance curves in a study of transfer of training effects between two tracking tasks. Group III performed on a following tracking task for Trials 1 to 8 and on a compensatory tracking task for Trials 9 to 16. Group IV experienced the two tasks in the opposite sequence. The triangular points are plotted to represent the hypothetical performance on Trials 9 to 16 of a Group IVe which is assumed to have performed on the same compensatory tracking task for all 16 trials. This extended performance curve provides a second basis for assessing the transfer effect displayed in the mean scores of Group III. (After Andreas, Green, and Spragg, 1954a.)

This would be our conclusion if the data from Group III, Trials 9 to 16 were significantly higher than those of Group IV, Trials 1 to 8 and significantly lower than the data for Group IVe, Trials 9 to 16.

Comparison with Extrapolated Curves

A considerable number of extra subjects are required in order to add extended practice control groups to an experimental design in which initial control data are provided by practice on the first task given to each group. The treatment of the data in a transfer of training experiment by Green (1955) illustrates another way of estimating how complete the degree of positive transfer may be. Subjects performed a following tracking task, switching from a large target to a small one, or vice versa, after 16 trials. Time on target scores in initial practice were markedly different for the different sizes of target used. Furthermore, transfer from either a large to a small target, or from a small to a large target, was very strong and positive.

The next problem in assessing the transfer was to determine if it was complete, that is, equivalent to the same amount of prior practice on the particular target size itself. Such an estimate was made by Green (1955) by fitting smooth curves to the initial performance data for each size of target. By extrapolating these fitted curves beyond the 16 trials of initial practice, he obtained a set of standards which enabled him to judge that the positive transfer effects were in all cases essentially complete. This was shown by the fact that points representing mean scores on each transfer task fell very close to the extrapolated curves.

Conversion to Per Cent Estimates

We have seen that transfer group scores on Task *B* may be compared with initial control group scores on the same task or with extended control performance measured empirically or obtained by curve-fitting and extrapolation. One difficulty with any such direct attempts at assessing the amount of transfer is that their numerical expression will reflect the units of measurement employed in scoring performance. In trying to compare the results of one transfer study with another, raw score expression may render meaningful comparison impossible if the studies involved different performance measures. Gagné, Foster, and Crowley (1948) have pointed out the desirability of expressing amount of transfer as a per cent, thus facilitating comparisons between different studies. The decision to express transfer as a per cent still permits considerable leeway, represented in the question, "Per cent of what?" After reviewing numerous studies of transfer of training, these authors present several alternative formulas for expressing amount of transfer as a per cent. The various limitations which they point out for each formula indicate that we need to consider, at the design stage of any transfer experiment, what way of expressing amount of transfer seems desirable. Then we can be sure to utilize the necessary groups, conditions, and measures. After discussing some of these formulas, Murdock (1957) has offered another way of computing per cent transfer. We shall examine some of these different computational guides without attempting to review the extensive discussion found in these two articles. We need to recall that a measurement of the amount of transfer may be taken for each performance measure obtained at each stage of practice. The per cent formulas we examine here are similarly applicable at more than one point in many experiments.

PER CENT DIFFERENCE FROM CONTROL GROUP. One way to express the amount of transfer is as a per cent of the accomplishment of the control group which performed the task without prior special training. We take the mean scores on Task *B* made by the experimental group,

E, and the control group, C, and express the difference between these two means as a per cent of the mean score made by the control group, C, at a similar point in Task B practice. The computational formula is as follows, assuming a score that increases with practice:

$$\text{Per Cent Transfer} = \frac{E - C}{C} \times 100 \qquad \text{Formula 17.1}$$

This arrangement of the formula is for scores like number of words correct or time on target—measures that increase as proficiency is gained. For behavior measures like errors or time to complete a task —scores that decrease as skill increases—the numerator is reversed: $C - E$.

Applying this formula to the first trial scores on Task B, compensatory tracking, taken from Table 17.1, we have $E = 758$ milliminutes and $C = 542$ milliminutes, yielding a transfer value of 40 per cent. This estimate of the initial transfer effect from the following to the compensatory tracking tasks used in the study was based on the Trial 9 mean score of Group III and the Trial 1 mean score of Group IV. If we use scores from Group III, Trial 16, and Group IV, Trial 8, we can compute the per cent transfer existing on the eighth trial of the compensatory task. These means, 852, and 752 milliminutes, respectively, indicate a transfer effect of 13 per cent, in agreement with the general principle that a transfer effect diminishes in its contribution to performance as Task B practice continues.

PER CENT GAIN TOWARD PERFECT SCORE. In assessing the positive transfer shown by Group III in the scores of Table 17.1, it may be convenient to consider the transfer effect as representing a boost toward perfect performance of the compensatory tracking task. We may express this gain as a per cent of the difference between the control group score and a perfect score by using the following formula:

$$\text{Per Cent Transfer} = \frac{E - C}{T - C} \times 100 \qquad \text{Formula 17.2}$$

where E and C are experimental and control means, as before, and T is the total possible score. For measures which decrease as skill is gained, both numerator and denominator would be reversed to $C - E$ and $C - T$, respectively.

To apply this formula to the description of the positive transfer from the following tracking task to the compensatory tracking task in the study by Andreas, Green, and Spragg (1954a), we would use $T = 1000$. A value of 1000 milliminutes represents a perfect time on target score for a 1-min tracking trial. For the first transfer trial $E = 758$

milliminutes made by Group III and $C = 542$ milliminutes, the mean score for first trial control performance by Group IV. Our computations give us

$$\frac{758 - 542}{1000 - 542} \times 100 = \frac{216}{4.58} = 47 \quad \text{per cent transfer}$$

On the eighth trial we calculate per cent transfer using $E = 852$ and $C = 752$ with T still, of course, equal to 1000 milliminutes. The formula we are now using gives us a value of 40 per cent transfer at this stage of Task B practice.

PER CENT OF DIRECT PRACTICE INCREMENT. Performance of many tasks will benefit maximally from prior *direct* practice on the task as compared with any positive transfer from an equal amount of practice on *another* task. We may take the increment in scores made through direct practice as a working estimate of 100 per cent transfer. An increment in mean score attributable to practice on a different task may then be compared with it to determine a per cent transfer value. The formula for this method of calculating amount of transfer is as follows:

$$\text{Per Cent Transfer} = \frac{E - C_i}{C_e - C_i} \times 100 \qquad \text{Formula 17.3}$$

where E is the experimental group score on a particular transfer trial, C_i is the mean score at the initial level of control group practice, and C_e is the mean score of a control group given extended direct prior practice on the task which is equivalent in amount to the practice on Task A in the transfer group.

In the experiment we are using illustratively, C_e would be a mean score for a hypothetical Group IVe on Trial 9 of practice on the compensatory tracking task alone. This assumes we are going to compute per cent transfer on Trial 9 of Group III, the initial transfer effect. Table 17.1 gives us $E = 758$ and $C_i = 542$, the mean score for Group IV at the initial trial of practice on the compensatory tracking task. We may assume $C_e = 765$ for illustrative purposes in the absence of an empirical value. The computation is

$$\frac{758 - 542}{765 - 542} \times 100 = \frac{216}{2.23} = 97 \quad \text{per cent transfer}$$

We would take the trouble to compute this per cent transfer only if the difference between mean scores E and C_e were shown to be statistically significant by some test like a t ratio. If these means did not differ significantly we could conclude that they differ only by chance or sampling error. In that case, the hypothesis would be tenable that 100 per cent transfer had occurred, that practice on Task *A* was equivalent to direct practice on Task *B*. In our earlier inspection of Figure 17.1 we assumed that the mean scores on Trials 9 to 16 did not differ significantly for Group III and the hypothetical Group IV*e*, so we spoke of transfer as complete.

A FORMULA FOR LIMITED, SYMMETRICAL PER CENT TRANSFER. In testing some of the formulas for per cent transfer with hypothetical data, Murdock (1957) found that some of them could yield values in excess of 100 per cent. In fact, when a score of zero had been recorded for either the transfer group or the control group, a value of infinity could be obtained as the index of amount of transfer. It would seem that a limit of 100% transfer in both positive and negative directions would have rational justification. In addition, the positive and negative per cent scales should be symmetrical around the zero point where such symmetry appears in the raw data. To meet these criteria of 100 per cent limits and symmetry, Murdock (1957) has devised the following computational formula:

$$\text{Per Cent Transfer} = \frac{E - C}{E + C} \times 100 \qquad \text{Formula 17.4}$$

where *E* and *C* represent, as before, the mean scores of the experimental and control group for a particular performance measure at a certain stage of practice on Task *B*. Applying this formula to the first trial on compensatory tracking in our illustrative experiment, we compute a value of

$$\frac{758 - 542}{758 + 542} \times 100 = \frac{216}{13.00} = 17 \quad \text{per cent transfer}$$

If we were dealing with a score such as number of errors, this formula would require that the numerator be reversed to $C - E$. Although it meets desirable criteria, this formula can also yield estimates of transfer which seem not to reflect the experimental findings with adequate sensitivity. We find, for example, that when the control group reaches a proficiency where their error score is zero, any number of errors made by the experimental group yields a transfer estimate of -100 per cent. This value is obtained even when this transfer group is making just a single error.

USING TRANSFER FORMULAS. It should not surprise us that different formulas yield different estimates of amount of transfer. Each formula is, in conjunction with experimental procedures, an operational definition of the term "transfer effect." The different computational operations lead to different transfer effects by definition, even when the raw data are the same.

In some instances the computed per cent transfer is quite sensitive to the values that can occur in the raw scores. It is probably of doubtful worth to compute the per cent transfer in two studies by carefully using the same formula in each case but applying it to different raw scores whose limiting values and functional relationships in the acquisition of proficiency may be quite divergent. Perhaps the various formulas are most useful in making us think about what we mean by transfer and in forcing us to choose behavior measures that will best serve our search for the quantitative description of transfer effects.

ILLUSTRATIVE TRANSFER STUDIES

To complete our discussion of transfer of training research we shall review certain aspects of selected reports of experiments. Our survey will include positive, negative, and zero transfer effects. It will reveal some of the areas of emphasis which have developed in the investigation of transfer.

Positive Effects

A survey of the literature on transfer of training would probably reveal that positive transfer effects have been more frequently predicted and found in experiments than have negative effects. Two possible reasons for this might be suggested. First, there are more different conditions or factors that can lead to a positive effect. Second, principles of positive transfer seemed eminently worth seeking because of their great potential value in education and in training applications.

TRANSFER FROM PART OF TASK TO WHOLE TASK. Positive transfer effects are usually found when performance of some complex task is preceded by practice on a part of that task. Investigations of this type have potential practical application to many training situations. If whole task training required the tying up of valuable production machines in industry, for example, the positive transfer effect from part task training on a training device might represent a great economy. Positive transfer effects of this sort may thus be beneficial even if they are not complete, that is, not equivalent to the same amount of whole task training.

Gagné and Foster (1949) studied part-whole transfer in an experiment where Task *B* required the operation of certain switches when one of four panel lights flashed on, providing a reaction time measure of performance. The panel lights were arranged in two pairs, an upper and a lower pair each having a red and a green light. The preliminary training, on part of the complete task, required practicing the proper switch-pressing response to each of two lights. For example, a subject might practice the proper response to make when either the upper green or the lower green light flashed on. During practice of the two reactions to these two stimuli, the switches corresponding to the other two stimuli were kept covered. In all the experimental groups part training consisted of practicing two reactions to two stimuli out of the four which would be involved in the whole task later. Different groups were given either 10, 30, or 50 trials of part training before performing on the whole task for 60 trials. A control group was given no part task training prior to performance on the whole task.

The experimenters noted the number of errors made during performance, and this was informative in their analysis of the transfer that took place from part training to whole task performance. We shall limit this brief review, however, to a consideration of the reaction time measure. We can immediately dismiss the experimental group which had just 10 trials of part practice. Its performance on the final task did not differ significantly in *RT* from that of the control group. When the groups given 30 or 50 trials of part training were switched to the whole task, they performed significantly better than the control group. Their mean scores indicated significantly speedier reactions, with superiority over the control group persisting into the fourth block of 10 trials.

Having seen a positive transfer effect when performance after 30 or 50 trials of part training was compared with the control group who began their whole-task performance from scratch, we may ask whether the part training was as effective as an equal amount of whole training would have been. The data of this study showed that transfer was not complete, in this sense. After 30 preliminary trials of part training, subjects began the whole task with scores representing 30 per cent of ultimate proficiency. In comparison, the control group was 46 per cent along toward complete mastery of the task after 30 trials of whole task training. For the group given 50 trials of preliminary training, positive transfer took them 54 per cent of the way toward the *RT* limit for the task. An equivalent amount of whole-task practice, however, gave the control group an 85 per cent advance toward the ultimate level of attainment. The fact that part-task practice yielded transfer that was positive but not complete in this study is a finding that may be obtained in many such experiments. Factors like task complexity, however, may occasionally lead to results that are quite divergent from these, including complete transfer in which practicing part of a task is just as efficient as early attempts to perform the entire task. We have seen, too, that the amount of part training will be a likely determinant of the amount of positive transfer that is observed.

STIMULUS PREDIFFERENTIATION. In performing a perceptual-motor task which has never been encountered before, subjects have to learn something about the stimuli, about the motor responses, and about how these two sets of elements must be associated. A number of studies have sought to examine the facilitation of such performance which may occur when subjects are given a prior opportunity to discriminate among the stimuli through working with them in a preliminary task. This *stimulus predifferentiation,* also termed *acquired distinctiveness of cues,* is supposed to counteract the confusion that would result from stimulus generalization if stimuli were initially encountered at the same time that responses were being learned in the final task.

A commonly used approach to stimulus predifferentiation is to have experimental subjects engage in paired associate learning in a preliminary task which involves the same stimuli as will be found later in the perceptual-motor task. In this final task each stimulus requires a discrete motor response, as we shall see, whereas in the preliminary task a verbal label or symbol must be associated with each cue. To control for the introduction of warm-up effects by this paired associate learning, control groups are provided which also associate symbolic responses with cues, but with cues which are different from those of the final test task.

A design such as we have outlined was used by Cantor (1955) to study how the expected positive transfer to the final task would be affected by different amounts of pretraining. The final task was the Star Discrimeter, on which a subject had to move a vertical wobble stick into one of six radiating channels in a horizontal panel. The cue indicating which channel was correct on any trial was a spot of colored light presented by means of a stimulus unit. A different hue in the red-orange-yellow range was used as the stimulus corresponding to each of the six response channels. Performance on this perceptual-motor task was subject-paced in that a new stimulus hue appeared only when the subject had moved the stick into the correct channel. The sequence of colors and of required responses was completely random. Performance scores were the number of correct responses and the number of errors made on each 20-sec trial.

Relevant pretraining involved the same six hues as the final task. Three groups of subjects had to practice, by the anticipation method, naming a letter of the alphabet as each hue was presented. Different groups received 2, 4, or 12 blocks of stimulus presentation, thus varying the amount of predifferentiation, with greater positive transfer expected to follow from greater amounts of relevant pretraining.

Irrelevant pretraining, needed to control for possible warm-up effects, also consisted of color-letter associations. For these three groups, however, the 2, 4, or 12 blocks of stimulus presentation involved blue-green hues. Learning to differentiate among these would presumably have no transfer value for the Star Discrimeter task which used the red-yellow series of six hues for all groups of subjects. A control group performed on the task without any preliminary training.

The results of the experiment showed evidence of positive transfer from relevant pretraining and no evidence of a warm-up effect due to irrelevant pretraining. The irrelevant pretraining groups did not differ from the control group, supporting the latter conclusion, but the relevant pretraining groups showed greater proficiency on the Star Discrimeter than did the irrelevant pretraining groups. It was not found, however, that the *amount* of relevant pretraining was related to final task performance.

BILATERAL TRANSFER. A special kind of positive transfer effect occurs when a task is first practiced with one hand and then performed with the other. This *bilateral transfer* or *cross education,* as it has been termed, has often been demonstrated in psychology laboratories by means of a mirror drawing task. A subject is required to look in a mirror for visual guidance as he traces a maze or star pattern, attempting to stay within printed lines. A small adjustable screen is arranged so as to prevent the use of direct vision. After one or more trials with one hand, the subject is required to perform the task with the other hand. Performance measures include time required to trace the pattern and the number of errors made, an error being counted whenever the subject's pencil line goes outside the guide lines.

Data from a study by Allen (1948) illustrate the usual positive bilateral transfer that is found in mirror drawing. One experimental group of subjects traced a maze pathway once with the left hand, then practiced with the right hand until a criterion of time less than a minute with not more than one error was reached. A second trial with the left hand then provided data for use in assessing bilateral transfer. Control data came from the second trial of a group given two successive trials with the left hand. First-trial performance showed the groups to be equal in skill, with experimental and control time scores of 74.6 and 72.9 sec, respectively. On the second trial with the left hand, the experimental group took 43.2 sec and the control group took 63.2 sec. This statistically significant difference demonstrates a positive transfer effect from the training with the right hand to the final test with the left hand. An analysis of errors gave similar evidence of positive transfer.

Numerous explanations have been offered for the positive bilateral transfer effects found in mirror drawing. One of these emphasizes the body symmetry of nerve and muscle structures and suggests that learning involving one hand actually activates a similar process of skill acquisition for the other hand, reduced in amount. A different explanation stresses the identical perceptual elements involved in performance with either hand; it is suggested that these form the basis for the positive transfer, possibly through learning how to react to certain visual percepts. Still another basis for the transfer might be learning to ignore visual cues to some extent, leaning heavily on kinesthetic guidance of hand movement over the pattern which has become familiar in performing with the first hand. This suggests the desirability of testing for bilateral transfer with a pattern different from that used in practice with the other hand. Additional control data would have to be obtained from a group which changed patterns but did not change hands. Such a study would be seeking the extent to which bilateral transfer involves skill or proficiency, and how much of it is due to specific habits whose exercise involves the use of a particular test pattern.

Negative Effects

Two tasks may be related in such a way that practice on one of them may prove detrimental to performance of the second one. Such negative transfer has not been studied as frequently as have positive effects. Among the reasons for paying greater attention to positive transfer may be the greater diversity of factors giving rise to it and its greater potential application in training situations. Negative transfer, arising from a somewhat more special set of conditions, provides a useful way of making a laboratory analysis of the transfer of training process.

It has been said that negative transfer arises when new responses to old stimuli have to be learned. If Task A requires learning a certain set of responses to a set of stimuli and Task B involves making a *different* set of responses to those *same* stimuli, the acquisition of proficiency at Task B will be retarded as a result of negative transfer in comparison with a control condition, the learning of Task B without prior practice on Task A. The source of the negative transfer effect is considered to be response competition. The experimental subjects tend to make the old Task A responses to the familiar stimuli they encounter as Task B is undertaken. These response tendencies interfere with the new response tendencies, slowing down the rate at which they acquire associative strength or habit strength linking them to the stimuli.

The paradigm for the experimental conditions in the type of transfer study we are discussing is $S_1-R_1 \ldots S_1-R_2$, where S_1 appears in both the first and second task to indicate that stimuli are kept the same for both tasks. The change from R_1 to R_2 indicates that a new set of responses is required when subjects switch from Task A to Task B.

Instead of introducing a new set of responses in establishing Task B, transfer experiments in perceptual-motor behavior have often required that the same responses made in Task A be retained in Task B, *but paired with different stimuli*. In this type of study, then, both stimuli and responses are carried over from Task A to Task B, but the stimulus-response pairings are realigned. In many experiments the new response required to be made to a particular stimulus is the opposite of the old one. For example, if the leftward drift of an indicator needle required a subject to turn a crank clockwise in Task A, the requirement in Task B would be for counterclockwise rotation of the crank in response to the same stimulus. Correspondingly, a rightward movement of the display indicator would demand clockwise cranking in Task B when it had called for counterclockwise cranking in Task A. Such a reversal of display-control relationships can be a potent source of negative transfer effect. In the case of a discriminative motor task where several discrete responses each had to be made to a specific stimulus, we might expect a negative transfer effect to arise from a re-pairing of stimuli and responses. Here Task B would call for a different response to each of the familiar stimuli, although this new response need not be opposite in any sense to the one originally elicited by that particular stimulus. If we use the subscript, R, to stand for either reversed or realigned responses we can write a paradigm for this relationship of Tasks A and B as follows: $S_1-R_1 \ldots S_1-R_R$.

Porter and Duncan (1953) studied transfer in a verbal learning situation using an experimental design which included both of the paradigms we have discussed. Their aim was to determine whether new responses or realigned responses would lead to more negative transfer when the same stimuli were carried over from Task *A* to Task *B*. Each task consisted of learning, by the anticipation method, a paired associate list composed of 12 pairs of two-syllable adjectives. For one group of 20 subjects Task *B* involved a new set of response adjectives but the same stimulus adjectives as in Task *A*. For another group of 20 subjects, both the stimulus and response items were identical in both tasks, but they were re-paired so that each stimulus was now followed by a different response adjective. Counterbalancing was used within groups so that either set of stimulus-response pairs was Task *A* for half the subjects and Task *B* for the others.

It was found that providing a completely new set of responses for Task *B* did not lead to negative transfer. It was only in the group given the realignment of the same responses that a negative transfer effect was observed. The performance of this group on Task *B* was characterized by a large number of intrusions, defined as responding to a stimulus with the response which had been associated with it in Task *A*. The tendency to make the old response in the new task was abundantly evident in this condition, but almost absent in the other condition.

Net Zero Effects

Occasionally a transfer of training experiment will result in no significant difference between experimental and control data for a particular measure of performance. This may be taken to indicate that a net transfer effect of zero magnitude is a tenable hypothesis as the two tasks were administered in the investigation. Such a zero effect may be given two possible interpretations. One is that there is simply no transfer between the two tasks as practiced by the subjects. The other interpretation is that both positive and negative transfer effects were present in such magnitudes as to cancel each other out in the experimental group's performance. Although it is seemingly more complex, this possibility may deserve careful consideration wherever the two tasks have elements in common which could yield both positive and negative effects. Other data from the investigation will often support this hypothesis.

AMOUNT OF PRACTICE. Whenever one task has both positive and negative transfer potential with respect to another task, a particular amount of training may result in a net transfer effect of zero magnitude. By giving different groups of subjects different amounts of practice on Task *A*, we may upset the balance between positive and negative contributions to transfer. Either a positive or a negative effect may be observed to follow a certain amount of training. This would then support the interpretation that the zero order effect had resulted from cancellation of positive and negative factors acquired in a particular amount of training.

By varying the amount of Task A practice over a considerable range and measuring transfer to Task B in the different experimental groups, we can learn something about how the positive and negative factors are acquired as Task A training proceeds. This approach to the analysis of transfer is illustrated in part of an experiment by Andreas, Green, and Spragg (1954b). Five different groups of subjects were given 1, 2, 4, 8, or 17 trials in practicing a following tracking task in which a "natural" display-control relationship existed between the directions of motion of the target follower and the directions of crank rotation causing its motion. After these differing amounts of experience with this display-control arrangement as Task A, subjects were required to perform Task B which required them to operate the same tracking apparatus with the directional relationships of crank rotation to target follower motion now reversed. Since Task B required that an opposite response be made to a given stimulus—any particular misalignment of target and follower—the task relationships fitted the paradigm for developing a negative transfer effect. Control data were provided by subjects who performed initially on the reversed display-control relationships of Task B.

When the first one-minute trial of Task B was examined for transfer effects in the different training groups, the results portrayed in Figure 17.2 were found. With the control group performance level representing a zero transfer effect, we see that small or great amounts of practice on Task A led to a negative transfer effect, whereas moderate amounts of practice yielded positive transfer effects. A net transfer effect of about zero magnitude is shown for the group given 2 previous trials on Task A. The functional relationship between first-trial performance on Task B and the amount of prior practice on Task A is thus seen to be curvilinear. It begins below the baseline performance of the control group, then crosses this baseline to rise to a significant positive transfer effect, and finally dips down to a significant negative effect. Transfer from Task A to Task B is either positive, negative, or zero, depending on the amount of Task A training.

Since the task relationships corresponded to the paradigm for negative transfer effects, we can ascribe the poor performance on Task B after 1 or 17 trials on Task A to interference of old response tendencies with the reversed responses required in the second task. Our problem is to indicate how 4 or 8 trials on Task A could lead to

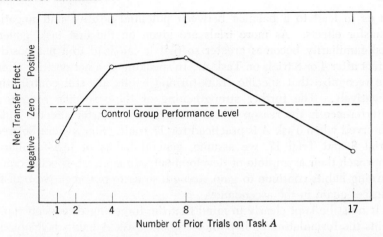

Fig. 17.2. Net transfer effect on Task *B*, tracking with one display-control relationship, as a function of the number of prior trials on Task *A*, tracking with the opposite display-control relationship. The plotted points represent first-trial performance levels of five different groups on Task *B*. (After Andreas, Green, and Spragg, 1954*b*.)

superior performance on Task *B* despite the reversal of display-control relationships. Clearly there are sources of positive transfer effects which must be postulated to exist for Tasks *A* and *B*. General task-familiarity was considered by the investigators to be a class of factors that could provide positive transfer potential. Familiarity with the target courses used in both tasks might be one such factor of a beneficial sort.

Having noted possibilities for both positive and negative transfer from Task *A* to Task *B*, we must now explain why one effect took place in some groups, with the effect of opposite sign occurring in others. We must also account for the occurrence of the net transfer effect of zero magnitude. Since Figure 17.2 represents a functional relationship between transfer effects and amount of Task *A* training, we center our attention on this variable. During Task *A* practice we assume that learning is taking place. The further assumption that different aspects of the task or different sorts of habit are being learned at different rates is the key to our explanation. During the first trial of Task *A* we assume, as the transfer data demand, that the specific direction-of-cranking habits are acquired to a greater degree than are the general task-familiarity habits. More potential for negative than for positive transfer is thus assumed. During 2 trials of Task *A* practice, we must assume, habits of the two sorts are acquired so as to lead to a balance between potential positive and negative transfer effects. As more trials are given on the first task, general task-familiarity becomes greater so that it can lead to a net positive effect after 4 or 8 trials on Task A. In speaking of a net positive effect, we recognize that specific crank-turning habits are still contributing negatively. The further strengthening of these specific sources of interference is the reason that a net negative transfer effect is again observed when Task A is practiced for 17 trials. Somewhere between Trial 8 and Trial 17, we assume, general habits of task-familiarity approach their asymptote of development. In contrast, specific crank-turning habits continue to gain strength so as to put negative transfer sources again in the ascendancy.

It must be kept clearly in mind that the foregoing discussion represents the formulating of hypotheses about Task A habit development that are actually inferences from the transfer of training data. The hypotheses about the growth of two classes of habit could be tested by providing different kinds of Task A experience for different groups of subjects. Instead of being given Task A to practice in its entirety, some groups could devote time merely to turning the control cranks and learning how their rotation related to target follower motion. This kind of training would strengthen the specific habits which we feel lead to negative transfer. Special training to augment positive transfer might take the form of having subjects familiarize themselves with the irregular target courses without actually operating the controls. By using a considerable number of groups given different combinations of special and regular training on Task A, we might use the transfer data from Task B to elucidate the different habit acquisitions involved in Task A practice.

Simultaneous Positive and Negative Effects

We have discussed how the study of transfer of training may be refined by using several experimental groups, each given different amounts of training on Task A. Another way of refining our analysis of transfer effects is to use more than one measure of performance. This provides the possibility that these different indices of proficiency will yield different sorts of information about the transfer processes between the two tasks being studied. Our choice of different measures to be used may often include a molar measure of over-all performance and one or more molecular indices which may show how specific associations or habits are contributing to, or opposing, the general effect.

In many instances two such measures as we are discussing might agree in showing, for example, positive transfer effects from Task A to Task B. It is also possible that a general index of proficiency might reveal a positive effect and a specific index might show a negative transfer effect. This possibility is illustrated in data presented by Lewis and Shephard (1950). These investigators were primarily interested in the associative interference effects appearing during relearning of a complex perceptual-motor task. Their experimental designs followed the paradigm for retroactive inhibition, OL-IL-RL.* Since we are presently concerned with proactive transfer effects we need examine only a part of their data, considering their OL task to be Task A and their IL task to be Task B.

These investigators used the Modified Mashburn Apparatus to provide both tasks in getting the data we shall cite. This apparatus requires a subject to use an airplane-type stick and rudder pedals to match a set of three green lights to a pattern of three red lights which appear on a display panel. The red and green lights are arranged correspondingly in two horizontal rows and one vertical row of each color. For each problem to be solved one red light in each row is illuminated, to be matched by the subject's illuminating the corresponding green lights. He does this by moving the controls until the required green light in each row lights up. The apparatus then presents the next set of red lights to be matched. A typically used score for general proficiency is the number of matches, green lights matched to the red ones, made during a 2-min trial.

In one experiment the standard display-control directional relationships were used in Task A. Under this arrangement moving the stick left or pushing the left rudder pedal would successively illuminate the green lights to the left of center in the top or bottom horizontal row, respectively. Opposite control movements would light up the green lights on the right side. Pushing the stick forward would successively illuminate green lights below the center one in the vertical row. Pulling back on the stick would operate the green lights above the center one, in a discrete sequence that corresponded to the stick position. Subjects practiced this Task A for 50 trials. Besides the number of matches on each 2-min trial, a count was made of the number of errors. An error occurred whenever an initial movement, upon receiving a new problem pattern of red lights, was in the wrong direction. As each new problem flashed on the panel a subject might

* OL = original learning of a task, IL = interpolated learning of a different task, and RL = relearning of the original task. This retroactive inhibition paradigm is discussed in Chapter 16.

make up to three initial direction-of-movement errors, one for each axis of stick movement and one for the rudder pedal operation.

After their training on Task A as described, subjects were given Task B which was similarly performed on the same apparatus with *reversed* display-control directional relationships. The successive illumination of the green lights in any row now required a movement of the same control as before but in an opposite direction. For example, the lights on the left of the lower row now were operated by pushing on the right rudder pedal. Both measures of performance, number of matches and number of errors, were again taken. Our earlier discussion indicated that requiring opposite responses to the same stimuli should lead to a negative transfer effect when Task B is undertaken.

In assessing transfer effects, Task A scores could be used as control data for Task B scores since previous studies had shown these two tasks to yield similar scores. At the outset of Task B performance, transfer effects were examined in both indices of performance. A positive transfer effect was indicated by the number of matches that were made. Subjects averaged 16.0 matches in 2 min compared with only 12.7 on Trial 1 of Task A. This facilitation is not in accord with our expectation of a negative transfer effect arising from reversal of required responses. If we turn to the mean number of errors made, we do find a negative transfer effect. Lewis and Shephard (1950) present data for Trial 3 on each task, for example, with a mean of 14.4 errors being made at this stage of Task A learning and 21.4 being made at the same point of Task B performance. This increase in errors of approximately 50 per cent provides evidence of a negative transfer effect.

The dual-measure analysis provides insight into the transfer processes involved when the display-control directional relationships are reversed. Requiring opposite responses in Task B does indeed yield a negative transfer effect as shown in the error scores. As each new problem appears on the panel, Task A response habits tend to be used, with resultant directional error providing a molecular measure of performance. Old habits interfere with performance of the new task. However, the 50 trials of practice on Task A have given subjects a general familiarity with the task and have trained habits like close watching of the display panel when controls are moved and quick correction of any wrong movement, so that Task B is facilitated according to the molar measure of number of matches accomplished during a trial. Direction-of-movement habits are only one sort of learning which occurred during Task A. Although they tended to introduce interference in Task B as shown in error scores, they were offset by other facilitative habits. Multiple performance measures in transfer studies can thus be useful in revealing the multiple habit development that occurs as complex tasks are practiced.

SUMMARY

Transfer of training is the effect, either beneficial or detrimental, that practice of one activity has upon the performance of another task. Experiments on transfer differentiate this process from learning and retention by introducing some difference in the two tasks to be performed successively. The sequence of performances which are required also differentiates studies of transfer, a proactive process, from retroactive inhibition. Laboratory experimentation permits the necessary controls and measurements to delineate transfer mechanisms in all kinds of tasks. The elements which are identical or similar from task to task are hypothesized to be important in transfer of training. Such elements foster the carryover from task to task of the same, or generalized, response tendencies which are the basis for the observed transfer effects. Various hypotheses concerning how transfer operates have also stressed the stimulus-response relationships within the two tasks as of prime importance. Reversed relationships are often demonstrated to underlie negative transfer. Some transfer effects may be mediated by implicit verbal behavior, with varied modes of operation possible.

A number of experimental designs have been generated in research on transfer. A simple design involves subjects randomly assigned to either an experimental group, experiencing both Task A and Task B, or a control group, doing Task B alone. If the latter group subsequently is given Task A, the design permits study of two-way transfer, Task B to Task A as well as Task A to Task B. A different design involves equated groups of subjects, pretested and matched on some performance related to Task B, the second task in the simple transfer paradigm. If this plan is used, considerable attention must be given to the pretest or matching factor and the amount of experience afforded the subjects as they are pretested. A transfer design in which the second task is varied requires the use of appropriate controls so that the experiment is actually composed of a pair of transfer studies of basic format.

A complete investigation of transfer mechanisms is likely to necessitate the running of more than two groups of subjects. Multiple groups permit the systematic manipulation of several different variables in the same study. Different variations of Task *A*, different performance measures on Task *B*, different amounts of training, and different inter-task intervals may all be possible sources of information about the processes underlying transfer.

Two principles of transfer measurement should be kept in mind as research is planned. One is that different indices of performance may yield different pictures of transfer. This principle suggests that multiple measures may enhance the description of transfer between two tasks, and that discrepancies in what the different indices portray need not be a cause for alarm. The second principle is that measured transfer effects can be expected to change as different stages in the practice of the second task are reached. Several comparisons of experimental and control data will usually show how transfer effect fades with continuing performance on the second task.

Besides comparison with control values, experimental measures may sometimes be compared with extrapolations of performance curves. Often the observed differences in any sort of comparison will be converted to per cent estimates of transfer. Transforming empirical findings to these per cent values may permit general comparisons of transfer effects between experiments in which different raw measures may have been employed. We noted several different formulas for converting group statistics to per cent estimates. A choice among these should be made in the planning stages of a research effort so that the required measurements may be taken properly.

A survey of illustrative studies of transfer of training revealed that positive, negative, and even zero net effects may be encountered in research. Certain special topics find a place in experimentation. Stimulus predifferentiation often involves transfer from a verbal performance to a perceptual-motor task. Bilateral transfer involves transfer from the accomplishing of a task with one hand to its performance with the other hand. Reversed stimulus-response alignments, or display-control relationships, is a special source of negative transfer effects.

REFERENCES

Allen, R. M. Factors in mirror drawing. *J. educ. Psychol.*, 1948, 39, 216–226.

Andreas, B. G., Green, R. F., & Spragg, S. D. S. Transfer effects between performance on a following tracking task (modified *SAM* Two-Hand Coordination Test) and a compensatory tracking task (modified *SAM* Two-Hand Pursuit Test). *J. Psychol.*, 1954, 37, 173–183. (*a*)

Andreas, B. G., Green, R. F., & Spragg, S. D. S. Transfer effects in following tracking (modified *SAM* Two-Hand Coordination Test) as a function of reversal of the display-control relationships on alternate blocks of trials. *J. Psychol.*, 1954, 37, 185–197. (*b*)

Cantor, Joan H. Amount of pretraining as a factor in stimulus predifferentiation and performance set. *J. exp. Psychol.*, 1955, 50, 180–184.

Gagné, R. M., & Foster, Harriet. Transfer of training from practice on components in a motor skill. *J. exp. Psychol.*, 1949, 39, 47–68.

Gagné, R. M., Foster, Harriet, & Crowley, Miriam E. The measurement of transfer of training. *Psychol. Bull.*, 1948, 45, 97–130.

Green, R. F. Transfer of skill on a following tracking task as a function of task difficulty (target size). *J. Psychol.*, 1955, 39, 355–370.

Lewis, D., & Shephard, A. H. Devices for studying associative interference in psychomotor performance: I. The Modified Mashburn Apparatus. *J. Psychol.*, 1950, 29, 35–46.

Murdock, B. B., Jr. Transfer designs and formulas. *Psychol. Bull.*, 1957, 54, 313–326.

Porter, L. W., & Duncan, C. P. Negative transfer in verbal learning. *J. exp. Psychol.*, 1953, 46, 61–64.

ADDITIONAL READINGS

Duncan, C. P. Transfer in motor learning as a function of degree of first-task learning and inter-task similarity. *J. exp. Psychol.*, 1953, 45, 1–11.

Vanderplas, J. M. Transfer of training and its relation to perceptual learning and recognition. *Psychol. Rev.*, 1958, 65, 375–385.

CHAPTER **18**

Problem
Solving

Like many other activities, problem solving is not a unitary behavior but a combination of psychological processes. A typical problem situation might demand that motivational, perceptual, associative, retentive, and transfer of training processes be used to arrive at a solution. Instead of attempting any psychological definition of problem solving, then, we need to consider briefly the essential aspects of a problem situation. These aspects tend to recur in the variety of problems or tasks employed in this area of behavioral study. As we list these elements, you may wish to relate them to problems encountered in real life to see if the psychologist is making an approach to problem solving which may have validity.

A situation that poses a problem to be solved generally involves these factors:

1. A specified goal or goals.
2. A variety of stimuli or cues.
3. A number of possible responses.
4. Varied associative strengths linking different stimuli and responses.
5. Sources of information indicating particular stimulus-response combinations to be correct or incorrect.

In research these elements are found in the instructions given to subjects and in the task materials as they are perceived and manipulated. Once the problem is posed, responses to the stimuli tend to occur sequentially with gains and losses in associative strength resulting from the information obtained. The trial-and-error variety of behavior may be quite prominent. The discovery or gradual acquiring of goal-attaining responses ends the behavioral sequence. This abstract survey of problem solving will take on specific meaning as we examine tasks used in laboratory studies.

MATERIALS AND METHODS USED IN RESEARCH

In order to study how people solve problems psychologists have employed a diversity of materials and methods. Essentially, we give a problem task to subjects and then observe and measure the behavior that follows. You may get a subject's-eye view of such investigations if you attempt to solve the problems posed for you here as illustrative examples.

Examples of Problem Tasks

Since we are using these sample tasks only for illustration, we are not considering them in a complete form. Some of the examples will, in fact, only suggest the nature of the problem as it might occur at some stage in an experiment. Several of the tasks are multidimensional, permitting the manipulation of more than one variable in research. Later we shall see how some of the problem tasks we pose here have actually been used by experimenters.

Task I. Concept Identification. From the examples given below, determine the stimulus characteristics which define a KEM, a FOV, a HAJ, and a YUG, each of these nonsense syllables designating one of four different concepts. *Hint:* Each concept is defined by *two* characteristics of the stimulus pattern.

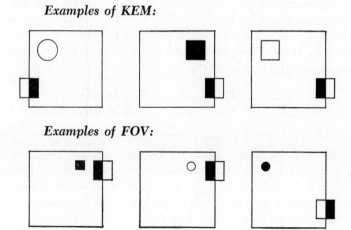

Examples of KEM:

Examples of FOV:

Examples of HAJ:

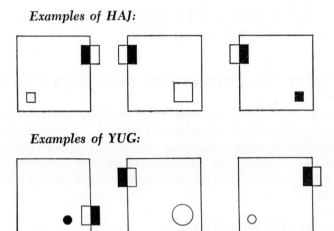

Examples of YUG:

The concepts presented here are based on those employed in a study by Kurtz and Hovland (1956). Their subjects were shown each example of a concept separately, a technique that differs very much from the way in which the problem was put to you.

Task II. Anagrams. Rearrange each group of five letters to form a meaningful word:

IHCLD   RAPTY   ERFSH

KAWEN   ACSRF   IRWTE

These anagrams were among those used by Maltzman and Morrisett (1953) in a study of the effect of instructions on such problem solving. As you unscrambled the six words, did you notice any rule by which each anagram could be quickly solved? Discovery of a principle or a workable formula is one aspect of problem solving in some instances.

Task III. Word Formation. Add the missing letters to these items to form meaningful words:

S__R__   P__ __G   M__L__G__

D__A__   CL__ __   __EM__ __IS__

The problems that are posed for you here represent possible stages in a task used by Battig (1957). Working on just one word at a time, a subject had to guess various letters while the experimenter showed him the location of each guessed letter if it did appear in the word. As given to you, each word problem is possibly open to more than one solution. Your task differs, too, in your not receiving any letter-by-letter information as you proceed to fill in the gaps.

Task IV. Twenty Questions. Read the sequence of questions and answers below and decide what question would be best to ask next in playing this familiar game.

Q: Is it human?
A: Yes
Q: Is it living?
A: Yes
Q: Is it a man?
A: Yes
Q: Is he in politics?
A: No
Q: Is he in show business?
A: Yes

This task has been used in several psychological experiments. For example, it was employed by Faust (1958) to investigate the improvement an individual shows as he repeatedly solves the problems posed in Twenty Questions. In your opinion, does the above series of questions represent a high or a low level of skill?

Task V. Water Jar Problems. For each problem below, decide how you would measure out the exact amount of water required, using the jars whose capacities are indicated:

Problem No.	Jar a	Jar b	Jar c	Amount Desired
1	6 pt	13 pt	2 pt	3 pt
2	10 pt	2 pt	9 pt	5 pt
3	4 pt	7 pt	2 pt	1 pt

Materials such as this have helped to reveal the habits formed as people solve many problems of a similar nature. Gardner and Runquist (1958) investigated how a particular way of solving such problems could be learned and then abandoned as the problem patterns changed.

Task VI. Verbal Puzzle. On the basis of the information which follows, match each senator with the state he represents.

In Washington, D.C., Senators Smith, Johnson, Jones, Miller, Jackson, and Robinson represent, but not respectively, the states of Oregon, California, Nevada, Idaho, Arizona, and Utah. All six of the senators live in the same hotel, but each resides on a different floor. The hotel has six floors.

The senators from Arizona and Utah are good friends and live on adjacent floors. The senator from Utah occupies the higher of the two adjacent floors.

Smith currently has a bill before the Senate and often goes down to the fourth floor to the Idaho senator's room to discuss the bill.

Jones must go up to get to any of the other senators' rooms.

Sometimes Jackson walks up four floors from his room to see the senator from Nevada. When Smith goes down to see Idaho's senator, who lives two floors above the senator from Utah, he never stops by to see Johnson.

Miller and the senator from Idaho belong to opposing political parties, but they both go up sometimes and talk with the senator from Oregon.

Match each senator with the state he represents.

This problem was given to subjects in a study carried out by Shaklee and Jones (1953). Various kinds of content can be used with this framework which presents numerous interrelationships and requires the discovery of other relationships in the network.

Task VII. Reaching a Decision. On the basis of the numbered cards which are presented here, decide whether the mean value of the entire set of 12 cards is positive or negative. Assume the cards were thoroughly shuffled before the eight were turned.

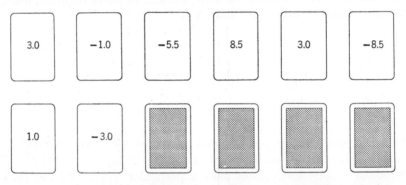

How confident are you in the correctness of your judgment? In a study by Irwin and Smith (1957) subjects were awarded a dollar prize for each time they made the proper decision about the means of decks of 100 such cards. To make it interesting, and to determine how cost as well as value affects decision-making, a subject had to pay a penny for each card he wished to see.

Task VIII. Trouble Shooting. Find the error in one of the sums of the addition problems given here. The error was introduced by *randomly* changing one digit of all those that appear in the answers. Did you succeed in locating the error? Which problem did you check first? With a simulated trouble-shooting task somewhat different from the one we have here, Detambel (1956) found that subjects

386	79,486	28	9	4182
924	81,384	93	4	9673
718	61,427	31	7	2895
842	13,726	56	8	5413
987	61,863	84	6	6614
435	34,199	33	2	4377
4292	332,085	325	36	33,254

looked first for the difficulty in the place where it had the highest probability of being found. Since our task here was set up by randomly designating one digit to be changed, the error had a greater probability of being in one of the problems with more columns of digits.

Aims of Research

In accordance with our general aim in psychological investigation, we wish to discover how the behavior of solving a problem depends upon antecedent conditions of various sorts. One approach is to vary task conditions and see how many subjects solve the problem under each condition. The number of solvers may be of less interest than the processes by which the solution is achieved. These processes could be explored, it might seem, by having subjects "think aloud" as they work with each problem. This introspective approach might reveal some of the verbal accompaniments of problem solving, but subjective reports cannot be trusted as valid indicators of the laws of the process. These laws must take the form of inferences based on extensive experimentation with numerous variables involved.

Ray (1955) is among those who have called for systematic manipulation of independent variables and measurement of different aspects of behavior in situations that require problem solution. His plea for dimensionalized task attributes and scaled response measurements accompanies a review of some of the tasks which have been employed in research.

It may be hoped that intensive empirical investigation will reveal functional relationships for behavior in problem situations. The relationships we seek are not necessarily primary behavior laws. For complex problems they may be higher order laws, based on more fundamental principles of perception, learning, and transfer of training, for example. Problem solving is an area of study where interactions among such basic processes may occur.

Desirable Task Attributes

Our aim of seeking functional relationships is the key to establishing criteria for tasks to be employed in experiments. An ideal task might have from two to four dimensions which can be manipulated quantitatively. If a task does not inherently contain such dimensions, independent variables may be sought in factors like the number of hints given for solving a difficult problem or the number of successive problems offered to the subjects. What aspects of the problems posed for you on pp. 503 to 507 could be given some sort of quantitative variation? A somewhat different rule for selecting tasks is to avoid those which demand special knowledge or special abilities on the subject's part.

In addition to discussing kinds of problems which may enrich research, Ray (1955) offers numerous suggestions for the observation and measurement of behavior in problem solving. A prime consideration is to be sure that the behavior *is* observable, at least in part. Many useful tasks require repeated overt responses as the subject proceeds toward solution of the problem. By having subgoals to be achieved before a final goal is reached, we may check a subject's progress. Using a problem which has just one *ultimate* solution insures that the frequency of those solving it will be one quantitative result of a study. More refined quantification, however, should be obtainable in most investigations.

Time spent in solving a problem may be a useful index in some instances. This measure may be less sensitive than others, however, in revealing the ongoing processes. These may be delineated better by recording the different responses that are made. We may accelerate our research progress if we use several different measures of performance as subjects solve problems. If we find that different indices do not agree completely, the discrepancies may actually serve to give us a bonus of information about the behavior under scrutiny. Different measures may reflect the different processes which actually comprise the problem solving.

In addition to those we have mentioned, Ray (1955) lists certain measures which may be useful in scoring problem-solving behavior of various sorts. Paraphrasing his listings, we may note the following measures for possible use in devising research tasks:

1. Number of steps correctly taken.
2. Number of successes in a series of problems.
3. Number of steps omitted.
4. Number of responses misplaced.
5. Number of unnecessary repetitions.
6. Number of wrong responses introduced.
7. Number of helps or hints required.
8. Closeness to goal achieved, if not successful.
9. Judged excellence of the solution.

Materials

It is already evident to you that materials of great variety may be used in research on problem solving, especially in the role of stimuli. In the sample problems given to you earlier, you saw symbolic material of verbal, numerical, and geometric kinds. We shall briefly discuss certain aspects of commonly employed material before going on to consider common methods of investigation.

GEOMETRIC OR PICTORIAL STIMULUS ITEMS. The geometric designs which we used in Task I, page 503, illustrate how stimulus material may incorporate several different aspects. These may figure in the concept a subject must define in order to solve the problem. In our example, the size, shape, and location of the small figure were attributes which might be used to identify and define a concept such as HAJ. In such a concept identification task, geometric stimuli may also include irrelevant aspects. A subject must learn to ignore such irrelevant attributes of complex stimuli while using the relevant cues as a basis for defining the different concepts.

To broaden the base of available stimulus material, Hovland (1953) has suggested a series of line drawings of flowers or plants. These may vary as to length of leaves or number of petals, for example. Their identification on the basis of such features closely resembles the classification task performed by the botanist.

The stimulus variations provided by geometric figures are often augmented by using different colors and by printing different numbers of such figures on each stimulus card. This is specifically illustrated in the Wisconsin Card Sorting Test where each card contains from one to four copies of a triangle, star, cross, or circle. These symbols are printed in either red, green, yellow, or blue on a particular card. In an earlier form of this test the concept of numerosity of symbols, one to four per card, was extra perceptible due to the regular patterning of symbol locations. When a single symbol appeared, for example, it was centered on the card, and when there were four identical symbols they formed a perfect square. Such systematic arrangements led to rapid sorting on the basis of quick perception of numerosity. Grant (1951) has described how the cards were revised by making locations of symbols unsystematic so that subjects must attend more closely to numerosity instead of responding on the basis of a perceptual configuration. This unsystematic arrangement has been used in subsequent research. Materials of this sort are often referred to as Weigl-type cards after an early experimenter.

VERBAL OR NUMERICAL MATERIALS. The first major advantage of

choosing verbal or numerical materials for a study of problem solving is that they are symbols which are commonly employed as problems are solved in everyday life. The thinking which occurs during problem solving is often described as the manipulation of symbols. By presenting symbols in controlled fashion and establishing the rules within which they must be manipulated, an experimenter can study the conditions that govern different kinds of problem-solving thought.

A second great advantage of these materials is that they lend themselves well to dimensional variations. Our system of cardinal numbers is actually a symbolic representation of an extensive dimension. We can use these symbols to represent relationships like "greater than" or "half" to experimental subjects. Our presentation may be an abstract one as in requiring mathematical problems or puzzles to be solved, or the numbers we present may be indicated as standing for quantitative aspects of a problem situation.

Verbal materials may be scaled along many dimensions. They represent an enormous pool of stimulus materials, great in variety yet capable of being classified into categories. Such classifications might involve characteristics like word length, grammatical part of speech, or frequency of usage. Another aspect of importance is meaning. The various scaling efforts in this realm offer promise for refining our studies of how verbal problems are solved. Besides manipulating semantic dimensions we may borrow from word association findings to tailor the stimulus-response associations which form parts of the problems we present to subjects. It seems likely that the realm of verbal behavior is one where the laws of perception, association, memory, and transfer may be interrelated. Some of these inter-relationships may come into focus in research on problem solving.

APPARATUS. Various kinds of apparatus and collections of objects and implements have been used to create problem situations in a realistic fashion. Beyond their realism, apparatus tasks offer possibilities for systematic variation of task dimensions. This is particularly true where an item of equipment is specifically designed to present problems to be solved.

We may consider one example of the flexibility in the devising of problem situations that is afforded by special apparatus. A specially constructed slot machine was used by Edwards (1956) to study the effect of reward probability and other factors on decision-making. Varying numbers of chips had to be inserted into the machine before a subject could "play" by pressing one of two buttons. The probabilities of either response leading to a payoff were completely controlled by the experimenter, of course. Sometimes either response would yield a reward but with one giving more chips than the other. Informing lights could signal the subject, if desired, of what reward would have followed his pressing of the other button on a particular trial. This simulated gambling situation thus gave the experimenter control over important antecedent conditions, represented in past experience with the machine, and over the information which followed a response. The research consequently offers promise for discovering how behavior patterns change as situational probabilities are varied systematically.

Common Research Methods

Our discussion has already touched upon some research methods in the study of problem solving. We need to attempt a reasonably inclusive listing of frequently employed techniques with comments on particular characteristics of each type. This will complete our background study of materials and methods and will enable us to understand key aspects of actual experiments which we examine.

CONCEPT IDENTIFICATION. The study of concept identification is one of the more frequently taken approaches to research on problem solving. Quite commonly the topic of investigation is labeled "concept formation" since the process of abstracting certain stimulus features and making a particular response to them is like the forming of an abstract concept by a child. Encountering many varied specimens of a class called "dog," the small child learns to give the verbal response "dog" to such creatures. The imperfect forming of the concept in a small child is shown when a toddler points to a Shetland pony and says, "big doggie." It seems more appropriate when using older subjects to refer to *identifying* concepts rather than to *forming* them, since the concepts involved are usually already in the behavior repertory of such subjects even though new names for the old ideas must be learned.

The usual experimental method involves presenting numerous examples of several concepts until the subject can discover which label is applicable to each one. Knowledge of results has to be given, of course, to guide the identification process. Numerous dimensions of the stimuli and their presentation can be varied in this research. It is also possible to choose stimulus materials so as to manipulate the pattern of response tendencies that are aroused in the early part of a study. The general features of concept identification tasks are thus congruent with our aims of finding functional relationships between observed responses and antecedent conditions.

A variant of concept identification is represented in tasks like the Wisconsin Card Sorting Test. The sorting bins are labeled by four stimulus cards bearing symbols such as three yellow crosses, one red triangle, four blue circles, and two green stars. A subject is told to sort a large number of different cards into the bins, but he is not told which concept—form, color, or number—to use as a guide. After each card is sorted the experimenter indicates whether its placement was correct or wrong. The subject gradually learns to use the proper concept as a basis for sorting. After a subject has learned to sort by number, for example, the experimenter may change the key concept to color without any warning. A few errors by the subject will inform him that he must seek a new guide to sorting the cards.

GAMES AND PUZZLES. Our classification of common methods of study must utilize a broad category which includes various games and puzzles which subjects may be asked to perform. Anagrams and wire puzzles are examples. Methods of using these in research often closely resemble their use for amusement purposes. Subjects are often familiar with the nature of such tasks and are interested in performing them. As investigators, our main concern is with manipulating the task materials systematically and setting up indices of performance.

TRAINING AND TRANSFER. One line of research in problem solving is closely parallel to studies of transfer of training. We may give subjects repeated experience in solving a series of similar problems. This may strengthen his response tendencies for a certain approach to such problems. A positive transfer effect will show up as improved efficiency as the series continues. If we next give a test problem which requires a different method of approach to its solution, we may find that solving is hindered in some way, a negative transfer effect.

PROBABILITY SITUATIONS. How to respond in the face of uncertainties is the essential question that defines one class of problem situation. As some of our earlier examples showed, psychologists have incorporated this paradigm in some of their research. These studies seek to describe how people behave when the outcome of their responses is, by the nature of the situation, uncertain. Both the probability of being correct and the cost of being incorrect are among the variables which may be manipulated. Through repeated experience a subject may learn some of these aspects of the problem he faces, adjusting his pattern of behavior accordingly. Alternatively, he may be informed of certain probabilities at the outset of the study, with the experimenter's aim being to see how such information leads to particular choices of response.

TASKS REQUIRING PRACTICAL ACCOMPLISHMENT. A simulated practical problem is often at the heart of an experimental study. The desired accomplishment is described to the subject and various objects or tools are made available for use in the task. The goal is not to be reached by making simple, direct use of these implements, however. A common requirement is that new relationships among the objects or a new utilization of a tool must be perceived before solution of the problem occurs. Making novel use of an item is sometimes hampered when a subject has to use it in a customary way first. For example, if a hammer is used to drive a nail from which a string is hung, the use of the hammer as a weight on the lower end of the string will be less likely to occur than in a situation where the hammer did not have to be employed first in its normal function. According to Duncker (1945, p. 85) the first use of the hammer would result in "functional fixedness," a strengthening of the tendency to perceive it for conventional employment. This recent strengthening of the perception of normal utilization would render a novel use less likely to occur later on.

A different interpretation of how novel use tends to be precluded by prior employment of an object might be considered. As he surveys all the articles provided for him, a subject might ask concerning each one, in effect, "What is the reason for giving me this article?" This question might elicit a series of responses tending to lead to some use of the article in solving the problem. In the case of the hammer, the question is answered when the hammer is employed to drive the nail. This tends to extinguish the question as far as the hammer is concerned. It may thus be the extinction of the verbal mediating response, the searching question, that underlies some of the failures to arrive at a novel use of the implement.

Tasks which require practical accomplishment have the merit of resembling problem situations which might confront the average person. Despite this aspect and the advantage of being an interesting challenge to subjects, this type of task often lacks features which are offered by some of the other kinds of problems we have considered for experimental employment. Simulations of practical problems tend to lack possibilities for dimensionalization of stimulus materials and of response measurement. They usually permit little observation of a sequence of behavior leading to final solution. Their characteristics make them well suited for testing certain special hypotheses, but less adaptable to delineating functional relationships among variables.

STUDIES OF CONCEPT IDENTIFICATION

As we undertake to review some illustrative experiments on concept identification, we may recall our attempt to learn what stimulus aspects of certain geometric figures defined the concepts KEM, FOV, HAJ, and YUG (p. 503). Subsequent discussion of materials and methods gave us a further acquaintance with this and other kinds of problem solving. We next extend this knowledge by reviewing some research efforts that will show some of the independent variables which have been manipulated in this area of study. The reports from which our review is taken will show us a diversity of experimental attacks on different aspects of concept identification. Nevertheless they offer but a glimpse of a broader research campaign which extends to such questions as how children form concepts. The extent of investigation in this and other directions is indicated in a review by Vinacke (1951).

Stimulus Aspects of the Task

It should not surprise us that experimenters have chosen stimulus material as a place to introduce experimental variables in concept identification studies. Concept identification hinges upon close examination of complex stimuli so that each response may be associated with the proper cues. In one study which we shall examine we find that irrelevant cues are employed to increase stimulus complexity to determine if concept identification is thus retarded. In the next experiment we shall see how concept learning is affected by the sequential arrangement in which the stimuli exemplifying different concepts are presented. Besides attacking different aspects of stimulus presentation, these two studies afford many contrasts in procedures used.

TASK COMPLEXITY. In an experiment by Brown and Archer (1956) the stimuli were geometric patterns projected on a screen, with possibilities for using two different colors and two degrees of shading. The patterns themselves incorporated several aspects: form of figures —either triangle or square; size of figures—large or small; number— one or two; and position on screen—top and bottom or left and right. For any particular subject only two of these paired aspects, like number and position, were relevant to concept identification. Other stimulus aspects were added in different amounts to provide the required condition for different groups of subjects. The concept-identifying responses were the pushing of four panel buttons, one corresponding to each concept. A simple motor response thus replaced the verbal label required as a response in many experiments.

Our understanding of this investigation will be aided if we examine the task as one subject might experience it under the simplest condition. Figure 18.1 indicates the stimuli which a subject might see in succession on the first trial, each pattern representing one stimulus presentation. The presentation of 16 stimulus patterns was considered to constitute one trial, so the figure represents just half a trial. The rectangle at the bottom of this figure is a schematic representation of the control panel, with the four buttons numbered for convenient reference. The subject was instructed to continue pushing these buttons on each stimulus presentation until he located the correct one —corresponding to the concept portrayed. Accuracy, rather than speed, was stressed. Whenever a subject's *first* response to a stimulus pattern was the proper button, he was credited with a correct response.

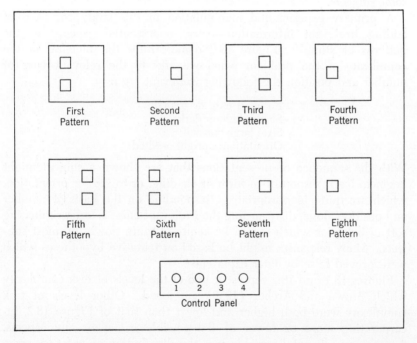

Fig. 18.1. Eight stimulus patterns which might have been presented successively to constitute half a trial in an experiment by Brown and Archer (1956). These stimuli exhibit only relevant stimulus aspects, number (one or two) and position (left or right) in this example. The control panel is also represented.

Performing merely on the basis of chance or random guessing should yield an average score of 4 correct responses per trial of 16 patterns, and 16 correct would represent perfect performance on a trial.

Suppose that our hypothetical subject discovered, after an error or two, that Response 3 was correct for the First Pattern shown in Figure 18.1. When the Second Pattern of Trial 1 was presented, he might find that Response 2 was correct. When the Third Pattern came along, he might remember his earlier discoveries but he would have to decide whether the number of squares or the position of the squares was the basis for associating a pattern and a response. He might discover that neither previously correct response was now the right one. Discovering that Response 1 was correct, he might realize that both stimulus aspects, number and position, constituted relevant information. Few subjects would approach the identification of the concepts quite as speedily as this, but a considerable amount of learning would take place on the 16 presentations of the first trial for some subjects.

A primary experimental manipulation in this study consisted of adding irrelevant information—extra, nonessential aspects—to the patterns of stimuli. Figure 18.2 demonstrates the increase in the complexity of the problem when we add to the relevant cues of number and position the following irrelevant cues:

> Form: square or triangle
> Shade: light or dark
> Size: large or small
> Orientation: upright or tilted

With the sequence of presentations that are shown a subject might begin to learn responses to form or shading, or to size or orientation, which are quite inappropriate. Responding on the basis of number and position alone, disregarding the irrelevant cues, is a discriminating sort of behavior which would be acquired quite slowly by most subjects. Many responses might be based on tentative hypotheses which were proved false by later experience.

Figures 18.1 and 18.2 represent two of the levels of task complexity which Brown and Archer (1956) employed. Other levels of task complexity were both higher and lower than that of Figure 18.2, incorporating more or fewer of the possible irrelevant cue aspects. Another experimental variable was the distribution of practice, some groups being given intertrial rests of 30 or 60 sec. However, since this variable did not significantly affect the mean number of correct responses, it will be ignored here as we examine the effects of task complexity.

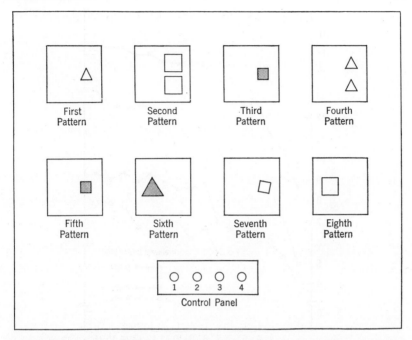

Fig. 18.2. Eight stimulus patterns representing a higher level of complexity in the study by Brown and Archer (1956). To the relevant aspects of the stimuli, number and position, have been added irrelevant cues such as form (triangle or square), shade (light or dark), size (large or small), and orientation (upright or tilted). This represents the introduction of four bits of irrelevant information.

The results of this experiment are portrayed in Figure 18.3 in which the mean number of correct responses is plotted as a function of trials. The rising curves indicate that the concept-identifying responses were being acquired under each task condition. It is clear, however, that concept identification is much more successful when the stimulus patterns are free of irrelevant cues—the condition represented in the top curve. The less satisfactory performance which results from the giving of irrelevant information is seen to be dependent on how many irrelevant cue aspects of the stimuli are manipulated at random. Poorest performance occurred when six cue aspects of the stimulus pattern were irrelevant to the concept identification task. Many subjects in this group performed at close to the chance level of expectancy for correct performance, and very few seemed to identify the relevant concepts in the 256 stimulus presentations made to them on the 16 trials.

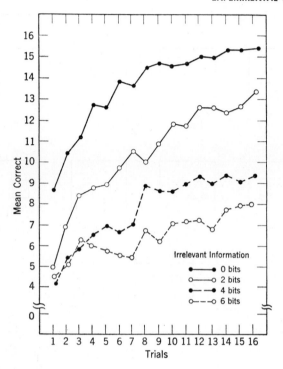

Fig. 18.3. Mean number of correct responses per trial as a function of repeated trials. The performance curves are differentiated by the amount of irrelevant information added to the relevant cues. (After Brown and Archer, 1956.)

SEQUENCES OF STIMULUS ITEMS. Suppose we consider that subjects are to be taught, through a series of sample presentations, to identify the concepts KEM, FOV, HAJ, and YUG which we encountered earlier in this chapter. There are various possibilities for arranging the series of stimulus patterns to be presented. We could group all instances of KEM together so that the several presentations of this concept followed in close succession. An alternative would be to avoid even two successive instances of the same concept by always having examples of one or more other concepts intervene. These two possible sequences of instances were the major conditions in an experiment by Kurtz and Hovland (1956).

Stimulus materials employed in this experiment were essentially the same as those presented in our illustrative Task I on p. 503. The characteristics of the four concepts may be summarized as follows:

Concept	Defining Aspects	Irrelevant Aspects
KEM	Up and circle	Black or white, large or small
FOV	Up and square	Black or white, large or small
HAJ	Down and small	Black or white, circle or square
YUG	Down and large	Black or white, circle or square

Additional irrelevant cues were provided by complicating the border square which enclosed each figure. This complication was itself a smaller square overlapping the border. It varied in placement and shading, but all of its variations were completely irrelevant. From the work of Brown and Archer (1956) we would assume that these various irrelevant aspects of the stimulus materials added to the task complexity and difficulty of identifying the concepts. Stimulus instances were drawn individually on 3 × 5 in. index cards.

Two groups of subjects were run through a similar series of training and testing procedures. Step 1 was preliminary training in identifying concepts based on geometric patterns of triangles, with both relevant and irrelevant cues involved. This preliminary training was continued through two problems to be sure each subject understood how to identify concepts on the basis of relevant cues. Step 2 started by acquainting the subject with the four relevant dimensions which would differentiate the concepts in the principal problem: position—up or down, and form—square or circle. Next, the four concept names were given to the subject on a card which remained in view throughout the remaining procedures. The presentation of concept instances then followed, with the experimenter naming the concept as each of 32 cards was displayed at a rate of 2 sec each. Each concept was represented eight times in this presentation, with irrelevant cues varied from card to card. For one group of subjects, this presentation was mixed, with one or more other concepts being presented between any two instances of a particular concept. For the other group, unmixed presentation was used, with all eight instances of a given concept grouped together in succession. Either of these arrangements constituted the training given to subjects on the concept identification task.

Step 3 consisted of a verbal description test in which each subject described the properties of KEM, FOV, HAJ, and YUG as he had learned them during the training of Step 2. The experimenter gave no comment on a subject's descriptions. Step 4 was a concept identification test in which 8 cards, 2 instances of each concept, were presented one at a time with the subject being required to name the concept shown on each card. Guesses were required if subjects were uncertain, and the experimenter again offered no comment as the test proceeded.

The experiment was concluded by repeating Steps 2 through 4 a second time. During Step 2 the specific sequence of the 32-card presentations was now made different, but the experimental condition of a mixed or unmixed sequence of concept instances was retained for subjects of the different groups. A different test pack of 8 cards was used in Step 4.

The completed experiment yielded 2 scores for each subject on the verbal description test, 1 for each repetition of Step 3. Also obtained were 2 scores on the identification test, 1 for each repetition of Step 4. On each administration of the verbal description test, a subject might receive 0, 1, or 2 points for each concept, depending on his describing none, one, or both of the relevant aspects of the concept. The total description score for all 4 concepts could thus range from 0 to 8. The score on the identification test was the number of correct identifications of concepts on the 8 cards of a test pack, with a possible range from 0 to 8 also.

When the mean scores for the two groups of subjects were compared, support was found for the hypothesis that the unmixed sequence of concept instances led to better concept learning. The results are presented in Table 18.1. On both concept identification tests,

TABLE 18.1

Scores on Concept Identification Tests Following Mixed or Unmixed Presentations of Concept Instances (After Kurtz and Hovland, 1956)

		Mixed Presentation	Unmixed Presentation
Mean number of correct identifications	First Test:	3.61	4.69
	Second Test:	4.38	5.54
Mean scores on verbal description	First Test:	2.92	4.84
	Second Test:	4.08	6.46

the group having the unmixed sequence of concept presentations scored higher, although their means did not exceed those of the mixed sequence group by an amount conventionally considered to be statistically significant. On both verbal description tests, however, the superior mean scores of the group having unmixed training sequences were significantly higher. These findings are interpreted as indicating interference in the mixed presentation arising from having other concept examples intervene between any two instances of the same concept. Proactive and retroactive inhibition in the memory process may be considered to hamper the problem solving that is required in learning several concepts concurrently.

Response Tendencies in the Task

As subjects undertake a concept identification task, their problem is to learn to make a certain response to each of the different stimuli presented. Studies of transfer of training suggest that the ease with which a stimulus and a response become associated is dependent on the previously developed tendency of the stimulus to evoke this response or to evoke other responses which may hinder the occurrence of this one. We are going to examine two experiments in which previously established response strengths were found to affect concept identification. Both studies employed verbal materials which had been scaled for associative strength or response dominance by other investigators. Accordingly we shall begin by reviewing this scaling effort.

RESPONSE DOMINANCE IN VERBAL CONCEPTUALIZATION. After some preliminary work, Underwood and Richardson (1956a) undertook to scale the associative strength between a large number of concrete nouns and various adjectives which were descriptive of the sensory impressions that might be aroused by the objects to which the nouns referred. It was found, for example, that the stimulus noun *baseball* elicited the adjectives *round, white, hard,* and *small* in a free association test. Since *round* was the response given to the word *baseball* by a great majority of subjects, this adjective is considered to have high response dominance to this stimulus. Such a high dominance level was found by the authors in a different experiment, which they mention, to lead to ready concept identification when the stimuli were concrete nouns and the concept categories were designated by adjectives of high dominance level with respect to those nouns. Adjectives of lower dominance level were less effective as concept identification was sought.

Having noted that these scaled verbal materials have been demonstrated to be useful in research on concept learning, we may examine the scaling procedure more closely. The experimental subjects, 153 college students, were first given instructions and preliminary training. These were aimed at insuring that the responses given were descriptive of *sense impressions*. A set of 328 nouns was then presented, being pronounced by the experimenter and flashed on a screen, each word being succeeded by the next one after a 6-sec exposure. Subjects wrote down the first sensory impression which they associated with each noun.

In categorizing the responses for tabulation, synonymous adjectives like *big* and *large* were combined. The final list of stimulus words tabulated by the authors contains 213 nouns, with 115 having been eliminated because they had been perceived ambiguously or had yielded too few common responses for categorization. For the 213 nouns, the per cent of subjects giving each adjective as a response is presented in the original article. Any response which was not given by at least 5 per cent of subjects was thrown into a miscellaneous category, along with responses which were not sense impressions. The distribution of responses to a sample of the nouns is presented in Table 18.2. In the original tabulation, a datum on frequency of usage of each noun in written English was also given.

TABLE 18.2

Selected Sample of Stimulus Nouns Scaled for Response Dominance on the Basis of Per Cent of Subjects Offering Different Sensory-Impression Responses in Word Association (After Underwood and Richardson, 1956a)

Stimulus Word	Response Categories and Per Cent Occurrence	Miscellaneous Responses
Aluminum	Shiny 59%; metallic 14%; light 12%	14%
Apple	Red 67; round 19; sweet 5	9
Atom	Small 87	13
Auditorium	Big 84	16
Barrel	Round 72; woody 15; big 6	7
Baseball	Round 70; white 11; hard 10; small 5	4
Bread	White 35; soft 31	28
Cave	Dark 66; deep 6; damp 14; hollow 5	9
City	Big 72; noisy 5	23
Dime	Round 30; metallic 23; small 15; shiny 13; thin 9	9
Ether	Smelly 70	30
Goat	White 29; smelly 20; hairy-furry 18; dirty 5	29
Ivory	White 65; hard 14; smooth 12	9
Lips	Red 59; soft 24	18
Needle	Sharp 53; pointed 15; small 9; metallic 5; thin 9	10
Pin	Sharp 55; small 22; pointed 10; metallic 5	9
Rice	White 54; small 24; hard 6	15
Stone	Hard 63; small 7; round 6; heavy 6	19
Zoo	Big 32; smelly 30; noisy 7	31

VARIANCE OF RESPONSE DOMINANCE. After scaling response dominance (1956a), Underwood and Richardson (1956b) went on to demonstrate that dominance level of adjectives designating categories or concepts was a determinant of the ease with which concepts are learned. Rather than reviewing their experiment, we shall go on to examine another study which makes further use of their scaled dominance levels. Noting that Underwood and Richardson (1956b) had kept the *variance* of dominance levels quite low while utilizing several different *mean* values of response dominance, Freedman and Mednick (1958) manipulated the variance of response dominance. With *mean* dominance level kept about constant, they sought to determine how the attainment of concepts would be affected when the response dominance of a particular adjective varied widely about this mean as different nouns were employed in constituting the categories to be learned by the subjects. For example, let us examine two sets of nouns which different subjects would have to group under the concept, *small*. Response dominance is measured by the per cent of subjects who gave the adjective *small* as a response in the scaling study by Underwood and Richardson (1956a). Both lists of nouns, given below, have *small* as a response with a mean response dominance of about 24%.

List 1	Response Dominance of *Small*	List 2	Response Dominance of *Small*
Gnat	76%	Cradle	24%
Needle	9	Closet	24
Stone	7	Rice	24
Canary	5	Pin	22

You can see from this tabulation that the dominance levels of *small* for List 1 vary quite widely about the mean value of 24 per cent, whereas in List 2 the variance in response dominance level is almost nil. It was predicted that the attainment of the concept *small* for List 1 would be accomplished more readily because the stimulus word *gnat* would elicit this response early and thus bring it into contiguity with the other nouns of the same concept.

Having noted the essential nature of the hypothesis and its method of testing, we may now examine the details of the study. List 1 and List 2, given to different groups of subjects, actually contained 12 nouns each. For purposes of counterbalancing, List 1 included 4 nouns, each of which had about 23% response dominance in the sense impression *smelly*. These nouns were *sauerkraut, hospital, tobacco,* and *gym*. The group getting List 1 would thus be working on a concept of high variance in response dominance, *small,* and one with low variance, *smelly.* List 2 was expanded by adding 4 nouns with high variance in response dominance in the concept *smelly.* With a mean dominance value of 24% these nouns and their values were *garlic* 58%, *vinegar* 14%, *daffodil* 12% and *coffee* 12%. It may be noted that Underwood and Richardson (1956*a*) categorized both good and bad smells together, and this is reflected in grouping *garlic* and *daffodil* together under one concept. Both Lists 1 and 2 were completed by adding 4 more nouns pertaining to the concept *round: apple, badge, collar, platter.*

The 12 nouns comprising a particular list were presented in random order to subjects of one group, run individually. Having been told that the nouns would be shown for 4 secs each in the window of a memory drum and that he must respond with a descriptive adjective, each subject was further told, "four of these can be described by the same adjective, four by another adjective, and four by a third adjective. In other words, there are three groups of four words and all of the words in each group can be described by the same adjective. It is your task to discover what four nouns go in each group and what adjective can be used to describe each group. . . . I will tell you if you are right or wrong. . . . If you learn the list completely you will be responding with only three words because each of the words is correct for four of the nouns" (Freedman and Mednick, 1958, p. 464). The subject was informed that adjectives descriptive of sensory impressions were required.

Each time through the list was a trial, and trials were continued until a criterion of a perfect trial was reached or until 20 trials had been given. By learning either list, each group of subjects was contributing data to test the hypothesis that concept attainment would be achieved more readily for the set of nouns with high variance in response dominance. Better learning was predicted for *small* in List 1 and *smelly* in List 2 than for *smelly* in List 1 and *small* in List 2. The concept *round* was used only to provide buffer items and did not enter into the performance measures.

Results of the study supported the hypothesis that high variance of response dominance levels would facilitate concept attainment. The high variance concept was attained by the fifth trial by 13 out of 40 subjects, whereas this quick learning was accomplished for the low variance concept by only 4 out of 40 subjects. It was found, further, that only 4 subjects failed to attain the high variance concept in 20 trials, whereas 11 out of the 40 subjects failed to master the low variance concept. The median number of trials to concept attainment was 8 for the high variance concept and 12 for the concept having low variance of response dominance.

Other measurements were congruent with number of trials to concept attainment in supporting the hypothesis. Fewer errors were made in attaining the high dominance concept. The assumption that the concept of high variance would be reached more quickly in the performance was also confirmed. The median trial for the first correct response was Trial 4 for the concept of high variance and Trial 10 for the concept of low variance. Under the high variance condition this correct response was presumably first made to the stimulus word *gnat* or *garlic* in most cases.

RESPONSE DOMINANCE OF IRRELEVANT WORDS. The response dominance levels scaled by Underwood and Richardson (1956a) were also used in a study of verbal concept identification by Kendler and Karasik (1958). Their experiment offers numerous procedural contrasts with that of Freedman and Mednick (1958) even though employing similar materials.

Elements of the experimental technique can be understood by examining some of the instructions given to subjects and the practice task which they performed prior to the experiment proper. In part, they were told, "In this experiment you will be shown eight cards, each with a different noun typed on it. Four of them will form a concept, in that they have a common sensory property. After looking at the eight cards for 15 sec you will be given one of the eight cards and asked to select the additional three cards that belong with it— and tell me the common sensory quality on which you have based your selection" (Kendler and Karasik, 1958, p. 279). A subject was next given a practice set of cards, each containing one of the following words: *mansion, pineapple, rabbit, city, pickle, auditorium, whale,* and *rod.* After a 15-sec inspection of these, he was handed the card bearing the word *city* and asked to pick out three more that shared a common sensory property with *city.* If *mansion, auditorium,* and *whale* were chosen, the experimenter said, "Right." The sensory quality, *big,* or a synonym, was given by the subject spontaneously or on request, or was stated by the experimenter if necessary. If the wrong three cards were selected, the subject was told, "Wrong—try again." If two additional wrong attempts were made, the experimenter explained the correct answer.

In the main part of the experiment, each subject had to try to solve a series of three such problems of concept identification. The three concepts and the stimulus nouns employed were *round: platter, derby, moon, bracelet; soft: flannel, kitten, moccasin, jellyfish;* and *small: pill, snail, minnow, thimble.* It was the 4 irrelevant words placed with any of these sets of 4 which provided the experimental test of the hypothesis. The hypothesis was that irrelevant words which have strong tendencies to evoke responses different from the required concept should facilitate concept formation. Irrelevant words were chosen on the basis of their response dominance, scaled by Underwood and Richardson (1956a), to provide three experimental conditions for each subject. Condition 1 was created by using 4 irrelevant words all of which had high dominance value in the same sensory impression category. Four irrelevant words of high dominance in the response *smelly,* for example, were *ether, garbage, gardenia,* and *manure.* These four words could be grouped with any set forming a desired concept—*round, soft* or *small*—when the identification of one of these was to be tested under Condition 1.

Condition 2 was created by a set of irrelevant words all of which had a low dominance value on a common response. One set of irrelevant nouns had low dominance for the response *white: enamel, fang, paste,* and *skull.* These should not permit as quick achievement of the concept required as would the high dominant irrelevant words of Condition 1. If this hypothesis were confirmed, the facilitation of concept identification under Condition 1 might be ascribed either to the *high* dominance of the irrelevant words or to the fact that they had *high dominance in a common concept.* To shed light on this possible question of interpretation, Condition 3 was added by the experimenters by selecting a set of 4 irrelevant words each of which had high dominance value in a different category of sense impression. One such set was *blood (red), night (dark), rhinestone (shiny),* and *spinach (green).* If high dominance itself is what makes the irrelevant words facilitating of achieving the concept common to the relevant words, then this Condition 3 should be like Condition 1 in exceeding Condition 2 performance. But if high dominance in a *common* concept is needed for such facilitation, then this condition should not lead to performance as good as that found under Condition 1.

The concepts to be identified—*round, soft,* or *small*—were presented to one-third of the 72 subjects in each possible order. Conditions 1, 2, and 3 were similarly given in different sequences to different subjects. Each condition was imposed by using irrelevant words, selected for dominance values as indicated in the samples we have considered—these samples actually having been among the irrelevant sets of words used in creating the appropriate condition. As they were individually run, the subjects were given each of the three problems in the same fashion as they had been presented with the practice set of eight cards in the sample problem. In the experiment proper, however, five attempts were allowed before proceeding to the next problem.

The extent to which concept identification was facilitated by the nature of the irrelevant items in the set of eight cards was assessed in two ways. The per cent of subjects performing the correct identifying responses on the first attempt was one measure. The number of incorrect sortings under each condition was the other index of performance. Both of these measures favored Condition 1 over the other two conditions, between which there was no significant difference on either index. Here is a summary of the results:

	Condition 1	Condition 2	Condition 3
	Irrelevant Words: High Dominance, Related	Irrelevant Words: Low Dominance, Related	Irrelevant Words: High Dominance, Unrelated
Per cent solving on first attempt	58.3%	29.2%	38.9%
Mean number of incorrect attempts	1.32	2.53	2.28

The outcome of the experiment confirms the hypothesis that high dominance in the irrelevant words facilitates the selection of the relevant words in forming the concept required. It is further shown that these irrelevant words must have their high dominance in the same sensory impression category, as in Condition 1. It would appear that the identifying of the relevant concept might be attained under Condition 1 by segregating the seven nouns under consideration. The subject may locate the three which go with the indicated one by noting that four of the seven pertain to a common concept, like *white* or *smelly*, so that the other three are identified by exclusion.

The findings of this experiment may be summarized by stating that relevant concept identification is facilitated when the irrelevant nouns have high response dominance *and* are related. High dominance or relatedness alone was less effective as a condition for the irrelevant material. To determine whether these two conditions are still somewhat facilitating would require that we run a test with irrelevant words that were of low response dominance *and* unrelated to each other. Comparison with this control condition would inform us as to the possible facilitation arising when the irrelevant words conform to Conditions 2 and 3 of this study.

ADDITIONAL STUDIES OF PROBLEM SOLVING

In the area of concept identification, which we have just examined, investigators have demonstrated trends toward the employment of standard methods and materials. Other regions of the vast realm of problem solving have been explored by a great diversity of techniques. In the remainder of this chapter we shall consider this research effort by examining a number of illustrative experiments.

Anagram Solution as a Function of Set

The course which problem solving takes has often been considered to be guided by relatively strong response tendencies which the solver brings to the situation. Heightened strength of a group of response tendencies is one thing that psychologists mean by the term "set." We establish a set by strengthening certain response tendencies. Our success in doing this may be revealed only later when these responses have a chance to occur in competition with others. The effect of different sets on the solution of five-letter anagrams was studied by Maltzman and Morrisett (1953).

Subjects were given 20 five-letter anagrams typed individually on 3×5 in. cards in a training series, followed by 15 similar anagrams in a test series. Two different kinds of set were established by the preliminary training. Under two conditions, this training was augmented by instructions to subjects designed to add even more strength to the set just before they undertook the test task. Ten subjects were run under each of the experimental conditions. Under Condition N subjects solved anagrams which had "nature" solutions like *peony,* *herbs,* and *grain* during preliminary training. They were tested on anagrams which offered either a nature solution or a non-nature solution, thus providing a means of assessing the strength of the set established during training. These test items included anagrams like ECAHP which could be solved as either PEACH or CHEAP. Under all conditions of training and testing a 2-min time limit was imposed on the individual as he worked on each anagram.

Under Condition O each anagram given during the training could be solved only by rearranging the letters in the order 32145. The anagram ERCAM, for example, could be rearranged in 32145 sequence to form the answer CREAM. During testing each anagram had at least two solutions, one involving the 32145 order of rearranging the given letters and one or two requiring some other rearrangement. For example, the test anagram UACSE permits a 32145 solution, CAUSE, or a different solution, departing from the set established in training, SAUCE.

It was assumed that subjects assigned to Conditions N and O would develop response sets as they solved the training anagrams which would carry over to the solving of the test items. No technique, aside from the training problems, was used to establish the set. Under Condition NI, however, certain instructions were given just before the training series. Subjects were told that "it will help you to look for words referring to flowers, growing things or their habitat" (Maltzman and Morrisett, 1958, p. 352). These instructions were intended to intensify the establishment of the set by the anagrams encountered in the training series, identical with those of Condition N.

Condition OI involved instructions intended to augment the effect of training on the anagrams scrambled in 32145 order. Subjects were alerted to look for a certain order of scrambled letters before they undertook the same training items as were used for Condition O.

The four conditions which we have thus far considered comprise a 2×2 factorial design for the experiment. There were two different types of training, nature words and special order. There were two different ways of establishing a set for these responses, training alone and instructions plus training. Condition ON utilized no special instructions, but it combined the training and testing arrangements for Conditions N and O. The anagrams were identical with those of Condition N, but they were arranged in 32145 order during training, and during testing the letters were located so that a 32145 solution would yield the nature word. The non-nature word would result from a different unscrambling of the letters.

The results of the various efforts to establish the different sets were assessed by noting the per cent of solutions of the test anagrams that were in accordance with the set intended by the experimenter. The mean per cent under each condition was as follows:

Condition	N	O	NI	OI	ON
Mean per cent of set solutions	54.7	63.3	60.7	76.0	85.3

Statistical analysis indicated that the conditions involving order led to significantly more solutions according to the set than were obtained under the nature set. A significant effect was also attributed to the addition of instructions prior to training. Finally, Condition

ON yielded significantly more solutions according to the training set than did Conditions *O*, *N*, or *NI*. The study leads to the conclusion that the course of anagram solution can be directed by prior training establishing a set and that this effect can be enhanced by adding instructions leading toward the same set.

Practice Effects in Playing Twenty Questions

Can a person learn to become a better problem solver? This question represents an extension of our interest in the learning process and it also is a matter of great practical importance. A specific investigation of this topic was made by Faust (1958) using an adaptation of the game of Twenty Questions. The experimenter began by identifying a topic as animal, vegetable, or mineral. Subsequently he answered the subject's questions by saying "Yes," "No," "Partly," "Sometimes," or "Not in the usual sense of the word." Each subject attempted four problems per day on 5 successive days, being permitted to ask 30 questions in identifying each topic instead of the traditional 20. The twenty subjects were given several different sequences of the same topics as the experiment progressed. The problem topics had been selected on the basis of earlier research to provide a strong likelihood that each one would be solved within the 30-question limit. The principal analyses of possible improvement were comparisons of performance on Day 1 and Day 5.

Twenty Questions provides its own quantitative index of efficient performance, the number of questions needed to reach a solution. Subjects showed a significant decrease in this measure from a mean of 19.6 questions required for the problems on Day 1 to a mean of 13.7 questions needed on Day 5. Also decreasing significantly was the mean time required to identify a topic, from 321 sec on Day 1 to 179 sec on Day 5. Time taken in solving each problem was a measurement that depended only in part on the number of questions which had to be asked, so it provided this second index of proficiency.

An attempt was made to discover other measures of performance which would reveal something of the nature of the improvement which subjects showed. Data analysis showed that, in comparison to Day 1, subjects on Day 5 asked a higher per cent of questions which were recurrent in the group as they tried to solve a particular problem. A question was classified as recurrent if it was asked by 8 out of 20 as they attempted to identify a topic. The trend toward using a higher per cent of these recurrent questions as practice continued could be interpreted as improvement since a supplementary study showed that a topic would be almost revealed for most people by the answers to such recurrent questions.

Still another analysis was directed at the questions which could *not* be classified as recurrent. These were rated by judges as good or bad on the basis of the information which they elicited. As subjects progressed from Day 1 to Day 5 it was found that the number of bad questions asked decreased far more than did the number of good questions. In its several ways of analyzing performance this study illustrates how research may help to clarify the process of problem solving and the improvement of skill as similar tasks are encountered repeatedly.

Work and Probability of Success in Trouble Shooting

A certain amount of trial-and-error behavior characterizes the problem-solving task of trouble shooting, or diagnosing, malfunctioning equipment. The diagnostic steps taken by the repairman do not follow a random sequence, however. The order in which various tests are made is guided by a number of factors. Among these are the probabilities that the trouble lies in different parts of the equipment and the amount of work or effort required in making each test. We shall examine a study by Detambel (1956) which investigated the role of these two factors as subjects were faced repeatedly with a simulated trouble-shooting situation.

Four component parts of a piece of equipment which was supposed to be working improperly were represented by four decks of playing cards. The ace of spades, which might be found in any deck, was an information card which represented the location of the trouble. The jokers were information cards which indicated that any of the four component decks in which one was found was a trouble-free part of the system. On every trial a subject's task was to turn over the cards of any deck he selected until he discovered an information card. If it was a joker, he had to go on to a different deck of his choice to continue looking for the trouble. The trial ended only when the ace of spades, indicating the locus of the trouble, was found. Each of 12 subjects had to go through this process of locating the trouble 120 times.

In each block of 15 trials, the ace of spades was put by the experimenter 8 times in Deck *A*, 4 times in Deck *B*, 2 times in Deck *C*, and 1 time in Deck *D*. This experimental manipulation simulated different empirical probabilities of the occurrence of the trouble in different parts of the equipment. On the basis of this factor alone, repeated trouble shooting would be most efficient if the order of searching the

decks were A–B–C–D. However, the work always involved in checking was different for the various decks.

In Deck A the information card was always the 16th card to be
turned, whereas it was the 8th card in Deck B, the 4th in Deck C, and
the 2nd in Deck D. Ignoring the probabilities cited earlier, this work
factor would dictate the sequence D–C–B–A as the most efficient.
In actual fact, the values of the two variables, probability and work,
were selected so that no sequence of checking would be more efficient
than any other, on the average. Using any one of the 24 possible
orders of checking the decks consistently would require that an average
of 20.67 cards be turned in order to locate the trouble. With no pattern
of behavior defensible as the best on mathematical grounds, the
experimenter was interested in seeing what trends in behavior might
develop as subjects were given a great number of trials.

Positional influences were counterbalanced by arranging the decks
in a different order in the row for each different subject. Deck A
was 1st from the left for 3 subjects, 2nd for 3, 3rd for 3, and 4th for
the other 3 subjects. Decks B, C, and D similarly appeared equally
often in each position. Of the 24 possible ways of arranging the decks,
12 of these permutations were used. For any one subject the particular
order of deck locations was maintained on every trial. The careful
treatment of the possible influence of deck position made it possible
for the experiment to reveal how trouble-shooting behavior was
affected as the work and probability factors were repeatedly encountered by each subject.

The principal behavior tendency in this situation is revealed by
noting the per cent of times that each deck was the first to be examined
in each block of 15 trials. As the first block of 15 problems was solved,
Decks A, B, C, and D were examined first about equally often. As
trials continued, the per cent of first choices for examination revealed
an increasing tendency to look through Deck A first. This deck continued to gain strength as the group's first choice throughout the experiment, despite the fact that it required that 16 cards be turned to locate
an information card. The fact that the trouble was located in Deck A
slightly more than half of the time seemed to lead to its popularity as
first choice for search.

The per cent of times that either Deck C or Deck D was investigated first declined as the experiment continued. Despite the speed
with which trouble would be found in either of these, the low probability of its being in one of them made them unpopular as places to
look. Deck B continued to be searched first about one trial out of
four throughout the experiment, on the average, although individuals

differed greatly in choosing this deck as in their choosing of the others.

For the final 30 trials, the mean number of first choices of Deck *A* was 17.0, whereas the means for Decks *B*, *C*, and *D* were 7.3, 3.2, and 2.4, respectively. Other analyses of performance also supported the conclusion that the probability of locating the trouble in a particular place was the principal guide to the searching behavior. The format of the experiment offers many possibilities for further research on essential factors in trouble shooting.

Training Methods and Transfer in Problem Solving

A study by Hilgard, Edgren, and Irvine (1954) dealt with transfer of training in problem solving as a function of several different methods of original training. A brief review of research which led to this experiment will help us to understand its aims. It had been found that learning a certain type of card trick, introduced to psychological research by Katona, resulted in better transfer to problems of performing similar tricks if the original learning had involved understanding and not mere rote memorization. Subjects who had learned by the understanding method had still made numerous errors on the transfer problem, however. The experiment we are considering here was designed to see if the transfer effects, especially in the errors made, would vary as a result of employing different methods of original training in the understanding approach to solving the card trick problem.

A typical problem requires a subject to place 8 playing cards, 4 red and 4 black, in such an order that they will turn out in alternating red and black when played in a certain manner: the cards must be dealt one face up and then the next to the bottom of the pack, then one face up, etc. The desired final arrangement on the table, *R–B–R–B–R–B–R–B*, is achieved only if the 8 cards are properly prearranged. The problem posed in this study was to learn how to do the trick and to perform other similar tricks.

Five different groups of subjects were first taught to do the trick, each group by a different method designed to impart clear understanding. Transfer of training to similar tasks was then required. Although we cannot describe them in detail, we may briefly indicate the 5 ways of teaching understanding:

Method 1. Katona Diagram. A written schema arranged in horizontal rows is prepared by the subject to indicate how the final pattern on the table stems from the prearrangement of the cards.
Method 2. Horizontal Row. A modified Katona diagram puts all the notations in a single horizontal row.

Method 3. Vertical Column. The subject puts all notations in a vertical row as he learns the order, thus simulating closely the physical arrangement of the cards.

Method 4. Slips of Paper. Slips are numbered in the order originally held, and then labeled as they are played with the designation of what each should be: *R–B–R–B*, etc.

Method 5. Working Backward. The cards are first laid out in their final desired arrangement and then picked up and manipulated in a complete reversal of performing the trick.

These different methods were intended to give subjects an understanding of how to work out an ordering of the cards which would result in proper performing of the trick. It was expected that they would also learn how to prepare the cards for similar tricks. In the various groups, these were expected to lead to different numbers of subjects who would successfully accomplish the successive tasks given to them and would make different numbers and types of errors whenever failing to do the trick properly.

Somewhat surprisingly, the different methods of training did not make very much difference in performance and transfer. The per cent of subjects who performed a given task without error differed significantly among the different groups of 30 subjects on only one of the transfer tasks. The transfer task which reflected some difference among training methods was the one for which the average number of successful performance in the different groups was lowest, compared to all other tasks assigned. For this most difficult task, Methods 1 and 4 led to correct performing of the trick by about 60 per cent of subjects in those groups. In other groups, the other training methods led to accomplishing this most difficult task by from 23 to 42 per cent of the subjects. This task, it may be noted, was the first one encountered where *two* cards had to be moved to the bottom of the pack each time that one was placed on the table.

Performance on this hardest task was examined closely to see if different types of errors had characterized the groups trained by the different methods. Such special error tendencies as well as general error tendencies were both reflected in the data. Generally, the commonest source of error was confusion based on the new requirement to skip two cards instead of one in dealing them out. This accounted for over half the errors made, indicating a negative transfer effect from prior training and practice which had involved skipping just one card at a time. Working backwards in arranging the cards, Method 5, gave the largest proportion of errors attributable to the method itself. For Method 4, with which 60 per cent of subjects were successful, those who did make a mistake sometimes did so by labeling some of the slips wrong or by failing to arrange the cards in exact conformity to the slips when these were correctly marked. The experimental approach of this study exemplifies how a detailed study of errors in problem solving can augment what is learned from merely tallying per cents of success and failure.

SUMMARY

Problem solving is not a single psychological process but a complex kind of behavior which is, in part, situationally defined. The elements of the situation usually include a specified goal, various stimuli or cues, several response possibilities, and some means of guiding progress toward the goal. Problem tasks of great variety, incorporating these basic aspects, have been used in laboratory experiments. These were introduced by means of samples ranging from Concept Identification to Trouble Shooting. Our research aims include the description of all the processes which interact as our subjects work at solving problems. These aims are best served through interrelated experiments that provide tasks with manipulable dimensions and permit one or more meaningful measures of behavior. Numerical, verbal, and pictorial materials, as well as apparatus tasks, can meet these criteria for laboratory studies. Commonly used research methods fall into classes which include concept identification, games and puzzles, probability situations, and tasks requiring practical accomplishment.

The heart of concept identification research is the manipulation of cues which are a part of complex stimulus patterns. One way to vary task complexity is by the addition of irrelevant cues to those needed in identifying the concepts. Another task characteristic is the sequence in which the different examples of the concepts are presented. Response tendencies, tested in prior research, may be woven into the fabric of a study by proper choice of stimulus items. These may be varied with respect to their dominance in eliciting specific verbal associations.

Besides reviewing research on concept identification we examined studies of many sorts which clearly showed the great number of experimental approaches to problem solving which may be taken. In some cases the illustrative experiments employed methods and variables which had already been partially tested. Our attention was given to the following examples of investigations: anagram solution as a function of set, practice effects in playing Twenty Questions, work and probability of success in trouble shooting, and training methods and transfer in problem solving.

REFERENCES

Battig, W. F. Some factors affecting performance on a word-formation problem. *J. exp. Psychol.*, 1957, 54, 96–104.

Brown, F. G., & Archer, E. J. Concept identification as a function of task complexity and distribution of practice. *J. exp. Psychol.*, 1956, 52, 316–321.

Detambel, M. H. Probabilities of success and amounts of work in a multichoice situation. *J. exp. Psychol.*, 1956, 51, 41–44.

Duncker, K. On problem-solving. *Psychol. Monogr.*, 1945, 58, No. 5 (Whole No. 270).

Edwards, W. Reward probability, amount, and information as determiners of sequential two-alternative decisions. *J. exp. Psychol.*, 1956, 52, 177–188.

Faust, W. L. Factors in individual improvement in solving Twenty-Questions problems. *J. exp. Psychol.*, 1958, 55, 39–44.

Freedman, J. L., & Mednick, S. A. Ease of attainment of concepts as a function of response dominance variance. *J. exp. Psychol.*, 1958, 55, 463–466.

Gardner, R. A., & Runquist, W. N. Acquisition and extinction of problem-solving set. *J. exp. Psychol.*, 1958, 55, 274–277.

Grant, D. A. Perceptual versus analytical responses to the number concept of a Weigl-type card sorting test. *J. exp. Psychol.*, 1951, 41, 23–29.

Hilgard, E. R., Edgren, R. D., & Irvine, R. P. Errors in transfer following learning with understanding: further studies with Katona's card-trick experiments. *J. exp. Psychol.*, 1954, 47, 457–464.

Hovland, C. I. A set of flower designs for experiments in concept-formation. *Amer. J. Psychol.*, 1953, 66, 140–142.

Irwin, F. W., & Smith, W. A. S. Value, cost, and information as determiners of decision. *J. exp. Psychol.*, 1957, 54, 229–232.

Kendler, H. H., & Karasik, A. D. Concept formation as a function of competition between response produced cues. *J. exp. Psychol.*, 1958, 55, 278–283.

Kurtz, K. H., & Hovland, C. I. Concept learning with differing sequences of instances. *J. exp. Psychol.*, 1956, 51, 239–243.

Maltzman, I., & Morrisett, L., Jr. Effects of task instructions on solution of different classes of anagrams. *J. exp. Psychol.*, 1953, 45, 351–354.

Ray, W. S. Complex tasks for use in human problem-solving research. *Psychol. Bull.*, 1955, 52, 134–149.

Shaklee, A. B., & Jones, B. E. Distribution of practice prior to solution of a verbal reasoning problem. *J. exp. Psychol.*, 1953, 46, 429–434.

Underwood, B. J., & Richardson, J. Some verbal materials for the study of concept formation. *Psychol. Bull.*, 1956, 53, 84–95. (*a*)

Underwood, B. J., & Richardson, J. Verbal concept learning as a function of instructions and dominance level. *J. exp. Psychol.*, 1956, 51, 229–238. (*b*)

Vinacke, W. E. The investigation of concept formation. *Psychol. Bull.*, 1951, 48, 1–31.

ADDITIONAL READINGS

Battig, W. F. Effects of previous experience and information on performance on a word-formation problem. *J. exp. Psychol.*, 1958, 56, 282–287.

Bruner, J. S., Goodnow, Jacqueline J., & Austin, G. A. *A study of thinking.* New York: Wiley, 1956.

Burack, B. The nature and efficacy of methods of attack on reasoning problems. *Psychol. Monogr.*, 1950, 64, No. 7 (Whole No. 313).

Detambel, M. H., & Stolurow, L. M. Stimulus sequence and concept learning. *J. exp. Psychol.*, 1956, 51, 34–40.

Galanter, E. H., & Smith, W. A. S. Some experiments on a simple thought-problem. *Amer. J. Psychol.*, 1958, 71, 359–366.

Goodnow, Jacqueline J., & Postman, L. Probability learning in a problem-solving situation. *J. exp. Psychol.*, 1955, 49, 16–22.

Hovland, C. I., & Weiss, W. Transmission of information concerning concepts through positive and negative instances. *J. exp. Psychol.*, 1953, 45, 175–182.

Mayzner, M. S., & Tresselt, M. E. Anagram solution times: a function of letter order and word frequency. *J. exp. Psychol.*, 1958, 56, 376–379.

Underwood, B. J. An orientation for research on thinking. *Psychol. Rev.*, 1952, 59, 209–220.

CHAPTER **19**

Social
Processes

Imagine for a moment a group of three hundred people listening
to a fiery political speech. Also, try to picture a somewhat different
situation in which a half dozen college students argue some controversy currently raging on the campus. Either one of these group
activities might seem too complex to permit objective behavioral
investigation. It is just such social processes, however—the persuasion
of an audience by a speaker, and free discussion of a problem in a
face-to-face group—that are among the targets of investigations which
social psychologists are conducting. Admittedly, a total description
of what is occurring in either of these situations would be so detailed
as to defy analysis, especially to the extent that the past experience
of each participant would have to be considered. The student of
social interaction, however, can follow the lead of those who investigate
other aspects of behavior, abstracting certain features to be measured
and to be examined for interrelationships, instead of trying to deal in
global fashion with a welter of phenomena.

AIMS AND METHODS OF RESEARCH
ON SOCIAL PROCESSES

The actions and interactions of individuals in a group constitute
a realm of behavior of great proportions. A major part of any person's
activity is carried on in a social context. Furthermore, our dealings
with other people often involve such major processes as perception,
motivation, learning, remembering, and problem solving. To some
extent, then, we are studying all these topics in complex relationship
when we investigate how people act and react in group situations.

Aims

Even a slight acquaintance with social psychology tends to suggest that a major aim of its research effort is to devise more effective techniques that groups may employ in striving toward their goals. Some investigators work consciously toward applicable principles for promoting group efficiency and harmony. Others seek basic knowledge, but the applications suggest themselves. The borderline between basic and applied research is thus insubstantial and devoid of any logical basis here as in other realms of behavior science.

Much of the research directed at social processes is aimed at bridging the territory between the two disciplines of sociology and psychology. We seek to determine the psychological mechanisms that underlie social phenomena which the sociologist may have observed in various groups in the community. Research efforts are often interdisciplinary. The specialists who pool their talents may come not only from psychology and sociology, but also from fields like economics and political science and from scenes of group action like government and industry. Our general aim of a unified science of behavior is thus more prominent here than in some special areas in psychology.

Another aim of research in the social realm is to investigate processes like perception and learning at a more complex level than is attempted in the usual laboratory investigation. Behavior science must work out the laws of behavior in the complexity of their interactions as well as in their simpler manifestations. We need to understand how a person perceives other persons, and how he learns attitudes as a result of communicating with others, before we can consider the psychology of perception and learning to be complete.

Methods

With aims as broad and diverse as those which we have briefly indicated, scholars who study behavior in groups use many methods. Social processes are complex enough to be approached by various techniques, often used conjointly to supplement one another. We may profit by examining briefly some of the major methods employed.

FIELD OBSERVATION. One way to study behavior in group situations is to investigate the composition and activities of groups already in existence. Numerous aspects of this approach have been discussed by Whyte (1951) who used it in an intensive study of a street corner gang. Such studies generally involve a long-term investigation rather than a brief perusal of the group's activity. This general method of field observation may employ one or more special techniques for gathering information, in addition to direct observation at gatherings of the group being studied. Besides recording the interactions of group members, we may employ opinion polls, attitude scaling, and depth interviews to obtain a picture of the psychological forces at work. The technicalities of these approaches, beyond the scope of our discussion, must be understood and carefully considered if these methods are to enhance a research effort.

SOCIOMETRY. Sociometry, a method of analyzing the interpersonal structure of an existent group, requires that individuals choose or reject other group members as potential associates. As a basis for choosing, rejecting, or ignoring other persons, the individual is asked to consider a hypothetical situation where he might be associated with those he indicates as his choices. This situation is often either a task requiring cooperative work or a period of leisure time which may be shared with others.

A tabulation of each individual's choices and rejections provides the raw data in sociometry. Together with the pattern of cases where neither choice nor rejection was made between two persons, these data can be used to construct a *sociogram*, which is a graphic representation of group structure based on the data of sociometric choice. Each individual is represented at one point, or circular symbol, in the sociogram, with solid lines indicating choices and dotted lines rejection. This schematic representation is further refined by having distances between the person-points represent the different degrees of choice and rejection between pairs of individuals. Two people who mutually chose each other would be represented close together, whereas a pair who mutually rejected each other would be widely separated. Intermediate relationships, like mutual ignoring and non-mutual choice and rejection, would be shown as intermediate distances in the diagram of the group. Such a graphic schema readily reveals the existence of subgroups or cliques, of highly popular group members, and of persons isolated in the structure of the group.

PERSUASIVE COMMUNICATION. A key role is played in social behavior processes by communication of many sorts: an officer gives orders to his subordinates, a small boy pesters his uncle with questions, a popular singer charms his hearers with a new tune. Still another sort of social interaction is the communication of a message from a speaker to an audience. In many cases the person speaking is attempting to persuade the audience to change their opinions on some set of issues, whether he be delivering a keynote political speech, a sermon, or a football pep talk, to say nothing of a sales pitch.

One analysis of research on persuasive communication points to three major aspects of the process as places where experimental manipulations of variables have been undertaken. These are the *communicator*, the *communication*, and the *audience*. A typical study involves choosing a particular group to serve as the audience. Various social and psychological characteristics of this group are noted. A specially selected communication—a speech, a tape-recorded panel discussion, or perhaps a motion picture—is presented to them. The communicator is either present as an element in the situation or he, or they, may be identified for the audience. Since we are dealing with persuasive communication, another procedural detail is the assessment of opinions of audience members after the communication has been delivered. This pattern of opinions is compared with that of the same group prior to receiving the message or with that of a different control group of similar composition.

GROUP DYNAMICS. The dynamic processes of interaction that occur when a small group of persons engages in a discussion or works on some assigned task have led to the development of a general method of study. Actually a set of methods, *group dynamics* refers to the careful observation and recording of the interactions of members as a group session proceeds. In its application to existing organized groups, this method overlaps with field observation. We shall concentrate on the use of group dynamics techniques in laboratory research.

Variations in this approach to behavior in small groups are found principally in the kinds of observations that observers are required to make. The observers view the scene from behind a one-way vision screen, or else they sit taking notes in the same room with the group. In either case, group members usually know that a record is being made. Obviously, it is impossible to record everything that goes on in the way of discussion, gestures, and facial expressions. Sound motion pictures are usually too costly and tape recordings of conversation do not get the directed feature of many remarks that are made. Although these aids have sometimes been employed, the trend in group dynamics has been in the development of categories of interaction which an observer can use in recording. A prearranged plan indicating which facets of group processes are to be noted makes the trained observer an effective instrument in their study. Some recording systems concentrate on actions and statements, and others indicate the quality of the interaction—as friendly, hostile, mature, etc. Besides recording activity, an observer may be required to rate certain aspects of the behavior of the group or its members.

Experimental variations in the laboratory use of group dynamics have centered in the formation of the groups to be observed and the task assigned to them. Groups may be created somewhat randomly by employing whatever experimental subjects are available, or the group's composition may be guided by careful study of the individuals assigned to it. In some experiments one or more group members have to be confederates of the experimenter, trained to play a certain role in the group activity. Leaders are appointed for some groups, whereas other groups begin in an unstructured fashion with leadership allowed to emerge as it will. Generally, groups are permitted to engage in face-to-face discussion, but one class of experiments features limited channels of communication as an imposed characteristic of group structure.

Among the tasks assigned to laboratory subjects, the conducting of a group discussion is one frequently chosen. We might ask a group to discuss, for example, the relative merits of coeducational universities and separate colleges for men and women. In some studies we might collect individual opinions before, after, and even during the discussion. The participants might be required to reveal their views during the session and in some cases their task would be to arrive at a consensus, if possible. In these respects, experiments in group dynamics may have features in common with studies of persuasive communication.

Widely used as an alternative to requiring discussion is the requirement that a group of subjects cooperate in solving a problem. Discussion will naturally take place, but the direction of group activity will be partly determined by the nature of the problem. Whether problem solving or discussion is required, groups brought into the laboratory provide a wealth of social processes for careful study. There is admittedly a certain artificiality to this method, with subjects aware that their statements and actions are being monitored. However, experience has shown that people soon turn to the task at hand with considerable interest and communication among themselves.

PERSUASIVE COMMUNICATION

Social processes are communicative processes, to a great extent. We noted earlier that the basic format for research on persuasive communication offers three possibilities for introducing independent variables: communicator, communication, and audience. As we consider them, we shall also be concerned with the problem of measuring the dependent variable, opinion change in the audience. The illustrative studies we shall examine have come from a program of investigation at Yale University, reported in a volume by Hovland, Janis, and Kelley (1953).

Some Methodological Considerations

In considering many types of research we have noted that an experimental situation is typically quite complex, even where a design of elegant simplicity is adopted for a study. Experimentation on persuasive communication might deserve our vote as one of the more treacherous areas in which to seek data that permit unequivocal interpretation. Hovland, Janis, and Kelley (1953, pp. 5-6) have noted that the generality of any relationships discovered in these studies must be tested in further experiments. The complexity of even a single study is such that a confounding of variables is virtually unavoidable. Additional testing serves to separate the relevant from the irrelevant factors.

THE COMMUNICATOR. If two or more communicators are brought separately into direct contact with the audience, any variable which is assumed to be introduced by the way in which each one delivers his speech may be confounded with numerous variables of his personality as the audience reacts to it. If the same person plays different communicator roles, his portrayal of one speaker may be more valid than his impersonation of another type of communicator. Again, a straightforward interpretation of results may be hindered.

Often the complexities introduced by using a speech delivered in person are avoided by using a tape-recorded presentation. In this way, an identical communication can be attributed to two or more sources. It thus becomes the task of the experimenter to persuade the audience, for each presentation, that the communication is coming from the source he names. If his attributing of the message to some source should be doubted for any reason, then the outcome of the experiment might be questionable in proportion to the existence of this doubt in one or more of the audience groups.

THE COMMUNICATION. It would seem that devising a communication to be used in research might pose less of a problem than creating a communicator's role. However, this part of an investigation can offer difficulties of its own. Primarily, these may stem from the fact that a communication is a multidimensional pattern of stimulation. Among the facets of the message which may represent important variables are its factual content, its motivational and emotional appeals, and its sequential organization as a series of persuasive arguments. For the investigator this wealth of variables again poses problems of interpreting results. It is unlikely that any one class of factor can be manipulated without some shift in the value of other factors.

Even prior to planning how we will vary a communication to suit our experimental purpose we must make a decision on the general topic of the message. Usually we will want the message to be one which has a fair amount of interest for the audience. Persuasion to the point of opinion change will hardly stem from exposure to a communication which fails even to arouse interest. Picking a very interesting topic has its pitfalls too, however. Such a topic may have been widely discussed among the audience to be employed. This may mean that many individuals have firmly held opinions on the issues involved. There may be general knowledge of the group's views, with attendant pressure to conform. If the topic is timely, it introduces the risk that day-to-day news stories may affect opinion strongly. Research on persuasive communication is obviously not very easy to plan and execute.

THE AUDIENCE. Having seen that a communication may be quite complex, we must now note that an audience is complex in the extreme. Each individual brings numerous perceptual, motivational, and associative predispositions to the experimental situation. We thus would face many unknowns if we tried to persuade even one person to alter his opinion on some matter. When we take great individual differences into account, we would face a formidable task if we tried to account in detail for the ongoing processes of the experiment. As in other research efforts in psychology, we take the easier course of treating group statistics, letting individual differences cancel out to some extent.

Most groups which constitute audiences for research in persuasive communication have a measure of homogeneity. Classroom groups, for example, would have a much narrower range on many psychological dimensions than would a random sample of persons from the general population. This similarity among individuals might even extend to the opinions which entered into the experiment. A degree of such convergence of viewpoints might be appropriate for some studies, whereas other experiments would benefit more from employing a group whose views diverged markedly, covering a broad spectrum of opinion.

Besides selecting a communication that is appropriate to the audience, the experimenter must create plausibility for his request that it be given their attention. Why should they listen to this tape-recording, and why should they fill out an opinion questionnaire on the topic? An ingenious investigator may invent some reason for conducting the experiment other than to see how the message causes opinion change. To admit his true purpose would invite resistance on the part of many people. Later, when the data have been collected, the experimenter may explain the study fully without danger of introducing distortion into his findings. The gaging of opinions must similarly be conducted in a way calculated not to alter response tendencies in an undesired way.

MEASURING OPINION. An opinion may be defined as an evaluative response which a subject makes, or indirectly indicates his readiness to make. Being evaluative, opinions are measured through psychological scaling techniques such as we considered in Chapter 6. Examples of items designed to assess an opinion are the following two:

Intercollegiate football . . .
_____ 1. should be given greater emphasis in college life.
_____ 2. should be maintained at the present level of emphasis in college life.
_____ 3. should be given less emphasis in college life.

Intercollegiate football should be abolished.
_____ Agree strongly
_____ Agree
_____ Neither agree nor disagree
_____ Disagree
_____ Disagree strongly

Either of these techniques for scaling opinion provides a means of measuring opinion change in a group. Some other scaling method, such as a graphic rating scale, might be selected instead if the experimental topic seemed to require it. In research on persuasive communication we may measure the average amount of shift along the opinion scale, or we may note the per cent of subjects who shift their opinion in either direction.

Opinion measurement cannot be regarded as simple to achieve. All stages of preparing and administering the testing instrument must be guided by the best technical advice available. Valid expressions of opinion must be encouraged by stressing the research orientation of the investigator. Anonymity may usually be promised to participants to elicit frank opinions. Communication topics may be chosen which do not arouse strong tendencies to shrink from revealing true opinions.

DESIGN OF THE EXPERIMENT. We may conclude our discussion of methodology by considering the design of a study in persuasive communication. Our considerations will be guided in large measure by parts of an article by Campbell (1957). His paper deals broadly with experimental designs for investigations in social science, but many of his points seem particularly appropriate for research in persuasive communication.

Suppose that we wish to determine the effect of a communication, X, on the opinions, O, held by a group. It might seem that measuring opinions before and after the presenting of the communication to a group of subjects would provide the needed data. Any difference between pretest and posttest opinion measures might be attributed to the effect of the message. This design may be schematized as follows:

$$\text{Only Group: } O_1 \text{——} X \text{——} O_2$$

where O_1 and O_2 represent the pretest and posttest of opinion, respectively, and X represents the persuasive communication.

This one-group pretest-posttest design has been shown by Campbell (1957, pp. 298–300) to yield data which are virtually impossible to interpret with scientific rigor. The crux of the difficulty is that the possible effect of X may be confounded with one or more other effects. Procedural details of a study would make some of these more likely to distort the data than others, but each of them is a potential threat as we evaluate the design in general. In listing the possible confounding effects we shall follow Campbell's nomenclature for these extraneous variables:

1. *History.* Other events, besides X, which occur during the time from O_1 to O_2 may influence opinion change. This class of factors is particularly suspect when the interval is great, when subjects do not remain in the experimental situation, and when the topic of the communication is one of current interest.

2. *Maturation.* This refers to any ongoing processes which are not linked to specific environmental events. Between O_1 and O_2 subjects may experience an increase in hunger or the desire for a cigarette. Such factors might contribute to changes in expressed opinion on some topics. For example, frustration might lead to aggression toward whatever was being evaluated.

3. *Testing.* Responses on O_2 may be affected by previous experience with O_1. Many psychological tests induce reactions in those who are tested. Such reactive effects can arise, for example, when O_1 leads subjects to focus their attention on a particular topic. These reactions to O_1 may be more complete by the time O_2 is experienced, thus providing potential confounding with the effect of X.

4. *Instrument Decay.* As a measuring device is used repeatedly, it may undergo changes which affect the data obtained. This effect would be virtually absent in a printed questionnaire or rating scale. If items look different the second time the subjects see them, this may be classified as a reactive effect of the previous testing. However,

an "instrument decay" effect might occur if we used judges to assess subjects' opinions in O_1 and O_2. The judges might be tired by the time O_2 took place, and this might affect their judgments.

The possible operation of one or more of these four types of factor—either introducing, augmenting, or reducing opinion change—leads Campbell to indicate that this plan for an investigation is not a true experimental design.

We shall briefly look at one more design in which a serious question of validity arises. An experimenter might present the communication, X, to one classroom group of subjects and try to compare their opinions subsequently with opinions measured in a different classroom group which had not been exposed to the message. This is a two-group design which yields a static group comparison, according to Campbell (1957, p. 300). The two groups, constituted in some way other than by random assignment of individuals to them, are treated as represented in the following schema:

$$\text{Experimental Group:} \quad X \text{——} O_E$$
$$\text{Control Group:} \qquad\qquad \text{——} O_C$$

where O_E and O_C represent the opinion measurement of the Experimental Group and Control Group, respectively, and X represents the persuasive communication.

The flaw in this design is that any differences in opinion revealed in the data of O_E and O_C may reflect differences in the two groups of subjects. This possible source of confounding is encountered whenever two ready-made groups are utilized or when groups are established on some basis which permits nonrandom factors to operate.

The schema we have just considered becomes the design for an acceptable experiment if we specify that the Experimental Group and Control Group are to be constituted by assigning individuals to them in a random fashion. A statistical test of a difference between O_E and O_C data is now valid because the analysis, perhaps a t ratio, is specifically intended to determine the likelihood that the difference might have stemmed by chance from the appointing of the various persons to serve in the groups.

It might happen that an experimenter would be forced to use existing classroom groups in a two-group study of persuasive communication. To be sure that differences of opinion at the end of the experiment were attributable to X and not to existing group characteristics, a pretest could be administered to both groups, as represented in this schema:

$$\text{Experimental Group:} \quad O_{1E} \underline{\hspace{1cm}} X \underline{\hspace{1cm}} O_{2E}$$
$$\text{Control Group:} \quad\quad\ O_{1C} \underline{\hspace{2.5cm}} O_{2C}$$

In this design we would compare the change from pretest to posttest in the experimental group with the corresponding change in opinion data in the control group. That is, the *difference* between O_{1E} and O_{2E} would be compared with the *difference* between O_{1C} and O_{2C}. The latter difference is assumed to contain the effects of such potential confounding factors as history, maturation, testing, and instrument decay, which we discussed earlier. This control is effective only if conditions and temporal spacing of the opinion tests are arranged so as to be equivalent for both groups of subjects.

If we use this design with existent groups, it represents a compromise with a more effective plan of setting up both groups on a random assignment basis. With existent groups, the pretesting of opinion, O_{1E} and O_{1C}, permits us to see if equivalent states of opinion characterized the two groups used. If equivalence is evident, our analysis of opinion change becomes more meaningful. If not, we can only consider the data on change of opinion as tentative findings. The operation of confounding factors might not be the same at the two different levels of opinions which distinguished the groups. There are additional complexities of the design problem in social science which are discussed by Campbell (1957, pp. 300–311), but the present discussion should be sufficient to alert us to possible pitfalls.

A Communicator Variable

As an illustration of how the communicator factor may be treated experimentally we shall review part of a study by Kelman and Hovland (1953). Their experiment dealt particularly with a delayed test of opinion change, administered three weeks after the communication, but we shall consider only the assessment of attitude immediately after presentation of the communication. Our interest centers in noting how the communicator variable was manipulated while communication and audience factors were equivalent in the different experimental conditions.

The persuasive communication was presented as a tape-recorded transcription of an educational radio program on juvenile delinquency. This interview between a moderator and a guest was prepared in three different forms, with the prestige and qualifications of the guest being varied. In one version, the guest was a positive communicator, introduced as a juvenile court judge of long experience. In a contrasting tape-recording, a negative communicator was established in the preliminary portion of the interview when it was brought out that the guest was a self-centered individual who had been in many scrapes with the law and was currently under indictment as a dope peddler. A neutral communicator was a guest who was presented as having been selected from the studio audience at random, with no information about him being given. After their identities and qualifications had been established in the first part of each tape-recording, the guests went on to give identically worded discussions of how juvenile delinquents should be treated. Their remarks advocated great leniency in treating such youthful offenders. Different classroom groups each listened to just one of the three tapes, involving either the positive, negative, or neutral communicator. It was predicted that the positive communicator would win more agreement with the advocated position than would the negative communicator, with the neutral speaker achieving intermediate success.

Ten classroom groups of high school students served as subjects with four classes listening to the positive communicator, four the negative communicator, and two the neutral guest. The content of the persuasive communication itself was identical in all cases. A questionnaire of eight multiple-choice items was given to all subjects before they heard their tape-recording. Analysis of these attitude indicators showed the different groups to be comparable in their attitude toward the treatment of juvenile delinquents. Immediately after hearing the recorded radio interview, subjects were given a set of twenty items from the Wang-Thurstone scale for attitude toward the treatment of criminals. These provided the data for assessing the effects of the different communicators. The different groups of subjects were also asked their opinions on how qualified the guest speaker seemed to be and how fair or one-sided they judged his remarks.

Analysis of the attitude scores showed that greatest agreement with the advocated position of leniency existed in the groups who had received the message from the positive communicator. A significantly lower degree of agreement was won by the negative communicator, delivering the same arguments. The neutral communicator achieved an intermediate degree of agreement as predicted, but the attitude level of these groups of subjects was much closer to that of the students who had heard the positive communicator, being not significantly lower. This neutral communicator did obtain a significantly greater measure of agreement than did the negative communicator. Attitudes toward the guest they had heard interviewed were similarly varied among the groups given the three experimental treatments. The speaker was judged to be highly qualified to discuss juvenile delinquency by 78% of those who heard the positive communicator, by

33% of those who heard the neutral guest, and by only 9% of the subjects who listened to the negative communicator. These data offer strong direct evidence that the communicators were perceived quite differently as intended. When asked for opinions on the fairness of the presentation, as opposed to one-sidedness, 73% of those who had heard the positive communicator responded favorably. Only 29% of those who had been exposed to the negative communicator felt that he had been fair, whereas this judgment of the communication was made by 63% of those who had listened to the neutral communicator. Again the evidence is that interrelated attitudes were being formed and shifted as the three different guests were introduced and as they gave the presentation.

A Communication Variable

Among the many variables which constitute dimensions of persuasive communications is the extent to which the message is studded with stimuli designed to arouse emotion or motivation. One form of motivational arousal which is widely employed is an appeal to fear or anxiety. Fear arousal may be employed in communications as diverse as "view-with-alarm" political speeches and "do-you-suffer-from" advertisements for patent medicines. What level of fear-arousal is most effective in bringing about sustained changes in attitudes and behavior? This question was the focus of an experiment which we shall review in concluding our discussion of research in persuasive communication.

Janis and Feshbach (1953) used three illustrated talks on dental hygiene which differed in the kind and amount of fear-arousing material that they contained. The three messages were similar in presenting basic information about causes of tooth decay, and they all contained the same recommendations concerning proper care of the teeth. Different randomly assigned high school freshmen served as subjects in the three experimental groups to which Strong, Moderate, or Minimal fear-arousing forms of the communication were presented. A similarly constituted fourth group served in the Control condition, being exposed to a completely irrelevant message. In the Strong form of the dental hygiene talk there was repeated emphasis on the grave dangers of neglecting the proper care of the teeth and the illustrative slides portrayed serious cases of oral infection and tooth decay. For the Moderate degree of fear-arousal the slides showed milder cases of dental difficulties and the talk included far fewer references to the more serious dangers of improper care of the teeth. The Minimal fear-arousal involved very little threatening reference to oral pathology either in the message or the accompanying slides.

The attitudes and ideas of the subjects concerning the care of the teeth were assessed at three different points during the experiment. One week prior to the presenting of the different forms of the communication, a general health questionnaire was administered to all the students. It included key items on their attitudes and practices in the realm of oral hygiene. Immediately after hearing one of the recorded talks and seeing the accompanying set of slides, subjects filled out a questionnaire designed to test the amount of information they had acquired and their reactions as they heard the lecture. One week later, all subjects were given a questionnaire which resembled the one administered a week before the talks. This was intended to reveal any changes which had occurred in the brushing of the teeth and in beliefs concerning proper dental care. The two post-communication tests of attitude were intended, of course, to reveal any differences among the three experimental groups as a result of the Strong, Moderate, or Minimal fear-arousing stimulation incorporated in their messages. Also comparisons of these three groups with the Control Group could be made.

Equivalence of the four randomly established groups of subjects was noted in age, mean IQ, and number of boys and girls in each group. The pre-communication questionnaire further showed that the groups did not differ significantly in their practices of dental care or in their attitudes on matters which were to be tested after they had received the different presentations.

When tested immediately after hearing the communication and viewing the slides, all experimental groups scored about the same on an information test concerning proper care of the teeth. If the experiment had ended at this point, the conclusion might have been that the different levels of fear-arousal had produced no significant effect, at least in the imparting of the factual material common to all the messages. The groups did differ at this point in their attitudes toward the communications. The most favorable general appraisal of the illustrated talk came from the group who had been subjected to the Strong degree of fear-arousal. At the same time, this group was most critical of certain aspects of the presentation, specifically the unpleasant nature of some of the accompanying photographs. Mixed reactions were often expressed in response to an open-end question, with students stating that the fear-arousal was unpleasant but probably a good way of impressing the important message on the audience.

One week later, further testing was intended to reveal whether fairly long-standing effects on attitudes had been achieved and whether the magnitude of these effects was dependent on the level of emotion intended to be aroused by the Strong, Moderate, or Minimal forms of the communication. A major part of this assessment dealt with the subjects' reports on their current practices in brushing their teeth. Identical questions about personal dental care had been asked two weeks earlier, so the data permitted the investigators to determine if an individual reported increased conformity or decreased conformity with the tooth-brushing recommendations which had been given in the communication, or if no change was reported. The authors of the report point out that their data were based on reports by the subjects and not on observed behavior. Any changes in reports may thus reflect only verbal conformity to the recommendations of the message. It remains a point of interest to see if such reported changes in dental care were influenced differentially by the three levels of fear-arousal in the different forms of the communication.

In every group some subjects showed increased conformity with the methods suggested in the message, some showed decreased conformity, and some showed no change from their former report of tooth-brushing practices. Between 34 and 56% of subjects in different groups indicated no change in conforming to the advocated practices. Ignoring these, and subtracting the per cent showing decreased conformity from that showing increased conformity, the investigators obtained a per cent indicating net change in conformity in each group. For example, in the Minimal fear-arousal group, 50% showed increased conformity and 14% showed decreased conformity, so that a net change in conformity of 36% was calculated. This preponderance of subjects changing their reported habits in the expected direction was the greatest obtained in any of the groups. The Moderate and the Strong fear-arousal groups showed net changes in conformity of 22 and 8%, respectively. In the Control Group, 22% showed increased conformity and exactly the same per cent showed decreased conformity, so the net change in conformity for these subjects was zero. Statistical analysis supported the conclusion that the change in reported conformity with recommendations of the communication was significantly greater in the Minimal Group than in either the Strong or the Control Groups. These latter two groups did not differ significantly from each other. The Moderate Group fell between the other two experimental groups, not differing significantly from either. This analysis of the data suggests a functional relationship, with reported changes in conforming behavior becoming more frequent as the level of fear-arousal in the communication is lessened. Milder degrees of emotional arousal appear more effective in winning acceptance of recommendations. The report of the study includes proper cautions against generalizing this finding too broadly. Under some conditions it is certainly possible that stronger emotional appeals would have the greater effect on attitudes or behavior.

Another part of the final questionnaire tested the resistance of the different groups of subjects to counterpropaganda. In the communication presented to the three experimental groups a particular kind of toothbrush had been recommended. Just before taking the final test of opinion all groups were exposed to counterpropaganda in which a well-known dentist was reported as stating that any sort of toothbrush is effective if used properly. How many subjects would show more agreement with this statement now than they had two weeks earlier? In the pre-communication testing there had been an item on the adequacy of any sort of toothbrush but the statement of this opinion by a dentist had not been used. Note that this view was counter to that presented in the major communication.

It was found that a net difference of 20 per cent occurred in the Control Group when those agreeing more and those agreeing less with this dentist's statement were counted. A greater number changed to a position of greater agreement with the view that any toothbrush was adequate. Of course this group had not received the message on care of the teeth. In the experimental groups the net changes in agreement with this counterpropaganda of the dentist were all negative. In other words, more of the subjects were swayed by their memories of the illustrated talk to reject his statement. The greatest resistance to this counterpropaganda occurred in the group which had been exposed to the Minimal fear-arousal form of the communication. In offsetting conflicting recommendations, then, as well as in eliciting reported conformity with advocated practices, the study indicates lesser emotional arousal to be more effective.

GROUP DYNAMICS

As we turn to group dynamics, the topic of communication as an important social process is by no means left behind. Rather, the one-way communication of speaker to audience is replaced by multiple channels of communication. In most research, group members are brought into face-to-face contact and each person can converse with everyone else. In some studies communication is given special attention by limiting the channels by which group members may deal with each other. In either form of experiment, the frequency, direction, and content of "messages" sent and received are of considerable interest to the investigator.

Earlier in this chapter we considered the general outlines of laboratory research in group dynamics. A small group of subjects is assembled, assigned a task, and carefully observed as interaction between group members continues. We noted that this general method is amenable to wide variation in the manipulation of experimental factors and in the observations and measurements which are made.

Methods of Study

Our methodological discussion of group dynamics research will take the simple form of considering first a sample of independent variables which have been manipulated and, second, a number of dependent variables used in assessing the group's behavior. We must omit any discussion of how group dynamics research is carried out in established groups in business and industry, in schools, and in the military. Within the domain of laboratory study of small groups assembled for experimentation, we shall further exclude from consideration those studies which center on the personal characteristics of the group members—age, sex, intelligence, abilities, and traits of personality. Factors which will occupy our attention will range from size of group to communication net imposed on the group.

SIZE OF GROUP. Among the early efforts in experimental social psychology were studies to determine whether individuals performing a given task would do better if they worked in a social setting, where others were similarly occupied, or in a solitary setting. The social setting proved to be facilitating for many performances. Somewhat different were attempts to determine if cooperative effort on a task like solving a problem would make a group more effective than an individual working alone. It was generally found that group problem solving was better than that accomplished by individuals. An extension of this sort of study is to determine what size of group is most effective in performing a given task cooperatively.

Taylor and Faust (1952) assigned a modified form of the Twenty Questions game as the problem to be solved by individuals and by groups of two and four experimental subjects. The groups tended to be superior to the individuals, but in most respects the groups did not differ, as a function of their size, in efficiency in solving the problems. The size of group made no difference, for example, in the number of questions asked or in the elapsed time before a solution was reached. One point at which a difference could be attributed to group size was in the number of failures. The groups of two persons failed to arrive at a solution in about 10 per cent of their attempts, whereas failures occurred in the groups of four subjects with less than half this frequency. With four people contributing ideas, a group was less likely to persist in pursuing an erroneous lead, as might be done by one or two persons.

In contrast to noting how size of group affects performance of the assigned task, some experimenters have sought the effects of group size on the ongoing processes of interaction as the group worked toward a goal. Hare (1953) assigned to groups of 5 and 12 Boy Scouts the task of discussing which items of camping equipment would prove most valuable to a scout sent out on his own into wild country. Each of the 18 discussion groups had to arrive at a consensus ranking of the 10 items of equipment. Individual rankings taken before and after the discussion provided correlational indices of how much general agreement had been engendered by the discussion. It was found that closer agreement was achieved in the groups of 5 than in the groups of 12. A questionnaire was employed to determine how the group leaders and followers had perceived their participation in the discussion. One perception that was widely shared in the groups of 12 was that there had been too little time available for discussion and exchange of views. Related to this was the judgment by members of groups of 12 that their own opinions had been of little importance as the group consensus was reached.

PRESSURE TO SOCIAL CONFORMITY. A social process of widespread occurrence is the tendency for individual opinions to be changed in the direction of group norms as views are exchanged in discussion. The mechanisms by which pressures toward conformity are exerted have been studied by three different methods with which we should be acquainted. In the first method, free discussion of a topic takes place among experimental subjects whose opinions are measured before and after the group exchange of views. Such experiments generally show the trend toward increased agreement, and they often reveal such aspects of the group interaction as the fact that most remarks tend to be directed toward those group members whose opinions are somewhat extreme.

A second experimental technique demonstrates the widespread extent to which individuals will abandon their asserted viewpoints or judgments in the face of divergent opinions expressed by others. In this type of study the experimenter often employs confederates who pose as subjects. These special assistants express judgments which are divergent from the viewpoint of the individual who is the true subject in the experiment. On repeated trials, if not in a single occurrence, the real subject tends to follow the lead of the confederates, even to the point of denying his own perceptual experience. For example, a subject might agree that a line was curved when others expressed this view, even when it appeared perfectly straight to him.

In the third method one or more confederates are also employed, but the majority of the group members are valid experimental subjects. It is usually the role of the special assistant to express opinions that are fairly extreme, quite divergent from the consensus of the legitimate subjects. This special technique enables the experimenter to note the reactions of the true subjects to the one whose viewpoint is deviant. He may also observe the efforts they make to induce conformity with their views. This attempt on their part is encouraged by the experimental instructions that the group is to arrive at a single opinion on the matter under discussion.

ASSIGNED TASK. The tasks assigned to experimental groups have tended to fall into two main classes—topics to be discussed and problems to be solved. In some instances a discussion may have a problem-solving aspect, as when a group is required to arrive at a consensus on how some problem should be solved. In these cases there is usually no right or wrong answer, so that these discussions still differ from attempts to solve problems where an objectively correct solution exists. In some discussion groups, performance data are sought in the opinion changes registered by individuals. We noted this experimental approach when we discussed methods for studying pressure to social conformity in the preceding section. Other studies may involve little interest in the outcome of the discussion but may concentrate attention on the social processes taking place as the group members interact.

Many experiments on problem solving by groups have used the number of groups achieving the solution or the time taken to solve the problem as indices of effectiveness, while varying such factors as size of group or channels of intragroup communication. Such molar measures of performance have often revealed little of the processes taking place as the group solved the problem. Furthermore, when a principle as to the most efficient group size or structure was sought, discussion of experimental results has often included the unhappy conclusion that it depends on the type of task or problem involved. It is precisely in this lament that we can detect a powerful resource for the investigator of social processes in recent and future studies. If the outcome of a problem-solving effort and the group interactions leading to that outcome differ as a function of the type of problem assigned, then the experimenter should be able to use problem tasks of such variety as to create a wealth of interactions of various sorts among the members of the group. Putting the matter somewhat more empirically, an investigator may hope to find numerous aspects of behavior varying as a function of the independent variables which he manipulates in devising problem tasks and presenting them to his subjects. As this approach is employed, more attention can be paid to measuring different facets of the individuals' behaviors as well as to the final outcome of the group effort.

Inspiration for the foregoing stress on the assigned problem as a pool of experimental variables has been largely derived from an article by Roby and Lanzetta (1958). These authors suggest the analysis of complex tasks into input variables of two kinds, those initiated by the experimenter and those which arise as group members receive communications from each other. They would also deal with output variables of two kinds, the communicative acts and the actions directed toward solving the problem. This detailed task analysis should lead to the identification of critical demands made on the group by different problem tasks. A program of research may incorporate tasks which feature different sets of critical demands so that different patterns of behavior are elicited from the group members. Some tasks, for example, might place special demands on group members for perceiving and remembering the stimulus information which might be gradually offered to them as the task progressed. Other tasks might stress a cooperative effort in logic to obtain a problem solution.

COMMUNICATION NET. A general method for studying the interactions of group members as they solve a problem has been to establish different communication nets which restrict the sending and receiving of messages. Certain group members are permitted to send messages directly to others. Contrastingly, direct communication between certain persons in the communication net is prohibited. They may exchange information only indirectly, transmitting messages through intermediaries in the net. Two-way communication over each of the channels which comprise the net is generally permitted, although one-way lines connecting certain persons may also be introduced as a variant in this method. Written messages are usually required so as to restrict communication to designated channels. This slows down the interaction processes and permits the experimenter to examine them in complete sequential detail. This experimental technique of

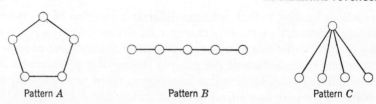

Pattern *A*   Pattern *B*   Pattern *C*

Fig. 19.1. Three sample patterns of communication net for a five-person group. Each circle is an individual and each line is a two-way communication channel. (After Bavelas, 1953.)

restricting the interaction of group members contrasts markedly with the free face-to-face discussion that is permitted in many experiments on group dynamics.

Bavelas (1953) has discussed several communication nets which have been compared with each other in a number of different experiments. Figure 19.1 illustrates three of the nets which have been commonly used. In Pattern *A* the channels of communication make every individual equally accessible to the others in general. Each person can communicate directly with two others and can reach the remaining two of the five-man group by using just one person as an intermediary. In Pattern *B* the individuals on the ends of the chain are so remote that their communications with most other group members are accomplished quite indirectly. Pattern *C* features one person who can communicate directly with each of the other four. Further, this same person must be used as an intermediary by any other two who wish to communicate.

Task Performance Measures

Having noted several methods for varying independent variables in research on group dynamics, we now turn to a brief survey indicating some of the ways in which behavior is assessed in the group situation. We begin by noting that the assigned task itself often provides measures of accomplishment which indicate how effectively each group performed under the imposed condition. Among the more molar performance measures are frequency data on how many groups under each condition arrive at a solution to the problem assigned them. An experimenter might also employ measures like the time or number of messages used in solving a problem and the frequency with which erroneous solutions are proposed. Communicative actions involved in the course of discussion or problem solving are also amenable to quantification and categorization. This possibility for analysis is especially strong where written messages have

been required, as in some studies of communication nets.   These
more molecular behavior measures should help to clarify the actual
dynamics of interaction among the members of a small group.

OBSERVATIONAL CATEGORY SYSTEMS.   Where a face-to-face inter-
change takes place among the experimental subjects, the common
research practice is to use trained observers to note the various facets
of their behavior.   These observers cannot be expected to obtain a
verbatim record of all discussion.   In some cases, tape-recording may
be employed for this purpose.   The observers' task is, rather, to get
a record of how the interactions among group members proceed
during the session.   The specific content of any interchanges of ideas
is usually not noted, but attention is directed instead to the nature
of the interactions.   To accomplish this, the trained observers employ
a system of interaction categories which has been prepared to cover
most of the aspects of group dynamics.

A set of interaction categories developed by Bales (1950) will
acquaint us with some of the features of a systematic observational
approach to group dynamics.   The trained observers classify every
interaction which they note into one of these categories:

1. *Shows solidarity,* raises other's status, gives help, reward.
2. *Shows tension release,* jokes, laughs, shows satisfaction.
3. *Agrees,* shows passive acceptance, understands, concurs, complies.
4. *Gives suggestion,* direction, implying autonomy for other.
5. *Gives opinion,* evaluation, analysis, expresses feeling, wish.
6. *Gives orientation,* information, repeats, clarifies, confirms.
7. *Asks for orientation,* information, repetition, confirmation.
8. *Asks for opinion,* evaluation, analysis, expression of feeling.
9. *Asks for suggestion,* direction, possible ways of action.
10. *Disagrees,* shows passive rejection, formality, withholds help.
11. *Shows tension,* asks for help, withdraws out of field.
12. *Shows antagonism,* deflates other's status, defends or asserts self.

Careful perusal of this list should convince you that an observer would
require extensive training and practice before hoping to employ these
categories in a reliable fashion.   The observations are not oriented
toward the content of the group's discussion but toward the social
interaction processes which comprise that discussion.   Frequency
tallies of the different interactions which take place, perhaps taken
separately for different time periods, can reveal the quality of the
dynamics exhibited by a group and by its individual members.   Some
groups may be strongly task-oriented and impersonal in their interactions, requiring an observer to make frequent use of Categories
4 through 9.   Another group might evidence considerable negative
emotionality, causing Categories 10 through 12 to be employed fre-

quently. One individual might be seen in the frequency tallies as one who repeatedly asked questions, Categories 7 through 9, whereas a different person often showed reactions of a positive emotional tone, Categories 1 through 3.

RATINGS. As a substitute or supplement for tallying the occurrence of various interactions, observers of a group may be required to rate the group on certain dimensions. This psychological scaling technique may be directed at the behavior of individuals as well as at the group's functioning. Dimensions of the group which might be rated include morale and degree of task orientation. Aspects of individual participation which might be scaled are amount of leadership exerted and intensity of interest exhibited. Observers' ratings of such a social-psychological trait as group morale can represent a facet of group dynamics which might not be readily apparent in tape-recorded group conversation or even in frequency counts of different interactions of group members. Of course, all the precautions concerning the use of ratings which we discussed in Chapter 6 on "Psychological Scaling" apply to their employment in group dynamics research. Raters require especially intensive training and practice since they must rate so many aspects of a complex situation that changes moment by moment.

The selection of numerous dimensions to be rated does not mean that interactions between group members need be conceptualized in as complex a fashion as appearances might dictate. Carter (1955) has reviewed a number of empirical studies in which the intercorrelations of ratings on various dimensions of individual behavior were examined. Using techniques of factor analysis it was found that about three factors could generally account for an individual's participation in the group session. The factor names which Carter assigned to these three aspects of a person's social behavior are *Individual Prominence*, the tendency to stand out from the group, *Group Goal Facilitation*, the tendency to promote group progress with the assigned task, and *Group Sociability*, a friendly interpersonal relationship to other group members.

Discussion and Decision-Making

A tremendous variety of possible experiments in group dynamics was indicated when our consideration of research methods revealed a number of ways of introducing independent variables and numerous techniques for describing and measuring behavior in the group situation. In the realm of discussion and decision-making the research which has actually been conducted has borne out the promise of this variety.

INTERACTION PROFILE AS A FUNCTION OF SIZE OF GROUP. Group size was the independent variable in a study by Bales and Borgatta (1955) who assigned similar discussion tasks to small groups of college students who met repeatedly for four sessions. Groups of two through seven men were formed from students drawn from a university employment bureau and paid for their time. Men previously acquainted were put into different groups. Once formed, every group was required to continue through four sessions, taking a new discussion task each time. Four different groups of each size were run.

Each discussion task was a case study or problem in human relations faced by an administrator. Copies of each problem were given to individual subjects to be read and were then put aside as the group discussion began. It was purposely not made clear whether the same range of facts had been presented to everyone. The discussion task was to bring all available information together, review the actions and motives of the people described, and decide a course of action which ought to be followed by the administrator. After about 40 min the group was supposed to make a tape-recording of their proposed solution.

For their analysis of the group dynamics of discussion groups as a function of size, the investigators made use of the interaction categories devised by Bales (1950) which we reviewed as an example of an observational system in our discussion of methods (p. 559). As the different interactions of individuals were tallied, how would these frequency tallies distribute themselves over the twelve categories of the system? To what extent would this distribution of interactions over the categories be affected by the size of the different discussion groups? This latter question was the heart of the investigation to which we shall devote our exclusive attention. Before reviewing the findings we need to note how the frequency data were combined and transformed.

In the principal analysis each individual's frequency tally over the twelve categories was first obtained by pooling all four sessions. Next, these twelve frequencies were converted to per cents for each subject. Then these per cents were treated by a mathematical transformation to obtain approximately normal distributions. Finally, a mean was computed, for each category of interaction, by pooling the individual's values according to the size of group in which they had participated. For example, mean values for each category were calculated for the twenty men who had been members of groups of five participants. Such means were compared within categories by tests of statistical significance to see how size of group affected the discussion process. We may take note of a few representative results.

As group size was increased, the investigators noted increases in the behaviors of exhibiting tension release (Category 2) and giving suggestion (Category 4). There were decreases in showing tension (Category 11) and showing agreement (Category 3). Such changes, occurring as the size of a discussion group grows larger, seem to reflect factors like the decreased talking time per participant which is available and the need to maintain good intragroup relationships as the number of persons interacting becomes larger.

The two-man discussion group showed a number of differences from the three-man group in the profile of interaction across the twelve categories. For example, the two-man groups were higher in frequency of showing tension (Category 11) but lower in showing disagreement (Category 10) and antagonism (Category 12). The authors suggest that this relative absence of overt antagonism in two-man groups is due to the need to proceed with caution when unanimity seems needed. In three-man groups such caution may be tossed aside when two participants arrive at a majority opinion and may hope to convince the third man of their view.

Although the two-man groups were fairly low in showing disagreement and antagonism, groups of four and six men were higher in these, Categories 10 and 12 respectively, than were the groups of three, five, and seven men, on the average. In this comparison, with the special two-man groups set aside, we need to ask why the groups containing an even number of men should generate more antagonism. The authors of the study suggest that it is due to the likelihood of even splits of opinion, which do not take place when an odd number of persons is involved in a discussion. In the latter instance, one view will have a majority which keeps discussion moving and avoids prolonged conflict.

SOCIAL SCALES OF JUDGMENT AND GROUP DECISIONS. A quantitative group decision will be more accurate if it is derived from a broad, rather than a narrow, reference scale developed in the group discussion. This was one hypothesis tested in an investigation by Ziller (1955) which we shall review partially to illustrate a basic experimental format for the study of group decision-making. Although the experimenter used organized air crews as groups in the experiment, the research techniques are largely applicable to any small groups two hypotheses we have stated. More coalitions were formed against the stooge subject when the task was considered to be very important. Likewise, more of these coalitions occurred under the peer condition in which the stooge was presented as a reasonable competitor for the others. These main effects were found to be statistically significant. The findings tended to be borne out by other data that were taken, such as the price in points which the stooge had to offer in order to break up a coalition against him. A greater number of points was demanded of him in the bargaining when the task was perceived as more important and when he was perceived as a peer against whom the real subjects ought to compete successfully.

THREE-MAN COMMUNICATION NETS. A series of experiments by Heise and Miller (1951) involved a variety of communication nets achieved by using both one-way and two-way channels between members of the group. The five different nets which were used are schematically represented in Figure 19.2. Among the features which distinguish these nets we may note that Net 1 permits each subject, A, B, or C, to communicate with each other person over a two-way channel; in Net 3 there is two-way communication between A and B as well as between A and C, but B and C are not joined directly by any channel; Net 5 involves three one-way channels, permitting A

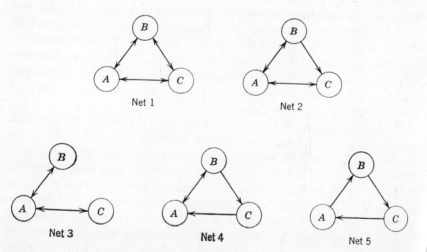

Fig. 19.2. **Five** three-person communication nets used by Heise and Miller (1951) with both one-way and two-way communication used in different net patterns as indicated by the arrowheads in the figure. (After Heise and Miller, 1951.)

which we might assemble for research purposes. In this brief review we shall omit discussion of how the factor of military status entered into the investigation as the different crews were studied.

Thirty-six crews ranging in size from ten to fifteen men served as the experimental groups. A quantitative task was devised for which there was an objectively true answer, but which would elicit a variety of individual estimates as a starting point for the group decision-making. With each group seated in a face-to-face arrangement, the experimenter dropped into their midst a 16 in. × 21 in. card on which were scattered, evenly but irregularly, exactly 3155 dots. The card was in view for only 15 sec, longer exposure times having led to unduly accurate techniques of estimation. Each group was given the task of arriving at a crew decision about the number of dots that had been displayed.

Under Conditions A and B, the group discussion was preceded by a public poll in which the experimenter called on each individual to announce his own personal estimate. Under Condition C the group discussion began without this requirement for individual estimates. This condition was expected to lead to less accurate group estimates on the assumption that these groups would carry on their discussion with a narrower reference scale of estimates. Conditions A and B were expected to develop broader scales of judgment as a result of polling individuals, and the hypothesis we stated earlier predicts that more accurate group decisions should ensue. This same hypothesis was testable by fractionating the groups under Conditions A and B into those exhibiting a broad scale and those showing a narrow scale of judgment when initial individual estimates were examined. In addition to this approach to group decision-making, the investigator concluded each session by surveying individual opinion on the influences each person had felt and the degree of agreement with the final group estimate. We may note this extension of the experimental procedure even though we shall not be able to consider this part of the results.

When the various group estimates were examined, it was found that Conditions A and B, with individual estimates having preceded the group discussion, had given rise to mean errors of about 1000 and 900 dots, respectively. These error magnitudes were compared with a mean error value of about 1500 dots made under Condition C, with no polling of individuals prior to group discussion. Although this much larger mean error was in the predicted direction, it was not statistically significant in comparison with the means for Conditions

A and *B* which had presumably come from broader scales of judgment. An analysis of the data from these two conditions alone did yield support for the hypothesis under discussion.

All groups under these Conditions *A* and *B* were examined as to the *SD* of the original individual estimates as publicly expressed. The groups showing an *SD* above the median were then compared to those exhibiting an *SD* of preliminary estimates which was below the median. In other words, the groups having a broad scale of judgment were compared with those having a narrower scale established in the initial poll. It was found that the mean error of group estimates based on the broader scales was only about 800 dots, whereas groups using narrower scales showed a mean group error of about 1400 dots. The difference in this case was statistically significant, offering support to the hypothesis under investigation.

Problem Solving

Investigations in which groups are required to solve problems are as varied in content and method as are studies of group discussions. Since we are not attempting a representative survey, we shall omit examples of the more straightforward experiments in which a face-to-face group is observed while it tries to solve an assigned problem. We shall look instead at some illustrative research featuring somewhat special methods.

DYNAMICS OF COMPETITIVE BARGAINING. In contrast to the usual study which calls for full cooperation in attacking a problem, Hoffman, Festinger, and Lawrence (1954) set up a situation in which three people bargained competitively to obtain points. Each individual was striving to earn points for himself, but the situation was arranged so that two people might form a coalition so as to win extra points. These points could then be shared in any way on which these two agreed. Such coalitions could be repeatedly formed and dissolved during a trial, so that the experimenters were afforded an excellent opportunity to see how competitive bargaining occurred under different conditions which they imposed.

A special aspect of this study was that one of the three college students in each group of subjects was a paid collaborator, assisting in the research. His role in the competition for points and in the forming of coalitions was designed to bring out the motivational and problem-solving patterns of behavior in the two *bona fide* subjects. Completing some geometric jigsaw puzzles was the first task required of the three persons, and on this task the confederate of the investigators always earned most points. On the subsequent four trials, points

could be earned only if any two subjects pooled certain jigsaw puzzle pieces. This set the stage for forming two-man coalitions. The two real subjects could cooperate with each other to earn the available points to be shared as they wished. Alternatively, either could form a coalition with the confederate who already held a commanding lead in points. The confederate would usually be required to offer a larger share of the potential points before either subject would cooperate with him in earning them. By bargaining according to a prearranged flexible plan, this special subject was able to test the strength of the coalitions which often were formed by the others to oppose him.

In their introduction of the subjects to the experiment, the investigators established two sets of conditions which they felt would affect the bargaining for points and the forming of the two-man coalitions. One set of conditions involved an indication of the assigned tasks as either very important or somewhat inconsequential in nature. On the one hand great importance was attached to the session by presenting it as a social intelligence test with each of the three students being evaluated as they bargained among themselves. Alternatively the session was minimized in importance by indicating it to be a routine check of a test whose validity was seriously doubted by the investigators. The second set of conditions involved the apparent status of the collaborating student posing as a subject. Under the peer condition he was indicated to be about equal in intelligence to the other students. Under the nonpeer condition he was shown to be their superior in intellectual functioning. The peer or nonpeer relations were combined with the high or low importance conditions in a 2×2 factorial design. Seven groups were run under each of the four combinations of these conditions.

It was hypothesized that high importance attaching to the task would induce more coalitions between the two *bona fide* subjects in an attempt to compete with the third man who held the lead as a result of his initial success. A second hypothesis was that these two subjects would cooperate more if the other were seen as a peer—an equal against whom they ought to make a good showing. If he were perceived as clearly superior, as in the nonpeer condition, then they should be less likely to cooperate in attempting to equal him. In this case, each of them should be more likely to join him in trying to beat the other regular subject who would appear to be appropriate competition.

Over the four critical trials the number of coalitions formed by the *bona fide* subjects under the two sets of conditions confirmed the

to communicate information to B, B to C, and C to A, without any chance for reversed communication over these three channels.

Microphones and earphones were employed in setting up the required nets for communication among the subjects who were located in different rooms. The equipment was arranged to permit the experimenters to introduce three different noise levels into the channels of any net. This varying of signal-to-noise ratio constituted a second major independent variable in addition to the different nets. A high ratio, with little noise, permitted subjects to make themselves understood quite readily over the channels provided. A low signal-to-noise ratio made it difficult to transmit information, causing many errors to occur. In this brief review we shall not deal extensively with the signal-to-noise ratio as a variable. We may note merely that the lower ratios impeded the solving of the assigned problems by interfering with accurate communication. These difficult conditions of message transmission also accentuated the differences between the nets as certain tasks were attempted.

Three experiments in this study differed in the task assigned to the subjects. In Experiment I each subject was given a number of pairs of words. Pairing indicated that the two words were consecutive items on a master list. The problem for the group to solve was to reconstruct this master list with the words in proper sequence, each subject contributing the information which his portions of the master list permitted. The problem was considered to be solved only when each subject had made a copy of the entire master list. In Experiment II a similar problem was involved except that a long sentence, instead of a list of unrelated words, had to be constructed from the portions given to each subject. Experiment III required each subject to form as many words as possible from a longer word assigned to the group. A bonus was offered for every word that was common to each of the three lists which were constructed in this problem-solving task. The communication net could be employed to exchange information on words formed.

Just as research has shown that the different net patterns which are illustrated in Figure 19.1 affect problem-solving efficiency, these experiments demonstrated that the nets of Figure 19.2 also differ in the speed with which they permit some problems to be solved. In Experiment I the number of words spoken and the time taken in arriving at the reconstructed master list both showed Net 1 to be the most efficient and Net 5 the least. The performance data were in general agreement with an analysis of how many spoken words would be needed to solve the problem, given each net with its own set of channels. Net 5, for example, does not permit any spoken word to reach two subjects at once, thus allowing no economy in transmitting information.

Experiment II, unlike Experiment I, showed Net 3 to be superior to Net 1. The experimenters suggest that the sentence construction task demands the sort of coordination which Subject A in Net 3 can supply. The more complete channels of Net 1 apparently introduce chaos, to some extent, when the sentence-building is attempted. The results for Experiment III contrast with those we have noted in that the nets did not differ in their effect on efficiency of performance. The task of constructing words did not require much exchange of information. Since each subject could go at the problem independently, the channels of communication played little differential role. This aspect of the findings emphasizes the contribution of type of task to research on group problem solving. In their discussion, the experimenters point out the desirability of classifying group problems along several dimensions as an aid to further study of group dynamics.

SUMMARY

From the complexities of the psychological processes occurring as people meet in groups, research workers abstract certain independent variables and aspects of behavior for special study. Their investigations may sometimes seek principles which can be applied in improving group functioning, or they may be aimed at studying laws of social interaction as a basic contribution to behavior science.

Social processes have been studied by field observation and by sociometry. Another method which has been employed in numerous studies is the group dynamics technique of giving a problem or discussion topic to a group of subjects whose interactions are then carefully observed, perhaps rated. An experimental approach to audience persuasion is made by measuring opinion before and after presenting a persuasive communication to a large group of subjects.

When we investigate the modification of opinion, or overt behavior, through persuasion, we may utilize independent variables from one of three aspects of the situation: communicator, communication, or audience. We are dealing with a research topic of undeniable complexity, and one which will not permit too much simplification. It appears that we need to use many interrelated studies, instead of single decisive experiments, to delineate the social processes which are operative. Proper employment of opinion-measuring techniques is another necessity for success in studying persuasion. Besides the complexities of experimental procedure in this realm of research, we face the need for rigor in the design of our experiments. We must be certain that any observed opinion change is validly attributable to the persuasive communication. Our review of illustrative studies demonstrated manipulations of a communicator variable, the positive or negative guest in the simulated radio interview, and a communication variable, the amount of fear-arousing material in the dental hygiene presentation.

In group dynamics research, certain aspects of the small group situation have been singled out for repeated exploration. Size of group, communication net, and assigned task are important ways of introducing independent variables which can serve to reveal some of the intricacies of social processes. Sometimes a particular process, like pressure to conformity, will be used by an experimenter as a means of studying reactions of experimental subjects.

The behavior of groups and of the individuals comprising them may be measured by various techniques. Frequency tallies of different interactions are guided by observational categories used by trained observers. Such observers may also rate the behavior of the group and its members. Certain dimensions of task accomplishment also provide means for assessing group efficiency.

Our discussion of group dynamics research was augmented by reviewing illustrative experiments. We saw how investigators have studied groups as they engaged in discussion, decision-making, problem solving, and competitive bargaining. Contrasting with these face-to-face groups, a group operating over a communication net was also the object of study.

REFERENCES

Bales, R. F. *Interaction process analysis: A method for the study of small groups.* Cambridge, Mass.: Addison-Wesley, 1950.

Bales, R. F., & Borgatta, E. F. Size of group as a factor in the interaction profile. In A. P. Hare, E. F. Borgatta, & R. F. Bales (Eds.), *Small groups.* New York: Knopf, 1955. Pp. 396–413.

Bavelas, A. Communication patterns in task-oriented groups. In D. Cartwright & A. Zander (Eds.), *Group dynamics research and theory.* Evanston, Illinois: Row, Peterson, 1953. Pp. 493–506.

Campbell, D. T. Factors relevant to the validity of experiments in social settings. *Psychol. Bull.,* 1957, 54, 297–312.

Carter, L. F. Recording and evaluating the performance of individuals as members of small groups. In A. P. Hare, E. F. Borgatta, & R. F. Bales (Eds.), *Small groups*. New York: Knopf, 1955. Pp. 492–497.

Hare, A. P. Interaction and consensus in different sized groups. In D. Cartwright & A. Zander (Eds.), *Group dynamics research and theory*. Evanston, Illinois: Row, Peterson, 1953. Pp. 507–518.

Heise, G. A., & Miller, G. A. Problem solving by small groups using various communication nets. *J. abn. soc. Psychol.*, 1951, 46, 327–336.

Hoffman, P. J., Festinger, L., & Lawrence, D. H. Tendencies toward group comparability in competitive bargaining. *Hum. Relat.*, 1954, 7, 141–159.

Hovland, C. I., Janis, I. L., & Kelley, H. H. *Communication and persuasion*. New Haven: Yale Univer. Press, 1953.

Janis, I. L., & Feshbach, S. Effects of fear-arousing communications. *J. abn. soc. Psychol.*, 1953, 48, 78–92.

Kelman, H. C., & Hovland, C. I. "Reinstatement" of the communicator in delayed measurement of opinion change. *J. abn. soc. Psychol.*, 1953, 48, 327–335.

Roby, T. R., & Lanzetta, J. T. Considerations in the analysis of group tasks. *Psychol. Bull.*, 1958, 55, 88–101.

Taylor, D. W., & Faust, W. L. Twenty questions: Efficiency in problem solving as a function of group size. *J. exp. Psychol.*, 1952, 44, 360–368.

Whyte, W. F. Observational field-work methods. In Marie Jahoda, M. Deutsch, & S. W. Cook (Eds.), *Research methods in social relations*. New York: Dryden, 1951. Pp. 493–513.

Ziller, R. C. Scales of judgment: a determinant of the accuracy of group decisions. *Hum. Relat.*, 1955, 8, 153–164.

ADDITIONAL READINGS

Campbell, D. T. The indirect assessment of social attitudes. *Psychol. Bull.*, 1950, 47, 15–38.

Green, B. F. Attitude measurement. In G. Lindzey (Ed.), *Handbook of social psychology. I. Theory and method*. Cambridge, Mass.: Addison-Wesley, 1954. Pp. 335–369.

Kelley, II. II., & Thibaut, J. W. Experimental studies of group problem solving and process. In G. Lindzey (Ed.), *Handbook of social psychology. II. Special fields and applications*. Cambridge, Mass.: Addison-Wesley, 1954. Pp. 735–785.

Miller, J. G. (Ed.) *Experiments in social process*. New York: McGraw-Hill. 1950.

Appendix

TABLE A

Table of Random Numbers

Col. 1	Col. 2	Col. 3	Col. 4	Col. 5	Col. 6	Col. 7	Col. 8
3831	7167	1540	1532	6617	1845	3162	0210
6019	4242	1818	4978	8200	7326	5442	7766
6653	7210	0718	2183	0737	4603	2094	1964
8861	5020	6590	5990	3425	9298	5973	9614
9221	6305	6091	8875	6693	8017	8953	5477
2809	9700	8832	0248	3593	4686	9645	3899
1207	0100	3553	8260	7332	7402	9152	5419
6012	3752	2974	7321	5964	7095	2855	6123
0300	0773	5128	0694	3572	5517	3689	7220
1382	2179	5685	9705	9919	1739	0356	7173
0678	7663	4425	6295	4158	6769	7253	8106
8966	0561	9341	8686	8866	2168	7951	9721
6293	3420	9752	9656	7191	1127	7783	2596
9097	7558	1814	0782	0310	7310	5951	8147
3362	3045	6361	4024	1875	4124	7396	3985
5594	1248	2685	1039	0129	5047	6267	0440
6495	8204	9251	1947	9485	3027	9946	7792
9378	0894	7233	2355	1278	8667	5810	8869
2932	4490	0680	8024	4378	9543	4594	8392
2868	7746	1213	0396	9902	4953	2261	8117
3047	6737	5434	9719	8026	9282	6952	1883
3673	2265	5271	4542	2646	1744	2684	4956
0731	8278	9597	0745	9682	8007	7836	2771
2666	3174	0706	6224	4595	2273	0802	9402
3379	3349	9239	2808	8626	8569	6660	9683
7228	8029	3633	6194	9030	1279	2611	3805
4367	2881	3996	8336	7933	6385	5902	1664
1014	9964	1346	4850	1524	1919	7355	4737
6316	4356	7927	6709	1375	0356	8855	3632
2302	6392	5023	8515	1197	9182	4952	1897
7439	5567	1156	9241	0438	0607	1962	0717
1930	7128	6098	6033	5132	5350	1216	0518
4598	6415	1523	4012	8179	9934	8863	8375
2835	5888	8616	7542	5875	2859	6805	4079

TABLE A *continued*

Col. 1	Col. 2	Col. 3	Col. 4	Col. 5	Col. 6	Col. 7	Col. 8
4377	5153	9930	0902	8208	6501	9593	1397
3725	7202	6551	7458	4740	8234	4914	0878
7868	7546	5714	9450	6603	3709	7328	2835
2168	2879	8000	8755	5496	3532	5173	4289
1366	5878	6631	3799	2607	0769	8119	7064
7840	6116	6088	5362	7583	6246	9297	9178
1208	7567	2984	1555	5633	2676	8668	9281
5492	1044	2380	1283	4244	2667	5864	5325
1049	9457	3807	8877	6857	6915	6852	2399
7334	8324	6028	6356	2771	1686	1840	3035
5907	6128	9673	4251	0986	3668	1215	2385
3405	6830	2171	9447	4347	6948	2083	0697
1785	4670	1154	2567	8965	3903	4669	4275
6180	3600	8393	5019	1457	2970	9582	1658
4614	8527	8738	5658	4017	0815	0851	7215
6465	6832	7586	3595	9421	9498	8576	4256
0573	7976	3362	1807	2929	0540	8721	3133
7672	3912	8047	0966	6692	4444	7690	8525
9182	1221	2215	0590	4784	5374	7429	5422
2118	5264	7144	8413	4137	6178	8670	4120
6478	5077	0991	3657	9242	5710	2758	0574
3386	1570	5143	4332	2599	4330	4999	8978
2053	4196	1585	4340	1955	6312	7903	8253
0483	3044	4609	4046	4614	4566	7906	0892
3825	9228	2706	8574	0959	6456	7232	5838
3426	9307	7283	9370	5441	9659	6478	1734
8365	9252	5198	2453	7514	5498	7105	0549
7915	3351	8381	2137	9695	0358	5163	1556
7521	7744	2379	2325	3585	9370	4879	6545
1262	0960	5816	3485	8498	5860	5188	3178
9110	8181	0097	3823	6955	1123	6794	5076
9979	5039	0025	8060	2668	0157	5578	0243
2312	2169	5977	8067	2782	7690	4146	6110
3960	1468	3399	4940	3088	7546	1170	6054
5227	6451	4868	0977	5735	0359	7805	8250
2599	3800	9245	6545	6181	7300	2348	4378
9583	3746	4175	0143	3279	0809	7367	2923
8740	4326	1105	0498	3910	2074	3623	9890
6541	2753	2423	4282	2195	1471	0852	6604
1237	2419	4572	3829	1274	9378	2393	4028
7397	4135	8132	3143	3638	0515	1133	9975
9105	3396	9469	0966	6128	3808	7073	7779
3348	5436	1171	5853	2392	7643	2011	0538

TABLE A *continued*

Col. 1	Col. 2	Col. 3	Col. 4	Col. 5	Col. 6	Col. 7	Col. 8
7792	4714	5799	1211	0409	5036	7879	6173
7523	0348	5237	2533	0635	2382	5092	3497
2674	2435	5979	7697	3260	2939	2511	7318
6825	3660	2688	9560	1329	4268	2532	5024
0639	6884	8337	5308	2054	3454	8745	1877
2467	2505	4916	1683	0034	7758	4458	9918
9513	2949	9337	7234	8458	3329	9691	4278
9116	6846	0205	1158	6112	9916	0723	3769
4012	3863	4817	6294	7865	1672	0137	6557
7698	0651	9756	1816	1154	6708	2522	8296
7158	8463	6406	0779	1185	7660	3065	8941
8412	5905	5612	7028	2545	2392	8434	1551
3134	3962	3147	9631	2881	3091	4678	4465
5840	1940	0754	0457	9533	0108	4523	8441
3237	4236	5504	3282	2838	5002	6614	2463
1990	9392	4943	9505	4925	8313	3108	7681
6724	8147	1557	1342	3352	4421	3707	2445
6521	8766	0654	2300	1696	0145	3257	3496
1888	6629	5385	8725	7185	6826	2279	5200
5567	1138	7139	8157	4906	2872	8842	0890
4511	3021	7370	0264	2690	6187	9110	0941
2188	3642	8905	8172	3930	0152	6931	4340
4086	8745	0988	4815	6192	9608	8686	7459
6817	9456	9157	3036	4769	9362	0074	0837
2914	8776	4833	3214	7643	4345	3304	6137
9122	4766	1599	5271	2257	8502	9560	2833
3558	1472	7664	7256	7181	0038	2257	2503
1928	8097	3520	2187	5124	7295	2525	1891
8032	1390	6606	7195	2724	7239	3888	5582
1846	9648	8699	9716	7752	9886	6299	9129
8691	5849	1005	6629	1632	1463	9288	8600
1884	3228	6397	1733	9543	9868	3611	4828
8211	8273	3941	1484	2627	8257	8493	6354
4070	3899	3121	6736	0668	0782	1398	7729
4463	5758	3905	1545	4699	4338	1235	9547
9961	4716	1687	2448	0815	3022	1220	4055
0420	8921	1593	4599	3401	7209	7877	6001
7927	6608	5190	9268	8431	0324	6619	6159
4007	1367	5975	8972	6629	1259	7204	6556
9515	5611	3025	2016	9209	0290	6236	7360
6670	0458	2062	7235	6818	7619	8698	0110
7485	8847	7234	9278	9453	4900	9119	9216
9177	4212	3238	2358	1109	9441	7591	3901

TABLE B

Values of the t Ratio Which Must Be Equalled or Exceeded for Statistical Significance at the .05 and .01 Levels of Confidence*

Col. 1	Col. 2	Col. 3
df	$t(p = .05)$	$t(p = .01)$
1	12.706	63.657
2	4.303	9.925
3	3.182	5.841
4	2.776	4.604
5	2.571	4.032
6	2.447	3.707
7	2.365	3.499
8	2.306	3.355
9	2.262	3.250
10	2.228	3.169
11	2.201	3.106
12	2.179	3.055
13	2.160	3.012
14	2.145	2.977
15	2.131	2.947
16	2.120	2.921
17	2.110	2.898
18	2.101	2.878
19	2.093	2.861
20	2.086	2.845
21	2.080	2.831
22	2.074	2.819
23	2.069	2.807
24	2.064	2.797
25	2.060	2.787
26	2.056	2.779
27	2.052	2.771
28	2.048	2.763
29	2.045	2.756
30	2.042	2.750
40	2.021	2.704
60	2.000	2.660
120	1.980	2.617
∞	1.960	2.576

* This table is abridged from Table III of *Statistical Tables for Biological, Agricultural and Medical Research* by Fisher and Yates, by permission of the publishers, Oliver and Boyd, Ltd., Edinburgh.

which we might assemble for research purposes. In this brief review we shall omit discussion of how the factor of military status entered into the investigation as the different crews were studied.

Thirty-six crews ranging in size from ten to fifteen men served as the experimental groups. A quantitative task was devised for which there was an objectively true answer, but which would elicit a variety of individual estimates as a starting point for the group decision-making. With each group seated in a face-to-face arrangement, the experimenter dropped into their midst a 16 in. × 21 in. card on which were scattered, evenly but irregularly, exactly 3155 dots. The card was in view for only 15 sec, longer exposure times having led to unduly accurate techniques of estimation. Each group was given the task of arriving at a crew decision about the number of dots that had been displayed.

Under Conditions A and B, the group discussion was preceded by a public poll in which the experimenter called on each individual to announce his own personal estimate. Under Condition C the group discussion began without this requirement for individual estimates. This condition was expected to lead to less accurate group estimates on the assumption that these groups would carry on their discussion with a narrower reference scale of estimates. Conditions A and B were expected to develop broader scales of judgment as a result of polling individuals, and the hypothesis we stated earlier predicts that more accurate group decisions should ensue. This same hypothesis was testable by fractionating the groups under Conditions A and B into those exhibiting a broad scale and those showing a narrow scale of judgment when initial individual estimates were examined. In addition to this approach to group decision-making, the investigator concluded each session by surveying individual opinion on the influences each person had felt and the degree of agreement with the final group estimate. We may note this extension of the experimental procedure even though we shall not be able to consider this part of the results.

When the various group estimates were examined, it was found that Conditions A and B, with individual estimates having preceded the group discussion, had given rise to mean errors of about 1000 and 900 dots, respectively. These error magnitudes were compared with a mean error value of about 1500 dots made under Condition C, with no polling of individuals prior to group discussion. Although this much larger mean error was in the predicted direction, it was not statistically significant in comparison with the means for Conditions

A and B which had presumably come from broader scales of judgment. An analysis of the data from these two conditions alone did yield support for the hypothesis under discussion.

All groups under these Conditions A and B were examined as to the SD of the original individual estimates as publicly expressed. The groups showing an SD above the median were then compared to those exhibiting an SD of preliminary estimates which was below the median. In other words, the groups having a broad scale of judgment were compared with those having a narrower scale established in the initial poll. It was found that the mean error of group estimates based on the broader scales was only about 800 dots, whereas groups using narrower scales showed a mean group error of about 1400 dots. The difference in this case was statistically significant, offering support to the hypothesis under investigation.

Problem Solving

Investigations in which groups are required to solve problems are as varied in content and method as are studies of group discussions. Since we are not attempting a representative survey, we shall omit examples of the more straightforward experiments in which a face-to-face group is observed while it tries to solve an assigned problem. We shall look instead at some illustrative research featuring somewhat special methods.

DYNAMICS OF COMPETITIVE BARGAINING. In contrast to the usual study which calls for full cooperation in attacking a problem, Hoffman, Festinger, and Lawrence (1954) set up a situation in which three people bargained competitively to obtain points. Each individual was striving to earn points for himself, but the situation was arranged so that two people might form a coalition so as to win extra points. These points could then be shared in any way on which these two agreed. Such coalitions could be repeatedly formed and dissolved during a trial, so that the experimenters were afforded an excellent opportunity to see how competitive bargaining occurred under different conditions which they imposed.

A special aspect of this study was that one of the three college students in each group of subjects was a paid collaborator, assisting in the research. His role in the competition for points and in the forming of coalitions was designed to bring out the motivational and problem-solving patterns of behavior in the two *bona fide* subjects. Completing some geometric jigsaw puzzles was the first task required of the three persons, and on this task the confederate of the investigators always earned most points. On the subsequent four trials, points could be earned only if any two subjects pooled certain jigsaw puzzle pieces. This set the stage for forming two-man coalitions. The two real subjects could cooperate with each other to earn the available points to be shared as they wished. Alternatively, either could form a coalition with the confederate who already held a commanding lead in points. The confederate would usually be required to offer a larger share of the potential points before either subject would cooperate with him in earning them. By bargaining according to a prearranged flexible plan, this special subject was able to test the strength of the coalitions which often were formed by the others to oppose him.

In their introduction of the subjects to the experiment, the investigators established two sets of conditions which they felt would affect the bargaining for points and the forming of the two-man coalitions. One set of conditions involved an indication of the assigned tasks as either very important or somewhat inconsequential in nature. On the one hand great importance was attached to the session by presenting it as a social intelligence test with each of the three students being evaluated as they bargained among themselves. Alternatively the session was minimized in importance by indicating it to be a routine check of a test whose validity was seriously doubted by the investigators. The second set of conditions involved the apparent status of the collaborating student posing as a subject. Under the peer condition he was indicated to be about equal in intelligence to the other students. Under the nonpeer condition he was shown to be their superior in intellectual functioning. The peer or nonpeer relations were combined with the high or low importance conditions in a 2×2 factorial design. Seven groups were run under each of the four combinations of these conditions.

It was hypothesized that high importance attaching to the task would induce more coalitions between the two *bona fide* subjects in an attempt to compete with the third man who held the lead as a result of his initial success. A second hypothesis was that these two subjects would cooperate more if the other were seen as a peer—an equal against whom they ought to make a good showing. If he were perceived as clearly superior, as in the nonpeer condition, then they should be less likely to cooperate in attempting to equal him. In this case, each of them should be more likely to join him in trying to beat the other regular subject who would appear to be appropriate competition.

Over the four critical trials the number of coalitions formed by the *bona fide* subjects under the two sets of conditions confirmed the two hypotheses we have stated. More coalitions were formed against the stooge subject when the task was considered to be very important. Likewise, more of these coalitions occurred under the peer condition in which the stooge was presented as a reasonable competitor for the others. These main effects were found to be statistically significant. The findings tended to be borne out by other data that were taken, such as the price in points which the stooge had to offer in order to break up a coalition against him. A greater number of points was demanded of him in the bargaining when the task was perceived as more important and when he was perceived as a peer against whom the real subjects ought to compete successfully.

THREE-MAN COMMUNICATION NETS. A series of experiments by Heise and Miller (1951) involved a variety of communication nets achieved by using both one-way and two-way channels between members of the group. The five different nets which were used are schematically represented in Figure 19.2. Among the features which distinguish these nets we may note that Net 1 permits each subject, A, B, or C, to communicate with each other person over a two-way channel; in Net 3 there is two-way communication between A and B as well as between A and C, but B and C are not joined directly by any channel; Net 5 involves three one-way channels, permitting A

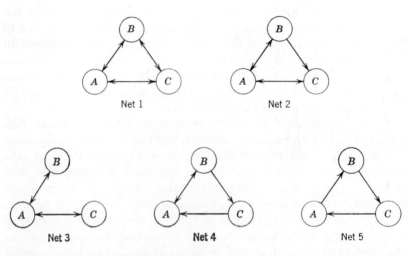

Fig. 19.2. Five three-person communication nets used by Heise and Miller (1951) with both one-way and two-way communication used in different net patterns as indicated by the arrowheads in the figure. (After Heise and Miller, 1951.)

to communicate information to B, B to C, and C to A, without any chance for reversed communication over these three channels.

Microphones and earphones were employed in setting up the required nets for communication among the subjects who were located in different rooms. The equipment was arranged to permit the experimenters to introduce three different noise levels into the channels of any net. This varying of signal-to-noise ratio constituted a second major independent variable in addition to the different nets. A high ratio, with little noise, permitted subjects to make themselves understood quite readily over the channels provided. A low signal-to-noise ratio made it difficult to transmit information, causing many errors to occur. In this brief review we shall not deal extensively with the signal-to-noise ratio as a variable. We may note merely that the lower ratios impeded the solving of the assigned problems by interfering with accurate communication. These difficult conditions of message transmission also accentuated the differences between the nets as certain tasks were attempted.

Three experiments in this study differed in the task assigned to the subjects. In Experiment I each subject was given a number of pairs of words. Pairing indicated that the two words were consecutive items on a master list. The problem for the group to solve was to reconstruct this master list with the words in proper sequence, each subject contributing the information which his portions of the master list permitted. The problem was considered to be solved only when each subject had made a copy of the entire master list. In Experiment II a similar problem was involved except that a long sentence, instead of a list of unrelated words, had to be constructed from the portions given to each subject. Experiment III required each subject to form as many words as possible from a longer word assigned to the group. A bonus was offered for every word that was common to each of the three lists which were constructed in this problem-solving task. The communication net could be employed to exchange information on words formed.

Just as research has shown that the different net patterns which are illustrated in Figure 19.1 affect problem-solving efficiency, these experiments demonstrated that the nets of Figure 19.2 also differ in the speed with which they permit some problems to be solved. In Experiment I the number of words spoken and the time taken in arriving at the reconstructed master list both showed Net 1 to be the most efficient and Net 5 the least. The performance data were in general agreement with an analysis of how many spoken words would be needed to solve the problem, given each net with its own set of channels. Net 5, for example, does not permit any spoken word to reach two subjects at once, thus allowing no economy in transmitting information.

Experiment II, unlike Experiment I, showed Net 3 to be superior to Net 1. The experimenters suggest that the sentence construction task demands the sort of coordination which Subject A in Net 3 can supply. The more complete channels of Net 1 apparently introduce chaos, to some extent, when the sentence-building is attempted. The results for Experiment III contrast with those we have noted in that the nets did not differ in their effect on efficiency of performance. The task of constructing words did not require much exchange of information. Since each subject could go at the problem independently, the channels of communication played little differential role. This aspect of the findings emphasizes the contribution of type of task to research on group problem solving. In their discussion, the experimenters point out the desirability of classifying group problems along several dimensions as an aid to further study of group dynamics.

SUMMARY

From the complexities of the psychological processes occurring as people meet in groups, research workers abstract certain independent variables and aspects of behavior for special study. Their investigations may sometimes seek principles which can be applied in improving group functioning, or they may be aimed at studying laws of social interaction as a basic contribution to behavior science.

Social processes have been studied by field observation and by sociometry. Another method which has been employed in numerous studies is the group dynamics technique of giving a problem or discussion topic to a group of subjects whose interactions are then carefully observed, perhaps rated. An experimental approach to audience persuasion is made by measuring opinion before and after presenting a persuasive communication to a large group of subjects.

When we investigate the modification of opinion, or overt behavior, through persuasion, we may utilize independent variables from one of three aspects of the situation: communicator, communication, or audience. We are dealing with a research topic of undeniable complexity, and one which will not permit too much simplification. It appears that we need to use many interrelated studies, instead of single decisive experiments, to delineate the social processes which are operative. Proper employment of opinion-measuring techniques is another necessity for success in studying persuasion. Besides the complexities of experimental procedure in this realm of research, we face the need for rigor in the design of our experiments. We must be certain that any observed opinion change is validly attributable to the persuasive communication. Our review of illustrative studies demonstrated manipulations of a communicator variable, the positive or negative guest in the simulated radio interview, and a communication variable, the amount of fear-arousing material in the dental hygiene presentation.

In group dynamics research, certain aspects of the small group situation have been singled out for repeated exploration. Size of group, communication net, and assigned task are important ways of introducing independent variables which can serve to reveal some of the intricacies of social processes. Sometimes a particular process, like pressure to conformity, will be used by an experimenter as a means of studying reactions of experimental subjects.

The behavior of groups and of the individuals comprising them may be measured by various techniques. Frequency tallies of different interactions are guided by observational categories used by trained observers. Such observers may also rate the behavior of the group and its members. Certain dimensions of task accomplishment also provide means for assessing group efficiency.

Our discussion of group dynamics research was augmented by reviewing illustrative experiments. We saw how investigators have studied groups as they engaged in discussion, decision-making, problem solving, and competitive bargaining. Contrasting with these face-to-face groups, a group operating over a communication net was also the object of study.

REFERENCES

Bales, R. F. *Interaction process analysis: A method for the study of small groups.* Cambridge, Mass.: Addison-Wesley, 1950.

Bales, R. F., & Borgatta, E. F. Size of group as a factor in the interaction profile. In A. P. Hare, E. F. Borgatta, & R. F. Bales (Eds.), *Small groups.* New York: Knopf, 1955. Pp. 396–413.

Bavelas, A. Communication patterns in task-oriented groups. In D. Cartwright & A. Zander (Eds.), *Group dynamics research and theory.* Evanston, Illinois: Row, Peterson, 1953. Pp. 493–506.

Campbell, D. T. Factors relevant to the validity of experiments in social settings. *Psychol. Bull.*, 1957, 54, 297–312.

Carter, L. F. Recording and evaluating the performance of individuals as members of small groups. In A. P. Hare, E. F. Borgatta, & R. F. Bales (Eds.), *Small groups.* New York: Knopf, 1955. Pp. 492–497.

Hare, A. P. Interaction and consensus in different sized groups. In D. Cartwright & A. Zander (Eds.), *Group dynamics research and theory.* Evanston, Illinois: Row, Peterson, 1953. Pp. 507–518.

Heise, G. A., & Miller, G. A. Problem solving by small groups using various communication nets. *J. abn. soc. Psychol.,* 1951, 46, 327–336.

Hoffman, P. J., Festinger, L., & Lawrence, D. H. Tendencies toward group comparability in competitive bargaining. *Hum. Relat.,* 1954, 7, 141–159.

Hovland, C. I., Janis, I. L., & Kelley, H. H. *Communication and persuasion.* New Haven: Yale Univer. Press, 1953.

Janis, I. L., & Feshbach, S. Effects of fear-arousing communications. *J. abn. soc. Psychol.,* 1953, 48, 78–92.

Kelman, H. C., & Hovland, C. I. "Reinstatement" of the communicator in delayed measurement of opinion change. *J. abn. soc. Psychol.,* 1953, 48, 327–335.

Roby, T. R., & Lanzetta, J. T. Considerations in the analysis of group tasks. *Psychol. Bull.,* 1958, 55, 88–101.

Taylor, D. W., & Faust, W. L. Twenty questions: Efficiency in problem solving as a function of group size. *J. exp. Psychol.,* 1952, 44, 360–368.

Whyte, W. F. Observational field-work methods. In Marie Jahoda, M. Deutsch, & S. W. Cook (Eds.), *Research methods in social relations.* New York: Dryden, 1951. Pp. 493–513.

Ziller, R. C. Scales of judgment: a determinant of the accuracy of group decisions. *Hum. Relat.,* 1955, 8, 153–164.

ADDITIONAL READINGS

Campbell, D. T. The indirect assessment of social attitudes. *Psychol. Bull.,* 1950, 47, 15–38.

Green, B. F. Attitude measurement. In G. Lindzey (Ed.), *Handbook of social psychology. I. Theory and method.* Cambridge, Mass.: Addison-Wesley, 1954. Pp. 335–369.

Kelley, H. H., & Thibaut, J. W. Experimental studies of group problem solving and process. In G. Lindzey (Ed.), *Handbook of social psychology. II. Special fields and applications.* Cambridge, Mass.: Addison-Wesley, 1954. Pp. 735–785.

Miller, J. G. (Ed.) *Experiments in social process.* New York: McGraw-Hill, 1950.

Appendix

TABLE A

Table of Random Numbers

Col. 1	Col. 2	Col. 3	Col. 4	Col. 5	Col. 6	Col. 7	Col. 8
3831	7167	1540	1532	6617	1845	3162	0210
6019	4242	1818	4978	8200	7326	5442	7766
6653	7210	0718	2183	0737	4603	2094	1964
8861	5020	6590	5990	3425	9298	5973	9614
9221	6305	6091	8875	6693	8017	8953	5477
2809	9700	8832	0248	3593	4686	9645	3899
1207	0100	3553	8260	7332	7402	9152	5419
6012	3752	2974	7321	5964	7095	2855	6123
0300	0773	5128	0694	3572	5517	3689	7220
1382	2179	5685	9705	9919	1739	0356	7173
0678	7663	4425	6295	4158	6769	7253	8106
8966	0561	9341	8686	8866	2168	7951	9721
6293	3420	9752	9656	7191	1127	7783	2596
9097	7558	1814	0782	0310	7310	5951	8147
3362	3045	6361	4024	1875	4124	7396	3985
5594	1248	2685	1039	0129	5047	6267	0440
6495	8204	9251	1947	9485	3027	9946	7792
9378	0894	7233	2355	1278	8667	5810	8869
2932	4490	0680	8024	4378	9543	4594	8392
2868	7746	1213	0396	9902	4953	2261	8117
3047	6737	5434	9719	8026	9282	6952	1883
3673	2265	5271	4542	2646	1744	2684	4956
0731	8278	9597	0745	9682	8007	7836	2771
2666	3174	0706	6224	4595	2273	0802	9402
3379	3349	9239	2808	8626	8569	6660	9683
7228	8029	3633	6194	9030	1279	2611	3805
4367	2881	3996	8336	7933	6385	5902	1664
1014	9964	1346	4850	1524	1919	7355	4737
6316	4356	7927	6709	1375	0356	8855	3632
2302	6392	5023	8515	1197	9182	4952	1897
7439	5567	1156	9241	0438	0607	1962	0717
1930	7128	6098	6033	5132	5350	1216	0518
4598	6415	1523	4012	8179	9934	8863	8375
2835	5888	8616	7542	5875	2859	6805	4079

TABLE A *continued*

Col. 1	Col. 2	Col. 3	Col. 4	Col. 5	Col. 6	Col. 7	Col. 8
4377	5153	9930	0902	8208	6501	9593	1397
3725	7202	6551	7458	4740	8234	4914	0878
7868	7546	5714	9450	6603	3709	7328	2835
2168	2879	8000	8755	5496	3532	5173	4289
1366	5878	6631	3799	2607	0769	8119	7064
7840	6116	6088	5362	7583	6246	9297	9178
1208	7567	2984	1555	5633	2676	8668	9281
5492	1044	2380	1283	4244	2667	5864	5325
1049	9457	3807	8877	6857	6915	6852	2399
7334	8324	6028	6356	2771	1686	1840	3035
5907	6128	9673	4251	0986	3668	1215	2385
3405	6830	2171	9447	4347	6948	2083	0697
1785	4670	1154	2567	8965	3903	4669	4275
6180	3600	8393	5019	1457	2970	9582	1658
4614	8527	8738	5658	4017	0815	0851	7215
6465	6832	7586	3595	9421	9498	8576	4256
0573	7976	3362	1807	2929	0540	8721	3133
7672	3912	8047	0966	6692	4444	7690	8525
9182	1221	2215	0590	4784	5374	7429	5422
2118	5264	7144	8413	4137	6178	8670	4120
6478	5077	0991	3657	9242	5710	2758	0574
3386	1570	5143	4332	2599	4330	4999	8978
2053	4196	1585	4340	1955	6312	7903	8253
0483	3044	4609	4046	4614	4566	7906	0892
3825	9228	2706	8574	0959	6456	7232	5838
3426	9307	7283	9370	5441	9659	6478	1734
8365	9252	5198	2453	7514	5498	7105	0549
7915	3351	8381	2137	9695	0358	5163	1556
7521	7744	2379	2325	3585	9370	4879	6545
1262	0960	5816	3485	8498	5860	5188	3178
9110	8181	0097	3823	6955	1123	6794	5076
9979	5039	0025	8060	2668	0157	5578	0243
2312	2169	5977	8067	2782	7690	4146	6110
3960	1468	3399	4940	3088	7546	1170	6054
5227	6451	4868	0977	5735	0359	7805	8250
2599	3800	9245	6545	6181	7300	2348	4378
9583	3746	4175	0143	3279	0809	7367	2923
8740	4326	1105	0498	3910	2074	3623	9890
6541	2753	2423	4282	2195	1471	0852	6604
1237	2419	4572	3829	1274	9378	2393	4028
7397	4135	8132	3143	3638	0515	1133	9975
9105	3396	9469	0966	6128	3808	7073	7779
3348	5436	1171	5853	2392	7643	2011	0538

TABLE A *continued*

Col. 1	Col. 2	Col. 3	Col. 4	Col. 5	Col. 6	Col. 7	Col. 8
7792	4714	5799	1211	0409	5036	7879	6173
7523	0348	5237	2533	0635	2382	5092	3497
2674	2435	5979	7697	3260	2939	2511	7318
6825	3660	2688	9560	1329	4268	2532	5024
0639	6884	8337	5308	2054	3454	8745	1877
2467	2505	4916	1683	0034	7758	4458	9918
9513	2949	9337	7234	8458	3329	9691	4278
9116	6846	0205	1158	6112	9916	0723	3769
4012	3863	4817	6294	7865	1672	0137	6557
7698	0651	9756	1816	1154	6708	2522	8296
7158	8463	6406	0779	1185	7660	3065	8941
8412	5905	5612	7028	2545	2392	8434	1551
3134	3962	3147	9631	2881	3091	4678	4465
5840	1940	0754	0457	9533	0108	4523	8441
3237	4236	5504	3282	2838	5002	6614	2463
1990	9392	4943	9505	4925	8313	3108	7681
6724	8147	1557	1342	3352	4421	3707	2445
6521	8766	0654	2300	1696	0145	3257	3496
1888	6629	5385	8725	7185	6826	2279	5200
5567	1138	7139	8157	4906	2872	8842	0890
4511	3021	7370	0264	2690	6187	9110	0941
2188	3642	8905	8172	3930	0152	6931	4340
4086	8745	0988	4815	6192	9608	8686	7459
6817	9456	9157	3036	4769	9362	0074	0837
2914	8776	4833	3214	7643	4345	3304	6137
9122	4766	1599	5271	2257	8502	9560	2833
3558	1472	7664	7256	7181	0038	2257	2503
1928	8097	3520	2187	5124	7295	2525	1891
8032	1390	6606	7195	2724	7239	3888	5582
1846	9648	8699	9716	7752	9886	6299	9129
8691	5849	1005	6629	1632	1463	9288	8600
1884	3228	6397	1733	9543	9868	3611	4828
8211	8273	3941	1484	2627	8257	8493	6354
4070	3899	3121	6736	0668	0782	1398	7729
4463	5758	3905	1545	4699	4338	1235	9547
9961	4716	1687	2448	0815	3022	1220	4055
0420	8921	1593	4599	3401	7209	7877	6001
7927	6608	5190	9268	8431	0324	6619	6159
4007	1367	5975	8972	6629	1259	7204	6556
9515	5611	3025	2016	9209	0290	6236	7360
6670	0458	2062	7235	6818	7619	8698	0110
7485	8847	7234	9278	9453	4900	9119	9216
9177	4212	3238	2358	1109	9441	7591	3901

TABLE B

Values of the *t* Ratio Which Must Be Equalled or Exceeded for Statistical Significance at the .05 and .01 Levels of Confidence*

Col. 1	Col. 2	Col. 3
df	$t(p = .05)$	$t(p = .01)$
1	12.706	63.657
2	4.303	9.925
3	3.182	5.841
4	2.776	4.604
5	2.571	4.032
6	2.447	3.707
7	2.365	3.499
8	2.306	3.355
9	2.262	3.250
10	2.228	3.169
11	2.201	3.106
12	2.179	3.055
13	2.160	3.012
14	2.145	2.977
15	2.131	2.947
16	2.120	2.921
17	2.110	2.898
18	2.101	2.878
19	2.093	2.861
20	2.086	2.845
21	2.080	2.831
22	2.074	2.819
23	2.069	2.807
24	2.064	2.797
25	2.060	2.787
26	2.056	2.779
27	2.052	2.771
28	2.048	2.763
29	2.045	2.756
30	2.042	2.750
40	2.021	2.704
60	2.000	2.660
120	1.980	2.617
∞	1.960	2.576

*This table is abridged from Table III of *Statistical Tables for Biological, Agricultural and Medical Research* by Fisher and Yates, by permission of the publishers, Oliver and Boyd, Ltd., Edinburgh.

TABLE C

Sigma Unit Values (x/σ) Corresponding to Per Cent of Area under the Normal Curve*

Col. 1	Col. 2	Col. 1	Col. 2	Col. 1	Col. 2
Per Cent of Area	x/σ	Per Cent of Area	x/σ	Per Cent of Area	x/σ
0.0000	0.00	0.3413	1.00	0.4772	2.00
0.0199	0.05	0.3531	1.05	0.4798	2.05
0.0398	0.10	0.3643	1.10	0.4821	2.10
0.0596	0.15	0.3749	1.15	0.4842	2.15
0.0793	0.20	0.3849	1.20	0.4861	2.20
0.0987	0.25	0.3944	1.25	0.4878	2.25
0.1179	0.30	0.4032	1.30	0.4893	2.30
0.1368	0.35	0.4115	1.35	0.4906	2.35
0.1554	0.40	0.4192	1.40	0.4918	2.40
0.1736	0.45	0.4265	1.45	0.4929	2.45
0.1915	0.50	0.4332	1.50	0.4938	2.50
0.2088	0.55	0.4394	1.55	0.4946	2.55
0.2257	0.60	0.4452	1.60	0.4953	2.60
0.2422	0.65	0.4505	1.65	0.4960	2.65
0.2580	0.70	0.4554	1.70	0.4965	2.70
0.2734	0.75	0.4599	1.75	0.4974	2.80
0.2881	0.80	0.4641	1.80	0.4981	2.90
0.3023	0.85	0.4678	1.85	0.4986	3·00
0.3159	0.90	0.4713	1.90	0.4990	3.10
0.3289	0.95	0.4744	1.95	0.4993	3.20

* One use of this table is to transform per cent values obtained in the method of constant stimulus differences to sigma unit values as described in the text, p. 119.

Name Index

Adams, J. A., 431, 433, 439, 440
Allen, R. M., 490, 500
Alprin, S. I., 412, 418
Ames, A., 283, 303
Ammons, C. H., 412, 418, 466, 469
Ammons, R. B., 405, 406, 412, 418, 430, 435, 439, 466, 469
Anderson, L. K., 303
Anderson, N., 281, 302, 303
Anderson, S. B., 373, 390
Andreas, B. G., 427, 440, 479, 480, 482, 484, 494, 495, 500, 501
Andreas, C. L., 453
Archer, E. J., 387, 391, 402, 412, 415, 418, 436, 437, 440, 514–519, 536
Arnoult, M. D., 281, 282, 302
Asch, S. E., 285–287, 302
Astin, H. S., 391
Austin, G. A., 537

Bahrick, H. P., 408, 409, 418
Bakan, P., 433, 440
Baker, L. M., 350, 368
Bales, R. F., 559, 561, 569, 570
Barclay, W. D., 354, 368
Bartlett, N. R., 420
Bartlett, S. C., 420
Battig, W. F., 504, 536, 537
Bavelas, A., 558, 569
Bendig, A. W., 171
Bennett, W. F., 408, 409, 418
Bergmann, G., 142, 205, 224
Bevan, W., 303
Bilodeau, E. A., 408, 418, 431, 432, 436, 440
Bilodeau, I. McD., 408, 418, 431, 440, 464, 469

Bindra, D., 333, 337
Blakely, W. A., 332
Bloch, E., 466, 469
Bogartz, W., 369
Boldt, R. F., 437, 440
Borgatta, E. F., 561, 569, 570
Boring, E. G., 224, 288, 302, 303
Bourne, L. E., Jr., 402, 412, 415, 418
Bousfield, W. A., 352–354, 368, 469
Boynton, R. M., 296, 297, 302
Brammer, L. M., 324, 337
Braun, H. W., 457, 458, 469
Breger, L., 369
Briggs, G. E., 102, 141, 460, 469
Brown, C. W., 25
Brown, F. G., 514–519, 536
Brown, J. S., 396, 397, 407, 408, 419
Brown, R., 369
Bruner, J. S., 453, 469, 537
Buchwald, A. M., 350, 368
Bunch, M. E., 375, 390
Bunsen, R. W. E., 244
Burack, B., 537
Bush, W. R., 296, 297, 302
Busiek, R. D., 453, 469

Campbell, D. T., 545–548, 569, 570
Campbell, N. R., 57
Cantor, J. H., 489, 501
Carter, L. F., 560, 569
Cartwright, D., 569, 570
Casperson, R. C., 280, 302
Caussé, R., 318, 337
Chalmers, E. L., Jr., 303
Chapanis, A., 237, 241, 267
Chase, A. M., 239, 267
Chavasse, P., 318, 337

Subject Index